2 cc
5.19

United States Edition

2015 Year B

Workbook for Lectors, Gospel Readers, and Proclaimers of the Word®

D0565218

Daniel J. Scholz

Marielle Frigge, OSB

Graziano Marcheschi, MA, DMIN

with Nancy Seitz Marcheschi

LTP
LITURGY
TRAINING
PUBLICATIONS

CONTENTS

New American Bible readings are taken from *Lectionary for Mass for Use in the Dioceses of the United States of America*, second typical edition © 1998, 1997, 1970 by the Confraternity of Christian Doctrine, Washington, DC, and are reproduced herein by license of the copyright owner. All rights reserved. No part of *Lectionary for Mass* may be reproduced in any form without permission in writing from the Confraternity of Christian Doctrine, Washington, DC.

WORKBOOK FOR LECTORS, GOSPEL READERS, AND PROCLAIMERS OF THE WORD® 2015, United States Edition © 2014 Archdiocese of Chicago. All rights reserved.

Liturgy Training Publications, 3949 South Racine Avenue, Chicago, IL 60609, 1-800-933-1800, fax 1-800-933-7094, orders@ltp.org, www.LTP.org.

Cover art: Barbara Simcoe

Printed in the United States of America.

ISBN: 978-1-61671-168-9
WL15

In accordance with c. 827, permission to publish was granted on May 15, 2014, by Most Reverend Francis J. Kane, DD, Vicar General of the Archdiocese of Chicago. Permission to publish is an official declaration of ecclesiastical authority that the material is free from doctrinal and moral error. No legal responsibility is assumed by the grant of this permission.

As a publisher, LTP works toward responsible stewardship of the environment. We printed the text of *Workbook for Lectors, Gospel Readers, and Proclaimers of the Word®* with soy-based ink on paper certified to the SFI (Sustainable Forestry Initiative) Certified Sourcing Standard CERT–0048284,

(continues on next page)

Ordinary Time

The Authors

Commentaries up through the Twelfth Sunday in Ordinary Time are by Daniel J. Scholz, dean of the College of Arts and Sciences at Cardinal Stritch University in Milwaukee, who has a PhD in biblical theology from Marquette University. He has taught Scripture for over twenty-five years in academic and pastoral settings, and his most recent publication is *The Pauline Letters*.

Remaining commentaries are by Marielle Frigge, OSB, teacher of Scripture and theology for thirty-three years at Mount Marty College in Yankton, SD, who has a PhD in theology and education from Boston College. She now directs ongoing formation for Sacred Heart Monastery and continues teaching in pastoral settings. Most recent publication: *Beginning Biblical Studies* (Anselm Academic, 2009; revised 2013).

The introduction and the proclamation advice in the margins are by Graziano Marcheschi with Nancy Seitz Marcheschi. Graziano has a DMin and has taught, spoken, and written nationally on Scripture, liturgy and the arts, and lay ecclesial ministry. He is the executive director of the Office for University Mission and Ministry, St. Xavier University, Chicago. Nancy is a choreographer, teacher of music and dance, and a school liturgist.

(continued from previous page)

and Chain-of-Custody Standard SAI-SFICOC-013349, confirming that the paper manufacturer takes a responsible approach to obtaining and managing the fiber. The wood fiber required for the making of this paper includes recycled content and was obtained from 100% responsible sources. Renewable and carbon-neutral biomass fuels are used for the energy needed in the paper manufacturing process, reducing the use of fossil fuels.

INTRODUCTION

The Role of the Reader

As readers of the Word, we share in a sacred process. "In Sacred Scripture, the Church constantly finds her nourishment and her strength, for she welcomes it not as a human word, but as what it really is, the Word of God" (1 Thessalonians 2:13; Second Vatican Council. *Dogmatic Constitution on Revelation [Dei Verbum]*, 24). "When the Sacred Scriptures are read in the Church, God himself speaks to his people, and Christ, present in his word, proclaims the Gospel. Therefore, the readings from the Word of God are to be listened to reverently by everyone, for they are an element of the greatest importance to the Liturgy" (*General Instruction of the Roman Missal*, 29). We who are privileged to read at the liturgy help to present the Word to the assembly.

We owe this privilege, as well as the insights just expressed, to the work of the Second Vatican Council, 1962–1965, which issued the *Dogmatic Constitution on Divine Revelation (Dei Verbum)* (quoted above) and the document that has most shaped our liturgical experience: the *Constitution on the Sacred Liturgy (Sacrosanctum Concilium)*. Among many contributions to the liturgy, it provided for a richer selection of Scripture to be read at Mass, it invited the laity into liturgical ministry, including the ministry of reader, and it urged everyone to listen attentively to the Word proclaimed, because "it is he [Christ] himself who speaks when the holy Scriptures are read in the Church" (7).

Our mission entails a great responsibility. At Mass, we serve as a bridge between the Scriptures and the faithful. In undertaking this sacred ministry, you are committing yourself to the preparation and discipline that enables Scripture to become a living Word. According to the Introduction to the *Lectionary for Mass*, this requires that "preparation must above all be spiritual, [though] . . . technical preparation is also needed" and "spiritual preparation presupposes at least a biblical and liturgical formation. . . . Biblical formation is to give readers the ability to understand the readings in context and to perceive . . . the central point of the revealed message. . . . Liturgical formation ought to equip readers to have some grasp of the meaning and structure of the liturgy of the word and of its connection with the Liturgy of the Eucharist. The technical preparation should make the readers more

skilled in the art of reading publicly" (55). Obviously, this responsibility requires serious effort.

Using This Book

Proclaiming Scripture is a ministry that involves your whole life. So make Scripture a part of your life each week, especially the week prior to proclaiming.

(1) Using this book, read all four Scriptures for your assigned Sunday. All were chosen for this day, so read them together. The Responsorial Psalm and Gospel can teach much about how the First Reading

> **In the beginning was the Word, and the Word was with God, and the Word was God.**

should be proclaimed. (2) Build your prayer for the week around the Scripture passage you will proclaim on Sunday. (3) As you are becoming familiar with your passage, read it directly from your Bible, reading also what comes before and after it to get a clear sense of its context. (4) Always read all three commentaries. Suggestions in each can help you with your own passage. As you read the commentaries, refer to the sections of the Scripture passage being discussed and make your own margin notations. (5) Read the Scriptures again using your margin notes and those printed in this book to remind you of the commentary suggestions. (6) Always read aloud, noticing suggestions for emphasis. After several readings, alter the emphasis markings to suit your own style and interpretation.

Workbook helps you prepare to *proclaim* your assigned reading, and it can also build your knowledge and skills when you use it every week to prepare to *hear* the readings. The commentaries deepen your understanding of Scripture and the proclamation advice in the margin notes helps you gradually absorb the skills you need to be a mature and seasoned proclaimer of the Word.

Using Additional Resources

The better you understand the meaning of your passage, the more effectively you will proclaim it and so help the assembly to understand it. Although the commentaries in this book will help you, readers may wish to dig deeper. Also, readers need to develop a lifelong habit of turning to the Scriptures for study and prayer. Additional resources that will help you to do this are listed in a downloadable file at http://www.ltp.org/t-productsupplements.aspx.

Appropriate Dramatic Technique

Good readers use techniques from the world of theater judiciously, not to draw attention to themselves, but to draw attention to the Word. When people experience good proclamation, they forget the reader in front of them and they hear the Scripture in a powerful way. That goal is best achieved by skillful use of all the available reading techniques. Of course, when readers are overly dramatic, and more focused on *how* they proclaim than on *what* they proclaim, listeners stop believing them. Artifice (an imitation of artfulness) can become an obstacle to good proclamation.

Avoiding artifice does not mean settling for colorless proclamation. Failing to use appropriate techniques can lead to mediocre reading that guarantees the Scripture will not be heard. Readers who cannot differentiate one character from another, who read too fast or too slowly, who have too little energy and don't use the colorful words of a passage, who read in a monotone without rising and falling dynamics and pacing—these readers only draw attention to themselves. The assembly cannot see beyond them. But really good proclaimers who utilize appropriate techniques draw the assembly into the reading.

True Humility. All readers need a model of true humility as they work toward excellence in proclamation. We look to Christ who "emptied himself, taking the form of a slave . . . [and] humbled himself, becoming obedient to death, even death on a cross" (Philippians 2:7–8). Jesus, the Word, humbles himself each Sunday by making himself dependent on us who proclaim him in the assembly. He depends on us to communicate him as a living and vital Word. Jesus, alive in every line of Scripture, is indeed obedient "unto death."

Reading as Interpretation

God's Word is "living and effective" (Hebrews 4:12) and it "goes forth from [God's] mouth . . . achieving the end for which [he] sent it" (Isaiah 55:11), yet we know that doesn't happen automatically. People must allow the Word to become a transforming influence in their lives. Before they can do that, readers must help them to hear it.

Reading is a form of interpretation. The same word spoken by two readers will not be "heard" in exactly the same way. Pacing, the words stressed, pauses, volume, tone color, and intensity are all elements that interpret the text. Your responsibility is to make sure your interpretation upholds the plain sense of the text, the author's clear intent, and that you enable the text to speak to everyone. God's Word can lose its power, beauty, and spiritual import if a reader fails to communicate the full content of a passage, which clearly consists of more than the words. Every text contains three kinds of content: intellectual-theological, emotional, and aesthetic.

Intellectual-theological content is what the text is about: the plot of the story, the points or details, behind which is a theological teaching or insight. Examples: Peter calls us to imitate Christ; Paul tells the Corinthians to stop feuding; Moses goes to Mt. Sinai to inaugurate the covenant; Jesus heals a blind man. **Emotional content** is how the author or characters "feel" (or want us to feel). When Juliet calls "O Romeo, Romeo! wherefore art thou, Romeo?" it is important to know she's not searching for him,

This is my commandment: love one another as I love you.

but lamenting that his name makes him one of her family's sworn enemies. The emotional content would be far different if she were searching for him. **Aesthetic content** refers to the artistic elements that make the writing pleasing, like metaphor, rhythm, repetition, suspense, picturesque language, and imagery. Shakespeare repeats Romeo's name as an aesthetic device to give emphasis. As readers, we must help our assemblies experience the beauty of the fine literature we call Scripture.

To acquire the intellectual-theological content, begin by reading the Scripture and the commentary. Next, search the text for the emotion the author is expressing: the emotional content. Finally, look for the author's aesthetic devices: repetition, simile, metaphor, irony, and so forth, the aesthetic content.

Tools of the Trade

Margin Notes serve as your coach, suggesting how to express the motivations of characters or author.

Build refers to increasing vocal intensity as you move toward a climactic point in the text. It calls for intensified emotional energy which can be communicated by an increase or decrease in volume or by speaking faster or slower. The point is to show more passion, greater urgency, or concern.

Stress (Bold Print) identifies words that are more important or expressive than others and require more stress. Use your judgment about the amount of stress so as to avoid an artificial delivery.

Echoes. Some words "echo" words that went before. For example, "You shall be a glorious crown . . . a royal diadem" (Isaiah 62:3). Here "diadem" echoes "crown" so it needs no stress. In such cases, emphasize the new idea: royal.

Words That Sound Like What They Mean don't require us to imitate the sound but to suggest it by stretching the word a bit. "Pop," "fizz," and "gulp" are obvious. Some are more subtle: "smashed," "vast," "in haste," "implore," "gleamed." They were chosen to convey meaning; let them do their work.

Word Value. "Shock" is always a more interesting word than "bean." "Shock" sounds like what it means and immediately conjures up vivid images. "Bean" won't even make your mouth water. Word value is also determined by context. The words "one, two, three" are neutral by themselves, but put in context they intensify: "Three seconds until lift-off! Three . . . two . . . !" If, in reading that sentence, "Three, two . . . " sounds the same as when followed by "buckle my shoe" you've got work to do. Words are your medium, like a painter's brush or a

sculptor's chisel. You must understand the words before you can communicate them. Most words have a dictionary meaning (denotative) and an associational meaning (connotative). "House" and "home" both mean "dwelling," yet they communicate different feelings. Be alert to subtle differences in connotative meanings and express them.

Separating Units of Thought with Pauses. Identify the units of thought in your text and use pauses to distinguish one from another. Running words together blurs meaning and fails to distinguish ideas. Punctuation does not always indicate clearly what words to group together or where to pause. The listener depends on you for this organization of ideas. With Paul, especially, carefully identify individual ideas and share them one at a time.

> **God so loved the world that he gave his only Son, so that everyone who believes in him might not perish but might have eternal life.**

Sense Lines. Scripture in this book is arranged (as in the Lectionary) in sense lines, one idea per line. Typically at least a slight pause should follow each line, but good reading requires you to recognize the need for other pauses within lines. Moving from one thought unit to another within a paragraph requires shifts in mood and pacing. Don't rush these transitions; honor them with a healthy pause.

Pauses are never "dead" moments. Something is always happening during a pause. Practice will teach you how often and how long to pause. Too many pauses make a reading choppy; too few cause ideas to run together. Too long a pause breaks the flow. If pauses are too short, your listeners will be struggling to keep up with you. A substantial pause always follows "A reading from . . ." and both precedes and follows "The word [Gospel] of the Lord."

Ritardando refers to the practice, common in music, of becoming gradually slower as you approach the end of a piece. On the final line of a song you automatically slow down and expand the words. Many readings end this way—with a decreased rate but increased intensity.

Characters. To distinguish the various characters that populate a passage, try to understand their thoughts, feelings, and motivations. Use subtle variations in pitch, pacing, and emotion to communicate them. But don't confuse proclamation with theatrics. Suggest characters, don't "become" them.

Narrator. Knowing the point of view the narrator is "rooting for" will help you more fully communicate the meaning of the text. The narrator always has a viewpoint, often speaking as a believer, not as an objective reporter. For this reason, the narrator is often the pivotal role in a passage. Using timbre, pitch, rate, and energy can help you convey the narrator's moods or meanings.

Openings and Closings are not part of the reading; they are liturgical dialogue between you and the assembly, so they differ in tone from the Scripture and require pauses, *after* the opening dialogue and *before* the closing dialogue. These formulas are prescribed, so don't vary the wording. **The opening:** First, establish eye contact and announce, from memory, "A reading from . . . ." Then take a pause (three full beats!) before starting the reading. The correct pronunciation is "A [uh] reading from . . ." instead of "A [ay] reading . . . ." **Character names** are often the first word of a reading, so lift out the names to ensure listeners don't miss who the subject is. **The closing:** Pause (three beats!) after ending the text, then, with sustained eye contact, announce from memory, "The word [Gospel] of the Lord." Always pronounce "the" as "thuh" except before words beginning with a vowel as in "thee Acts of the Apostles." Maintain eye contact while the assembly makes its response.

Follow the custom of your parish, but a substantial period of silence after each reading is recommended. Approach and depart from the ambo with reverence—neither too fast nor too slow.

Eye Contact and Eye Expression. Eye contact connects you with those to whom you minister. Look at the assembly during the middle and at the end of every thought or sentence. That means you look down at the beginning, look up in the middle, look down quickly as you approach the end, and then look up again as you finish the sentence. This "down, up, down, up" pattern must not appear mechanical or choppy. Keep a finger on the page to mark your position. Through meaningful "eye expression" you help the listeners enter the story.

Pace. The rate at which you read is influenced by the size of your church, the size of the congregation, and the complexity of the text. As each increases, rate decreases. Too slow is better than too fast. Your listeners have not spent time with this reading as you have. They need time to absorb it—to catch your words and comprehend what they mean.

However, too slow can also be deadly. Besides being boring and making every text sound the same, it erases the reading's natural cadences and makes it impossible to impart the passion of the author.

You'll read more naturally if you read ideas rather than words, if you share images rather than sentences. Dialogue imitates real conversation, so it often moves faster than the rest of the passage.

Lists. Whether proclaiming a genealogy or one of Paul's enumerations of virtues and sins, avoid the extremes of too much stress (slowly punctuating each word with equal stress) or too little (rushing through as if each item were the same).

Magnify the LORD with me; let us exalt his name together.

Using the Microphone. Know your public address system. If it echoes, speak even more slowly. If you hear "popping," you're probably standing too close to the microphone. If you are the first reader, go to the ambo before the start of Mass to adjust the height of the microphone. If you are proclaiming the second reading or Gospel, adjust the microphone position when you reach the ambo.

Gestures and Posture. Using gestures is not part of the task of proclamation; within the liturgy, gestures are an unnecessary distraction. However, your body language is always communicating. Avoid leaning on the ambo or standing on one foot. And don't let your face or body contradict the good news you announce. Readers are allowed to smile!

Pronunciation. Mispronunciations can be distracting for your listeners. Pronunciation aids are provided in the margin notes (see the key at the end of this introduction). You may also want to consult the LTP publication, *Pronunciation Guide to the Lectionary*. Various Internet pronunciation guides allow you to hear the word spoken aloud. Do a simple search such as: "Bible pronunciation guide."

The Responsorial Psalm

Because preparation for proclamation requires familiarity with all the day's texts, *Workbook* includes the psalm. Reflecting on it helps you see the connections among the texts and discern what to stress in your reading. In Sunday worship, the psalm should be sung, and its inclusion here is not meant to encourage its proclamation.

Giving Voice to God's Word

It is helpful to identify the literary form or genre of your reading. Is it a narrative (story or history), letter, or poetry (such as parts of Genesis or the prophets; the Psalms)? Each form possesses distinct characteristics that will influence your approach to the

Blessed are the poor in spirit, for theirs is the kingdom of heaven.

reading: plotlines and characters in stories; rhythm and rhyme in poetry. But simply identifying the form won't tell you all you need to know about the reading. One key to better understanding Scripture is to know who is speaking within a particular text. Recognizing the form puts you in the right neighborhood; next you want to pinpoint the house—the person speaking. The answer may not be obvious.

For example, even knowing you're reading from a letter by Paul doesn't tell you all you need to know, for Paul may be in various states of mind, even within the same letter. The circumstances about which Paul writes, his age and health at the time of writing, whether or not he is imprisoned at the time, and the emotions surrounding the situation he addresses all determine who the speaker is at that given moment. The Paul who writes to one community is not the same Paul who writes to another. That is also true of the prophets, and even of Jesus.

So determining that a text is a narrative, prophecy, or poetry is just your starting point. Next you must determine who the speaker is, why he or she is speaking, and how the speaker feels about what is spoken. By identifying the speaker, you automatically fine-tune your proclamation so that you avoid the all-too-common problem of delivering two different passages in the same way. You will adjust your tone, pacing, energy, and mood to fit the identity and mood of the speaker. With that in mind, read the following discussions of the "neighborhoods" we call stories, epistles, prophecy, and poetry. Remember that your goal is not simply finding the right neighborhood but entering the home of the one who speaks your text.

Stories. Stories must be "told," not "read." You don't have to memorize them, but you do have to tell them. You are the storyteller. Make the story yours, then share it with your listeners.

Know the story and its context—what precedes and follows it. Know the significance of the events for the characters involved. Understand the chronology of the plot. Identify the climax and employ your best energy there. Use the language. Don't throw away any good words.

Settings give context for the action and usually appear at the beginning. Don't rush the description.

Characters must be believable. Understand their motivation: why they feel, act, and speak as they do. Characters are often identified in relationship to another character: "the parents of the one who had gained his sight" (John 9:18). Stress those identifying words. Create the characters as distinct individuals, changing inflection and tone of voice for each one.

Dialogue reveals character. What a character says and how are nearly infallible clues to personality. Besides subtly distinguishing one character from another with your voice, learn to let the speakers listen to and answer one another as in real conversation. Bring the dialogue to life and build suspense in the story, revealing one detail at a time.

Epistles. Epistles are simply letters. Know who wrote the letter and who received it. Many biblical resources explain the circumstances in which the letter was written. Whether addressed to an individual or to a community, each epistle is also addressed to the faithful gathered in your church. *The tone* of each letter may vary, but the delivery is always direct. Letters are like conversations between the writer and the person or community addressed. *The purpose* or intent of each letter dictates the tone. Very often Paul is the writer. As teacher and spiritual leader, he is motivated by multiple concerns: to

The LORD's word is true; all his works are trustworthy.

instruct, console, encourage, chastise, warn, settle disputes, and more. When reading from one of his letters, be aware of what he's trying to accomplish and which hat he's wearing: teacher, coach, father-figure, disciplinarian, and so forth. Paul is always direct and earnest; even when he exhorts, he never stops loving his spiritual children.

Go slowly in the epistles. The assembly needs time to catch the ideas you toss at them. Paul's theology can be tricky, and the style is often a tangle of complex sentences. Many times his mood and purpose change within a single passage. Remembering how seriously Paul took his role will help keep you from rushing. Love your listeners and desire their good as much as Paul and the other letter-writers do.

Prophetic Writing. The intensity of emotion and degree of urgency required in proclaiming the writing of the prophets make some readers uncomfortable. But their urgency can't be compromised. A pervasive theme in the Old Testament is that we are chosen. With election comes responsibility. Prophets were to remind the Chosen People about those responsibilities—not a popular task. Though not shown in the text, prophetic words are spoken with vocal exclamation points. One must work up courage to tell people what they don't want to hear. With equal passion the great seers spoke threat and consolation, indictment and forgiveness. You must do the

same for the Chosen People you call "parish." It is a grave disservice to the prophets and their ministry to fail to distinguish consolation from indictment, letting all their words sound the same.

As with the epistles, use resources to learn the situation in which a prophet ministers. Prophets vary; be attentive to style as well as content. Beware of fast transitions, instant climaxes, and the frequent lack of conclusions. Willingly or reluctantly prophets were compelled to speak for God. Don't rob them of their intensity. We need to hear their words.

Poetry. The Old Testament contains much poetry—a marvelously effective and economical form of communication. Because the carefully crafted words and images are so rich and evocative, poetry makes special demands on the proclaimer.

Take time. Poetry is gourmet food, eaten slowly and savored. Go slowly with readings like this passage from Baruch for the Second Sunday of Advent, Year C (Baruch 5:8-9): "The forests and every fragrant kind of tree / have overshadowed Israel at God's command; / For God is leading Israel in joy / by the light of his glory, / with his mercy and justice for company." You need to respond to images by letting yourself "hear" and "feel" as well as "see." Word choice in poetry affects meaning because it affects sound and rhythm.

Sound and meaning go hand in hand in poetry. Even in a language you don't understand, the sound of well-recited poetry should touch your emotions.

Rhythm is what distinguishes poetry from prose. It's what makes words sound like music. Compare these two verses: "In times past, God spoke in partial and various ways to our ancestors through the prophets" (Hebrews 1:1), and "For Zion's sake I will not be silent, for Jerusalem's sake I will not be quiet" (Isaiah 62:1). The first line is smooth and flat, but the second has a rhythmic beat flowing through it that makes it exciting.

Repetition abounds in poetry. Yet instead of feeling redundant, repetitions intensify our emotional experience.

In Hebrew poetry, *parallelism* is a technique used to repeat, balance, and develop ideas in a poem. Consider this first verse of Psalm 19: "The heavens declare the glory of God; / the sky proclaims its builder's craft." Two parallel images express *one* idea. Since the two thoughts mean the same thing, this is *synonymous parallelism*. In *antithetic parallelism*, opposing images express one idea. Proverbs 15:15 says: "Every day is miserable for the depressed, / but a lighthearted person has a continual feast."

Contrasting ideas make a similar point. Identifying such parallelism helps you decide what words to stress or balance. Look for these and other forms of poetry. Enjoy the language and give it time to do its work.

Graziano Marcheschi

An Option to Consider

The third edition of *The Roman Missal* encourages ministers of the Word to chant the introduction and conclusion to the readings ("A reading from . . . "; "The word of the Lord."). For those parishes wishing to use these chants, they are demonstrated in audio files that may be accessed either through the QR codes given here (with a smart phone) or through the URL indicated beneath the code. (This url is case sensitive, and be careful to distinguish between the letter l (lower case L) and the numeral 1.)

The first QR code contains the tones for the First Reading in both a male and a female voice.

http://bit.ly/l2mjeG

The second QR code contains the tones for the Second Reading in both a male and a female voice.

http://bit.ly/krwEYy

The third QR code contains the simple tone for the Gospel.

http://bit.ly/iZZvSg

The fourth QR code contains the solemn tone for the Gospel.

http://bit.ly/lwf6Hh

A fuller explanation of this new practice, along with musical notation for the chants, is provided in a downloadable PDF file found at http://www.ltp. org/t-productsupplements.aspx. Once you arrive at this web page, scroll until you find the image of the cover of *Workbook*, click on it, and the PDF file will appear.

Pronunciation Key

bait = bayt	thin = thin
cat = kat	vision = VIZH*n
sang = sang	ship = ship
father = FAH-<u>th</u>er	sir = ser
care = kayr	gloat = gloht
paw = paw	cot = kot
jar = jahr	noise = noyz
easy = EE-zee	poison = POY-z*n
her = her	plow = plow
let = let	although = ahl-<u>TH</u>OH
queen = kween	church = cherch
delude = deh-L<u>OO</u>D	fun = fuhn
when = hwen	fur = fer
ice = īs	flute = fl<u>oo</u>t
if = if	foot = foot
finesse = fih-NES	

Recommended Works

Find a list of recommended reading in a downloadable PDF file at http://www.ltp.org/t-product supplements.aspx.

FIRST SUNDAY OF ADVENT

LECTIONARY #2

READING I   Isaiah 63:16b–17, 19b; 64:2–7

A reading from the Book of the Prophet Isaiah

You, LORD, are our **father**,
    our **redeemer** you are named **forever**.
Why do you let us **wander**, O LORD, from your ways,
    and harden our **hearts** so that we fear you **not**?
Return for the sake of your **servants**,
    the tribes of your **heritage**.
Oh, that you would rend the heavens and come down,
    with the mountains quaking before you,
while you wrought awesome deeds we could not hope for,
    such as they had not **heard** of from of old.
No ear has ever heard, no eye ever seen, any God but you
    doing such deeds for those who wait for him.
Would that you might meet us doing **right**,
    that we were **mindful** of you in our ways!
Behold, you are **angry**, and we are **sinful**;
    all of us have become like **unclean** people,
    all our good **deeds** are like polluted **rags**;
we have all **withered** like leaves,
    and our **guilt** carries us away like the **wind**.
There is **none** who calls upon your **name**,
    who **rouses** himself to **cling** to you;
for you have **hidden** your face from us
    and have delivered us up to our **guilt**.

Isaiah = ī-ZAY-uh
From the start, the tone is one of repentance.

The anger is self-directed, not aimed at God. Think of a child saying to a parent, "Why didn't you stop me?"

The people's awareness of their guilt fuels the passion in these lines. It's the plea of those desperately seeking another chance.

"No ear . . . no eye" is one idea; stress instead God's unique character.

From repentance, the cry shifts to desire for a sharp turn away from sin.

Note and use the strong language: "polluted rags," "withered . . . leaves."

The passage reaches a more serious and sobering tone.

God never withdraws from us; these lines reflect the attitude of the speaker who is admitting guilt.

READING I The season of Advent begins our new liturgical year. Advent focuses on the two "comings" of Christ: his birth (Incarnation) and his return (Second Coming). It is a season of waiting for the presence of the Lord.

So it is fitting that our First Reading for Advent is a prayer of petition for the Lord to reveal his presence. Speaking probably near the end of Israel's exile in Babylon (587–538 BC), Isaiah prays for the Lord to reveal himself to the captive Israelites. In his prayer, Isaiah recalls how God made his presence known in past mighty deeds and implores the Lord to make his presence known once again to his people. Having been in exile for many years, Isaiah acknowledges Israel's collective sense of guilt and shame over the sins that led to their captivity in Babylon: "All of us have become like unclean people, all our good deeds are like polluted rags." In his prayer, Isaiah captures the despair of a people in captivity: "There is none who calls upon your name, who rouses himself to cling to you; for you have hidden your face from us."

Isaiah draws his prayer to a close with a beautiful metaphor for Israel's relationship with the Lord: "We are the clay, and you are our potter; we are all the work of your hands." Isaiah concedes Israel must wait for the Lord to reveal his presence according to his own timeline.

READING II Paul's letters routinely open with a greeting and a thanksgiving. Most of today's reading is taken from Paul's thanksgiving to the members of the church in Corinth. Although this letter is titled "First Corinthians," it is not

God's true nature is presented here; our sins never cancel God's love or willingness to forgive.

Yet, O LORD, you are our **father**;
  we are the **clay** and you the **potter**:
  we are **all** the work of your **hands**.

For meditation and context:

RESPONSORIAL PSALM   Psalm 80:2–3, 15–16, 18–19 (4)

R. Lord, make us turn to you; let us see your face and we shall be saved.

O shepherd of Israel, hearken,
  from your throne upon the cherubim,
    shine forth.
Rouse your power,
  and come to save us.

Once again, O LORD of hosts,
  look down from heaven, and see;
take care of this vine,
  and protect what your right hand
    has planted,
  the son of man whom you yourself
    made strong.

May your help be with the man of your
    right hand,
  with the son of man whom you yourself
    made strong.
Then we will no more withdraw from you;
  give us new life, and we will call upon
    your name.

TO KEEP IN MIND
Dialogue imitates real conversation, so it often moves faster than the rest of the passage.

READING II   1 Corinthians 1:3–9

Corinthians = kohr-IN-thee-uhnz

The greeting is upbeat and joyful. Deliver it from memory, sustaining eye contact.

This long sentence contains seven clauses that build toward the end. You could remove the lines between the first and last and have a complete sentence, so those in between are subordinate clauses that can be read at a somewhat faster pace. Paul is praising the people whom he holds dear, so keep the tone light and hopeful.

A reading from the first Letter of Saint Paul to the Corinthians

Brothers and sisters:
Grace to you and **peace** from God our Father
  and the Lord Jesus **Christ**.

I give **thanks** to my God **always** on your account
  for the **grace** of God bestowed on you in Christ **Jesus**,
  that in **him** you were **enriched** in every way,
  with all **discourse** and all **knowledge**,
  as the testimony to Christ was **confirmed** among you,
  so that you are not **lacking** in any spiritual **gift**
  as you wait for the **revelation** of our Lord Jesus **Christ**.

---

the first letter exchanged between Paul and the Corinthians. Later in First Corinthians, Paul indicates that he wrote a previous letter to them ("I wrote to you in my letter not to associate with immoral people," 5:9), and the Corinthians themselves wrote to Paul ("Now in regard to the matters about which you wrote . . ." 7:1). These letters, unfortunately, have been lost.

The references to these previous exchanges indicate that Paul had some considerable history with the Christians

in Corinth even prior to writing First Corinthians. In the thanksgiving, Paul's flattering descriptions of the Corinthians as "enriched in every way, with all discourse and all knowledge . . . not lacking in any spiritual gift" likely come from his direct and personal experience of the congregation. But Paul makes it clear that while the Corinthians have much to be proud of, the gifts of the Church come from "the grace of God" and are intended to prepare the Corinthians for "the day of our Lord Jesus Christ," the return of Christ at the end of time.

In this regard, Paul asserts a central component to his overall theological framework: "God is faithful." In the Death, Resurrection, and final return of Christ, God has fulfilled the covenants he established with Israel. God's desire is for everyone to share "fellowship with his Son," both now in the present moment, and in the future, at the Second Coming.

He will keep you **firm** to the **end**,
    irreproachable on the day of our Lord Jesus Christ.
God is **faithful**,
    and by **him** you were called to **fellowship** with his **Son**,
Jesus **Christ** our **Lord**.

Like a coach before a game, Paul assures them they can hold "firm to the end." But the reason is God's faithful love, not our abilities.

GOSPEL   Mark 13:33–37

A reading from the holy Gospel according to Mark

Jesus said to his **disciples**:
"Be **watchful**! Be **alert**!
You do not **know** when the time will come.
It is like a man traveling **abroad**.
He **leaves** home and places his **servants** in charge,
    each with his own **work**,
    and orders the gatekeeper to be on the **watch**.
Watch, therefore;
    you do not **know** when the lord of the house is coming,
    whether in the **evening**, or at **midnight**,
    or at **cockcrow**, or in the **morning**.
May he not come **suddenly** and find you **sleeping**.
What I say to **you**, I say to **all**: '**Watch**!'"

Jesus's tone is intentionally alarmist: he wants us to be ready for the unexpected hour, so he shakes us up to wake us up!

Don't lapse into a neutral tone; the urgency perdures.

Tell the story in the persona of the homeowner giving orders to the "servants" and "gatekeeper." Each of the four time-words ("evening," "midnight," "cockcrow," "morning") conveys a distinctive mood. Use them to reinforce our inability to predict the master's return.

Here, "sleeping" carries a negative connotation of being unaware and negligent.

Take a substantial pause before speaking the word, "Watch!" Don't forget that great love is what motivates Jesus's urgent call to vigilance.

TO KEEP IN MIND
Stress (Bold Print): identifies words that are more important or expressive than others and require more stress. Use your judgment about the amount of stress so as to avoid an artificial delivery.

GOSPEL   This Gospel Reading is the ending of Jesus's eschatological (eschaton = end time) discourse with his Apostles. (see Mark 13:3-37 for the full discourse). According to Mark, prior to his Passion, Death, and Resurrection, Jesus spoke to Peter, Andrew, James, and John about events associated with the end of time, including signs of the times (false messiahs, wars, earthquakes, and famines), persecutions, tribulations, and finally the return of the Son of Man to gather his elect and begin the new age.

In today's reading, Jesus forewarns the four apostles, "Be watchful! Be alert!" since no one knows when the end-time will arrive. He offers the Apostles, by way of example, the parable of the wise traveler who properly arranges for his house to be safely guarded while away. The servants and the gatekeepers are trusted to watch over the house until the man's return. They will receive their just reward provided they remain diligent in their duties until the Lord of the house returns. Jesus concludes by offering a sobering prayer of petition: "May he not come suddenly and find you sleeping."

Jesus's command to his original Apostles applies to Christians of all ages, since by our baptismal call we are the "servants" and "gatekeepers" of the Lord's house. We, too, are challenged to remain alert and "Watch!" for the coming of the Lord at the end-time. The season of Advent reminds us at the start of each new liturgical year to remain faithful to our fundamental duty to be watchful and alert for the coming of our Lord Jesus Christ.

SECOND SUNDAY OF ADVENT

LECTIONARY #5

READING I   Isaiah 40:1–5, 9–11

A reading from the Book of the Prophet Isaiah

Comfort, give **comfort** to my people,
    says your God.
Speak **tenderly** to Jerusalem, and **proclaim** to her
    that her **service** is at an **end**,
    her **guilt** is **expiated**;
indeed, she has received from the hand of the Lord
    double for all her sins.

    A **voice** cries out:
In the desert **prepare** the way of the Lord!
    Make **straight** in the wasteland a **highway** for our **God**!
Every **valley** shall be filled **in**,
    every **mountain** and **hill** shall be made **low**;
the **rugged** land shall be made a **plain**,
    the **rough** country, a broad **valley**.
Then the **glory** of the Lord shall be **revealed**,
    and all people shall see it **together**;
    for the mouth of the Lord has **spoken**.

Isaiah = i-ZAY-uh

The sound of words always carries a large percentage of a text's meaning, especially when the text is poetry. Isaiah's poetry is meant to "comfort" and it should be spoken "tenderly."

These words announce the end of Israel's collective guilt and national exile, but they also speak to us as individuals about God's mercy and readiness to forgive.

Be sure to stress the bounty of God's mercy.

Take a substantial pause to transition to the new unit that begins here.

Note the voice is not in the "desert": the "desert" is the place within our hearts where we must make a "way" for the Lord.

The good news of God's coming should rouse us to action, clearing away any clutter that stands between us and God.

The joyful sound of these metaphors is more important than their literal meaning.

Imagine this glorious scene and call us to believe because "the mouth of the *Lord* has spoken."

READING I The Book of Isaiah, the longest book of the Bible, contains sixty-six chapters divided into three sections, each written at different times in Israel's history. Chapters 1–39 contain oracles and prophecies from the prophet Isaiah who was active in the southern kingdom of Judah, around the years 740–700 BC. The material included in the "Immanuel Prophecies" (Isaiah 7–12) is familiar to many Christians from Scripture readings heard in late Advent and Christmas Time. Chapters 40–55 were written about 200 years later, toward the end of Israel's exile in Babylon,

around 550 BC. The oracles and songs from these chapters are attributed to an unknown prophet commonly called Second Isaiah. This section contains the four well-known "Servant of the Lord" oracles (Isaiah 42:1–4, 49:1–7, 50:4–11, heard on Palm Sunday; and 52:13—53:12, heard on Good Friday). The remaining chapters of the book, Isaiah 56–66 (also heard at Advent-Christmas Time), are a compilation of oracles and prophecies written soon after the return of the Israelites from captivity in Babylon, post-538 BC.

Knowing about this historical division of the Book of Isaiah helps us see why today's reading is significant: these are the opening words of Second Isaiah. It's likely that the final editors who arranged the prophetic books saw Second Isaiah's message of comfort and expiation of sin in today's reading as part of the central theme of his prophetic ministry.

During their time of exile in Babylon, Israel had two prophets in their midst: Ezekiel (early in the exile) and Second Isaiah (late in the exile). These two prophets stand unique in Israel's classical prophetic period:

As these words were once addressed to "Zion" and "Jerusalem," they are now addressed to your assembly.

Speak with the authority and conviction of the prophet.

Isaiah blends images of God's power and mercy.

Stress the nouns, not the prepositions in these two lines.

The shepherd is known by his sheep, who recognize his voice and trust him; it is an image of authority and tenderness.

Go up onto a high **mountain**,
   Zion, herald of glad **tidings**;
cry out at the top of your voice,
   Jerusalem, herald of good **news**!
Fear **not** to cry out
   and **say** to the cities of Judah:
   Here is your **God**!
Here comes with **power**
   the Lord G**OD**,
   who rules by his strong **arm**;
here is his **reward** with him,
   his **recompense** before him.
Like a **shepherd** he feeds his **flock**;
   in his **arms** he gathers the **lambs**,
carrying them in his **bosom**,
   and **leading** the ewes with **care**.

For meditation and context:

RESPONSORIAL PSALM   Psalm 85:9–10, 11–12, 13–14 (8)

R. Lord, let us see your kindness, and grant us your salvation.

I will hear what God proclaims;
   the LORD—for he proclaims peace to
      his people.
Near indeed is his salvation to those who
      fear him,
   glory dwelling in our land.

Kindness and truth shall meet;
   justice and peace shall kiss.
Truth shall spring out of the earth,
   and justice shall look down from heaven.

The LORD himself will give his benefits;
   our land shall yield its increase.
Justice shall walk before him,
   and prepare the way of his steps.

TO KEEP IN MIND

When practicing, **read Scriptures aloud**, taking note of stress and pause suggestions. After several readings, alter the stress markings to suit your style and interpretation.

---

they were the only two called to prophecy outside Jerusalem or its surrounding region. Second Isaiah prophesied an almost unthinkable message of hope to the captive Israelites: the time of exile had come to a close. God had forgiven Israel of her sins, and was calling Israel back to the Promised Land. Israel's long wait in exile, spanning two generations, was finally coming to an end.

 READING II Second Peter is widely regarded by scholars as the last written book of the New Testament,

produced in the early second century, around AD 125. The focus of today's reading is one reason scholars date this letter so late: an explanation for the "delay" in the return of Christ.

The first generation of Christians, which included Peter and Paul, had a strong conviction in the imminent return of Christ within their own lifetime. With the death of most of the original Apostles in the 60s (around thirty years after the Resurrection), and the destruction of the city of Jerusalem and the Temple in AD 70 during the Jewish-Roman War, expectations for an imminent

return of Christ began to fade into an indeterminate future. This, in part, motivated the writing of the New Testament Gospel accounts by the next generation of Christians. With the Apostles gone, and Jesus not yet returned, Christians were eager to keep the Good News of Jesus Christ alive, and the Gospel writers were obviously successful in doing so.

But as the Second Letter of Peter shows, questions still remained about the "delay" on the return of Christ, even among third-generation Christians. The author of Second Peter addresses the concerns first

The first point comes immediately, so read the first line slowly to set it up.

Don't overstress the time-related words; it's not the literal meaning that matters but the point that God's measure differs from ours. This is reassuring instruction.

The urgency intensifies here and your tempo can quicken as you move through the sentence with increased volume.

The mood shifts back to instruction. Imagine a question mark after "ought you to be," and then offer what follows as the answer to the question.

This is not a pretty picture!

Despite the warning that just preceded, we remain hopeful and upbeat.

The final line is an exhortation. Make eye contact and speak with conviction that all must work diligently to be ready when he comes.

> TO KEEP IN MIND
> **Pauses are never "dead" moments.** Something is always happening during a pause. Practice will teach you how often and how long to pause. Too many pauses make a reading choppy; too few cause ideas to run into one another.

READING II   2 Peter 3:8–14

A reading from the second Letter of Saint Peter

Do not **ignore** this one fact, beloved,
　　that with the **Lord** one **day** is like a thousand **years**
　　and a **thousand** years like one day.
The Lord does not **delay** his promise, as **some** regard "delay,"
　　but he is **patient** with you,
　　not wishing that **any** should perish
　　but that **all** should come to **repentance**.
But the **day** of the Lord will come like a **thief**,
　　and then the heavens will pass **away** with a mighty **roar**
　　and the **elements** will be dissolved by **fire**,
　　and the **earth** and everything **done** on it will be found **out**.

Since everything is to be **dissolved** in this way,
　　what sort of **persons** ought you to be,
　　conducting yourselves in **holiness** and **devotion**,
　　waiting for and **hastening** the coming of the day of God,
　　because of which the **heavens** will be dissolved in **flames**
　　and the **elements** melted by **fire**.
But according to his **promise**
　　we await **new** heavens and a new **earth**
　　in which **righteousness** dwells.
Therefore, beloved, since you **await** these things,
　　be **eager** to be found without **spot** or **blemish** before him,
　　　at **peace**.

---

by assuring his readers that "the Lord does not delay his promise." Time is a matter of perspective. Although it may seem to have been a long time since the promise of Christ's return, from God's perspective, "a thousand years [are] like one day." Second Peter employs a second strategy: he reminds his readers of the tradition they received about the return of Christ: "the day of the Lord will come like a thief." So, be prepared by living a good and holy life until that day when the Lord does return in glory.

Second Peter concludes his response to concerns about the delay in the Second Coming by imploring his readers to "await" patiently, trusting in the Lord's promise. And most importantly, be found "at peace" when the Lord does return to usher in "new heavens and a new earth."

GOSPEL   Each of the four Gospel writers was faced with the decision of how to begin telling their story of the Good News of Jesus Christ. Mark opens his account, not with the birth stories of Jesus (as in the Gospel accounts of Matthew 1:1—2:23 and Luke 1:5—2:52), or with a Christological hymn (the Gospel according to John 1:1–18), but with the figure of John the Baptist. Whether Mark does not know the details of the birth and early years of Jesus, or knows and chooses not to include these details about Jesus, is uncertain. What is known is that Mark begins his Gospel account with Jesus as an adult, connecting Jesus with the preaching and activities of John the Baptist in Judea.

Mark sees the ministry of John the Baptist, characterized by "a baptism of

GOSPEL   Mark 1:1–8

A reading from the holy Gospel according to Mark

The **beginning** of the **gospel** of Jesus Christ the Son of **God**.

As it is written in **Isaiah** the **prophet**:
> **Behold**, *I am sending my **messenger** ahead of you;*
> *he will **prepare** your way.*
> *A **voice** of one crying out in the **desert**:*
> *"Prepare the way of the **Lord**,*
> *make **straight** his paths."*

John the **Baptist** appeared in the **desert**
> proclaiming a baptism of **repentance** for the forgiveness of **sins**.

People of the whole Judean countryside
> and all the inhabitants of **Jerusalem**
> were going **out** to him
> and were being **baptized** by him in the Jordan **River**
> as they acknowledged their **sins**.

John was clothed in **camel's** hair,
> with a leather **belt** around his waist.

He fed on **locusts** and wild **honey**.

And this is what he **proclaimed**:
> "One **mightier** than I is coming **after** me.

I am not **worthy** to stoop and loosen the thongs of his **sandals**.

I have baptized you with **water**;
> **he** will baptize you with the Holy **Spirit**."

Mark's simple but elegant opening should be spoken with dignity.

Pause after introducing the Isaiah quotation, and then speak his words in a slow and deliberate manner.

Note the difference in the quote from Isaiah: here the "desert" is where the prophet speaks rather than the place where we prepare the way.

John is a major figure in the Advent season and in Jesus's early ministry.

Judean = joo-DEE-un

Jerusalem = juh-ROO-suh-lem

Let your tone convey the significance of John's ministry.

Make good use of the details Mark provides about John's appearance and lifestyle.

These words reveal the depth of insight and humility with which John was graced. Don't rush.

Contrast "water" (unremarkable) with Jesus's "Holy Spirit" (life-changing).

> **TO KEEP IN MIND**
> You'll read more naturally if you read **ideas rather than words**, and if you share **images rather than sentences**.

---

repentance for the forgiveness of sins," as fulfilling the prophecies of Isaiah and Malachi. He also describes the appearance of John the Baptist in a way reminiscent of the prophet Elijah (see 2 Kings 1:8). Connecting John the Baptist to the greatest of Israel's prophets lays the foundation for Mark's theological conviction that the message and activities of John the Baptist were to be understood in the context of Israel's prophetic tradition. Further, John the Baptist's humility ("One mightier than I is coming after me. I am not worthy to stoop and loosen the thongs of his sandals.") highlights his role in salvation history as the forerunner to announce the good news that Israel's long wait for the Messiah was nearly over.

John's insistence that "I have baptized you with water; he will baptize you with the Holy Spirit" points to a clear distinction between John and the coming Messiah. John's baptism merely *cleanses* one from sin, but Jesus comes to *purify* us for God's holy presence. This was an important distinction to be made, since many of those original eyewitnesses wondered and even questioned whether John himself was the Messiah (see Luke 3:15; John 1:20). In the first century AD, many in Israel longed for the Messiah and the messianic age that would reveal God's presence in a new and definitive way. We Christians structure our liturgical year to begin with this same hope. During Advent, we continue to wait in eager expectation for God's holy presence.

THE IMMACULATE CONCEPTION OF THE BLESSED VIRGIN MARY

LECTIONARY #689

READING I   Genesis 3:9–15, 20

Genesis = JEN-uh-sis

This familiar story is a privilege to proclaim. As you tell the story, create characters, not caricatures. Adam and Eve are fully aware and very good at passing the buck. God's voice conveys divine disappointment and clear authority.

The opening question betrays no divine agenda.

Adam is hiding his guilt as well as his "nakedness"; that's the word that gives him away, so stress it.

God's reply might be as much a question as a statement.

Adam is not posturing; he really believes Eve is to blame.

Eve makes no effort to deny, but lithely shifts the blame.

The consequences of their disobedience are visited first upon the serpent. Avoid a menacing tone in God's voice; instead, let the tone convey God's solicitousness for the woman and man who were deceived.

This punishment is well deserved. It is justice, not retribution.

A reading from the Book of Genesis

After the man, **Adam**, had **eaten** of the **tree**,
    the LORD God **called** to the man and **asked** him,
        "Where **are** you?"
He answered, "I **heard** you in the **garden**;
    but I was **afraid**, because I was **naked**,
    so I **hid** myself."
Then he asked, "Who **told** you that you were naked?
You have **eaten**, then,
    from the **tree** of which I had **forbidden** you to eat!"
The man **replied**, "The **woman** whom **you** put here with me—
    she **gave** me fruit from the tree, and so I **ate** it."
The LORD God then asked the **woman**,
    "Why did you **do** such a thing?"
The woman **answered**, "The **serpent tricked** me into it,
    so I **ate** it."

Then the LORD God said to the **serpent**:
    "Because you have **done** this, you shall be **banned**
        from all the **animals**
        and from all the wild **creatures**;
    on your **belly** shall you crawl,
        and **dirt** shall you eat
        all the **days** of your **life**.

READING I The Bible begins with two creation stories. The first (Genesis 1:1–2:4a) presents God's six-day creation of the universe. The second (Genesis 2:4b—3:24) focuses on God's creation of humanity and humanity's subsequent fall and expulsion from the Garden of Eden. The First Reading is an excerpt from the second creation story, where God discovers that Adam and Eve, tricked by the serpent, disobeyed him and ate fruit from the tree of the knowledge of good and bad. Although Adam and Eve experienced consequences from God for their sin of disobedience (Genesis 3:16–19), today's reading highlights the consequence for the serpent of his deception: an eternal "enmity" (hostility, antagonism) between the woman and her offspring and the serpent and its offspring.

It is no accident that the Bible begins with these two creation stories. When, around 400 BC, the first five books of the Bible (often referred to as the Pentateuch) were assembled, the unknown, inspired ancient editors arranged these texts in the order we find today. From these two creation stories, we learn numerous important lessons that frame the interpretation of the rest of the Bible. First, God is the source and creator of all things. Second, everything that God created is "good." Third, humanity—man and woman—is created in God's "image." Fourth, although made in God's image, humanity is marked with the sin of disobedience. Fifth, there are forces outside ourselves that seek to separate us from God.

These lines are the reason this text is read today. Mary is "the woman" (the new Eve) who will help repair the damage done in the garden.

Contrast the snake's *futile* strikes at "his heel" with the offspring's damaging blows to the serpent's "head."

Pause before this final line. As Eve became mother of all, so the new Eve, Mary, becomes the universal Mother.

I will put **enmity** between you and the **woman**,
  and between **your** offspring and **hers**;
he will strike at your **head**,
  while **you** strike at his **heel**."

The man called his wife **Eve**,
  because she became the **mother** of **all** the **living**.

RESPONSORIAL PSALM   Psalm 98:1, 2–3ab, 3cd–4 (1a)

R. Sing to the Lord a new song, for he has done marvelous deeds.

Sing to the LORD a new song,
  for he has done wondrous deeds;
His right hand has won victory for him,
  his holy arm.

The LORD has made his salvation known:
  in the sight of the nations he has revealed
    his justice.
He has remembered his kindness and his
    faithfulness
  toward the house of Israel.

All the ends of the earth have seen
  the salvation by our God.
Sing joyfully to the LORD, all you lands;
  break into song; sing praise.

For meditation and context:

TO KEEP IN MIND

Know who wrote the letter and who received it. Discover the circumstances. **The intent of each letter dictates the tone.** Often Paul is the writer; he is motivated by multiple concerns: to instruct, console, encourage, chastise, warn, settle disputes, and more. When reading from one of his letters, be aware of what he's trying to accomplish.

Ephesians = ee-FEE-zhuhnz

The text begins as a prayer, so pray it. The words are full of gratitude.

Don't rush these lines that tell us what to be grateful for.

By pausing after "in love," you will draw attention to what it is that motivates God.

This is a long, tricky sentence. The main point is at the start: God "destined us for adoption . . . through Jesus Christ." The clauses that follow are explanations that can be read briskly.

READING II   Ephesians 1:3–6, 11–12

A reading from the Letter of Saint Paul to the Ephesians

Brothers and **sisters**:
Blessed be the **God** and **Father** of our Lord Jesus **Christ**,
  who has **blessed** us in Christ
  with every spiritual **blessing** in the heavens,
  as he **chose** us in him, before the **foundation** of the world,
  to be **holy** and without **blemish** before him.
In **love** he destined us for **adoption** to himself through
    Jesus **Christ**,
  in accord with the favor of his **will**,
  for the **praise** of the **glory** of his **grace**
  that he **granted** us in the **beloved**.

The story of Adam and Eve teaches us that the struggle we all face in our daily living, to obey God and order our lives according to his will, is fundamental to our human nature. This tension connects us as a human family—to ourselves, and to each other, all the way back to Eve, "the mother of all the living."

READING II The Second Reading is taken from the opening verses to Paul's Letter to the Ephesians. The tone and tenor of this reading is quite a

contrast to the First Reading. Words such as "banned" and "enmity" are replaced with "chose" and "spiritual blessing."

Unlike most of Paul's letters that open with a greeting and a thanksgiving, Ephesians substitutes the thanksgiving with an extended blessing that recounts God's plan of salvation for us (see Ephesians 1:3–14). The blessing has a three-fold structure, addressing God the Father (verses 3–6), Christ (verses 7–12), and the Holy Spirit (verses 13–14). Over time, the early Church drew upon these types of Pauline formulas in developing a clear Trinitarian

theology—our belief in God as Three Persons in One: Father, Son, and Holy Spirit.

Ephesians begins with exuberance, blessing *God* for the abundance of the blessings that we have received in Christ. The letter then makes a remarkable claim: God "chose us . . . before the foundation of the world, to be holy and without blemish." Our state of holiness is not obtained, however, by our own merit or simply by our human nature; rather, through our faith in Jesus Christ, we receive an "adoption" as children of God. Ephesians speaks of this

Don't let "Chosen" and "destined" sound redundant; build from one to the other. "In him" and "the One" refer to Christ and God the Father respectively.

Our acceptance of grace glorifies God

In **him** we were also **chosen**,
　　destined in accord with the purpose of the One
　　who **accomplishes** all things according to the intention
　　　　of his **will**,
　　so that we might **exist** for the praise of his **glory**,
　　we who **first** hoped in **Christ**.

GOSPEL　Luke 1:26–38

A reading from the holy Gospel according to Luke

There are eight pieces of information shared in this first sentence. Don't rush, but avoid a choppy delivery as well.

The name "Mary" climaxes this sentence. Take a brief pause.

The angel's words are a greeting, not the prayer formula we're used to.

The narration should communicate the distress the angel's words evoke in Mary.

"Do not be afraid" is a frequent New Testament theme. The angel's goal is to reassure so that Mary can hear his unsettling message.

The angel **Gabriel** was sent from **God**
　　to a town of **Galilee** called **Nazareth**,
　　to a **virgin** betrothed to a man named **Joseph**,
　　of the house of **David**,
　　and the virgin's name was **Mary**.
And **coming** to her, he said,
　　"**Hail**, full of **grace**! The **Lord** is with you."
But she was greatly **troubled** at what was said
　　and **pondered** what sort of greeting this might be.
Then the angel **said** to her,
　　"Do not be **afraid**, Mary,
　　for you have found **favor** with God.

TO KEEP IN MIND
Pace: The rate at which you read is influenced by the size of your church, the size of the congregation, and the complexity of the text. As each increases, rate decreases.

adoption as divine providence: "destined in accord with the purpose of the One."

GOSPEL　Each year, during the season of Advent, we celebrate the Solemnity of the Immaculate Conception. This Marian solemnity teaches us that God, from the moment of Mary's conception, preserved her from original sin and, at that moment, blessed her like no other, with sanctifying grace. The Church's understanding of Mary (Mariology) took centuries to develop, continuing well

beyond the period of the writings of the New Testament.

　　Most of what we know about Mary in the New Testament comes from the Gospel account of Luke. In the opening chapters, the so-called "infancy narrative" (Luke 1:5—2:52), Luke presents many of the details surrounding the conceptions and births of Jesus and John the Baptist from Mary's point of view. (This is nicely balanced with the Gospel account of Matthew, which presents the birth of Jesus largely from Joseph's perspective). Within Christian tradition, today's Gospel reading is known

as "the Annunciation," that moment in history when the angel Gabriel visited Mary and announced to her that she would conceive the Son of God.

　　Gabriel appears twice in the Old Testament, both times in the Book of Daniel. He comes first to the prophet Daniel to present an interpretation of the vision of the ram and he-goats that Daniel received from God (Daniel 8:15–26). Gabriel appears a second time to Daniel to announce the time of seventy weeks for God's revelation to Israel (Daniel 9:21–27). The archangel also appears twice in the New Testament,

These words are not a sales pitch, but a profound announcement of God's decisive action in history.

The references to "David" and "Jacob" emphasize the regal nature of her offspring.

Mary is not struck dumb like Zechariah because her question asks "how," not "if," the promise will be fulfilled.

Here is a solemn promise spoken with authority and reassurance.

The angel compounds the good news with the announcement of Elizabeth's pregnancy, a sure sign of God's awesome power.

Is it at this very moment that Jesus is conceived in her womb? Whether strong or hushed, Mary's words convey inner strength and amazing courage.

Pause, before announcing the angel's departure.

TO KEEP IN MIND

A substantial pause always follows "A reading from" and both precedes and follows "The word [Gospel] of the Lord."

Behold, you will **conceive** in your womb and bear a **son**,
and you shall name him **Jesus**.
He will be **great** and will be called **Son** of the Most **High**,
and the Lord God will give him the **throne** of **David**
his **father**,
and he will **rule** over the house of Jacob **forever**,
and of his **Kingdom** there will be no **end**."
But **Mary** said to the angel,
"How can this **be**,
since I have no relations with a **man**?"
And the angel said to her in **reply**,
"The Holy **Spirit** will come upon you,
and the power of the Most **High** will **overshadow** you.
Therefore the **child** to be born
will be called **holy**, the **Son** of **God**.
And behold, **Elizabeth**, your relative,
has **also** conceived a son in her old **age**,
and this is the **sixth** month for her who was called **barren**;
for **nothing** will be **impossible** for God."
Mary said, "Behold, I am the **handmaid** of the Lord.
May it be **done** to me according to your **word**."
Then the angel **departed** from her.

---

both times in Luke's Gospel account. He comes the first time to inform Zechariah of the upcoming birth of John the Baptist to Zechariah's barren wife, Elizabeth (Luke 1:5–25), and he then visits Mary, telling her the good news of Jesus (Luke 1:26–38).

The first words that Mary speaks in Luke's account are a question to the angel Gabriel: "How can this be, since I have no relations with a man?" With this simple question, Luke brings to the forefront Mary's status as a virgin, allowing Luke to emphasize that Jesus was not conceived by man and woman, but rather through the Holy Spirit and "the power of the Most High." Gabriel's further revelation to Mary, that Jesus would receive from God "the throne of David his father," solidified Jesus's identity as both Son of God and Son of David.

In addition to what this Gospel Reading tells us about Jesus, we also learn something important about Mary. Despite being "greatly troubled" and questioning the meaning of Gabriel's announcement, Mary accepts God's will for her life: "Behold, I am the handmaid of the Lord. May it be done to me according to your word." From the moment of her conception, preserved from sin, Mary's will was oriented to the will of God. Mary's free-will choice to obey God is juxtaposed with Eve's sin of disobedience. As we hear in the Letter to the Ephesians, God's desire for us is "to be holy and without blemish." Mary provides all of us with a model of how to obey God and order our lives according to his will.

THIRD SUNDAY
OF ADVENT

LECTIONARY #8

READING I   Isaiah 61:1–2a, 10–11

A reading from the Book of the Prophet Isaiah

Isaiah = ī-ZAY-uh

This robust and joyous text lays out the prophet's job description. At the start of Luke's account, Jesus applies these words to himself. Let your energy build as you paint images of "liberty," "release," and "favor."

Each of these actions ("proclaim," "release," "announce") is distinct. Imagine those in need of liberation and vindication (family, neighbors, you!) and speak these words for them.

The sound of joy should fill these lines. It is a joy born of recognizing the privilege of serving God and his people.

In a culture where wardrobe was scant, these clothing images speak of God's lavish generosity. "Salvation" and "justice" will enfold and adorn us like the finest garments and jewelry.

The abundance of a fertile harvest is compared to the abundance of God's mercy. Speak with joyful conviction.

The **spirit** of the Lord God is upon me,
    because the Lord has **anointed** me;
he has **sent** me to bring glad **tidings** to the **poor**,
    to **heal** the **brokenhearted**,
to proclaim **liberty** to the **captives**
    and **release** to the **prisoners**,
to announce a year of **favor** from the Lord
    and a day of **vindication** by our **God**.

I rejoice **heartily** in the Lord,
    in my **God** is the joy of my **soul**;
for he has **clothed** me with a robe of **salvation**
    and **wrapped** me in a mantle of **justice**,
like a **bridegroom** adorned with a **diadem**,
    like a **bride** bedecked with her **jewels**.
As the **earth** brings forth its **plants**,
    and a **garden** makes its **growth** spring up,
so will the Lord God make **justice** and **praise**
    spring up before all the **nations**.

TO KEEP IN MIND
Read all three commentaries. Suggestions in each can give you insight into your own passage.

READING I Within their original historical context, the words of the prophet Isaiah in today's reading were heard as an oracle of comfort for the Israelite people returning from exile in Babylon in late sixth century BC. Isaiah presents to Israel the scope of God's call for him, summarizing his task as announcing "a year of favor from the Lord." Isaiah found true happiness in this good news, proclaiming, "my God is the joy of my soul." Using the analogy of plants growing in a garden, Isaiah foresaw a future in which Israel would witness how the Lord God will "make justice and praise spring up before all the nations."

For many Christians, the opening words to this reading are better known from an episode in Luke's Gospel account. (See Luke 4:16–30, especially verses 18–19.) According to Luke, at the start of his public ministry, Jesus quoted Isaiah 61:1–2 in his synagogue in Nazareth as a means of announcing that his ministry was the fulfillment of Israel's prophetic tradition. For Luke, Isaiah's prophecy, spoken nearly 500 years earlier, foreshadowed God's salvation to "all the nations" in the person of Jesus Christ.

READING II Paul's First Letter to the Thessalonians is widely regarded by scholars as the New Testament's earliest piece of written literature, composed in the year AD 50. This letter bears witness to one of the main

For meditation and context:

TO KEEP IN MIND

Separating units of thought with pauses: Identify the units of thought in your text and use pauses to distinguish one from another. Running words together blurs meaning and fails to distinguish ideas. Punctuation does not always indicate clearly what words to group together or where to pause. The listener depends on you for this organization of ideas.

Thessalonians = thes-uh-LOH-nee-unz
This brief text is comprised of many short imperative sentences. Avoid a choppy, shopping list delivery by keeping in mind the first two commands: "rejoice" and "pray." Thinking of a specific listener to whom the words are addressed (a college-bound student . . . someone being installed into a position of great responsibility), and speaking the words as if to them, will be helpful.

Speak these commands with full awareness of how difficult it can be to carry them out.

Two "do not" commands are followed by two positive admonitions.

You are no longer giving orders but praying. Pause to shift mood, then make eye contact as you share these lines.

"Spirit," "soul," and "body" are distinct aspects of each individual. Don't blur them into one.

End boldly, speaking out of your own experience of God's fidelity.

RESPONSORIAL PSALM   Luke 1:46–48, 49–50, 53–54 (Isaiah 61:10b)

R. My soul rejoices in my God.

My soul proclaims the greatness of the Lord;
  my spirit rejoices in God my Savior,
for he has looked upon his lowly servant.
  From this day all generations will call
    me blessed.

The Almighty has done great things for me,
  and holy is his Name.
He has mercy on those who fear him
  in every generation.

He has filled the hungry with good things,
  and the rich he has sent away empty.
He has come to the help of his servant Israel
  for he has remembered his promise
    of mercy.

READING II   1 Thessalonians 5:16–24

A reading from the first Letter of Saint Paul to the Thessalonians

Brothers and sisters:
Rejoice always. Pray without **ceasing.**
In all circumstances give **thanks,**
  for this is the will of **God** for you in Christ **Jesus.**
Do not **quench** the Spirit.
Do not **despise** prophetic utterances.
Test everything; retain what is **good.**
Refrain from every kind of **evil.**

May the God of **peace** make you perfectly **holy**
  and may you **entirely, spirit, soul,** and **body,**
    be preserved **blameless** for the coming of our Lord
      Jesus **Christ.**
The one who **calls** you is **faithful,**
  and he will also **accomplish** it.

concerns of the first generation of Christians: when would Christ return again? 1 Thessalonians 4:13—5:11 addresses this issue directly. Today's reading is taken from Paul's concluding comments in his letter to members of the Christian congregation in Thessalonica. Here, too, we see some of the real challenges of community life among the earliest believers in Christ.

Paul gives a series of eight directives (six in the positive and two in the negative) for the Thessalonian community members.

In the positive, Paul asserts: "Rejoice always. Pray without ceasing. In all circumstances give thanks. . . . Test everything; retain what is good. Refrain from every kind of evil." In the negative, Paul emphasizes: "Do not quench the Spirit. Do not despise prophetic utterances." Paul's call to high ethical standards and conduct among believers in Christ helped define the early Pauline Christian communities.

Paul closes his letter to the Thessalonians with a prayer, which is included at the end of this Second Reading. The prayer returns to one of the themes of the letter, the Parousia (Second Coming of Christ): "Be preserved blameless for the coming of our Lord Jesus Christ." There remained among the earliest Christians a firm conviction in the imminent return of Christ. We do not know when Christ will come, but like the Christians in Thessalonica, we, too, wait in hope for his return.

GOSPEL   John 1:6–8, 19–28

A reading from the holy Gospel according to John

The opening is rather stylized and contains much repetition. Don't resist the stylization or rush through it. Read slowly and let the words do their work.

A man named **John** was sent from God.
He came for **testimony**, to testify to the **light**,
    so that all might **believe** through him.
He was not the light,
    but came to **testify** to the light.

John's was a critical role in God's plan of salvation. He came to "testify."

Levites = LEE-vīts

And **this** is the testimony of John.
When the Jews from Jerusalem sent **priests** and **Levites** to him
    to ask him, "Who **are** you?"
    he **admitted** and did not **deny** it,
    but admitted, "I am not the **Christ**."
So they **asked** him,
    "What **are** you then? Are you **Elijah**?"
And he said, "I am **not**."
"Are you the **Prophet**?"
He answered, "**No**."
So they said to him,
    "Who **are** you, so we can give an **answer** to those who **sent** us?

Stress only the first "admitted."

John's three negations set the stage for his affirmation that follows. His tone should be authoritative and he doesn't seem to like the questions.

Elijah = ee-LIH-juh

The priests' frustration grows as they question John.

Though they try to bully him, John does not provide the direct answer they seek. Proclaim the quote from Isaiah without fanfare, as if it were everyday speech. But speak with authority.

TO KEEP IN MIND

Narrator: Knowing the point of view that the narrator is "rooting for" will help you more fully communicate the meaning of the text. The narrator always has a viewpoint, often speaking as a believer, not as an objective reporter. For this reason, the narrator is often the pivotal role in a passage. Using timbre, pitch, rate, and energy can help you convey the narrator's moods or meanings.

GOSPEL   Each year the Gospel readings for the second and third Sundays of Advent focus on John the Baptist, the desert prophet and forerunner to Christ who announced to Israel, "Make straight the way of the Lord." Within the four Gospel accounts of the New Testament, a consistent portrait of John the Baptist emerges. But each of the Gospel writers also brings a distinctive theological and historical perspective to the presentation of John the Baptist. Today's reading from the Gospel according to John illustrates this well.

Throughout his account, John tries to help his audience understand who Jesus is, often through metaphors. For example, John presents Jesus as the living water (see John 4:4–42), as the light of the world (John 8:12–59), and as the Good Shepherd (see John 10:1–18). One of John's favorite metaphors is Jesus as "the light." We hear this in the opening of today's reading as John clarifies that John the Baptist was "not the light, but came to testify to the light."

The Gospel Reading also gives us a glimpse into how others perceived the activity of John the Baptist. Some thought John the Baptist was "the Christ." Others believed he was a Jewish prophet, similar to Elijah, or perhaps even "the Prophet" that Moses prophesied about in Israel's forty-year desert wanderings (see Deuteronomy 18:15). But John made it clear he was none of these; rather, he was "the voice of one crying out in the desert." The ministry of John the Baptist was to "baptize" the people in preparation for the coming of the Messiah. In this way, John the Baptist laid the framework for the celebration of Advent to this very day.

Are the Pharisees more or less hostile than his other questioners?

John's reply is cryptic; it's not meant to satisfy, but to rouse curiosity: whom is it among us that we don't recognize?

John's last words are self-effacing as he stares down his audience.

Bethany = BETH-uh-nee

The final lines situate John's ministry in the same area where Jesus will soon begin his.

TO KEEP IN MIND

The closing: Pause (three beats!) after ending the text. Then, with sustained eye contact, announce from memory, "The word [Gospel] of the Lord." Always pronounce "the" as "thuh" except before words beginning with a vowel, as in "thee Acts of the Apostles." Maintain eye contact while the assembly makes its response.

What do you have to **say** for yourself?"
He said:
 "I am *the* **voice** *of one crying out in the* **desert**,
 'Make **straight** *the way of the* **Lord**,'
 as Isaiah the **prophet** said."
Some **Pharisees** were also sent.
They asked him,
 "Why then do you **baptize**
 if you are not the **Christ** or **Elijah** or the **Prophet**?"
John **answered** them,
 "I baptize with **water**;
 but there is one **among** you whom you do not **recognize**,
 the one who is coming **after** me,
 whose **sandal** strap I am not worthy to **untie**."
This happened in **Bethany** across the **Jordan**,
 where John was **baptizing**.

FOURTH SUNDAY OF ADVENT

LECTIONARY #11

READING I   2 Samuel 7:1–5, 8b–12, 14a, 16

A reading from the second Book of Samuel

When King **David** was settled in his **palace**,
    and the LORD had given him **rest** from his enemies
        on every side,
    he said to **Nathan** the prophet,
    "Here **I** am living in a house of **cedar**,
    while the ark of **God** dwells in a **tent**!"
Nathan **answered** the king,
    "**Go**, do whatever you have in mind,
    for the LORD is with you."
But that **night** the LORD **spoke** to Nathan and said:
    "**Go**, tell my servant **David**, 'Thus says the LORD:
    Should you build **me** a house to dwell in?

"'It was **I** who took you from the **pasture**
    and from the care of the **flock**
    to be **commander** of my people Israel.
I have been with you **wherever** you went,
    and I have destroyed all your **enemies** before you.
And I will make you **famous** like the **great** ones of the earth.
I will fix a **place** for my people Israel;
    I will **plant** them so that they may **dwell** in their place
    without further **disturbance**.

Read the Gospel to appreciate why this text is read during Advent.
Enjoying peace and prosperity, David nonetheless senses something is out of balance in his kingdom. Your tone can reveal his uneasiness.

One can wonder if David wants to please God or impress royal visitors to his kingdom.

Nathan is as convinced as David that the plan will meet with God's approval.

As you speak "But that night," your tone should immediately signal that the plan is ill-fated.

Without anger, these lines teach David who has done what for whom. True gratitude is shown through a holy life lived in obedience to God's will; God doesn't need David's favors.
First, God recounts what he has already *done* for David and his house.

Here is a list of what God will *do* for David. Let your tone be confident and persuasive, like an employer who revels in doling out end-of-year perks and bonuses.

READING I One way of making sense of the long and complex storyline of the Old Testament is to think about it in terms of a long series of *covenantal promises* that God establishes with his people. Sometimes these covenants are between God and an individual, such as the covenant between God and Abraham in Genesis 15:1–21, the promise to Abraham of land and descendents. Other times, the covenant is between God and the people of Israel; for example, the covenant at Mount Sinai (Exodus 19:1—23:33), the delivery of

the Mosaic Law. In today's reading, God makes a covenant with both an individual (King David) and with the people of Israel. This covenant from 2 Samuel 7:8–16 is commonly referred to as the "Davidic covenant," dated by scholars to about the year 1000 BC.

The covenant in this reading originates in David's concern for a proper location for "the ark of God." The Old Testament makes many references to this structure (sometimes called the ark of the covenant). Dating back to the time of Moses and the Israelites' forty-year sojourn in the desert (about 1200 BC), the ark was a chest,

thought to contain (among other things, such as Aaron's rod and a jar of manna) the stone tablets upon which the Ten Commandments were inscribed. Most importantly, "the ark of God" was believed to represent God's presence with the people of Israel. Given its history and this belief, David's concern for the proper placement of, and appropriate housing for, the ark is quite understandable.

As David discerns how best to honor the ark of God, the prophet Nathan reveals a new covenant that God will establish with

"Judges" were ad hoc charismatic leaders who led the nation in times of crises before Israel had any kings.

Pause before beginning this last section; this is a grand announcement of God's enduring favor on the house of David.

These lines brim with affection for David.

In the context of today's liturgy we hear these words in reference to Jesus. Think of that as you speak "father" and "son."

The final promise is the grandest; proclaim it with great dignity.

For meditation and context:

Neither shall the **wicked** continue to **afflict** them as they did
    of **old**,
  since the time I first appointed **judges** over my people Israel.
I will give you **rest** from all your enemies.
The Lord **also** reveals to you
    that he will establish a house for **you**.
And when your **time** comes and you rest with your **ancestors**,
    I will raise up your **heir** after you, sprung from your **loins**,
    and I will make his kingdom **firm**.
I will be a **father** to him,
    and he shall be a **son** to me.
Your **house** and your **kingdom** shall endure **forever** before me;
    your **throne** shall stand firm **forever**.'"

RESPONSORIAL PSALM   Psalm 89:2–3, 4–5, 27, 29 (2a)

R. Forever I will sing the goodness of the Lord.

The promises of the Lord I will sing forever;
    through all generations my mouth shall
    proclaim your faithfulness.
For you have said, "My kindness is
    established forever";
    in heaven you have confirmed your
    faithfulness.

"I have made a covenant with my chosen one,
    I have sworn to David my servant:
forever will I confirm your posterity
    and establish your throne for all
    generations."

"He shall say of me, 'You are my father,
    my God, the rock, my savior.'
Forever I will maintain my kindness
    toward him,
    and my covenant with him stands firm."

> **TO KEEP IN MIND**
> **Separating units of thought with pauses:** Identify the units of thought in your text and use pauses to distinguish one from another. Running words together blurs meaning and fails to distinguish ideas. Punctuation does not always indicate clearly what words to group together or where to pause. The listener depends on you for this organization of ideas.

Israel and with Israel's king, David. God's covenantal promise to Israel is to "fix a place" (that is, give Israel land upon which to settle and call their own), free from "further disturbance" by "enemies." To David, God's covenantal promise was twofold. The first aspect of the covenant had to do with David's house, kingdom, and throne: "Your house and your kingdom shall endure forever before me" and "your throne shall stand firm forever." The second aspect of the covenant had to do with David's direct descendent: "I will raise up your heir after you, sprung from your loins, and I will make

his kingdom firm." And God not only promises descendants in David's own family line but also to continue a close father-son relationship with them.

Christians throughout the ages have come to believe that the birth of Jesus fulfilled the "Davidic covenant": the promise God made to King David.

READING II   Today's reading is composed of the closing verses from Paul's Letter to the Romans. It is a doxology; that is, a hymn of praise to God.

Paul addresses his praise "to him" who is able to "strengthen you." Paul saw two main channels of God's strength for the Christians in Rome: "my gospel" and "the proclamation of Jesus Christ." This is a bold assertion by Paul, and a somewhat risky one. The Letter to the Romans is one of the few Pauline letters addressed to a community that Paul himself did not establish. The congregation in Rome was founded by other Christian missionaries besides Paul and his co-workers. It was founded on teaching a "gospel" most likely different from Paul's. Part of Paul's motivation for

One long sentence of seventy-three words with multiple subordinate clauses to make a simple declaration: to God be glory forever. Between the first and the final lines are explanatory clauses which, though important, should not keep this from being a bold declaration of praise to our merciful God.

Anticipate where you will pause and take catch-breaths.

The second "according to" = "which is"

"But now" = "But which is now"

"Made known" = "which is made known"

Catch your breath and increase your energy as you remind us of whom you are speaking. Don't just speak of glory; give it!

READING II   Romans 16:25–27

A reading from the Letter of Saint Paul to the Romans

Brothers and sisters:
To him who can **strengthen** you,
    according to my **gospel** and the proclamation of Jesus **Christ**,
    according to the revelation of the **mystery** kept secret
      for long **ages**
    but now **manifested** through the prophetic **writings** and,
    according to the command of the eternal **God**,
    made known to all **nations** to bring about the **obedience**
      of **faith**,
    to the only **wise** God, through Jesus **Christ**
    be **glory** forever and **ever**. **Amen**.

The pericope opens with an exposition that offers several important details about who came, where, and to whom. The exposition climaxes with the identification of Mary.

The angel's greeting immediately "troubles" Mary. Contrast the joyful salutation with the sober narration that follows it.

Gabriel perceives Mary's concern and immediately seeks to comfort.

GOSPEL   Luke 1:26–38

A reading from the holy Gospel according to Luke

The angel **Gabriel** was sent from **God**
    to a town of **Galilee** called **Nazareth**,
    to a **virgin** betrothed to a man named **Joseph**,
    of the house of **David**,
    and the virgin's **name** was **Mary**.
And **coming** to her, he said,
    "**Hail**, full of **grace**! The **Lord** is with you."
But she was greatly **troubled** at what was said
    and **pondered** what sort of greeting this might be.
Then the angel said to her,
    "Do not be **afraid**, Mary,
    for you have found **favor** with God.

writing to the Roman Christians was to solicit their support (politically and financially) for his missionary work in the western half of the Roman Empire—a territory yet to be evangelized by Paul. He wanted to establish a home base in Spain (Romans 15:24) and begin his evangelization of the west from there. By concluding his letter highlighting "my gospel" (rather than the Gospel message preached in the Roman congregation) as a source of strength from God himself, Paul was risking some degree of alienation from the believers in Rome.

In this doxology, Paul also speaks of "the revelation of the mystery kept secret for long ages . . . now . . . made known to all the nations." Mention of the "revelation of the mystery" at the conclusion of the letter draws attention to the main thesis of the Letter to the Romans and the heart of Paul's Gospel message: God offers salvation to everyone, Jew and Gentile alike, who has faith in Jesus Christ (Romans 1:16–17). Although this universal call to salvation is widely held by Christians today

and celebrated as an integral aspect to the season of Advent, among the first generation of believers in Christ, Paul's Gospel message was quite controversial.

GOSPEL   The Gospel Reading for the Fourth Sunday of Advent is "the Annunciation," the angel Gabriel's visit and announcement to Mary that she would conceive the Son of God. Recall this was the same Gospel reading for the Solemnity of the Immaculate Conception, celebrated on December 8. Read in the context of the First and Second Readings, this passage

Keep the announcement upbeat and joyful, speaking with energy without rushing the details.

Ancient prophecy will be fulfilled in the birth of her son. Make it dignified without sounding imperious.

Mary has listened well and believes what she's heard, but asks "how" it will happen, not "if."

Consider a hushed delivery of these lines so you can be reassuring while also communicating awareness of God's awesome power.

This final revelation will be the *most* persuasive detail!

Slow down for this declaration.

Pause after "Mary said . . . " Her response is deliberate and strong: she surrenders without reserve.

Pause before announcing the angel's departure.

"Behold, you will **conceive** in your womb and bear a **son**,
    and you shall name him **Jesus**.
He will be **great** and will be called **Son** of the Most **High**,
    and the Lord **God** will give him the **throne** of David
        his **father**,
    and he will **rule** over the house of Jacob **forever**,
    and of his **kingdom** there will be no **end**."
But **Mary** said to the angel,
    "How can this **be**,
    since I have no relations with a **man**?"
And the angel said to her in **reply**,
    "The Holy **Spirit** will come upon you,
    and the power of the Most **High** will **overshadow** you.
Therefore the **child** to be born
    will be called **holy**, the Son of **God**.
    And behold, **Elizabeth**, your relative,
    has **also** conceived a son in her old **age**,
    and this is the **sixth** month for her who was called **barren**;
    for **nothing** will be **impossible** for God."
Mary said, "Behold, I am the **handmaid** of the Lord.
May it be **done** to me according to your **word**."
Then the angel **departed** from her.

THE 4 STEPS OF *LECTIO DIVINA* OR PRAYERFUL READING

1. *Lectio:* Read a Scripture passage aloud slowly. Notice what phrase captures your attention and be attentive to its meaning. Silent pause.

2. *Meditatio:* Read the passage aloud slowly again, reflecting on the passage, allowing God to speak to you through it. Silent pause.

3. *Oratio:* Read it aloud slowly a third time, allowing it to be your prayer or response to God's gift of insight to you. Silent pause.

4. *Contemplatio:* Read it aloud slowly a fourth time, now resting in God's word.

---

from Luke's "infancy narrative" (Luke 1:5—2:52) offers some interesting insights and connections.

The First Reading, which narrates the terms of the Davidic covenant, is clearly connected to the Gospel Reading. Not only does Luke tell us that Joseph is "of the house of David," but we also hear from Gabriel's words to Mary that through the conception and birth of Jesus, God will fulfill his covenantal promise to David. Of David's throne, house, and kingdom, "there will be no end." The Davidic covenant reaches fruition in the birth of Jesus, "called Son of the Most High."

In the Second Reading from the Letter to the Romans, we hear Paul speak about the "revelation of the mystery . . . now manifested through the prophetic writings and, according to the command of the eternal God, made known to all nations." Luke informs us that "the angel Gabriel was sent by God to a town in Galilee called Nazareth." Here we see the "command" of the "eternal God" being carried out by the angel Gabriel. Further, Gabriel reveals to Mary how the conception and birth of Jesus fulfills the "prophetic writings" from the prophet Nathan as recorded in 2 Samuel.

As the season of Advent draws to a close, "all nations" wait in eager expectation for the celebration of the birth of Christ and remain ever-vigilant for his return.

THE NATIVITY OF THE LORD (CHRISTMAS): VIGIL

LECTIONARY #13

Isaiah = Ī-ZAY-uh;

Zion = Zī-ahn

In the opening lines the prophet assumes God's own voice. This declaration can be rendered with bold energy or with hushed and muted joy.

The text is comprised of couplets (two-line verses) that state and restate a single idea ("I will not be silent"/"I will not be quiet"; "Nations shall behold your vindication"/"kings your glory"). This literary device requires that you increase your energy from the first expression to the second.

Diadem = Dī-uh-dem

These lines are part of a divine pep talk that offers hope to those who have nearly lost it.

You are contrasting what *was* with what *will be.*

The last four couplets utilize spousal imagery to communicate God's passionate love for Israel. In each couplet, the second line receives greater stress.

The objective of these lines is to persuade and offer hope. Speak them with conviction as if to an individual who needs reassurance.

READING I   Isaiah 62:1–5

A reading from the Book of the Prophet Isaiah

For **Zion's** sake I will not be **silent**,
for **Jerusalem's** sake I will not be **quiet**,
until her **vindication** shines forth like the **dawn**
and her **victory** like a burning **torch**.

Nations shall **behold** your vindication,
and all the **kings** your **glory**;
you shall be called by a **new** name
pronounced by the mouth of the **Lord**.
You shall be a glorious **crown** in the hand of the Lord,
a royal **diadem** held by your God.
No **more** shall people call you "**Forsaken**,"
or your land "**Desolate**,"
but you shall be called "My **Delight**,"
and your **land** "**Espoused**."
For the Lord **delights** in you
and makes your land his **spouse**.
As a young **man** marries a **virgin**,
your **Builder** shall marry **you**;
and as a **bridegroom** rejoices in his **bride**
so shall your **God** rejoice in **you**.

READING I Throughout the four Masses of Christmas, we hear the words of the prophet Isaiah in the first readings. As previously discussed with the readings for the Second Sunday of Advent, the sixty-six chapters of the Book of Isaiah span about 200 years in Israel's history: Isaiah 1–39 from the period associated with the Assyrian crisis (740–700 BC), Isaiah 40–55 from the time of Israel's captivity in Babylon (about 550 BC), and Isaiah 56–66 from shortly after Israel's return from exile in Babylon (post-538 BC). These two centuries were among Israel's most turbulent times—politically, militarily, and religiously. The First Readings for the vigil and dawn Masses belong to the period of Israel's return from exile in Babylon and adjustment to life in a post-exilic world.

In tonight's First Reading, we hear Isaiah use the language of a people freed from war and captivity ("vindication" and "victory"). This surely resonated with the Israelites' return from seventy years of exile in Babylon. To celebrate this historical turning point for Israel, Isaiah speaks of new beginnings, grounded in divine decree: "You shall be called by a new name pronounced by the mouth of the Lord." Isaiah reminds the Israelites of the names they and their land had been called ("Forsaken" and "Desolate") by allies and enemies alike when they were captured and their land was destroyed by the Babylonian Empire. But after two generations of captivity and eventual return from exile, the people of Israel are now renamed "My Delight" and the land of Israel as "Espoused." Isaiah then states the reason for this name-change: "For the Lord delights in you and makes

For meditation and context:

TO KEEP IN MIND

Pronunciation: Mispronunciations can be distracting for your listeners. Pronunciation aids are provided in the margin notes (see the key at the end of this introduction). You may also want to consult the LTP publication, *Pronunciation Guide to the Lectionary*.

Antioch = ANN-tee-ahk

Pisidia = pih-SID-ee-uh

Paul motions "with his hand" to ask for silence.

"and you others": Paul would have needed to increase volume to get their attention.

Ever the teacher, Paul provides a history lesson to delineate the "thread" that has run through their entire history. Paul addresses a congregation, as you are doing.

As you relate the history, keep in mind where you're headed: Jesus! Paul always has a goal in mind.

The mention of David is purposeful because Jesus is his descendant. Speak of David with affection and pride.

RESPONSORIAL PSALM   Psalm 89:4–5, 16–17, 27, 29 (2a)

R. Forever I will sing the goodness of the Lord.

I have made a covenant with my chosen one,
   I have sworn to David my servant:
forever will I confirm your posterity
   and establish your throne for all
      generations.

Blessed the people who know the
   joyful shout;
   in the light of your countenance, O Lord,
      they walk.
At your name they rejoice all the day,
   and through your justice they are exalted.

He shall say of me, "You are my father,
   my God, the rock, my savior."
Forever I will maintain my kindness toward
      him,
   and my covenant with him stands firm.

READING II   Acts of the Apostles 13:16–17, 22–25

A reading from the Acts of the Apostles

When **Paul** reached Antioch in Pisidia and entered the **synagogue**,
   he **stood** up, motioned with his **hand**, and said,
   "Fellow **Israelites** and you **others** who are God-fearing, **listen**.
The God of this people Israel chose our **ancestors**
   and **exalted** the people during their sojourn in the land
      of **Egypt**.
With uplifted **arm** he led them **out** of it.
Then he removed **Saul** and raised up **David** as king;
   of him he **testified**,
   'I have found **David**, son of **Jesse**, a man after my own **heart**;
   he will carry out my every **wish**.'

your land his spouse." Isaiah retrieves from Israel's prophetic tradition the imagery of marriage between God and Israel to characterize this new reality (see, for example, Hosea 2:21–25). In this prophecy, Isaiah helps Israel realize God's fidelity to his covenantal people and contributes to the ongoing prophetic tradition that will prepare Israel for the arrival of the Messiah.

READING II The Second Reading, taken from the Acts of the Apostles, presents part of the speech that Paul delivered in the city of Antioch in the region of Pisidia during his first missionary journey. Today's reading is the beginning of Paul's speech to both the Jews and the Gentiles (the "God-fearers") present in the Antioch synagogue. Paul starts with a historical overview of God's relationship with Israel, beginning with Moses and the Exodus, highlighting David and the Davidic covenant, and culminating in Jesus, the descendent of David, the "Savior." Luke, author of both the Gospel and Acts, includes this speech because it connects God's historic relationship to Israel with the saving work accomplished in the Death and Resurrection of Christ. One of Luke's main theological themes running through the storyline of Acts is that Jesus is the Savior of both Jew and Gentile alike, and this theme often surfaces in the many speeches delivered in Acts by Peter and Paul. Throughout the readings for the Christmas Masses, we will hear that the good news of the birth of the Messiah is meant for all people to hear.

Paul reaches his intended goal. Speak with greater energy and pause before speaking "Jesus."

Paul presumes knowledge of John. Set off his name for your assembly.

John was forever having to explain who he was and *wasn't*. His denial should be forceful, but the last line can be delivered simply and sincerely, as if John were watching Jesus walking on the opposite shore.

From this man's **descendants** God, according to his **promise**,
　has brought to Israel a **savior**, **Jesus**.
John **heralded** his coming by proclaiming a **baptism** of **repentance**
　to all the people of Israel;
　and as John was **completing** his course, he would say,
　'What do you suppose that I **am**? I am not **he**.
Behold, one is coming **after** me;
　I am not **worthy** to unfasten the **sandals** of his feet.'"

GOSPEL　Matthew 1:1–25

A reading from the holy Gospel according to Matthew

Rehearse reading this listing several times and don't rush the "litany" of ancestral names. genealogy = jee-nee-OL-uh-jee

The book of the **genealogy** of Jesus **Christ**,
　the son of **David**, the son of **Abraham**.

Abraham = AY-bruh-ham

Isaac = Ī-zik

Judah = JOO-duh

Perez = PAYR-ez

Zerah = ZEE-rah

Tamar = TAY-mahr: see Genesis 38.

Hezron = HEZ-ruhn

Ram = ram

Amminadab = uh-MIN-uh-dab

Nashon = NAH-shun

Salmon = SAL-muhn

Boaz = BOH-az

Rahab = RAY-hab: see Joshua 2:1–7

Obed = OH-bed

Ruth was the great-grandmother of King David.

Jesse = JES-ee

Abraham became the father of **Isaac**,
　Isaac the father of **Jacob**,
　Jacob the father of **Judah** and his brothers.
Judah became the father of **Perez** and **Zerah**,
　whose **mother** was **Tamar**.
Perez became the father of **Hezron**,
　Hezron the father of **Ram**,
　Ram the father of **Amminadab**.
Amminadab became the father of **Nahshon**,
　Nahshon the father of **Salmon**,
　Salmon the father of **Boaz**,
　whose **mother** was **Rahab**.
Boaz became the father of **Obed**,
　whose **mother** was **Ruth**.
Obed became the father of **Jesse**,
　Jesse the father of **David** the **king**.

GOSPEL　The Gospel according to Matthew provides the opening words of the entire New Testament. It is by no accident that the early Church placed Matthew's account first in the twenty-seven books of the New Testament. Of the four Gospel accounts that were ultimately included in the New Testament, the early Church concluded that Matthew's offered the best transition from the Old Testament to the New Testament. This was partly because the community to whom Matthew was writing was a largely Jewish Christian congregation. Also, Matthew's

overarching aim was to show the continuity and connection between God's saving work with Israel and with Jesus.

At tonight's Mass we hear the opening verses of Matthew's Gospel account. This lengthy reading falls into three parts: the opening line of the Gospel, the genealogy of Jesus, and the story of Jesus's birth.

All four Gospel writers had various questions that needed to be answered as they assembled and ordered the oral and written materials available to them in telling the story of the life, Death, and

Resurrection of Christ: what material should be included and what words of Jesus will be presented first? The question of the opening verses of the Gospel warranted special attention. Matthew was quite deliberate in his opening verse: "The book of the genealogy of Jesus Christ, the son of David, the son of Abraham." In the ancient world, one's identity was largely understood by gender, geography, and genealogy—the three g's. Whether you were male or female, where you came from, and who your ancestors were all defined your identity and relationship to others. Matthew's opening

Uriah = yoo-RĪ-uh. His "wife" is Bathsheba: 2 Samuel 11:1–27.

Rehoboam = ree-huh-BOH-uhm

Abijah = uh-BĪ-juh

Asaph = AY-saf

Jehoshaphat = jeh-HOH-shuh-fat

Joram = JOHR-uhm

Uzziah = yuh-ZĪ-uh: Struck with leprosy for usurping role of priests: 2 Chronicles 26:16–20.

Jotham = JOH-thuhm

Ahaz = AY-haz

Hezekiah = hez-eh-KĪH-uh: One of the few "good" kings; a reformer.

Manasseh = muh-NAS-uh: The nation's worst king.

Josiah = joh-SĪ-uh: One of Judah's best kings; a reformer. Ascended the throne at age eight.

The exile was the nation's greatest trial.

Jechoniah = jek-oh-NĪ-uh

Shealtiel = shee-AL-tee-uhl

Zerubbabel = zuh-ROOB-uh-b*l

Abiud = uh-BĪ-uhd

Eliakim = ee-LĪ-uh-kim

Azor = AY-sohr

Zadok = ZAD-uhk

Achim = AH-kim

Eliud = ee-LĪ-uhd

Eleazar = el-ee-AY-zer

Matthan = MATH-uhn

"Fourteen" is a *deliberate* redundancy. Stress each recurrence.

David became the father of **Solomon**,
   whose **mother** had been the wife of **Uriah**.
Solomon became the father of **Rehoboam**,
   Rehoboam the father of **Abijah**,
   Abijah the father of **Asaph**.
Asaph became the father of **Jehoshaphat**,
   Jehoshaphat the father of **Joram**,
   Joram the father of **Uzziah**.
Uzziah became the father of **Jotham**,
   Jotham the father of **Ahaz**,
   Ahaz the father of **Hezekiah**.
Hezekiah became the father of **Manasseh**,
   Manasseh the father of **Amos**,
   Amos the father of **Josiah**.
Josiah became the father of **Jechoniah** and his brothers
   at the time of the Babylonian **exile**.

After the Babylonian exile,
   Jechoniah became the father of **Shealtiel**,
   Shealtiel the father of **Zerubbabel**,
   Zerubbabel the father of **Abiud**.
Abiud became the father of **Eliakim**,
   Eliakim the father of **Azor**,
   Azor the father of **Zadok**.
Zadok became the father of **Achim**,
   Achim the father of **Eliud**,
   Eliud the father of **Eleazar**.
Eleazar became the father of **Matthan**,
   Matthan the father of **Jacob**,
   Jacob the father of **Joseph**, the husband of **Mary**.
Of her was born **Jesus** who is called the **Christ**.

Thus the total number of **generations**
   from **Abraham** to **David**
   is **fourteen** generations;
   from **David** to the Babylonian **exile**,

verse addressed two of the major components of Jesus's identity (his gender and his genealogy): Jesus is "the son." Where Jesus was born and raised—his geography—is addressed early on by Matthew as well (see Matthew 2:1, 23).

But before launching into a more detailed accounting of Jesus's genealogy, Matthew offers us in summary form the two main ancestors from whom Jesus descends: David and Abraham. This is significant. Each represents a covenantal promise established by God that was being fulfilled

in the birth of Jesus. Through Christ, the Davidic covenant is fulfilled: an "heir" of David assures that his house, kingdom, and throne will endure forever (see 2 Samuel 7:12–16). Likewise through Christ, the Abrahamic covenant is fulfilled: "And in your descendants all the nations of the earth shall find blessing" (see Genesis 22:18). All believers in Christ—Jews and Gentiles—would have been able to identify with one, or both, of these fulfilled covenants.

The extended genealogy of Jesus is highly structured and strategically designed. Structurally, Matthew 1:17 informs us that

salvation history has been divinely orchestrated through key people (Abraham, David and Christ) and key events (the Babylonian exile) in Israel's history, easily recognizable through three sets of fourteen generations. The inclusion of five women in Jesus's genealogy (Tamar, Rahab, Ruth, the wife of Uriah, and Mary) would have stood out as a unique feature. Each of these women had unusual relations with their husbands. This may have helped Matthew's community be more receptive to the virginal conception of Jesus by Mary.

fourteen generations;
from the Babylonian exile to the **Christ**,
fourteen generations.

Now this is how the **birth** of Jesus Christ came about.
When his mother **Mary** was betrothed to **Joseph**,
    but before they **lived** together,
    she was found with **child** through the Holy **Spirit**.
Joseph her **husband**, since he was a **righteous** man,
    yet unwilling to expose her to **shame**,
    decided to divorce her **quietly**.
Such was his **intention** when, **behold**,
    the **angel** of the Lord appeared to him in a **dream** and said,
    "**Joseph**, son of David,
    do not be **afraid** to take Mary your **wife** into your **home**.
For it is through the Holy **Spirit**
    that this child has been **conceived** in her.
She will bear a **son** and you are to name him **Jesus**,
    because he will **save** his people from their **sins**."
All this took place to **fulfill**
    what the Lord had said through the **prophet**:
        *Behold, the **virgin** shall **conceive** and bear a **son**,*
            *and they shall name him **Emmanuel**,*
        which means "**God** is **with** us."
When Joseph **awoke**,
    he **did** as the angel of the Lord had **commanded** him
    and took his **wife** into his **home**.
He had no **relations** with her until she bore a **son**,
    and he **named** him Jesus.

[Shorter: Matthew 1:18–25]

Margin notes

Emphasis on Joseph and the details regarding Jesus's conception serves Matthew's agenda.

Speak the words "before they lived together" with concern for the "delicacy" of the situation.

Stress "righteous man"; his conscience required him not to dismiss her presumed infidelity. Insert a brief pause before the word "quietly."

Dreams were seen as means of divine revelation. This dream reveals Jesus's divine origin and his messianic destiny.

Don't let the angel's instruction sound like items on a to-do list.

Make a subtle vocal shift when quoting from Isaiah.

The word "Emmanuel" climaxes the reading, so don't rush the translation of the name.

Stressing "until" would suggest they had "relations" after the birth of Jesus, so note carefully the words marked for stress. The Church affirms the perpetual virginity of Mary.

After speaking "Jesus," take a substantial pause before announcing the end of the Gospel reading.

Matthew's account of the birth of Jesus offers us Joseph's perspective on the events that transpired. Scholars often note that this balances nicely with Luke's infancy narrative, which presents Mary's perspective on the birth of Christ (see Luke 1:26–38; 2:1–38).

It is clear that Joseph, a "righteous man," recognizes the gravity of Mary being pregnant. To spare Mary the "shame" and penalty for adultery, Joseph decides "to divorce her quietly." Reminiscent of the Old Testament Joseph who became famous for dreams (see, for example, Genesis 37:5–11; 40:1–23), Joseph discovers a different resolution to his dilemma after having a dream in which an "angel of the Lord" informs him of the truth of Mary's conception. Joseph is also instructed by the angel to name the child "Jesus" (the Greek equivalent of "Joshua" in Hebrew), which literally translates as "the LORD saves."

Joseph further learns that Mary's conception of Jesus fulfills the prophecy of Isaiah 7:14, which confirms Jesus's divine identity: "God is with us." Herein lies one of Matthew's favorite themes, the abiding presence of God. He reinforces this central concept at the beginning of his Gospel account in the birth narrative (1:23), at the center of his Gospel account in Jesus's teachings to his disciples (18:20), and at the end of the Gospel account with the resurrected Christ's final words: "And behold, I am with you always, until the end of the age" (28:20b).

THE NATIVITY OF THE LORD (CHRISTMAS): NIGHT

Isaiah = Ī-ZAY-uh

This classic text is a privilege to proclaim. Dedicate adequate time to preparation.

The Church reads this most famous of the Old Testament messianic prophecies through the eyes of Christian faith.

Those who "walked in darkness" and have now "seen a great light" are sitting before you.

Persuade your assembly that these words are addressed to them.

Imagine the sentence without the first "as" and the meaning will become clearer.

Read each phrase with growing intensity, as if piling one stone upon another, to await the hammer blow on the word "smashed."

Repeat the pattern of building intensity on the two clauses that climax on "burned as fuel."

The mood changes as "yokes" and "battles" yield to a newborn who will shoulder a nation. Speak with awe, great pride, and joy.

These titles can be spoken boldly or with hushed intensity.

LECTIONARY #14

READING I   Isaiah 9:1–6

A reading from the Book of the Prophet Isaiah

The people who walked in **darkness**
    have seen a great **light**;
upon those who dwelt in the land of **gloom**
    a light has **shone**.
You have brought them abundant **joy**
    and great **rejoicing**,
as they rejoice before you as at the **harvest**,
    as people make **merry** when dividing **spoils**.
For the **yoke** that **burdened** them,
    the **pole** on their **shoulder**,
and the **rod** of their **taskmaster**
    you have **smashed**, as on the day of **Midian**.
For every **boot** that tramped in **battle**,
    every **cloak** rolled in **blood**,
    will be **burned** as fuel for **flames**.
For a **child** is born to us, a **son** is given us;
    upon his shoulder **dominion** rests.
They name him **Wonder-Counselor**, **God-Hero**,
    Father-Forever, **Prince** of **Peace**.

READING I | The First Reading for the Mass during the night is a well-know oracle from the prophet Isaiah. It belongs to some of the earliest prophecies recorded in the Book of Isaiah, dating to the period of the eighth-century BC Assyrian crisis, which ultimately resulted in the capture and destruction of the northern kingdom of Israel in 721 BC. Scholars commonly date this prophecy (and the larger set of messianic oracles comprising Isaiah 7–12 known as the "Immanuel Prophecies") during the twenty-year reign of King Ahaz (735–715 BC).

Isaiah's prophecy about the people who were walking in darkness, seeing "a great light," emerged during a time when King Ahaz was attempting to forge an alliance with the Assyrians. Rather than trust in the Lord, as Isaiah urged, Ahaz tried to lessen the damage Assyria could cause Israel by placing his faith in the strength of the Assyrian army. But Assyria was not interested in an alliance with the Israelites living in the northern kingdom. In fact, the opposite occurred: they were treated ruthlessly by the Assyrians, who were described graphically as "the yoke that burdened" Israel, "the pole on their shoulder," and "the rod of their taskmaster."

The sense of the sentence that begins here is: his dominion, which he exercises from David's throne and over David's kingdom and which he confirms and sustains by judgment and justice both now and forever, is vast and forever peaceful.

Think of the miracle we celebrate this night as you speak of what God "will do."

His dominion is **vast**
   and forever **peaceful**,
from **David's** throne, and over his **kingdom**,
   which he **confirms** and **sustains**
by **judgment** and **justice**,
   both **now** and **forever**.
The **zeal** of the LORD of hosts will **do** this!

For meditation and context:

TO KEEP IN MIND

Build: refers to increasing vocal intensity as you work toward a climactic point in the text. It calls for intensified emotional energy, which can be communicated by an increase or decrease in volume, or by speaking faster or slower. The point is to show more passion, greater urgency, or concern.

RESPONSORIAL PSALM   Psalm 96:1–2, 2–3, 11–12, 13 (Luke 2:11)

R. Today is born our Savior, Christ the Lord.

Sing to the LORD a new song;
   sing to the LORD, all you lands.
Sing to the LORD; bless his name.

Announce his salvation, day after day.
   Tell his glory among the nations;
   among all peoples, his wondrous deeds.

Let the heavens be glad and the
   earth rejoice;
   let the sea and what fills it resound;
   let the plains be joyful and all that is
   in them!
Then shall all the trees of the forest exult.

They shall exult before the LORD,
   for he comes;
   for he comes to rule the earth.
He shall rule the world with justice
   and the peoples with his constancy.

Titus = TĪ-tuhs

Let "Beloved" set the tone. This birth announcement is full of delight: "The grace of God" is Isaiah's "great light" that transforms all of life.

The entire text is one sentence; plan your pauses and breaths and don't let the absence of periods cause you to rush.

The changes that God's "grace" brings are a source of great joy!

"the blessed hope, the appearance" = "the blessed hope which is the appearance"

The word "cleanse" is an allusion to Baptism.

The word "eager" should not only characterize our commitment to Christ but the tone of your delivery!

READING II   Titus 2:11–14

A reading from the Letter of Saint Paul to Titus

Beloved:
The grace of **God** has appeared, **saving** all
   and training us to **reject** godless ways and **worldly** desires
   and to live **temperately**, **justly**, and **devoutly** in this age,
as we await the blessed **hope**,
   the **appearance** of the glory of our great **God**
   and **savior** Jesus **Christ**,
who **gave** himself for us to **deliver** us from all **lawlessness**
   and to **cleanse** for himself a people as his **own**,
eager to do what is **good**.

But in the midst of these dark days for Israel, the prophet Isaiah foresaw a new day for Israel, one that rested its hope in a newborn son who would rule righteously and faithfully over Israel. Scholars suspect that Isaiah may have originally believed that Israel's next ruler, King Hezekiah (715–687 BC), was the fulfillment of his prophecy. History would show that Israel would have to wait another 700 years before Isaiah's prophecies were truly fulfilled in the birth of Jesus.

READING II   At both the night and dawn Masses, we hear from Paul's Letter to Titus for the Second Reading. Titus was one of Paul's trusted co-workers and field delegates in his missionary outreach to the Gentiles. Titus is mentioned by Paul in other letters. For example, in his Letter to the Galatians, we hear that Titus was a Gentile who came to believe in Christ and that he accompanied Paul and Barnabas to meet with the Apostles in Jerusalem for the Church's first council (Galatians 2:1–3). In the Second Letter to the Corinthians, we read that Paul felt close to Titus (2 Corinthians 2:13; 7:6, 13–14). He relied on Titus to help organize the collection of money for the poor people in Corinth (2 Corinthians 8:6, 16–23) and to resolve a conflict between Paul and the church in Corinth (2 Corinthians 12:17–18).

In his letter to Titus, Paul refers to Christ as "the grace of God." "Grace" (in Greek, *charis*) means favor, often divine favor freely given. It is an interesting way to define Christ—as a divine favor freely given

GOSPEL   Luke 2:1–14

A reading from the holy Gospel according to Luke

In those days a **decree** went out from Caesar **Augustus**
   that the whole **world** should be **enrolled**.
This was the **first** enrollment,
   when **Quirinius** was governor of **Syria**.
So all went to be **enrolled**, **each** to his own **town**.
And **Joseph** too went up from **Galilee** from the town
    of **Nazareth**
   to **Judea**, to the city of **David** that is called **Bethlehem**,
   because he was of the **house** and **family** of David,
   to be enrolled with **Mary**, his **betrothed**, who was with **child**.
While they were there,
   the time came for her to **have** her child,
   and she gave **birth** to her firstborn **son**.
She wrapped him in **swaddling** clothes and laid him in a **manger**,
   because there was no **room** for them in the **inn**.

Now there were **shepherds** in that region living in the **fields**
   and keeping the **night** watch over their flock.
The **angel** of the Lord **appeared** to them
   and the **glory** of the Lord **shone** around them,
   and they were struck with great **fear**.
The angel **said** to them,
   "Do not be **afraid**;
   for **behold**, I proclaim to you good **news** of great **joy**
   that will be for **all** the people.
For **today** in the city of **David**
   a **savior** has been born for you who is **Christ** and **Lord**.

The details set a historical context for this familiar story. Use the concrete information without fanfare, speaking with confidence and conviction.

Quirinius – kwih-RIN-ee-uhs

Mention of Joseph is significant for it is through his adoptive father that Jesus receives his royal lineage. Syria = SEER-ee-uh; Galilee = GAL-ih-lee; Judea = joo-DEE-uh.

Mary's name emerges from the listing of geographic names; make it stand out.

Narrate the birth simply, with peaceful joy. Stress "son" instead of "firstborn" so as not to suggest that there were later children. "Firstborn" is more of a title than a birth order reference.

Don't rush these tender images.

The mood shifts as the shepherds are introduced. Angels dominate the rest of the story.

Take a slight pause before the sudden declaration of the angelic announcement.

Speak the angel's greeting with confident reassurance.

From the hushed "manger" we have moved out into the open night sky and a grand angelic announcement of the Savior's birth. Stress "savior," "Christ," and "Lord."

---

to us. Paul informs Titus of a threefold favor from God given to us in Christ: universal salvation; "training" to know how best to live; deliverance and purification from "all lawlessness."

| GOSPEL | Matthew and Luke each present their own narratives on the birth of Christ. For the Vigil Mass, we heard Matthew's account of Jesus's birth (Matthew 1:18–25). Tonight, we hear Luke's report: Luke 2:1–14.

Scholars have long noted Luke's interest in historical detail. This is evident in Luke beginning his narration of the birth of Jesus by placing it within historical context. By identifying Augustus as the Roman Emperor (Caesar) who sent out a "decree" to determine the population of the Roman Empire ("that the whole world should be enrolled"), Luke provides us with the timeframe of 27 BC–AD 14 for the birth of Christ, since these were the years within which Augustus ruled. Luke further narrows the date of Jesus's birth by referring to the enrollment that occurred while "Quirinius was governor of Syria." This census occurred in the latter years of Augustus's reign as Caesar. With this limited information, Jesus's birth is commonly dated by scholars to the years 6–4 BC.

Luke provides additional background on Mary and Joseph beyond what we hear from Matthew's Gospel narrative. He notes that Nazareth was the village in which Joseph resided and Bethlehem was Joseph's city of origin "because he was of the house

No need to reprise the tender quality of the first mention of "swaddling clothes."

Mood shifts again as the skies fill with angelic beings. Don't rush these familiar lines.

Your hearers should detect here the antecedent of our liturgical "Glory to God."

And this will be a **sign** for you:
> you will find an **infant** wrapped in **swaddling** clothes
> and lying in a **manger**."
And **suddenly** there was a **multitude** of the heavenly host with the angel,
> **praising** God and saying:
>> "**Glory** to God in the **highest**
>>> and on **earth peace** to those on whom his **favor** rests."

TO KEEP IN MIND

Each text contains **three kinds of content**: intellectual-theological, emotional, and aesthetic. The plot and details of the story and the theological teaching behind them comprise the intellectual-theological content. How the author or characters feel (or want us to feel) is the emotional content. Elements that make the writing pleasing—rhythm, repetition, suspense, and picturesque language—are the aesthetic content.

---

and family of David." We hear that Jesus was Mary's "firstborn son," forced to be delivered in a stable "because there was no room for them in the inn."

But Luke's aims in narrating the birth of Jesus are not merely historical. They are also theological. By including what the shepherds in a nearby field experienced when "an angel of the Lord" appeared to them, Luke is able to communicate the divine identity of this newborn son. He refers to the baby Jesus as "Savior," "Christ," and "Lord." For Luke, this was the heart of the "good news of great joy for all the people": in the birth of the son of Mary, we find our salvation.

THE NATIVITY OF THE LORD (CHRISTMAS): DAWN

LECTIONARY #15

Isaiah = Ī-ZAY-uh

Pause after the word "see." "Behold" is a better exclamation.

This short reading is an opportunity to do much with few words: announce the savior's coming and the transformation of the nation into a "holy" people!

Proclaim with authority and conviction.

Pause after "comes!" and then begin rebuilding your energy.

The second term ("redeemed"), as always, receives more energy than the first ("holy people").

"Frequented" is an unexpected name for Jerusalem. Announce joyfully that the land will no longer be "forsaken" but will be overrun with returning exiles!

For meditation and context:

READING I   Isaiah 62:11–12

A reading from the Book of the Prophet Isaiah

See, the LORD proclaims
    to the **ends** of the **earth**:
say to daughter **Zion**,
    your **savior** comes!
Here is his **reward** with him,
    his **recompense** before him.
They shall be called the **holy** people,
    the **redeemed** of the LORD,
and you shall be called "**Frequented**,"
    a city that is **not forsaken**.

RESPONSORIAL PSALM   Psalm 97:1, 6, 11–12

R. **A light will shine on us this day: the Lord is born for us.**

The LORD is king; let the earth rejoice;
    let the many isles be glad.
The heavens proclaim his justice,
    and all peoples see his glory.

Light dawns for the just;
    and gladness, for the upright of heart.
Be glad in the LORD, you just,
    and give thanks to his holy name.

TO KEEP IN MIND

Pray the Scriptures: Make reading these Scriptures a part of your prayer life every week, and especially during the week prior to the liturgy in which you will proclaim.

READING I   Once again we hear from the prophet Isaiah. As with the First Reading for the vigil Mass, this is one of the later prophecies in the Book of Isaiah—one from the period of Israel's return after Babylonian captivity, sometime shortly after 538 BC. It is, in fact, a continuation of Isaiah's oracle heard from the First Reading of the vigil Mass.

In this passage the people rejoice in their newfound status of deliverance and restoration from exile. Isaiah speaks of Jerusalem whose "savior" has come.

Continuing with the language of new beginnings, Isaiah shares the good news that the citizens of Jerusalem shall once again "be called the holy people," "redeemed," a people "frequented," "a city . . . not forsaken". In the aftermath of the Babylonian exile, this period of restoration was like a new birth for Israel. For Christians, the birth of Christ fulfilled Isaiah's prophecy: "Your savior comes!"

READING II   The Second Reading is taken again from Paul's Letter to Titus. We learn from the opening section of this letter that Titus was a leader among the Christian communities on the island of Crete. Much of the letter focuses on church order (the duties and tasks of bishops) and on how to deal with false teachings. Today's excerpt contains some of the "sound doctrine" (Titus 1:9) that Paul instructed Titus to teach the Christians on Crete.

Paul reminds Titus to pass onto the Cretans "our common faith" (Titus 1:4) and understanding of Christ. First, the gift of Christ stems not from human endeavors

READING II   Titus 3:4–7

A reading from the Letter of Saint Paul to Titus

Beloved:
When the **kindness** and generous **love**
    of God our savior appeared,
not because of any righteous **deeds** we had done
    but because of his **mercy**,
he **saved** us through the **bath** of **rebirth**
    and **renewal** by the Holy **Spirit**,
whom he richly **poured** out on us
    through Jesus **Christ** our **savior**,
so that we might be **justified** by his grace
    and become **heirs** in hope of eternal **life**.

Titus = Tī-tuhs

Short readings always call for slow reading.

You are announcing salvation that arrived in the person of Christ.

This is *why* we were saved: because of God's mercy, not our merit.

Speak with joy of the "bath of rebirth" (Baptism) and the gift of the Spirit (Confirmation).

This is catechetical instruction that must sound like good news.

Let your own gratitude echo in your voice.

TO KEEP IN MIND
Know who wrote the letter and who received it. Discover the circumstances. **The intent of each letter dictates the tone.** Often Paul is the writer; he is motivated by multiple concerns: to instruct, console, encourage, chastise, warn, settle disputes, and more. When reading from one of his letters, be aware of what he's trying to accomplish.

---

but from God's mercy and love for us. Second, Christ and the Holy Spirit work together for our salvation. Third, as believers in Christ, we are justified before God, "heirs" to the promise of eternal life. Paul's words to Titus help us contextualize the meaning of Christmas morning.

GOSPEL   The Gospel reading continues Luke's birth narrative, heard at the Mass during the night. The core details of Luke's entire infancy narrative (Luke 1:5—2:52) are found only in Luke. One of the unique features is the angelic

visitations to Zechariah and Mary (1:5–20; 1:26–38) and to the shepherds in the field (2:8–20), heard, in part, in today's reading. These angelic appearances serve to reveal the true identity of Jesus as Son of the Most High, the Lord and Messiah.

The inclusion of the angels visiting the shepherds serves an important theological function for Luke. Shepherds were culturally devalued, seen by many as having low social rank and little honor. The great Canticles of Mary (1:46–55) and Zechariah (1:68–79) speak to God's past promises,

now fulfilled in the births of John and Jesus, and bringing about a great reversal of fortune for the strong and the weak, the privileged and the marginalized. For Luke, the revelation of Christ's birth to the shepherds in the fields aptly demonstrates the great reversal of God's empowerment of the weak and marginalized. Further, the shepherds' faith in the Word of God to them and their determination to communicate this good news to Mary and Joseph confirms the reversed status of those previously held in low regard. The shepherds' reaction to these events, "glorifying and praising

The disappearance of the angels is not a natural phenomenon; it's part of a miracle!

The shepherds want to go not to "verify" but to revel in what was revealed to them.

Begin "in haste," but slow your pace when you mention "Mary and Joseph"and shift to a hushed tone as if in deference to the sleeping child. After naming the parents, pause so it doesn't sound like all three are in the manger.

The shepherds' excitement grows and continues till we hear of Mary.

Don't rush the narration of this precious moment.

The shepherds exit joyfully. Distinguish "heard" (expectation) from "seen" (fulfillment).

TO KEEP IN MIND

Tell the story: Make the story yours, then share it with your listeners. Use the language; don't throw away any good words. Settings give context; don't rush the description. Characters must be believable; understand their motivation. Dialogue reveals character; distinguish one character from another with your voice.

GOSPEL   Luke 2:15–20

A reading from the holy Gospel according to Luke

When the **angels** went **away** from them to **heaven**,
    the **shepherds** said to one another,
    "Let us **go**, then, to **Bethlehem**
    to **see** this thing that has taken place,
    which the Lord has made **known** to us."
So they went in **haste** and found **Mary** and **Joseph**,
    and the **infant** lying in the **manger**.
When they **saw** this,
    they made known the **message**
    that had been **told** them about this child.
All who heard it were **amazed**
    by what had been **told** them by the shepherds.
And Mary **kept** all these things,
    reflecting on them in her **heart**.
Then the shepherds **returned**,
    glorifying and **praising** God
    for all they had **heard** and **seen**,
    just as it had been **told** to them.

God for all they had heard and seen," reinforces the Lukan theme of universal salvation for all people who believe in Christ.

Twice in Luke's infancy narrative, at the end of today's reading and in the report of Jesus in the Temple at age twelve (Luke 2:51), Luke informs us, "Mary kept all these things, reflecting on them in her heart." Of the four Gospel writers, Luke offers us the most insights into Mary, allowing us to formulate somewhat of a character sketch of her. In his infancy narrative, Luke presents Mary as a woman of courage, trusting that the message from the angel Gabriel was of divine origin. She is also presented as a woman of faith, connecting the events taking place in her life with the past promises God had made to Israel. In today's Gospel Reading, she is presented as a woman of deep contemplation, reflecting on the meaning of the birth of her newborn son.

Luke returns to this characterization of Mary as a woman of prayer and reflection in his presentation of the twelve-year-old boy Jesus being found by Mary and Joseph in the Temple in Jerusalem (Luke 2:41–51). Here Luke comments that "his mother kept all these things in her heart." Given the narrative time that elapses within the opening chapters of Luke's Gospel account—a span of twelve years in Luke 1 and 2—Luke is presenting an important point here: Mary, the mother of the Messiah, has been prayerfully discerning the course of her son's life from newborn child to young man.

THE NATIVITY OF THE LORD (CHRISTMAS): DAY

LECTIONARY #16

READING I   Isaiah 52:7–10

A reading from the Book of the Prophet Isaiah

How **beautiful** upon the **mountains**
    are the **feet** of him who brings glad **tidings**,
announcing **peace**, bearing good **news**,
    announcing **salvation**, and saying to **Zion**,
    "Your **God** is **King**!"

Hark! Your sentinels raise a **cry**,
    together they shout for **joy**,
for they see **directly**, before their **eyes**,
    the LORD **restoring** Zion.
Break out together in **song**,
    O **ruins** of Jerusalem!
For the LORD **comforts** his people,
    he **redeems** Jerusalem.
The LORD has **bared** his holy arm
    in the sight of all the **nations**;
all the ends of the **earth** will behold
    the **salvation** of our **God**.

Isaiah = ī-ZAY-uh

This is musical poetry that must *sound* like it means, i.e. joy must echo in every line.

"Feet" is a *synecdoche*, a poetic device that uses a part to represent the whole person.

The news he bears even makes the messenger "beautiful"!

Without overdoing, take a brief pause before and after "Hark!"

Isaiah stresses the reality ("before their eyes") of God's presence among the people.

A new beat begins at "Break out." Increase your energy and volume.

Note the words marked for stress: "ruins" and "redeemed," not "Jerusalem."
bared = bayrd

The final lines tell us what God has done and what God will do. On this day, we see "salvation" lying in the manger. Speak with that awareness.

| READING I | Today's reading comes from around the year 550 BC, during the period of Israel's captivity in Babylon. Isaiah was one of two prophets who arose during the long years of Israel's exile (597-538 BC). In the early stages of captivity, Ezekiel was called to be a prophet; in the latter period, the prophet we now call "Second Isaiah" took up his work.

The collection of oracles and prophecies of "Second Isaiah" are found in chapters 40–55 in the Book of Isaiah. Scholars are uncertain as to the exact identity of this second prophet who emerged during the Babylonian exile. The name "Second Isaiah," commonly applied to him, acknowledges that his message resembles that of his predecessor, Isaiah of Jerusalem (who lived during the period of the Assyrian crisis, 740–700 BC), and it differentiates between these two historical figures who lived centuries apart.

Second Isaiah was a prophet of great hope whose fundamental message is succinctly presented in the opening verse of chapters 40–55: "Comfort, give comfort to my people, says the Lord" (Isaiah 40:1). (We heard those words on the Second Sunday of Advent). This tone of unthinkable optimism occurs again in today's reading: "Break out together in song, O ruins of Jerusalem! For the Lord comforts his people, he redeems Jerusalem." Isaiah spoke this message to the Israelites who were now in their second generation of captivity in Babylon. Words such as "peace," "good news," and "salvation" were long gone from the vocabulary of an exiled people. Yet Second Isaiah envisioned a new beginning, a time in which Israel would proclaim once again, "Your God is King!"

For meditation and context:

TO KEEP IN MIND

The opening: Establish eye contact and announce, from memory, "A reading from . . . ." Then take a pause (three full beats!) before starting the reading. The correct pronunciation is "A [uh] reading from" instead of "A [ay] reading from."

RESPONSORIAL PSALM   Psalm 98:1, 2–3, 3–4, 5–6 (3c)

R. All the ends of the earth have seen the saving power of God.

Sing to the LORD a new song,
    for he has done wondrous deeds;
his right hand has won victory for him,
    his holy arm.

The LORD has made his salvation known:
    in the sight of the nations he has revealed
        his justice.
He has remembered his kindness and his
        faithfulness
    toward the house of Israel.

All the ends of the earth have seen
    the salvation by our God.
Sing joyfully to the LORD, all you lands;
    break into song; sing praise.

Sing praise to the LORD with the harp,
    with the harp and melodious song.
With trumpets and the sound of the horn
    sing joyfully before the King, the LORD.

Give this theological oratory the joyful sound it needs on Christmas: before, God spoke indirectly, now he speaks through his Son!

Contrast "times past" with "these last days" and "prophets" with "Son."

These descriptive clauses (probably from a hymn of praise) describe the "Son" whose birth we celebrate. Give them the tonal quality of a birthday toast.

"Refulgence" = radiance or reflection. The second term ("the very imprint") requires greater emphasis.

"Accomplished purification" means his Death and Resurrection through which he saved *us*.

Jesus is Lord even of the angels. Jesus's "inherited" name is "Son."

You press the point of his superiority with a logical argument.

The logical reasoning continues, but give it a tone fitting for this grand solemnity.

READING II   Hebrews 1:1–6

A reading from the Letter to the Hebrews

Brothers and sisters:
In times **past**, God spoke in **partial** and **various** ways
    to our **ancestors** through the **prophets**;
    in these **last** days, he has spoken to us through the **Son**,
    whom he made **heir** of all things
    and **through** whom he created the **universe**,
    who is the **refulgence** of his **glory**,
        the very **imprint** of his **being**,
    and who **sustains** all things by his mighty **word**.
    When he had accomplished purification from **sins**,
    he took his **seat** at the **right** hand of the **Majesty** on high,
    as far **superior** to the **angels**
    as the **name** he has inherited is more **excellent** than theirs.

For to **which** of the angels did God ever say:
    You are my **son***; this day I have* **begotten** *you*?
Or again:
    I will be a **father** *to him, and he shall be a* **son** *to me*?
And again, when he leads the **firstborn** into the world, he says:
    Let all the **angels** *of God* **worship** *him*.

Israel was, historically, only a few years away from release from captivity in Babylon. The rest of the world would wait another 500 years before seeing Isaiah's words fulfilled in the birth of Christ: "All the ends of the earth will behold the salvation of our God."

 Today's reading for Mass comes from the opening words of the Letter to the Hebrews. While the authorship of Hebrews was traditionally attributed to Paul, scholars no longer believe he wrote this letter. Its style, vocabulary,

and theological vision are too different from the letters of Paul to support the claim of Pauline authorship. The early Church may have, in part, attributed Hebrews to Paul because from very early on the thirteen letters of Paul in the New Testament were collected and circulated together to various Christian communities. In later manuscripts, the Letter to the Hebrews was often attached to the collection of the thirteen letters of Paul, commonly known as the Pauline Corpus. Today, the real author of Hebrews remains unknown.

The Letter to the Hebrews begins with the assertion that Christ is the climax of God's revelation to the world, the culmination of God's Word spoken through Israel's prophets. Today's reading (and this letter in general) contains some of the New Testament's highest Christology, referring to Jesus as the "refulgence" of God's glory, the "very imprint" of God's being, "far superior to the angels."

The reading ends with the first two proofs (in a series of seven proofs) of Jesus's superiority to the angels based on excerpts from Old Testament texts. The

John uses staircase parallelism (where the last word of one phrase becomes the first word of the next—less apparent here in the English translation) to introduce his dominant themes: Christ's preexistence, life, light and darkness, the world, and witness.

Stress John's obvious echo of Genesis. Don't rush the opening lines that artfully proclaim Christ's identity.

Don't narrate words, but a person. Don't let this sound like theology, but like someone describing their beloved.

"Life" refers to the abundance Christ came to share.

Let this be a powerful statement of faith!

Pause before introducing John. Speak of him with the same reverence Jesus used for his cousin.

Stress the word "testimony" but not "testify." Testimony nourishes faith.

"He was not" is just a clarification that doesn't need stress.

Don't overdo the irony in these lines or assume a judgmental attitude.

> **TO KEEP IN MIND**
> **Poetry** is gourmet food, eaten slowly and savored. Go slowly. Pay attention to the sounds, rhythms, and repetitions.

GOSPEL   John 1:1–18

A reading from the holy Gospel according to John

In the **beginning** was the **Word**,
 and the **Word** was with **God**,
 and the Word **was** God.
He was in the **beginning** with God.
All things came to be **through** him,
 and without him **nothing** came to be.
What came to be through him was **life**,
 and this life was the **light** of the human race;
 the light **shines** in the **darkness**,
 and the darkness has not **overcome** it.
A man named **John** was sent from **God.**
He came for **testimony**, to testify to the **light**,
 so that all might **believe** through him.
He was not the light,
 but came to **testify** to the light.
The **true** light, which enlightens **everyone**,
 was coming into the world.
He was **in** the world,
 and the world came to **be** through him,
 but the world did not **know** him.
He came to what was his **own**,
 but his own people did not **accept** him.

---

author's focus on this matter stems from a conviction in the divinity of Christ that was clearly shown in Christ's Death, Resurrection, and Ascension into heaven.

 GOSPEL John 1:1–18, the longer version of today's Gospel Reading, contains two different literary forms. Verses 1–5, 10–11, 14 are poetic in structure (in fact, they appear to be lines from a hymn). Verses 6–9, 12–13, 15–18 are in narrative prose. Parallels to this Johannine hymn concerning the identity of Christ are found in the letters of Paul; for example, Philippians 2:6–11 and Colossians 1:15–20. Scholars suspect that these hymns may have been originally used in liturgical settings of the early Christians.

All four New Testament Gospel writers begin their narratives of the life of Christ differently: Matthew begins with Jesus's genealogy, Mark opens up with the preaching of John the Baptist, Luke provides an introduction that mimics Greek classical literature, and John starts with a Christological hymn. Each Gospel writer presents a different portrait of Jesus. Matthew portrays Jesus as the new Moses, Mark as the suffering Messiah, Luke as the universal savior, and John speaks of Jesus as the Word made flesh. In today's Gospel Reading, we see John presenting his fundamental portrait of Jesus in the opening words of his account: "And the Word became flesh."

John's description of Jesus uses the Greek word *ho logos* ("the Word"). In the first-century Mediterranean world, "the Word" had both a religious and a philosophical meaning. Judaism taught that God's

Speak with awe of the great privilege of becoming "children of God."

Your pace quickens and intensifies as you move through the "not," "nor," and "but" phrases.

Speak these lines as if you were narrating the birth in the manger.

"And we saw" contrasts with "his own people" who did not accept him.

The testimony of John reminds us, even on this Christmas day, that we celebrate not just a babe in arms, but the Lord of life.

"Fullness" echoes "life" in the opening verses of this text. It is a life he gives in abundance.

"Law" and "Moses" contrast with "grace" and "Jesus." The emphasis goes to the "grace and truth" we've received in Christ.

The final sentence is a solemn declaration of the unique relationship between Father and Son.

But to those who **did** accept him
  he gave power to become **children** of **God**,
  to those who **believe** in his name,
  who were born not by **natural** generation
  nor by human **choice** nor by a **man's** decision
  but of **God**.
    And the **Word** became **flesh**
      and made his **dwelling** among us,
      and we saw his **glory**,
      the glory as of the Father's only **Son**,
      full of **grace** and **truth**.
John **testified** to him and cried out, saying,
  "This was he of whom I said,
  'The one who is coming **after** me ranks **ahead** of me
  because he existed **before** me.'"
From his **fullness** we have all received,
  grace in place of **grace**,
  because while the **law** was given through **Moses**,
  grace and **truth** came through Jesus **Christ**.
No one has ever **seen** God.
The only **Son**, **God**, who is at the Father's **side**,
  has **revealed** him.

[Shorter: John 1:1–5, 9–14]

TO KEEP IN MIND
Eye contact connects you with those to whom you minister. Look at the assembly during the middle and at the end of every thought or sentence.

"Word" was the creative force that generated everything into being (see, for example, the creation story of Genesis 1:1–2:4a) and was personified as God's Wisdom in the world (see, for instance, Wisdom of Solomon 7–8). Greek philosophy taught that *Logos* was the force that governed all intelligible reality. Consequently, people who had both Jewish and Gentile backgrounds could derive different meanings from John's identifying Jesus as "the Word."

Today's Gospel is an apt culmination of the four Gospel readings heard throughout the Masses of Christmas. John sets before us an important perspective on who this newborn son of Mary is. Jesus, "the Word," has been God and with God from the very "beginning." He is the source of all "life," "the light" that "shines in the darkness." This life and light has been "in the world" even though "the world did not know him" nor did "his own people" accept him. But for those who believe in Jesus as "the Word," then and now, we are "children of God."

Throughout Christmas, we celebrate the birth of Jesus and the reality that Christ "made his dwelling among us." We honor this newborn child as both the son of Mary and as "the Father's only Son." We acknowledge that in Christ we find the Son of God, our Lord and Messiah, the one "full of grace and truth."

THE HOLY FAMILY OF JESUS, MARY, AND JOSEPH

LECTIONARY #17

READING I   Genesis 15:1–6; 21:1–3

A reading from the Book of Genesis

The word of the **Lord** came to **Abram** in a **vision**, saying:
    "Fear **not**, Abram!
        I am your **shield**;
        I will make your **reward** very **great**."
But **Abram** said,
    "O Lord God, what **good** will your gifts be,
    if I keep on being **childless**
    and have as my **heir** the **steward** of my house, **Eliezer**?"
Abram continued,
    "**See**, you have given me no **offspring**,
    and so one of my **servants** will be my heir."
Then the word of the Lord came to him:
    "**No**, that one shall **not** be your heir;
    your own **issue** shall be your heir."
The Lord took Abram **outside** and said,
    "Look up at the **sky** and count the **stars**, if you can.
Just **so**," he added, "shall your **descendants** be."
Abram put his **faith** in the Lord,
    who **credited** it to him as an act of **righteousness**.

Margin notes:

Genesis = JEN-uh-sis

Abram = AY-br*m

Let your tone suggest this is not an ordinary encounter, but a "vision" of divine encounter.

God's first words are of reassurance. "Fear not" is a constant biblical theme that Jesus will take up. Speak God's promise with authority.

Because Abram believes, he's all the more distressed that God's gifts will benefit his "servant" instead of his own progeny.

Abram's relationship with God is intimate, so he doesn't hesitate to make his case!

This narration should signal that God's reply will shift Abram's thinking.

Speak with conviction.

Narrate slowly to suggest passage of time.

There is much implied in God's few words of promise. Don't rush them.

Your tone should reveal the great significance of Abram's decision to trust in God.

Pause before starting the final paragraph focused on Sarah.

Today options are given for the readings. Contact your parish staff to learn which readings will be used.

READING I | **GENESIS.** Genesis 12–25 contains the cycle of stories about Abraham (called Abram, in this early part of the story), a long saga of covenantal blessings and journey. God promised Abraham land and descendants in response to Abraham's trust. Genesis 15:6 in today's reading, is the key to understanding the rest of the story: "Abram put his faith in the Lord, who credited it to him as an act of righteousness." It was Abraham's *faith* that made him righteous in God's eye, deserving to be the recipient of God's covenant.

In today's First Reading we hear about God's covenant with Abraham and the birth of Abraham's son, Isaac. But the story of God's promise is actually presented four times in the Book of Genesis (12:1–4; 15:1–21; 17:1–27; 22:1–19), each with varying elements. Scholars commonly account for these four versions of the story by saying that the final composition of the entire Pentateuch (the first five books of the Bible) resulted from a smaller number of more extensive works ("documents") written independently, at different periods, covering the same ground. These were woven together by different editors over a period of about 500 years, from about 950-450 bc. Genesis 15 (today's reading) was recorded around 700 bc, shortly after the fall of the northern kingdom of Israel to Assyria.

In it, God comes to Abraham in a vision, offering him a divine commitment: "Fear not, Abram! I am your shield; I will make your reward very great." Given his

Few words relate major details and events of salvation history. Use every word of the sentence.

Abraham's age reinforces God's fidelity to his promises and the miraculous nature of Isaac's birth.

This is joyful news. Note, Sarah's role is restated for emphasis.

The LORD took note of **Sarah** as he had **said** he would;
  he **did** for her as he had **promised**.
Sarah became **pregnant** and bore Abraham a **son** in his old **age**,
  at the set **time** that God had **stated**.
Abraham gave the name **Isaac** to this son of his
  whom Sarah **bore** him.

Or:

READING I   Sirach 3:2–6, 12–14

Sirach = SEER-ak; Sī-ruhk

A reading from the Book of Sirach

  God sets a **father** in **honor** over his **children**;
    a **mother's authority** he **confirms** over her **sons**.
  Whoever honors his **father** atones for **sins**,
    and **preserves** himself from them.
  When he **prays**, he is **heard**;
    he stores up **riches** who reveres his **mother**.
  Whoever honors his **father** is gladdened by **children**,
    and, when he **prays**, is **heard**.
  Whoever reveres his **father** will live a long **life**;
    he who **obeys** his father brings **comfort** to his **mother**.

  My son, take **care** of your father when he is **old**;
    grieve him **not** as long as he **lives**.
  Even if his **mind** fail, be **considerate** of him;
    revile him **not** all the days of his **life**;
  kindness to a **father** will not be **forgotten**,
    firmly **planted** against the debt of your **sins**
    —a house raised in **justice** to you.

Each couplet names a benefit that results from honoring one's parents. Don't deliver the couplets like items in a sales pitch extolling the qualities of a new car. These are noble consequences of righteous and noble behavior.

Note the carefully balanced reasoning: "father/children" and "mother/sons."

Imagine a loving grandparent offering this wise advice to beloved grandchildren.

Note the repetition of "when he prays." These benefits are not interest on an investment but merciful grace lavished on those who obey God's holy will.

Honor in the home establishes peace and brings abundant blessing.

Pause before the second paragraph. The tone has become more personal as the advice is spoken directly to "my son."

The challenges of caring for aged parents are acknowledged, but the responsibility of tender care remains.

Imagine the words "it will be" and "it becomes" initiating the last two lines respectively.

"old age," Abraham was nearly despondent over his childless state. So God assured Abraham that one day his descendants would be as numerous as the stars. In spite of his deep sadness, Abraham believed God. The reading ends with Sarah (called Sarai here) giving birth to Isaac, and God fulfilling his "promise."

  In the story of Abraham, Sarah, and Isaac, we see God ever-present in the struggle, faithful to his covenantal promises. During periods of doubt and fear, the faith of Abraham and Sarah sustains them.

With this family, we see the foreshadowing of the holy family that is to come—Jesus, Mary, and Joseph.

  SIRACH. Written about 200 years before the birth of Jesus, the Book of Sirach offers moral instruction for Jewish daily life and human relationships. The Jewish sage who wrote this text is clearly male, as is seen throughout the writing (see, for example, Sirach 9:1–9; 30:1–13). One of the recurring themes taken up in Sirach, and throughout Israel's wisdom literature, is that of family relations. Today's reading

offers a prime example of the ideal family structure, one in which "honor" governs family ties. Children are clearly expected to obey and revere their parents, while parents are to support each other and exercise authority over their children with care.

  From the Jewish perspective, living out proper family relations is not an end in itself. How one honors and respects parents has a direct impact on one's relationship with God. According to Sirach, when a child "honors" and "reveres" his father, especially in old age, various divine rewards

For meditation and context:

TO KEEP IN MIND

When practicing, **read Scriptures aloud**, taking note of stress and pause suggestions. After several readings, alter the stress markings to suit your style and interpretation.

RESPONSORIAL PSALM   Psalm 105:1–2, 3–4, 5–6, 8–9 (7a , 8a)

R. The Lord remembers his covenant forever.

Give thanks to the Lord, invoke his name;
    make known among the nations
       his deeds.
Sing to him, sing his praise,
    proclaim all his wondrous deeds.

Glory in his holy name;
    rejoice, O hearts that seek the Lord!
Look to the Lord in his strength;
    constantly seek his face.

You descendants of Abraham, his servants,
    sons of Jacob, his chosen ones!
He, the Lord, is our God;
    throughout the earth his
       judgments prevail.

He remembers forever his covenant
    which he made binding for a thousand
       generations
which he entered into with Abraham
    and by his oath to Isaac.

Or:

For meditation and context:

TO KEEP IN MIND

Know who wrote the letter and who received it. Discover the circumstances. **The intent of each letter dictates the tone.** Often Paul is the writer; he is motivated by multiple concerns: to instruct, console, encourage, chastise, warn, settle disputes, and more. When reading from one of his letters, be aware of what he's trying to accomplish.

RESPONSORIAL PSALM   Psalm 128:1–2, 3, 4–5 (1)

R. Blessed are those who fear the Lord and walk in his ways.

Blessed is everyone who fears the Lord,
    who walks in his ways!
For you shall eat the fruit of your handiwork;
    blessed shall you be, and favored.

Your wife shall be like a fruitful vine
    in the recesses of your home;
your children like olive plants
    around your table.

Behold, thus is the man blessed
    who fears the Lord.
The Lord bless you from Zion:
    may you see the prosperity of Jerusalem
       all the days of your life.

In light of the First Reading from Genesis, it's easy to see why the author emphasizes, through repetition, the "faith" of Abraham. Three major stages in Abraham's life are named, and each is characterized "by faith." Stress those words each time they recur, following them with a slight pause for emphasis, and employing greater stress on each recurrence.

Abraham left his original home to seek God's promised land.

READING II   Hebrews 11:8, 11–12, 17–19

A reading from the Letter to the Hebrews

Brothers and sisters:
By faith Abraham obeyed when he was called to go out
     to a place
    that he was to **receive** as an **inheritance**;
    he went out, not **knowing** where he was to **go.**

are accorded: sins are atoned, prayers are heard, children are forthcoming, and long life is granted. Jesus himself would have been familiar with these Jewish wisdom traditions on family relations. They certainly governed and guided his relationship with Mary and his foster-father, Joseph.

READING II   **HEBREWS.** Toward the end of his Letter to the Hebrews, the author draws upon some of the most important and well-known figures from the Old Testament to emphasize the importance of faith and perseverance in

the face of the many challenges of life. Today's reading excerpts verses about Abraham, but in addition to him, others such as Abel, Enoch, and Noah are also upheld as models of those who have pleased God by their obedience and faith within their life circumstances.

In today's reading, the first instance from Abraham's life that is reported is God's call to Abraham to "go forth from your land . . . to a land that I will show you," a land unknown to him (see Genesis 12:1–4). By faith, Abraham proceeded, trusting in the word of the Lord. The second

act of faith Hebrews cites is when Abraham believed that God would bring forth a descendent for him and his wife Sarah, despite their lifetime of infertility (see Genesis 15:1–5). Abraham unconditionally believed in God's promise. A third time in Abraham's life when his faith was tested was in his willing sacrifice of his son, Isaac (see Genesis 22:1–18). This may have been Abraham's ultimate test of faith, since so much of his hope rested upon his son Isaac.

The author of Hebrews presents Abraham's faith in the context of his family life. In his decision about where to live, in

Abraham trusted God's promise to give him a son through his wife Sarah. The author is arguing a case, like a lawyer, to persuade. Use the details to reinforce the premise that Abraham consistently trusted God's word.

This is an elaboration on the previous point: because Abraham trusted, the whole people of Israel came into being.

The case strengthens with each "by faith." The strongest point is the last: because of his faith, Abraham was even able to offer up his son.

The author explains why Abraham had such radical trust: he believed God could raise Isaac from the dead. The Church sees here a clear anticipation of Christ's Resurrection.

By **faith** he received power to **generate**,
    even though he was **past** the normal age
    —and Sarah **herself** was **sterile**—
    for he thought that the one who had made the **promise**
        was **trustworthy**.
So it **was** that there came forth from **one man**,
    himself as good as **dead**,
    descendants as **numerous** as the stars in the **sky**
    and as **countless** as the **sands** on the **seashore**.

By **faith** Abraham, when put to the **test**, offered up **Isaac**,
    and he who had received the **promises** was ready to offer his
        only **son**,
    of whom it was said,
    "Through **Isaac** descendants shall bear your **name**."
He reasoned that **God** was able to raise even from the **dead**,
    and he received Isaac **back** as a **symbol**.

Or:

READING II   Colossians 3:12–21

A reading from the Letter of Saint Paul to the Colossians

Brothers and sisters:
Put **on**, as God's **chosen** ones, **holy** and **beloved**,
    heartfelt **compassion**, **kindness**, **humility**, **gentleness**,
        and **patience**,
    bearing with one another and **forgiving** one another,
    if one has a **grievance** against another;
    as the Lord has forgiven **you**, so must you **also** do.
And over **all** these put on **love**,
    that is, the **bond** of **perfection**.
And let the **peace** of Christ **control** your hearts,
    the **peace** into which you were **also** called in one **body**.

Colossians = kuh-LOSH-uhnz

The tone of this instruction should match the advice given: "compassion . . . humility . . . gentleness."

Avoid a rote recitation of virtues. The goal is to persuade as well as instruct.

"if one has a grievance" is a subordinate clause that explains the previous phrase: "forgiving one another."

Note all the imperatives: "Put on; so must you . . . let the peace . . . be thankful . . . let the word." They are spoken by a caring teacher, not a drill sergeant.

his relationship with his wife Sarah, and in his relationship with his son, Isaac, Abraham consistently drew upon his faith to assist him in the challenges he faced in his life. The Holy Family, as well, drew upon their faith in God as they journeyed together through successive trials. In these stories, sacred Scripture offers us a pathway to living as a family of faith in the midst of our contemporary challenges.

COLOSSIANS. Today's reading focuses on virtues to be applied within Christian communities as well as characteristics of

the ideal relationships between husbands, wives, and children. Paul sees the key to living the Christian moral life, in the community and in the family, in Christ. He speaks of letting "the peace of Christ control your hearts" and "the word of Christ dwell in you richly." With Christ as the moral compass, humility, kindness, forgiveness, and gratitude will abound within the congregation at Colossae. Paul urges the Colossians, "whatever you do, in word or deed, do everything in the name of the Lord Jesus."

Numerous letters of Paul contain lists of virtues and vices (for example, Romans 1:29–31; 2 Corinthians 12:20–21). But only in the letters to the Colossians and the Ephesians are there household codes of conduct. Each letter pairs off members of the Christian household—wife/husband, child/parent, and slave/master—and offers a similar parallel set of instructions, first addressing the subordinate and then

This instruction should be set off with a pause.

The admonition is not to "heed" or "obey" God's word, but to let it live in us!

"Psalms, hymns, and spiritual songs" comprise one idea and don't need to be distinguished. The emphasis goes to "gratitude."

This is a much beloved exhortation. Stress that it applies to both "word" and "deed."

The operative words here are "as is proper," "love," and "avoid bitterness."

Establish eye contact before speaking this line (preferably from memory) and joyfully announce what it brings about.

Avoid ending on a down note by stressing the *reason* to avoid provoking children.

And be **thankful**.
Let the **word** of Christ dwell in you **richly**,
    as in all **wisdom** you **teach** and **admonish** one another,
    singing **psalms**, **hymns**, and spiritual **songs**
    with **gratitude** in your hearts to **God**.
And **whatever** you do, in **word** or in **deed**,
    do **everything** in the name of the Lord **Jesus**,
    giving **thanks** to God the **Father** through **him**.

Wives, be **subordinate** to your husbands,
    as is **proper** in the Lord.
Husbands, **love** your wives,
    and avoid any **bitterness** toward them.
Children, obey your **parents** in **everything**,
    for this is **pleasing** to the Lord.
Fathers, do not **provoke** your children,
    so they may not become **discouraged**.

[Shorter: Colossians 3:12–17]

GOSPEL   Luke 2:22–40

A reading from the holy Gospel according to Luke

When the days were completed for their **purification**
    according to the law of **Moses**,
    they took him up to **Jerusalem**
    to **present** him to the **Lord**,
    just as it is **written** in the **law** of the Lord,
    *Every **male** that opens the **womb** shall be **consecrated**
        to the **Lord**,*
    and to offer the **sacrifice** of
    *a pair of **turtledoves** or two young **pigeons**,*
    in accordance with the **dictate** in the law of the **Lord**.

The use of the plural in "*their* purification" is ambiguous: does it refer to Joseph and Mary or to Mary and Jesus? What is clear is that Joseph and Mary are following the Law, though travel to the Temple was not required for the firstborn son's consecration to the Lord.

"A pair of turtledoves" could substitute for the sacrifice of a year-old lamb for those who could not afford it.

the main member. While many modern Christians may find the language of "subordinate" unsettling, it is important to remember that these letters reflect the cultural values of the ancient world, governed by the norms of patriarchy.

One striking feature of the household code in Colossians is its departure from Paul's more countercultural view of women and slaves. Whereas Colossians speaks of the submission of slaves and women/wives, Paul acknowledged women's leadership roles within Christian congregations

(for example, Philippians 4:2–3) and advocated treating believers who were slaves as brothers (Philemon 16).

Because Colossians departs from Paul's more countercultural view of women and slaves, as well as differences in style, language, and theology, scholars deduce that it was likely written by an unknown author(s), a generation or two after Paul's death, applying aspects of this theology and ethics to a contemporary situation.

The household code of conduct in Colossians reflects the new, unprecedented challenges faced by the next generation of

believers within the Christian congregations. Given that the code of conduct more closely aligns to household behavior of the larger society in the Roman Empire, it is likely that this next generation of Christians was attempting to assimilate into Greco-Roman life. This interesting historical context aside, the expectations for family life described in Colossians (husbands and wives loving each other, avoiding bitterness, and children obeying their parents) certainly characterize what we surmise of

Simeon = SIM-ee-uhn

Speak with reverence of Simeon and Anna who represent the long frustrated but never abandoned hopes of faithful Jews for the coming of the Messiah.

The "Holy Spirit" is a major theme in Luke. Note the triple mention here.

Speak these lines with the joy that would have been welling up in Simeon's heart at the sight of the boy.

Remember, this is a beloved prayer of the Church. Allow yourself to experience it as for the first time.

The "salvation" he beholds is the child he holds, who will impact both Jews and Gentiles.

The "revelation" of this child's special destiny is made first to his *parents*.

These words carry a weighty message, especially for Mary. Speak the prophecy with great dignity.

Phanuel = FAN-yoo-el
Asher = ASH-er

Make a slight vocal shift to introduce Anna. Your tone is upbeat, as if saying, "There was yet another significant noble figure who recognized the child!"

These are remarkable details about her asceticism.

Jesus is the fulfillment of Israel's longing.

Now there was a man in Jerusalem whose name was **Simeon**.
This man was **righteous** and **devout**,
    awaiting the consolation of Israel,
    and the Holy **Spirit** was upon him.
It had been **revealed** to him by the Holy Spirit
    that he should not see **death**
    before he had seen the **Christ** of the **Lord**.
He came in the Spirit into the **temple**;
    and when the **parents** brought in the child **Jesus**
    to perform the custom of the **law** in regard to him,
    he took him into his **arms** and blessed **God**, saying:
        "**Now**, Master, you may let your servant **go**
            in **peace**, according to your **word**,
        for my eyes have **seen** your **salvation**,
            which you prepared in sight of all the **peoples**,
        a light for **revelation** to the **Gentiles**,
            and **glory** for your people **Israel**."
The child's father and mother were **amazed** at what was said
        about him;
    and Simeon **blessed** them and said to **Mary** his **mother**,
    "**Behold**, this child is destined
    for the **fall** and **rise** of **many** in Israel,
    and to be a **sign** that will be **contradicted**
    —and you **yourself** a **sword** will pierce—
    so that the thoughts of **many** hearts may be **revealed**."
There was also a **prophetess**, **Anna**,
    the daughter of **Phanuel**, of the tribe of **Asher**.
She was **advanced** in years,
    having lived **seven** years with her husband after her **marriage**,
    and then as a **widow** until she was **eighty-four**.
She never **left** the temple,
    but worshiped **night** and **day** with **fasting** and **prayer**.
And coming **forward** at that very **time**,
    she gave **thanks** to God and **spoke** about the child
    to **all** who were awaiting the **redemption** of **Jerusalem**.

---

the relationships that Joseph, Mary, and Jesus enjoyed within their family.

GOSPEL Today's Gospel Reading offers a glimpse of the holy family at a threshold moment in their lives. Luke is alone among the Gospel writers in offering this portrait. In it he emphasizes how Joseph and Mary "fulfilled all the prescriptions of the law of the Lord," specifically the circumcision and naming of the infant Jesus and the purification of Mary after childbirth. Luke makes it clear that Joseph and Mary were law-abiding Jews.

After completing the prescriptions of the Jewish law, the couple brought Jesus to the Temple in Jerusalem to offer an animal sacrifice and "to present him to the Lord." Here they encountered two people, Simeon, a "righteous and devout" man, and Anna, a "prophetess." This male-female pairing is seen elsewhere in Luke's infancy narrative; for example, in Gabriel's visits to Zechariah (1:5–20) and Mary (1:26–38) and in the great canticles (songs) of Mary (1:46–55) and Zechariah (1:68–79).

For Luke, Simeon and Anna are important figures for advancing his theological goal, so carefully laid out in the opening chapters of his Gospel account. First, the words of the prophets Simeon and Anna speak to God's salvation, offered to both Jews and Gentiles, and they also point to the "contradiction" (controversy) that will mark the public ministry of Jesus and the Apostles. In the Gospel, Jesus's outreach and offer of salvation to the Gentiles (see, for example, Luke 4:16–30) and in Acts, the Apostles' mission to the Gentiles (see,

Fidelity to the Law is again emphasized, but the tone takes on a prosaic quality: they returned to normal, everyday life in Nazareth.

Even during his "hidden years," Jesus was "filled" with God's wisdom and in full conformity with the divine will.

When they had **fulfilled** all the prescriptions
of the law of the Lord,
they returned to **Galilee**,
to their **own** town of **Nazareth**.
The child **grew** and became **strong**, filled with **wisdom**;
and the favor of **God** was upon him.

[Shorter: Luke 2:22, 39–40]

TO KEEP IN MIND

Tell the story: Make the story yours, then share it with your listeners. Use the language; don't throw away any good words. Settings give context; don't rush the description. Characters must be believable; understand their motivation. Dialogue reveals character; distinguish one character from another with your voice.

---

for instance, Acts 13:44–52) stirred much controversy.

Second, by saying that Simeon came "in the Spirit" into the Temple to prophesy about the child Jesus, Luke suggests that the ministry of Jesus and of the early Church is divinely guided. Simeon says, "My eyes have seen your salvation, which you have prepared in sight of all the peoples." Anna, too, confirms to all that in the infant Jesus, she sees God's presence, "the redemption of Jerusalem."

The Gospel Reading ends with a summary statement about Jesus growing up in his hometown of Nazareth: "The child grew and became strong, filled with wisdom; and the favor of God was upon him." Luke is filling in one of the major gaps of time in Jesus's life—the time from his birth and infancy to the age of twelve. Nowhere else in the New Testament are details offered about the boy Jesus. But even such limited comments suggest that Mary and Joseph, by providing a rich and reverent family life, were instrumental in Jesus's growth and strength.

THE OCTAVE DAY OF THE NATIVITY OF THE LORD / SOLEMNITY OF MARY, THE HOLY MOTHER OF GOD

LECTIONARY #18

A short reading always means a slow reading. Establish eye contact before starting.

"Aaron and his sons" are priests who will carry out this command.

There is a double set-up to the words of the blessing. Use the set-ups to suggest the importance of what will follow.

Pause at the end of each part of the blessing, noting each is distinct and ends with an exclamation point.

The tone of the blessing conveys a blend of parental love and royal favor.

Render these words slowly: "and give . . . you . . . peace."

Pause after "peace," then summarize the instruction, stressing the word "name" not "my." Note that the summary ends with a promise of blessing.

For meditation and context:

READING I   Numbers 6:22–27

A reading from the Book of Numbers

The **Lord** said to **Moses**:
  "**Speak** to **Aaron** and his sons and **tell** them:
  This is how you shall **bless** the **Israelites**.
Say to them:
  The Lord **bless** you and **keep** you!
  The Lord let his face **shine** upon
    you, and be **gracious** to you!
  The Lord look upon you **kindly** and
    give you **peace**!
So shall they invoke my **name** upon the **Israelites**,
  and I will **bless** them."

RESPONSORIAL PSALM   Psalm 67:2–3, 5, 6, 8 (2a)

R. May God bless us in his mercy.

May God have pity on us and bless us;
  may he let his face shine upon us.
So may your way be known upon earth;
  among all nations, your salvation.

May the nations be glad and exult
  because you rule the peoples in equity;
  the nations on the earth you guide.

May the peoples praise you, O God;
  may all the peoples praise you!
May God bless us,
  and may all the ends of the earth
    fear him!

READING I — Today's celebration of Mary as *Theotokos* (in Greek, literally, "God-bearer") dates back to the Council of Ephesus in 431. This Marian title both affirms the divinity of Christ and proclaims Mary's motherhood of Jesus, the Son of God.

The First Reading is taken from the Book of Numbers. This fourth book of the Bible continues the storyline of the Israelites' forty-year journey in the desert that began in the Book of Exodus. Numbers begins with the Israelites at the base of Mount Sinai and ends with their arrival at the border of the promised land. For first-century law-abiding Jews like Mary, the story of Moses receiving of the Law was the center of Israel's sacred narrative.

Today's reading, a blessing prayer, likely would have been well-known to Mary. She and other ancient Jews would have heard in this prayer God's providential care for the Israelite people. As we ponder this reading, we give thanks that God, in choosing to come into the world through Mary, has extended his divine Providence and blessing to all people through her Son, Jesus Christ.

READING II — The Letter to the Galatians contains the only reference to Mary in all of Paul's letters. And here Paul does not even refer to her directly by her name. This passing reference to Mary ("born of a woman") is part of Paul's larger discussion of Jesus and his Jewish identity and roots ("born under the law"), as well as his identity as Son of God whose purpose it was to "ransom those under the law."

Paul's belief that Jesus came in "the fullness of time" speaks to his apocalyptic world-view ("apocalypse," in Greek, meaning "revelation" of the end-times). Further,

Galatians = guh-LAY-shunz

"Fullness of time" means God's timing.

After "Son," pause and mentally insert "who was born."

Jesus became subject to the Law in order to save us from the tyranny of the Law.

Don't let "proof" sound like courtroom argumentation. It is gentle persuasion that reveals God's surprisingly tender love.

Pause between "Abba," ("Daddy") and "Father!" placing equal emphasis on both words.

Stress both "slave" and "son" to emphasize our *former* and *current* status before God. Then build your energy to make the final point that being children of God gives us a claim on his mercy.

> **TO KEEP IN MIND**
> Each text contains **three kinds of content**: intellectual-theological, emotional, and aesthetic. The plot and details of the story and the theological teaching behind them comprise the intellectual-theological content. How the author or characters feel (or want us to feel) is the emotional content. Elements that make the writing pleasing—rhythm, repetition, suspense, and picturesque language—are the aesthetic content.

READING II   Galatians 4:4–7

A reading from the Letter of Saint Paul to the Galatians

Brothers and sisters:
When the **fullness** of time had **come**, **God** sent his **Son**,
   born of a **woman**, born under the law,
   to **ransom** those under the law,
   so that **we** might receive **adoption** as **sons**.
As **proof** that you are sons,
   God sent the **Spirit** of his **Son** into our **hearts**,
   crying out, "**Abba**, **Father**!"
So you are no longer a **slave** but a **son**,
   and if a **son** then also an **heir**, through **God**.

Paul was convinced of Christ's imminent return, his Second Coming. Both Christ's arrival and his return constituted for Paul God's decisive intervention into history that was bringing about the end of the age.

In Paul's theological vision, Jesus, being both born of a woman (Mary) and being God's Son, allows believers in Christ to "receive adoption"—through faith, to be a "son," an "heir" to all of God's possessions. For Paul, one's heartfelt confession of faith, inspired by the Spirit, was evidence of this adoption.

It may surprise us to know that Paul had almost nothing to say about Mary in his letters to the various Christian congregations. However, Paul's letters were "occasional;" he wrote to address specific situations—the particular problems and concerns of certain congregations. Paul's surviving letters never give a systematic summary of his theology. From what we see here, however, Mary's role is crucial to our adoption, to the presence of the Spirit in our hearts "crying out, Father!" It is that role we celebrate today.

GOSPEL   This is the same Gospel reading proclaimed at the dawn Mass on Christmas. Heard within the context of this Solemnity of Mary, the Mother of God, new insights can be gleaned from this text.

One of the reasons the Gospel according to Luke was important to the early Church was its fundamental portrait of Jesus as the universal savior. Luke presented God's offer of salvation through Christ to all people of all cultures—Jews and Gentiles alike—and to all classes. The

GOSPEL   Luke 2:16–21

A reading from the holy Gospel according to Luke

The **shepherds** went in **haste** to **Bethlehem** and found **Mary**
       and **Joseph**,
    and the **infant** lying in the **manger**.
When they saw this,
    they made **known** the message
    that had been **told** them about this child.
All who **heard** it were **amazed**
    by what had been **told** them by the **shepherds**.
And **Mary** kept all these things,
    reflecting on them in her **heart**.
Then the **shepherds** returned,
    glorifying and **praising** God
    for all they had **heard** and **seen**,
    just as it had been told to them.

When **eight** days were completed for his **circumcision**,
    he was named **Jesus**, the name given him by the **angel**
    before he was **conceived** in the womb.

Review commentary and notes for Christmas Mass at Dawn.

The narrative pattern in this text looks like this: the shepherds rush; they pause and share; all are amazed and Mary reflects; they rush off again. Note the key words in each scene of this brief text: "saw" and "made known"; "kept . . . reflecting"; "glorifying and praising."

This is a quiet amazement, in the depths of the heart.

Speak reverently of Mary's life-long reflection on these events.

Fill these lines with joyful energy, speaking at a faster pace on the middle lines and with a slower pace at the end.

Pause to suggest the passage of time. Speak reverently of the divinely given name revealed before his miraculous conception.

TO KEEP IN MIND

Narrator: Knowing the point of view that the narrator is "rooting for" will help you more fully communicate the meaning of the text. The narrator always has a viewpoint, often speaking as a believer, not as an objective reporter. For this reason, the narrator is often the pivotal role in a passage. Using timbre, pitch, rate, and energy can help you convey the narrator's moods or meanings.

---

economically poor and socially marginalized would receive God's salvation as well.

In today's Gospel reading, Luke makes a point of emphasizing that the news from the shepherds "amazed" all the people who heard it. Part of the surprise of the shepherd's report was the source of the information—the shepherds. Socially, shepherds had a low honor rating. Initially, at least, Luke's audience may have wondered if this report could be trusted.

In Luke's description of Mary's reaction to the visit of the shepherds, "And Mary kept all these things, reflecting on them in her heart," we see Mary's human but faithful response to a puzzling situation. In details presented earlier in his infancy narrative, Luke shows that Mary was already a young woman of deep faith before the birth of Jesus. (See, for example, Mary's response at the Annunciation, Luke 1:26–38). In today's Gospel reading, we learn that Mary, even as Mother of God, had to grow in understanding of the role that her newborn son Jesus was to have in God's plan for the salvation of all people.

THE EPIPHANY OF THE LORD

LECTIONARY #20

READING I   Isaiah 60:1–6

Isaiah = ī-ZAY-uh

The images of light and darkness should be stressed and *contrasted*.

The text uses synonymous parallelism (see the Introduction) in which the first line of each couplet (paired lines) makes a point that is repeated, balanced, or developed in the second. This intentional repetition requires a *rise in energy* in the *second* line.

Don't let the rhythmic lines lure you into a singsong delivery. Avoid that problem by focusing on the content of each line.

All the "nations" and "kings" will take notice of Israel's impact.

Move slowly through these tender images.

Pause to renew your energy. "Riches" and "wealth" are metaphors representing the abundance of God's mercy; increase energy from one to the other.

Dromedaries are single-humped camels.

Midian = MID-ee-uhn

Ephah = EE-fuh

The camels associated with the wise men of Christ's birth narrative derive from this text, not from the Gospel accounts.

The reading ends as it began—in joyful praise.

A reading from the Book of the Prophet Isaiah

Rise up in **splendor**, Jerusalem! Your **light** has **come**,
    the **glory** of the Lord **shines** upon you.
See, **darkness** covers the earth,
    and thick **clouds** cover the **peoples**;
but upon **you** the Lord **shines**,
    and **over** you appears his **glory**.
Nations shall walk by your **light**,
    and **kings** by your shining radiance.
Raise your **eyes** and **look** about;
    they all **gather** and **come** to you:
your **sons** come from **afar**,
    and your **daughters** in the arms of their **nurses**.

Then you shall be **radiant** at what you see,
    your **heart** shall throb and **overflow**,
for the **riches** of the sea shall be emptied out **before** you,
    the **wealth** of nations shall be **brought** to you.
Caravans of camels shall **fill** you,
    dromedaries from **Midian** and **Ephah**;
all from **Sheba** shall come
    bearing **gold** and **frankincense**,
    and proclaiming the **praises** of the Lord.

READING I	The same set of powerful readings is used each year

for the celebration of the Epiphany of the Lord. Each of these readings speaks to the reality that God wills his Son to be made manifest to all nations of the world.

The First Reading comes from Second Isaiah, who prophesied during Israel's exile in Babylon around 550 BC. Often considered the prophet of great hope, Second Isaiah offered the captured Israelites a vision not only of better days to come, but also of a future of unimaginable joy. What Second Isaiah foresaw for Israel was a complete disconnect from their experiences of exile. The proclamation, "Rise up in splendor, Jerusalem!" would have felt very unnatural after nearly seventy years in captivity. Words such as "the glory of the Lord shines upon you" and "nations shall walk by your light" were concepts now almost foreign to the Israelites after two generations in Babylon away from their promised land, their capital city of Jerusalem, and their Temple worship.

But Second Isaiah offered more than mere words of hope; he presented the captive Israelites with images from their sto-ried past: "All from Sheba shall come bearing gold and frankincense and proclaiming the praises of the Lord" (see 1 Kings 10:1–13). He challenged them to believe that the God of Israel would once again restore them to glory as he had done with their ancestors. Although many Jews would have seen their return from Babylonian exile as verification of Isaiah's prophecies, not until the birth of Christ would all nations see the prophesies of Second Isaiah reach complete fulfillment.

For meditation and context:

RESPONSORIAL PSALM   Psalm 72:1–2, 7–8, 10–11, 12–13 (11)

R. Lord, every nation on earth will adore you.

O God, with your judgment endow the king,
  and with your justice, the king's son;
he shall govern your people with justice
  and your afflicted ones with judgment.

Justice shall flower in his days,
  and profound peace, till the moon be no
  more.
May he rule from sea to sea,
  and from the River to the ends of the earth.

The kings of Tarshish and the Isles shall
  offer gifts;
  the kings of Arabia and Seba shall bring
  tribute.
All kings shall pay him homage,
  all nations shall serve him.

For he shall rescue the poor when he cries out,
  and the afflicted when he has no one to
  help him.
He shall have pity for the lowly and the poor;
  the lives of the poor he shall save.

TO KEEP IN MIND

Word value: Words are your medium, like a painter's brush or a sculptor's chisel. You must understand the words before you can communicate them. Most words have a dictionary meaning (denotative) and an associational meaning (connotative). "House" and "home" both mean "dwelling," yet they communicate different feelings. Be alert to subtle differences in connotative meanings and express them.

Ephesians = ee-FEE-zhuhnz

This sentence can be perplexing: Paul asserts that God gave him a special insight by direct revelation; namely, that Gentiles are coheirs with the Jews to the promises of Christ.

Use "namely" to draw attention to what follows.

The "revelation" is still unnamed. Former ages did not know it, but now Apostles (like Paul) have glimpsed it.

The hidden truth now made known is named in the final lines. Distinguish his three categories: "coheirs," "same body," "copartners." A slow delivery will keep the three terms from blurring into one.

READING II   Ephesians 3:2–3a, 5–6

A reading from the Letter of Saint Paul to the Ephesians

Brothers and sisters:
You have heard of the **stewardship** of God's **grace**
  that was **given** to me for your **benefit**,
  namely, that the **mystery** was made **known** to me by **revelation**.
It was not made known to people in **other** generations
  as it has **now** been revealed
  to his holy **apostles** and **prophets** by the **Spirit**:
  that the **Gentiles** are **coheirs**, **members** of the same **body**,
  and **copartners** in the promise in Christ **Jesus** through
    the **gospel**.

The story begins with positive energy.

"East" suggests the magi's foreign, exotic identity. With eagerness and sincerity they inquire about the newborn king.

GOSPEL   Matthew 2:1–12

A reading from the holy Gospel according to Matthew

When **Jesus** was born in **Bethlehem** of **Judea**,
  in the days of King **Herod**,
  behold, **magi** from the **east** arrived in **Jerusalem**, saying,

---

READING II   Paul's Letter to the Ephesians is widely recognized by scholars as a Deutero-Pauline letter. That is, the unknown author(s) of the letter wrote in Paul's name and drew upon his authority, applying his theology and ethics to a contemporary situation. Keeping this in mind, and also the date of this text (between AD 80 and 110) can help us understand the import of this reading—that Paul's theology was working its way into common belief.

Obviously, the author of Ephesians considered himself a Pauline Christian, seeking to preserve and apply the foundational message of Paul to a new generation of Christians. We hear repeated in today's reading one of the central tenets of Paul's original message: "the mystery was known to me by revelation." (See, for example, Romans 16:25; Galatians 1:11–12.) And what was originally revealed to Paul, is here reinforced to the next generation of believers: "The Gentiles are coheirs, members of the same body, and copartners in the promise in Christ Jesus through the gospel."

This language of Paul and the Pauline Christians who followed after him, describing Jews and Gentiles as "coheirs" and "copartners," expresses the insight, the epiphany, that many Christians were coming to realize through their faith in Christ. All believers in Christ are members of the "same body." This is one of the enduring legacies of Paul's theology and ethics: God makes himself manifest to all the nations through the life, Death, and Resurrection of his divine Son, Jesus.

GOSPEL   The story of the visit of the magi from Matthew's Gospel account has some parallels to the

Herod's name introduces a tone of threat.

"All Jerusalem" refers to the power elite.

Herod is methodical in his research.
The priests and scribes are eager to inform
the king.

This text is from Micah 5:1, but Matthew
alters it slightly.

Your narration should suggest the brewing
danger. Make full use of the words "secretly"
and "ascertained"

Don't overplay these lines. Herod is a
convincing deceiver who persuades them of
his sincerity.

We forget about the threat as these familiar
and comforting images take the stage.

"House" is unexpected. They find him safe in
Mary's arms.

They don't kneel but "prostrate" themselves
in a remarkable sign of respect. The gifts
contain textured meaning.

There is both relief and delight in these final
lines: God intervenes and reroutes the magi,
leaving Herod in the dark.

"Where is the newborn **king** of the **Jews**?
We saw his **star** at its **rising**
    and have **come** to do him **homage**."
When King Herod **heard** this,
    he was greatly **troubled**,
    and all **Jerusalem** with him.
Assembling all the chief **priests** and the **scribes** of the people,
    he **inquired** of them where the Christ was to be **born**.
They said to him, "In **Bethlehem** of **Judea**,
    for **thus** it has been written through the **prophet**:
        And **you**, *Bethlehem, land of* **Judah**,
            are by no means **least** *among the rulers of Judah;*
        since from you shall come a **ruler**,
            who is to **shepherd** *my people* **Israel**."
Then Herod called the magi **secretly**
    and **ascertained** from them the **time** of the star's appearance.
He sent them to **Bethlehem** and said,
    "**Go** and search **diligently** for the child.
When you have **found** him, bring me **word**,
    that I **too** may go and **do** him **homage**."
After their **audience** with the king they **set** out.
And **behold**, the **star** that they had seen at its rising
        preceded them,
    until it came and **stopped** over the place where the **child** was.
They were **overjoyed** at seeing the star,
    and on entering the **house**
    they saw the **child** with **Mary** his **mother**.
They **prostrated** themselves and did him **homage**.
Then they opened their **treasures**
    and **offered** him gifts of **gold**, **frankincense**, and **myrrh**.
And having been **warned** in a **dream** not to **return** to Herod,
    they **departed** for their country by another **way**.

story of the visit of the shepherds in Luke's story. First, both the magi and the shepherds are used as witnesses to the birth of Christ. Second, both stories present the God of Israel as controlling the events associated with the witness of the magi and the shepherds.

Despite some important similarities, however, the *identity* of the witnesses speaks to the different theologies of Matthew and Luke. For Luke, the shepherds represent one of the major theological themes of his account: the birth of Christ signals a great reversal in the regular order of human events. God comes into the world to empower the weak and marginalized. In Matthew, the "magi from the east" represent the other nations of the world (that is, the Gentiles), who come to pay "homage" to the "newborn king of the Jews." This recurring Matthean theme of including Gentiles in the historic promises and covenants made between God and Israel even appears in the final words of the resurrected Christ to his disciples: "Go, therefore, and make disciples of all nations, baptizing them in the name of the Father, and of the Son, and of the Holy Spirit" (Matthew 28:19).

The prophecy of Second Isaiah from the First Reading (Isaiah 60:1–6) is fulfilled in the magi's long journey from the east, in their presentation of the treasures and gifts to the newborn child, and in the "homage" paid for God's gift to the world.

THE BAPTISM OF THE LORD

LECTIONARY #21

READING I   Isaiah 55:1–11

A reading from the Book of the Prophet Isaiah

> **Thus** says the *Lord*:
> All you who are **thirsty**,
>   come to the **water**!
> You who have no **money**,
>   **come**, receive **grain** and **eat**;
> come, without **paying** and without **cost**,
>   drink **wine** and **milk**!
> Why spend your **money** for what is not **bread**,
>   your **wages** for what fails to **satisfy**?
> Heed **me**, and you shall eat **well**,
>   you shall delight in **rich** fare.
> Come to me **heedfully**,
>   **listen**, that you may have **life**.
> I will **renew** with you the everlasting **covenant**,
>   the **benefits** assured to **David**.
> As I made him a **witness** to the peoples,
>   a **leader** and commander of **nations**,
> so shall **you** summon a nation you knew **not**,
>   and nations that knew **you** not shall **run** to you,
> because of the *Lord*, your **God**,
>   the **Holy** One of **Israel**, who has **glorified** you.
>
> **Seek** the Lord while he may be **found**,
>   **call** him while he is **near**.

Isaiah = Ī-ZAY-uh

Except for the opening, the entire text is in the voice of the Lord.

As was the case in last week's text from Isaiah, this passage uses synonymous parallelism (see the Introduction) in which the first line of each couplet (paired lines) makes a point that is repeated, balanced, or developed in the second. The repetition is intentional and requires a *rise in energy* in the *second* line.

There is urgency in these lines, like that of a parent coaxing a runaway to return home.

As if resisted, God reasons and cajoles till we come to our senses.

Responding to God's call is not optional; it is a matter of life or death.

"David" is often the measure against which all who follow are considered.

What was true of David is now made true of all God's people. The sense of urgency does not let up.

Increase your intensity on "the Holy One of Israel."

A pause precedes this new section in which the urgency climbs yet again.

Today options are given for the readings. Contact your parish staff to learn which readings will be used.

READING I **ISAIAH 55:1–11.** "All you who are thirsty, come to the water!" These opening words of the First Reading will lead us directly to the Gospel, where John the Baptist is preaching and baptizing. But to recover the text's original meaning for its audience, we need some background. Around the year 200 BC, the prophetic books of the Old Testament were arranged in the final order and form that we know today. The sixty-six chapters of the Book of Isaiah were aligned to the different time periods from which they emerged: chapters 1–39 from 740–700 BC; chapters 40–55 from around 550 BC; chapters 56–66 from the period when Israelite exiles returned from Babylon, post-538 BC. Isaiah 55, from which most of the First Reading is drawn, is the final chapter of the prophetic oracles and songs attributed to the prophet of the Babylonian exile, Second Isaiah.

In these words, it is easy to feel Second Isaiah's sense of impending release from captivity in Babylon. Images of rebirth ("I will renew with you the everlasting covenant") and new beginnings ("Let the scoundrel forsake his way, and the wicked man his thoughts") abound in these prophesies. It is no accident that Second Isaiah drew upon images of water. One of the defining moments in Israel's historic relationship with God was the release from Egyptian slavery and the crossing of the Red Sea. Scholars date this event to around

Here are specific strategies for surrendering to God's will.

The tone begins to shift. You are now characterizing God's tender and merciful ways that contrast so plainly with ours.

Don't let the sound of these words turn harsh; the poetry continues to contrast our ways with God's.

A new beat (section) begins here. Note the balance of the text comprises one sentence. Speak it one thought at a time, keeping in mind the single analogy: my word, like the rain that falls, achieves the end for which I sent it. Everything in between is in apposition, all are phrases describing both the "rain and snow" *and* God's word. The imagery is important because it characterizes God's word as fertile and life-giving.

> **TO KEEP IN MIND**
> Proclaiming the **words of the prophets** requires intensity and urgency. With equal passion, they spoke threat and consolation, indictment and forgiveness. You must do the same for the chosen people you call "parish."

Let the scoundrel **forsake** his way,
    and the wicked man his **thoughts**;
let him **turn** to the LORD for **mercy**;
    to our **God**, who is **generous** in **forgiving**.
For **my** thoughts are not **your** thoughts,
    nor are **your** ways **my** ways, says the LORD.
As high as the **heavens** are above the **earth**
    so high are **my** ways above **your** ways
    and **my** thoughts above **your** thoughts.

For just as from the **heavens**
    the **rain** and **snow** come down
and do not **return** there
    till they have **watered** the earth,
    making it **fertile** and **fruitful**,
giving **seed** to the one who **sows**
    and **bread** to the one who **eats**,
so shall my **word** be
    that goes forth from my **mouth**;
my **word** shall **not** return to me **void**,
    but shall **do** my will,
    achieving the **end** for which I **sent** it.

Or:

1200 BC. For Second Isaiah and the exiled Israelites, this would have been nearly 700 years in their past. Yet, the hope and the glory of those days still filled the imagination of the prophets and the people of Israel.

Just as the first words of this reading prepare us for Jesus's baptism, the last words set us up for the preaching of John the Baptist and the public ministry of Jesus. The word of God that "goes forth" from the mouth of the prophets "shall not return to me void, but shall do my will, achieving the end for which I sent it." John's words and

God's own words after the baptism of Jesus, launch the public ministry of Jesus that will bring the Good News of the Kingdom of God to the world.

ISAIAH 42:1–4, 6–7. This "Servant-of-the-Lord" oracle was first spoken by Second Isaiah around the year 550 BC while Israel was still in captivity in Babylon. It was, in fact, a song of unimaginable hope for a people in exile, thought to have been long-forgotten by their God. Scholars remain uncertain as to who Second Isaiah

was speaking of in his reference to "my servant" and "my chosen one with whom I am pleased." Obviously, the early Christians came to believe this prophecy was fulfilled in Jesus Christ, as expressed by the Gospel writers, when they record God's words at Jesus's baptism: "You are my beloved Son; with you I am well-pleased" (Mark 1:11; compare Matthew 3:17; Luke 3:22).

Second Isaiah foreshadowed God's "servant" bringing forth and establishing "justice on earth" and being "a light for the nations." He would open "the eyes of the

READING I   Isaiah 42:1–4, 6–7

Isaiah = ī-ZAY-uh

Let the introductory narration signal God's solicitous attitude toward the "servant."

Speak with pride of the faithful servant who does great things through the power of God's spirit.

These words are often seen as an anticipation of the mercy of Christ. Compassion will be a chief characteristic of God's servant.

"Coastlands" are the nations surrounding the Mediterranean Sea, which, at this time, were pagan lands.

Stress God's initiative in calling the servant to this ministry of justice.

The energy continues to climb from here to the end of the passage. Speak the words as a message of encouragement telling the servant he will bring light to the blind and freedom to the imprisoned.

Use ritardando (a gradual slowing) on "those who live in darkness."

For meditation and context:

A reading from the Book of the Prophet Isaiah

Thus says the LORD:
Here is my **servant** whom I **uphold**,
    my **chosen** one with whom I am **pleased**,
upon whom I have put my **spirit**;
    he shall bring forth **justice** to the nations,
not **crying** out, not **shouting**,
    not making his voice **heard** in the **street**.
A **bruised reed** he shall not **break**,
    and a smoldering **wick** he shall not **quench**,
until he establishes **justice** on the earth;
    the **coastlands** will **wait** for his **teaching**.

I, the LORD, have **called** you for the victory of **justice**,
    I have **grasped** you by the **hand**;
I **formed** you, and set you
    as a **covenant** of the people,
    a **light** for the **nations**,
to open the eyes of the **blind**,
    to bring out **prisoners** from **confinement**,
    and from the **dungeon**, those who live in **darkness**.

RESPONSORIAL PSALM   Isaiah 12:2–3, 4bcd, 5–6 (3)

R. You will draw water joyfully from the springs of salvation.

God indeed is my savior;
    I am confident and unafraid.
My strength and my courage is the LORD,
    and he has been my savior.
With joy you will draw water
    at the fountain of salvation.

Give thanks to the LORD, acclaim his name;
    among the nations make known his deeds,
    proclaim how exalted is his name.

Sing praise to the LORD for his glorious
    achievement;
    let this be known throughout all the earth.
Shout with exultation, O city of Zion,
    for great in your midst
    is the Holy One of Israel!

Or:

blind" and free "prisoners" and those "who live in darkness." It may be that the captive Israelites in Babylon believed that Second Isaiah himself was God's "chosen one" in his prophecy of hope for a new future. Within the lifetime of many exiled Israelites, they saw King Cyrus of Persia defeat the Babylonians and release them from captivity. Some probably saw King Cyrus as at least partially fulfilling Second Isaiah's prophecy. (See Isaiah 44:28; 45:1–3.) It is certainly the case that the Gospel writers and early Christians saw in Jesus's public ministry the blind healed, the lame walk,

and the lepers cleansed, leading them to see in Jesus the fulfillment of Second Isaiah's prophecies.

READING II | **1 JOHN 5:1–9.** The three letters attributed to John in the New Testament (1 John, 2 John, and 3 John) are closely associated with the Gospel according to John because of their similarities in theology, style, and vocabulary. Because of this, scholars conclude that the same community of Christians who were the recipients of John's Gospel account were also the intended audience for these

Johannine letters. Scholars debate about whether the Gospel or the letters were written first. But most date the composition of the letters to the late first century AD.

Today's reading from 1 John falls into two parts: first, the notion that loving the Father and the Son and keeping the commandments enables the faithful to conquer the world, and second, the "three that testify" that Jesus is the Son of God. The idea that the Christian is one who "conquers the world" and that believers are "children of God" suggests that members of the Johannine community saw themselves as

For meditation and context:

RESPONSORIAL PSALM   Psalm 29:1–2, 3–4, 3, 9–10 (11b)

R. The Lord will bless his people with peace.

Give to the LORD, you sons of God,
  give to the LORD glory and praise,
give to the LORD the glory due his name;
  adore the LORD in holy attire.

The voice of the LORD is over the waters,
  the LORD, over vast waters.
The voice of the LORD is mighty;
  the voice of the LORD is majestic.

The God of glory thunders,
  and in his temple all say, "Glory!"
The LORD is enthroned above the flood;
  the LORD is enthroned as king forever.

> **TO KEEP IN MIND**
> **Build:** refers to increasing vocal intensity as you work toward a climactic point in the text. It calls for intensified emotional energy, which can be communicated by an increase or decrease in volume, or by speaking faster or slower. The point is to show more passion, greater urgency, or concern.

READING II   1 John 5:1–9

A reading from the first Letter of Saint John

Beloved:
Everyone who **believes** that **Jesus** is the **Christ** is **begotten**
    by **God**,
  and everyone who loves the **Father**
  loves **also** the one **begotten** by him.
In **this** way we **know** that we love the **children** of God
  when we love **God** and obey his **commandments**.
For the love of God is **this**,
  that we **keep** his commandments.
And his commandments are **not burdensome**,
  for whoever is begotten by **God** conquers the **world**.
And the **victory** that conquers the world is our **faith**.
Who indeed is the **victor** over the world
  but the one who **believes** that Jesus is the Son of God?

This is the one who came through **water** and **blood**, Jesus **Christ**,
  not by water **alone**, but by water and **blood**.
The **Spirit** is the one who **testifies**,
  and the **Spirit** is **truth**.

The word "Beloved" sets the tone.

Declare this solemn teaching with conviction and authority.

Love of God and God's people is equated with obedience to God's will and with keeping the commandments.

This truth is restated; don't soften, but strengthen your delivery here.

Reflect on this line during your preparation: why are God's commands *not* burdensome?

Faith in Christ gives us victory over the deceitful world. Yielding to Christ is far less burdensome than the weight the world would place on our shoulders.

"Water and blood" refer to Jesus's baptism and his Death on the Cross. Note the repetition.

God's Spirit fills us with confidence.

separate from the larger society, perhaps even against the dominant culture, and were most likely a minority group. However this congregation fit within the larger fabric of the Greco-Roman world, it is clear they saw their faith in Christ and love of God as defining characteristics within their community.

Most notable in today's reading is the community's firm belief in the divine sonship of Jesus. The emphasis on "water and blood" as testimony that Jesus is the Son of God is a Johannine reference to Jesus's

baptism (water) and his Death on the cross (blood). For the author of 1 John, these events, along with the confirmation of "the Spirit," are the ultimate witness to Jesus as God's Son.

ACTS 10:34–38. The entire speech that Peter delivers in the house of Cornelius, the Gentile centurion (Acts 10:34–43), can be summed up in Peter's opening remarks: "In truth, I see that God shows no partiality." No phrase better captures the fundamental

tension between Jewish and Gentile believers in Christ and the struggle of the early Church. For many ethnic Jews, their fundamental religious and cultural identity was defined by being "separate" from the nations (that is, the Gentiles). For many Gentiles, the Jewish Law was viewed as an impediment to their newfound faith in Jesus as the Messiah and Son of God.

In his speech, Peter attempts to find common ground for Jews and Gentiles by returning to the focus of Jesus as "Lord of all." He reminds his audience of the

Name each of the "three" with equal emphasis.

"If we accept" sets up an if/then clause: if we are willing to believe humans, then how much more reliable is God? Let your own faith shine through!

TO KEEP IN MIND
Context: Who is speaking in this text? What are the circumstances?

As narrator, you are aware that Peter has been profoundly changed by a great epiphany.

These are words Peter never expected to proclaim with such conviction.

These are words Peter never expected to proclaim with such conviction.

Speak with enthusiasm and conviction of God's work in the life of Jesus.

Peter was witness to all this. He speaks with authority and great reverence for Jesus.

Speak this final sentence not as a past event but as a joyful promise of what Christ continues to do in the lives of believers.

So there are **three** that testify,
the **Spirit**, the **water** and the **blood**,
and the **three** are of **one accord**.
If we accept **human** testimony,
the testimony of **God** is surely **greater**.
Now the testimony of **God** is **this**,
that he has testified on **behalf** of his **Son**.

Or:

READING II   Acts of the Apostles 10:34–38

A reading from the Acts of the Apostles

Peter proceeded to speak to those gathered
in the house of **Cornelius**, saying:
"In **truth**, I see that **God** shows no **partiality**.
Rather, in **every** nation whoever **fears** him and acts **uprightly**
is **acceptable** to him.
You **know** the word that he sent to the **Israelites**
as he proclaimed **peace** through Jesus **Christ**, who is Lord of **all**,
what has happened all over **Judea**,
beginning in **Galilee** after the baptism
that **John** preached,
how God anointed **Jesus** of **Nazareth**
with the Holy **Spirit** and **power**.
He went about doing **good**
and **healing** all those oppressed by the **devil**,
for **God** was with him."

Baptism that unites them all, beginning with the preaching of John the Baptist and the baptism of Jesus himself that "anointed" him "with the Holy Spirit and power." In all the good that Jesus did, "God was with him."

Peter and Paul both preached that for all those who have faith in Christ, the Holy Spirit descends upon them at Baptism—Jew *and* Gentile. In this way, God shows no partiality to those who believe in Jesus and are baptized in the Holy Spirit—all are saved in Christ.

GOSPEL   The Gospel according to Mark carries the distinction of being the first written narrative on the life of Jesus among the four New Testament Gospel accounts. It was likely composed around AD 65–70. Mark does not open his account with the birth stories of Jesus, as Matthew and Luke do; rather, Mark begins his story with the preaching and activities of John the Baptist. He saw the work of John the Baptist as so closely associated with the ministry of Jesus that he decided to start the story of Jesus by focusing on John's baptism of repentance for the forgiveness of sins.

John was likely active for months, if not years, preaching and baptizing Jews from Jerusalem and the surrounding region of Judea before his encounter with Jesus. Mark offers only a brief character sketch of the Baptist. He is fully aware of his duty, proclaiming a baptism of forgiveness and baptizing repentant Jews in the waters of the Jordan River. Despite his popularity, John is also aware of his subordinate role: "One mightier than I is coming after me.

GOSPEL   Mark 1:7–11

A reading from the holy Gospel according to Mark

Name John with reverence and announce his quotation with confident pride.

John's words are redolent of sincerity and humility.

Contrast "water" and "Spirit."

Pause before starting this new section.

The mood shifts to fit the theophany that will now be manifested.

Don't rush this important line; it is full of mystery and divine love.

This is what John the **Baptist** proclaimed:
  "One **mightier** than I is coming **after** me.
I am **not worthy** to stoop and loosen the **thongs** of his **sandals**.
I have baptized you with **water**;
  he will baptize you with the Holy **Spirit**."

It **happened** in those days that **Jesus** came from **Nazareth**
    of **Galilee**
  and was **baptized** in the **Jordan** by **John**.
On coming up out of the **water** he saw the **heavens** being
    torn **open**
  and the **Spirit**, like a **dove**, **descending** upon him.
And a **voice** came from the heavens,
  "**You** are my beloved **Son**; with **you** I am well **pleased**."

TO KEEP IN MIND

Tell the story: Make the story yours, then share it with your listeners. Use the language; don't throw away any good words. Settings give context; don't rush the description. Characters must be believable; understand their motivation. Dialogue reveals character; distinguish one character from another with your voice.

I am not worthy to stoop and loosen the thongs of his sandals."

Mark then reports that Jesus "was baptized in the Jordan by John." For some in the early Church, Jesus receiving from John "a baptism of repentance for the forgiveness of sins" (Mark 1:4) led to the conclusion that Jesus himself had his own sins forgiven before the start of his public ministry. It would take some time for the Church to correct this line of thinking that developed into a heresy known as adoptionism

(the belief that Jesus was "adopted" as God's Son only after his baptism).

Mark goes on to describe what Jesus himself experienced after "coming up out of the water." Images of the heavens "being torn" and the Spirit like a dove "descending upon him" create the idea of a divine anointing. This concept is solidified in God himself speaking, "You are my beloved Son; with you I am well pleased." Torah-observant Jews from Mark's community would have recognized in this scene the fulfillment of numerous prophecies from Isaiah (see Isaiah 11:2; 42:1; 61:1).

For Mark, Jesus's baptism by John in the Jordan River was the initiating event that launched his public ministry. Little else is said by Mark about John the Baptist, except to report on the circumstances surrounding his death in 6:17–29. For Mark, John's mission of preparing Israel for the arrival of the Messiah was accomplished through his baptism of Jesus.

SECOND SUNDAY IN ORDINARY TIME

LECTIONARY #65

READING I   1 Samuel 3:3b–10, 19

A reading from the first Book of Samuel

Samuel was **sleeping** in the **temple** of the LORD
  where the **ark** of **God** was.
The LORD **called** to Samuel, who answered, "**Here** I am."
Samuel ran to **Eli** and said, "**Here** I am. You **called** me."
"I did not **call** you," Eli said. "Go back to **sleep**."
So he **went** back to sleep.
Again the LORD called Samuel, who **rose** and went to **Eli**.
"**Here** I am," he said. "You **called** me."
But Eli answered, "I did **not** call you, my **son**. Go back to **sleep**."

At **that** time **Samuel** was not **familiar** with the LORD,
  because the LORD had not **revealed** anything to him as yet.
The LORD called Samuel **again**, for the **third** time.
Getting **up** and going to **Eli**, he said, "Here I **am**. You **called** me."
Then Eli understood that the LORD was calling the youth.
So he **said** to Samuel, "Go to **sleep**, and **if** you are **called**, reply,
  '**Speak**, LORD, for your servant is **listening**.'"
When Samuel **went** to sleep in his place,
  the LORD **came** and revealed his **presence**,
  calling out as before, "**Samuel, Samuel!**"
Samuel answered, "**Speak**, for your servant is **listening**."

Samuel grew up, and the LORD was **with** him,
  not permitting any **word** of his to be without **effect**.

TO KEEP IN MIND

Names of characters: Often the first word of a reading. Lift out the names to ensure listeners don't miss who the subject is.

Samuel is living in the house of the Lord, close to the "ark." Don't rush these details.

"Here I am" is a familiar Old Testament response to God's call.

Samuel's pace is brisk, while Eli (roused from sleep) responds with less energy.

The urgency rises with the second call.

Samuel speaks an eager "Here I am." Eli remains patient and calm.

This is not an inconsequential aside. It tells us that Samuel was still spiritually naïve.

Place emphasis on "the third time." Samuel speaks with conviction that finally gets Eli's attention.

"Eli understood" marks a turning point in the story.

Eli has thought this through and gives careful instructions to the boy.

God's voice is full of authority, but not fearsome. The second "Samuel" gets greater stress. Pause before starting the final sentence. Use a persuasive tone. These weighty lines suggest the encounter with God will transform the boy. There are three distinct pieces of information in the sentence. Don't run them together.

READING I | Samuel lived during a major transitional period in Israel's history. After Israel had arrived in the promised land around 1200 BC and conquered the Canaanites under the leadership of Joshua, the land was eventually divided into twelve regions, one for each of the twelve tribes of Israel. After the death of Joshua, who died at the age of 110 (Joshua 24:29), "judges" were assigned as military leaders of the tribes. This system of governance, commonly called "the period of the Judges," lasted about 200 years, until the establishment of Israel's monarchy around 1020 BC. The final two judges in Israel, Eli and Samuel, bore witness to this transition from the period of the Judges to the period of the monarchy.

Samuel had the distinctive role of being the last judge in Israel (in the period of the Judges), as well as the prophet at the beginning stages of the monarchy. The opening chapters of the First Book of Samuel detail Samuel's birth, including the well-known song of Hannah, the mother of Samuel (1 Samuel 2:1–10, which can be compared with Mary's song in Luke 1:46–55). We also learn in these chapters that Hannah gave Samuel to the Lord in thanksgiving for receiving him when she was thought to be barren. All of this background helps us understand why it was so important that Samuel learn to hear and respond to God's call, and this is the subject of today's reading.

Eli, the priest of the temple in Shiloh, raised Samuel from his youth "in the service of the Lord" (1 Samuel 2:11) after receiving him from Hannah. It is to Eli that Samuel first turns as he begins to make sense of the voice he has heard. And it is Eli who instructs Samuel on how to respond

For meditation and context:

TO KEEP IN MIND

Sense lines: Scripture in this book is arranged (as in the Lectionary) in sense lines, one idea per line. Typically at least a slight pause should follow each line, but good reading requires you to recognize the need for other pauses within lines.

Corinthians = kohr-IN-thee-uhnz

Paul's message is blunt and lacks nuance, but it is spoken in love for the welfare of those listening.

Contrast the word "immorality" with the word "Lord."

"Members" is not used like "members of a club," but refers to actual parts, like arms and hands, of Christ's body.

This strong injunction results from the reality of being "one Spirit" with Christ. Make eye contact as you speak.

Employ a persuasive tone. Defiling our body is serious because our body is united to Christ.

Though Paul's intent is to persuade, not intimidate, you mustn't dilute his authority.

For Paul the logic is clear: you have been "purchased," therefore you must "glorify God."

RESPONSORIAL PSALM   Psalm 40:2, 4, 7–8, 8–9, 10 (8a and 9a)

R. Here am I, Lord; I come to do your will.

I have waited, waited for the LORD,
    and he stooped toward me and heard my cry.
And he put a new song into my mouth,
    a hymn to our God.

Sacrifice or offering you wished not,
    but ears open to obedience you gave me.
Holocausts or sin-offerings you sought not;
    then said I, "Behold I come."

"In the written scroll it is prescribed for me,
    to do your will, O my God, is my delight,
    and your law is within my heart!"

I announced your justice in the vast assembly;
    I did not restrain my lips, as you,
    O LORD, know.

READING II   1 Corinthians 6:13c–15a, 17–20

A reading from the first Letter of Saint Paul to the Corinthians

Brothers and sisters:
The body is not for **immorality**, but for the **Lord**,
    and the **Lord** is for the **body**;
    God **raised** the Lord and will also raise **us** by his **power**.

Do you not **know** that your bodies are **members** of **Christ**?
But whoever is **joined** to the Lord becomes one **Spirit** with him.
Avoid immorality.
Every **other** sin a person commits is **outside** the body,
    but the **immoral** person sins against his own **body**.
Do you not **know** that your body
    is a **temple** of the Holy **Spirit** within you,
    whom you have from **God**, and that you are not your **own**?
For you have been **purchased** at a **price**.
Therefore **glorify** God in your **body**.

to it by saying, "Speak, Lord, for your servant is listening." Samuel does as Eli taught him, and Samuel receives a revelation.

Today's reading excludes the details of this first revelation (1 Samuel 3:11–18), probably because, as we see by this reading's pairing with today's Gospel, the preparers of the Lectionary want us to focus on how God's faithful servants respond to his call. In fact, Samuel's first revelation was a sad one: Eli, Samuel's mentor, is about to be punished by God because Eli allowed his own sons to "blaspheme the Lord" and Eli did not admonish them. But as

we learn from the last lines of today's reading, Samuel faithfully continues to answer the Lord's call, and "the Lord was with him, not permitting any word of his to be without effect."

READING II Between the Feast of the Baptism of the Lord (last Sunday) and Ash Wednesday, there is a short stretch of five Sundays in Ordinary Time. The Second Reading for each of these Sundays is taken from Paul's First Letter to the Corinthians, chapters 6–10. We begin

today in 1 Corinthians 6 with Paul responding to one of the slogans heard among the community members in Corinth: "Everything is lawful for me" (6:12). Clearly, some in the community have misunderstood his teaching, probably concerning the believer's newfound freedom in Christ (see, for example, Galatians 2:4; 4:21–31; 5:1; Romans 8:21). Now he hastens to correct this, laying out his position on sexual morality.

Paul counters the notion of everything being lawful by presenting his theology of the body. He is consistent in his theological framework oriented to Christ; in this case,

Name the characters and locations with familiarity and affection.

Don't rush the introduction. Imagine John watching his cousin and being *filled* with the insight that he was "the Lamb of God."

The disciples listen to John with their hearts as well as their ears.

As he does other times, Jesus plays "dumb" and asks leading questions. He seems to be enjoying the exchange with these men.

This is a significant line, spoken to each of us as well as these disciples.

After naming the hour, the mood shifts. The narration suggests the evangelistic fervor that early on grabbed Andrew's heart.

This is a bold (and risky) declaration!

Give this life-altering line ("he brought him to Jesus") the import it requires.

"Jesus looked at him" should suggest the length and depth with which Jesus looked *into* Peter. Don't overdo Jesus's line. You can't give it its full import, which would only later become apparent to Peter and the others.

TO KEEP IN MIND

Openings and Closings: differ in tone from the Scripture and require pauses, after the opening dialogue and before the closing dialogue. These formulas are prescribed, so don't vary the wording.

GOSPEL   John 1:35–42

A reading from the holy Gospel according to John

John was standing with two of his **disciples**,
    and as he watched **Jesus** walk by, he said,
    "**Behold**, the **Lamb** of **God**."
The two disciples **heard** what he said and **followed** Jesus.
Jesus **turned** and **saw** them following him and **said** to them,
    "What are you **looking** for?"
They said to him, "**Rabbi**"—which translated means **Teacher**—,
    "where are you **staying**?"
He said to them, "**Come**, and you will **see**."
So they **went** and **saw** where Jesus was staying,
    and they **stayed** with him that day.
It was about **four** in the afternoon.
Andrew, the brother of Simon **Peter**,
    was **one** of the two who **heard** John and **followed** Jesus.
He **first** found his own brother **Simon** and told him,
    "We have found the **Messiah**" —which is translated **Christ**—.
Then he **brought** him to Jesus.
Jesus **looked** at him and said,
    "You are **Simon** the son of **John**;
    you will be called **Cephas**"—which is translated **Peter**.

---

the connection of the body of the individual believer with the body of Christ: "Do you not know that your bodies are members of Christ?" Here Paul issues a strong assertion: "Avoid immorality." Paul views our physical bodies as "a temple of the Holy Spirit within you," owned, in fact, by God and meant to "glorify God."

GOSPEL   The Gospel reading is John's account of the call of the first disciples. Each Gospel writer provides a distinctive version of how this

event took place. John alone includes these features in his story: John the Baptist points Jesus out to two of his disciples and calls Jesus the "Lamb of God"; Jesus's first spoken words are "What are you looking for?"; Andrew is identified as a disciple of John the Baptist; and Jesus, upon meeting Simon, immediately renames him Cephas ("Peter"). This renaming of Simon, in part, foreshadows the leadership role that Simon Peter will assume among the followers of Jesus.

Those first words of Jesus in the Gospel according to John ("What are you looking for?") function as both an invitation and a challenge—to the disciples and to us. They set the stage for one of the main ways that John defines discipleship. True disciples are those who bring others to Christ to see and believe the revelation that Jesus is "the Word made flesh" (John 1:14). Like Samuel in the First Reading and the disciples here in the Gospel, we must decide how to respond to the revelation.

THIRD SUNDAY IN ORDINARY TIME

LECTIONARY #68

Jonah = JOH-nuh

The book of Jonah is only two pages. Reading it will give you the context of this reading.

Nineveh = NIN-uh-vuh

God sends Jonah on a "rescue" mission.

Jonah went, but reluctantly!

Jonah is dragging his heels, and his success surprises him most of all.

Convey the sincerity and totality of their repentance.

Pause to shift to the slower pace and more pensive mood of the final sentence.

Let the merciful love of God echo in this line.

READING I   Jonah 3:1–5, 10

A reading from the Book of the Prophet Jonah

The **word** of the LORD came to **Jonah**, saying:
    "**Set** out for the great city of **Nineveh**,
    and **announce** to it the message that I will **tell** you."
So Jonah made **ready** and **went** to Nineveh,
    according to the LORD's **bidding**.
Now Nineveh was an **enormously large** city;
    it took three **days** to go through it.
Jonah began his **journey** through the city,
    and had gone but a **single** day's walk announcing,
    "**Forty** days more and Nineveh shall be **destroyed**,"
    when the people of Nineveh **believed** God;
    they proclaimed a **fast**
    and **all** of them, **great** and **small**, put on **sackcloth**.

When God **saw** by their actions how they **turned** from their
        evil way,
    he **repented** of the evil that he had **threatened** to do to them;
    he did **not** carry it out.

TO KEEP IN MIND
Read all three commentaries.
Suggestions in each can give you insight into your own passage.

READING I   The prophet Jonah is one of the more interesting biblical characters. Disobedient to God's call to prophesy, miraculously rescued in his flight from prophetic duties, and later frustrated by the successful conversion of the Ninevites, Jonah is truly a prophet like no other in the Old Testament. Some scholars even see the Book of Jonah as closer in literary form to a prophetic parable than to a historical account.

In today's reading, this is actually the second time the Lord has requested Jonah to preach repentance to the citizens of Nineveh. Upon the first request, Jonah fled to the city of Tarshish (Jonah 1:1–3). After much delay, Jonah finally preaches repentance to the Ninevites. Much to the surprise and disappointment of the prophet (see Jonah 4:1), all the citizens of Nineveh, "great and small," repented of their sins against God. Jonah's somewhat perplexing reaction to God's show of mercy to the Ninevites stems from two probable factors. First, the Ninevites did not belong to the Chosen People; they were counted among the other "nations" (that is, they were Gentiles). Second, and perhaps more importantly, Nineveh was the capital city of Assyria, the historic enemies of Israel.

The call for repentance from sin was a consistent strand in Israel's prophetic tradition. We see in today's reading from Jonah the divine invitation extended to other nations, including those counted among Israel's enemies. It anticipated one of the basic teachings of Jesus: "Repent, and believe in the gospel."

For meditation and context:

TO KEEP IN MIND
Pace: The rate at which you read is influenced by the size of your church, the size of the congregation, and the complexity of the text. As each increases, rate decreases.

RESPONSORIAL PSALM   Psalm 25:4–5, 6–7, 8–9 (4a)

R. Teach me your ways, O Lord.

Your ways, O LORD, make known to me;
    teach me your paths,
guide me in your truth and teach me,
    for you are God my savior.

Remember that your compassion, O LORD,
    and your love are from of old.
In your kindness remember me,
    because of your goodness, O LORD.

Good and upright is the LORD;
    thus he shows sinners the way.
He guides the humble to justice
    and teaches the humble his way.

Corinthians = kohr-IN-thee-uhnz

Be sure your assembly is settled and ready to listen before you begin.

Deliver the entire first line from memory, with sustained eye contact.

Though the text is brief, there is no need for an overly slow reading. The activities named (weeping, rejoicing, buying, etc.) are less important than the message that *all* worldly things will pass away. Better to convey urgency through brisk pacing than to belabor the specific life situations.

A clear pause precedes the final sentence which, like the beginning, should be spoken from memory with sustained eye contact.

READING II   1 Corinthians 7:29–31

A reading from the first Letter of Saint Paul to the Corinthians

I **tell** you, brothers and sisters, the **time** is running **out**.
From **now** on, let those having **wives** act as **not** having them,
    those **weeping** as **not** weeping,
    those **rejoicing** as **not** rejoicing,
    those **buying** as **not** owning,
    those **using** the world as **not** using it **fully**.
For the world in its **present** form is passing **away**.

GOSPEL   Mark 1:14–20

A reading from the holy Gospel according to Mark

After **John** had been **arrested**,
    Jesus came to **Galilee** proclaiming the gospel of **God**:
    "**This** is the time of **fulfillment**.
The kingdom of **God** is at **hand**.
Repent, and **believe** in the **gospel**."

John's incarceration sounds a somber note and impacts the tone of the lines that follow.

Jesus speaks with authority, not like the scribes and Pharisees. His words are sober; the "good news" demands repentance.

READING II This reading from First Corinthians offers a good example of Paul's eschatological (end-time) worldview: "I tell you, brothers and sisters, the time is running out." Paul saw all around him signs of the imminent return of Christ (the Parousia), which would usher in the new age: "For the world in its present form is passing away." Jesus and John the Baptist held a similar end-time view of the world. As we will hear in the Gospel Reading today, Mark tells us that Jesus preached at the start of his public ministry, "This is the time of fulfillment."

Paul's eschatological worldview was likely part of the message that he preached to the Christians during his time in Corinth. However, this perspective raised some very practical questions for the Corinthians, not the least of which were, how should they live in this eschatological tension? How should they carry on with their lives waiting for the Second Coming of Christ? Paul urged them in today's reading to live radically different lives: "From now on, let those having wives act as not having them, those weeping as not weeping."

GOSPEL Mark tells us that after his baptism and temptation in the desert (Mark 1:9–13), Jesus officially began his public ministry in Galilee. The village in which Jesus was raised, Nazareth, was located in Galilee, the northern region of Palestine. Mark places the start of Jesus's public ministry after John's arrest. We hear later from Mark that John was arrested by Herod Antipas (and eventually executed) for speaking out against Herod's unlawful marriage to his sister-in-law (see Mark 6:17–29).

The tone is upbeat as you describe these fishermen.

As he passed by the Sea of **Galilee**,
    he saw **Simon** and his brother **Andrew** casting their **nets**
        into the sea;
    they were **fishermen**.
Jesus **said** to them,

Note that Jesus doesn't ask; his words take the form of an imperative.

    "Come after **me**, and I will make you fishers of **men**."
Then they **abandoned** their nets and **followed** him.

Their decision is instant and so is their response.

He walked along a little **farther**
    and saw **James**, the son of **Zebedee**, and his brother **John**.

Speak of these brothers with familiarity and stress the familial relationship of sons and father.

They **too** were in a boat mending their **nets**.
Then he **called** them.

"Then he called them" says much more than the bald words would suggest.

So they **left** their father Zebedee in the boat
    along with the hired men and followed him.

Pause briefly after speaking "the hired men," and then announce their bold decision.

TO KEEP IN MIND

Using the Microphone: Know your public address system. If it echoes, speak even more slowly. If you hear "popping," you're probably standing too close to the microphone.

The Gospel Reading also presents the first words spoken by Jesus in the Gospel of Mark: "This is the time of fulfillment. The kingdom of God is at hand. Repent, and believe in the gospel." Mark sees this as the basic summary of Jesus's "gospel of God." In the Gospel according to Mark, the Kingdom of God is the centerpiece of Jesus's preaching. The Greek word used here for "kingdom" (*basileia*) may be more actually translated as "reign" or "rule." The idea of the "reign of God" better captures the active sense of God's presence in and through Jesus and his ministry that is conveyed so effectively, for example, in the parables of Jesus.

Also captured in Jesus's first words is the call to repentance. The Greek word used here by Mark for "repent" is *metanoia*, which can be translated as change of heart/mind. Jesus challenged his would-be followers to begin thinking and feeling differently in light of the good news of the arrival of the reign of God. As heard in the First Reading, the call to repentance was firmly grounded in Israel's prophetic tradition.

This reading concludes with the call of the first disciples. Mark offers a different description of the call than John's account reported last Sunday. According to John, John the Baptist played a key role in connecting Peter and Andrew with Jesus. In Mark, John the Baptist had already been arrested by the time Jesus calls the two sets of fishermen brothers, Peter and Andrew, James and John. The brothers immediately accept Jesus's invitation to follow him: "Come after me, and I will make you fishers of men."

FOURTH SUNDAY IN ORDINARY TIME

TO KEEP IN MIND

Names of characters: Often the first word of a reading. Lift out the names to ensure listeners don't miss who the subject is.

Deuteronomy = d<u>oo</u>-ter-AH-nuh-mee

But for the first line, the entire text is spoken in Moses' voice.

First, Moses tells the people what God will do, and then he explains that God is giving them just what they asked for.

Moses reminds them of how fearful they were (at Horeb) of direct encounter with the awesome God. Therefore, God is accommodating the people.

God was pleased by the request for an intermediary (a prophet).

These words came to be understood as a great prophecy of the coming Messiah.

There is warning and threat in these lines: if you ignore the prophet, woe to you; if the prophet ignores me, woe to the prophet!

This is an intentionally strong and blunt declaration. Don't try to soften it.

LECTIONARY #71

READING I   Deuteronomy 18:15–20

A reading from the Book of Deuteronomy

Moses spoke to all the **people**, saying:
  "A **prophet** like me will the LORD, your God, raise **up** for you
  from among your own **kin**;
  to **him** you shall **listen**.
This is exactly what you **requested** of the LORD, your God,
    at **Horeb**
  on the day of the **assembly**, when you said,
  'Let us not **again** hear the voice of the LORD, our God,
  nor see this great **fire** any more, lest we **die**.'
And the *LORD* said to me, 'This was **well** said.
I will **raise** up for them a **prophet** like you from among their **kin**,
    and will put my **words** into his mouth;
  he shall tell them **all** that I **command** him.
Whoever will not **listen** to my words which he speaks
    in my name,
  I **myself** will make him **answer** for it.
But **if** a prophet **presumes** to speak in my name
    an **oracle** that I have **not** commanded him to speak,
  or speaks in the name of **other** gods, he shall **die**.'"

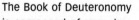 **READING I**   The Book of Deuteronomy is composed of speeches delivered by Moses to the Israelites on the plains of Moab at the end of the forty-year desert wanderings. Moses is preparing the Israelites for their long-awaited entry into the promised land, reminding them of key aspects of the Law.

In today's reading, Moses foretells the arrival of a prophet who will guide the people and deliver God's words to them: "A prophet like me will the Lord, your God, raise up for you from among your own kin." Early in the desert journey, the people had asked Moses to speak for God, since communicating directly with God was so terrifying (Exodus 20:19). Moses is assuring them that they will continue to have an intermediary. He knows they will need such a leader to keep them from turning to the "soothsayers and fortune-tellers" (Deuteronomy 18:14) of the other native people occupying the promised land. Israel must not assimilate the cultural practices of other peoples, for that would threaten the covenantal relationship between God and Israel so clearly laid out in the giving of the Law.

Moses's news of a future prophet is intended to assure them of God's ongoing presence: "[I ,God] will put my words into his mouth; he shall tell them all that I command him." But there is also a warning in this prophecy: "Whoever will not listen to my words which he speaks in my name, I myself will make him answer for it." Israel would continue to look to a long line of prophets to speak for God to the people. Some would connect this reading's promise with a messiah, and Christians see a foreshadowing of Christ.

For meditation and context:

TO KEEP IN MIND

When practicing, **read Scriptures aloud**, taking note of stress and pause suggestions. After several readings, alter the stress markings to suit your style and interpretation.

RESPONSORIAL PSALM   Psalm 95:1–2, 6–7, 7–9 (8)

R. If today you hear his voice, harden not your hearts.

Come, let us sing joyfully to the LORD;
    let us acclaim the rock of our salvation.
Let us come into his presence with
        thanksgiving;
    let us joyfully sing psalms to him.

Come, let us bow down in worship;
    let us kneel before the LORD who made us.
For he is our God,
    and we are the people he shepherds,
        the flock he guides.

Oh, that today you would hear his voice:
    "Harden not your hearts as at Meribah,
        as in the day of Massah in the desert,
where your fathers tempted me;
    they tested me though they had seen
        my works."

Corinthians = kohr-IN-thee-uhnz

Remember, Paul's intent is to make recommendations for how best to be ready for the Lord's return.

Don't stress "anxious," but "Lord."

Paul says a less complicated life is easier to live than one laden with the responsibilities of children, home, and spouse.

Paul is not denigrating married life but endorsing stability, i.e., maintaining one's current state rather than embracing new responsibilities and their attendant tensions.

The responsibilities of marriage, says Paul, can distract a woman from a life of prayer and focus on the Lord.

Paul offers suggestions and options, not commands.

Reading this entire chapter of 1 Corinthians will clarify the context and Paul's intent.

READING II   1 Corinthians 7:32–35

A reading from the first Letter of Saint Paul to the Corinthians

Brothers and sisters:
I should like you to be free of **anxieties**.
An **unmarried** man is anxious about the things of the **Lord**,
    how he may **please** the Lord.
But a **married** man is anxious about the things of the **world**,
    how he may please his **wife**, and he is **divided**.
An unmarried **woman** or a **virgin** is anxious about the things
        of the **Lord**,
    so that she may be holy in both **body** and **spirit**.
A **married** woman, on the other hand,
    is anxious about the things of the **world**,
    how she may please her **husband**.
I am telling you this for your own **benefit**,
    not to impose a **restraint** upon you,
    but for the sake of **propriety**
    and **adherence** to the Lord without **distraction**.

READING II First Corinthians 7 opens with the line: "Now in regard to the matters about which you wrote." The Corinthians apparently had a variety of questions they hoped Paul could address in a letter to them. Marriage and sexuality are the first issues that Paul formally addresses in his response to Corinthians' questions. This likely indicates its importance for both Paul and the Corinthian congregation. Paul offers advice to the married (7:1–16), the unmarried

(7:25–38), and the widowed (7:39–40). Today's reading picks up on Paul's advice to the unmarried.

Two important factors should be considered when reflecting on Paul's advice to the unmarried. First, Paul makes clear that his advice is offered in his desire for believers in Corinth "to be free anxieties." Second, and not mentioned directly in today's reading, but part of Paul's eschatological worldview heard last Sunday, the return of Christ is imminent; therefore, Paul is always thinking in terms of the short

term. Paul's concerns are about divided loyalties. Although he himself was not married (1 Corinthians 7:7–8), he knows well that a good marriage requires a husband and wife to be devoted to each other, first and foremost. Spouses are anxious about how "to please" each other. But the unmarried are more focused on "the things of the Lord." With the Second Coming soon to arrive, Paul, understandably, recommends that the unmarried stay in that state so as to live "without distraction."

GOSPEL   Mark 1:21–28

A reading from the holy Gospel according to Mark

Capernaum = kuh-PER-nee-*m

Then they came to **Capernaum**,
    and on the **sabbath Jesus** entered the **synagogue** and **taught**.
The people were **astonished** at his teaching,
    for he taught them as one having **authority** and not as
        the **scribes**.
In their synagogue was a man with an **unclean spirit**;
    he cried out, "What have you to **do** with us, Jesus of Nazareth?
Have you come to **destroy** us?
I **know** who you are—the **Holy** One of **God**!"
Jesus **rebuked** him and said,
    "**Quiet**! Come **out** of him!"
The unclean spirit **convulsed** him and with a loud **cry** came **out**
    of him.
All were **amazed** and asked one another,
    "What **is** this?
A new **teaching** with **authority**.
He commands even the unclean **spirits** and they **obey** him."
His **fame** spread **everywhere** throughout the whole region
    of **Galilee**.

Don't rush, but create a sense of Jesus's riveting presence.

This is a significant detail; don't gloss over it.

Slowly set up the scene, then quicken the pace and build the intensity as the "spirit" rails and attempts to "out" Jesus.

Pause after "Quiet!" Then deliver his next command.

Narrate their amazement slowly, and then deliver their comments with energy and brisk pacing.

After a brief pause, narrate with admiration the news of his rising notoriety.

TO KEEP IN MIND

Pray the Scriptures: Make reading these Scriptures a part of your prayer life every week, and especially during the week prior to the liturgy in which you will proclaim.

GOSPEL   In the opening chapters of his Gospel account, Mark presents Jesus performing many miracles, especially healings and exorcisms. In fact, the first and most often performed miracle by Jesus in Mark is exorcism. As we hear in today's reading, Mark presents Jesus in conversation with demons, controlling them and commanding them to follow his orders (see also, for example 1:34; 5:1–20; 6:7; 9:14–29).

One of the interesting features of Jesus's dialogues with the demons is that the demons know Jesus's true identity: "What have you to do with us, Jesus of Nazareth? Have you come to destroy us? I know who you are—the Holy One of God!" (see also 1:34; 3:11; 5:7). The demons do not waiver in their understanding of Jesus, unlike the crowds and even, at times, his own disciples (4:41), who fail to recognize Jesus as the Messiah and Son of God.

Not surprisingly, those in the synagogue who heard Jesus's teaching and witnessed the exorcism were "amazed." They were reacting both to the miracle and to the teachings. Curiously, Mark does not include any details about what Jesus was teaching that day in the Capernaum synagogue. But clearly the crowds viewed Jesus as someone "with authority." According to Mark, it is Jesus's teachings and his ability to control the demons that helped him gain widespread fame throughout Galilee early on in his public ministry.

FIFTH SUNDAY IN ORDINARY TIME

LECTIONARY #74

Job = johb

Don't look for the silver lining here; this is a plaintive text about life's hopelessness.

The specific complaints are less important than the overall tone of weariness and despondency. Job complains without embarrassment.

Often, verbalizing our woes can be therapeutic. Job seems to understand this.

Contrast his long, restless *nights* with *days* that go too fast and bring no relief.

Don't hold back from making eye contact.

Job claims license to focus on life's futility. His depression is palpable, but he speaks with resignation.

TO KEEP IN MIND

Names of characters: Often the first word of a reading. Lift out the names to ensure listeners don't miss who the subject is.

READING I Job 7:1–4, 6–7

A reading from the Book of Job

Job spoke, saying:
Is not man's life on earth a **drudgery**?
    Are not his days those of **hirelings**?
He is a **slave** who longs for the **shade**,
    a hireling who waits for his **wages**.
So **I** have been assigned months of **misery**,
    and **troubled** nights have been allotted to me.
If in **bed** I say, "When shall I **arise**?"
    then the night **drags** on;
    I am filled with **restlessness** until the dawn.
My days are **swifter** than a weaver's **shuttle**;
    they come to an end without **hope**.
Remember that my life is like the **wind**;
    I shall not see **happiness** again.

READING I Written sometime between the seventh and fifth centuries BC, the Book of Job is widely considered one of the finest works of Israel's wisdom tradition contained in the Old Testament. The main question raised in Job is: why do innocent people suffer?

The plot of the story is established in the opening twelve verses of this lengthy book: Job, a wise man "blameless and upright" with many blessings from God, including children and wealth, is suddenly put to the test by Satan. Will Job remain strong in his faith when all is lost and suffering ensues? Job's response in the face of many calamities makes up the remainder of the book.

Today's reading is part of Job's reaction to one of his friends, Eliphaz, who attempts to comfort and console Job, offering various sound and rational explanations for his recent misfortunes. But Job finds no relief in Eliphaz's words; his pain is too great. "I shall not see happiness again."

At the end of the book, after Job's deep questioning and God's thought-provoking reply, Job does find resolution and reward. But that is not where this reading leaves us. We are left with a stark sense of our mortality and helplessness.

READING II Today's reading is a continuation of Paul's responses to various questions raised by the Corinthian Christians (1 Corinthians 7:1; 8:1). This short excerpt from 1 Corinthians is somewhat disjointed because it includes two related topics: Paul's rationale for not charging for his preaching of the Gospel and Paul's freedom as an Apostle.

For meditation and context:

TO KEEP IN MIND

Know who wrote the letter and who received it. Discover the circumstances. **The intent of each letter dictates the tone.** Often Paul is the writer; he is motivated by multiple concerns: to instruct, console, encourage, chastise, warn, settle disputes, and more. When reading from one of his letters, be aware of what he's trying to accomplish.

Corinthians = kohr-IN-thee-uhnz

For Paul, preaching the Gospel is a privilege, not a burden. He says "Woe to me" not out of fear, but because he would lose his identity if he were mute about the Gospel.

Preaching willingly is its own reward; preaching unwillingly means I'm at least fulfilling my responsibility.

Paul was criticized by opponents who claimed his refusal to accept money for preaching reflected a lack of confidence in his own authority. He claims it as a badge of honor.

Paul's careful reasoning is conveyed through carefully balanced statements. Balance "*free* in regard to all" with "a *slave* to all"; and balance "all things to *all*" with "to save at least *some*."

Here Paul reveals his ultimate motivation: by sharing the Gospel he receives a share of its blessing.

RESPONSORIAL PSALM   Psalm 147:1–2, 3–4, 5–6 (3a)

R. Praise the Lord, who heals the brokenhearted.
or
R. Alleluia.

Praise the LORD, for he is good;
   sing praise to our God, for he is gracious;
   it is fitting to praise him.
The LORD rebuilds Jerusalem;
   the dispersed of Israel he gathers.

He heals the brokenhearted
   and binds up their wounds.
He tells the number of the stars;
   he calls each by name.

Great is our Lord and mighty in power;
   to his wisdom there is no limit.
The LORD sustains the lowly;
   the wicked he casts to the ground.

READING II   1 Corinthians 9:16–19, 22–23

A reading from the first Letter of Saint Paul to the Corinthians

Brothers and sisters:
If I preach the **gospel**, this is no reason for me to **boast**,
   for an **obligation** has been **imposed** on me,
   and **woe** to me if I do **not** preach it!
If I do so **willingly**, I have a **recompense**,
   but if **unwillingly**, then I have been entrusted with
      a **stewardship**.
What then is my **recompense**?
That, when I **preach**,
   I offer the gospel free of **charge**
   so as not to make full use of my **right** in the gospel.

Although I am **free** in regard to all,
   I have made myself a **slave** to all
   so as to win over as **many** as **possible**.
To the **weak** I became **weak**, to win **over** the weak.
I have become all things to **all**, to save at least **some**.
All this I do for the sake of the **gospel**,
   so that I **too** may have a **share** in it.

A larger discussion in this section of the letter is Paul's defense of his apostleship. While Paul does, in fact, have the lawful right to charge a fee for his preaching, he chooses not to, because he views his preaching of the Gospel more as a "stewardship" authorized by the Lord than an occupation deserving a just wage. In fact, Paul's sense of mission is so great that his outreach must include all people. This demands extreme measures, even if, in the end, he can only reach some: "I have become all things to all, to save at least some." Paul's life is completely attuned to his work for, and his participation in, the Gospel

GOSPEL | We continue to hear today about Jesus's many healings and exorcisms at the start of his public ministry in Galilee. Mark begins his Gospel account with a strong emphasis on Jesus's "powerful deeds" (in Greek, *dunameis*). In fact, the extensive focus on Jesus's miracles, especially during his Galilean ministry (Mark 1–8), seems to emphasize Jesus's deeds more than his words. There are four

movements to this reading: the healing of Peter's mother-in-law, evening healings of all the sick and possessed in Capernaum, Jesus at prayer, and Jesus's departure from Capernaum.

Some interesting details emerge from today's Gospel; for instance we learn that Simon Peter was married, and that he and his brother Andrew lived in Capernaum, a town about twenty miles northeast of Nazareth where Jesus was raised. But what else is going on in this passage? Jesus cured many people who were ill from various causes, ranging from disease to demonic

GOSPEL   Mark 1:29–39

A reading from the holy Gospel according to Mark

On leaving the **synagogue**
>   **Jesus** entered the house of **Simon** and **Andrew** with **James**
>   and **John**.
Simon's **mother-in-law** lay sick with a **fever**.
They immediately **told** him about her.
He **approached**, **grasped** her hand, and helped her **up**.
Then the fever **left** her and she **waited** on them.

When it was **evening**, after **sunset**,
>   they brought to him all who were **ill** or possessed by **demons**.
The whole **town** was gathered at the door.
He cured **many** who were **sick** with various **diseases**,
>   and he drove out many **demons**,
>   not permitting them to **speak** because they **knew** him.

Rising very **early** before dawn, he **left**
>   and went off to a **deserted** place, where he **prayed**.
Simon and those who were with him **pursued** him
>   and on **finding** him said, "Everyone is **looking** for you."
He **told** them, "Let us go on to the nearby **villages**
>   that I may preach there **also**.
For this **purpose** have I come."
So he went into their **synagogues**,
>   **preaching** and driving out **demons** throughout the **whole**
>   of **Galilee**.

Take care not to rush the naming of characters and setting.

Speaking of Simon's "mother-in-law" should differ from speaking about some anonymous person in need.

Savor these very specific and personal details. That she immediately waits on them is a surprise.

Note the time references that initiate each division of this text. Pause before starting in order to suggest the passage of time and to shift mood.

The intimate scene is left behind as the crowd gathers at their doorstep. Jesus is fully in charge healing, driving out demons, and commanding their silence.

The mood shifts again; now it is early morning, and Jesus quietly leaves for solitary prayer.

But not for long! "Pursued" and "finding" suggest the eagerness with which the disciples sought him out and scolded him for going off alone.

Without complaint, Jesus returns to his "purpose": to preach God's word.

Speak the final sentence suggesting the authority with which Jesus entered the synagogues to preach and cast out demons. What he did then, you still do today.

> **TO KEEP IN MIND**
> **Eye contact** connects you with those to whom you minister. Look at the assembly during the middle and at the end of every thought or sentence.

---

possession. The majority of those receiving miraculous cures remain anonymous figures. When Mark (or any of the Gospel writers) does record the healing of an individual, such as Peter's mother-in-law (or the leper in next Sunday's Gospel), the writer is telling us something theologically significant, in this case, about Jesus and his effect on people. Not only did Jesus cure the mother-in-law, he "helped her up." The verb used in Greek is the same often used to describe Jesus's Resurrection. So he raises her, and as a result of being raised/saved, she serves. This is the ideal outcome of Jesus's work, healing that creates servant-minded disciples.

In the next movement Jesus continues his work of healing and exorcizing en mass, careful to keep the demons quiet since "they knew him." This seeming afterthought of a phrase can be seen as another clue about Mark's purpose in writing: to help us know Jesus. Next, in the midst of Jesus's solitary prayer, his intimate communication with his Father, the disciples come to tug him back to his public work. And from Jesus himself we hear the main "purpose" for his public ministry: to "preach" the Gospel to the "nearby villages" of the lower Galilee. Mark makes an important assertion here: while Jesus's deeds are truly amazing and astonishing, it is his words that also communicate the Good News of the Kingdom of God. Both Jesus's words and deeds left an impact on those he touched in his public ministry.

SIXTH SUNDAY IN ORDINARY TIME

LECTIONARY #77

READING I   Leviticus 13:1–2, 44–46

A reading from the Book of Leviticus

The LORD said to **Moses** and **Aaron**,
  "If someone has on his skin a **scab** or **pustule** or **blotch**
  which appears to be the sore of **leprosy**,
  he shall be brought to **Aaron**, the **priest**,
  or to one of the priests among his **descendants**.
If the man **is** leprous and unclean,
  the priest shall **declare** him unclean
  by reason of the **sore** on his head.

"The one who **bears** the sore of leprosy
  shall keep his garments **rent** and his head **bare**,
  and shall muffle his **beard**;
  he shall cry out, '**Unclean, unclean!**'
As long as the sore is on him he shall **declare** himself unclean,
  since he is in **fact** unclean.
He shall dwell **apart**, making his abode **outside** the camp."

Leviticus = lih-VIT-ih-kuhs

Save for the opening line, it is God who speaks throughout.

Aaron = AYR-uhn
leprosy = LEP-ruh-see

Submission to the priests ensured a proper diagnosis and accurate determination of whether one was rendered "unclean."

These are matters of great concern for the health of the community. Speak without judgment, but not without concern.

By stressing words like "rent," "bare" and "muffle," you will emphasize the serious nature of these matters. Increase your volume and energy on the words "unclean, unclean," but don't approach the level expected of one afflicted with leprosy.

The uncompromising order in the final line is motivated by concern for the community's well-being. Allow pathos and regret to color your tone.

READING I The Book of Leviticus stands at the center of the five books of the Pentateuch: Genesis, Exodus, Leviticus, Numbers, and Deuteronomy. This placement is by design. Leviticus is a book teaching Israel how to be clean and holy in God's presence—a major aspect to Israel's covenantal obligations with God. To that end, much of the material in the Book of Leviticus deals with legal matters around purity. Today's reading is taken from an entire section dealing with purity laws (Leviticus 11–6), addressing topics that range from food to personal hygiene. The issue of leprosy receives extensive treatment (Leviticus 13:1–14:57). Today's First Reading sets up the background for appreciating the Gospel.

Purity laws dating back to the ancient Israelites were intended to separate the clean from the unclean, and ultimately, the sacred from the profane, in religious ritual observances. These purity laws kept unclean Jews (such as men or women infected with leprosy) separated from clean Jews. While it may seem cruel by modern standards of medicine to treat those infected with the disease of leprosy by separating them from the community ("He shall dwell apart, making his abode outside the camp"), there did exist the very real possibility of the spread of the disease.

People suffering from leprosy were affected spiritually by the disease (since many saw it as a curse from God) as well as emotionally and psychologically. Alienation from the community was especially painful since the Israelites had a strong sense of collective identity.

For meditation and context:

TO KEEP IN MIND

Pace: The rate at which you read is influenced by the size of your church, the size of the congregation, and the complexity of the text. As each increases, rate decreases.

Corinthians = kohr-IN-thee-uhnz

Paul has been discussing the eating of meat sacrificed to idols. He concludes this way: Whatever you choose to do, do it for "the glory of God."

His concern is not about what is lawful to eat, but about not scandalizing others who may be naïve or more scrupulous.

In trying to "please everyone," Paul is not being two-faced. His advice is a variation of "when in Rome . . ."

Paul does not hesitate to offer himself as a model if it will benefit others. By imitating Paul we imitate Christ. Deliver the last line from memory, sustaining eye contact.

RESPONSORIAL PSALM Psalm 32:1–2, 5, 11 (7)

R. I turn to you, Lord, in time of trouble, and you fill me with the joy of salvation.

Blessed is he whose fault is taken away,
  whose sin is covered.
Blessed the man to whom the LORD imputes
    not guilt,
  in whose spirit there is no guile.

Then I acknowledged my sin to you,
  my guilt I covered not.
I said, "I confess my faults to the LORD,"
  and you took away the guilt of my sin.

Be glad in the LORD and rejoice, you just;
  exult, all you upright of heart.

READING II 1 Corinthians 10:31—11:1

A reading from the first Letter of Saint Paul to the Corinthians

Brothers and sisters,
Whether you **eat** or **drink**, or **whatever** you do,
  do **everything** for the glory of **God**.
Avoid giving **offense**, whether to the **Jews** or **Greeks** or the
    church of **God**,
  just as **I** try to please **everyone** in every **way**,
  not seeking my **own** benefit but that of the **many**,
  that they may be **saved**.
Be **imitators** of **me**, as I am of **Christ**.

READING II Today's brief reading from First Corinthians contains Paul's concluding remarks to the various questions raised by the Corinthian congregation. His answers have been lengthy, taking up four chapters (see 1 Corinthians 7:1—11:1). But now he summarizes succinctly. Paul is offering what he sees as solid advice, applicable to probably most of the future questions raised by the Christians in Corinth. First, "do everything for the glory of God." Second, "avoid giving offense" to everyone. And last, "be imitators of me, as I am of Christ." In this last sentence, Paul provides a practical model. As Paul works to imitate Christ, so they should follow his lead and also imitate Christ. Most likely, Paul considered these three prescriptions to be his universal standards of conduct for all believers in Christ, regardless of their congregation.

GOSPEL Mark's story of the cleansing of the leper is set against the actual and symbolic value of purity at the time of Jesus, a value that rested on the tradition we learned about in the First Reading: lepers were to be separated from the community because their contagious disease made them unclean.

Notice that upon healing this man of leprosy, making him "clean," Jesus tells the man to go to the priest, for it is the priest alone who determines whether the man can return to the community. When Jesus tells the man to "offer for your cleansing what Moses prescribed," he is referring to Leviticus 14:1–9, which prescribes an offering and several bathing rituals. In his healing ministry, Jesus clearly worked within the context of Jewish purity laws.

Here is a poignant human encounter. You don't need melodrama to reveal the touching aspects of this story.

"Moved with *pity*," Jesus responds. Stress his motivation and the physical contact between Jesus and leper.

From a slow delivery on "I do will it . . . clean," shift to a faster pace and joyful tone to announce the healing.

Jesus commands with authority and compassion. The priests don't need "proof" of Jesus's power but of the fact that the man was *healed* so he can return to community life.

"He" refers to Jesus who, futilely, seeks the quiet of the desert for reflection and prayer.

TO KEEP IN MIND

Characters: To distinguish the various characters that populate a passage, try to understand their thoughts, feelings, and motivations. Use subtle variations in pitch, pacing, and emotion to communicate them. But don't confuse proclamation with theatrics. Suggest characters, don't "become" them.

GOSPEL   Mark 1:40–45

A reading from the holy Gospel according to Mark

A **leper** came to **Jesus** and kneeling down **begged** him and said,
    "If you **wish**, you can make me **clean**."
Moved with **pity**, he stretched out his **hand**,
    touched him, and **said** to him,
    "**I do** will it. Be made **clean**."
The leprosy left him **immediately**, and he was made **clean**.
Then, warning him **sternly**, he **dismissed** him at once.

He **said** to him, "See that you tell **no** one **anything**,
    but **go**, show yourself to the **priest**
    and **offer** for your cleansing what Moses **prescribed**;
    that will be **proof** for them."

The man went away and began to **publicize** the whole matter.
He **spread** the report abroad
    so that it was **impossible** for Jesus to enter a town **openly**.
He remained **outside** in **deserted** places,
    and people kept **coming** to him from **everywhere**.

The Gospel Reading concludes with two rather remarkable comments by Mark. First, the cleansed leper directly violates Jesus's "stern warning" to remain silent about the healing: "The man went away and began to publicize the whole matter." This secrecy motif is a prominent feature in the first eight chapters of the Gospel of Mark. Jesus commands many to be silent about his activities and his identity: the disciples (5:43; 8:30; 9:9), the demons (1:34; 3:12), and many of those whom he healed (1:44; 7:36; 8:26). While the demons obey, many whom Jesus heals are unable or unwilling to remain silent, like the leper in today's Gospel.

This leads to the second extraordinary comment by Mark. Jesus's fame had spread so quickly throughout Galilee that soon it was no longer possible for Jesus "to enter a town openly." Jesus may have foreseen this when he requested silence from those whom he healed. Now Jesus had to remain "outside in deserted places." He has put himself "outside" in place of the lepers he healed.

And yet Jesus is hardly alone. People come to him. The conclusion to the Gospel reading leaves the impression of a very difficult situation for Jesus and the four disciples: "People kept coming to him from everywhere." Mark provides virtually nothing of what Jesus was preaching to the people of these villages in the opening chapter of his Gospel. We hear instead about his healing actions. These actions seem to constitute his teaching and, most significantly, establish an important aspect of his identity.

ASH WEDNESDAY

LECTIONARY #219

READING I   Joel 2:12–18

A reading from the Book of the Prophet Joel

Even **now**, says the LORD,
   return to me with your **whole heart**,
   with **fasting**, and **weeping**, and **mourning**;
Rend your hearts, not your **garments**,
   and **return** to the LORD, your God.
For **gracious** and **merciful** is he,
   slow to anger, **rich** in kindness,
   and **relenting** in **punishment**.
Perhaps he will **again** relent
   and leave behind him a **blessing**,
Offerings and **libations**
   for the LORD, your God.

Blow the **trumpet** in Zion!
   proclaim a **fast**,
   call an **assembly**;
Gather the people,
   notify the congregation;
Assemble the elders,
   gather the **children**
   and the **infants** at the **breast**;
Let the bridegroom **quit** his room
   and the bride her **chamber**.

Joel = JOH-*l

There are three sections in this text, each with a distinctive mood. The first is a long, earnest plea to soften our hearts and change our ways.

First state the goal: "return . . . rend your hearts . . . return." Then provide the motivation: "merciful is he . . . perhaps he will again relent."

"Rend your hearts . . . " expresses God's desire for *sincere* contrition, not a false outward show but genuine, *heart* rending sorrow.

A hopeful tone fills these lines that lead to the rousing second section that follows.

After a short pause, use the imperatives ("blow," "proclaim," "call," "gather," "notify," "assemble," "gather") to call your assembly to action.

The inclusion of "Elders," "children," "infants" underscores the urgency of the situation.

Let your tone suggest that even bride and groom must sacrifice their pleasure to entreat the Lord's mercy.

READING I | The prophecies of Joel are dated around 400 BC, toward the end of the period of Israel's great prophets. The prophets of Israel are commonly divided into three periods: early, classical, and post-exilic (after the exile). Early prophecy covers the period from the birth of Moses to the rise of the monarchy, 1250–1020 BC. Classical prophecy spans Israel's time in the Promised Land, both as a united Monarchy and as a divided kingdom, 1020–587 BC. Included in this period are the three great writing prophets: Isaiah, Jeremiah, and Ezekiel. Post-exilic prophecy covers the time of Israel's return from exile in Babylon (after 538 BC) to around 300 BC. Joel belongs to this last group, which includes Haggai, Zechariah, and Malachi.

Because of his emphasis on "the coming day of the Lord" at the end of time, Joel is often considered an eschatological (*eschaton* = end-time) prophet. Those prophets envisioned God's divine judgment at the end of time when Israel would be vindicated and the historic enemies of Israel would be punished.

The Book of Joel opens with the report of an invasion of swarms of locusts on the land of Judah, an event Joel saw as a sign that "the day of the Lord" was near—God's judgment on the world was imminent. He believed that this day could bring about divine blessings for the Jewish people, but it was critical that the people repent. They must return to God "with your whole heart, with fasting and weeping, and mourning." Joel believed that for Israel's repentance to be sincere, it must involve all the people, from the elders and priests to the children

The priests' role is to intercede for the people. Here they attempt to rouse God's pride, suggesting that if the people don't prosper the Lord will lose respect before the nations.

Speak the question, "Where is their God?" in the mocking voice of the nations.

Pause before the brief final section. The Lord heard the people's prayer and responds with mercy.

For meditation and context:

> **TO KEEP IN MIND**
> **Read all four Scriptures** for your assigned Sunday. Because all were chosen for this day, it is important to look at them together.

Between the **porch** and the **altar**
    let the **priests**, the **ministers** of the LORD, **weep**,
And say, "**Spare**, O LORD, your people,
    and make not your **heritage** a **reproach**,
    with the nations **ruling** over them!
Why should they say among the peoples,
    '**Where** is their God?' "

Then the LORD was stirred to **concern** for his land
    and took **pity** on his people.

RESPONSORIAL PSALM   Psalm 51:3–4, 5–6ab, 12–13, 14 and 17 (3a)

R. Be merciful, O Lord, for we have sinned.

Have mercy on me, O God, in your goodness;
    in the greatness of your compassion wipe
    out my offense.
Thoroughly wash me from my guilt
    and of my sin cleanse me.

For I acknowledge my offense,
    and my sin is before me always:
"Against you only have I sinned,
    and done what is evil in your sight."

A clean heart create for me, O God,
    and a steadfast spirit renew within me.
Cast me not out from your presence,
    and your Holy Spirit take not from me.

Give me back the joy of your salvation,
    and a willing spirit sustain in me.
O Lord, open my lips,
    and my mouth shall proclaim your praise.

Corinthians = kohr-IN-thee-uhnz

Address the assembly with affection, and then speak the second line from memory. There is clear urgency in these lines.

What Christ did is our motivation to seek "reconciliation": Jesus, the innocent, sinless one, took *all* sin upon himself.

Paul's urgent tone continues. His reasoning is that we must not squander the gift purchased at so great a price!

READING II   2 Corinthians 5:20—6:2

A reading from the second Letter of Saint Paul to the Corinthians

Brothers and sisters:
We are **ambassadors** for **Christ**,
    as if **God** were **appealing** through us.
We **implore** you on behalf of Christ,
    be **reconciled** to God.
For **our** sake he made him to **be** sin who did not **know** sin,
    so that we might become the **righteousness** of God in him.

and parents. As we hear at the end of today's First Reading, God was moved by Israel's "whole heart[ed]" conversion: "Then the Lord was stirred to concern for his land and took pity on his people."

The words of the prophet Joel are heard each Ash Wednesday because he spoke so forcefully about the people's need to repent. In this regard, prayer, fasting, and almsgiving have become important spiritual practices during the season of Lent.

| READING II | There are three separate ideas woven together in this reading from Second Corinthians. Paul begins by using the language of reconciliation to define the nature of his ministry to the Christians in Corinth. He holds up God's reconciliation to the world through Christ as the model for his own ministry of reconciliation. Paul speaks of himself and Timothy as "ambassadors for Christ," calling all to reconciliation with God and with each other. Paul presents his reconciliation with the Corinthians as emblematic of humanity's reconciliation with God in Christ.

Next, Paul speaks of God making Christ, although sinless in nature, "to be sin" for our sake. In other words, Christ voluntarily suffered Death on the Cross as the penalty for our sin. According to the Jewish Law, any criminal who dies "hung on a tree" is an abomination to God (Deuteronomy 21:22–23). Paul tells the Corinthian Christians that Christ died on the Cross "so that we might become the righteousness of God in him." When Paul refers to "the righteousness of God," he is speaking of God's fidelity to his covenants with Israel. In other

Paul is quoting Isaiah 49:8.

Paul is telling the Corinthians (and us) that God's grace is flowing down upon us at this very moment, as his words are proclaimed among us.

Working **together**, then,
    we **appeal** to you not to receive the grace of God in **vain**.
For he says:

    In an **acceptable** time I **heard** you,
        and on the day of **salvation** I **helped** you.

Behold, **now** is a very **acceptable** time;
    behold, **now** is the **day** of salvation.

GOSPEL Matthew 6:1–6, 16–18

A reading from the holy Gospel according to Matthew

Jesus's advice is straightforward and practical: do this and don't do that. Avoid a stern judgmental tone. But don't pull punches either.

The repeated reference to the "hypocrites" is for the purpose of illustration, to make his point using *contrast*, not to condemn scribes and Pharisees.

We can hear Jesus's frustration. His words are a warning to us to avoid this trap.

"And your father" is a thrice-repeated refrain. Refrains don't require variation; it's the repetition, not variation, which makes them effective. So, stress "Father . . . sees . . . repay" each time.

Jesus said to his **disciples**:
    "Take care not to perform righteous deeds
    in order that people may **see** them;
    otherwise, you will have no **recompense** from your heavenly
        Father.
When you give **alms**,
    do not blow a **trumpet** before you,
    as the **hypocrites** do in the **synagogues** and in the **streets**
    to win the praise of **others**.
Amen, I say to you,
    they have **received** their reward.
But when **you** give alms,
    do not let your **left** hand know what your **right** is doing,
    so that your almsgiving may be **secret**.
And your **Father** who sees in secret will **repay** you.

---

words, Christ's Death on the Cross, which saves all who believe, fulfills God's promises to Israel.

Finally, Paul's plea to the Corinthians to accept "the grace of God" offered through Christ is urgent, because he believes that salvation in Christ belongs to the present moment. They, and we, as we enter Lent, must act directly, for "*now* is the day of salvation!"

GOSPEL | Matthew 5–7 is commonly referred to as the "Sermon on the Mount." This is the first of five major discourses that Jesus delivers in the Gospel according to Matthew. The other four discourses are Matthew 10 (Jesus's missionary discourse), Matthew 13 (Jesus's parables discourse), Matthew 18 (Jesus's community discourse), and Matthew 24–25 (Jesus's eschatological discourse). Throughout his account, Matthew alternates between narrative material (characterized by action that propels the plot) and discourse material (speeches that Jesus delivers at various points in the narrative).

Jesus's first discourse, the Sermon on the Mount, develops Matthew's fundamental portrait of Jesus as the new Moses. The setting for the sermon, on a mountain with crowds of people, sets the stage for Matthew to present Jesus as the new Lawgiver who has to fulfill the Mosaic Law. It is likely that Matthew's intended audience of mostly Jewish Christians would have connected the setting of this speech with the

Don't assume the haughty airs of the hypocrites when you speak these lines. A simple delivery will be more effective.

Let your tone tell us that this is the better way.

Stress the same words as before.

Again, the sin lies in turning repentance into a self-aggrandizing show.

There is greater sacrifice in hidden mortification; your tone calls us to this level of self-sacrifice and humility.

Make sure this sounds like more than ample reward for the authentic mortification we are called to embrace.

"When **you** pray,
 do not be like the **hypocrites**,
 who love to stand and pray in the **synagogues** and on **street**
  corners
 so that others may **see** them.
Amen, I say to you,
 they have **received** their reward.
But when **you** pray, go to your **inner** room,
 close the door, and pray to your Father in **secret**.
And your Father who **sees** in secret will **repay** you.

"When **you** fast,
 do not look **gloomy** like the **hypocrites**.
They **neglect** their appearance,
 so that they may **appear** to others to be **fasting**.
Amen, I say to you, they have **received** their reward.
But when **you** fast,
 anoint your head and **wash** your face,
 so that you may not **appear** to be fasting,
 except to your **Father** who is **hidden**.
And your Father who **sees** what is hidden will **repay** you."

TO KEEP IN MIND

Each text contains **three kinds of content**: intellectual-theological, emotional, and aesthetic. The plot and details of the story and the theological teaching behind them comprise the intellectual-theological content. How the author or characters feel (or want us to feel) is the emotional content. Elements that make the writing pleasing—rhythm, repetition, suspense, and picturesque language—are the aesthetic content.

---

setting of Moses delivering the Law to the people of Israel at the base of Mount Sinai.

In today's reading, an excerpt from the larger sermon, Jesus speaks of the "righteous deeds" of almsgiving, praying, and fasting—three spiritual exercises common to Jewish tradition and adopted by the early Christians. Using both positive and negative examples, Jesus challenges the disciples to have the proper mind-set and motivation with these spiritual practices.

He begins each time with the negative, citing the behavior of "the hypocrites" (that is, the scribes and the Pharisees) as actions to be avoided. Their mind-set is self-serving, motivated by the praise of others. Jesus then offers the disciples an alternative way—righteous deeds characterized by a positive attitude and sincerity of heart.

Jesus speaks of performing almsgiving, prayer, and fasting "in secret," hidden from the view of others. For each of these spiritual exercises, Jesus repeats the phrase, "And your Father who sees in secret will repay you." The secrecy motif underscores the importance of maintaining the correct perspective in doing these types of "righteous deeds." Prayer, fasting, and almsgiving are centered on our relationship with God. Understood correctly, these are acts of repentance that seek to reconcile us to God. They ground us during the journey of Lent, preparing us to embrace the mystery of the life, Death, and Resurrection of Christ.

FIRST SUNDAY OF LENT

LECTIONARY #23

READING I   Genesis 9:8–15

A reading from the Book of Genesis

God said to **Noah** and to his **sons** with him:
"**See**, I am now establishing my **covenant** with you
  and your **descendants** after you
  and with every living **creature** that was with you:
  all the **birds**, and the various tame and wild **animals**
  that were with you and came out of the **ark**.
I will establish my **covenant** with you,
  that **never** again shall all bodily creatures be **destroyed**
  by the waters of a **flood**;
  there shall not be **another** flood to devastate the earth."
God **added**:
"This is the **sign** that I am giving for all ages to come,
  of the **covenant** between me and you
  and every living creature with you:
  I set my **bow** in the clouds to serve as a **sign**
  of the covenant between **me** and the **earth**.
When I bring **clouds** over the earth,
  and the bow **appears** in the clouds,
  I will **recall** the covenant I have made
  between me and you and all living beings,
  so that the waters shall never again become a flood
  to destroy **all** mortal beings."

Genesis = JEN-uh-sis

Repetitions prompt us to pay attention to language, for there is more language than *content* here.

"Covenant" is the key word. Its repetition reinforces God's initiative toward humanity and God's good will.

Naming of the animals is not information but ritual language that heightens the dignity of the covenant God makes with humanity.

Don't rush the repetitions. Refrains in a song receive the same amount of time with each recurrence. Let the repetitions speak, with unadorned sincerity, of God's mercy and fidelity.

Speak this promise with solemn authority. The language remains stylized and lofty. God offers a special sign as if to remove all doubt.

bow = boh. God does not set "a" bow but "my" bow "in the clouds."

"I will recall": as is typical in the Old Testament, God receives anthropomorphic qualities.

Of course, God needs no reminding. Let your tone convey God's tenderness and long-suffering fidelity.

READING I The story of Noah and the Ark (Genesis 6:5–9:29) covers a major portion of Genesis 1–11, the opening section of the Book of Genesis. The pattern set in these first eleven chapters (creation, sin, destruction, recreation) is the template through which the entire storyline of the Bible can be understood. God creates, human sin affects that creation, destruction ensues, and God recreates. We see this four-fold pattern throughout the history of Israel as recorded in the Old Testament. And we see this pattern in the incarnation, life, Death, and Resurrection of Christ in the New Testament.

Today's reading is the covenantal promise that God established with Noah after the flood waters receded from the earth. It is part of God's "recreation" in the pattern of creation, sin, destruction, and recreation. God's promise to Noah and his sons is clear: "Never again shall all the bodily creatures be destroyed by the waters of a flood." Further, this covenant will be accompanied by a "sign," a rainbow, which will serve to remind God of his promise to Noah.

This is the Bible's first explicit covenant offered by God. In the story line of the Old Testament, numerous covenants are to follow with the major historical figures of Israel such as Abraham, Moses, David, and Isaiah. One of the interesting features of this first covenant is its unconditional terms. God simply promises never again to "devastate" the entire earth with a flood. Many future covenants with individuals and with the people of Israel will be conditional; for example, the covenant of circumcision with Abraham (Genesis 17) and the covenant of the Law with Israel (Exodus 20–24).

For meditation and context:

RESPONSORIAL PSALM   Psalm 25:4–5, 6–7, 8–9 (10)

R. Your ways, O Lord, are love and truth to those who keep your covenant.

Your ways, O LORD, make known to me;
   teach me your paths,
guide me in your truth and teach me,
   for you are God my savior.

Remember that your compassion, O LORD,
   and your love are from of old.
In your kindness remember me,
   because of your goodness, O LORD.

Good and upright is the LORD,
   thus he shows sinners the way.
He guides the humble to justice,
   and he teaches the humble his way.

TO KEEP IN MIND
Stress (Bold Print): identifies words that are more important or expressive than others and require more stress. Use your judgment about the amount of stress so as to avoid an artificial delivery.

READING II   1 Peter 3:18–22

A reading from the first Letter of Saint Peter

Beloved:
Christ **suffered** for sins **once**,
   the **righteous** for the sake of the **unrighteous**,
   that he might lead you to **God**.
Put to **death** in the **flesh**,
   he was brought to **life** in the **Spirit**.
In it he also went to preach to the **spirits** in **prison**,
   who had once been **disobedient**
   while God patiently waited in the days of **Noah**
   during the building of the **ark**,
   in which a **few** persons, **eight** in all,
   were **saved** through water.
This prefigured **baptism**, which saves you **now**.

The word "beloved" sets the tone.

The text begins and ends with lines that may be drawn from an ancient Christological hymn. Give them the sound of joyful worship.

You have two rhetorical balances at the start of the reading: the "*righteous*" one suffered for the "*unrighteous*"; he died in the "*flesh*" but was raised in the "*spirit*." Be sure to emphasize those contrasting words.

"It" refers to the "Spirit." This cryptic reference may allude to the sinners of Noah's day or to the angelic spirits who rebelled against God from time immemorial.

Lift out the mention of Noah that connects this text to the First Reading.

The *destructive* waters of the flood prefigured the *saving* waters of Baptism.

But the Bible's first covenant between God and humanity is presented in the simplest of terms.

 This brief excerpt from the First Letter of Peter offers some important theological insights as well as a direct connection to our First Reading. Theologically, this letter informs us that Christ "suffered" so that "he might lead you to God." We see here how the early Christians began to make sense of Jesus's agonizing Death on the Cross.

The letter further asserts that Jesus's Death not only served to connect us with God, it also allowed Jesus to "preach to the spirits in prison." Scholars remain uncertain as to the exact meaning of the reference "spirits in prison." Theories range from those who died in the flood in the days of Noah to demonic forces conquered by Christ through his Resurrection and Ascension. Despite this indeterminate allusion, it seems clear that the letter wants us to know Jesus continued his message of salvation beyond the time of his life on earth.

The reading concludes with a discussion of Noah and the practice of early Christian baptismal rites and rituals. The flood waters in the days of Noah "prefigured" (that is, foreshowed) the baptismal water that initiates the believer into the Christian faith. Just as Noah and his family were "saved through water," so, too, believers in Christ are now saved through the water of Christian Baptism.

God's saving of Noah and his family was an important message to communicate to the Gentile Christians of Asia Minor to whom the letter is addressed (1 Peter 1:1). Because Jesus was both the Son of God and the *Jewish* Messiah, early evangelization efforts of Gentiles often sought ways to connect Gentiles to figures from

Make eye contact on "an appeal . . . conscience."

It is not a removal of **dirt** from the body
  but an **appeal** to God for a clear **conscience**,
  through the **resurrection** of Jesus Christ,
  who has gone into **heaven**
  and is at the right hand of **God**,
  with **angels**, **authorities**, and **powers subject** to him.

These final hymn-like lines should convey and extol the dignity of the one who sits at God's right hand.

GOSPEL   Mark 1:12–15

A reading from the holy Gospel according to Mark

Give your assembly time to hear and absorb this brief text that's comprised of two distinct sections: the desert temptations and the kerygma.

Mark gives you few words with which to establish setting and mood.

The **Spirit** drove **Jesus** out into the **desert**,
  and he **remained** in the desert for **forty** days, **tempted**
    by **Satan**.
He was among wild **beasts**,
  and the **angels ministered** to him.

Be sure to contrast his presence among "*beasts*" with the ministry of "*angels*."

After **John** had been **arrested**,
  Jesus came to **Galilee** proclaiming the gospel of **God**:
  "This is the time of **fulfillment**.
The **kingdom** of God is at **hand**.
  Repent, and **believe** in the **gospel**."

Pause to suggest the passage of time. The word "arrested" sets the context for Jesus's inaugural preaching.

Jesus is mindful of his cousin's death and takes up his message. Speak with a sense of urgency, aware of the import of your declaration. A brief pause after "Repent."

> TO KEEP IN MIND
> **Openings and Closings:** differ in tone from the Scripture and require pauses, after the opening dialogue and before the closing dialogue. These formulas are prescribed, so don't vary the wording.

---

the Old Testament who were not exclusively Jewish, such as Noah, thereby connecting Gentile Christians to God's covenantal promises to all people. Relating Noah and the flood waters to the Christian baptism of Gentiles served this purpose well. Such a reminder of God's offer of salvation to all people provides a perfect introduction to the season on this First Sunday of Lent.

 GOSPEL Within the first fifteen verses of the Gospel according to Mark, we hear about John the Baptist and his preaching, the baptism of Jesus, and, in today's reading, the temptation of Jesus and the beginning of his public ministry in Galilee. More so than the other Gospel writers, Mark is truly economical with his words. In fact, Mark tells the entire story of Jesus in only 678 total verses, by far the shortest of the New Testament Gospel accounts.

Each year, the Gospel Reading for the First Sunday of Lent begins with the story of Jesus's temptation in the desert. Not surprisingly, Mark's account of the temptation offers us the sparsest of details. But the critical point is not lost. Like his Israelite ancestors (Moses and the Israelites wandering the desert for forty years), Jesus, too, had his desert experience. As Mark reports, Jesus emerged from the desert victorious, defeating Satan and proclaiming the Good News of the Kingdom of God throughout Galilee.

The season of Lent calls us as well to enter into a journey through the "desert," to repent and seek reconciliation with God, ourselves, and each other.

SECOND SUNDAY OF LENT

Genesis = JEN-uh-sis

Before all else, this is a story that must be told in direct and simple style, without melodrama. But that doesn't mean leave out the emotion and suspense. If you hold your listeners' attention, then you'll be doing your job.

The first line is critical to understanding the text, especially the word "test."

"Here I am" is the response of one ready to do God's will.

The poignancy of this situation is heightened by the words, "your *only* one …whom you *love*."

Speak the words simply and the horror of God's command will stand out all the more starkly.

Stressing the word "came" will suggest the passage of time.

Abraham struggles mightily and silently to do as God commanded.

Narrate Abraham's handling of the "knife" one phrase at a time. A rushed, careless delivery would make him seem heartless.

Quicken your pace on the narration that precedes the calling of Abraham's name. When a name is twice stated, the second iteration is spoken with more intensity (though, not necessarily more volume).

There is great relief in this narration, especially on the words "in place of his son."

LECTIONARY #26

READING I   Genesis 22:1–2, 9a, 10–13, 15–18

A reading from the Book of Genesis

God put **Abraham** to the **test**.
He **called** to him, "**Abraham**!"
"**Here** I am!" he replied.
Then God said:
> "Take your son **Isaac**, your **only** one, whom you **love**,
> and go to the land of **Moriah**.
There you shall **offer** him up as a **holocaust**
> on a height that I will point out to you."

When they **came** to the place of which God had told him,
> Abraham built an **altar** there and arranged the **wood** on it.
Then he **reached** out and took the knife to **slaughter** his son.
But the LORD's messenger **called** to him from heaven,
> "**Abraham, Abraham**!"
"**Here** I am!" he answered.
"Do not lay your **hand** on the boy," said the messenger.
"Do not do the least **thing** to him.
I **know** now how **devoted** you are to God,
> since you did not **withhold** from me your own beloved **son**."
As Abraham looked **about**,
> he spied a **ram** caught by its horns in the **thicket**.
So he went and **took** the ram
> and **offered** it up as a **holocaust** in place of his **son**.

READING I The opening line to today's reading ("God put Abraham to the test") requires some context for understanding. In the Book of Genesis, chapters 12–25 are dedicated to stories about Abraham and Sarah, and they contain numerous chronological markers. We learn, for example, that when God first established a covenant with him (Genesis 12:4), Abraham was seventy-five years old. At the birth of Ishmael, Abraham's son through Hagar, Abraham was eighty-six (Genesis 16:16). When Abraham was ninety-nine the covenant of circumcision began

(Genesis 17:1), and Abraham was one hundred years old at the birth of Isaac, the only son of Abraham and Sarah (Genesis 21:5). Abraham lived to the age of one hundred and seventy-five (Genesis 25:7); Sarah lived to be one hundred and twenty-seven years old (Genesis 23:1). It should be noted that scholars do not think these are exact year references; rather, it is the ancient authors' way of speaking of the depth of God's blessings upon Abraham and Sarah—old age was considered a divine gift.

In today's reading, Isaac is about thirteen years of age, making Abraham about

one hundred and thirteen years old when God put him to "the test." Since Abraham first met God at the age of seventy-five, this "test" occurred after a nearly forty-year relationship between God and Abraham. In other words, throughout Abraham's life, his faith was tested. The test in today's reading centers on whether or not Abraham will sacrifice Isaac at God's request. It is the ultimate test of Abraham's faith.

Even within the full reading of the story of the testing of Abraham, Genesis 22:1–19, the narrator never reveals Abraham's inner struggle over the impending sacrifice of his

A pause before this section will suggest the passage of time.

Again the LORD's messenger called to Abraham from heaven
    and said:
"I **swear** by **myself**, declares the LORD,
that because you **acted** as you did
in not **withholding** from me your beloved son,
I will **bless** you **abundantly**
and make your **descendants** as countless
as the **stars** of the sky and the **sands** of the seashore;
your descendants shall take **possession**
of the gates of their **enemies**,
and in your **descendants** all the nations of the **earth** shall
    find **blessing**—
all this because you **obeyed** my **command**."

The voice of God swells with authority, but also with pride and gratitude over Abraham's obedience.

Don't simply narrate but *pray* this blessing. It falls not only upon Abraham and his descendants, but on your assembly as well.

The Bible views obedience as a major component of a positive relationship with God.

For meditation and context:

RESPONSORIAL PSALM   Psalm 116:10, 15, 16–17, 18–19 (9)

R. I will walk before the Lord, in the land of the living.

I believed, even when I said,
  "I am greatly afflicted."
Precious in the eyes of the LORD
  is the death of his faithful ones.

O LORD, I am your servant;
  I am your servant, the son of your
    handmaid;
you have loosed my bonds.
To you will I offer sacrifice of thanksgiving,
  and I will call upon the name of the LORD.

My vows to the LORD I will pay
  in the presence of all his people,
in the courts of the house of the LORD,
  in your midst, O Jerusalem.

TO KEEP IN MIND

Tell the story: Make the story yours, then share it with your listeners. Use the language; don't throw away any good words. Settings give context; don't rush the description. Characters must be believable; understand their motivation. Dialogue reveals character; distinguish one character from another with your voice.

READING II   Romans 8:31b–34

A reading from the Letter of Saint Paul to the Romans

Brothers and sisters:
If **God** is for us, who can be **against** us?
He who did not spare his own **Son**
    but handed him over for us **all**,
    how will he not also give us everything **else** along with him?

These are some of Scripture's most comforting words. Be sure they sound like it.

Let yourself marvel at God's unwavering goodness toward us.

only son through whom God's covenantal promises would be realized. Abraham is presented as unwavering in his trust and his duty to follow God's command and sacrifice Isaac as a holocaust, a burnt offering to the Lord. For his unconditional obedience and faithfulness to God, Isaac was spared and Abraham was rewarded "abundantly" with countless descendents and blessings. For this reason, Abraham is one of the greatest role models of faith within both Jewish and Christian traditions.

READING II In this short reading, Paul assures the Christians in the city of Rome of God's complete and total commitment to them. The rhetorical questions Paul raises ("Who will bring a charge against God's chosen ones?") were very real concerns for the first generation of Jews and Gentiles who believed in Christ. Persecution for expressing faith in Christ was a constant threat, as is seen most clearly in Paul's life (see, for example 2 Corinthians 11:24–28).

Paul offers the example of God's sacrifice of his own Son for our salvation as the ultimate proof of God's fidelity and love. From Paul's perspective, Christians have not only God, but also Christ, who, raised from the dead, now intercedes for us. For Paul, faith in Christ "acquits" one from sins and spares one from condemnation.

GOSPEL Each year, the Gospel reading for the Second Sunday of Lent is the Transfiguration of Jesus. Matthew, Mark, and Luke (the Synoptic Gospel writers) all record this event following Jesus's first Passion prediction. In fact,

The goal is to persuade your listeners that "No" is the only true answer to these questions.

Having made your point about God's mercy, drive it home with the final sentence that stresses Christ's constant intercession.

> **TO KEEP IN MIND**
> **Names of characters:** Often the first word of a reading. Lift out the names to ensure listeners don't miss who the subject is.

Be sure you lift out who is accompanying Jesus.

You have four words to set the scene: "up a high mountain." Mountaintops are biblical sites of divine revelation.

Don't use an exaggerated tone to describe the transformation of Jesus. A simple, sincere delivery will work best.

Speak of "Elijah" and "Moses" with a sense of awe and respect.

Peter never feigns. His statement is pure sincerity.

His talk of tents, however, is excited mumble spoken with energetic pacing.

The theophany narrated here requires a tone of great dignity. God's voice, though authoritative, must also convey divine love.

Let a pause suggest the passage of time. Jesus is insistent that they not discuss this event.

Despite the word "suddenly," narrate this sentence slowly.

Let the final sentence convey their confusion over Jesus's cryptic words.

Who will bring a **charge** against God's chosen ones?
　It is **God** who **acquits** us, who will **condemn**?
Christ Jesus it is who **died**—or, rather, was **raised**—
　who also is at the right hand of **God**,
　who indeed **intercedes** for us.

GOSPEL   Mark 9:2–10

A reading from the holy Gospel according to Mark

Jesus took **Peter**, **James**, and **John**
　and led them up a high **mountain** apart by **themselves**.
And he was **transfigured** before them,
　and his clothes became **dazzling** white,
　such as no **fuller** on earth could **bleach** them.
Then **Elijah** appeared to them along with **Moses**,
　and they were **conversing** with Jesus.
Then **Peter** said to Jesus in reply,
　"**Rabbi**, it is **good** that we are here!
Let us make three **tents**:
　one for **you**, one for **Moses**, and one for **Elijah**."
He hardly knew what to **say**, they were so **terrified**.
Then a **cloud** came, casting a **shadow** over them;
　from the cloud came a **voice**,
　"This is my beloved **Son**. **Listen** to him."
Suddenly, looking **around**, they no longer saw **anyone**
　but Jesus **alone** with them.

As they were coming **down** from the mountain,
　he **charged** them not to **relate** what they had seen to **anyone**,
　except when the Son of Man had **risen** from the **dead**.
So they kept the matter to **themselves**,
　questioning what rising from the dead **meant**.

---

the details from each account of the Transfiguration are remarkably consistent.

One of the more notable features of the Transfiguration is the presence of God's voice in the narrative. God speaks directly only twice in the storyline of the New Testament Gospels: at Jesus's baptism and at Jesus's Transfiguration. Both times, God identifies Jesus as his "beloved Son." At Jesus's baptism, God adds, "With you I am well pleased." At the Transfiguration, God then says, "Listen to him."

Within the immediate narrative context of the Transfiguration, this divine command to "listen to him" is seen in Jesus's command to the disciples not to tell others of his Transfiguration until after he rose from the dead. Within the larger narrative context of Mark's entire Gospel, the command to "listen to him" is understood as the totality of the Good News of the Kingdom of God that Jesus came to proclaim.

The appearance of Elijah and Moses at Jesus's Transfiguration is another stable element present in all three versions of this story. Many scholars today agree that

Moses symbolically represents the Law and Elijah symbolically represents the Prophets. For first-century Jews, the Law and the Prophets embodied the Old Testament. The presence of Moses and Elijah shows Jesus deeply rooted in the sacred Scriptures that shaped his life and his understanding of God and Israel. It calls all of us to enter more intentionally in our own sacred Scriptures heard throughout the season of Lent.

THIRD SUNDAY OF LENT

LECTIONARY #29

READING I   Exodus 20:1–17

A reading from the Book of Exodus

In those days, **God** delivered all these **commandments**:
"I, the LORD, am your **God**,
who brought you out of the land of **Egypt**, that place of **slavery**.
You shall not have **other** gods besides me.
You shall not carve **idols** for yourselves
in the shape of anything in the sky **above**
or on the earth **below** or in the waters **beneath** the earth;
you shall not **bow** down before them or **worship** them.
For **I**, the LORD, your **God**, am a **jealous** God,
inflicting **punishment** for their fathers' wickedness
on the **children** of those who hate me,
down to the **third** and **fourth** generation;
but bestowing **mercy** down to the **thousandth** generation
on the children of those who **love** me and **keep**
my commandments.

"You shall not take the **name** of the LORD, your God, in **vain**.
For the LORD will not leave **unpunished**
the one who **takes** his name in vain.

"**Remember** to keep **holy** the sabbath day.
Six days you may labor and do all your work,
but the **seventh** day is the **sabbath** of the LORD, your God.

Exodus = EK-suh-duhs
Keep in mind, Scripture views the Commandments not as confinements but as liberation from the tyranny of our moral frailty.

God first reminds the people of his merciful and saving love.

God speaks with authority and dignity. In the Old Testament, idolatry was Israel's greatest and most consistent failing.

The surprising word "jealous" refers to God's solicitousness for his people, the way a mother would be jealous for the welfare of her child.

God doesn't relish punishment but wants people to realize that certain behaviors have consequences. Stress both God's eagerness to shower "mercy to the thousandth generation" and God's desire to teach us through the consequences of our decisions.

The elaborations on the Commandments require the same dignified tone as the Commandments themselves.

This elaboration is important to hear for people in a work-obsessed culture like ours.

Today options are given for the readings: Year A or Year B. Contact your parish staff to learn which readings will be used.

READING I The receiving of the Law at Mount Sinai was one of the defining moments within Israel's collective identity and historic relationship with God. Today's reading lists the "Ten Commandments," which are only a portion of the many laws Moses received from God at Mount Sinai. Beyond the Ten Commandments, chapters 20:22 to 23:33 of Exodus, as well as the entire Book of Leviticus, present literally hundreds of laws governing the social, religious, and civic dimensions for the newly formed people of Israel. These laws were given by God as guidelines for Israel to achieve the status of a great and holy nation.

The Law became one of the major cultic markers that Israel believed separated them from the other nations. Over time, other aspects of Israelite culture, such as the practice of male circumcision, worship in the Temple in Jerusalem, belief in a single God (the LORD), and a strict dietary code served to solidify Israel's collective identity as God's Chosen People.

Eight of the Ten Commandments are in the negative ("you shall not") and address matters the Israelites must avoid; for example, killing, stealing, bearing false witness. Only two Commandments are in the positive: keep holy the Sabbath and honor your father and mother. These two affirm the importance of family and worship in the daily life of the ancient Israelites.

Additionally, among the Ten, only the first three speak to Israel's relationship with God. The remaining seven Commandments

Note that Sabbath rest is extended even to "slave" and "alien" and to all of God's creatures.

Begin this sentence, "In six days" at a good clip, but slow your pace at "but on the seventh."

No **work** may be done then either by **you**, or your **son** or **daughter**,
    or your male or female **slave**, or your **beast**,
    or by the **alien** who lives with you.
In **six** days the LORD made the **heavens** and the **earth**,
    the **sea** and all that is **in** them;
    but on the **seventh** day he **rested**.
That is why the LORD has **blessed** the sabbath day and made
        it **holy**.

Of the seven Commandments that deal with human relationships (rather than our relationship with God), only the fourth Commandment gets elaborated. Don't rush that teaching.

The "shall not" Commandments call us to freedom from fear of each other and freedom to love one another. Without rushing, these can be spoken at a faster rate. Note that the stress falls almost always on the last word of each line.

Read the final Commandment more slowly. Tell us how *futile* it is to covet these things.

"**Honor** your **father** and your **mother**,
    that you may have a long **life** in the land
    which the LORD, your God, is giving you.
You shall not **kill**.
You shall not commit **adultery**.
You shall not **steal**.
You shall not bear **false** witness against your neighbor.
You shall not **covet** your neighbor's **house**.
You shall not **covet** your neighbor's **wife**,
    nor his male or female **slave**, nor his **ox** or **ass**,
    nor anything **else** that belongs to him."

[Shorter: Exodus 20:1–3, 7–8, 12–17]

For meditation and context:

RESPONSORIAL PSALM   Psalm 19:8, 9, 10, 11 (John 6:68c)

R. Lord, you have the words of everlasting life.

The law of the LORD is perfect,
    refreshing the soul;
the decree of the LORD is trustworthy,
    giving wisdom to the simple.

The precepts of the LORD are right,
    rejoicing the heart;
the command of the LORD is clear,
    enlightening the eye.

The fear of the LORD is pure,
    enduring forever;
the ordinances of the LORD are true,
    all of them just.

They are more precious than gold,
    than a heap of purest gold;
sweeter also than syrup
    or honey from the comb.

TO KEEP IN MIND

The opening: Establish eye contact and announce, from memory, "A reading from . . . ." Then take a pause (three full beats!) before starting the reading. The correct pronunciation is "A [uh] reading from" instead of "A [ay] reading from."

---

focus on the Israelites' relationships with each other. The disproportionate weight and emphasis on laws regulating social norms among themselves indicates that was a concern for the Israelites as they sought to build a great and holy nation.

READING II   Paul had a formidable task on his hands as he wrote First Corinthians in the spring of AD 55. There were serious problems within the congregation in Corinth, ranging from the believers' moral conduct and sexual practices to inappropriate behavior at liturgies.

Believers were also engaged in theological debates on such topics as the purpose and meaning of the Lord's Supper and the meaning of the resurrection of the dead. These issues may well have existed before Paul's departure, but the problems apparently became more acute after he left.

One of the overriding concerns Paul had for the church in Corinth was the divisions within the community. Today's reading highlights one of the sources of tension: the confusing of human wisdom with divine

wisdom. Paul likely suspected that the Corinthian Christians were interested in the teachings of the philosophical schools.

Paul recognized that preaching "Christ crucified" did not, at face value, make sense to Jews or Gentiles in Corinth. In fact, his Gospel message offered "a stumbling block to Jews and foolishness to Gentiles." For Paul, human reasoning overriding faith failed to recognize that God's wisdom is revealed to us, not by human wisdom or knowledge, but "through the Spirit" (1 Corinthians 2:10). Further, the wisdom of individuals should not be valued over the

Corinthians = kohr-IN-thee-uhnz

Jewels need careful and prolonged examination. This jewel of a reading requires a slow pace and careful diction to draw in your listeners.

There is pride in claiming the foolishness of Christ!

Imagine the word "is" between "Christ" and "the power of God."

Try memorizing this final sentence and speak it with confidence and joy.

READING II 1 Corinthians 1:22–25

A reading from the first Letter of Saint Paul to the Corinthians

Brothers and sisters:
Jews demand **signs** and **Greeks** look for **wisdom**,
    but **we** proclaim Christ **crucified**,
    a **stumbling** block to Jews and **foolishness** to Gentiles,
    but to those who are **called**, Jews and Greeks **alike**,
    Christ the **power** of God and the **wisdom** of God.
For the **foolishness** of God is **wiser** than human wisdom,
    and the **weakness** of God is **stronger** than human strength.

The opening gives no hint of what's to come. But your tone as you speak of "oxen, sheep, and doves" should suggest the brewing storm.

The mood shifts suddenly and becomes surprisingly violent. Make the narration energetic, suggesting the passion that drives Jesus to such extreme behavior.

Jesus clearly remains in control of himself, but he will not be stopped.

This key line states his motivation, which is confirmed by the quotation of Psalm 69:10: *"Zeal* for your house will *consume* me."

The leaders challenge his seeming arrogance and presumption, trying to cow him into retreat.

GOSPEL John 2:13–25

A reading from the holy Gospel according to John

Since the **Passover** of the Jews was **near**,
    Jesus went up to **Jerusalem**.
He found in the **temple** area those who sold **oxen**, **sheep**,
    and **doves**,
    as well as the **money** changers seated there.
He made a **whip** out of **cords**
    and **drove** them all out of the temple area, with the **sheep**
      and **oxen**,
    and spilled the **coins** of the money changers
    and overturned their **tables**,
    and to those who sold **doves** he said,
    "Take these **out** of here,
    and stop making my Father's **house** a **marketplace**."
His **disciples** recalled the words of **Scripture**,
    Zeal for your house will **consume** *me.*
At this the Jews **answered** and said to him,
    "What **sign** can you show us for **doing** this?"

community's unity. Paul stood by his conviction that Christ crucified embodied "the power of God and the wisdom of God"—a power and wisdom incomparable to human power and wisdom.

GOSPEL The Gospel Reading from John is about the cleansing of the Temple in Jerusalem. Scholars have long been intrigued by John's placement of this incident in the narrative design of his Gospel account. Whereas the Synoptics place the cleansing of the Temple in the final week of Jesus's life (compare Matthew

21:12–17; Mark 11:15–19; Luke 19:45–48), John records this event near the beginning of his public ministry. While there is no unanimous consensus among scholars about which Gospel account better represents the historicity of this event, many scholars place the cleansing in Jesus's final days, siding with the synoptic account.

Of the four Gospel writers, John offers the most graphic description of Jesus's reaction to the merchants and money-changers buying and selling animals in the Temple area: "He made a whip out of cords and drove them all out of the temple area,

with the sheep and oxen, and spilled the coins of the money changers and overturned their tables." The source of Jesus's anger is clear: "Stop making my Father's house a marketplace."

The debate between Jesus and the Jews that follows his actions in the Temple is filled with irony. Even though the Jews miss it, we recognize the irony of the Jews challenging Jesus about resurrecting the Temple in three days. To make sure we don't miss the point, John even informs us that Jesus "was speaking about the temple of his body."

Jesus's reply is intentionally cryptic, but it's stated with strength, as if daring them.

Taking Jesus literally, they scoff at him.

This aside is spoken as if by an insider confiding in fellow partisans. There is a catechetical thrust to the statement.

Jesus is not satisfied with faith based on signs. Let your tone tell us that.

These lines give us a rare insight into Jesus: while willing to spend himself for the crowds, he remains cautious and will not "trust himself to them." The text ends soberly, with hints of anger and sadness. Yet with this full knowledge of human nature, Jesus walked willingly to the Cross.

TO KEEP IN MIND

Narrator: Knowing the point of view that the narrator is "rooting for" will help you more fully communicate the meaning of the text. The narrator always has a viewpoint, often speaking as a believer, not as an objective reporter. For this reason, the narrator is often the pivotal role in a passage. Using timbre, pitch, rate, and energy can help you convey the narrator's moods or meanings.

Jesus **answered** and said to them,
 "**Destroy** this temple and in **three days** I will raise it **up**."
The Jews said,
 "This **temple** has been under construction for forty-six **years**,
 and **you** will raise it up in three **days**?"
But he was speaking about the temple of his **body**.
Therefore, when he was raised from the **dead**,
 his disciples **remembered** that he had said this,
 and they came to **believe** the Scripture
 and the word Jesus had spoken.

While he was in **Jerusalem** for the feast of **Passover**,
 many began to **believe** in his name
 when they saw the **signs** he was doing.
But Jesus would not **trust** himself to them because he **knew**
  them all,
 and did not need anyone to testify about human **nature**.
He himself understood it **well**.

[Shorter: John 4:5–15, 19b–26, 39a, 40–42]

In the Gospel according to John, there is a very liberal use of the literary devices of symbolism, misunderstanding, and irony. We as readers are able to understand the symbolism and appreciate the misunderstanding and irony because its intent is to reveal Jesus's true origins as "the Word made flesh" (John 1:14) from and with God, and his identity as the Son of God.

John concludes the story of the cleansing of the Temple with an interesting commentary about those in Jerusalem who came "to believe in his name." In John's Gospel account, there is an emphasis on the importance of believing in Jesus. Very often Jesus's miracles, or signs, inspire belief in his followers. Yet believing occurs not only by signs Jesus performs but also by encounters with him. The Samaritan woman at the well, and especially the Samaritan villagers (John 4:4–42), for example, come to believe in Jesus through their encounters with him more so than by any signs he performs. John appears to be saying that followers of Jesus in Jerusalem believed in Jesus largely, or exclusively, because of the signs he performed. The fact that Jesus "would not trust himself to them" suggests that there were not authentic encounters between Jesus and the Jews in Jerusalem at that time.

The Johannine emphasis on *encountering* Jesus serves as an important reminder that the season of Lent should focus on an authentic desire for an encounter with the divine.

THIRD SUNDAY
OF LENT, YEAR A

LECTIONARY #28

READING I   Exodus 17:3–7

A reading from the Book of Exodus

In those days, in their **thirst** for **water**,
  the people **grumbled** against Moses,
  saying, "**Why** did you ever make us **leave** Egypt?
Was it just to have us **die** here of **thirst**
  with our **children** and our **livestock**?"
So Moses **cried** out to the LORD,
  "What shall I **do** with this people?
A little **more** and they will **stone** me!"
The LORD **answered** Moses,
  "Go over there in front of the **people**,
  along with some of the **elders** of Israel,
  holding in your hand, as you go,
  the **staff** with which you struck the **river**.
I will be **standing** there in front of you on the rock in **Horeb**.
Strike the rock, and the **water** will flow from it
  for the people to **drink**."
This Moses **did**, in the presence of the **elders** of Israel.
The place was called **Massah** and **Meribah**,
  because the Israelites **quarreled** there
  and **tested** the LORD, saying,
  "Is the LORD in our **midst** or **not**?"

Exodus = EK-suh-duhs
Moses = MOH-ziz; MOH-zis

The Lord is the only "adult" in this text reacting to the adolescent whining of both people and Moses. "Thirst for water" establishes the premise of the complaints. Grumbling takes various forms—greater stridency or intense, soft-spoken anger.

Their fear is as palpable as their immature faith.

Moses is both fearful and angry, perhaps at the people, or God, or both.

God, like a patient parent or teacher, gives clear, reasonable directions.

"Staff . . . river" alludes to the plague that turned the Nile's water to blood. The staff that deprived Egypt of fresh water will now provide water for Israel.

The miracle takes place before all the people, so they witness the power and love of their God.

Meribah = MAYR-ih-bah and means "the place of the quarreling."

The final question could be spoken in the anxious voice of the people or with the narrator's regret over the lack of faith demonstrated here.

Today options are given for the readings: Year A or Year B. Contact your parish staff to learn which readings will be used.

READING I   "Is the Lord in our midst or not?" Today's reading ends with this provocative question posed to Moses by the Israelites early in their desert wanderings. In the larger narrative of the Book of Exodus, the story of the miracle of water from the rock occurs within a few months of the Israelites' release from Egyptian slavery. It speaks to the fragile nature of the newly formed community under Moses's leadership.

This group had yet to arrive at Mount Sinai, where Moses would receive the revelation of the Law from the LORD. Uncertain of Moses's leadership and quick to question whether or not the God who miraculously brought them out of Egypt would remain with them in the desert, the Israelites challenge Moses: "Why did you ever make us leave Egypt?"

In the Israelites' challenge, the relationship between Moses and God comes into focus. God answers Moses's prayer of petition: "What shall I do with this people? A little more and they will stone me!" He instructs Moses on how to save the Israelites from dying of thirst. With his staff in hand, Moses provides water from a rock for the people to drink. With the elders of Israel as witness, the peoples' thirst is quenched and confidence in Moses's leadership is restored. The Israelites were learning early in their forty-year journey to trust that the Lord was in their midst and that Moses was their worthy, prophetic leader.

For meditation and context:

RESPONSORIAL PSALM   Psalm 95:1–2, 6–7, 8–9 (8)

R. If today you hear his voice, harden not your hearts.

Come, let us sing joyfully to the LORD;
    let us acclaim the Rock of our salvation.
Let us come into his presence with
        thanksgiving;
    let us joyfully sing psalms to him.

Come, let us bow down in worship;
    let us kneel before the LORD who made us.
For he is our God,
    and we are the people he shepherds, the
        flock he guides.

Oh, that today you would hear his voice:
    "Harden not your hearts as at Meribah,
        as in the day of Massah in the desert.
Where your fathers tempted me;
    they tested me though they had seen
        my works."

TO KEEP IN MIND
Go slowly in the epistles. Paul's style is often a tangle of complex sentences; his mood can change within a single passage.

On many Sundays, Paul addresses the assembly with truth and convictions he's acquired through experience. Root these words in your experience, not in abstract theology.

Your tone and conviction are more critical than the specific words. Paul says faith gives us peace and access to grace. And this grace fills us with confident hope that enables us to stand tall. Note that we "boast" of this hope with confident joy.

We can "hope" because we've known the "love" of God given to us by God's "Holy Spirit."

While the diction here is rather stiff, give it the resonance of John 3:16, which it echoes.

The tone is persuasive. He's saying: "Rarely does anyone die for even a just person, but truly unusual is God's willingness to die for us while we were still steeped in sin."

Speak with joy these words that comprise the heart of the Gospel.

READING II   Romans 5:1–2, 5–8

A reading from the Letter of Saint Paul to the Romans

Brothers and sisters:
Since we have been **justified** by **faith**,
    we have **peace** with God through our Lord Jesus **Christ**,
    through whom we have gained **access** by faith
    to this **grace** in which we stand,
    and we boast in **hope** of the glory of **God**.

And hope does not **disappoint**,
    because the **love** of God has been poured out into our **hearts**
    through the Holy **Spirit** who has been **given** to us.
For **Christ**, while we were still **helpless**,
    died at the appointed time for the **ungodly**.
Indeed, only with **difficulty** does one die for a **just** person,
    though perhaps for a **good** person one might even find **courage**
        to die.
But God **proves** his love for us
    in that while we were still **sinners** Christ **died** for us.

Today's reading ends with the Hebrew words *Massah* (meaning, "the test") and *Meribah* (meaning, "the quarreling"). The location from where the water miraculously flowed from the rock was to be forever remembered by the Israelites as the place where they tested the Lord and where they quarreled with Moses. It served to teach future generations the simultaneous lessons of God's fidelity, Moses's leadership, and the Israelites' fragility that often threatened to make them unfaithful.

READING II | This excerpt from the fifth chapter of Paul's Letter to the Romans contains three interrelated Pauline themes: "justified by faith," "peace with God," and "hope of the glory of God." Unpacking the meaning of this passage offers significant insight into Paul's theological thinking.

One of the central themes in the Letter to the Romans is the idea that believers in Christ are "justified by faith." Paul spends a so much time discussing this concept in Romans that some scholars claim "justification by faith" is the *center* of Paul's

thought, not only in his Letter to the Romans, but in his entire theological worldview. Being "justified" means, for Paul, that when a person has *faith in Christ*, that person receives all of God's graces that flow through Christ (forgiveness of sins, eternal redemption, salvation, and so forth).

As a result of being "justified," one receives the additional divine gift of being at "peace with God." Because of one's faith in Christ, the sin that alienates us from God no longer defines our relationship with God. Through faith in Christ, we are reconciled with God; we have "peace with God."

GOSPEL　John 4:5–42

A reading from the holy Gospel according to John

Jesus came to a town of **Samaria** called **Sychar**,
　near the plot of land that **Jacob** had given to his son **Joseph**.
Jacob's **well** was there.
Jesus, **tired** from his journey, sat down there at the well.
It was about **noon**.

A **woman** of Samaria came to draw **water**.
Jesus **said** to her,
　"Give me a **drink**."
His **disciples** had gone into the **town** to buy **food**.
The **Samaritan** woman said to him,
　"How can **you**, a **Jew**, ask me, a **Samaritan woman**, for a **drink**?"
—For **Jews** use nothing in **common** with Samaritans.—
Jesus **answered** and said to her,
　"If you knew the **gift** of God
　and **who** is saying to you, 'Give me a drink,'
　you would have asked **him**
　and he would have given you **living** water."
The woman **said** to him,
　"**Sir**, you do not even have a **bucket** and the cistern is **deep**;
　where then can you **get** this living water?
Are you **greater** than our father Jacob,
　who **gave** us this cistern and drank from it himself
　with his **children** and his **flocks**?"
Jesus **answered** and said to her,
　"Everyone who drinks **this** water will be **thirsty** again;
　but whoever drinks the water **I** shall give will **never** thirst;
　the water I shall give will become in him
　a **spring** of water **welling** up to eternal **life**."

Place yourself in this story as if this were your town, the woman your neighbor, and her testimony life-changing for you.

Samaria = suh-MAYR-ee-uh

Sychar = SĪ-kahr

Jesus comes here because of *his* need.

Immediately, we encounter the unconventional—a woman out alone and Jesus addressing a woman who is not his relative.

His request is simple and unnuanced. Her reply reveals deep-seated resentment toward the presumed superior attitude of the Jews.

Speak the aside quickly.

Sustain a conversational tone; Jesus will enjoy the repartee.

Clearly not intimidated, the woman is confident and challenging.

She has no patience for his *chutzpah*.

As above, go for a conversational rather than a theological tone. He is drawing her in and not wanting to alienate her.

Although sin remains, it no longer has the sting of separating us from God.

It is in being justified by faith and experiencing peace with God that Paul can "boast" of the certain future "hope of the glory of God." Paul often speaks of the three virtues of faith, hope, and love that Christians enjoy. (See, for example, First Thessalonians 1:3; 5:8; Galatians 5:5–6; First Corinthians 13:13.) In this context, "hope" is not something believers simply wish will happen as a result of their faith in Christ; rather, Christian hope is grounded in the certainty that the "love of God has been poured into our hearts through the Holy Spirit," and that upon Christ's return, his Second Coming, all believers will share and participate in the "glory of God" at the end of time.

The reading ends with an interesting assertion by Paul. He appears concerned that some might want to limit Jesus's Death to a courageous act—one man laying down his life for "a just person." But Paul maintains that the Death of Christ reaches far beyond simple heroism. Christ "died for us," the "ungodly," "while we still were sinners." This is a critical point for Paul because it "proves" the depth of God's love for us.

> **GOSPEL**　All four Gospel accounts present Jesus as a teacher. In the synoptic accounts of Matthew, Mark, and Luke, Jesus often teaches in parables or with one-liners that cover a variety of topics ranging from the Kingdom of God to the Mosaic Law. But in John's Gospel account, Jesus teaches primarily through extended discourses in which he himself is often the focal point of the discussion. These discourses often explain aspects of

She sees an opportunity and jumps at it.

The **woman** said to him,
   "Sir, **give** me this water, so that I may not be **thirsty**
   or have to keep **coming** here to draw water."

Jesus doesn't comment on her misunderstanding, but takes the conversation to a new and deeper level.

Jesus said to her,
   "**Go** call your **husband** and come **back**."
The woman **answered** and said to him,
   "I do not **have** a husband."
Jesus answered her,
   "You are **right** in saying, 'I do not have a **husband**.'

She seems to trust him and lets down her guard.

Jesus's blunt reply should not be so harsh as to provoke defensiveness.

For you have had **five** husbands,
   and the one you have **now** is not your **husband**.
What you have said is **true**."
The woman said to him,
   "Sir, I can see that you are a **prophet**.

She's impressed by his prescient knowledge, but steers him to a safer subject.

Our **ancestors** worshiped on this **mountain**;
   but you people say that the place to worship is in **Jerusalem**."
Jesus said to her,
   "**Believe** me, woman, the hour is **coming**
   when you will **worship** the Father
   neither on this mountain **nor** in **Jerusalem**.

Jesus is fully engaged; she has become a true conversation partner.

Jesus is clearly teaching, but strive to sustain a conversational tone.

You people worship what you do not **understand**;
   we worship what we **understand**,
   because **salvation** is from the **Jews**.
But the hour is **coming**, and is now **here**,
   when **true** worshipers will worship the Father in **Spirit**
      and **truth**;
   and **indeed** the Father **seeks** such people to worship him.

These words should not take on an accusatory tone or smack of arrogance. The solicitous and compassionate quality of "the father seeks" characterizes Jesus's teaching about where to worship.

God is **Spirit**, and those who **worship** him
   must worship in **Spirit** and **truth**."

TO KEEP IN MIND
Context: Who is speaking in this text? What are the circumstances?

---

his identity as the Word made flesh (John 1:14). Today's discourse in the encounter with the Samaritan woman at the well reveals Jesus as the living water. Other self-revealing discourses in John's account include Jesus as the Son of the Father (5:19–47), Jesus as the bread of life (6:22–71), Jesus as the light of the world (8:12–59), and Jesus as the good shepherd (10:1–18).

From its opening setting and rich dialogue between Jesus and the feisty Samaritan woman to its unexpected conclusion, this has become one of the most well-known stories in the Gospel according

to John. Jesus's encounter with the Samaritan woman at the well offers a prime example of the Johannine definition of discipleship: true disciples are those who believe in Jesus and bring others to Christ.

Three aspects of the setting of this story stand out. First, the encounter between Jesus and the woman occurs in Sychar, a town in the region of Samaria. Galilean Jews (like Jesus and his disciples) and Judean Jews routinely avoided the territory of Samaria, deeming it too unclean to enter or even pass through. Second, the dialogue between Jesus and the Samaritan

woman takes place at "Jacob's well." Jacob, one of Israel's great patriarchs, met his wife Rachael at this well and fell in love with her. For many Israelites, Jacob's well conjured romantic images. (See Genesis 29:1–30.) Third, Jesus meets and talks to a woman of Samaria by herself, at the noon of the day. The fact that this woman is a Samaritan, often regarded by Jews as half-breeds (neither full-blooded Jews nor Gentiles) and therefore ritually impure, was bad enough. But the fact that she was alone, without any other women from her kinship group, indicates that this woman was an outcast

Is she sensing the identity of the one who stands before her?

> The woman **said** to him,
>> "I know that the **Messiah** is coming, the one called the **Christ**;
>> when he **comes**, he will tell us **everything**."
> Jesus said to her,
>> "I am **he**, the one **speaking** with you."

Here begins the second act of this drama. The disciples' return changes the mood. They seem skeptical about the woman.

> At that moment his disciples **returned**,
>> and were **amazed** that he was talking with a **woman**,
>> but still no one said, "What are you **looking** for?"
>> or "Why are you **talking** with her?"

Her conversion is almost complete. Like the Apostles, she abandons all to assume a missionary role.

"Could he possibly be?" is more a joyful declaration than a question.

> The woman **left** her water jar
>> and went into the town and said to the people,
>> "**Come** see a man who told me **everything** I have done.
> Could he possibly be the **Christ**?"
> They went out of the town and **came** to him.

They assume a parental tone: "Rabbi . . . EAT!"

> Meanwhile, the disciples **urged** him, "Rabbi, **eat**."
> But he said to them,
>> "I have **food** to eat of which you do not **know**."
> So the disciples **said** to one another,
>> "Could someone have **brought** him something to eat?"

Jesus's response hints at his deep relationship with the Father.

> Jesus said to them,
>> "My **food** is to do the will of the one who **sent** me
>> and to **finish** his work.

Jesus summarizes his single-minded mission.

> Do you not **say**, 'In four months the **harvest** will be here'?
> I tell you, look up and see the fields **ripe** for the harvest.
> The reaper is **already** receiving **payment**
>> and gathering crops for eternal **life**,
>> so that the **sower** and **reaper** can rejoice **together**.

As always, Jesus offers familiar, practical images to ground his teaching. Here it is harvest imagery.

> For here the saying is verified that 'One **sows** and another **reaps**.'

even to the Samaritans. She was, in other words, unclean in the extreme.

The initial exchange between Jesus and the woman is tense, as the woman challenges Jesus for even asking her a question, then accuses Jesus of dishonoring "our father Jacob." Despite the tension, Jesus begins to reveal himself to the woman as "the living water." As the dialogue continues, it becomes clear why she is isolated even from the other women of Sychar: she has been married (and presumably divorced) five times and is currently living in an unlawful union with a man. The Samaritan woman initially identifies Jesus as a prophet, since Jesus knew about her misconduct. But Jesus then reveals to her his true identity as the long-awaited Christ.

The story concludes with the woman informing the villagers of Sychar about her encounter with Jesus. Upon hearing the woman's testimony, the Samaritans invite Jesus to stay with them for two days, after which many of the Samaritans also came to believe in Jesus as "the savior of the world."

For John, the Samaritan woman who came to believe in Jesus exemplifies true discipleship in her witness to the villagers of Sychar. Despite her extreme unclean state, the woman underwent an honest conversion and expressed faith in Jesus as the Christ. And she brought the Good News of Jesus to her fellow Samaritans, inviting them to a similar encounter with Christ.

Each of the readings reveals that despite our sinfulness, God continually seeks a means to be reconciled with us. What a message of hope as we continue our journey in the season of Lent!

This is not a chastisement, but a wise insight gleaned from various Old Testament sources including Deuteronomy 20:6 and 28.30; Job 31:8; and Micah 6:15.

Here begins the final act. The woman has sparked much interest in Jesus. They plead for him to remain with them.

The people are grateful to the woman who introduced them to Jesus. Don't rush the title they assign to Jesus.

I sent you to **reap** what you have not **worked** for;
  others have done the work,
  and **you** are sharing the **fruits** of their work."

Many of the **Samaritans** of that town began to **believe** in him
  because of the word of the **woman** who testified,
  "He told me **everything** I have done."
When the Samaritans **came** to him,
  they invited him to **stay** with them;
  and he stayed there two **days**.
Many **more** began to believe in him because of his word,
  and they **said** to the woman,
  "We no longer believe because of **your** word;
  for we have heard for **ourselves**,
  and we **know** that this is **truly** the **savior** of the **world**."

[Shorter: John 4:5–15, 19b–26, 39a, 40–42]

TO KEEP IN MIND

Characters: To distinguish the various characters that populate a passage, try to understand their thoughts, feelings, and motivations. Use subtle variations in pitch, pacing, and emotion to communicate them. But don't confuse proclamation with theatrics. Suggest characters, don't "become" them.

FOURTH SUNDAY
OF LENT

LECTIONARY #32

READING I   2 Chronicles 36:14–16, 19–23

A reading from the second Book of Chronicles

In those days, all the **princes** of **Judah**, the **priests**, and the **people**
    added **infidelity** to **infidelity**,
    practicing all the **abominations** of the **nations**
    and **polluting** the Lord's **temple**
    which he had **consecrated** in **Jerusalem**.

Early and **often** did the Lord, the God of their **fathers**,
    send his **messengers** to them,
    for he had **compassion** on his people and his **dwelling** place.
But they **mocked** the messengers of God,
    despised his warnings, and **scoffed** at his prophets,
    until the **anger** of the Lord against his people was so **inflamed**
    that there was no **remedy**.
Their enemies **burnt** the house of God,
    tore down the walls of **Jerusalem**,
    set all its **palaces afire**,
    and **destroyed** all its precious **objects**.
Those who **escaped** the **sword** were carried **captive** to **Babylon**,
    where they became **servants** of the king of the **Chaldeans** and
        his **sons**
    until the kingdom of the **Persians** came to power.

Chronicles = KRAH-nih-k*ls

There is pain and frustration in these
opening lines.

"Polluting" is a strong word. Let it express
frustration turned to contempt.

Imagine legislators who ignored warnings
about an impending natural disaster. How
would you speak of their indifference and
neglect? The author wants to vindicate God,
saying the Lord did all that was possible to
warn the people.
Speak with a degree of disbelief about this
reprehensible behavior.

Don't recite this news with regret because
it is the well-deserved consequence of
their infidelity.

The exile was Israel's greatest trial. Suggest
its devastating impact.

Today options are given for the readings:
Year A or Year B. Contact your parish staff
to learn which readings will be used.

READING I The Second Book of
Chronicles offers a historical account of Israel's time in the promised land from the reign of King Solomon (960–922 BC) to the period of the divided kingdom (922–597 BC), highlighting the reforms of King Hezekiah (715–687 BC) and King Josiah (641–609 BC), and concluding with the collapse of the southern kingdom of Judah and the exile to Babylon (597–538 BC). Today's reading comes from the final chapter of 2 Chronicles, detailing events that led to Judah's exile to Babylon.

The chronicler makes a clear case against all the people of Judah, from the ruling elites to the common people, that God's exile of Judah to Babylon was justified. In fact, the chronicler offers somewhat of an abbreviated history of the Old Testament's witness to God's continuous sending of "messengers" and "prophets" to forewarn Israel to change its ways. Despite God's nearly unlimited patience, conditions in Jerusalem had become so deplorable that there was "no remedy." Just as the prophet Jeremiah forewarned, eventually the Babylonians captured the southern kingdom of Judah, ransacked Jerusalem and the Temple, and sent the Israelites into exile to Babylon in two separate deportations, 597 BC and 587 BC.

The concluding remarks in today's reading about Cyrus, king of Persia, are the final verses of 2 Chronicles. Interestingly, this great chronicle does not end with the catastrophe of Israel exiled in Babylon. The final verses (2 Chronicles 36:22–23)

To compensate for their defilement of the Sabbath, the land will lie abandoned and fallow for seventy years.

God uses this pagan king to achieve a divine purpose. Speak of Cyrus with dignity for he was in the grip of God's will.

Shift to a proclamatory tone, slightly louder. Cyrus is sincerely seeking God's will.

The last sentence is both an invitation and a blessing.

All this was to fulfill the **word** of the Lord spoken by **Jeremiah**:
    "Until the land has **retrieved** its lost **sabbaths**,
    during all the time it lies **waste** it shall have **rest**
    while **seventy** years are fulfilled."

In the first year of **Cyrus**, king of **Persia**,
    in order to **fulfill** the word of the Lord spoken by Jeremiah,
    the Lord **inspired** King Cyrus of **Persia**
    to issue this **proclamation** throughout his kingdom,
    both by word of **mouth** and in **writing**:
    "Thus says **Cyrus**, king of **Persia**:
    All the kingdoms of the **earth**
    the Lord, the God of **heaven**, has **given** to me,
    and he has also **charged** me to build him a **house**
    in **Jerusalem**, which is in **Judah**.
Whoever, therefore, among you belongs to **any** part
        of his **people**,
    let him go **up**, and may his God be with him!"

For meditation and context:

RESPONSORIAL PSALM   Psalm 137:1–2, 3, 4–5, 6 (6ab)

R. Let my tongue be silenced, if I ever forget you!

By the streams of Babylon
    we sat and wept when we
        remembered Zion.
On the aspens of that land
    we hung up our harps.

For there our captors asked of us
    the lyrics of our songs,
and our despoilers urged us to be joyous:
    "Sing for us the songs of Zion!"

How could we sing a song of the Lord
    in a foreign land?
If I forget you, Jerusalem,
    may my right hand be forgotten!

May my tongue cleave to my palate
    if I remember you not,
if I place not Jerusalem
    ahead of my joy.

TO KEEP IN MIND
Go slowly in the epistles. Paul's style is often a tangle of complex sentences; his mood can change within a single passage.

offer hope for a better future. The rise of the Persian Empire and its defeat of the Babylonian Empire facilitated the release of the captive Israelites. The ending of 2 Chronicles and the beginning of the Book of Ezra (the book following 2 Chronicles in the Old Testament) makes it clear that the rise of King Cyrus and the Persian Empire and the return of the exiled Israelites was part of God's plan for salvation, reflecting the depth of God's mercy and forgiveness.

READING II   In his Letter to the Ephesians, Paul describes God as being "rich in mercy" and having "great love" for us. God's mercy and love is most evident in that, despite being "dead in our transgressions," God "brought us to life with Christ." Paul sees this simple phrase as saying it all: "By grace you have been saved."

Paul is consistent in his letters, and here in Ephesians, that our salvation, which comes from faith in Christ, is a free "gift of God," not earned by us or granted as a special favor to a select few who might find it a reason to "boast." For Paul, this gift of God serves the larger purpose to prepare us for "the good works" that God has in store for us.

GOSPEL   As today's Gospel Reading opens, Jesus is speaking to Nicodemus, recalling that Moses had "lifted up the serpent in the desert." Jesus rightly

Look up another translation of this passage (the NRSV reads well) for help understanding Paul's message.

Ephesians = ee-FEE-zhunz

An initial sentence of multiple clauses opens this text. Each clause communicates a valuable piece of information, so read carefully with awareness of the message you are delivering.

"By grace" is a reminder that salvation is not earned but is God's free gift.

Paul's message was stated in the first line, "God . . . is rich in mercy." Here he underscores the message declaring that God greatly desires to share "immeasurable riches" with us.

Paul says it again: our salvation is not our own doing!

We are the fruit of God's loving labor, crafting us into the likeness of Christ.

Free grace leads us to making good works our way of life.

READING II   Ephesians 2:4–10

A reading from the Letter of Saint Paul to the Ephesians

Brothers and sisters:
God, who is **rich** in **mercy**,
    because of the great **love** he had for us,
    even when we were dead in our **transgressions**,
    brought us to **life** with **Christ**—by **grace** you have
        been **saved**—,
raised us up with him,
    and **seated** us with him in the **heavens** in Christ **Jesus**,
    that in the ages to come
He might show the immeasurable **riches** of his **grace**
    in his **kindness** to us in Christ **Jesus**.
For by **grace** you have been saved through **faith**,
    and this is not from **you**; it is the **gift** of **God**;
    it is not from **works**, so no one may **boast**.
For we are his **handiwork**, created in Christ **Jesus** for the
        good **works**
    that God has prepared in **advance**,
    that we should **live** in them.

Light and darkness, good news and bad—the text is a mixture of both. Don't emphasize one to the exclusion of the other.

Nicodemus = nik-uh-DEE-muhs

See Numbers 21:9. Jesus employs this subtle analogy to make a serious point about his destiny and our salvation.

GOSPEL   John 3:14–21

A reading from the holy Gospel according to John

Jesus said to **Nicodemus**:
    "Just as Moses lifted up the **serpent** in the **desert**,
    so must the Son of **Man** be lifted up,
    so that everyone who **believes** in him may have eternal **life**."

assumes that Nicodemus, a "Pharisee" and "ruler of the Jews" (John 3:1), would immediately recognize this as an excerpt from Numbers 21:4–9. It is a brief and somewhat shocking story of God's reaction to the Israelites' continual complaints in the desert.

The Israelites, once again lacking faith in God and trust in Moses's leadership, and "disgusted" by the food provided to them, challenged both God and Moses, and

expressed regret over leaving Egypt. As punishment, God sent poisonous snakes to bite those who complained. The venomous snake bite often resulted in death. Repentant of their sins, the Israelites implored Moses to save them from the snakes. Following God's commands, Moses mounted on a pole a bronze serpent. Snake-bitten Israelites who were repentant and looked up at the bronze serpent on the pole recovered from their snake bite.

Knowing Numbers 21:4–9, Jesus's words to Nicodemus ("so must the Son of Man be lifted up, so that everyone who believes in him may have eternal life") are to be interpreted as God once again offering salvation, but this time through the Cross of Christ and with the promise of eternal life. We see here the Johannine emphasis on believing in Jesus and on God's desire to save the world.

Give the assembly time to hear and recognize this beloved text.

God's purpose is always our salvation.

A faster pace for what God did *not* intend and slower pace to assert what he *did* intend.

This is a "hard saying." Don't soften its impact.

These words are as true now as then. Don't blunt their ability to jolt us.

Evil hides in darkness; only goodness seeks the light.

Speak the final, hopeful sentence as an invitation to live in the light.

TO KEEP IN MIND
Names of characters: Often the first word of a reading. Lift out the names to ensure listeners don't miss who the subject is.

For God so **loved** the world that he **gave** his only Son,
    so that everyone who **believes** in him might not **perish**
        but might have eternal **life**.
For God did not **send** his Son into the world to **condemn**
        the world,
    but that the world might be **saved** through him.
Whoever **believes** in him will **not** be condemned,
    but whoever does **not** believe has **already** been condemned,
    because he has not believed in the name of the only Son
        of **God**.
And **this** is the **verdict**,
    that the **light** came into the **world**,
    but people preferred **darkness** to light,
    because their works were **evil**.
For **everyone** who does **wicked** things **hates** the light
    and does not come **toward** the light,
    so that his works might not be **exposed**.
But whoever lives the **truth** comes to the light,
    so that **his** works may be clearly seen as done in **God**.

[Shorter: John 9:1, 6–9, 13–17, 34–38]

John is also fond of presenting Jesus as the symbol of light, often as "the light of the world" seen in today's reading. (See also, for example, 1:5; 8:12, 12:46.) Jesus, the light, is often presented in contrast to darkness, suggesting a clear choice for the path to eternal life.

Each of the three readings for today, read in the context of the season of Lent, speaks to both the human condition of sin and to God's unlimited mercy. The journey through Lent challenges us to balance these realities as we seek reconciliation with God through his Son, Jesus Christ.

FOURTH SUNDAY OF LENT, YEAR A

LECTIONARY #31

READING I   1 Samuel 16:1b, 6–7, 10–13a

A reading from the first Book of Samuel

The LORD said to **Samuel**:
  "Fill your horn with **oil**, and be on your way.
I am sending you to **Jesse** of **Bethlehem**,
  for I have chosen my **king** from among his **sons**."

As Jesse and his sons came to the **sacrifice**,
  Samuel looked at **Eliab** and thought,
  "**Surely** the LORD's anointed is here before him."
But the LORD said to Samuel:
  "Do not judge from his **appearance** or from his lofty **stature**,
  because I have **rejected** him.
Not as **man** sees does **God** see,
  because man sees the **appearance**
  but the LORD looks into the **heart**."
In the **same** way Jesse presented **seven** sons before Samuel,
  but Samuel said to Jesse,
  "The LORD has not chosen any **one** of these."
Then Samuel **asked** Jesse,
  "Are these **all** the sons you have?"
Jesse replied,
  "There is still the **youngest**, who is tending the **sheep**."
Samuel said to Jesse,
  "**Send** for him;
  we will not **begin** the sacrificial banquet until he **arrives** here."

Immediately, your tone hints at the significance of the mission given to Samuel.

Jesse = JES-ee

Bethlehem = BETH-luh-hem

Eliab = ee-Lī-uhb

Don't rush Jesse's name or his hometown. These will become cornerstones of Israel's history.

Suggest the scrutiny with which Samuel gazes upon Eliab and speak his assessment with self-satisfied confidence.

The tone of "But the Lord" immediately signals that Samuel has misjudged.

God's dialogue is a lesson in the difference between God's ways and ours; it is not a reproach. Don't overstress "rejected him," because Eliab is not being passed over due to sinfulness or flaws.

Speak this truth like a wise, old teacher.

Eliminating all *seven* sons was a long and tedious process. Stress "seven."

Samuel can't make sense of coming up short. Let us hear his exasperation.

Jesse alludes to David, but clearly without confidence.

But Samuel immediately sees a ray of hope.

Today options are given for the readings: Year A or Year B. Contact your parish staff to learn which readings will be used.

READING I David ruled over the united monarchy of Israel for forty years (1000–961 BC) and is regarded as the greatest king in Israel's history. Much attention is given to David in the historical books of the Old Testament. In fact, the life of David is discussed in four different books: First and Second Samuel, First Kings, and First Chronicles. First Samuel, from where our First Reading is taken, introduces David and records the turbulent relationship between David and Israel's first king of the monarchy, Saul. Second Samuel covers the forty-year reign of King David. The opening chapters of First Kings report the final days and death of David. Most of First Chronicles provides a favorable retelling of the life and reign of David, using First and Second Samuel and First Kings as three sources.

Today's reading opens with the Lord instructing the prophet Samuel to anoint the new king of Israel. According to 1 Samuel, God is replacing Saul as king of Israel because of Saul's disobedience to God's command (see 1 Samuel 15). Samuel was a key figure in the transitioning of Israel into a united monarchy. He served as one of the last judges of Israel during the period of the judges (1200–1020 BC), and remained influential during the entire reign of Saul, dying in the early stages of David's reign as king.

The story of Samuel anointing David as the next king of Israel is presented with some interesting details. First, of all the sons of Jesse of Bethlehem—eight in all— the Lord does not choose someone who, by

Speak slowly and with great reverence of David. This *is* God's chosen one . . . and he's "handsome" to boot.

David is God's choice!

This is a moment of great consequence. Fill it with dignity. David is clearly open to the movement of God's spirit.

For meditation and context:

> **TO KEEP IN MIND**
> **Tell the story:** Make the story yours, then share it with your listeners. Use the language; don't throw away any good words. Settings give context; don't rush the description. Characters must be believable; understand their motivation. Dialogue reveals character; distinguish one character from another with your voice.

Ephesians = ee-FEE-zhuhnz

Light and darkness are major themes today. Pay close attention to the contrasts in this text.

Speak this imperative with authority. "Goodness," "righteousness," and "truth" are three *distinct* outcomes of living in the light. Don't blur them.

"Try" suggests that doing right is not easy to master.

Jesse **sent** and had the young man **brought** to them.
He was **ruddy**, a youth **handsome** to behold
    and making a **splendid** appearance.
The LORD said,
    "**There—anoint** him, for **this** is the one!"
Then Samuel, with the horn of **oil** in hand,
    anointed David in the presence of his **brothers**;
    and from **that** day **on**, the **spirit** of the LORD **rushed**
        upon David.

RESPONSORIAL PSALM   Psalm 23:1–3a, 3b–4, 5, 6 (1)

R. The Lord is my shepherd; there is nothing I shall want.

The LORD is my shepherd; I shall not want.
    In verdant pastures he gives me repose;
beside restful waters he leads me;
    he refreshes my soul.

He guides me in right paths
    for his name's sake.
Even though I walk in the dark valley
    I fear no evil; for you are at my side
with your rod and your staff
    that give me courage.

You spread the table before me
    in the sight of my foes;
you anoint my head with oil;
    my cup overflows.

Only goodness and kindness follow me
    all the days of my life;
and I shall dwell in the house of the LORD
    for years to come.

READING II   Ephesians 5:8–14

A reading from the Letter of Saint Paul to the Ephesians

Brothers and sisters:
You were once **darkness**,
    but now you are **light** in the **Lord**.
Live as **children** of light,
    for **light** produces every kind of **goodness**
        and **righteousness** and **truth**.
Try to learn what is **pleasing** to the Lord.

human standards, would best meet the criteria for kingly office. God chooses the youngest son, David, who was relegated simply to tending the family's sheep.

Another notable aspect of this story is the initial character sketch of David, describing him as "ruddy, a youth handsome to behold and making a splendid appearance." But beyond his physically attractive features, God saw in David a young man with the right "heart" to lead Israel.

The reading concludes with the comment that "from that day on, the spirit of the Lord rushed upon David." The historical

books dedicated to telling the story of David are consistent in portraying the spirit of the Lord present to David throughout his life.

The relationship between David and God reaches its pinnacle in the establishment of the Davidic covenant (2 Samuel 7:8–16), where God vows to have David's house and kingdom endure "forever" and to raise up an heir after David whose throne will also stand firm "forever." The New Testament writers believed God fulfilled his covenantal promise to David in the birth of Jesus.

READING II This excerpt from Ephesians is taken from Paul's concluding remarks in his letter (4:25—6:20), where he addresses the matter of Christian moral behavior. Paul begins this final section with instructions for proper Christian conduct, emphasizing compassion, love, and forgiveness for one another. In the line just before today's reading begins he urges the Ephesians to disassociate from the disobedient because Paul believes God's wrath is coming upon them.

One of the clues that Paul is primarily, if not exclusively, addressing Gentile

"Take no part . . ." Speak this as sage advice imparted from an elder to a beloved younger person.

What is exposed to and absorbs the light of Christ itself becomes light.

Taken from an early Christian hymn, this poetic, well-cadenced line ends the passage in joy and hope.

> **TO KEEP IN MIND**
> **Eye contact** connects you with those to whom you minister. Look at the assembly during the middle and at the end of every thought or sentence.

It is critical that we hear the opening line.

The disciples reflect contemporary thinking that suffering and sin were directly related.

Jesus enunciates a new and unexpected teaching.

Jesus speaks with a sense of urgency regarding his mission.

Don't rush into the healing section. The graphic details ("spat . . . clay . . . saliva . . . smeared . . . ") add texture to the story. Don't waste them.

Siloam = sih-LOH-uhm

Speak of the miracle with conviction and awe.

The mood shifts with the entrance of the "neighbors." The differing opinions can be spoken at a faster rate than the narration. The energy and controversy are more important than their specific objections.

Take no part in the fruitless works of **darkness**;
　rather **expose** them, for it is shameful even to **mention**
　the things done by them in secret;
　but everything **exposed** by the light becomes **visible**,
　for everything that **becomes** visible is **light**.
Therefore, it says:
　"**Awake**, O sleeper,
　and **arise** from the **dead**,
　and **Christ** will give you **light**."

GOSPEL　John 9:1–41

A reading from the holy Gospel according to John

As **Jesus** passed by he **saw** a man **blind** from **birth**.
His **disciples** asked him,
　"**Rabbi**, who **sinned**, **this** man or his **parents**,
　that he was born **blind**?"
Jesus answered,
　"Neither **he** nor his **parents** sinned;
　it is so that the works of **God** might be made **visible**
　　through him.
We have to do the works of the one who sent me while it is **day**.
Night is coming when **no** one can work.
While I am in the **world**, I am the **light** of the world."
When he had said this, he **spat** on the ground
　and made **clay** with the saliva,
　and **smeared** the clay on his **eyes**, and said to him,
　"Go **wash** in the **Pool** of **Siloam**"—which means **Sent**—.
So he **went** and **washed**, and came back able to **see**.

His **neighbors** and those who had **seen** him earlier
　as a **beggar** said,
　"Isn't this the one who used to sit and **beg**?"

Christians in his letter to the Ephesians is the reference: "You were once darkness, but now you are light in the Lord." Formerly living in "darkness" is likely an allusion to the Ephesians' past religious practices and beliefs. His assertion that "it is shameful even to mention the things done by them in secret" may well be an implicit commentary on the rites and rituals practiced by participants of the mystery religions in many cities of the Roman Empire.

　Paul uses the dichotomy of light and darkness to differentiate between right and wrong conduct. He implores believers in Christ to live as "children of light," intentionally seeking and living the virtues of "goodness and righteousness and truth." He directs the Ephesians not only to "take no part in the fruitless works of darkness," but also actively to "expose" these works of darkness. It is unclear whether this means to expose one's own darkness to scrutiny or that of others in the community who still practiced the mystery religions.

　The reading concludes with what scholars suspect is an early Christian hymn used in initiation (Baptism) ceremonies: "Awake, O sleeper, and arise from the dead, and Christ will give you light." Paul inserts this hymn to link his moral exhortations to the liturgical practices of the Christian congregation in Ephesus.

> GOSPEL The first half of the Gospel according to John (1:19—12:50) chronicles Jesus's public ministry in Galilee, Samaria, and Judea, and is punctuated with seven signs and numerous dialogues that reveal the identity and meaning of Jesus as the Son of God and the Word made flesh.

The man leaves no room for doubt!

Some said, "It **is**,"
    but **others** said, "**No**, he just **looks** like him."
He said, "I **am**."
So they said to him, "How were your eyes **opened**?"
He replied,
    "The man called **Jesus** made **clay** and **anointed** my eyes
        and told me, 'Go to **Siloam** and **wash**.'
So I went there and **washed** and was able to **see**."
And they said to him, "Where **is** he?"
He said, "I don't **know**."

He still can't quite believe it all happened
so simply.

The sudden realization that he's unaware
of Jesus's whereabouts even takes him
by surprise.

Here, the operative word is "Sabbath."
Your tone should signal where the Pharisees
are heading.

The man is reserved at first and ends joyfully.

The Pharisees are not all cut from the same
cloth. One is angry; the other open-minded.

They brought the one who was once blind to the **Pharisees**.
Now Jesus had made clay and opened his eyes on a **sabbath**.
So then the Pharisees **also** asked him how he was able to see.
He **said** to them,
    "He put **clay** on my eyes, and I **washed**, and now I can **see**."
So some of the **Pharisees** said,
    "This man is not from **God**,
        because he does not keep the **sabbath**."
But **others** said,
    "How can a **sinful** man do such **signs**?"
And there was a **division** among them.
So they said to the blind man **again**,
    "What do **you** have to say about him,
        since he opened **your** eyes?"
He said, "He is a **prophet**."

He must be aware of the risk of making this
declaration. He does it anyway.

No amount of evidence is enough for those
who refuse to see.

Now the Jews did not **believe**
    that he had been **blind** and gained his **sight**
    until they summoned the **parents** of the one who had gained
        his sight.
They **asked** them,
    "Is this your **son**, who you say was **born** blind?
How does he now **see**?"
His parents answered and said,
    "We **know** that this is our **son** and that he was born **blind**.

Their tone intimidates the parents.

The parents are wary of falling into a trap and
give only what they must.

Today's story of Jesus healing the man born blind is the sixth of seven "signs" that Jesus performs in John's Gospel account. Those seven signs include turning water into wine at Cana (2:1–11), curing the royal official's son (4:46–54), curing a paralytic on the Sabbath (5:1–18), feeding the five thousand (6:1–15), walking on the water of the Sea of Galilee (6:16–21), curing the man born blind (9:1–41), and raising Lazarus from the dead (11:1–44).

John uses the Greek word *semeia* ("signs") to describe Jesus's miracles. See,

for example, John 2:11; 3:12 and the epilogue of John's account that tells us: "Jesus did many other signs (*semeia*) in the presence of [his] disciples that are not written in this book" (20:30–31). These signs or miracles point to his divine glory. By comparison, in the synoptic Gospel accounts, Jesus performs *dunameis* ("mighty deeds") as proof of his authority and of the authority of the disciples to act in Jesus's name.

The longer version of the story (9:1–41) of Jesus curing the man born blind begins with the disciples asking a perfectly logical question from the ancient Jewish point of

view: "Rabbi, who sinned, this man or his parents, that he was born blind?" Sickness and disease, even physical disabilities such as blindness, were thought to be rooted in sin. (See, for example, Exodus 20:5.) Jesus does not respond to the principle behind the disciples' question; rather, he indicates that sin plays no part in this particular man's blindness from birth and that it was serving a higher purpose: "so that the works of God might be made visible through him."

They're protecting themselves, not slighting their son.

This aside explains the parents' seemingly cold behavior.

Speak in the persona of the leaders who greet the man with clenched-teeth exasperation.

The man doesn't back away from his bold posture. He's saying: Don't draw me into your schemes. All I know is I'm healed!

He's clearly emboldened, but this time he will cross the line.

He affronted their dignity and they react with hostility and defensiveness.

He dares first to *mock* them and then to *teach* them.

He intuits a truth that has escaped the experts.

We do **not** know how he **sees** now,
    nor do we know **who** opened his eyes.
Ask **him**, he is of **age**;
    he can speak for **himself**."
His parents said this because they were **afraid**
    of the Jews, for the Jews had already **agreed**
        that if anyone **acknowledged** him as the **Christ**,
    he would be **expelled** from the **synagogue**.
For this reason his **parents** said,
    "He is of **age**; question **him**."

So a **second** time they called the man who had been **blind**
    and said to him, "Give **God** the praise!
We **know** that this man is a **sinner**."
He replied,
    "If he is a **sinner**, I do not **know**.
One thing I **do** know is that I was **blind** and now I **see**."
So they said to him,
    "What did he **do** to you?
    How did he open your eyes?"
He answered them,
    "I told you **already** and you did not **listen**.
Why do you want to hear it **again**?
Do **you** want to become his disciples, **too**?"
They **ridiculed** him and said,
    "**You** are that man's disciple;
    we are disciples of **Moses**!
We **know** that God spoke to **Moses**,
    but we do **not** know where this one is from."
The man answered and said to them,
    "This is what is so **amazing**,
    that you do not know where he is **from**, yet he opened my **eyes**.
We **know** that God does not listen to **sinners**,
    but if one is **devout** and does his **will**, he **listens** to him.
It is **unheard** of that anyone ever **opened** the eyes of a person
        born blind.

Given the extended length of the story, the cure itself of the blind man occurs relatively quickly, within the first few verses. Jesus "smeared" clay on the blind man's eyes, and the man followed Jesus's instructions to "go wash in the Pool of Siloam." The man then returned, able to see. The interaction between Jesus and the different groups of people following the healing of the blind man develops the larger point of the story.

As the story unfolds, various reactions to the cure come from the Jewish neighbors and the Pharisees, even from the man's parents. The neighbors debated among themselves the legitimacy of the miracle, even after the blind man accurately reported to them the details of his cure. The Pharisees were divided among themselves, with some arguing that no man from God would heal on the Sabbath. Neither questioning the cured man directly nor interrogating his parents satisfied the Pharisees. Throughout the deliberations and debates, the healed blind man remains consistent in reporting accurately the details of the cure, and confessing Jesus as a prophet sent from God.

The story turns when Jesus encounters the healed blind man after the Pharisees "threw him out." Jesus asks him the pointed question: "Do you believe in the Son of Man?" The healed man responds, "'I do believe, Lord,' and he worshiped him." No longer did the man perceive Jesus as just a prophet sent by God; rather, the man came to fully see Jesus's true identity as Lord and Son of Man.

The longer version of the story ends with the Pharisees and Jesus in a final tense exchange of words. The Pharisees were willing neither to accept the blind

This declaration, made publicly, must be repudiated. And they don't hesitate.

Speak the "threw him out" narration in the angry voice of the leaders. Then pause to suggest passage of time.
Remember, the man has not yet "seen" Jesus.

His question is full of gratitude and anticipation.

A pause after "He said" will suggest his moment of decision.

Jesus's words and his tone summon the defensive Pharisees.

Are they so blind that they actually mean this?

Jesus's words are direct and confrontational. His motive, however, is a desire that they, too, come to "see."

> **TO KEEP IN MIND**
> **Characters:** To distinguish the various characters that populate a passage, try to understand their thoughts, feelings, and motivations. Use subtle variations in pitch, pacing, and emotion to communicate them. But don't confuse proclamation with theatrics. Suggest characters, don't "become" them.

man's testimony nor to believe in Jesus. The sixth sign of John's Gospel account reveals the blindness of the Pharisees to the revelation of Jesus as "the light of the world." Although the man's faith in Jesus (9:38) allows him to see, the Pharisees lack of faith in Jesus keeps them blind (9:40–41).

As the season of Lent reaches its fourth Sunday, we are reminded of God's orchestration of salvation history from King David to Jesus Christ. The Lenten journey challenges us to live as "children of light," offering penance and seeking reconciliation with the true "light of the world."

If this man were not from **God**,
   he would not be able to **do** anything."
They answered and said to him,
   "You were born totally in **sin**,
   and are you trying to teach **us**?"
Then they **threw** him out.

When Jesus **heard** that they had thrown him out,
   he **found** him and said, "Do you **believe** in the Son of Man?"
He answered and said,
   "Who **is** he, sir, that I may **believe** in him?"
Jesus said to him,
   "You have **seen** him,
   and the one **speaking** with you is **he**."
He said,
   "I **do** believe, Lord," and he **worshiped** him.
Then Jesus said,
   "I came into this world for **judgment**,
   so that those who do **not** see **might** see,
   and those who **do** see might become **blind**."

Some of the **Pharisees** who were with him **heard** this
   and said to him, "Surely **we** are not also blind, **are** we?"
Jesus said to them,
   "If you **were** blind, you would have no **sin**;
   but now you are saying, 'We **see**,' so your sin **remains**."

[Shorter: John 9:1, 6–9, 13–17, 34–38]

FIFTH SUNDAY OF LENT

LECTIONARY #35

Jeremiah = jayr-uh-MĪ-uh

This is a hope-filled and joyous declaration.

This brief backward glance at previous wrongdoing should not be emphasized. But the tone does contrast with the joy of the rest of the text.

"But *this*" revives the energetic and positive tone that began the reading.

God speaks of a radically new relationship with Israel. It is a parent's voice declaring unconditional love; it is not an imposition of divine will, but God's total self-giving.

"All" and "least to greatest" say the same thing. Give the second term the greater stress. God never tires of forgiving and enfolding us in his love once more.

READING I   Jeremiah 31:31–34

A reading from the Book of the Prophet Jeremiah

The days are **coming**, says the LORD,
    when I will make a **new** covenant with the house of **Israel**
    and the house of **Judah**.
It will **not** be like the covenant I made with their **fathers**
    the day I **took** them by the **hand**
    to lead them forth from the land of **Egypt**;
    for they **broke** my covenant,
    and I had to show myself their **master**, says the LORD.
But **this** is the covenant that I will **make**
    with the house of Israel after those days, says the LORD.
I will place my law **within** them and write it upon their **hearts**;
    I will be their **God**, and **they** shall be my **people**.
No **longer** will they have need to **teach** their friends and relatives
    how to **know** the LORD.
All, from **least** to **greatest**, shall **know** me, says the LORD,
    for I will **forgive** their **evildoing** and **remember** their sin
      no **more**.

Today options are given for the readings: Year A or Year B. Contact your parish staff to learn which readings will be used.

READING I Jeremiah was called to be a prophet at the age of twenty-two in 628 BC. His destiny was to shepherd the southern kingdom of Judah through some of the darkest days in Israel's history. The rise of the Babylonian Empire and its growing power in the seventh century BC soon became a threat to Judah. Jeremiah saw only one option for survival—the people needed to repent of their sins and seek God's mercy and forgiveness. For Jeremiah, nothing short of the people's complete conversion could assure Judah of God's protection from this new enemy.

As was the case with the northern kingdom of Israel facing the Assyrian threat a century earlier (721 BC), the rulers and people of Judah did not heed the words of the prophet sent to them. Jeremiah was unable to convince his fellow Judeans to repent of their sinful ways. In 598 BC, King Nebuchadnezzar of Babylon captured Jerusalem and sent the leading citizens of Judah—the religious and political rulers—into exile in what would be the first of two deportations. Rather than follow Jeremiah's counsel and return to the Lord, Zedekiah, the king of Judah appointed by Nebuchadnezzar, eventually sought a military alliance with Egypt to overthrow the Babylonians. In retaliation, Nebuchadnezzar destroyed the city of Jerusalem and the Temple, exiling the remaining Judeans to Babylon in 587 BC. It was during this period when Jeremiah prophesied a "new covenant" between God and his people Israel.

Jeremiah's prophecy, heard in today's reading, emerged during this national

For meditation and context:

TO KEEP IN MIND
Proclaiming the **words of the prophets** requires intensity and urgency. With equal passion, they spoke threat and consolation, indictment and forgiveness. You must do the same for the chosen people you call "parish."

RESPONSORIAL PSALM   Psalm 51:3–4, 12–13, 14–15 (12a)

R. Create a clean heart in me, O God.

Have mercy on me, O God, in your goodness;
    in the greatness of your compassion wipe
        out my offense.
Thoroughly wash me from my guilt
    and of my sin cleanse me.

A clean heart create for me, O God,
    and a steadfast spirit renew within me.
Cast me not out from your presence,
    and your Holy Spirit take not from me.

Give me back the joy of your salvation,
    and a willing spirit sustain in me.
I will teach transgressors your ways,
    and sinners shall return to you.

Short readings always call for slower reading.

Don't overdramatize, but keep in mind this refers to Jesus's agony in the garden. The author's point is that even God's son "learned obedience" through *suffering*. It's not enough to read slowly. Read with awareness of the suffering you are describing.

Jesus can be a model for us because his divine nature did not spare him the need to accept God's will, even when it included suffering.

Deliver this line from memory, sustaining eye contact. Some of those who "obey him" are in your assembly.

READING II   Hebrews 5:7–9

A reading from the Letter to the Hebrews

In the days when Christ **Jesus** was in the **flesh**,
    he offered **prayers** and **supplications** with loud **cries** and **tears**
    to the one who was able to **save** him from **death**,
    and he was **heard** because of his **reverence**.
Son though he **was**, he learned **obedience** from what he **suffered**;
    and when he was made **perfect**,
    he became the source of eternal **salvation** for all who
        obey him.

The request to see Jesus is unusual coming from Gentiles.

Bethsaida = beth-SAY-uh-duh

GOSPEL   John 12:20–33

A reading from the holy Gospel according to John

Some **Greeks** who had come to worship at the **Passover** Feast
    came to **Philip**, who was from **Bethsaida** in **Galilee**,
    and **asked** him, "**Sir**, we would like to see **Jesus**."

---

trauma of the Babylonian destruction of the southern kingdom of Judah. For the first time since Moses led the Israelites to the promised land 600 hundred years earlier, Israel found itself completely exiled from the promised land. Through the prophet Jeremiah, the Lord offered the people of Judah the hope and divine promise of a new beginning.

Scholars commonly refer to Jeremiah's new-covenant oracle, heard in today's reading, as "the Gospel before the Gospel." For Christians, Jeremiah's prophecy is fulfilled in the life, Death, and Resurrection of Christ.

READING II   The Letter to the Hebrews contains some of the most remarkable theology in the New Testament. Images of Jesus as a "great high priest" and "mediator of a new covenant" (Hebrews 9:11–15) places this letter in a category all its own. Today's brief reading offers some other good examples of the letter's distinctive theological perspective.

The author of Hebrews presents two rather remarkable claims. First, Jesus "learned obedience from what he suffered." The notion that Jesus's suffering helped him "learn" to be "obedient" is intriguing. In

Luke's Gospel account, we hear of the young Jesus learning (2:40a: "The child grew and became strong, filled with wisdom"), but other examples of Jesus learning are not explicit.

The second notable assertion from Hebrews is that through this suffering "he was made perfect" and "became the source of eternal salvation." Many Christians routinely connect Jesus's sinless nature with the idea of being "perfect." This reading invites a different idea. In his humanity, he "was made" perfect through obedience, and modeled that process for us.

Seemingly unrelated to the Greeks' request, Jesus's reply actually reveals what "seeing" him truly means.

Sometimes a dying person offers more reassurance to loved ones than they can offer him. Read these lines from that point of view.

Jesus expounds the profound ironies of the Kingdom, which clearly apply to his own life as he faces death. Don't rush them.

Philip went and told **Andrew**;
   then Andrew and Philip went and told **Jesus**.
Jesus **answered** them,
   "The hour has **come** for the Son of Man to be **glorified**.
Amen, **amen**, I **say** to you,
   unless a grain of **wheat** falls to the ground and **dies**,
   it **remains** just a **grain** of wheat;
   but if it **dies**, it produces much **fruit**.
Whoever **loves** his life **loses** it,
   and whoever **hates** his life in **this** world
   will **preserve** it for **eternal** life.
Whoever **serves** me must **follow** me,
   and where **I** am, there also will my **servant** be.
The Father will **honor** whoever serves me.

This brief dialogue is considered John's attempt at a "garden scene." Don't ignore Jesus's genuine anguish.

Jesus is saying "Yes" to God's will.

The power of the divine voice impacts the people like thunder.

"I am **troubled** now. Yet what should I say,
'Father, **save** me from this **hour**'?
But it was for **this** purpose that I **came** to this hour.
Father, **glorify** your **name**."
Then a **voice** came from heaven,
   "I **have** glorified it and will glorify it **again**."
The crowd there **heard** it and said it was **thunder**;
   but **others** said, "An **angel** has spoken to him."
Jesus answered and said,
   "This **voice** did not come for **my** sake but for **yours**.

Note the points Jesus is making: the time of judgment has come; Satan's hold on the world is about to be broken; "everyone" will benefit from his Death and Resurrection.

Now is the time of **judgment** on this world;
   now the **ruler** of this world will be **driven** out.
And when I am **lifted** up from the **earth**,
   I will draw **everyone** to **myself**."

The final line should be spoken as Jesus spoke of his Death: it is the doorway to glory.

He said this indicating the kind of **death** he would **die**.

[Shorter: John 11:3–7, 17, 20–27, 33b–45]

GOSPEL | In today's Gospel Reading, "some Greeks" (Gentiles) approach one of the disciples, Philip, asking to meet Jesus. Although Philip and Andrew (who have Greek names) present the request, Jesus seems to ignore it, responding, "The hour has come for the Son of Man to be glorified." Some scholars interpret his remark to mean that only after his Resurrection can the Gospel be shared with non-Jews, through his disciples. The metaphor of the coming "hour" is one of the distinctive ways in which John presents Jesus's impending suffering, Death, Resurrection, and Ascension. In fact, throughout John's account, the verb tenses associated with Jesus's "hour" change as the story moves toward the Passion narrative. (See John 2:4, the first mention of Jesus's coming hour, and subsequent references: 4:21; 7:30; 8:20; 12:23; 13:1; 16:25; 17:1.)

Jesus explains his impending suffering with the grain of wheat metaphor, and then concludes, "I am troubled now." This leads to his rhetorical question: "Yet what should I say? 'Father, save me from this hour'?" Now Jesus reveals his upcoming Passion as his destiny: "But it was for this purpose that I came to this hour."

In the Gospel according to John, this is the only place we hear God's voice: "I have glorified it and will glorify it again." In the synoptic Gospels, God's voice enters the narrative at Jesus's baptism and Transfiguration, but John reserves God's voice for this single event of the foreshadowing of Jesus's Death on the Cross, where he will be "lifted up from the earth" (that is, nailed and elevated on the Cross), and where he "will draw everyone" to himself as the Savior.

FIFTH SUNDAY OF LENT, YEAR A

LECTIONARY #34

Read all twenty-eight verses of Chapter 37 to better understand the context of this striking prophecy.

Ezekiel = ee-ZEE-kee-uhl

Twice stated in God's own voice, "O my people," sets the tone of the prophecy. Declared boldly or with quiet intensity, speak these lines as if to a community that has experienced recent devastation and offer them vision and hope.

On both the first and second sentences, a slower pace for the first and third lines and a faster pace on the second may work best.

Three promises are made here: conferring of the Spirit; settlement on the land; knowledge of the Lord.

Speak the last line with authority first ("I have promised") and compassion second ("and I will do it").

For meditation and context:

READING I   Ezekiel 37:12–14

A reading from the Book of the Prophet Ezekiel

Thus says the LORD **God**:
  O my **people**, I will **open** your **graves**
  and have you **rise** from them,
  and bring you **back** to the land of **Israel**.
Then you shall **know** that **I** am the LORD,
  when I **open** your graves and have you **rise** from them,
  O my people!
I will put my **spirit** in you that you may **live**,
  and I will **settle** you upon your land;
  thus you shall know that **I** am the LORD.
I have **promised**, and I will **do** it, says the LORD.

RESPONSORIAL PSALM   Psalm 130:1–2, 3–4, 5–6, 7–8 (7)

R. With the Lord there is mercy and fullness of redemption.

Out of the depths I cry to you, O LORD;
  LORD, hear my voice!
Let your ears be attentive
  to my voice in supplication.

If you, O LORD, mark iniquities,
  LORD, who can stand?
But with you is forgiveness,
  that you may be revered.

I trust in the LORD;
  my soul trusts in his word.
More than sentinels wait for the dawn,
  let Israel wait for the LORD.

For with the LORD is kindness
  and with him is plenteous redemption;
and he will redeem Israel
  from all their iniquities.

TO KEEP IN MIND

Ritardando: refers to the practice, common in music, of becoming gradually slower and expanding the words as you approach the end of a piece. Many readings end this way—with a decreased rate but increased intensity.

Today options are given for the readings: Year A or Year B. Contact your parish staff to learn which readings will be used.

READING I This brief reading is an excerpt from Ezekiel's larger prophetic vision of the dry bones and two sticks, Ezekiel 37:1–28. The prophecy dates to the early stages of Israel's seventy-year exile in Babylon, around 575 BC.

Ezekiel was trained as a priest, and during his apprenticeship he worked among the priestly elite in the city of Jerusalem.

When the Babylonian king, Nebuchadnezzar, laid siege to the southern kingdom of Judah in 598 BC, Ezekiel was captured and brought to Babylon along with the other religious and political leaders of Jerusalem. It was in his fifth year of exile, in 593 BC, that Ezekiel received his call to be a prophet (see Ezekiel 1–3). Ezekiel and Second Isaiah are unique among the Old Testament prophets, being the only two to receive their call outside of Jerusalem and its surrounding region. Ezekiel was the prophet to the exiled Israelites in Babylon. No prophet before him faced such an enormous challenge.

Ezekiel's prophetic message can be divided into two distinct phases. The Babylonian siege and ultimate destruction of Jerusalem and the Temple in 586 BC is the pivotal event that separates the content and tone of Ezekiel's prophecies. For the Israelite leadership already in exile in Babylon since 598 BC, and for the majority of Israelites still in Judah, the annihilation of their capital city of Jerusalem and their sacred Temple was an unimaginable event. For many Israelites, this event was the sure sign that God had abandoned his people.

This is a classic "progressive reasoning" text in which Paul lays out a logical argument building each successive point on the one that went before. But while reasoned and logical, it is not dispassionate. Paul is arguing about the salvation of souls.

Color "flesh" (our "old self" that resists God) with a negative tone and immediately shift to positive color on "But you are not."

Contrast the negative tone color of "does not belong to him" with the enthusiasm of "But if Christ." Though the subordinate clause "although . . . because of sin" is important, don't lose the link between "But if Christ" and "the spirit is alive."

Because the final sentence employs an "if-then" construct ("then" is implied, not stated) it requires a sense of urgency and an effort to persuade that this good news ("will give life to your mortal bodies") truly applies to us.

Confidence in your voice will express Paul's conviction that our bodies *will* rise from the dead.

TO KEEP IN MIND

Tell the story: Make the story yours, then share it with your listeners. Use the language; don't throw away any good words. Settings give context; don't rush the description. Characters must be believable; understand their motivation. Dialogue reveals character; distinguish one character from another with your voice.

READING II   Romans 8:8–11

A reading from the Letter of Saint Paul to the Romans

Brothers and sisters:
Those who are in the **flesh** cannot **please** God.
But **you** are not in the flesh;
      on the **contrary**, you are in the **spirit**,
      if only the Spirit of God **dwells** in you.
Whoever does not **have** the Spirit of Christ does not **belong**
          to him.
But **if** Christ is **in** you,
      although the **body** is dead because of **sin**,
      the **spirit** is **alive** because of **righteousness**.
If the **Spirit** of the one who raised Jesus from the dead **dwells**
          in you,
      the **One** who raised Christ from the **dead**
      will give life to **your** mortal bodies also,
      through his **Spirit dwelling** in **you**.

All hope for the overthrow of the Babylonian Empire was now lost.

On a more personal note, these two phases are also marked by two traumatic events in Ezekiel's life: the death of his wife on the day that the siege of Jerusalem had begun (24:1, 15–18), and a two-year period of dumbness following his wife's death (24: 25–27; 33: 21–22). The division of the forty-eight chapters of the Book of Ezekiel reflects these two phases and personal events: chapters 1–24 covering the years 593–589 BC, and chapters 25–48 spanning a larger period of time, 585–572 BC. Today's

reading comes from this latter period and represents one of the recurring themes in Ezekiel's visions: hope for a future beyond captivity for the exiled Israelites, a new beginning in which the community itself will have an inner renewal and a new spirit.

Ezekiel 37 records two visions: the vision of the dry bones (verses 1–14), the ending of which is today's reading, and the vision of the two sticks (verses 15–28), not included in our reading, concerning a future union of the northern and southern kingdoms of Israel and Judah. In the dramatic vision of the dry bones, Ezekiel is led to a

plain filled with human bones, remains of Israelites long dead. He bears witness to their collective resurrection from the dead. And, as heard in today's reading, Ezekiel hears God's commitment to one day raise the people from their "graves" and return them "to the land of Israel." He bears witness to God's promise to the exiled Israelites: "I will put my spirit in you that you may live." It is a vision of the restoration of Israel, and, for many early Christians, Jesus's Resurrection from the dead was understood as the fulfillment of Ezekiel's vision of the dry bones.

GOSPEL   John 11:1–45

A reading from the holy Gospel according to John

Now a man was **ill**, **Lazarus** from **Bethany**,
   the village of **Mary** and her sister **Martha**.
Mary was the one who had **anointed** the Lord with perfumed **oil**
   and dried his **feet** with her **hair**;
   it was her **brother** Lazarus who was ill.
So the sisters sent **word** to Jesus saying,
   "**Master**, the one you **love** is **ill**."
When Jesus **heard** this he said,
   "This illness is **not** to end in **death**,
   but is for the **glory** of **God**,
   that the **Son** of God may be **glorified** through it."
Now Jesus **loved** Martha and her sister and Lazarus.
So when he **heard** that he was ill,
   he **remained** for two **days** in the place where he was.
Then **after** this he said to his disciples,
   "Let us go back to **Judea**."
The disciples said to him,
   "**Rabbi**, the Jews were just trying to **stone** you,
   and you want to go **back** there?"
Jesus answered,
   "Are there not **twelve** hours in a day?
If one walks during the **day**, he does not **stumble**,
   because he sees the **light** of this world.
But if one walks at **night**, he **stumbles**,
   because the light is not **in** him."
He said this, and then told them,
   "Our friend **Lazarus** is **asleep**,
   but I am going to **awaken** him."

The opening introduces familiar (and beloved) characters and reminds us of Jesus's special relationship with these siblings.

Bethany = BETH-uh-nee. The name means "house of the lowly."

Speak tenderly of this seminal moment in the relationship.

They've learned to count on Jesus, but their anxiety is real.

Jesus's reply shifts to a different plane than the sisters' concern for Lazarus's health.

This declaration takes the sting out of Jesus's seeming lack of response, but doesn't explain his intentional delay.

The disciples don't like this decision. Danger awaits in Judea.

Don't give Jesus's words a philosophical tone; keep them conversational. Jesus articulates John's familiar theme of "day and night."

Let us hear the resolve in Jesus's voice. He gives no hint of his real purpose.

READING II   Paul often wrote about the dichotomy between the spirit and the flesh in the life of believers in Christ. Today's reading is a good example of the tension Paul notes between the spirit (the in-dwelling of God's Spirit, Romans 8:9) and the flesh (not literally our bodies, but "our sinful passions," Romans 7:5). It is a subject that Paul frequently turned to in his letters (see, for example, Romans 7:4–6; 8:3–14; 1 Corinthians 3:14; Galatians 3:2–3; 5:16–25; 6:7–8; Philippians 3:3).

One of the important connections between today's reading from Romans and the First Reading from Ezekiel is the discussion of God's Spirit. Ezekiel prophesied to the exiled Israelites that "I [God] have promised" so that in the future "I will put my spirit in you." Paul sees this promise fulfilled for believers in Christ. Non-believers remain "in the flesh" and "cannot please God." But for believers, "You are not in the flesh; on the contrary, you are in the spirit, if only the Spirit of God dwells in you."

An equally significant connection between Paul and Ezekiel is Paul's conviction that the Spirit dwelling within believers will also raise us from the dead: "The One who raised Christ from the dead will give life to your mortal bodies also, through his Spirit dwelling in you." Here we find fulfilled Ezekiel's prophecy that God will "open your graves and have you rise from them."

GOSPEL   The raising of Lazarus from the dead is the seventh and final sign Jesus performs in the Gospel according to John. It shows Jesus's ability to exercise his divine power even over life and death, revealing Jesus as the Resurrection and the life. Unlike the synoptic Gospel accounts, in which the cleansing

They think he's not making sense. Their tone says, "What?!"

He's getting them on board, but he's not grieving.

Didymus = DID-uh-muhs. Thomas is willing to pay the price of discipleship, even if his reply smacks of melodrama.
In Jewish belief the soul left the body after three days, so Lazarus is beyond the reach of hope and prayer.

Contrast the responses of Martha and Mary.

Mary doesn't hide her disappointment; but she still has hope in Jesus.

Jesus's remarks continue to be intentionally cryptic.

Her misunderstanding leads to Jesus's bold self-identification, which is central to this Gospel text.

These lines parallel the "light of the world" pronouncement in last week's (Year A) Gospel Reading.

So the disciples said to him,
   "Master, if he is **asleep**, he will be **saved**."
But Jesus was talking about his **death**,
   while **they** thought that he meant **ordinary** sleep.
So then Jesus said to them **clearly**,
   "**Lazarus** has **died**.
And I am **glad** for you that I was not there,
   that you may **believe**.
Let us **go** to him."
So **Thomas**, called **Didymus**, said to his fellow disciples,
   "Let us **also** go to **die** with him."

When Jesus **arrived**, he found that Lazarus
   had already been in the **tomb** for **four days**.
Now Bethany was **near** Jerusalem, only about two miles away.
And many of the **Jews** had come to Martha and Mary
   to **comfort** them about their brother.
When Martha **heard** that **Jesus** was coming,
   she went to **meet** him;
   but **Mary** sat at home.
Martha said to Jesus,
   "Lord, if you had **been** here,
   my brother would not have **died**.
But even **now** I know that **whatever** you ask of God,
   God will **give** you."
Jesus said to her,
   "Your brother will **rise**."
Martha said to him,
   "I **know** he will rise,
   in the **resurrection** on the last **day**."
Jesus told her,
   "**I** am the resurrection and the **life**;
   whoever **believes** in me, even if he **dies**, will **live**,
   and everyone who **lives** and believes in me will **never** die.

---

of the Temple triggers the events that lead to Jesus's execution, in John's narrative, it is Jesus glorifying God through the raising of his friend Lazarus that ironically facilitates his own Death by the Sanhedrin (see John 11:45–53).

At the beginning of this miraculous sign, we learn the main purpose of the sign (Lazarus's return to life) described in this lengthy story: "so that the Son of God may be glorified through it." This indeed is the overarching theme. But John incorporates many other notable features into the story. In the shorter version of the raising of Lazarus, there are three: the dialogue between Jesus and Martha; Jesus's range of emotions at the death of Lazarus; and the Jews' reaction to Jesus raising Lazarus.

Upon seeing Jesus, the grief-stricken Martha begs him to raise her brother, Lazarus. But Jesus must first lay some groundwork for a deeper understanding on her part of his true identity as the Messiah and Son of God. Referring to himself as "the resurrection and the life," Jesus asks of Martha: "Do you believe this?" Martha responds, "Yes, Lord. I have come to believe that you are the Christ, the Son of God, the one who is coming into the world." Martha's confession of faith reveals faith and insight known to few others within the four-fold Gospel tradition. In the synoptic Gospel accounts, it is Peter, who, speaking for the Twelve Apostles, confesses his faith in Jesus as the Christ and Son of God (Matthew 16:13–20; Mark 8:27–30; Luke 9:18–21).

In the shorter version of this story, immediately following Martha's confession of faith, the story moves abruptly to John's report that Jesus "became perturbed and deeply troubled." The Greek word used here, and again when Jesus approaches the

Jesus's blunt question elicits an earnest and unreserved response from Martha.

> Do **you** believe this?"
> She said to him, "**Yes**, Lord.
> I have come to believe that you are the **Christ**, the Son of **God**,
>   the one who is **coming** into the **world**."

Use a quieter tone for the secret conversation between the sisters. Martha may have been coaxing Mary, but finally Mary goes eagerly.

> When she had **said** this,
>   she went and called her sister Mary **secretly**, saying,
>   "The **teacher** is here and is **asking** for you."
> As soon as she **heard** this,
>   she rose **quickly** and **went** to him.
> For Jesus had not yet come into the **village**,
>   but was still where Martha had **met** him.

These are likely family and friends, not the professional mourners who were not uncommon in the Middle East.

> So when the Jews who were with her in the house **comforting** her
>   **saw** Mary get up quickly and go out,
>   they **followed** her,
>   presuming that she was going to the **tomb** to **weep** there.
> When Mary came to where **Jesus** was and **saw** him,
>   she fell at his **feet** and said to him,

Mary echoes her sister's line. The emotion is sincere.

> "**Lord**, if you had **been** here,
>   my brother would not have **died**."

This rare glimpse of Jesus's profound emotion is stirring. The *New American Bible* points out that in the Greek the line is startling: "He snorted in spirit."

> When Jesus saw her **weeping** and the **Jews** who had come with
>   her weeping,
>   he became **perturbed** and deeply **troubled**, and said,
>   "Where have you **laid** him?"

Recall that Jesus gave the same response when the disciples of John the Baptist joined him.

> They said to him, "**Sir**, come and **see**."
> And Jesus **wept**.
> So the Jews said, "See how he **loved** him."

Contrast vividly the crowds' conflicting perspectives.

> But some of them said,
>   "Could not the one who opened the eyes of the **blind** man
>   have **done** something so that this man would not have **died**?"

Don't gloss over this second mention of Jesus's distress. Speak these simple but dramatic details with significance.

> So Jesus, perturbed **again**, came to the **tomb**.
> It was a **cave**, and a **stone** lay across it.
> Jesus said, "Take away the **stone**."

---

tomb, *embrimaomai*, is literally translated in English as "snort" (in anger). It offers a rather shocking image of Jesus, certainly one not seen elsewhere in the Gospel story lines. The longer version of the story makes it a little clearer that Jesus is not reacting to Martha's confession of faith, as the shorter version could imply. (Avoid that implication by pausing briefly after Martha's confession before moving on.) Jesus is actually responding to the deep grief of Lazarus's other sister, Mary, and the other Jews who knew and loved Lazarus. Scholars have debated about where exactly Jesus's anger is directed. A common conclusion is that Jesus is angry at death itself that brings such sorrow and anguish to loved ones.

We then hear, "And Jesus wept." Jesus moves quickly from extreme anger to grief, only to shift back into anger: "So Jesus, perturbed again, came to the tomb." The range of emotions we see Jesus experience is startling, but not uncommon for grieving loved ones.

In response to Jesus raising Lazarus from the dead, we hear that "many of the Jews who had come to Mary and seen what he had done began to believe in him." In his Gospel account, John emphasizes the importance of *believing* in Jesus. Here, the Jews who began "believing" in Jesus were reacting not only to the sign he performed (raising Lazarus from the dead), but also to their encounter with Jesus and their shared experience of a genuine love and grief for Lazarus.

At the beginning of this reading, the shorter version excludes the concern expressed by the disciples when Jesus announced his plan to go back to the village

Martha is back to practical concerns, perhaps wavering in her reliance on Jesus's intervention.

Jesus offers a real but gentle reproach for this lapse.

As ever, Jesus demonstrates compassionate concern for others.

Boldly or softly, the command conveys Jesus's divine authority.

You might try a delivery like this: "the dead man / came out / bound / hand / and foot / with burial bands / and his face / was wrapped in a cloth." Practice till the delivery sounds natural.

If this was a proclamation of hope rather than a recitation of history, it should rouse deeper faith in your assembly as it did in the townspeople.

TO KEEP IN MIND
Pace: The rate at which you read is influenced by the size of your church, the size of the congregation, and the complexity of the text. As each increases, rate decreases.

Martha, the dead man's **sister**, said to him,
"Lord, by **now** there will be a **stench**;
he has been dead for **four days**."
Jesus said to her,
"Did I not tell you that if you **believe**
you will see the **glory** of **God**?"
So they **took** away the stone.
And Jesus raised his **eyes** and said,
"**Father**, I **thank** you for **hearing** me.
I know that you **always** hear me;
but because of the **crowd** here I have said this,
that they may believe that you **sent** me."
And when he had **said** this,
he cried out in a **loud** voice,
"**Lazarus**, come **out**!"
The **dead** man **came** out,
tied **hand** and **foot** with **burial** bands,
and his face was wrapped in a **cloth**.
So Jesus said to them,
"**Untie** him and let him **go**."

Now **many** of the Jews who had come to Mary
and **seen** what he had done began to **believe** in him.

[Shorter: John 11:3–7, 17, 20–27, 33b–45]

of Bethany in Judea to see Lazarus: "Rabbi, the Jews were just trying to stone you, and you want to go back there?" The disciples' apprehension is not unwarranted, since as it turns out, in reaction to this seventh and final sign of Jesus revealing himself as the Resurrection and the life, some reported to the Pharisees, and the Sanhedrin began planning to kill Jesus.

PALM SUNDAY OF THE PASSION OF THE LORD

LECTIONARY #37

GOSPEL AT THE PROCESSION   Mark 11:1–10

A reading from the holy Gospel according to Mark

When **Jesus** and his **disciples** drew near to **Jerusalem**,
   to **Bethphage** and **Bethany** at the Mount of **Olives**,
   he sent two of his **disciples** and said to them,
   "Go into the village **opposite** you,
   and immediately on **entering** it,
   you will find a **colt** tethered on which no one has ever sat.
Untie it and **bring** it here.
If anyone should **say** to you,
   'Why are you **doing** this?' reply,
   'The **Master** has need of it
   and will send it back here at **once**.'"
So they **went** off
   and **found** a colt tethered at a gate outside on the street,
   and they **untied** it.
Some of the **bystanders** said to them,
   "What are you **doing**, untying the colt?"
They **answered** them just as Jesus had **told** them to,
   and they **permitted** them to do it.
So they **brought** the colt to Jesus
   and put their **cloaks** over it.
And he **sat** on it.

Margin notes (left column)

Bethphage = BETH-fuh-jee. Practice this pronunciation.

Bethany = BETH-uh-nee, the home of Mary and Martha, was the town where Jesus most often stayed when visiting Jerusalem.

"The Mount of Olives" was the spot popularly associated with the coming of the Messiah.

These details suggest an intentional reenactment of the prophecy found in Zechariah 9:9.

Keep the tone of Jesus's dialogue straightforward and conversational. The deeper significance of what they will find and Jesus's foreknowledge of it won't become apparent till later.

Now it dawns on the disciples that Jesus had prescient knowledge of these matters.

Create the brief scene of scolding bystanders and timid disciples who parrot Jesus's words.

"And they permitted them . . . " rings with their surprise that the owners did as Jesus predicted.

Let your tone convey the mounting excitement that soon will engulf Jesus.

Today, options are given for the processional Gospel.

PROCESSION GOSPEL This reading from the Gospel according to Mark, the first-written and most succinct Gospel account, comes from the beginning of Mark's Passion narrative (Mark 11:1–10). In Mark's version of Jesus's entry into Jerusalem, he places much emphasis on the detailed, mysterious instructions Jesus gives to the disciples and the effortless way the men are able to carry them out. According to Mark, as Jesus approached the outer limits of the city of Jerusalem (Bethphage and Bethany), he was deliberate in wanting to ride into the city of Jerusalem on a colt. Mark includes this important detail because the image of Jesus riding a colt into Jerusalem fulfills the messianic prophecy of Zechariah 9:9 ("Rejoice heartily, O daughter Zion, shout for joy, O daughter Jerusalem! See, your king shall come to you; a just savior is he, Meek, and riding on an ass, on a colt, the foal of an ass.").

Zechariah was a prophet in Israel in the immediate aftermath of the return from exile in Babylon, around 520 BC. He prophesied about a coming Messiah who would embrace peace, (unlike previous kings of Judah, who behaved more like conquering warriors). Zechariah's image of the "meek" Messiah riding into Jerusalem on a colt rather than a horse and chariot captured this idea well.

Relate this scene like an on-the-scene reporter watching the remarkable events play out before you.

Stress "Those *preceding* . . . those *following*" to tell us that Jesus is now enveloped in the adoring crowd. The second "Blessed" declaration requires more energy than the first. The final "Hosanna" doesn't need to be shouted, but it does require intensity. A pause between "Hosanna" and "in the highest" will add emphasis.

Many people spread their **cloaks** on the **road**,
    and others spread leafy **branches**
    that they had cut from the **fields**.
Those preceding him as well as those following kept **crying** out:
    "**Hosanna!**
        Blessed is he who comes in the name of the **Lord!**
        Blessed is the **kingdom** of our father **David** that is to **come!**
    Hosanna in the **highest!**"

Or

The "great crowd" came for the "feast" but quickly turns its interest on Jesus.

In contrast to Mark, the events here unfold much more spontaneously.
Of course, mention of the palms needs emphasis, as does the crowd's initiative.
Let the crowd's energy mount through the three lines of praise.

Here, Jesus finds his own donkey to ride.

The prophecy from Zechariah 9:9 needs a formal, regal tone.

Contrast their lack of understanding "at first" with the awareness that comes after he was "glorified."
Without prompting, the crowd has fulfilled prophecy.

GOSPEL AT THE PROCESSION   John 12:12–16

A reading from the holy Gospel according to John

When the great **crowd** that had come to the **feast** heard
    that **Jesus** was coming to Jerusalem,
    they took **palm** branches and went out to **meet** him, and
        cried out:
    "**Hosanna!**
    Blessed is he who **comes** in the name of the Lord, the **king**
        of **Israel.**"
Jesus found an **ass** and **sat** upon it, as is written:
    Fear no more, O daughter Zion;
    see, your king comes, seated upon an ass's colt.
His disciples did not **understand** this at first,
    but when Jesus had been **glorified**
    they **remembered** that these things were **written** about him
    and that they had **done** this for him.

In highlighting the shouts from the crowds ("Hosanna! Blessed is he who comes in the name of the Lord! Blessed is the kingdom of our father David that is to come! Hosanna in the highest!"), Mark portrayed the people's heightened expectation that Jesus would usher in the coming messianic kingdom. For Mark, Jesus's entry into Jerusalem as a prince of peace was triumphal, fulfilling prophecy, and setting the stage for the dramatic events about to unfold in this historic city.

JOHN. John's account of Jesus's final entry into Jerusalem has a slightly different focus than that of the synoptic accounts. Whereas in Matthew, Mark, and Luke, the disciples are instrumental in following Jesus's directives and organizing his triumphal entry into Jerusalem, in John, a "great crowd" spontaneously reacts to the news of Jesus approaching Jerusalem, greeting him with "palm branches." And the animal on which Jesus will ride seems to appear at

the right moment without prior arrangements. John's comment, "His disciples did not understand this at first" further diminishes their role in Jesus's Jerusalem entry. John's de-emphasis on the disciples in this scene is representative of his entire Gospel account where the focus is squarely on Jesus's identity and power.

Another difference between John's treatment of the entry scene and the synoptics' treatment relates to the pacing and ordering of events. In John, the anointing at

LECTIONARY #37

READING I   Isaiah 50:4–7

Isaiah = ī-ZAY-uh

This is a grand and eloquent text that requires your best reading. It swells with gratitude for God's special call that brought both joy and great suffering to God's servant.

The servant's mission is to fill God's people, especially those "weary" from life's burdens, with expectant hope!

"Morning after morning": God is faithful and consistent, thus the servant does not falter. Speak with pride of this steely resolve to endure.

These vivid details anticipate the indignities of Christ's Passion. Having one's beard "plucked" was a grave insult at that time.

Despite suffering and opposition, the servant rejoices in God's mercy.

There is more gratitude than grit in this final line.

A reading from the Book of the Prophet Isaiah

The Lord **God** has **given** me
    a **well**-trained **tongue**,
that I might **know** how to speak to the **weary**
    a **word** that will **rouse** them.
Morning after **morning**
    he **opens** my **ear** that I may **hear**;
and I have not **rebelled**,
    have not turned **back**.
I gave my **back** to those who **beat** me,
    my **cheeks** to those who plucked my **beard**;
my **face** I did not **shield**
    from **buffets** and **spitting**.

The Lord **God** is my **help**,
    therefore I am not **disgraced**;
I have set my face like **flint**,
    knowing that I shall **not** be put to shame.

For meditation and context:

TO KEEP IN MIND
Poetry is gourmet food, eaten slowly and savored. Go slowly. Pay attention to the sounds, rhythms, and repetitions.

RESPONSORIAL PSALM   Psalm 22:8–9, 17–18, 19–20, 23–24 (2a)

R. My God, my God, why have you abandoned me?

All who see me scoff at me;
    they mock me with parted lips, they wag
        their heads:
"He relied on the LORD; let him deliver him,
    let him rescue him, if he loves him."

Indeed, many dogs surround me,
    a pack of evildoers closes in upon me;
they have pierced my hands and my feet;
    I can count all my bones.

They divide my garments among them,
    and for my vesture they cast lots.
But you, O LORD, be not far from me;
    O my help, hasten to aid me.

I will proclaim your name to my brethren;
    in the midst of the assembly I will
        praise you:
"You who fear the LORD, praise him;
    all you descendants of Jacob, give glory
        to him;
    revere him, all you descendants of Israel!"

Bethany occurs before Jesus's entry into Jerusalem. Once John's entry occurs, the focus intensifies on Jesus's identity and the question of who will believe in him. When we pick up John's version of the story again on Holy Thursday, we will find ourselves at the Last Supper, hearing of Jesus washing the feet of the disciples. This contrasts with Mark's structure, in which the suspense after the entry builds more slowly, through various events, parables, and teachings.

The Lectionary skips over two chapters of these, picking up again with the anointing at Bethany, which will be the prelude to the Passion story that we hear today. Despite these differences, certain elements remain the same. All four Gospel accounts see Jesus's entry on a colt into Jerusalem as fulfilling the prophecy of Zechariah 9:9 and present the shouts from crowds as fulfilling Psalm 118:25–26. Furthermore, each of the accounts portrays Jesus's entry as triumphal, setting the stage for the drama of Jesus's Passion.

READING I This prophecy from Isaiah is the First Reading every Palm Sunday. It is the third of four "Servant of the Lord" oracles found in Isaiah 40–55. The four Isaiah prophesies, often called messianic oracles, are Isaiah 42:1–4; 49:1–7; 50:4–11; 52:13—53:12. Each belongs to the period of Second Isaiah, the prophet of the Babylonian Exile (597–538 BC). Scholars date these servant songs to around 550 BC.

Philippians = fih-LIP-ee-uhnz

There is more gratitude than grit in this final line.

Contrast what he "was" with his willingness to set it aside (for our sakes!).

Here is what Christ did in place of clinging to his divinity: he "emptied" himself, obeyed, and accepted death—on a *cross*!

Jesus was not a player in a drama; his pain was real.

"Because of this" signals a shift in the text. Your rate and volume climb to match the energy of these lines.

No name is holier than this name. Paul is citing Isaiah 45:23.

The song rises to a crescendo on "Jesus Christ is Lord." The final line can be delivered in a quieter tone and with measured cadence: "to the glory / of God the Father."

READING II   Philippians 2:6–11

A reading from the Letter of Saint Paul to the Philippians

Christ **Jesus**, though he was in the form of **God**,
  did **not** regard **equality** with God
  something to be **grasped**.
Rather, he **emptied** himself,
  taking the form of a **slave**,
  coming in **human** likeness;
  and found human in **appearance**,
  he **humbled** himself,
  becoming **obedient** to the point of **death**,
  even death on a **cross**.
Because of this, God greatly **exalted** him
  and **bestowed** on him the **name**
  which is above **every** name,
  that at the name of **Jesus**
  every **knee** should bend,
  of those in **heaven** and on **earth** and **under** the earth,
  and every **tongue confess** that
  Jesus **Christ** is **Lord**,
  to the **glory** of God the **Father**.

GOSPEL   MARK 14:1—15:47

The Passion of our Lord Jesus Christ according to Matthew

The **Passover** and the Feast of Unleavened **Bread**
  were to take place in two days' **time**.
So the chief **priests** and the **scribes** were seeking a way
  to **arrest** him by **treachery** and put him to **death**.
They said, "**Not** during the **festival**,
  for fear that there may be a **riot** among the people."

The leaders want to do away with Jesus *before* the Passover feast. Their minds are made up and their hearts are steeled.

Jesus still has much support among the crowds.

A feature worth pondering in the four songs of the suffering servant is the different voices articulating the song. Whereas in the first oracle, Isaiah 42:1–4, God himself speaks of *Israel* as the "servant" to the whole world, in the second and the third oracle (today's reading), the prophet ("Second Isaiah") speaks about himself, his call to bring his message to distant peoples, and how he has been targeted for persecution in doing so. The final servant song, Isaiah 52:13—53:12, heard as the first

reading every Good Friday, is actually the community's testimony about Second Isaiah, bearing witness to his suffering and their hope.

As Mark's Passion narrative unfolds, it is easy to understand how the early Christians came to see that this third suffering servant oracle was fulfilled in the Passion and Death of Jesus. As with Second Isaiah before him, even though Jesus suffered an agonizing death, he was "not disgraced" nor was he "put to shame." Rather, Jesus faced his destiny with the sure belief that "the Lord God is my help."

READING II Traditionally, scholars have dated the writing of Paul's Letter to the Philippians to his imprisonment in Rome, about the year AD 60. If this is the case, then Philippians would have been one of Paul's final letters.

Paul appears to have had a personal and long-lasting relationship with the Christian congregation in Philippi. According to Luke, who wrote both a Gospel account and the Acts of the Apostles as a two-part narrative chronicling the first seventy years of the early Church, Paul established a

Bethany (BETH-uh-nee) is also the home of Mary, Martha, and Lazarus. This tender scene and the woman's ministrations contrast mightily with his later treatment. Don't rush.

The solicitude for Jesus turns to controversy; the peaceful scene is already shattered.

Are they angered by the "waste" or her access to the Lord?

Don't hold back on Jesus's words in defense of the woman. She alone has anticipated his time of greatest need.

In all the New Testament, future glory is promised to no one other than Jesus's mother, Mary, and this woman.

Mention of Judas immediately sounds a somber note. Slow your pace, especially when you mention his being "one of the Twelve."

Let the line suggest that Judas has sealed his fate.

Don't rush these details.

When he was in Bethany reclining at table
    in the house of **Simon** the **leper**,
    a **woman** came with an alabaster jar of perfumed **oil**,
        costly genuine **spikenard**.
She **broke** the alabaster jar and **poured** it on his **head**.
There were some who were **indignant**.
"Why has there been this **waste** of perfumed **oil**?
It could have been **sold** for more than three **hundred** days' wages
    and the money given to the **poor**."
They were **infuriated** with her.
Jesus said, "Let her **alone**.
Why do you make **trouble** for her?
She has done a **good** thing for me.
The **poor** you will **always** have with you,
    and whenever you **wish** you can do **good** to them,
    but you will **not** always have **me**.
She has done what she **could**.
She has **anticipated** anointing my body for **burial**.
Amen, I **say** to you,
    wherever the **gospel** is **proclaimed** to the whole **world**,
    what she has **done** will be told in **memory** of her."

Then Judas **Iscariot**, one of the **Twelve**,
    went off to the chief **priests** to hand him **over** to them.
When they heard him they were **pleased**
        and promised to pay him **money**.
Then he looked for an **opportunity** to hand him over.

On the **first** day of the Feast of Unleavened **Bread**,
    when they sacrificed the Passover **lamb**,
    his **disciples** said to him,
    "Where do you want us to go
    and **prepare** for you to eat the **Passover**?"

community of Gentile believers in Philippi during his second missionary journey, likely around AD 49 or 50 (Acts 16:11–12). This would have made the Philippians one of Paul's first congregations established in Macedonia. If all of these dates are accurate, by the time Paul wrote his letter to the Philippians in AD 60, the church in Philippi would have been about ten years old.

In contrast to his relationship with some other congregations (for example, the Gentile churches of Galatia), Paul and the Philippians shared a bond of trust and "partnership" (1:5) such that, even after ten years, Paul could refer to his original founding community as "partners with me . . . in the defense and confirmation of the gospel" (1:7). In this regard, Paul's Letter to the Philippians is commonly referred to as Paul's "letter of joy." The word "joy" or "rejoice" (in Greek, *chara* or *chairō*) appears throughout the letter (1:4, 5, 18, 25: 2:2, 17, 28, 29; 3:1; 4:1, 4, 10), and Paul is grateful for their support of his ministry from the very beginning (4:15).

The reading for today is the well-known Christological hymn of Philippians 2:6–11. Read in the context of Palm Sunday, the hymn presents to us how some of the first generation of Christians defined Christ in light of the Cross. Scholars have debated for nearly two centuries who wrote the hymn of Philippians 2:6–11. Was it Paul's own composition, or was it a preexisting text that Paul inserted into the letter? Other New Testament writers appear to

As with the "colt," Jesus speaks confidently, with prescient knowledge, of the events that will unfold.

He sent two of his disciples and said to them,
    "Go into the **city** and a man will **meet** you,
    carrying a jar of **water**.
Follow him.
Wherever he **enters**, say to the **master** of the house,
    'The **Teacher** says, "Where is my **guest** room
    where I may eat the Passover with my **disciples**?"'
Then he will show you a large **upper** room **furnished** and **ready**.
Make the preparations for us **there**."
The disciples then **went** off, **entered** the city,
    and **found** it just as he had **told** them;
    and they **prepared** the Passover.

Your tone can tell us the disciples delighted in finding things as Jesus stated and that they were eager to *minister* to him through attending to these details.

"Evening" shifts the tone to a more philosophical mood. Jesus is with his special "Twelve."

Typical of Mark, few words set the scene before we are hit with the shocking news of a traitor in their midst.

Their concern is for themselves, not for him.

When it was **evening**, he came with the **Twelve**.
And as they reclined at **table** and were **eating**, Jesus said,
    "**Amen**, I say to you, **one** of you will **betray** me,
    one who is **eating** with me."
They began to be **distressed** and to **say** to him, one by one,
    "**Surely** it is not **I**?"
He said to them,
    "One of the **Twelve**, the one who **dips** with me
        into the **dish**.

In John, Jesus dips the bread and gives it to Judas, something a host would do for an *honored* guest.

For the Son of Man indeed **goes**, as it is **written** of him,
    but **woe** to that man by **whom** the Son of Man is betrayed.
It would be **better** for that man if he had never been **born**."

Jesus speaks no harder words than these of friend or enemy.

The mood shifts suddenly again. Don't speak these words as ritual language, but as loving, compelling conversation with intimate friends.

While they were **eating**,
    he took **bread**, said the **blessing**,
    broke it, and **gave** it to them, and said,
    "**Take** it; this is my **body**."
Then he took a **cup**, gave **thanks**, and **gave** it to them,
    and they all **drank** from it.
He said to them,
    "This is my **blood** of the **covenant**,
    which will be **shed** for **many**.

"Many" is expansive and inclusive, not a restrictive or limiting word.

have added preexisting texts to their writing (see, for example, Colossians 1:15–20; John 1:1–4; 1 Timothy 3:16; 2 Timothy 2:11–13; Ephesians 5:14). So apparently it was a common practice. These texts, along with Philippians 2:5–11, date to the oral period of the New Testament, AD 30–70. It appears that Paul and other New Testament writers strategically placed these texts into their writing to support their theology. Paul may have done so with 2:6–11. It flows well within the context of his appeal to the Philippians for unity and humility.

It is likely that verse 5, immediately preceding today's reading ("Have among yourselves the same attitude that is also yours in Christ Jesus") was written by Paul to serve as an introduction and transition to the hymn itself. Paul hopes the Philippian Christians will embrace Jesus's "attitude" of humility and, in doing so, receive a similar exaltation (reward) from God as did Jesus.

The six-verse hymn is divided equally between Jesus's humility and obedience (verses 6-8) and the resulting exaltation of Jesus by God (verses 9-11). The text's opening comment that Jesus "did not regard

equality with God something to be grasped" may be a reference to Adam who attempted to do so in the Garden of Eden (Genesis 3:5-6). The first human's arrogance and disobedience is sharply contrasted here with Christ's humility. In other letters, Paul is fond of drawing upon the Adam-Christ comparison/contrast (see, for example, Romans 5:12–21; 1 Corinthians 15:21–28, 42–49). The image of Jesus as a "slave" speaks to Jesus's unconditional obedience to God and the humiliating fate of death by crucifixion, an agonizing end awaiting all

For a moment, Jesus somersaults over the Passion and anticipates the glory of the Kingdom.

Jesus goes, singing, toward his Death.

They are now at the Mount of Olives. Jesus quotes Zechariah 13:7 not to shame or chastise but to *prepare* them.

Peter never feigns; he's convinced he won't let Jesus down.

Another hard truth for Jesus to share, but again he does it to prepare Peter for his great failing.

Peter is affronted and probably hurt, yet his avowal is sincere and full of love.

In the garden, Jesus struggles mightily, but his grief is contained and muted.

Make sure we hear who his intimates are.

His dark hour has begun. He *needs* the presence and support of his friends.

Amen, I say to you,
    I shall not **drink** again the fruit of the **vine**
    until the day when I drink it **new** in the kingdom of **God**."
Then, after singing a **hymn**,
    they went out to the Mount of **Olives**.

Then Jesus said to them,
    "**All** of you will have your **faith** shaken, for it is **written**:
        *I will **strike** the shepherd,*
            *and the **sheep** will be **dispersed**.*
But after I have been **raised** up,
    I shall go before you to **Galilee**."
Peter said to him,
    "Even though **all** should have their faith **shaken**,
    mine will **not** be."
Then Jesus said to him,
    "**Amen**, I say to you,
    this very **night** before the cock crows **twice**
    you will **deny** me **three** times."
But he **vehemently** replied,
    "Even though I should have to **die** with you,
    I will not **deny** you."
And they **all** spoke similarly.

Then they came to a place named **Gethsemane**,
    and he said to his disciples,
    "**Sit** here while I **pray**."
He took with him **Peter**, **James**, and **John**,
    and began to be **troubled** and **distressed**.
Then he **said** to them, "My soul is **sorrowful** even to **death**.
Remain here and keep **watch**."

---

slaves found guilty of capital offenses in the Roman Empire.

Unlike Adam, who was banned from the garden, or slaves, whose bodies were left to decay on the cross, Jesus was exalted by God because he submitted to God's will. With Jesus's Resurrection and Ascension into heaven, all in the created order ("those in heaven and on earth and under the earth") "confess that Jesus Christ is Lord." The hymn concludes where it began, with a focus on God. The twofold action of Jesus's humiliation and exaltation ultimately point us to "the glory of God the Father."

GOSPEL Well over a century ago, the German biblical scholar Martin Kähler referred to the Gospel according to Mark as "a passion narrative with an extended introduction." This description has stuck in the minds of subsequent scholars because it so aptly fits Mark's story line. The central event for Mark is the Passion, or suffering and Death, of Jesus. From the very beginning of his Gospel account, Mark places Jesus's impending Death in the minds of his readers. We are informed that after Jesus healed a man's withered hand, "the Pharisees went out immediately and took counsel with the Herodians against him to put him to death" (Mark 3:6).

Mark's focus on Jesus's suffering and Death creates the fundamental portrait of Jesus as the suffering Messiah. Today, scholars recognize that each Gospel writer paints a distinctive picture of Jesus. Matthew presents Jesus as the new Moses.

Note the words marked for stress: "if it were *possible . . . all* things are possible." He truly desires to escape this fate.

He **advanced** a little and **fell** to the ground and **prayed**
    that if it were **possible** the hour might **pass** by him;
    he said, "**Abba**, **Father**, **all** things are possible to **you**.
Take this cup **away** from me,
    but not what **I** will but what **you** will."
When he **returned** he found them **asleep**.

His disappointment is real and poignant. Like an elder brother, Jesus warns them for their own good, not out of anger.

He said to **Peter**, "**Simon**, are you **asleep**?
Could you not keep **watch** for one **hour**?
Watch and **pray** that you may not undergo the **test**.
The **spirit** is **willing** but the **flesh** is **weak**."
Withdrawing **again**, he **prayed**, saying the same **thing**.

Mark offers a weak excuse for the disciples' lack of vigilance.

Then he **returned** once more and found them **asleep**,
    for they could not keep their **eyes** open
    and did not know what to **answer** him.

Still marveling at their lack of discipline, Jesus is now resolved and ready to move toward his destiny.

He returned a **third** time and said to them,
    "Are you **still** sleeping and taking your rest?
It is **enough**. The hour has **come**.
Behold, the Son of Man is to be handed **over** to **sinners**.
Get **up**, let us **go**.
See, my **betrayer** is at hand."

Jesus doesn't shy from identifying Judas by his sinister role.

Judas is intentionally identified as one of the "Twelve."

Then, while he was still **speaking**,
    Judas, one of the Twelve, **arrived**,
    accompanied by a **crowd** with **swords** and **clubs**
    who had come from the chief **priests**,
    the **scribes**, and the **elders**.
His betrayer had arranged a **signal** with them, saying,
    "The man I shall **kiss** is the one;
    arrest him and lead him away **securely**."

Quote Judas speaking to the priests with bravado.

Pause briefly before and after "Rabbi."

He came and **immediately** went over to him and said,
    "**Rabbi**." And he **kissed** him.
At this they laid **hands** on him and **arrested** him.

In Luke, Jesus is the universal Savior. For John, Jesus is the Word made flesh. These various images of Jesus reflect the needs and interests of the different communities for whom the authors wrote.

The full Passion narrative in Mark runs from 14:1—16:8, which begins with the chief priests and scribes plotting to put Jesus to death (14:1–2) and concludes with the report of the empty tomb (16:1–8). Today's reading, however, stops after Jesus

is laid in the tomb. Mark places the Passion of Jesus within the Jewish feast days of Passover and Unleavened Bread. These days commemorated the defining moments in Israel's history and identity, when God led Israel out of Egyptian slavery under Moses's leadership. (See Exodus 12:3–20 and Deuteronomy 16:1–8.) For Mark, that setting provides an opportunity to wield one of his favorite literary devices—irony. In fact, irony will be the most significant literary device driving the story line of Jesus's suffering and Death.

Sometimes, Mark's irony is subtle, as with this opening to the Passion narrative. The very reason for the Jewish celebration, commemorating God's intervention in history to save Israel, is now completely missed by the religious leaders of Jerusalem. They fail to see that in Jesus, God once again comes to save Israel. Other times in Mark, the irony is dramatic, as when the very same chief priests and scribes mock Jesus as he is dying on the cross, saying, "He saved others; he cannot save himself."

The "bystander" reacts with anger and violence. Let your tone convey his fury.

Jesus holds a mirror up to the leaders and crowd, forcing them to face their cowardice and hypocrisy.

Those who "left" were his disciples, not the crowd.

The young man who runs off naked (abandons him) is unique to Mark.

Those most threatened by Jesus are gathering to judge him.

Peter is lagging behind, hoping to fade into the crowd. Let your tone suggest his desire to be invisible.

Sanhedrin = san-HEE-druhn

As narrator, you are a believer relating the history of your beloved protagonist. Here you can enjoy their futile efforts to make the tales "agree."

The high priest is thwarted in his effort to provoke Jesus into speaking.

Feeling himself affronted, the high priest speaks angrily.

One of the **bystanders** drew his **sword**,
    struck the high priest's **servant**, and cut off his **ear**.
Jesus said to them in **reply**,
    "Have you come out as against a **robber**,
    with **swords** and **clubs**, to **seize** me?
Day after day I was with you **teaching** in the **temple** area,
    yet you did not **arrest** me;
    but that the Scriptures may be **fulfilled**."
And they all **left** him and **fled**.
Now a young **man** followed him
    wearing nothing but a linen **cloth** about his body.
They **seized** him,
    but he left the cloth **behind** and ran off **naked**.

They led **Jesus** away to the high **priest**,
    and all the **chief** priests and the **elders** and the **scribes**
        came **together**.
Peter followed him at a **distance** into the high priest's **courtyard**
    and was seated with the **guards**, **warming** himself at the **fire**.
The chief **priests** and the entire **Sanhedrin**
    kept trying to obtain **testimony** against Jesus
    in order to put him to **death**, but they found **none**.
Many gave **false** witness against him,
    but their testimony did not **agree**.
Some took the **stand** and testified **falsely** against him,
    alleging, "We **heard** him say,
    'I will **destroy** this **temple** made with **hands**
    and within **three days** I will build **another**
    not made with hands.'"
Even **so** their testimony did not **agree**.
The **high** priest rose before the assembly and **questioned** Jesus,
    saying, "Have you no **answer**?
What are these men **testifying** against you?"
But he was **silent** and answered **nothing**.
Again the high priest asked him and **said** to him,
    "Are you the **Christ**, the son of the **Bessed** One?"

Let the Messiah, the King of Israel, come down from the cross that we may see and believe" (Mark 15:31b–32). Here again, the Jewish religious leaders of Jerusalem fail to grasp that it is *because* of his suffering and Death on the Cross that Jesus is the Messiah, the King of Israel.

The shorter version of the Gospel reading for today is Mark 15:1–39, excluding such events as the betrayal of Judas (14:10–11), the agony in the garden (14:32–42), Jesus

on trial before the Sanhedrin (14:53–65), and Peter's denial of Jesus (14:66–72). One of the most dramatic ironies in Mark's Passion account occurs during Jesus's trial before the Sanhedrin, and it is closely connected to one of Mark's more enigmatic features: the secrecy motif.

According to Mark, Jesus spoke to the Twelve about "the mystery of the kingdom of God" (4:11), explaining only to them, in private, about the meaning of his publicly spoken parables (4:34). Furthermore, Jesus

commands silence about his activities and his identity: to the disciples (5:43; 8:30; 9:9), the demons (1:34; 3:12), even those whom he healed (1:44; 7:36; 8:26). Jesus's "secret" identity as the Messiah and Son of God comes to a climactic point when the high priest asks Jesus directly at his trial: "Are you the Messiah, the son of the Blessed One?" For the first time in Mark's narrative, Jesus openly declares his true identity with the words, "I am." Ironically, it is Jesus's

Jesus responds confidently with the divine "I am." But this response seals his fate.

Jesus has provided the blasphemy they need to indict him. The high priest makes a great show of his indignation.

Use the verbs "condemned," "spit," blindfolded," "struck," "prophesy" to suggest the fury with which they attacked this supposed blasphemer who has finally exposed himself.

In the garden, Peter too is put on trial—and becomes his own judge and jury.

The maid is at first motivated by simple curiosity.

Peter's denial is deliberate and strongly stated.

Speak slowly and with significance of the "cock" crowing.

The maid may believe she was lied to and insists on outing Peter.

The bystanders have joined the cause of exposing Peter; they press him.

Peter has no defense left but panicked cursing.

Then Jesus answered, "I **am**;
  and 'you will **see** the Son of Man
    seated at the **right** hand of the **Power**
    and **coming** with the **clouds** of **heaven**.'"
At **that** the high priest **tore** his garments and said,
  "What further **need** have we of **witnesses**?
You have **heard** the blasphemy.
What do you **think**?"
They all **condemned** him as deserving to **die**.
Some began to **spit** on him.
They **blindfolded** him and **struck** him and **said** to him,
    "**Prophesy**!"
And the **guards** greeted him with **blows**.

 While **Peter** was below in the **courtyard**,
  one of the high priest's **maids** came along.
Seeing Peter **warming** himself,
  she looked **intently** at him and said,
  "You **too** were with the Nazarene, **Jesus**."
But he **denied** it saying,
  "I neither **know** nor **understand** what you are talking about."
So he went out into the **outer** court.
Then the **cock** crowed.
The maid **saw** him and began **again** to say to the **bystanders**,
  "This man is **one** of them."
Once **again** he denied it.
A little **later** the **bystanders** said to Peter once more,
  "**Surely** you are one of them; for you too are a **Galilean**."
He began to **curse** and to **swear**,
  "I do not **know** this man about whom you are talking."
And **immediately** a cock **crowed** a **second** time.

revelation of his divinity to the Jewish leaders that seals his fate: "At that the high priest tore his garments and said, 'What further need have we of witnesses? You have heard the blasphemy. What do you think?' They all condemned him as deserving to die."

Mark injects irony at other moments in the story as well. In Pilate's attempt at leniency for Jesus, he offers the crowds the opportunity to release one prisoner (a custom by which the Roman Empire acknowledged the Jewish feast day of Passover and unleavened bread.) Rather than choose Jesus, the crowds shout for the release of a prisoner named Barabbas. But ironically, the Aramaic name *Bar-abbas* means, "son of the father." And in the most climactic and revealing moment of the story, the Roman centurion, upon seeing that Jesus "breathed his last" on the Cross and died, said, "Truly this man was the Son of God!" In Mark's ironic vision, it is a Gentile soldier who makes this critical connection.

For Mark, Jesus's true identity as the Messiah and the Son of God is most truly recognized in his suffering and Death. In fact, in Mark's view, Jesus is best understood as the *suffering* Messiah. In creating the first written narrative on the life of Jesus, Mark brilliantly weaves together a received tradition largely in oral form and creates a written theological document that both faithfully hands on what he receives and offers a context for understanding Jesus in light of the Cross.

Deliver these lines aware of the heaviness in Peter's heart. The emotion is underplayed; as if remembering tears, not shedding them.

Then Peter **remembered** the word that Jesus had **said** to him,
"Before the cock crows **twice** you will deny me **three** times."
He broke **down** and **wept**.

This brief episode suggests the desire of the priests to be done with this business.

As soon as **morning** came,
the chief **priests** with the **elders** and the **scribes**,
that is, the whole **Sanhedrin**, held a **council**.
They **bound** Jesus, led him **away**, and handed him **over** to **Pilate**.
Pilate **questioned** him,
"Are you the **king** of the **Jews**?"

Jesus is a problem prisoner who opens no doors for Pilate to acquit him.

He said to him in reply, "**You** say so."
The chief priests accused him of **many** things.
Again Pilate questioned him,
"Have you no **answer**?
See how many things they **accuse** you of."

Is it Jesus's silence or his confidence that amazes Pilate?

Jesus gave him no further **answer**, so that Pilate was **amazed**.

Speak hopefully of the feast, as if there might be a chance things will work out after all.

Now on the occasion of the **feast** he used to **release** to them
one **prisoner** whom they **requested**.
A man called **Barabbas** was then in prison
along with the **rebels** who had committed **murder**
in a **rebellion**.
The crowd came forward and began to **ask** him
to do for them as he was **accustomed**.
Pilate **answered**,
"Do you want me to **release** to you the **king** of the **Jews**?"

Pilate is looking for a way out. Convey his sympathy in the narration that follows.

For he **knew** that it was out of **envy**
that the chief priests had handed him **over**.
But the chief priests **stirred** up the crowd
to have him release **Barabbas** for them **instead**.

TO KEEP IN MIND
Dialogue imitates real conversation, so it often moves faster than the rest of the passage.

Pilate persists in his effort, despite the danger to himself.

Yet Pilate can't commandeer his authority to take decisive action.

His patience is spent. His tone suggests, "Fine, have it your way!"

Now comes the humiliation. Read without emotion but with steely awareness of the indignities inflicted upon the Lord of life.

Pilate **again** said to them in reply,
  "Then what do you want me to do
  with the man you call the **king** of the **Jews**?"
They **shouted** again, "**Crucify** him."
Pilate said to them, "**Why**? What **evil** has he done?"
They only shouted the **louder**, "**Crucify** him."
So Pilate, wishing to **satisfy** the crowd,
  released **Barabbas** to them and, after he had Jesus **scourged**,
  handed him over to be **crucified**.

The **soldiers** led him away inside the **palace**,
  that is, the **praetorium**, and **assembled** the whole **cohort**.
They **clothed** him in **purple** and,
  weaving a crown of **thorns**, **placed** it on him.
They began to **salute** him with, "**Hail**, King of the Jews!"
  and kept **striking** his head with a **reed** and **spitting** upon him.
They **knelt** before him in **homage**.
And when they had **mocked** him,
  they **stripped** him of the purple cloak,
  dressed him in his **own** clothes,
  and led him out to **crucify** him.

A slow, measured delivery that distinguishes the hostile actions ("mocked," "stripped," "dressed") will reveal the scorn heaped upon Jesus.
Speak of Simon as someone known and respected.
Cyrenian = si-REE-nee-uhn
Rufus = ROO-fuhs
Simon's forced service is more privilege than burden.
Golgotha = GAWL-guh-thuh

(16) They **pressed** into service a **passer-by**, **Simon**,
  a **Cyrenian**, who was coming in from the **country**,
  the father of **Alexander** and **Rufus**,
  to carry his **cross**.

They **brought** him to the place of **Golgotha**
  —which is translated **Place** of the **Skull**—.
They gave him **wine** drugged with **myrrh**,
  but he did not **take** it.
Then they **crucified** him and divided his **garments**
  by casting **lots** for them to see what each should **take**.
It was **nine** o'clock in the **morning** when they **crucified** him.

Pause after "crucified him" and then let the casting of lots contrast with the horror of his agony.

Speak the inscription in the mocking tone of the soldiers.

Jesus is treated like just one more troublesome revolutionary.

Jesus is mocked by three groups of detractors: *bystanders*, *scribes,* and *priests*, and the two *insurgents* who hang alongside him. Jesus's accusers feel vindicated in their disdain of him. They are emboldened by his defenselessness.

There is no "good thief" in this telling. Share this final detail with regret.

The Aramaic can be delivered with pained emotion, but the translation should be rendered in hushed and neutral tones.

The bystanders are thick and derisive.

Pause before you speak this line, and then, with reverence and without any show of emotion, announce Jesus's death.

The torn veil suggests the greater access to God won for us by Christ's Death.

Centurion = sen-TOOR-ee-uhn

Speak the centurion's declaration simply and sincerely.

The **inscription** of the **charge** against him read,
    "The **King** of the **Jews**."
With him they crucified two **revolutionaries**,
    one on his **right** and one on his **left**.
Those passing by **reviled** him,
    shaking their **heads** and **saying**,
    "**Aha**! You who would destroy the temple
    and **rebuild** it in three **days**,
    save yourself by coming **down** from the cross."
Likewise the chief **priests**, with the **scribes**,
    mocked him among themselves and said,
    "He saved **others**; he cannot save **himself**.
Let the **Christ**, the King of **Israel**,
    come down now from the cross
    that we may **see** and **believe**."
Those who were **crucified** with him **also** kept abusing him.

At **noon darkness** came over the whole land
    until **three** in the afternoon.
And at three o'clock Jesus cried out in **a loud** voice,
    "*Eloi, Eloi, lema sabachthani?*"
    which is **translated**,
    "My **God**, my **God**, **why** have you **forsaken** me?"
Some of the bystanders who **heard** it said,
    "**Look**, he is calling **Elijah**."
One of them **ran**, soaked a **sponge** with **wine**, put it on a **reed**
    and **gave** it to him to drink saying,
    "**Wait**, let us **see** if Elijah comes to take him down."
Jesus gave a loud **cry** and breathed his **last**.

    [Here all kneel and pause for a short time.]

The **veil** of the **sanctuary** was torn in **two** from top to **bottom**.
When the **centurion** who stood **facing** him
    saw how he breathed his last he said,
    "**Truly** this man was the Son of **God**!"
There were also **women** looking on from a **distance**.

Mention the women with affection and familiarity. They have remained while the men dispersed.

Among them were Mary **Magdalene**,
  Mary the mother of the younger **James** and of **Joses**,
    and **Salome**.
These women had **followed** him when he was in **Galilee**
  and **ministered** to him.
There were also many **other** women
  who had come up with him to **Jerusalem**.

Joseph is another of the heroes of this sad history. Speak of him with respect.

When it was already **evening**,
  since it was the day of **preparation**,
  the day before the **sabbath**, **Joseph** of **Arimathea**,
  a **distinguished** member of the **council**,
  who was **himself** awaiting the kingdom of **God**,
  came and **courageously** went to **Pilate**
  and **asked** for the body of **Jesus**.

His courage should evoke a tone of admiration.

Only Mark's account speaks of Pilate's *surprise*.

Stress Pilate's desire for confirmation of Jesus's Death.

Pilate was **amazed** that he was already **dead**.
He summoned the **centurion**
  and **asked** him if Jesus had already died.
And when he **learned** of it from the **centurion**,
  he **gave** the body to Joseph.
Having bought a linen **cloth**, he took him **down**,
  wrapped him in the linen cloth,
  and laid him in a **tomb** that had been hewn out of the **rock**.
Then he rolled a **stone** against the **entrance** to the tomb.

Joseph is granted the solemn privilege of ministering to the lifeless body of the Lord.

Joses = JOH-sez. Again, these are familiar and beloved names. Speak of them, and of their vigil, with a note of hope. ("spat . . . clay . . . saliva . . . smeared . . . ") add texture to the story. Don't waste them.

Mary **Magdalene** and Mary the mother of **Joses**
  watched where he was **laid**.

[Shorter: Mark 15:1–39]

TO KEEP IN MIND
Eye contact connects you with those to whom you minister. Look at the assembly during the middle and at the end of every thought or sentence.

THURSDAY OF HOLY WEEK (HOLY THURSDAY): EVENING MASS OF THE LORD'S SUPPER

LECTIONARY #39

READING I   Exodus 12:1–8, 11–14

A reading from the Book of Exodus

The **Lord** said to **Moses** and **Aaron** in the land of **Egypt**,
  "This **month** shall stand at the **head** of your **calendar**;
  you shall reckon it the **first** month of the year.
Tell the whole **community** of **Israel**:
  On the **tenth** of this month every one of your families
  must procure for itself a **lamb**, one apiece for each **household**.
If a family is too **small** for a whole lamb,
  it shall **join** the **nearest** household in procuring one
  and shall **share** in the lamb
  in **proportion** to the number of persons who **partake** of it.
The lamb must be a year-old **male** and without **blemish**.
You may **take** it from either the **sheep** or the **goats**.
You shall **keep** it until the **fourteenth** day of this month,
  and **then**, with the whole assembly of Israel **present**,
  it shall be **slaughtered** during the evening **twilight**.
They shall take some of its **blood**
  and apply it to the two **doorposts** and the **lintel**
  of every **house** in which they **partake** of the lamb.
That same **night** they shall **eat** its roasted **flesh**
  with **unleavened** bread and bitter **herbs**.

Exodus = EK-suh-duhs

While still in captivity, Israel receives these ritual instructions. Right worship is never out of season for God's people.

These ceremonial details may seem less than vital, but in the life of Israel this *night* was like no other night and this *meal* like no other meal.

It is God's authoritative voice that speaks these commands.

Note that God does not intend for the requirements of the ritual to burden the needy; rather, they help form community.

For your reading, the specifics are less essential than communicating God's providence and the people's willing compliance. So maintain a brisk pacing.

Again, the ritual forms community.

Here you should slow your delivery: these details anticipate the blood of the messianic lamb and relate more directly to tonight's celebration.

READING I In this First Reading from the twelfth chapter of Exodus, we hear God instructing Moses and his brother Aaron on how the people of Israel are to observe the Passover Meal. Why are the instructions so detailed and solemn? This is a ritual meal with an important backstory. The first twelve chapters in the Book of Exodus introduce the oppression of Israel under Egyptian rule (Exodus 1), the birth, youth, and call of Moses (Exodus 2–3), Moses's preparation for his initial encounters with the Pharaoh of Egypt (Exodus 4–6), and the series of plagues intended to coerce the Egyptian Pharaoh into releasing the Israelites he had enslaved (Exodus 7–12). The tenth and final plague was the death of the firstborn of all the people of Egypt, including the firstborn male animals. Even Pharaoh's own firstborn son was not to be spared.

Following the instructions for the Passover meal was an essential preparation that would ensure the people's survival through the tenth plague that God was delivering upon Egypt. These preparations involved the sacrifice of a lamb, with the blood of the lamb marking the two doorstops and the lintel. The blood of the slaughtered lamb that marked the doorposts was key to Israel's rescue from Egypt: "The blood will mark the houses where you are. Seeing the blood, I will *pass over* you; thus when I strike the land of Egypt, no destructive blow will come upon you."

The death of the firstborn in all of Egypt ultimately led to Israel's freedom from slavery. Neither the Pharaoh of Egypt nor the gods of Egypt could stop the God of Israel. This event set in motion Israel's journey toward freedom in the promised land.

These are remarkable details that underscore the need for vigilance and urgency. Such preparedness should characterize our longing for the return of the Messiah.

This is a solemn declaration.

These stark images communicate God's sovereign authority and God's vigilance on behalf of his people.

"But the blood" requires that you slow down. Speak of God's reaction to seeing the blood on the doorposts with compassion.

This feast is celebrated per divine command. Pause before this last sentence; establish eye contact and then deliver God's instruction.

"This is **how** you are to **eat** it:
    with your loins **girt**, **sandals** on your feet and your **staff**
      in **hand**,
    you shall eat like those who are in **flight**.
It is the **Passover** of the LORD.
For on this **same** night I will go through **Egypt**,
    striking down every **firstborn** of the land, both **man** and **beast**,
    and executing **judgment** on all the **gods** of Egypt—**I**, the LORD!
But the **blood** will mark the houses where **you** are.
Seeing the blood, I will pass **over** you;
    thus, when I **strike** the land of Egypt,
    no destructive blow will come upon **you**.

"**This** day shall be a **memorial feast** for you,
    which all your generations shall **celebrate**
    with **pilgrimage** to the LORD, as a **perpetual** institution."

For meditation and context:

RESPONSORIAL PSALM   Psalm 116:12–13, 15–16bc, 17–18
(1 Corinthians 10:16)

R. Our blessing-cup is a communion with the Blood of Christ.

How shall I make a return to the LORD
  for all the good he has done for me?
The cup of salvation I will take up,
  and I will call upon the name of the LORD.

Precious in the eyes of the LORD
  is the death of his faithful ones.
I am your servant, the son of your handmaid;
  you have loosed my bonds.

To you will I offer sacrifice of thanksgiving,
  and I will call upon the name of the LORD.
My vows to the LORD I will pay
  in the presence of all his people.

TO KEEP IN MIND
Ritardando: refers to the practice, common in music, of becoming gradually slower and expanding the words as you approach the end of a piece. Many readings end this way—with a decreased rate but increased intensity.

The commemoration of Passover recalls God's historic intervention in Israel's history, an event scholars date to around the year 1250 BC. We listen as God instructs our ancestors in faith to "tell the whole community of Israel" how to prepare for this unprecedented moment in their history. Because the people followed God's precepts, the ritual of Passover became over time a "memorial feast" and a "perpetual institution" defining the nation of Israel. And we participate in the memorial feast by retelling the story that would shape Jesus and continue to form his followers.

READING II Embedded within his First Letter to the Corinthians is a tradition that Paul "received from the Lord" and now "handed on" to the congregation of believers in Corinth. Many Christians today are familiar with this tradition (commonly referred to as the institution of the Eucharist) from the Gospel narratives. Matthew, Mark, and Luke each present these words of Jesus within the context of the "Last Supper" that Jesus shared with his disciples (compare Matthew 26:26–29; Mark 14:22–25; Luke 22:14–20). The synoptic Gospel writers composed

their accounts between AD 70 and 90. Paul wrote First Corinthians in the spring of AD 55. From a historical perspective, this means that the tradition of the institution of the Eucharist is first recorded by Paul decades earlier than the Gospel writers, and a mere twenty years after the Death and Resurrection of Jesus. In other words, Paul's First Letter to the Corinthians contains the New Testament's earliest attestation of the institution of the Eucharist at the Last Supper.

Paul, however, does not include this received tradition within a vacuum. He is

Corinthians = kohr-IN-thee-uhnz

The text begins *in media res*, so start slowly as if confiding a great secret to beloved companions. Don't rush the separate moments: "took . . . given thanks . . . broke."

Only Paul and Luke record Jesus's command to "do this." Speak it less as an order and more as a plea from Jesus—despite being physically absent—to remain with the community.

"In the same way" does not signal a redundancy, but another opportunity to proclaim Christ's love outpoured. "Do this" reiterates the desire to be one with the gathered believers.

The final sentence declares Paul's great insight. Begin with clear eye contact and then, simply and from memory, speak directly to your assembly.

John's "Eucharist" is the washing of feet. Proclaim this Gospel with tenderness, remembering that the object lesson Jesus teaches culminates a *habitual* ministry of service that climaxes in this night's dramatic action.

Jesus's awareness of the "hour" is an important theme in John.

Jesus's love of "his own" contrasts with the malice of the betrayer who has succumbed to the influence of the "devil."

Iscariot = ih-SKAYR-ee-uht

Again, Jesus's awareness is highlighted.

Imagine the disciples' resistance to Jesus's service and use his words (paying careful attention to the verbs) to refute their objections and discomfort.

READING II   1 Corinthians 11:23–26

reading from the first Letter of Saint Paul to the Corinthians

Brothers and sisters:
I **received** from the Lord what I also handed on to **you**,
    that the Lord **Jesus**, on the **night** he was handed **over**,
    took **bread**, and, after he had given **thanks**,
    broke it and said, "This is my **body** that is for **you**.
Do this in **remembrance** of me."
In the **same** way also the **cup**, after supper, saying,
    "This cup is the new **covenant** in my **blood**.
Do this, as often as you **drink** it, in **remembrance** of me."
For as often as you **eat** this bread and **drink** the cup,
    you proclaim the **death** of the **Lord** until he **comes**.

GOSPEL   John 13:1–15

A reading from the holy Gospel according to John

Before the feast of **Passover**, Jesus knew that his hour had **come**
    to pass from **this** world to the **Father**.
He loved his **own** in the world and he loved them to the **end**.
The **devil** had already induced **Judas**, son of Simon the **Iscariot**,
    to hand him **over**.
So, during **supper**,
    fully **aware** that the Father had put **everything** into his power
    and that he had **come** from God and was **returning** to God,
    he **rose** from supper and took off his outer **garments**.
He took a **towel** and **tied** it around his **waist**.
Then he poured **water** into a **basin**
    and began to **wash** the disciples' **feet**
    and **dry** them with the towel around his waist.

---

speaking in the larger context of liturgical abuses occurring within the community in Corinth. (See First Corinthians 11–14.) Paul sees "harm" (11:17) occurring at liturgies (the eating of the Lord's Supper). The Corinthians had been gathering in separate groups rather than sharing the liturgy together. Apparently they were dining within their own socioeconomic groups, further exasperating the already existing divisions within the congregation. In addition to eating separately, some were also getting "drunk" at the celebration (11:21). Reminding the Corinthians of the received

tradition on the Lord's Supper that Paul brought to the community (today's reading, 11:23–26), he condemns this behavior as "unworthy" of Christian conduct.

We see within the New Testament itself that Jesus's institution of the Eucharist at the Last Supper quickly became a "memorial feast" and a "perpetual institution" just as Passover had become for the Jewish people. The words spoken and the meal shared between Jesus and his disciples on the night before he suffered and died has helped define us as a Christian

community, just as the night that the angel of death *passed-over* the Hebrew households marked with the blood of the lamb defined ancient Israel as God's Chosen People.

GOSPEL   The Gospel Reading for Holy Thursday is the opening scene from Jesus's farewell discourse (John 13–17), in which Jesus washes the feet of the disciples. Unlike the synoptic tradition, in which the institution of the Eucharist is established at the Last Supper, John does not have a formal institution of

The identity of this disciple is critical.

Is Peter being dismissive, or rather is he overwhelmed?

It's of utmost importance to Jesus that Peter, most of all, understand this gesture.

Jesus is teaching not rebuking Peter.

As always, when Peter "gets it," he dives in!

Note the baptismal allusion: one who has received baptismal cleansing, like someone who has just bathed, needs no further cleansing, except for the *washing of feet* (a metaphor for removing the grime of *daily* sin).

Shift the mood for this last section. The work is done, and Jesus leads them in theological reflection on his enacted parable.

These pronouns are key to understanding this sentence, and his enacted parable.

Though they all will follow his lead in laying down their lives, perhaps the harder challenge is this call to selfless service.

He came to Simon **Peter**, who said to him,
    "**Master**, are you going to wash my **feet**?"
Jesus **answered** and said to him,
    "What I am **doing**, you do not understand **now**,
    but you **will** understand **later**."
Peter said to him, "You will **never** wash my **feet**."
Jesus answered him,
    "Unless I **wash** you, you will have no **inheritance** with me."
Simon Peter said to him,
    "**Master**, then not only my **feet**, but my **hands** and **head**
        as well."
Jesus said to him,
    "Whoever has **bathed** has no **need** except to have his
        feet washed,
    for he is clean all **over**;
    so **you** are clean, but not **all**."
For he knew who would **betray** him;
    for this **reason**, he said, "Not **all** of you are clean."

So when he had **washed** their **feet**
    and put his **garments** back on and reclined at **table** again,
    he **said** to them, "Do you **realize** what I have **done** for you?
You call me '**teacher**' and '**master**,' and **rightly** so, for indeed I **am**.
If **I**, therefore, the **master** and **teacher**, have washed **your** feet,
    you ought to wash one **another's** feet.
I have given you a **model** to follow,
    so that as **I** have done for **you**, you should **also** do."

TO KEEP IN MIND
Pauses are never "dead" moments. Something is always happening during a pause. Practice will teach you how often and how long to pause. Too many pauses make a reading choppy; too few cause ideas to run into one another.

---

the Eucharist (although see John 6 which contains Eucharistic rituals [6:11] and language [6:22–59]). Furthermore, whereas Matthew, Mark, and Luke narrate the Lord's Supper within a few short verses (Matthew 26:26–30; Mark 14:22–26; Luke 22:14–20), John takes a full five chapters to present Jesus's final meal with his disciples.

Just as the ancient Israelites had to prepare for the "pass over" of the angel of death who would spare the life of their firstborn, likewise did Jesus have to prepare his disciples for his own Death, and he begins his preparation with an act of care—by washing their feet. Simon Peter objects, taking an act of humility and love for an unthinkable self-abasement. But Jesus insists that he, as teacher and master of the disciples, must model and demonstrate to them how to be a servant. After the washing of the disciples' feet, Jesus says, "I have given you a model to follow, so that as I have done for you, you should also do."

Within the first two generations of Christians, it is uncertain if this practice of washing each others' feet spread far beyond the Johannine community. What is more certain is that the Johannine community saw the preservation of this commandment as an important expression of love for one another, as an outward sign of their commitment to their faith in Jesus Christ, and as a commemoration of the suffering, Death, and Resurrection of Christ.

FRIDAY OF THE PASSION OF THE LORD (GOOD FRIDAY)

LECTIONARY #40

READING I   Isaiah 52:13—53:12

A reading from the Book of the Prophet Isaiah

> **See**, my servant shall **prosper**,
>   he shall be raised **high** and greatly **exalted**.
> Even as many were **amazed** at him—
>   so **marred** was his look beyond human **semblance**
>   and his **appearance** beyond that of the sons of **man**—
> so shall he **startle** many **nations**,
>   **because** of him **kings** shall stand **speechless**;
> for those who have not been **told** shall **see**,
>   those who have not **heard** shall **ponder** it.
>
> Who would **believe** what we have heard?
>   To **whom** has the **arm** of the LORD been **revealed**?
> He grew up like a **sapling** before him,
>   like a **shoot** from the parched **earth**;
> there was in him no **stately** bearing to make us **look** at him,
>   nor **appearance** that would **attract** us to him.
> He was **spurned** and **avoided** by people,
>   a man of **suffering**, accustomed to **infirmity**,
> one of those from whom people **hide** their faces,
>   **spurned**, and we held him in no **esteem**.

Isaiah = ī-ZAY-uh

"See" means "behold" and calls us to attention.

God speaks of the "servant" with conviction and pleasure. Even when describing the servant's suffering, God's voice doesn't weaken or betray anything but support and gratitude.

The sense of the verses is: just as those who saw him in his suffering were shocked by how disfigured and unhuman he looked, nations and kings will be rendered speechless when he is revealed in his glory.

This section is spoken in the "voice" of the foreign nations that marvel that this unremarkable "servant" was in fact the instrument of God.

There's a dual thrust here: the servant's unexceptional appearance and behavior, but also the people's own blindness for failing to recognize him, and their regret for gravely mistreating him.

READING I   In the Lectionary, certain solemnities are assigned the same set of readings each year, regardless of the Lectionary cycle (A, B, or C) and that is the case for Good Friday. The Church has established these readings for exploring the mystery of the Passion, suffering, and Death of Jesus Christ.

The First Reading for Good Friday is the fourth in the series of four Servant of the Lord songs from the Book of Isaiah, and

is thought to have been composed around 550 BC. The three earlier suffering servant oracles—Isaiah 42:1-4, 49:1-7, 50:4-11—clearly build toward this fourth and final oracle. Given that Isaiah 52:13–53:12 narrates the persecution and death of the anonymous prophet (named by scholars as "Second Isaiah," active during Israel's captivity in Babylon), it is rather jarring to hear the opening words to this song: "See, my servant shall prosper, he shall be raised up and greatly exalted."

One of the features that makes this fourth suffering servant song unique is that it was composed by the *community* of believers exiled in Babylon. The first person singular ("I"), used in the three previous oracles, is the voice of God in the first song (42:1-4), and the voice of the prophet himself in the second and third (49:1-7 and 50:4–11). This fourth song speaks in the first person plural ("we"): "We held him in no

While we thought him spurned for his own offenses, it was for *our* sins that he suffered!

Speak these lines with awareness that we did great harm to one whose only goal was our good and our salvation.

"Stripes" are the residue of brutal whipping; they should evoke gratitude.

His lack of resistance and his innocent suffering evoke sincere admiration and genuine regret. "Lamb" and "sheep" are one metaphor, but the "sheep" reference suggests more conscious acceptance of his fate.

"Oppressed" and "condemned" are strong and *distinct* words; don't blur them together.

Speak of this final indignity with mild anger and deep regret that climaxes on "though he had done no wrong."

"The Lord was pleased" in no way suggests the servant deserved punishment, but declares all that happened was within God's permissive will.

God's voice, not the nations', speaks in this final section. The "if . . . then" clause that starts the section reminds us death alone is not salvific without the *intentionality* of the one who gives his life.

Your tone softens; speak persuasively both of the servant's sacrifice and of those who benefit from it.

Yet it was **our** infirmities that he bore,
　　our **sufferings** that he endured,
while we thought of him as **stricken**,
　　as one **smitten** by God and **afflicted**.
But he was **pierced** for our **offenses**,
　　crushed for our **sins**;
upon **him** was the chastisement that makes us **whole**,
　　by his **stripes** we were **healed**.
We had all gone astray like **sheep**,
　　each following his **own** way;
but the Lord laid upon **him**
　　the guilt of us **all**.

Though he was **harshly** treated, he **submitted**
　　and opened **not** his mouth;
like a **lamb** led to the **slaughter**
　　or a **sheep** before the **shearers**,
　　he was **silent** and opened not his mouth.
Oppressed and **condemned**, he was taken **away**,
　　and who would have thought any more of his **destiny**?
When he was cut **off** from the land of the living,
　　and **smitten** for the sin of his people,
a **grave** was assigned him among the **wicked**
　　and a **burial** place with **evildoers**,
though he had done **no wrong**
　　nor spoken any **falsehood**.
But the *Lord* was **pleased**
　　to **crush** him in **infirmity**.

If he gives his **life** as an offering for **sin**,
　　he shall see his **descendants** in a **long** life,
　　and the **will** of the Lord shall be **accomplished**
　　　　through him.

Because of his **affliction**
　　he shall see the **light** in fullness of days;

esteem . . . we thought of him as stricken." This last Servant of the Lord text is a communal reflection on the suffering and death of one innocent among them.

As the words of the song demonstrate, Israel gained two important insights from the suffering and death of this prophet. First, Israel-in-exile came to a deeper understanding of *atonement* for sins: "But he was pierced for our offenses,

crushed for our sins; upon him was the chastisement that makes us whole, by his stripes we were healed." Second, the captive Israelites saw that suffering can be *redemptive*: "And he shall take away the sins of many, and win pardon for their offenses."

These two insights—that the suffering and death of this innocent prophet brought about atonement for sins and that it also brought the redemption of the people— became an important interpretive key for

the early Christian community to help make sense of the suffering and death of Jesus. And only in light of the Resurrection of Christ could the earliest Christians make sense of the opening line of this prophetic oracle: "See, my servant shall prosper, he shall be raised up and greatly exalted."

through his **suffering**, my servant shall justify **many**,
> and their **guilt** he shall **bear**.
Therefore I will give him his **portion** among the **great**,
> and **he** shall divide the **spoils** with the **mighty**,
because he **surrendered** himself to **death**
> and was counted among the **wicked**;
and he shall take **away** the sins of **many**,
> and win **pardon** for their **offenses**.

Make this climactic announcement with a strong, proclamatory tone. The servant receives glory because of his *willing* suffering.

The text slows toward the conclusion and ends with *good* news, not with mourning.

For meditation and context:

RESPONSORIAL PSALM   Psalm 31:2, 6, 12–13, 15–16, 17, 25 (Luke 23:46)

R. Father, into your hands I commend my spirit.

In you, O LORD, I take refuge;
> let me never be put to shame.
In your justice rescue me.
Into your hands I commend my spirit;
> you will redeem me, O LORD,
> > O faithful God.

For all my foes I am an object of reproach,
> a laughingstock to my neighbors, and a
> > dread to my friends;
> they who see me abroad flee from me.
I am forgotten like the unremembered dead;
> I am like a dish that is broken.

But my trust is in you, O LORD;
> I say, "You are my God.
In your hands is my destiny; rescue me
> from the clutches of my enemies and my
> > persecutors."

Let your face shine upon your servant;
> save me in your kindness.
Take courage and be stouthearted,
> all you who hope in the LORD.

TO KEEP IN MIND

Word value: Words are your medium, like a painter's brush or a sculptor's chisel. You must understand the words before you can communicate them. Most words have a dictionary meaning (denotative) and an associational meaning (connotative). "House" and "home" both mean "dwelling," yet they communicate different feelings. Be alert to subtle differences in connotative meanings and express them.

READING II   Hebrews 4:14–16; 5:7–9

A reading from the Letter to the Hebrews

Brothers and sisters:
Since we have a great high **priest** who has passed through
> the **heavens**,
> **Jesus**, the Son of **God**,
> let us hold **fast** to our **confession**.
For we do not have a high priest
> who is unable to **sympathize** with our **weaknesses**,
> but one who has similarly been tested in every way,
> yet without **sin**.

The reading utilizes progressive reasoning to make the case for clinging to Christ.

"Great high priest" asserts Christ's superiority over the human priests of the old Law.

Because he was one like us, Jesus understands and "sympathize(s)" with our "weaknesses."
But he was also *unlike* us in his total freedom from sin.

READING II   The language with which Hebrews speaks of the suffering of Jesus ("he learned obedience from what he suffered" and "was made perfect" by his suffering) is unique within the New Testament. The author of Hebrews uses this language in connection with Jesus as "a great high priest," a figure that would have appealed to his original Jewish audience.

Within Jewish tradition, the high priest served as a mediator between God and the people, a relationship broken by sin. The tradition of atonement for sin through the mediation of a priest dated back to the days of Moses and the Israelites in the desert where Aaron (as the original high priest) was instructed on how to make atonement for himself and his household, as well as for the whole Israelite community. (See Leviticus 16.) Central to the ritual was the recognition that sin separates everyone from God, including the high priest. It was precisely because the high priest, too, sinned and repented that he could sympathize with the believing community and effectively mediate for the people.

"Confidently" tells you how to read. Differentiate "mercy" from "grace"; and pause between the two clauses.

The "prayers and supplications" of Jesus are likely allusions to more than Gethsemane; the death of Lazarus, Judas's betrayal, and Peter's denial were sources of real suffering that gave him insight into ours.

"Learned obedience" and "was made perfect" may strike us as odd, but they reinforce the humanity of Jesus and our kinship with him.

In learning to accept even those things he preferred to avoid, Jesus became our model. Make eye contact as you announce that obedience is not a burden but a joy.

So let us **confidently** approach the throne of **grace**
to receive **mercy** and to find grace for timely **help**.

In the days when Christ was in the **flesh**,
he offered **prayers** and **supplications** with loud **cries** and **tears**
to the one who was able to **save** him from **death**,
and he was **heard** because of his **reverence**.
Son though he **was**, he learned **obedience** from what he suffered;
and when he was made **perfect**,
he became the **source** of eternal **salvation** for all who
obey him.

GOSPEL   John 18:1—19:42

The Passion of our Lord Jesus Christ according to John

Kidron = KID-ruhn

The peace of the familiar garden lasts but a moment.

The mention of "Judas" sounds a note of threat.

"Lanterns" symbolize the hour of darkness.

In John, Jesus is not a helpless victim, but fully aware and in control of his destiny.

Don't gloss over the significant and deliberate "I AM."

Jesus possesses divine power to avert this crisis but freely submits, yet only when he *chooses* to be taken.

Jesus went out with his **disciples** across the Kidron **valley**
to where there was a **garden**,
into which he and his disciples entered.
Judas his **betrayer also** knew the place,
because Jesus had **often** met there with his disciples.
So Judas got a band of **soldiers** and **guards**
from the chief **priests** and the **Pharisees**
and went there with **lanterns**, **torches**, and **weapons**.
Jesus, knowing **everything** that was going to happen to him,
went out and said to them, "Whom are you **looking** for?"
They **answered** him, "**Jesus** the **Nazorean**."
He said to them, "**I AM**."
Judas his betrayer was **also** with them.
When he said to them, "**I AM**,"
they turned away and fell to the **ground**.
So he **again** asked them,
"**Whom** are you looking for?"
They said, "**Jesus** the **Nazorean**."

With our author to Hebrews referring to Jesus as "a great high priest," the early Christian believers were in a bit of a quandary, wondering how Jesus, who was "tested in every way, yet without sin," could mediate for them in heaven on the level of sin. Here is where Hebrews speaks of Jesus mediating our relationship with God on a level other than sin. It is through Jesus's *suffering*, rather than sin, that Jesus is now able to "sympathize with our weaknesses." For the author of Hebrews, it is because of Jesus's suffering that believers can "confidently approach the throne of grace." Through that suffering, we now have direct access to God.

The Letter to the Hebrews asserts that Jesus, the final and greatest high priest, who was made perfect through suffering, "became the source of eternal salvation for all who obey him." That assertion helped the early Christians make sense of the Cross, and making sense of the idea of a *suffering Messiah* was one of the early Church's greatest challenges. This reading expresses that key insight about Jesus Christ that we reaffirm tonight.

GOSPEL   The sequence of events in John's Passion narrative is consistent with what is presented in the synoptic accounts of Matthew, Mark, and Luke. No other events in the fourfold Gospel tradition can make such a claim

Again, Jesus uses the theologically significant (and dangerous) response.

Quote Scripture with a slower and more deliberate tone.

"Then Simon Peter / who had a sword / drew it . . . struck . . . and cut": speak the line a phrase at a time to mitigate the sudden and surprising narration. "Struck" and "cut off" help convey the violence. Malchus = MAL-kuhs Jesus's words are a rebuke to Peter.

Annas = AN-uhs

Caiaphas = KAY-uh- fuhs or KĪ-uh-fuhs

The attribution of this quote to Caiaphas is significant.

A hushed tone can suggest their effort to go undetected.

The amount of detail signals the importance of what occurs here.

She makes it easy for him to deny it, so he does, but without fanfare lest he be *overheard* denying Jesus.

The warmth of the "fire" will contrast with his cold denials.

Jesus answered,
  "I **told** you that **I AM.**
So if you are looking for **me,** let these men **go.**"
This was to **fulfill** what he had said,
  "I have not lost **any** of those you gave me."
Then Simon **Peter,** who had a **sword, drew** it,
  struck the high priest's slave, and **cut** off his right ear.
The slave's name was **Malchus.**
Jesus said to Peter,
  "Put your sword into its **scabbard.**
Shall I not **drink** the cup that the Father gave me?"

So the band of **soldiers,** the **tribune,** and the Jewish **guards**
    seized Jesus,
  bound him, and brought him to **Annas** first.
He was the **father-in-law** of **Caiaphas,**
  who was high **priest** that year.
It was **Caiaphas** who had **counseled** the Jews
    that it was better that **one** man should die rather than
      the **people.**

Simon **Peter** and **another** disciple **followed** Jesus.
Now the **other** disciple was **known** to the high **priest,**
    and he entered the **courtyard** of the high priest with **Jesus.**
But **Peter** stood at the gate **outside.**
So the other **disciple,** the **acquaintance** of the high priest,
    went out and spoke to the **gatekeeper** and brought Peter **in.**
Then the **maid** who was the gatekeeper said to Peter,
  "You are not one of this man's **disciples,** are you?"
He said, "I am **not.**"
Now the slaves and the **guards** were standing around a char-
    coal **fire**
    that they had made, because it was **cold,**
    and were **warming** themselves.
Peter was **also** standing there keeping warm.

because most of the material, like the stories of Jesus's miracles and parables, circulated as individual oral units for decades (around AD 30–70) prior to their incorporation into the longer Gospel narratives. The survival of these individual units was assured because they proved to be useful in the daily life and worship of the early Christian communities.

Prior to the Gospel according to Mark, composed in AD 70, scholars agree that it is likely no single coherent narrative existed on the life of Jesus. There is one exception to this rule, however: the Passion narrative. The events from the Last Supper to the Death on the Cross are stable elements in all four written Gospel accounts, suggesting that the Passion narrative was the earliest written attempt to put the events of

Jesus's life and Death within a larger context. A written and circulating Passion narrative gave context and conveyed meaning in a way that these incidents, if reported in isolation, could not.

Every Palm Sunday, Catholics hear the Passion narrative from one of the synoptic Gospel accounts, depending on cycle A (Matthew), B (Mark), or C (Luke) in the Catholic Lectionary. Regardless of the cycle,

This is a new beat in the narrative. Note, Jesus is questioned about the "disciples." Peter would clearly have interest in hearing this.

Jesus exposes the weakness of their case, speaking with confidence and without fear.

Jesus's bravado is too much for the guard. Deliver the line like a slap—fast and hard.

Jesus is not cowed, but responds with energy. Announce his delivery to Caiaphas with the frustration of Annas.

Another narrative beat begins here. With Jesus out of earshot, Peter's denials grow bolder.

He is unequivocal.

John spares Peter the embarrassment of too much detail, but the crowing "cock" suggests the lasting impact left on Peter.

praetorium = prih-TOHR-ee-uhm. Read slowly of the transference of Jesus "from Caiaphas (the religious leader) to the praetorium (the political authority)."

The hypocrisy is blatant.

Inconvenienced at an early hour, Pilate comes out to *them*.

The high priest **questioned** Jesus
    about his **disciples** and about his **doctrine**.
Jesus **answered** him,
    "I have spoken **publicly** to the world.
I have always taught in a **synagogue**
    or in the **temple** area where all the Jews **gather**,
    and in **secret** I have said **nothing**. Why ask **me**?
Ask those who **heard** me what I said to them.
    They know what I said."
When he had **said** this,
    one of the temple guards standing there **struck** Jesus and said,
    "Is this the way you answer the high **priest**?"
Jesus answered him,
    "If I have spoken **wrongly**, **testify** to the wrong;
    but if I have spoken **rightly**, why do you **strike** me?"
Then Annas sent him **bound** to **Caiaphas** the high priest.

Now Simon **Peter** was standing there keeping warm.
And they **said** to him,
    "**You** are not one of his disciples, **are** you?"
He **denied** it and said,
    "I am **not**."
One of the **slaves** of the high priest,
    a **relative** of the one whose **ear** Peter had cut **off**, said,
    "Didn't I see you in the **garden** with him?"
Again Peter denied it.
And **immediately** the **cock** crowed.

Then they brought Jesus from **Caiaphas** to the **praetorium**.
It was **morning**.
And they themselves did not **enter** the praetorium,
    in order not to be **defiled** so that they could eat the **Passover**.
So **Pilate** came out to **them** and said,
    "What **charge** do you bring against this man?"

however, every Good Friday, Catholics hear the Passion narrative according to John. While many similarities exist within the Passion narratives of the four Gospel accounts, there are also many differences between John and the synoptics, which often reflect John's rhetorical style and theology.

In terms of similarities, much of the plot of the Passion narrative is the same. Broadly speaking, it unfolds as follows: Judas betrays Jesus after the final meal

together; Jesus is arrested in the garden; Peter denies Jesus three times; Jesus is interrogated before Jewish leaders and the Roman official, Pontius Pilate; Jesus is sentenced to die by crucifixion; Jesus dies on the Cross; and Jesus is buried in a tomb. It is widely held by scholars that these plot similarities result from the writers' use of a common written source circulating at an early point in the formation of the Gospel tradition.

There are numerous differences found in John's Passion narrative, which often provide insight into John's portrayal of Christ's identity and nature and into John's literary skills. John is notable for including a mysterious character, the "beloved disciple." This enigmatic figure is first introduced into John's Gospel account at Jesus's farewell discourse, in which he is presented as "the one whom Jesus loved . . . reclining at Jesus's side" (13:23). Twice the beloved disciple appears in the Passion

There is no attempt among these political adversaries to hide their animus.

Pilate's impatience is palpable.

They give away their intent to "execute" Jesus. This detail is unique to John.

Pilate takes a breath and starts over again. He's clearly not characterized as a villain.

Jesus is alone before Pilate, who plays both accuser and occasional advocate.

Pilate's patience is being tested.

Jesus does not withdraw, but engages the Governor.

Stress "are," not "king." Pilate is drawn in by Jesus's compelling power. Though not fully won over, he's willing to spar with the prisoner.

Let Jesus's voice resound with confidence.

They **answered** and said to him,
  "If he were not a **criminal**,
  we would not have handed him over to you."
At this, **Pilate** said to them,
  "Take him **yourselves**, and **judge** him according to your **law**."
The Jews **answered** him,
  "We do not have the right to **execute** anyone,"
  in order that the word of Jesus might be **fulfilled**
  that he said indicating the kind of **death** he would die.
So **Pilate** went back into the **praetorium**
  and **summoned** Jesus and said to him,
  "Are you the **King** of the **Jews**?"
Jesus answered,
  "Do you say this on your **own**
  or have **others** told you about me?"
Pilate answered,
  "I am not a **Jew**, am I?
Your own **nation** and the chief **priests** handed you over to me.
What have you **done**?"
Jesus answered,
  "My **kingdom** does not belong to **this** world.
If my kingdom **did** belong to this world,
  my attendants would be **fighting**
  to **keep** me from being handed over to the Jews.
But as it **is**, my kingdom is not **here**."
So Pilate said to him,
  "Then you **are** a king?"
Jesus answered,
  "**You** say I am a king.
For this I was **born** and for **this** I came into the **world**,
  to **testify** to the **truth**.
Everyone who **belongs** to the truth **listens** to my voice."
Pilate said to him, "What is **truth**?"

narrative. He helps Peter gain access to Pilate's court where Jesus stands trial (18:15–16) and, standing at the foot of the Cross, he is entrusted by Jesus with the care of Jesus's mother, Mary: "'Woman, behold, your son.' Then he said to the disciple, 'Behold, your mother'" (19:26–27).

Other differences include John's dramatic presentation of Jesus's arrest. In the garden arrest scene, as the soldiers seek out Jesus, twice Jesus identifies himself to them as "I AM" (18:5, 8). For John, this is a reference to Christ's divinity. (See Exodus 3:11–15, where God identifies himself to Moses as "I AM.") This is contrasted with Peter twice denying Jesus, saying "I am not" (18:17, 25). (Johannine irony is in full display here.)

John uses "I am" sayings for Jesus throughout his account as metaphors for his identity. Echoing the seven "signs" of Jesus in John 1–12, John presents seven metaphorical "I am" sayings, indicating the fullness of Jesus's identity as the Word made flesh: "I am the bread of life" (6:35); "I am the light of the world" (8:12), "I am the gate for the sheep" (10:7), "I am the good shepherd" (10:11), "I am the resurrection and the life" (11:25), "I am the way and the truth and the life" (14:6), and "I am the true vine" (15:1). Having read all of these metaphoric statements about Jesus's identity, the reader is not taken by surprise as the arresting soldiers in the garden are: they "turned away and fell to the ground" in reaction to Jesus's divine presence.

Another new beat begins. Pilate is proactive in trying to save Jesus.

When he had **said** this,
  he **again** went out to the Jews and said to them,
  "I find no **guilt** in him.
But you have a custom that I release one **prisoner** to you
    at **Passover**.
Do you want me to release to you the **King** of the **Jews**?"
They cried out again,
  "Not **this** one but **Barabbas**!"
Now Barabbas was a **revolutionary**.

Pilate wants to be done with this and even seems to be putting words in their mouths.

Barabbas = buh-RAB-uhs

Then Pilate took Jesus and had him **scourged**.
And the soldiers wove a **crown** out of **thorns** and placed it
    on his **head**,
  and clothed him in a **purple** cloak,
  and they came to him and said,
  "**Hail**, **King** of the **Jews**!"
And they **struck** him **repeatedly**.

Your tone can convey reluctance on Pilate's part, as if he's thinking, "Maybe *this* will satisfy them!"

Once **more** Pilate went out and said to them,
  "**Look**, I am bringing him out to you,
  so that you may **know** that I find no **guilt** in him."
So Jesus came out,
  wearing the crown of **thorns** and the purple **cloak**.

Speak of the disrespect and indignities without overdramatizing. Simple sincerity is best.

And he said to them, "**Behold**, the man!"
When the chief priests and the guards saw him they **cried** out,
  "**Crucify** him, **crucify** him!"

Pilate seems to be saying, "Look what you made me do!" "Behold the man . . . " can be spat out scornfully at the crowd.

Pilate said to them,
  "Take him **yourselves** and crucify him.
I find no **guilt** in him."
The Jews **answered**,
  "We have a **law**, and according to that law he ought to **die**,
  because he made himself the **Son** of **God**."

The drama between religious leaders and governor intensifies. He doesn't want more blood on his hands.

Now when Pilate **heard** this statement,
  he became even **more** afraid,
  and went back into the praetorium and said to **Jesus**,
  "Where are you **from**?"

With heightened energy and louder voices, the leaders make their case.

Pilate is gripped with fear. They've played him well!

Only John reports that the inscription on the Cross ("Jesus the Nazorean, the King of the Jews") is written in Hebrew, Latin, and Greek (19:20). These were three spoken languages in the Roman Empire at that time: Hebrew, the ancestral language of the Jews; Latin, the official language of the Roman rulers; and Greek, the common language of citizens of the Roman Empire. It is from the Latin inscription, *Iesus Nazarenus Rex Iudaeroum* ("Jesus of Nazareth, King of the Jews") that the acronym "INRI" comes. Interestingly, the language that Jesus himself spoke, Aramaic, is not included in the inscription. It may be that Pilate considered this a language of the slave class, and therefore, irrelevant.

A final notable difference between the Passion narratives of John and the synoptics is the Death of Jesus. According to John, Jesus is pierced in his side with a lance while on the Cross, and blood and water flow out (19:33–34). John uses bread, water, and light as three recurring symbols associated with Jesus, so his emphasis on blood and water flowing from Jesus's side points symbolically to Jesus as the wellspring of eternal waters. The symbol of water is first associated with Jesus in his encounter with the Samaritan woman at the well, where he tells her: "Whoever drinks the water I shall give will never

Jesus knows words are of no further use.

Pilate turns his anger on Jesus.

Unapologetic, Jesus speaks simply, not to save himself but to let Pilate know who's really in charge.

Pilate is impressed with Jesus, but the religious leaders play on his insecurities. "Friend of Caesar" is a ceremonial title given by Rome to high-ranking officials; Pilate might jeopardize his standing if he mishandles this situation.

In John, Pilate's tenacity is most remarkable. Gabbatha = GAB-uh-thuh

"Behold your king" betray Pilate's frustration with both the priests and the troublesome Jesus.

Pilate makes a final effort to forestall.

Another new narrative beat begins here.

Golgotha = GAWL-guh-thuh

The identity of those crucified with Jesus is not given.

Jesus did not **answer** him.
So Pilate said to him,
  "Do you not speak to **me**?
Do you not know that I have power to **release** you
  and I have power to **crucify** you?"
Jesus answered him,
  "You would have **no** power over me
  if it had not been **given** to you from **above**.
For this reason the one who handed me **over** to you
  has the **greater** sin."
Consequently, Pilate tried to **release** him; but the **Jews** cried **out**,
  "If you **release** him, you are not a **Friend** of **Caesar**.
Everyone who makes himself a **king** opposes Caesar."

When Pilate heard these words he brought Jesus out
  and **seated** him on the **judge's** bench
  in the place called **Stone Pavement**, in **Hebrew**, **Gabbatha**.
It was **preparation** day for **Passover**, and it was about **noon**.
And he said to the **Jews**,
  "**Behold**, your **king**!"
They **cried** out,
  "**Take** him away, **take** him away! **Crucify** him!"
Pilate said to them,
  "Shall I crucify your **king**?"
The chief priests answered,
  "We have no king but **Caesar**."
Then he **handed** him over to them to be **crucified**.

So they **took** Jesus, and, **carrying** the cross **himself**,
  he went out to what is called the **Place** of the **Skull**,
    in **Hebrew**, **Golgotha**.
There they **crucified** him, and with him two **others**,
  one on either **side**, with Jesus in the **middle**.

thirst; the water I shall give will become in him a spring of water welling up to eternal life" (4:14).

The challenge for each of the Gospel writers was to work with a received written tradition about the Passion and Death of Jesus in a way that would not disrupt the fundamental integrity of the plot, while still weaving in their particular theological perspective on the mystery of the Christ's Passion. What we have in the Passion narratives is the original "Gospel" among the

first generation of believers, the embryonic stage of what would later become full-blown narratives on the life of Jesus. John's incorporation of such features as the role of the beloved disciple, the "I AM" sayings, the mention of the multiple languages, and the report of the blood and water flowing from Jesus's side all point to John's theological and literary contributions to the Passion narrative of Christ. And they all intensify our meditation on this foundational mystery of our faith.

Read the inscription slowly and with authority, as if it were Pilate's last effort to provoke the priests.

Pilate also had an **inscription** written and put on the cross.
It read,
> "**Jesus** the **Nazorean**, the **King** of the **Jews**."
Now many of the Jews **read** this inscription,
>   because the place where Jesus was crucified was near the **city**;
>   and it was written in **Hebrew**, **Latin**, and **Greek**.
So the chief **priests** of the Jews said to Pilate,
>   "Do not write 'The **King** of the Jews,'
>   but that he **said**, 'I am the King of the **Jews.'"
Pilate answered,
>   "What I have **written**, I have **written**."

Pilate's effort elicits a response that he won't entertain: "What I have written, / I / have / written!"

When the soldiers had **crucified** Jesus,
>   they took his **clothes** and **divided** them into four **shares**,
>   a share for each **soldier**.
They also took his **tunic**, but the tunic was **seamless**,
>   woven in one **piece** from the top down.
So they said to one another,
>   "Let's not **tear** it, but cast **lots** for it to see whose it will be,"
>   in order that the passage of **Scripture** might be **fulfilled**
>   that says:
>   *They divided my **garments** among them,*
>   *and for my **vesture** they cast **lots**.*
This is what the soldiers **did**.

Speak slowly and with sorrow of the soldiers' cruel self-interest.

The seamless tunic has value they don't want to compromise.

Quote Scripture with a sense of how it's been fulfilled.

Standing by the **cross** of Jesus were his **mother**
>   and his mother's **sister**, **Mary** the wife of **Clopas**,
>   and Mary of **Magdala**.
When Jesus **saw** his mother and the **disciple** there whom
>   he **loved**
>   he said to his mother, "**Woman**, behold, your **son**."
Then he said to the **disciple**,
>   "Behold, your **mother**."
And from that hour the disciple took her into his **home**.

The silent presence of the women has gone unmentioned. Probably there are four women identified if (as some maintain) "his mother's sister" is different from "Mary the wife of Clopas."

Clopas = KLOH-puhs
Magdala = MAG-duh-luh

Don't rush the tender scene between the dying Jesus, his mother, and "the disciple."

In this new beat of the narrative, John's effort to present Christ as sovereign and in control of circumstances is much apparent.

Relate these final moments as you would the experience of being at the bedside of a beloved relative. Hyssop = HIS-uhp

Jesus both surrenders his life and hands on the Holy Spirit. Take a substantial pause for silence and prayer.

Don't rush the significant details regarding the "preparation day" and "Sabbath."

Breaking the legs assured a faster death by asphyxiation.

That they *don't* break his legs is a significant detail. The men whose legs they break are still alive.

That eyewitness testimony supported the story of Christ's Death was important to the early Christian community.

The issue of "blood and water" was a certain sign of death. Cite the Scripture with reverence and authority.

After this, aware that everything was now **finished**,
    in order that the Scripture might be **fulfilled**,
    Jesus said, "I **thirst**."
There was a **vessel** filled with common **wine**.
So they put a sponge **soaked** in wine on a sprig of **hyssop**
    and put it up to his **mouth**.
When Jesus had **taken** the wine, he said,
    "It is **finished**."
And bowing his **head**, he handed over the **spirit**.

[Here all kneel and pause for a short time.]

Now since it was **preparation** day,
    in order that the bodies might not **remain**
    on the cross on the **sabbath**,
    for the sabbath day of that week was a **solemn** one,
    the Jews asked Pilate that their legs be **broken**
    and that they be taken **down**.
So the **soldiers** came and **broke** the legs of the **first**
    and then of the **other** one who was crucified with Jesus.
But when they came to Jesus and saw that he was already **dead**,
    they did **not** break **his** legs,
    but **one** soldier thrust his **lance** into his **side**,
    and immediately **blood** and **water** flowed out.
An **eyewitness** has **testified**, and his testimony is **true**;
    he **knows** that he is speaking the **truth**,
    so that you **also** may come to **believe**.
For this happened so that the **Scripture** passage might
        be **fulfilled**:
*Not a **bone** of it will be **broken**.*
And again **another** passage says:
*They will **look** upon him whom they have **pierced**.*

Arimathea = ayr-ih-muh-THEE-uh

Joseph and, later, Nicodemus, are revered for their courage and their love of the Lord. Speak of them with reverence.

Nicodemus = nik-uh-DEE-muhs

Myrrh = mer

Aloes = AL-ohz

The synoptics do not have these ministrations occurring on Friday.

It is the simplicity of the final sentence that lends dignity and solemnity to the scene of his entombment.

After this, **Joseph** of **Arimathea**,
  secretly a **disciple** of Jesus for **fear** of the **Jews**,
  asked Pilate if he could **remove** the body of Jesus.
And Pilate **permitted** it.
So he came and **took** his body.
Nicodemus, the one who had first come to him at **night**,
  also came bringing a mixture of **myrrh** and **aloes**
  weighing about one hundred **pounds**.
They took the **body** of Jesus
  and bound it with **burial** cloths along with the **spices**,
  according to the Jewish burial custom.
Now in the place where he had been crucified there was
    a **garden**,
  and in the garden a **new tomb**, in which no one had yet
    been **buried**.
So they laid Jesus **there** because of the Jewish **preparation** day;
  for the tomb was close by.

THE 4 STEPS OF *LECTIO DIVINA* OR PRAYERFUL READING

1. *Lectio:* Read a Scripture passage aloud slowly. Notice what phrase captures your attention and be attentive to its meaning. Silent pause.

2. *Meditatio:* Read the passage aloud slowly again, reflecting on the passage, allowing God to speak to you through it. Silent pause.

3. *Oratio:* Read it aloud slowly a third time, allowing it to be your prayer or response to God's gift of insight to you. Silent pause.

4. *Contemplatio:* Read it aloud slowly a fourth time, now resting in God's word.

HOLY SATURDAY: EASTER VIGIL

This epic text conveys both God's cosmic power and solicitous love for creation, especially man and woman. Each day consists of five-recurring refrains: 1) an *introduction*: "Then God said"; 2) God's spoken *command*: "Let there be"; 3) announcement of the *accomplishment* of the command: "And so it happened"; 4) an *affirmation* of the goodness of each day's work: "God saw how *good* it was"; 5) *identification* of the day: "Evening came, and morning followed the first . . . second . . . day [etc.]." This repetition is intentional, so you don't need novel inflection on the recurrences of the refrains. Their familiarity, regularity, and predictability lend power to the reading.

On each day, give greater stress to refrains that declare God's command was accomplished and the goodness of creation.

Throughout, focus less energy on the details of what was made when, and more on the loving God who made it all.

Help us sense God's *delight* in bringing order and beauty into the world.

Remember, *tone* is more important than detail; God's surging power animating the cosmos and earth's plants and animals is what your listeners should hear and remember.

Establish eye contact and renew your energy at the start of each narrative beat ("Then God said")

LECTIONARY #41

READING I   Genesis 1:1—2:2

A reading from the Book of Genesis

In the **beginning**, when God created the **heavens** and the **earth**,
    the earth was a formless **wasteland**, and **darkness** covered
        the **abyss**,
    while a mighty **wind** swept over the **waters**.

Then God **said**,
    "Let there be **light**," and there **was** light.
God saw how **good** the light was.
God then **separated** the light from the **darkness**.
God called the light "**day**," and the darkness he called "**night**."
Thus **evening** came, and **morning** followed—the **first** day.

Then God said,
    "Let there be a **dome** in the **middle** of the waters,
    to **separate** one body of water from the **other**."
And so it **happened**:
    God **made** the dome,
    and it separated the water **above** the dome from the water
        below it.
God called the dome "the **sky**."
Evening came, and **morning** followed—the **second** day.

Then God said,
    "Let the **water** under the sky be gathered into a single **basin**,
    so that the dry **land** may appear."

READING I   The set of readings we hear at the Easter Vigil presents some of the defining moments in salvation history. Beginning with the story of creation and revisiting some of the Old Testament's greatest figures—Abraham, Moses, Isaiah, Baruch, and Ezekiel—the Scriptures then lead us to Paul and his Letter to the Romans and to Jesus's empty tomb. We see revealed in these readings God's great love for the people and the gradual unfolding of the mystery of salvation, culminating in the Death and Resurrection of Christ.

The readings begin at the beginning, of course, and the Bible opens with two accounts of creation, Genesis 1:1–2:4a and Genesis 2:4b–3:24. The first is commonly known as the six-day creation story; it presents a grand, poetic vision of creation in contrast to the second account, a narrative that personifies God and his creation in very earthly terms. The more cosmic, poetic account is the one we hear tonight.

This long, stately, rhythmic proclamation of the creation of the universe signals that the story unfolding in the dark of this night is an exalted one. Even in the shorter version of this reading, which includes the opening words of the first creation story and moves directly to the sixth day of creation, when God created man and woman, the key theme of human blessedness is

Convey God's mother love for each creation: "the earth, the sea."

And so it **happened**:
   the water under the sky was **gathered** into its basin,
   and the dry **land** appeared.
God called the **dry land** "the **earth**,"
   and the **basin** of the **water** he called "the **sea**."
God saw how **good** it was.
Then God said,
   "Let the **earth** bring forth **vegetation**:
   every kind of **plant** that bears **seed**
   and every kind of **fruit** tree on earth
   that bears fruit with its **seed** in it."

Read of the "third day" with much energy without getting caught up in the profusion of details. A jubilant tone is most important.

And so it **happened**:
   the earth brought forth every kind of plant that bears **seed**
   and every kind of **fruit** tree on earth
   that bears fruit with its **seed** in it.
God saw how **good** it was.

Relate these events with a sense of awe, as if watching them spring forth from the ground.

Evening came, and morning **followed**—the **third** day.

Vary your volume and pacing: perhaps a bit softer and slower for day four. But let your tone suggest God's choices are all for the good of the woman and man who will people this world.

Then God said:
   "Let there be **lights** in the dome of the sky,
   to separate **day** from **night**.
Let them mark the fixed **times**, the **days** and the **years**,
   and serve as **luminaries** in the dome of the sky,
   to shed **light** upon the earth."
And so it **happened**:
   God made the **two** great lights,
   the **greater** one to govern the **day**,
   and the **lesser** one to govern the **night**;
   and he made the **stars**.

Think of your own enjoyment of sunny days and moonlit nights as you speak these lines.

God set them in the **dome** of the sky,
   to shed **light** upon the earth,
   to **govern** the day and the night,
   and to separate the **light** from the **darkness**.
God saw how **good** it was.

"And he made the stars" evokes the wonder of a child who for the first time sees the brilliant stars against a darkened sky.

Each repetition of the great refrain "Evening came, and morning followed" ends an entire epoch of time and creation. Convey the sense of accomplishment, joy, and peace experienced by the Creator, who takes a very active role in creation.

Evening came, and **morning** followed—the **fourth** day.

lifted up: God has made us the *imago dei* ("image of God"): "God created man in his image, in the divine image he created him; male and female he created them." Humans have been given the "image" and "likeness" of God in that they have "domin-ion" over the rest of God's creation: "Be fer-tile and multiply; fill the earth and subdue it." God places on humanity the divine duty to care for all that he created.

This six-day creation story, originally heard among the captive Israelites in Babylon, helped the people see beyond their immediate situation to a God with grand purposes in which they would have a future role. It must have seemed to that original audience as if the Babylonian Empire had full control over them; but in fact, the story asserted, God is creator and ruler of the world since the beginning of time. In addition, the message that human-ity was made in God's "image" and "like-ness" brought a new sense of dignity to the otherwise demoralized Israelites, enslaved in a foreign land.

Water and its teeming creatures spark renewed energy and delight.

First God "blesses" and then orders the creatures to *multiply*," which forever is made a way of honoring the divine will.

Continue narrating with joy God's creation of earth's large land animals.

Even "creeping" things issue from the creative hand of God.

The reading reaches a subclimax midway thorough day six. Pronouncing all creation good, God prepares for creation's culmination.

Slow your pacing for the pinnacle of God's creative action. With a tone that is dignified and full of compassion relate how humans are made a reflection of God's own goodness and beauty! Note God's use of plural pronouns: "us . . . our." Don't rush the three "created man . . . created him . . . created them" phrases. These repetitions cast a significant spotlight on humanity's kinship with its creator.

Speak these words as a *blessing;* God's instruction becomes humanity's best means of honoring its creator: being creative like the Lord; caring for all that God fashioned.

Then God said,
"Let the water **teem** with an **abundance** of living **creatures,**
and on the **earth** let **birds** fly beneath the **dome** of the sky."
And so it **happened:**
God created the great **sea** monsters
and all kinds of **swimming** creatures with which the
water **teems,**
and all kinds of winged **birds.**
God saw how **good** it was, and God **blessed** them, saying,
"Be **fertile, multiply,** and **fill** the water of the seas;
and let the birds **multiply** on the earth."
Evening came, and morning **followed**—the **fifth** day.

Then God said,
"Let the **earth** bring forth all kinds of living **creatures:**
cattle, creeping things, and wild **animals** of all kinds."
And so it **happened:**
God made all kinds of wild **animals,** all kinds of **cattle,**
and all kinds of **creeping** things of the earth.
God saw how **good** it was.

Then God said:
"Let us make **man** in our **image,** after our **likeness.**
Let them have **dominion** over the **fish** of the sea,
the **birds** of the air, and the **cattle,**
and over all the wild **animals**
and all the creatures that crawl on the **ground.**"
God created **man** in his **image;**
in the image of **God** he created him;
male and **female** he created them.
God **blessed** them, saying:
"Be **fertile** and **multiply;**
fill the earth and **subdue** it.
Have **dominion** over the fish of the **sea,** the birds of the **air,**
and all the **living** things that move on the earth."

Don't miss the opportunity to give God the loving quality of a parent bequeathing all to beloved children.

God **also** said:

"**See**, I give you every **seed**-bearing plant all over the earth
   and every **tree** that has seed-bearing **fruit** on it to be your **food**;
   and to all the **animals** of the land, all the **birds** of the air,
   and all the living creatures that crawl on the **ground**,
   I give all the **green** plants for food."
And so it **happened**.
God looked at **everything** he had made, and he found it
   very good.
Evening came, and **morning** followed—the **sixth** day.

In this summary statement, God pronounces creation as *very* good!

Thus the **heavens** and the **earth** and all their array
   were **completed**.
Since on the **seventh** day God was **finished**
   with the work he had been doing,
   he **rested** on the seventh day from all the work he
   had undertaken.

Announce the completion of heaven and earth with a sense of accomplishment and pride. Then pause before announcing God's Sabbath rest.

Here and in Israel's understanding of the Sabbath "rest" means a great deal more than refraining from work or being idle. It means really *seeing* the beauty and goodness of creation and delighting in it in a way that renews and refreshes the spirit.

For meditation and context:

[Shorter: Genesis 1:1, 26–31a]

RESPONSORIAL PSALM   Psalm 104:1–2, 5–6, 10, 12, 13–14, 24, 35 (30)

R. Lord, send out your Spirit, and renew the face of the earth.

Bless the LORD, O my soul!
   O LORD, my God, you are great indeed!
You are clothed with majesty and glory,
   robed in light as with a cloak.

You fixed the earth upon its foundation,
   not to be moved forever;
with the ocean, as with a garment, you
      covered it;
   above the mountains the waters stood.

You send forth springs into the watercourses
   that wind among the mountains.
Beside them the birds of heaven dwell;
   from among the branches they send forth
      their song.

You water the mountains from your palace;
   the earth is replete with the fruit
      of your works.
You raise grass for the cattle,
   and vegetation for man's use,
producing bread from the earth.

How manifold are your works, O LORD!
   In wisdom you have wrought them all—
the earth is full of your creatures.
   Bless the LORD, O my soul!

Or:

TO KEEP IN MIND
Lists: Whether proclaiming a genealogy or one of Paul's enumerations of virtues and sins, avoid the extremes of too much stress (slowly punctuating each word with equal stress) or too little (rushing through as if each item were the same).

READING II   In the Bible, after Genesis 1–11 (the creation accounts, the fall of Adam and Eve, Noah and the flood, and the tower of Babel), the cycle of Abraham stories is presented in Genesis 12–25. We first meet Abraham when he is seventy-five years old (Genesis 12:4) as God is calling him to migrate from his homeland. Here God makes his first covenantal promise to "bless" Abraham and make of him a "great nation." The Book of Genesis records events in the life of Abraham for the next one hundred years, until his death at the age of one hundred and seventy-five (Genesis 25:7). Scholars date these events around 2000 BC.

One of the recurring themes running through the stories of Abraham is the promises God made to him. Because Abraham put his trust in the Lord (Genesis 15:6), God established a covenant with him, which included the assurance of land and descendants—two markers of true wealth and divine blessings in the ancient world. When Abraham and Sarah finally gave birth to their firstborn son Isaac (Abraham was one hundred years old at the time, Genesis 21:5), it seemed that God's promise of descendants had been realized. This is the

For meditation and context:

TO KEEP IN MIND

Characters: To distinguish the various characters that populate a passage, try to understand their thoughts, feelings, and motivations. Use subtle variations in pitch, pacing, and emotion to communicate them. But don't confuse proclamation with theatrics. Suggest characters, don't "become" them.

Genesis = JEN-uh-sis

The crucial first line alerts your listeners to God's intent.

"Here I am" betrays Abraham's eagerness and naiveté regarding what's about to unfold.

God's voice is sober but not stern. The poignancy of Abraham's dilemma is heightened by the words "only" and "whom you love."
Moriah = moh-RĪ-uh

Abraham must keep his dire mission secret; he works hard to hide the pain, so don't let this sound like a weekend outing for father and son.

The "third" day will not bring death but "resurrection" for the grieving Abraham.

Deliver Abraham's dialogue without emotion.

RESPONSORIAL PSALM   Psalm 33:4–5, 6–7, 12–13, 20–22 (5b)

R. The earth is full of the goodness of the Lord.

Upright is the word of the LORD,
  and all his works are trustworthy.
He loves justice and right;
  of the kindness of the LORD the earth
  is full.
By the word of the LORD the heavens
  were made;
  by the breath of his mouth all their host.
He gathers the waters of the sea as in a flask;
  in cellars he confines the deep.

Blessed the nation whose God is the LORD,
  the people he has chosen for his own
  inheritance.
From heaven the LORD looks down;
  he sees all mankind.

Our soul waits for the LORD,
  who is our help and our shield.
May your kindness, O LORD, be upon us
  who have put our hope in you.

READING II   Genesis 22:1–18

A reading from the Book of Genesis

God put **Abraham** to the **test**.
He called to him, "**Abraham!**"
"**Here** I am," he replied.
Then God said:
  "Take your son **Isaac**, your **only** one, whom you **love**,
  and go to the land of **Moriah**.
There you shall **offer** him up as a **holocaust**
  on a **height** that I will point **out** to you."
Early the next **morning** Abraham saddled his **donkey**,
  took with him his son **Isaac** and two of his **servants** as well,
  and with the **wood** that he had cut for the **holocaust**,
  set out for the place of which God had told him.

On the **third** day Abraham got **sight** of the place from afar.
Then he **said** to his servants:
  "Both of you stay here with the **donkey**,
  while the **boy** and I go on over **yonder**.
We will **worship** and then come **back** to you."

---

backdrop that makes today's story of Abraham's near-sacrifice of his son, Isaac so dramatic. When God "put Abraham to the test," not only was the life of Abraham's "beloved son" Isaac at stake, but also the validity of God's promise of descendants for Abraham. Yet Abraham's depth of faith in God was so profound that he was willing to follow God's command to offer his only son as a "holocaust."

Abraham's unconditional trust in God and his obedience to God's command led to the renewed covenant: "I will bless you abundantly and make your descendants as countless as the stars of the sky and the sands of the seashore; . . . in your descendants all the nations of the earth shall find blessings." Abraham's passing of the test God put before him led generations of Abraham's descendants to consider him their "great Patriarch."

Isaac carrying the wood on his shoulders foreshadows Jesus's carrying his own Cross. Don't rush.

The father/son dialogue is poignant. Isaac's childish naiveté and curiosity contrasts with the pained and weighty words choking in Abraham's throat.

"Then the two" contains the ominous tone of what's about to unfold.

Don't overdo these stark images, but preparing Isaac for the holocaust can't sound like Abraham is buttoning his coat.

Don't describe the events as a "close call" but as if the sacrifice were about to occur.

"But" shatters the tension. The second "Abraham" is more urgent than the first.

"Here I am" is terror-filled, not a cry of relief. God's "Do not" commands are spoken with calm and reassuring tenderness.

"I know now" conveys the majesty of a merciful God who is well pleased with this humble servant.

Tone livens and pacing quickens as you speak of the "ram."

"Yahweh-yireh" (YAH-way-YEER-ay) means "the Lord will see [to it]."

Thereupon Abraham took the wood for the holocaust
    and **laid** it on his son **Isaac's** shoulders,
    while he himself carried the **fire** and the **knife**.
As the two walked on **together**, Isaac **spoke** to his
        father Abraham:
    "**Father!**" Isaac said.
"**Yes**, son," he replied.
Isaac continued, "Here are the **fire** and the **wood**,
    but where is the **sheep** for the holocaust?"
"**Son**," Abraham answered,
    "God **himself** will provide the sheep for the holocaust."
Then the two **continued** going forward.

When they **came** to the place of which God had told him,
    Abraham built an **altar** there and arranged the **wood** on it.
Next he **tied** up his son **Isaac**,
    and put him on **top** of the wood on the altar.
Then he **reached** out and took the **knife** to **slaughter** his son.
But the LORD's **messenger** called to him from **heaven**,
    "**Abraham, Abraham!**"
"**Here** I am," he answered.
"Do not lay your **hand** on the boy," said the **messenger**.
"Do not do the least **thing** to him.
I **know** now how **devoted** you are to God,
    since you did not **withhold** from me your own beloved **son**."
As Abraham looked **about**,
    he spied a **ram** caught by its horns in the **thicket**.
So he went and **took** the ram
    and offered **it** up as a holocaust in **place** of his son.
Abraham **named** the site **Yahweh-yireh**;
    hence people now say, "On the mountain the LORD will **see**."

A consistent pace, whether fast or slow, works against effective proclamation. Variety in pacing better communicates meaning and sustains interest. Here, God's declaration should sound like a parent reassuring and praising a child.

Because God honored these promises, we are celebrating this night.

In the final line we can hear God calling each of us to fidelity and obedience (and therefore reward) like Abraham's.

For meditation and context:

Again the Lord's messenger **called** to Abraham from heaven
    and said:
  "I **swear** by myself, declares the Lord,
  that because you **acted** as you **did**
  in not **withholding** from me your beloved **son**,
  I will bless you **abundantly**
  and make your **descendants** as **countless**
  as the **stars** of the **sky** and the **sands** of the seashore;
  your descendants shall take **possession**
  of the gates of their **enemies**,
  and in your **descendants** all the nations of the earth shall
    find **blessing**—
all this because you **obeyed** my **command**."

[Shorter: Genesis 22:1–2, 9a, 10–13, 15–18]

RESPONSORIAL PSALM   Psalm 16:5, 8, 9–10, 11 (1)

R. You are my inheritance, O Lord.

O Lord, my allotted portion and my cup,
    you it is who hold fast my lot.
I set the Lord ever before me;
    with him at my right hand I shall not
        be disturbed.

Therefore my heart is glad and my soul
        rejoices,
    my body, too, abides in confidence;
because you will not abandon my soul to the
        netherworld,
    nor will you suffer your faithful one to
        undergo corruption.

You will show me the path to life,
    fullness of joys in your presence,
    the delights at your right hand forever.

TO KEEP IN MIND
Tell the story: Make the story yours, then share it with your listeners. Use the language; don't throw away any good words. Settings give context; don't rush the description. Characters must be believable; understand their motivation. Dialogue reveals character; distinguish one character from another with your voice.

Exodus = EK-suh-duhs

Repetitions and refrains are common in tonight's readings. Have faith in the ability of refrains to communicate effectively. Your confidence and energy will make the difference.

You begin with God's strong voice calling Moses to task.

"And you" initiates three strong directives to take decisive action. Let your tone say that as well as your words.

In view of the sacred writer, even Pharaoh's obstinacy is within God's will.

"Pharaoh . . . army . . . chariots . . . charioteers" becomes a powerful refrain that communicates God's supremacy over all earthly powers. Don't let your energy wane on the repetitions of the refrain.

The "angel of God" and the "column of cloud" both manifest God's powerful presence and defense of Israel. Build suspense as the action intensifies.

Let the tone of "But the cloud" prepare for the awesome feat God is about to work through Moses's outstretched arm.

As often happens in literature, the sound of your words conveying God's sweeping power is more important than the specific words.

READING III   Exodus 14:15—15:1

A reading from the Book of Exodus

The **LORD** said to **Moses**, "**Why** are you crying out to me?
Tell the Israelites to go **forward**.
And **you**, lift up your **staff** and, with hand outstretched
        over the **sea**,
    split the sea in **two**,
    that the Israelites may pass **through** it on dry **land**.
But I will make the **Egyptians** so **obstinate**
    that they will go in **after** them.
Then I will receive **glory** through **Pharaoh** and all his **army**,
    his **chariots** and **charioteers**.
The Egyptians shall know that **I** am the Lord,
    when I receive glory through **Pharaoh**
    and his **chariots** and **charioteers**."

The **angel** of God, who had been **leading** Israel's camp,
    now **moved** and went around **behind** them.
The column of **cloud** also, leaving the **front**,
    took up its place **behind** them,
    so that it came **between** the camp of the **Egyptians**
    and that of **Israel**.
But the cloud now became **dark**, and thus the **night** passed
    without the rival camps coming any closer together all
        night long.
Then Moses **stretched** out his hand over the **sea**,
    and the LORD **swept** the sea
    with a **strong** east **wind** throughout the night
    and so **turned** it into **dry** land.
When the **water** was thus **divided**,
    the **Israelites** marched into the **midst** of the sea on **dry** land,
    with the water like a **wall** to their **right** and to their **left**.

READING III | The story of Moses and the Israelites' crossing of the Red Sea was the final event in a series of miraculous activities associated with Israel's liberation from Egyptian slavery, around 1200 BC. From the ten plagues brought upon the land of Egypt to the culmination of the death of the first-born on Passover, God relentlessly worked through Moses to lead his chosen people to freedom.

The ancient Near East was dominated by the belief in many gods, what we call today polytheism. The gods were often viewed hierarchically, with the gods of war and the gods of fertility believed to be the most powerful deities. The mention in today's reading of "the column of cloud . . .

between the camp of the Egyptians and that of Israel" presents a military encounter between these two groups. Since the Egyptian army was so large and powerful, it was thought that the Egyptian gods of war were likewise dominant among the many gods. Conversely, the gods of enslaved people (like the LORD of the Israelites) were thought to have been

Your tone tells us they pursue in vain and at their great peril.

Your pace quickens as you describe the chaos and the destruction.

Let this statement be more about God's intervention than Egypt's retreat.

Restoring the waters to their normal levels is as impressive a miracle as the first.

The sacred author sees God's justice as uncompromising. Don't hold back in narrating the devastating price paid by Egypt.

This is justice, not revenge. Let there be no vindictiveness in your tone.

These lines underscore that this event is about God's solicitous care for Israel, not punishment of Egypt.

TO KEEP IN MIND

Ritardando: refers to the practice, common in music, of becoming gradually slower and expanding the words as you approach the end of a piece. Many readings end this way—with a decreased rate but increased intensity.

The Egyptians **followed** in **pursuit**;
   all Pharaoh's **horses** and **chariots** and **charioteers** went
      after them
  right into the **midst** of the sea.
In the **night** watch just before **dawn**
  the LORD **cast** through the column of the fiery cloud
  upon the Egyptian force a **glance** that threw it into a **panic**;
  and he so **clogged** their chariot wheels
  that they could hardly **drive**.
With **that** the Egyptians sounded the **retreat** before Israel,
  because the LORD was fighting for them **against** the Egyptians.

Then the LORD told **Moses**, "**Stretch** out your **hand** over the **sea**,
  that the **water** may flow **back** upon the Egyptians,
  upon their **chariots** and their **charioteers**."
So Moses **stretched** out his hand over the sea,
  and at **dawn** the sea flowed **back** to its normal **depth**.
The Egyptians were fleeing head **on** toward the **sea**,
  when the LORD **hurled** them into its midst.
As the water flowed **back**,
  it **covered** the **chariots** and the **charioteers** of Pharaoh's
     whole **army**
  which had followed the Israelites into the sea.
Not a single **one** of them escaped.
But the **Israelites** had marched on dry **land**
  through the **midst** of the sea,
  with the water like a **wall** to their **right** and to their **left**.
Thus the LORD **saved** Israel on that day
  from the power of the **Egyptians**.

---

weak, incapable of mounting much of a defense. God's utter destruction of the Egyptian army in the final rescue of his people would have been an extraordinary display of the immense strength of the LORD defeating the Egyptian gods.

The song of Miriam sung at the end of this reading, reflects Israel's joy in the LORD's utter victory over the powerful gods of Egypt: "Who is like to you among the gods, O Lord? Who is like to you, magnificent in holiness? O terrible in renown, worker of wonders, when you stretched out your right hand, the earth swallowed them!" With the defeat of the army of Egypt, Israel marched forth toward the promised land with confidence in the Lord and in the leadership of Moses.

The works of God inspire reverential fear among the Israelites. Speak in softer tones of their response to God and Moses.

Their awe turns to rejoicing. Let your face convey the joy as much as your voice.

When Israel **saw** the Egyptians lying **dead** on the **seashore**
and beheld the great **power** that the LORD
had shown **against** the Egyptians,
they **feared** the LORD and **believed** in him and in his
servant Moses.

Then **Moses** and the **Israelites** sang this **song** to the LORD:
I will **sing** to the LORD, for he is **gloriously triumphant;**
horse and **chariot** he has cast into the **sea.**

For meditation and context:

RESPONSORIAL PSALM   Exodus 15:1–2, 3–4, 5–6, 17–18 (1b)

R. Let us sing to the Lord; he has covered himself in glory.

I will sing to the LORD, for he is gloriously
  triumphant;
  horse and chariot he has cast into the sea.
My strength and my courage is the LORD,
  and he has been my savior.
He is my God, I praise him;
  the God of my father, I extol him.

The LORD is a warrior,
  LORD is his name!
Pharaoh's chariots and army he hurled into
  the sea;
  the elite of his officers were submerged
  in the Red Sea.

The flood waters covered them,
  they sank into the depths like a stone.
Your right hand, O LORD, magnificent
  in power,
  your right hand, O LORD, has shattered
  the enemy.

You brought in the people you redeemed
  and planted them on the mountain of
  your inheritance—
the place where you made your seat,
  O LORD,
  the sanctuary, LORD, which your hands
  established.
The LORD shall reign forever and ever.

TO KEEP IN MIND

Word value: Words are your medium, like a painter's brush or a sculptor's chisel. You must understand the words before you can communicate them. Most words have a dictionary meaning (denotative) and an associational meaning (connotative). "House" and "home" both mean "dwelling," yet they communicate different feelings. Be alert to subtle differences in connotative meanings and express them.

Isaiah = ī-ZAY-uh

This text is essentially a "mood" reading that expresses in the stunning imagery of human love and reconciliation the depths of God's love for his people. Practice it several times to appreciate fully the profound love it expresses.

"Husband" and "maker" both express deep affection. The sense is: your creator has become your beloved.

READING IV   Isaiah 54:5–14

A reading from the Book of the Prophet Isaiah

The One who has become your **husband** is your **Maker;**
  his **name** is the LORD of **hosts;**
your **redeemer** is the **Holy** One of Israel,
  called **God** of all the **earth.**

READING IV The next two readings from Isaiah are dated to the period of the Babylonian Exile, around 550 BC, and attributed to the prophet of the exile, Second Isaiah. The image of the relationship between God and the exiled Israelites as husband and wife ("The One who has become your husband is your Maker") is best understood in the context of the revelation from Isaiah that Israel was soon to be released from exile. Israel, the unfaithful wife, was justifiably "cast off." But God, as the ever-faithful husband, shows mercy and forgiveness: "For a brief moment I abandoned you, but with great tenderness I will take you back."

Isaiah presents the Lord's offer for reconciliation in almost unimaginable terms. He speaks of a rebuilt city of Jerusalem, war-torn and destroyed by the Babylonians decades earlier, now restored to a city constructed of the valuable minerals and stones treasured in the ancient world: "I lay your pavements in carnelians, and your foundations in sapphires; I will make your battlements of rubies, your gates of carbuncles, and all your walls of precious stones."

This new beginning initiated by God extends even to the next generation of Israelites: "All your children shall be taught by the Lord, and great shall be the peace of your children."

Your task is to persuade us, through a tone that matches the sincerity of Isaiah's poetry, that God really loves us this much.

God's anger was temporary and "brief," but God's love is "enduring."

God compares the exile to the chastisement visited on the earth in the time of Noah. God is saying: "As I swore to Noah, so now I swear never to 'be angry' or 'rebuke' you again."

My love, says the Lord, is more stable than the mountains and more durable than the hills.

Imagine a lover holding in his hands the face of his beloved. Here, God speaks *directly* to Jerusalem.
carnelians = kahr-NEEL-yuhnz

Semi-precious stones, carnelians are brownish-red quartz and carbuncles are smooth, round, deep-red garnets.

"All your children": God will instruct Israel in the ways of righteousness. Your tone must offer hope, renewal, and salvation, so speak with strength and confidence.

The metaphor of God's relationship to Israel as that of a husband to a wife was not new within Israel's prophetic tradition. Past prophets such as Hosea, Jeremiah, and Ezekiel spoke of Israel as an unfaithful spouse to God. But here, with Isaiah, God has decided resolutely to meet Israel's infidelity with unswerving faithfulness: "I have sworn not to be angry with you, or to rebuke you. . . . My love shall never leave you nor my covenant of peace be shaken."

The LORD calls you **back**,
   like a wife **forsaken** and grieved in **spirit**,
   a wife married in **youth** and then cast **off**,
   says your God.
For a brief **moment** I **abandoned** you,
   but with great **tenderness** I will take you **back**.
In an outburst of **wrath**, for a **moment**
   I **hid** my face from you;
but with enduring **love** I take **pity** on you,
   says the LORD, your **redeemer**.
This is for me like the days of **Noah**,
   when I **swore** that the waters of Noah
   should never **again** deluge the earth;
so I have sworn not to be **angry** with you,
   or to **rebuke** you.
Though the mountains **leave** their place
   and the hills be **shaken**,
my **love** shall **never** leave you
   nor my covenant of peace be **shaken**,
   says the LORD, who has **mercy** on you.
O **afflicted** one, **storm-battered** and **unconsoled**,
   I lay your **pavements** in **carnelians**,
   and your **foundations** in **sapphires**;
I will make your **battlements** of **rubies**,
   your **gates** of **carbuncles**,
   and all your **walls** of precious **stones**.
All your **children** shall be taught by the LORD,
   and **great** shall be the **peace** of your children.
In **justice** shall you be established,
   far from the fear of **oppression**,
   where destruction cannot come **near** you.

For meditation and context:

RESPONSORIAL PSALM   Psalm 30:2, 4, 5–6, 11–12, 13 (2a)

R. I will praise you, Lord, for you have rescued me.

I will extol you, O LORD, for you drew
  me clear
  and did not let my enemies rejoice over me.
O LORD, you brought me up from the
  netherworld;
  you preserved me from among those
  going down into the pit.

Sing praise to the LORD, you his faithful ones,
  and give thanks to his holy name.
For his anger lasts but a moment;
  a lifetime, his good will.
At nightfall, weeping enters in,
  but with the dawn, rejoicing.

Hear, O LORD, and have pity on me;
  O LORD, be my helper.
You changed my mourning into dancing;
  O LORD, my God, forever will I give
  you thanks.

TO KEEP IN MIND

Echoes: Some words echo words that went before. For example, "You shall be a glorious crown . . . a royal diadem" (Isaiah 62:3). Here "diadem" echoes "crown" so it needs no stress. In such cases, emphasize the new idea: royal.

Isaiah = ī-ZAY-uh

Because the text is comprised of short, poetic lines, failing to appreciate the poetic meaning and structure will lead to a choppy, droning delivery. Remember throughout that God is inviting us to turn to him for all our needs, because only he can offer what truly satisfies.

You are inviting the malnourished and starving to a feast they cannot see; so you must paint an inviting picture for them.

Ask these questions simply and directly.

Finding true nourishment requires us to "heed" and "listen." Only God can lead us to this saving banquet; on our own we would not find it. Slow your pace and increase your urgency.

READING V   Isaiah 55:1–11

A reading from the Book of the Prophet Isaiah

Thus says the LORD:
All you who are **thirsty**,
  come to the **water**!
You who have no **money**,
  come, receive **grain** and **eat**;
come, without **paying** and without **cost**,
  drink **wine** and **milk**!
Why spend your money for what is not **bread**,
  your **wages** for what fails to **satisfy**?
Heed me, and you shall eat **well**,
  you shall **delight** in **rich** fare.
Come to me **heedfully**,
  listen, that you may have **life**.
I will **renew** with you the everlasting **covenant**,
  the benefits assured to **David**.

READING V This Fifth Reading is again from Second Isaiah and is part of the oracles spoken around 550 BC during Israel's exile in Babylon. This prophecy extends beyond Israel; God invites all nations to find rest in him: "All you who are thirsty, come to the water!" Although Isaiah presents God's invitation to the exiled Israelites as a renewal of the covenant made to their ancestor, King David—"I will renew with you the everlasting covenant,

the benefits assured to David"—(see 2 Samuel 7:12–16), there is also a more universal dimension to the fulfillment of this prophecy: "So shall you summon a nation you knew not, and nations that knew you not shall run to you, because of the Lord, your God, the Holy One of Israel, who has glorified you."

The reading concludes with God's assurance that his Word will be fulfilled: "My word shall not return to me void, but

shall do my will, achieving the end for which I sent it." After nearly seventy years of captivity in Babylon, and beginning a third generation of exile, the Israelites likely clung to these prophetic words of hope, praying they would see the prophecy's fulfillment in their lifetime, or in the lifetime of their children.

Despite her former infidelity, God will turn Israel into a witness to the nations, like their great king David.

Pause after "has glorified you" and renew your energy.

These words suggest urgency about embracing what God is offering. Delay may mean a tragically missed opportunity.

The "scoundrel" is not being accused but *enticed*.

We struggle to imagine love so "generous in forgiving" because our ways are so far removed from God's. This is not a courtroom argument but a profession of love.

This is a seminal teaching about the efficacy of God's word. Don't rush it. The comparison is long and says essentially that God's word accomplishes what it sets out to do. Each clause is *not* as important as every other; some clauses explain or elaborate what went before. Avoid making *every* word sound important.

Here's the point: God's word works like the rain: it falls and doesn't evaporate and return to the sky without first watering the earth and making it fruitful.

End on a note of divine authority.

As I made him a **witness** to the peoples,
　　a **leader** and commander of **nations**,
so shall you **summon** a nation you knew **not**,
　　and nations that knew you not shall **run** to you,
because of the Lord, your **God**,
　　the **Holy** One of Israel, who has **glorified** you.

Seek the Lord while he may be **found**,
　　call him while he is **near**.
Let the scoundrel **forsake** his way,
　　and the **wicked** man his **thoughts**;
let him **turn** to the Lord for **mercy**;
　　to our **God**, who is **generous** in **forgiving**.
For **my** thoughts are not **your** thoughts,
　　nor are **your** ways **my** ways, says the Lord.
As high as the **heavens** are above the **earth**,
　　so high are **my** ways above **your** ways
　　and **my** thoughts above **your** thoughts.

For just as from the **heavens**
　　the **rain** and **snow** come down
and do not **return** there
　　till they have **watered** the **earth**,
　　making it **fertile** and **fruitful**,
giving **seed** to the one who **sows**
　　and **bread** to the one who **eats**,
so shall my **word** be
　　that goes forth from my mouth;
my **word** shall not return to me **void**,
　　but shall do my **will**,
　　achieving the end for which I **sent** it.

For meditation and context:

RESPONSORIAL PSALM   Isaiah 12:2–3, 4, 5–6 (3)

R. You will draw water joyfully from the springs of salvation.

God indeed is my savior;
　I am confident and unafraid.
My strength and my courage is the LORD,
　and he has been my savior.
With joy you will draw water
　at the fountain of salvation.

Give thanks to the LORD, acclaim his name;
　among the nations make known his deeds,
　proclaim how exalted is his name.

Sing praise to the LORD for his glorious
　achievement;
　let this be known throughout all the earth.
Shout with exultation, O city of Zion,
　for great in your midst
　is the Holy One of Israel!

> **TO KEEP IN MIND**
> **Context:** Who is speaking in this text? What are the circumstances?

Baruch = buh-ROOK

This is another poetic text that challenges the novice reader whose comfort zone is limited to prose. Baruch requires awareness of the devices and the sound of poetry. Don't read this like an excerpt from the editorial pages. It is an *entreaty* to center oneself in the realms of Wisdom grounded in knowledge of God.

The opening exhortation is motivated entirely by love.

The five lines following "How is it" ask Israel to figure out why it is in crisis. The sixth line provides the blunt answer!

Speak "You have forsaken" as a tough-love indictment that's meant to awaken and motivate.

Now you offer a better way: take this path and find peace! Like a good friend, spouse, or parent, you are coaxing, exhorting, pushing for change. "Who has found . . . entered?" are rhetorical questions meant to provoke thought.

READING VI   Baruch 3:9–15, 32—4:4

A reading from the Book of the Prophet Baruch

Hear, O Israel, the **commandments** of **life**:
　listen, and know **prudence**!
How is it, Israel,
　that you are in the land of your **foes**,
　grown old in a **foreign** land,
defiled with the **dead**,
　accounted with those destined for the **netherworld**?
You have **forsaken** the fountain of **wisdom**!
　Had you walked in the way of **God**,
　you would have dwelt in enduring **peace**.
Learn where **prudence** is,
　where **strength**, where **understanding**;
that you may know also
　where are length of **days**, and **life**,
　where light of the **eyes**, and **peace**.
Who has **found** the place of wisdom,
　who has entered into her **treasuries**?

READING VI | Baruch was the scribe of the prophet Jeremiah. He is mentioned by name in the Book of Jeremiah (36:1–8) and is credited with writing down many of Jeremiah's prophesies. Both men bore witness to the Babylonian siege on the city of Jerusalem in 587 BC and the deportation of many of its citizens to Babylon. The Book of Baruch itself is actually five different compositions from varying time periods, with the reading for today being a hymn of praise for the wisdom revealed in the Law of Moses.

Baruch lays blame for the state of exile in Babylon squarely at the feet of the Israelites; he sees their lack of fidelity to the Mosaic Law as the cause for their captivity in a foreign land: "You have forsaken the fountain of wisdom! Had you walked in the way of God, you would have dwelt in enduring peace." Baruch urged the captive Israelites to return to the Law of Moses for "all who cling to her (that is, the wisdom of God revealed in the Law) will live."

He concludes with a dire warning: "Give not your glory to another, your privileges to an alien race." What did he mean by this? It may well have been the case that some of the exiled Israelites were marrying Babylonians and worshipping the gods of Babylon. For Baruch, this would have been a tragedy, since through the Mosaic Law "what pleases God is known to us!" There is simply no excuse for not doing what we know pleases God.

The mood shifts dramatically to a song of praise extolling Wisdom. "The One" is the God of creation; you're retelling the story of God speaking the world into existence. Your tempo is brisk and joyful. "Dismisses light" and "calls it" allude to the sun's setting and rising.

Your voice rings with joy and gratitude on "Such is our God." In the phrase "given her," "her" refers to "understanding." "Jacob" and "Israel" are not individuals but the nation.

"She has appeared on earth" refers to wisdom, here personified as "the book of the precepts" (the Law).

"All who cling" makes the same statement twice using contrasting words "live" and "die."

Imagine speaking "Turn, O Jacob" to a youngster who needs a gentle nudge.

"Glory" refers to God's law, and "privileges" to knowing and heeding the Law's commands. You are pleading that they not squander the treasure they've received. End with joyful gratitude.

The One who knows **all** things knows **her**;
    he has probed her by his **knowledge**—
the One who **established** the earth for all time,
    and **filled** it with four-footed **beasts**;
he who **dismisses** the light, and it **departs**,
    calls it, and it obeys him **trembling**;
before whom the **stars** at their posts
    shine and **rejoice**;
when he **calls** them, they answer, "Here we **are**!"
    shining with **joy** for their Maker.
Such is our **God**;
    no other is to be **compared** to him:
he has traced out the whole way of **understanding**,
    and has given her to **Jacob**, his **servant**,
    to **Israel**, his beloved **son**.

Since then she has **appeared** on earth,
    and **moved** among people.
She is the **book** of the **precepts** of God,
    the **law** that endures **forever**;
all who **cling** to her will **live**,
    but those will **die** who **forsake** her.
Turn, O Jacob, and **receive** her:
    walk by her **light** toward **splendor**.
Give not your glory to **another**,
    your **privileges** to an **alien** race.
Blessed are we, O Israel;
    for what **pleases** God is **known** to us!

For meditation and context:

TO KEEP IN MIND

When practicing, **read Scriptures aloud**, taking note of stress and pause suggestions. After several readings, alter the stress markings to suit your style and interpretation.

Ezekiel = ee-ZEE-kee-uhl

God is anthropomorphized in this text, given human attributes that suggest reluctance to show mercy, which in the end is given less to benefit Israel and more to redeem God's good name.

"In their land" means "in their own land." The tone is plainspoken. Make good use of the strong words that convey God's disappointment and anger: "fury," "scattered," "dispersing," "judged," and "profane."

"The blood that they poured" is a reference to reverencing idols.

God bluntly states that the exile was God's punishment for Israel's many infidelities.

The punishment had the unintended consequence of making the foreign nations questions God's fidelity to the covenant with Israel.

Speak this taunt in the mocking tones of the foreigners.

God's anger was righteous, but God relents nonetheless.

God ensures the people know he acted not for their sake but to restore his "good name."

RESPONSORIAL PSALM   Psalm 19:8, 9, 10, 11 (John 6:68c)

R. Lord, you have the words of everlasting life.

The law of the LORD is perfect,
   refreshing the soul;
the decree of the LORD is trustworthy,
   giving wisdom to the simple.

The precepts of the LORD are right,
   rejoicing the heart;
the command of the LORD is clear,
   enlightening the eye.

The fear of the LORD is pure,
   enduring forever;
the ordinances of the LORD are true,
   all of them just.

They are more precious than gold,
   than a heap of purest gold;
sweeter also than syrup
   or honey from the comb.

READING VII   Ezekiel 36:16–17a, 18–28

A reading from the Book of the Prophet Ezekiel

The word of the LORD came to me, saying:
   Son of **man**, when the house of **Israel** lived in their **land**,
   they **defiled** it by their **conduct** and **deeds**.
Therefore I poured out my **fury** upon them
   because of the **blood** that they poured out on the ground,
   and because they defiled it with **idols**.
I **scattered** them among the nations,
   dispersing them over **foreign** lands;
   according to their **conduct** and **deeds** I judged them.
But when they came among the nations **wherever** they came,
   they served to **profane** my holy name,
   because it was said of them: "These are the people of the LORD,
   yet they had to **leave** their land."
So I have **relented** because of my holy name
   which the house of Israel **profaned**
   among the nations where they came.
Therefore **say** to the house of Israel: Thus says the Lord **GOD**:
   Not for **your** sakes do I act, house of Israel,
   but for the sake of my holy **name**,
   which you **profaned** among the nations to which you came.

| READING VII | The final Old Testament reading for the Easter |

READING VII — The final Old Testament reading for the Easter Vigil is from the prophet Ezekiel. During the Babylonian Exile (597–538 BC), Israel experienced two prophets: Ezekiel and Second Isaiah. Ezekiel was a priest in Jerusalem and, as such, was part of the first deportation to Babylon by King Nebuchadnezzar in 597 BC. The Babylonians initially deported only the leading citizens of Jerusalem in an effort to seize control of the larger, less educated masses. Five years into captivity (593 BC), Ezekiel received his call to be a prophet (see Ezekiel 1–3). In this regard, Ezekiel is the first prophet to be called when he was outside the city and region of Jerusalem. Like Second Isaiah after him, these were the only prophets to be called in a foreign land.

In this reading, Ezekiel offers God's perspective on Israel's captivity in Babylon, as well as God's motive for redeeming his Chosen People. We first hear God's justification for sending Israel into exile: "The house of Israel lived in their land, they defiled it by their conduct and deeds." Simply put, Israel "profaned" God's "holy name." As a result, Israel was expelled from the promised land, "scattered . . .

But as always, God yields to mercy;
he will prove *his* "holiness" by acting in
their best interest.

Speak these lines reassuringly, as a
divine promise.

God's use of water to purify the people is
important within the baptismal context of
tonight's liturgy.

This beloved and classic line might well be
delivered from memory.

Like a parent with a child, God vows to
"make" them live by his law.

There are three promises in the final
sentence. Make them distinct and speak with
loving assurance.

For meditation and context:

TO KEEP IN MIND
Pray the Scriptures: Make reading
these Scriptures a part of your
prayer life every week, and especially during the week prior to the
liturgy in which you will proclaim.

I will prove the **holiness** of my great name, profaned among
    the nations,
  in whose midst you have **profaned** it.
Thus the nations shall **know** that **I** am the LORD, says the
    Lord GOD,
  when in their sight I prove my holiness through **you**.
For I will take you **away** from among the nations,
    gather you from all the foreign lands,
  and bring you **back** to your **own** land.
I will sprinkle **clean water** upon you
    to **cleanse** you from all your **impurities**,
  and from all your **idols** I will cleanse you.
I will give you a **new** heart and place a new **spirit** within you,
    taking from your bodies your **stony** hearts
  and giving you **natural** hearts.
I will put my **spirit** within you and make you live by my **statutes**,
    careful to observe my **decrees**.
You shall **live** in the land I gave your **fathers**;
    you shall be my **people**, and **I** will be your **God**.

RESPONSORIAL PSALM   Psalm 42:3, 5; 43:3, 4 (2)

R. Like a deer that longs for running streams, my soul longs for you, my God.

Athirst is my soul for God, the living God.
  When shall I go and behold the face
    of God?

I went with the throng
  and led them in procession to the house
    of God,
amid loud cries of joy and thanksgiving,
  with the multitude keeping festival.

Send forth your light and your fidelity;
  they shall lead me on
and bring me to your holy mountain,
  to your dwelling-place.

Then will I go in to the altar of God,
  the God of my gladness and joy;
then will I give you thanks upon the harp,
  O God, my God!

Or:

among the nations." Eventually, God "relented," and decided to bring back his Chosen People. Lest Israel return to its former idolatry, God's purpose in redeeming Israel is clearly set forth: "Not for your sakes do I act, house of Israel, but for the sake of my holy name."

The good news for Israel is that God's plan of salvation will result not only in being freed from Babylon and returned to their promised land. More importantly, Israel will experience a complete break from the past: God will "cleanse" Israel from its sins that led to their "impurities" and idolatry. Israel will know a complete conversion: "I will give you a new heart and place a new spirit within you."

Ezekiel offered the exiled Israelites an unimaginable future while still living as captives in Babylon. He foresaw a time in salvation history when both the people and the land of Israel would live in perfect union with the divine. In doing so, Ezekiel set forth God's divine promise: "You shall live in the land I gave your fathers; you shall be my people, and I will be your God."

For meditation and context:

RESPONSORIAL PSALM   Isaiah 12:2–3, 4bcd, 5–6 (3)

R. You will draw water joyfully from the springs of salvation.

God indeed is my savior;
   I am confident and unafraid.
My strength and my courage is the LORD,
   and he has been my savior.
With joy you will draw water
   at the fountain of salvation.

Give thanks to the LORD, acclaim his name;
   among the nations make known his deeds,
   proclaim how exalted is his name.

Sing praise to the LORD for his glorious
   achievement;
   let this be known throughout all the earth.
Shout with exultation, O city of Zion,
   for great in your midst
   is the Holy One of Israel!

Or:

For meditation and context:

RESPONSORIAL PSALM   Psalm 51:12–13, 14–15, 18–19 (12a)

R. Create a clean heart in me, O God.

A clean heart create for me, O God,
   and a steadfast spirit renew within me.
Cast me not out from your presence,
   and your Holy Spirit take not from me.

Give me back the joy of your salvation,
   and a willing spirit sustain in me.
I will teach transgressors your ways,
   and sinners shall return to you.

For you are not pleased with sacrifices;
   should I offer a holocaust, you would not
   accept it.
My sacrifice, O God, is a contrite spirit;
   a heart contrite and humbled, O God, you
   will not spurn.

TO KEEP IN MIND
Know who wrote the letter and who received it. Discover the circumstances. **The intent of each letter dictates the tone.** Often Paul is the writer; he is motivated by multiple concerns: to instruct, console, encourage, chastise, warn, settle disputes, and more. When reading from one of his letters, be aware of what he's trying to accomplish.

Paul's rhetorical question calls us to attention. Use it to command the consideration of your assembly.

"We were indeed" calls for clear eye contact and a direct delivery spoken with conviction.

Paul's point: Christ died, was buried, and rose. We die and are buried in Baptism, and we, too, rise to new life.

EPISTLE   Romans 6:3–11

A reading from the Letter of Saint Paul to the Romans

Brothers and sisters:
Are you **unaware** that we who were **baptized** into Christ **Jesus**
   were baptized into his **death**?
We were indeed **buried** with him through baptism into death,
   so that, just as Christ was **raised** from the dead
   by the glory of the **Father**,
   we **too** might live in newness of **life**.

EPISTLE | The first New Testament reading for the Easter Vigil comes from Paul's Letter to the Romans. Christians throughout the ages have recognized Romans as Paul's most detailed letter in terms of theology and ethics. Written in the spring of AD 56, about twenty-five years after the Death and Resurrection of Christ, Paul writes to a Christian congregation he has yet to meet personally. With this letter,

Paul introduces himself and his Gospel of Jesus Christ to the Christians living in Rome. Today's reading offers some insights into Paul's conviction about God's salvation offered to us through Christ.

Paul saw an inextricable link between Christian Baptism and the Death and Resurrection of Christ. He believed that baptized Christians are called to "live in the newness of life" that Jesus himself experi-

enced through his own Death and Resurrection. In Baptism, the faithful experience a "union," a literal participation between believers and Christ in both his Death and his Resurrection. Because Christ's Death on the Cross put an end to sin, "death no longer has power over him" or us. And through his Resurrection, we are now free to live for God. Paul urged the Christians in Rome to imitate the life of

Work as hard here as above to convey Paul's meaning: we became one with Christ by dying like him in Baptism; we also become one with him by experiencing Resurrection.

"We know": for the believer "faith" equals knowledge. We *know* these things to be true!

"Died" and "live" both are spoken with a positive attitude, for death (Baptism) in Christ leads to life in Christ.

"We know" means we would stake our lives on this!

"Dies no more" and "death no longer has power" is a double statement of a single idea; the second statement receives more stress.

With solid eye contact announce that we are no longer slaves to sin, but alive in the freedom of God.

For meditation and context:

TO KEEP IN MIND
Eye contact connects you with those to whom you minister. Look at the assembly during the middle and at the end of every thought or sentence.

For if we have grown into **union** with him through a **death**
    like his,
   we shall also be **united** with him in the **resurrection**.
We know that our **old** self was **crucified** with him,
   so that our **sinful** body might be done away with,
   that we might no longer be in **slavery** to sin.
For a **dead** person has been **absolved** from sin.
If, then, we have **died** with Christ,
   we believe that we shall also **live** with him.
We know that **Christ**, **raised** from the dead, dies no **more**;
   death no longer has **power** over him.
As to his **death**, he died to sin once and for **all**;
   as to his **life**, he lives for **God**.
Consequently, you **too** must think of yourselves as being **dead**
    to **sin**
   and **living** for **God** in Christ **Jesus**.

RESPONSORIAL PSALM   Psalm 118:1–2, 16–17, 22–23

R. Alleluia, alleluia, alleluia.

Give thanks to the LORD, for he is good,
   for his mercy endures forever.
Let the house of Israel say,
   "His mercy endures forever."

The right hand of the LORD has struck
    with power;
   the right hand of the LORD is exalted.
I shall not die, but live,
   and declare the works of the LORD.

The stone which the builders rejected
   has become the cornerstone.
By the LORD has this been done;
   it is wonderful in our eyes.

Christ: "You too must think of yourselves as being dead to sin, and living for God in Christ Jesus."

For Paul, the Death and Resurrection of Christ were the fulfillment of God's promises made to Israel's patriarchs and prophets. All of salvation history was directed to God's saving acts in Christ. All baptized believers, Jew and Gentile alike, now share in the newness of life that God offers through his own Beloved Son.

GOSPEL   Tonight's Gospel Reading is Mark's narration of the empty tomb. The tradition of the empty tomb is reported by each of the Gospel writers with a remarkable degree of consistency. For example, Mary Magdalene and other women are reported as the first witnesses of the Resurrection in each account. But each evangelist also includes some details unique to his account, features that often reflect each author's theological vision.

In the Gospel according to Mark, one of the curious elements is the presence of a "young man" testifying to the women about Jesus's Resurrection. The other synoptic writers report an "angel of the Lord" (Matthew) and "two men in dazzling clothes" (Luke) at the empty tomb. Mark uses the Greek term *neanias* ("young man") only twice in his Gospel account: in the garden arrest scene (14:51–52) and at the empty tomb (16:5). Mark reports that a "young man" in the garden of Gethsemane

The women, weary and heavy-laden, come with sadness, wondering how they will even gain access to Jesus's body.

Magdalene = MAG-duh-luhn

The details of day and time are important for establishing the veracity of the Resurrection.

They are musing about an impossible task.

Mark notes the size of the stone to increase the capacity for faith.

Your unnuanced tone should not give away the identity of the "young man."

The women's reaction elicits the "young man's" admonition to "not be amazed."

The women examine the very spot where Jesus lay; the witness of the empty tomb was an essential aspect of the early Christian *kerygma*.

Significantly, Peter is singled out from among the disciples. It is not giddy joy that fills these final lines, but swelling hope.

TO KEEP IN MIND

Using the Microphone: Know your public address system. If it echoes, speak even more slowly. If you hear "popping," you're probably standing too close to the microphone.

GOSPEL   Mark 16:1–7

A reading from the holy Gospel according to Mark

When the **sabbath** was over,
    Mary **Magdalene**, Mary, the mother of **James**, and **Salome**
    bought **spices** so that they might go and **anoint** him.
Very **early** when the **sun** had risen,
    on the **first** day of the week, they came to the **tomb**.
They were **saying** to one another,
    "Who will roll back the **stone** for us
    from the entrance to the **tomb**?"
When they looked **up**,
    they saw that the stone **had** been rolled back;
    it was very **large**.
On **entering** the tomb they saw a young **man**
    sitting on the right **side**, clothed in a white **robe**,
    and they were utterly **amazed**.
He **said** to them, "Do **not** be amazed!
You seek **Jesus** of **Nazareth**, the **crucified**.
He has been **raised**; he is not **here**.
Behold the place where they **laid** him.
But **go** and tell his **disciples** and **Peter**,
    'He is going before you to **Galilee**;
    there you will **see** him, as he **told** you.'"

was among the followers of Jesus whom the soldiers tried to arrest, but in his struggle to be freed, he "ran off naked." At the empty tomb, Mark recounts a "young man" now sitting on the right side of the tomb, "clothed in a white robe," bearing witness to Christ's Resurrection. Scholars have wondered if this "young man" may serve part of Mark's theological aims to draw parallels between Christ and Adam. The original man (Adam) naked in a garden and clothed only in shame from disobedience

contrasts with the new Adam (Christ), now clothed in a glorified body from his obedience to the Father, even to the point of Death on a Cross.

In Mark's rapidly paced style, the women are not left to wonder what the empty tomb could mean. This witness in white immediately states that "he has been raised." He instructs the women to take the news to "his disciples and Peter" and reassures them that they will see him in Galilee. What could be more joyful for the Easter Vigil?

What remains constant in each of the empty tomb narratives is the revelation that Jesus "has been raised; he is not here." With the empty tomb, God shows himself definitively in salvation history as the God of the living, inviting all believers into the newness of life offered in the Death and Resurrection of Christ.

EASTER SUNDAY OF THE RESURRECTION OF THE LORD

LECTIONARY #42

READING I   Acts of the Apostles 10:34a, 37–43

A reading from the Acts of the Apostles

Peter proceeded to **speak** and said:
  "You know what has happened all over **Judea**,
    beginning in **Galilee** after the baptism
    that **John** preached,
    how God **anointed** Jesus of **Nazareth**
    with the Holy **Spirit** and **power**.
He went about doing **good**
    and **healing** all those oppressed by the **devil**,
    for **God** was with him.
We are **witnesses** of all that he did
    both in the country of the **Jews** and in **Jerusalem**.
They put him to **death** by hanging him on a **tree**.
This man God **raised** on the **third** day and granted that he
      be **visible**,
    not to **all** the people, but to **us**,
    the witnesses **chosen** by God in **advance**,
    who **ate** and **drank** with him **after** he rose from the **dead**.
He **commissioned** us to preach to the people
    and **testify** that he is the one appointed by God
    as **judge** of the **living** and the **dead**.
To him all the **prophets** bear witness,
    that everyone who **believes** in him
    will receive **forgiveness** of **sins** through his **name**."

Peter is making a public address in the private home of a new convert. He speaks with the conviction of one who has witnessed Christ's Resurrection.

Peter presumes at least a cursory knowledge among his listeners of the ministry of John and Jesus.

Let his voice ring not only with knowledge of Jesus but also with love.

"Spirit" and "power" are manifested in Jesus's healings and exorcisms. All this information is important and supports Peter's witness to Jesus.

"We are witnesses" is a powerful declaration of Peter's authority and of the reliability of his testimony.

Because he has experienced the Resurrection, Peter can speak of Jesus's Crucifixion without apology.

"Witnesses chosen by God" is not braggadocio but confident awareness that the disciples are instruments of God.

Peter's tone is upbeat and full of gratitude.

"Preach" and "testify" are different words. Build energy from the one to the other.

End strong and confident, speaking what you "know," not just what you believe.

Today options are given for the readings. Contact your parish staff to learn which readings will be used.

READING I The Scriptures for Easter Sunday begin with an excerpt from one of Peter's numerous speeches from the Acts of the Apostles. Speeches are, in fact, one of the prominent literary features of Acts, making up nearly one-third of the story line. Peter delivers a total of six speeches: 2:14–36; 3:12–26; 4:8–12; 5:29–32; 10:34–43; 15:7–11.

Today's reading is taken from a speech that Peter delivers in Cornelius's household. Significant to this speech is that Cornelius and the members of his household are Gentiles. In the story line of Acts, it took Peter some time to fully realize the Gentile mission. The visions that he and Cornelius experience in Acts 10 define a turning point in the mission of the Church after Jesus's Ascension. They helped convince Peter that "in truth, I see God shows no partiality" (10:34b).

Another significant aspect of Peter's speech is that Luke, the author of Acts of the Apostles, preserves for us some of the Church's earliest kerygma (preaching) about Christ. In fact, we see in Peter's speech the core of the early Church's preaching about Christ. First, Jesus began his ministry with John's baptism at which God "anointed" him with the Holy Spirit and power. Second, Jesus had a healing ministry of which there were many witnesses. Third, Jesus's Death on the Cross and Resurrection from the dead is also grounded in eyewitness testimony. Fourth, the resurrected Jesus "commissioned" his Apostles to preach and to testify to others that he is "appointed by

For meditation and context:

TO KEEP IN MIND

Know who wrote the letter and who received it. Discover the circumstances. **The intent of each letter dictates the tone.** Often Paul is the writer; he is motivated by multiple concerns: to instruct, console, encourage, chastise, warn, settle disputes, and more. When reading from one of his letters, be aware of what he's trying to accomplish.

Colossians = kuh-LOSH-uhnz

Paul is full of enthusiasm, but you must deliver his words without rushing.

"If then you were raised" means "because you were raised up."

Paul is giving life-saving advice and he does it with conviction.

Paul is referring to Christ's appearance at the Second Coming.

RESPONSORIAL PSALM   Psalm 118:1–2, 16–17, 22–23 (24)

R. This is the day the Lord has made; let us rejoice and be glad. orR. Alleluia.

Give thanks to the LORD, for he is good,
   for his mercy endures forever.
Let the house of Israel say,
   "His mercy endures forever."

"The right hand of the LORD has struck
     with power;
   the right hand of the LORD is exalted.
I shall not die, but live,
   and declare the works of the LORD.

The stone which the builders rejected
   has become the cornerstone.
By the LORD has this been done;
   it is wonderful in our eyes.

READING II   Colossians 3:1–4

A reading from the Letter of Saint Paul to the Colossians

Brothers and sisters:
If then you were **raised** with Christ, seek what is **above**,
   where Christ is seated at the right hand of **God**.
Think of what is **above**, not of what is on **earth**.
For you have **died**, and your life is **hidden** with Christ in **God**.
When Christ your life **appears**,
   then you **too** will appear with him in **glory**.

Or:

God as judge of the living and the dead." Last, one's belief in the crucified and resurrected Christ is directly linked to the "forgiveness of sins." It was largely in light of the Resurrection that the disciples were able to fully understand Jesus as the Messiah and Son of God.

READING II | **COLOSSIANS.** The Christian community at Colossae was not founded by Paul, but by a Colossian "minister of Christ" named Epaphras who formed the people in faith. This letter was apparently written after Epaphras visited

Paul in prison and reported on the situation at Colossae. Other teachers had come to town, preaching a false doctrine that is described in the letter as "a seductive philosophy according to human tradition, according to the elemental powers of the world and not according to Christ." The false teachings also included certain physical practices related to diet, festivals, and astronomical observances. The letter is intended to lead the Colossians back onto the true path by reminding them of the essentials about Christ and Christian life.

Today's excerpt from the letter introduces a section laying out the ethical consequences of being a disciple of Christ. The list of behaviors to be avoided and those to be cultivated is not part of the reading. Instead, the Lectionary offers for our contemplation the logical proposition out of which Christian behavior flows—that if we are Christians, we must be focused on "what is above, not what is on earth"—on ultimate spiritual truths rather than on the immediate physical world.

In the first verse, the "if" part of the proposition describes the Christian's bond

READING II   1 Corinthians 5:6b–8

A reading from the first Letter of Saint Paul to the Corinthians

Brothers and sisters:
Do you not **know** that a little **yeast** leavens **all** the dough?
Clear out the **old** yeast,
      so that you may become a **fresh** batch of dough,
      inasmuch as you are **unleavened**.
For our paschal **lamb**, **Christ**, has been **sacrificed**.
Therefore, let us **celebrate** the feast,
      not with the **old** yeast, the yeast of **malice** and **wickedness**,
      but with the **unleavened** bread of **sincerity** and **truth**.

Corinthians = kor-in-THEE-uhnz

Paul is urging vigilance in the moral life. His tone is not stern, but hopeful and buoyant.

For Paul, yeast is symbolic of the subtle and menacing spread of "malice and wickedness."

In Christ, we become a batch of "unleavened," which for Paul means uncorrupted, dough.

The penultimate line states the negative: "Don't do this" (spoken with greater volume) and the last line states the positive: "Do this instead" (spoken with greater intensity).

For meditation and context:

SEQUENCE   Victimae paschali laudes

Christians, to the Paschal Victim
      Offer your thankful praises!
A Lamb the sheep redeems;
      Christ, who only is sinless,
      Reconciles sinners to the Father.
Death and life have contended in that
      combat stupendous:
      The Prince of life, who died, reigns
      immortal.

Speak, Mary, declaring
      What you saw, wayfaring.
"The tomb of Christ, who is living,
      The glory of Jesus' resurrection;
Bright angels attesting,
      The shroud and napkin resting.
Yes, Christ my hope is arisen;
      to Galilee he goes before you."
Christ indeed from death is risen, our new
      life obtaining.
      Have mercy, victor King, ever reigning!
      Amen. Alleluia.

TO KEEP IN MIND
Gestures and Posture: Using gestures is not part of the task of proclamation; within the liturgy, gestures are an unnecessary distraction. However, your body language is always communicating. Avoid leaning on the ambo or standing on one foot. And don't let your face or body contradict the Good News you announce. Readers are allowed to smile!

---

with Christ. "If then you were raised with Christ" is a phrase that becomes more clear in the light of a verse from an earlier chapter (2:12): "You were buried with him in baptism, in which you were also raised with him through faith in the power of God, who raised him from the dead." So it is our Baptism that binds us to Christ so firmly that when we go down into the waters we experience symbolically Christ's burial, and when we come up out of the water we are symbolically raised, just as God raised his Son. This experience drastically changes

hearts and minds, making us capable of seeking spiritual values in place of our physical concerns. How do we do this? By setting our minds on spiritual realities instead of remaining consumed by the earthly. This new capacity of mind and heart enables us to live the ethical life expected of disciples.

1 CORINTHIANS. When Paul wrote his First Letter to the Corinthians, he was deeply concerned about the factions that developed within the congregation in Corinth. In fact, Paul committed the opening four chapters of his letter to addressing

this problem, urging the Corinthian church to find its unity in Christ. Paul then turns to some unethical behavior being reported in the community. It is within this context that we hear in today's reading of the importance of clearing out the "old yeast."

The "old yeast" to which Paul is referring is connected to reports he heard that one of their community members was "a man living with his father's wife" (1 Corinthians 5:1). Paul's metaphor of clearing out all the old yeast to create "a fresh batch of dough" speaks directly to this

GOSPEL John 20:1–9

A reading from the holy Gospel according to John

On the **first** day of the **week**,
    Mary of **Magdala** came to the **tomb** early in the **morning**,
    while it was still **dark**,
    and saw the **stone removed** from the **tomb**.
So she **ran** and went to Simon **Peter**
    and to the **other** disciple whom Jesus **loved**, and told them,
    "They have taken the **Lord** from the **tomb**,
    and we don't know where they **put** him."
So **Peter** and the **other** disciple went out and **came** to the tomb.
They both **ran**, but the **other** disciple ran **faster** than Peter
    and arrived at the tomb **first**;
    he **bent** down and saw the **burial** cloths there, but did not go **in**.
When Simon **Peter** arrived **after** him,
    he went **into** the tomb and **saw** the burial cloths there,
    and the cloth that had covered his **head**,
    not with the **burial** cloths but rolled up in a **separate** place.
Then the **other** disciple **also** went in,
    the one who had arrived at the tomb **first**,
    and he **saw** and **believed**.
For they did not yet **understand** the Scripture
    that he had to **rise** from the dead.

Begin low-key, mindful that Mary approaches the tomb with weariness and great sadness.

Magdala = MAG-duh-luh

"It was still dark" not in the tomb, but in the recesses of Mary's heart.

She hurries to share the bad news of Jesus's presumed abduction.

"The other disciple" can't be a throwaway identification; speak it with as much reverence as Peter's name.

Distinguish the activities of running, arriving, bending down, seeing, and not going in.

Peter is all action; John is pensive and full of awe.

"Saw and believed" name two distinct actions; don't run them together.

The final sentence has no trace of admonishment. It is understandable that they would not yet fully "understand."

TO KEEP IN MIND

Ritardando: refers to the practice, common in music, of becoming gradually slower and expanding the words as you approach the end of a piece. Many readings end this way—with a decreased rate but increased intensity.

---

man's immoral behavior, "the yeast of malice and wickedness." Because of the Resurrection of Christ, "our paschal lamb," Paul viewed the Corinthian congregation as capable of being a "fresh batch of dough," a new opportunity to be "the unleavened bread of sincerity and truth." But to do so, all members of the Christian community must recognize that they are called to a higher ethical standard. Christian faith, in light of the resurrected Christ, demands a certain norm of moral conduct.

GOSPEL The Gospel Reading for the Easter Vigil was Mark's account of the empty tomb. On Easter Sunday, we hear the first part of John's story. Mark and John share only a few details in common: Mary of Magdala (Mary Magdalene) is the first to approach the tomb of Jesus (accompanied, in Mark, by two other women); the stone covering the tomb was removed; and the tomb where Jesus was laid was empty. John offers his own version of what happened next.

In John's version, Peter and the Beloved Disciple investigate the tomb where Jesus's

body was laid to rest. The Beloved Disciple defers to Peter, allowing Peter to discover Jesus's burial cloths (his head and body covering) "rolled up in a separate place." Yet the Beloved Disciple, upon entering the empty tomb after Peter, "saw and believed." The importance of believing in Jesus is a major theme running throughout the Gospel according to John. In fact, John contrasts believing with understanding, for he follows the report of the Beloved Disciple's immediate belief with the comment: "For they did not yet understand the Scripture

AFTERNOON GOSPEL   Luke 24:13–35

A reading from the holy Gospel according to Luke

That **very** day, the **first** day of the week,
    two of Jesus' **disciples** were going
    to a village seven **miles** from Jerusalem called **Emmaus**,
    and they were **conversing** about all the things that
        had **occurred**.
And it **happened** that while they were **conversing** and **debating**,
    Jesus **himself** drew near and **walked** with them,
    but their eyes were **prevented** from **recognizing** him.
He asked them,
    "What are you **discussing** as you walk along?"
They **stopped**, looking **downcast**.
One of them, named **Cleopas**, said to him in reply,
    "Are you the **only** visitor to Jerusalem
    who does not **know** of the **things**
    that have taken place there in these days?"
And he replied to them, "What **sort** of things?"
They **said** to him,
    "The **things** that happened to **Jesus** the **Nazarene**,
    who was a **prophet** mighty in **deed** and **word**
    before **God** and all the **people**,
    how our chief **priests** and **rulers both** handed him over
    to a sentence of **death** and **crucified** him.
But we were **hoping** that **he** would be the one to **redeem** Israel;
    and **besides** all this,
    it is now the **third** day since this took place.
Some **women** from our group, however, have **astounded** us:
    they were at the **tomb** early in the **morning**
    and did not find his **body**;
    they came back and reported
    that they had indeed seen a **vision** of angels
    who announced that he was **alive**.

Naming the "day" is important.

Emmaus = eh-MAY-uhs

The words "conversing and debating" suggest a spirited conversation and perhaps some theological reflection on the jarring events of Christ's Passion.

Don't overlook the irony of not recognizing the very one they long to see.

Jesus goads them on by playing dumb.

Cleopas = KLEE-uh-puhs

His grief has made him short-tempered.

Jesus has an agenda and prods further. Though initially annoyed, they're soon into their storytelling.

We can sense hope surging anew in their hearts as they relate their story.

They lay Jesus's Death at the feet of both "priests" and "rulers."

Many have known the sadness of watching their hopes dashed to pieces.

Are they lending credence to the testimony or dismissing it because it came from women?

Is there hope building in their hearts as they relate these events?

that he had to rise from the dead."(John may have been referring here to Psalm 16:10 and Hosea 6:2.)

In the very personal, touching scene between the risen Lord and Mary Magdalene, John also shows us the power of love in bridging the seeming chasm between death and life, body and spirit. Mary's role as the first to see the Lord, as apostle to the Apostles, has made her an inspiring figure for both women and men.

AFTERNOON GOSPEL Luke is the only Gospel writer to preserve the Resurrection story of Jesus's appearance to the two disciples on the road to Emmaus. Catholic scholars have long recognized that this story falls into parts reflecting the two essential actions of the Mass: the Liturgy of the Word (where Jesus interpreted for the two disciples "what referred to him in all the Scriptures") and the Liturgy of the Eucharist (where Jesus revealed himself "in the breaking of the bread").

In preserving this Resurrection story, Luke provides for us some insights into the beliefs and traditions of the earliest Christians that can be seen in the two parts of the story. In the first part of the story, Jesus, in his resurrected body, was unrecognizable (the disciples' eyes "were prevented from recognizing him"), and Jesus was acknowledged as "a prophet mighty in deed and word before God and all the people." (Whether, at the time of the Resurrection, one believed that Jesus was

By now, awareness should be dawning, but they remain obtuse.

Jesus does not hide his disappointment.

"Then beginning" initiates a new narrative beat. Jesus resumes his former role of teacher.

Jesus feigns needing to go further, but they plead for him to stay!

Pause after "went in to stay with them."
Lift out the Eucharistic language.

The pace quickens once their eyes are "opened."

Their words express the joy-filled awareness that floods their hearts.

The conviction with which they relate their tale in Jerusalem should characterize your telling of this pivotal story.

The final sentence states the basis of all Christian liturgy. Speak with care, with gradual slowing on the words "in the breaking of the bread."

"Then some of those with us **went** to the tomb
and found things just as the women had **described**,
but **him** they did not **see**."
And he said to them, "Oh, how **foolish** you are!
How **slow** of heart to believe all that the **prophets** spoke!
Was it not **necessary** that the Christ should **suffer** these things
and enter into his **glory**?"
Then beginning with **Moses** and all the **prophets**,
he **interpreted** to them what **referred** to him
in **all** the **Scriptures**.
As they approached the **village** to which they were **going**,
he gave the impression that he was going on **farther**.
But they **urged** him, "**Stay** with us,
for it is nearly **evening** and the day is almost **over**."
So he went in to **stay** with them.
And it **happened** that, while he was with them at **table**,
he took **bread**, said the **blessing**,
broke it, and **gave** it to them.
With **that** their **eyes** were **opened** and they **recognized** him,
but he **vanished** from their **sight**.
Then they **said** to each other,
"Were not our **hearts burning** within us
while he **spoke** to us on the way and opened the **Scriptures**
to us?"
So they set out at **once** and returned to **Jerusalem**
where they found gathered together
the **eleven** and those with them who were saying,
"The Lord has truly been **raised** and has appeared to **Simon**!"
Then the **two** recounted
what had taken place on the **way**
and how he was made **known** to them in the **breaking**
of **bread**.

the Christ and Son of God or not, no one could argue against his healing and preaching ministry.) In addition, the reference in Scripture to Jesus's Passion ("Was it not necessary that the Messiah should suffer?") does not seem to come from an explicit "suffering Messiah" text in the Old Testament, although close parallels can be found; for example, in the four suffering servant songs in Isaiah 40–55, especially Isaiah 52:13—53:12.

In the second part of the story, two traditions are apparent. First, the fourfold action of the Eucharistic meal is already well known: "While he was with them at table, he took the bread, said the blessing, broke it, and gave it to them." Second, the Apostles' witness to the Resurrection was being preached as a core element in the Gospel message: "The Lord has truly been raised and has appeared to Simon!"

The story of the road to Emmaus has become one of the most well-known Resurrection narratives. Catholics often see in it the "first Mass," with its clear divisions between proclaiming and expounding on Scripture and celebrating the Eucharist. Catholics believe that the resurrected Christ is present in the Mass in the sacred Scriptures and in the consecrated bread and wine that we eat and drink. In the Emmaus story, Luke provides the scriptural basis for this Church teaching.

SECOND SUNDAY OF EASTER (OR SUNDAY OF DIVINE MERCY)

LECTIONARY #44

READING I   Acts of the Apostles 4:32–35

A reading from the Acts of the Apostles

The community of **believers** was of one **heart** and **mind**,
> and **no** one claimed that any of his **possessions** was his **own**,
> but they had everything in **common**.
With great **power** the apostles bore **witness**
> to the **resurrection** of the Lord Jesus,
> and great **favor** was accorded them all.
There was no **needy** person among them,
> for those who owned **property** or **houses** would **sell** them,
> bring the **proceeds** of the sale,
> and put them at the feet of the **apostles**,
> and they were **distributed** to each according to **need**.

A pause to establish eye contact will help establish the mood of harmony with which the text begins.

Relate this information with awareness of how remarkable it was to enjoy such accord.

The Apostles bore "witness" and did it with "power." Be sure to convey both realities.

Throughout, your tone is saying, "Difficult as it may be to believe, this is how they lived." The generosity attested to here is remarkable.

Convey joyous admiration for these exemplary role models of Christian faith.

For meditation and context:

RESPONSORIAL PSALM   Psalm 118:2–4, 13–15, 22–24 (1)

R. Give thanks to the Lord, for he is good; his love is everlasting. orR. Alleluia.

Let the house of Israel say,
  "His mercy endures forever."
Let the house of Aaron say,
  "His mercy endures forever."
Let those who fear the LORD say,
  "His mercy endures forever."

I was hard pressed and was falling,
  but the LORD helped me.
My strength and my courage is the LORD,
  and he has been my savior.
The joyful shout of victory
  in the tents of the just.

The stone which the builders rejected
  has become the cornerstone.
By the LORD has this been done;
  it is wonderful in our eyes.
This is the day the LORD has made;
  let us be glad and rejoice in it.

TO KEEP IN MIND

Openings and Closings: differ in tone from the Scripture and require pauses, after the opening dialogue and before the closing dialogue. These formulas are prescribed, so don't vary the wording.

READING I Today's reading is an example of the numerous summary statements that Luke provides in Acts of the Apostles, his account of the growth of the early Church. (Others include: 2:42–47; 4:32–35; 5:12–16; 6:7; 9:31; 16:5; and 19:20.) These summaries present an idealized portrait of the early Church: a Church united under apostolic leadership, guided by the Holy Spirit, growing and spreading throughout the Roman Empire.

Today's is the second such summary in Acts, and it describes the original "community of believers" in Jerusalem. The

Church was "of one heart and mind," no longer concerned about personal "possessions," and guided by the leadership of the apostles. In other words, Luke portrays the followers of Jesus living just as Jesus had commanded them during his ministry (see, for example, Luke 12:33; 16: 9, 11, 13; 18:24–25, 28–30).

Equally important, the Apostles followed the command of the resurrected Christ to bear witness to the Resurrection and to preach repentance for the forgiveness of sins in Jesus's name to all the nations, beginning in Jerusalem (Luke

24:47–48): "With great power the apostles bore witness to the resurrection of the Lord Jesus." In return, members of the Jerusalem congregation were loyal to the Apostles' leadership, trusting in their judgment, and laying the "proceeds" from the sale of their possessions "at the feet of the apostles." Through Luke's writing, we see a model of Christian life and evangelism that continues to inspire discipleship.

READING II In this excerpt from John's letter, the Lectionary has inserted the author's characteristic way of

This is the first of six consecutive weeks we read from 1 John.

Each sentence relies on the one before and sets up the one after it, repeating information from the previous sentence before advancing the thought with new information. Use the repetitions like bricks that support the new idea.

"Everyone who believes . . . loves also the one begotten by him" is the key teaching of the text. Proclaim it with conviction.

Here is a stark truth: you can obey without loving, but you can't love without obeying.

Don't rush this sentence; note it communicates two distinct ideas.

"Who indeed" is oratorical language designed to make a point. Use it as intended.

Don't overlook the intentional repetitions of "water and blood." "Water" (Christ's baptism) and "blood" (his Death) are both necessary parts of Christ's saving work.

Through your proclamation, you too testify to Christ.

READING II   1 John 5:1–6

A reading from the first Letter of Saint John

Beloved:
Everyone who **believes** that Jesus is the **Christ** is **begotten**
    by **God**,
    and everyone who loves the **Father**
    loves also the one **begotten** by him.
In this way we know that we **love** the **children** of God
    when we love **God** and obey his **commandments**.
For the love of God is this,
    that we keep his **commandments**.
And his commandments are not **burdensome**,
    for whoever is begotten by God **conquers** the **world**.
And the **victory** that conquers the world is our **faith**.
Who indeed is the **victor** over the world
    but the one who **believes** that Jesus is the Son of **God?**

This is the one who came through **water** and **blood**, Jesus **Christ**,
    not by water **alone**, but by **water** and **blood**.
The **Spirit** is the one that **testifies**,
    and the **Spirit** is **truth**.

Remember, the narrator is not a neutral bystander but a proactive proselytizer.

The opening narration offers significant information: first day of the week; locked doors; fear of the Jews.

Jesus's proffer of peace can be spoken with strength, like an imperative.

GOSPEL   John 20:19–31

A reading from the holy Gospel according to John

On the evening of that **first** day of the week,
    when the doors were **locked**, where the disciples were,
    for fear of the **Jews**,
    Jesus came and stood in their midst
    and said to them, "**Peace** be with you."

addressing his community—"Beloved" and we hear him speak of believers in this community as "children of God." More than terms of endearment, these designations carry with them the ethical obligation to "love God," and "obey his commandments." Further, as children of God, all Christians share a theology that asserts the divinity of Christ, proclaiming, "Jesus is the Son of God."

For John, it is our faith in Christ and love of God and his Commandments that give us "the victory that conquers the world." Faith and love in the life of a

Christian provide a certain kind of power in the world against all that is evil. Scholars suspect that John's concern about conquering "the world" is likely rooted in persecutions that his congregation was experiencing, as well as certain heretical ideas about Jesus that had emerged in the community. The letter lifts up community love and solidarity based on true ideas about Jesus and fidelity to his teachings.

The reading closes with John asserting that the power and the presence of "the Spirit" in their midst confirms the truth of his words: "The Spirit is the one that testi-

fies, and the Spirit is truth." The language of "Spirit" and "truth" mentioned here and throughout this letter is also found in the Gospel according to John (see, for example, John 15:26; 16:13; 18:38). This leads to the conclusion that the Gospel according to John and the three letters of John may have been intended for the same community of believers.

GOSPEL   All four Gospel writers preserve as the opening to their Resurrection narratives the story of the empty tomb. And all share some features

To these ten, Jesus immediately shows "his hands and his side." The second offer of peace shifts their focus from celebration to commissioning.

Don't rush this critical moment of receiving the Spirit and the power to forgive sins.

Quicken your pacing for this new narrative beat.

Thomas asks for what the others have already seen. Their testimony is not enough for him.

The narrator knows where the story is going: speak with that awareness. Again, the doors are locked.

Jesus satisfies Thomas's need for proof, but turns it into an object lesson.

Rather than "rejoicing" like the other ten, Thomas declares his faith and worships.

Looking at your assembly, let these words honor them rather than chide Thomas.

This is not a throwaway summary, but an effort to bolster faith. Speak it directly to the assembly.

When he had said this, he showed them his **hands** and his **side**.
The disciples **rejoiced** when they saw the Lord.
Jesus said to them **again**, "**Peace** be with you.
As the **Father** has sent me, so **I** send **you**."
And when he had said this, he **breathed** on them and said
  to them,
 "**Receive** the Holy **Spirit**.
Whose **sins** you **forgive** are **forgiven** them,
  and whose sins you **retain** are **retained**."

Thomas, called **Didymus**, one of the **Twelve**,
 was not **with** them when Jesus came.
So the **other** disciples said to him, "We have **seen** the Lord."
But he said to them,
 "Unless I **see** the mark of the **nails** in his **hands**
 and put my **finger** into the nailmarks
 and put my **hand** into his **side**, I will not **believe**."

Now a week **later** his disciples were again inside
 and Thomas **was** with them.
Jesus **came**, although the doors were **locked**,
 and stood in their midst and said, "**Peace** be with you."
Then he said to **Thomas**, "Put your **finger** here and see my **hands**,
 and bring your **hand** and put it into my **side**,
 and do not be **unbelieving**, but **believe**."
Thomas **answered** and said to him, "My **Lord** and my **God**!"
Jesus said to him, "Have you come to **believe** because you have
  seen me?
Blessed are those who have **not** seen and have **believed**."

Now Jesus did many **other** signs in the presence of his disciples
 that are not **written** in this book.
But **these** are written that you may come to **believe**
 that Jesus is the **Christ**, the Son of **God**,
 and that **through** this belief you may have **life** in his name.

of the story, such as the first witness of Mary Magdalene and the general concern over Jesus's body being absent. But after the report of the empty tomb, the evangelists offer distinctive features in their Resurrection stories. Today's reading, the story of "doubting Thomas," is found only in the Gospel according to John.

In this Resurrection account, when Jesus appeared to the disciples with the greeting, "Peace be with you," John remarks twice that "the doors were locked." Jesus, in his resurrected body, defied some physical realities as we know them. Yet, when attempting to assuage Thomas's doubts over his corporeal Resurrection, Jesus challenged Thomas, "Put your fingers here and see my hands, and bring your hand and put it into my side." Upon seeing Jesus's physical body and hearing his invitation, Thomas believed. "Belief" in Jesus is a major theme running throughout the Gospel according to John, and it is affirmed here in Jesus's words to all who have not seen the resurrected Christ: "Blessed are those who have not seen and have believed." This is reinforced with the concluding remark in today reading: "These are written that you may come to believe that Jesus is the Christ, the Son of God."

In the synoptic Gospel accounts, it is Peter's confession that lays claim to Jesus's true identity, "You are the Messiah, the Son of the living God" (Matthew 16:16, which can be compared to Mark 8:29 and Luke 9:20). In the same category, Thomas's confession of faith in the resurrected Jesus, "My Lord and my God!" stands as one of the New Testament's most powerful Christological claims.

THIRD SUNDAY
OF EASTER

LECTIONARY #47

TO KEEP IN MIND
Read all three commentaries.
Suggestions in each can give you
insight into your own passage.

There is an unmistakable oratorical quality
signaled by the repetitions at the start of the
text. Let your voice match the oratorical style.

Peter has worked a miracle just prior to this
address, so he's emboldened and the
audience is riveted.

There is more regret than accusation in
these lines.

He doesn't want to turn them away, but
to help them understand who Jesus was.
The titles he gives Jesus were reserved
for God.

Like a parent who has said what needed
to be said, he now softens his tone
and acknowledges the mitigating factor
of their "ignorance."

The witness of the prophets confirms Jesus
as Messiah.

The entire reading leads to this last line: it is a
heartfelt call to conversion, not just for them
then, but for us now.

READING I   Acts of the Apostles 3:13–15, 17–19

A reading from the Acts of the Apostles

Peter said to the **people**:
"The God of **Abraham**,
    the God of **Isaac**, and the God of **Jacob**,
    the God of our **fathers**, has **glorified** his servant **Jesus**,
    whom **you** handed over and **denied** in Pilate's presence
    when he had decided to **release** him.
You denied the **Holy** and **Righteous** One
    and asked that a **murderer** be released to you.
The author of **life** you put to **death**,
    but God **raised** him from the dead; of this we are **witnesses**.
Now I **know**, brothers,
    that you acted out of **ignorance**, just as your **leaders** did;
    but God has thus brought to **fulfillment**
    what he had announced **beforehand**
    through the mouth of all the **prophets**,
    that his **Christ** would **suffer**.
Repent, therefore, and be **converted**, that your **sins** may be
    wiped **away**."

READING I   This reading from the Acts of the Apostles is an excerpt from the second major speech that Peter delivers in the streets of Jerusalem. The focus is on the meaning of the Death and Resurrection of Jesus. (See Acts 3:11–26 for the full speech.) Peter's speech follows his healing of a crippled man, accomplished by Peter in the name of "Jesus Christ the Nazorean" (Acts 3:6). Like all the speeches from Acts, this reflects the *kerygma* (oral proclamations) of the early Church that Luke, the author of Acts, wanted to preserve.

One of the consistent themes in these speeches is the connection between the Resurrection of Jesus and the God of the historical figures of ancient Israel. Peter connects Jesus to "the God of Abraham, the God of Isaac, and the God of Jacob, the God of our fathers." In this speech, Peter refers to Jesus as God's servant ("his servant") and God's Christ ("his Christ"). The pronouns make it clear that the early Church proclaimed Jesus as God's instrument for salvation: "God has thus brought to fulfillment what he had announced

beforehand through the mouth of all the prophets."

The speech concludes with a call to conversion: "Repent, therefore, and be converted that your sins may be wiped away." Simply listening to, and perhaps even believing, Peter and the other Apostles was not enough—an active response was required. God's salvific work in raising Jesus from the dead required repentance of one's sins. Peter called his audience into a participation in God's covenantal fulfillment. For Luke, the dramatic events of salvation history required more than passive

For meditation and context:

TO KEEP IN MIND

Stress (Bold Print): identifies words that are more important or expressive than others and require more stress. Use your judgment about the amount of stress so as to avoid an artificial delivery.

This is the second of six consecutive weeks we read from John's letter.

Imagine the Apostle, at an advanced age, writing with compassion, but pulling no punches.

He writes to "children" in need of instruction.

Because we will always be sinners, we will always have an "Advocate" to intercede for us. This is *good* news.

He speaks of an intimate, not a passing, kind of *knowing*, and it is equated with keeping the Commandments.

This is the kind of hard teaching best delivered by a loving grandparent or beloved teacher. Yet the message is blunt: they are "liars" and are void of "truth."

After a pause, announce this good news in a gentle, hopeful tone.

These are the two disciples, with hearts still burning, whom Jesus encountered on the road to Emmaus.

READING II Although the author to the First Letter of John never directly identifies himself in this letter, he does use the first person singular ("I") and states clearly his intention for writing: "My children, I am writing this to you so that you may not commit sin." In the Second and Third Letter of John, however, the author refers to himself as the "Presbyter" (2 John 1:1; 3 John 1:1), suggesting some type of leadership role within the congregation.

RESPONSORIAL PSALM   Psalm 4:2, 4, 7–8, 9 (7a)

R. Lord, let your face shine on us. orR. Alleluia.

When I call, answer me, O my just God,
   you who relieve me when I am in distress;
   have pity on me, and hear my prayer!

Know that the LORD does wonders for his
      faithful one;
   the LORD will hear me when I call
      upon him.

O LORD, let the light of your countenance
      shine upon us!
   You put gladness into my heart.

As soon as I lie down, I fall peacefully asleep,
   for you alone, O LORD,
   bring security to my dwelling.

READING II   1 John 2:1–5a

A reading from the first Letter of Saint John

My **children**, I am **writing** this to you
   so that you may not commit **sin**.
But if anyone **does** sin, we have an **Advocate** with the Father,
   Jesus **Christ** the **righteous** one.
He is **expiation** for our sins,
   and not for **our** sins only but for those of the whole **world**.
The way we may be **sure** that we know him
   is to keep his **commandments**.
Those who say, "I **know** him," but do **not** keep his
      commandments
   are **liars**, and the **truth** is not in them.
But whoever **keeps** his word,
   the love of God is truly **perfected** in him.

GOSPEL   Luke 24:35–48

A reading from the holy Gospel according to Luke

The two disciples **recounted** what had taken place on the way,
   and how Jesus was made **known** to them
   in the **breaking** of **bread**.

---

receptivity; rather, they demanded a very specific response from all people.

Today's reading calls Jesus "an Advocate" and "the righteous one," and speaks of Jesus as the "expiation for our sins." John emphasizes the importance of knowing Christ and calls believers to a high ethical standard: "Keep his commandments." Within the writings of John's community—the Gospel according to John and the three letters—Jesus's "commandment" is explicit: "Love one another" (for example, John 13:34; 1 John 3:14; 2 John 5; 3 John 6). For the author of 1 John, failure to follow this fundamental charge renders one a "liar." But rising daily to this challenge to love one another has a supreme reward: "the love of God is truly perfected" in the believer.

GOSPEL The Gospel Reading is taken from the final Resurrection appearance in the Gospel according to Luke. Since Luke wrote both the Gospel account and the Acts of the Apostles, it is not surprising that a similar theme arises in both: the Death and Resurrection of Christ fulfills God's covenants with Israel.

Jesus's offer of peace is almost a command.

The opposite of peace ensues; they are panicked and frightened.

Jesus's response betrays impatience and disappointment.

Despite previous appearances, he needs to escalate his proofs that it is really he.

We sense Jesus thinking these close disciples should know better.

This detail not only persuades them but also depicts his ongoing pastoral concern for his disciples.

Ever the teacher, Jesus resumes his ministry and educates them. He wants the "words that I spoke to you" to be the foundation of their faith. But he must "open their minds" to ensure understanding.

Each line of this sentence imparts a new piece of information. Spotlight those teachings by lifting out the operative words: "suffer," "rise," "repentance," "preached," and "nations."

The final line is as true of your assembly as it was of the Apostles. Look right at them as you speak.

While they were still **speaking** about this,
   he **stood** in their midst and said to them,
   "**Peace** be with you."
But they were **startled** and **terrified**
   and thought that they were seeing a **ghost**.
Then he **said** to them, "Why are you **troubled**?
And why do **questions** arise in your hearts?
Look at my **hands** and my **feet**, that it is I **myself**.
Touch me and **see**, because a **ghost** does not have flesh and bones
   as you can see I have."
And as he **said** this,
   he **showed** them his hands and his feet.
While they were still incredulous for **joy** and were **amazed**,
   he asked them, "Have you anything here to **eat**?"
They gave him a piece of baked **fish**;
   he took it and **ate** it in **front** of them.

He said to them,
   "These are my words that I spoke to you while I was still
      with you,
   that everything written about me in the law of **Moses**
   and in the **prophets** and **psalms** must be **fulfilled**."
Then he opened their minds to **understand** the Scriptures.
And he said to them,
   "Thus it is written that the Christ would **suffer**
   and **rise** from the dead on the third **day**
   and that **repentance**, for the forgiveness of **sins**,
   would be preached in his name
   to all the **nations**, beginning from **Jerusalem**.
You are **witnesses** of these things."

The Resurrection stories heard last week in John's account and this week in Luke's story share some elements. First, in both, the resurrected Christ greets his disciples with the phrase, "Peace be with you." It is a greeting of comfort and support to the group so traumatized by the events of the past few days. Second, both Luke and John place much emphasis on the physical presence of the resurrected Christ. Jesus encourages the disciples to touch him "because a ghost does not have flesh and bones as you can see I have." Jesus even asks for food to eat, indicating the complete restoration of his corporeal existence. Third, both Resurrection narratives discuss the element of "doubt" among the disciples. Recall doubting Thomas in John. In Luke, Jesus asks all his disciples, "Why do questions arise in your hearts?"

In today's Gospel reading, we hear the final words spoken by Jesus in Luke's account, and they convey two important elements in the *kerygma* (proclamation) of the early Church. First, the life, Death and Resurrection of Christ fulfill Sacred Scripture ("the law of Moses and in the prophets and psalms"). In other words, God is faithful to his covenantal promises. Second, the disciples receive their final instructions: they are to preach "repentance, for the forgiveness of sins . . . to all nations, beginning from Jerusalem." With these words, the Church receives its divine directive to evangelize the world.

FOURTH SUNDAY OF EASTER

LECTIONARY #50

READING I   Acts of the Apostles 4:8–12

A reading from the Acts of the Apostles

Peter, filled with the Holy **Spirit**, said:
  "**Leaders** of the people and **elders**:
  If we are being **examined** today
  about a good **deed** done to a **cripple**,
  namely, by what **means** he was saved,
  then all of **you** and all the people of **Israel** should know
  that it was in the name of Jesus **Christ** the **Nazorean**
  whom you **crucified**, whom God **raised** from the **dead**;
  in **his** name this man stands before you **healed**.
He is *the stone **rejected** by you, the **builders**,*
  *which has become the **cornerstone**.*
There is no **salvation** through anyone **else**,
  nor is there any **other** name under heaven
  given to the human race by which we are to be **saved**."

TO KEEP IN MIND
Names of characters: Often the first word of a reading. Lift out the names to ensure listeners don't miss who the subject is.

That Peter was "filled with the Holy Spirit" is critical information. The Spirit enables him to speak with confidence and authority.

Peter had healed a cripple shortly before being questioned. His attitude is: if we have to justify ourselves, then here it is!
Lift your voice as you say, "and all the people of Israel."

Increase your intensity from the first modifying clause ("whom you crucified") to the second ("whom God raised").

He is quoting Psalm 118:22. While the Resurrection has vindicated the "stone rejected by you," don't suggest arrogance or defiance.

This is why martyrs shed their blood and saints sacrificed their lives: only in Jesus—and in no other name—can one find salvation.

TO KEEP IN MIND
Eye contact connects you with those to whom you minister. Look at the assembly during the middle and at the end of every thought or sentence.

READING I The effects of Peter's healing of the crippled man in Jesus's name (see Acts 3:1–10, especially verse 6) began with Peter's speech (3:11–26), which we heard last Sunday. Consequences continue in today's reading with Peter and John on trial before the Sanhedrin. For Luke, the author of Acts, speeches and trials were ideal occasions to insert the early Church's oral preaching (*kerygma*) about Jesus. Scholars debate about how much Luke is preserving an already established and received *kerygma* in these speeches and trials, and how much he may be shaping and defining it. Either way, we see some of the Church's earliest beliefs and assertions about Jesus in light of his Death and Resurrection.

In his speech before the Sanhedrin, Peter makes two declarations about "Jesus Christ the Nazorean." First, it was God himself who "raised [Jesus] from the dead," thus confirming Jesus's innocence before the very group that condemned him. Second, "there is no salvation through anyone else"; therefore, Jesus is the universal savior. Christ as savior to all is the fundamental portrait of Jesus in Luke-Acts.

Luke also presents Peter citing prophetic texts that are fulfilled in the Death and Resurrection of Christ, such as Isaiah 28:16 and Psalm 118:22: "He is the stone rejected by you, the builders, which has become the cornerstone." The conviction that the resurrected Christ was the foretold "cornerstone" from Israel's prophetic tradition proved to be a very effective way of explaining the resurrected Christ as the foundation of the Church.

For meditation and context:

RESPONSORIAL PSALM   Psalm 118:1, 8–9, 21–23, 26, 28, 29 (22)

R. The stone rejected by the builders has become the cornerstone. orR. Alleluia.

Give thanks to the LORD, for he is good,
   for his mercy endures forever.
It is better to take refuge in the LORD
   than to trust in man.
It is better to take refuge in the LORD
   than to trust in princes.

I will give thanks to you, for you have
   answered me
   and have been my savior.
The stone which the builders rejected
   has become the cornerstone.
By the LORD has this been done;
   it is wonderful in our eyes.

Blessed is he who comes in the name of
   the LORD;
   we bless you from the house of the LORD.
I will give thanks to you, for you have
   answered me
   and have been my savior.
Give thanks to the LORD, for he is good;
   for his kindness endures forever.

TO KEEP IN MIND
Read all four Scriptures for your assigned Sunday. Because all were chosen for this day, it is important to look at them together.

READING II   1 John 3:1–2

A reading from the first Letter of Saint John

Beloved:
See what **love** the Father has bestowed on us
   that we may be called the **children** of **God**.
Yet so we **are**.
The **reason** the world does not **know** us
   is that it did not know **him**.
Beloved, we are God's children **now**;
   what we **shall** be has not yet been **revealed**.
We **do** know that when it **is** revealed we shall be **like** him,
   for we shall **see** him as he **is**.

This is the third of six consecutive weeks we read from John's first letter.

A considered pause before you begin reading will be an integral part of your proclamation. Survey the assembly, and then begin in a loving tone that befits the salutation "Beloved."

Sustain the eye contact and speak with deep gratitude of God's love outpoured.

Make this claim with pride and appreciation.

The pace quickens as you critique the world's blindness.

You are saying: Appreciate our current state; our future is not fully known.

Note *all* the content in the final sentence: we will *resemble* him and we will *see* him for who he truly *is*.

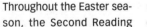 Throughout the Easter season, the Second Reading is taken from the First Letter of John. Throughout that letter, we can hear the author referring to believers within his community as "children" and "children of God." Although in this First Letter the author never reveals himself directly, in the Second and Third Letters of John he refers to himself as the "Presbyter," So the designation "children" expresses the familial relationship between the author and his community, and the "Presbyter," by extension, sees the community in a familial relationship with God the Father.

The congregation to whom the author writes sees itself as somehow separated and rejected from the world, "the world does not know us." This alienation from the world, however, becomes the source of unity with the resurrected Christ, since "it [the world] did not know him [Christ]" either. The community's estrangement from the world further unites the believer in Christ in the unknown future life to come: "What we shall be has not yet been revealed. We do know that when it is revealed we shall be like him."

Language used throughout the letter (see, for example, 2:15–16; 5:19) indicates that the author sees the world as filled with "evil" and the presence of "the evil one." To be rejected from such a world is, understandably for this author, a source of pride and affirmation of Christian identity.

GOSPEL   John 10:11–18

A reading from the holy Gospel according to John

Jesus said:
"I am the **good shepherd**.
A **good** shepherd lays down his **life** for the sheep.
A **hired** man, who is **not** a shepherd
    and whose sheep are not his **own**,
        sees a **wolf** coming and leaves the sheep and runs **away**,
        and the wolf **catches** and **scatters** them.
This is because he works for **pay** and has no **concern** for
        the sheep.
I am the **good** shepherd,
    and I know **mine** and mine know **me**,
    just as the **Father** knows **me** and I know the **Father**;
    and I will lay down my **life** for the sheep.
I have **other** sheep that do not **belong** to this fold.
These **also** I must lead, and they will **hear** my voice,
    and there will be **one** flock, **one shepherd**.
This is **why** the Father loves me,
    because I **lay** down my **life** in order to take it **up** again.
No one **takes** it from me, but I lay it down on my **own**.
I have **power** to lay it down, and power to take it **up** again.
This **command** I have received from my **Father**."

Don't let this striking discourse sound like courtroom reasoning: I do this, the hired hand does that; these are my motives, those are his, and so forth. Jesus describes a laying-down-my-life kind of love. Let his words echo that love.

Don't let this sound like oratory, but like conversation between friends.

Jesus judges harshly the Pharisees he considers self-serving hired hands.

Being a *good* shepherd means *knowing* and being *known*; or, as Pope Francis says, "smelling like the sheep."

"Other sheep" may refer to Gentiles or perhaps Christians in conflict with John's community.

His desire for unity is strong and urgent.

John's presentation of Jesus as firmly in control of his fate, not a victim but a willing player in God's drama, is consistent throughout his Gospel.

Your tone should convey that Jesus is proclaiming his love for us more than speaking about himself.

TO KEEP IN MIND

Openings and Closings: differ in tone from the Scripture and require pauses, after the opening dialogue and before the closing dialogue. These formulas are prescribed, so don't vary the wording.

GOSPEL   Numerous times in the Gospel according to John (4:26; 8:24, 28, 58; 13:19; 18:5, 6, 8), Jesus describes himself with the phrase *egō eimi*, in Greek, "I am." Today's reading begins with Jesus saying, "I am the good shepherd." Jesus and his Jewish audience, and especially the Pharisees listening to this discourse, would have been well aware that the Law and the Prophets refer to the Lord as their "shepherd." (See, for example Genesis 48:15; Isaiah 40:11; Micah 7:14; Psalm 23:1–4; 80:1.) In John, Jesus's metaphorical "I am" sayings indicate the fullness of his divine identity as "the Word [who] became flesh" (John 1:14).

In referring to himself as the "good shepherd," Jesus makes two important assertions. First, as shepherd to his flock, Jesus is no mere "hired man." Jesus's relationship with his sheep is as intimate as his relationship with the Father, assured with the commitment: "I will lay down my life for the sheep." Second, "other sheep" from another "fold" belong to the flock that Jesus leads. This is likely a reference to his Gentile followers. For both the Jewish and the Gentile followers, there is "one shepherd," Jesus.

Jesus concludes his "good shepherd" discourse by foreshadowing of his own Death and Resurrection: "I lay down my life in order to take it up again." He presents himself and his Father in complete control of his destiny: "I have the power to lay it down, and the power to take it up again. This command I have received from my Father." In this way, the shepherd leads his entire flock to Resurrection and new life.

FIFTH SUNDAY
OF EASTER

LECTIONARY #53

TO KEEP IN MIND

Context: Who is speaking in this text? What are the circumstances?

Paul's history gave them good reason to fear him.

Barnabas = BAHR-nuh-buhs

Introduce Barnabas with a tone that suggests he will help remedy the situation.

Let this dialogue sound like Barnabas pleading Paul's cause before the Apostles.

Damascus = duh-MAS-kuhs

Paul finds acceptance, but not among all.

The Hellenists (Greek-speaking Jews) still suspected Paul's motives and feared him.

Speak of the efforts of "the brothers" in a tone that suggests their fraternal concern.

Caesarea = sez-uh-REE-uh
Tarsus = TAHR-suhs
Judea = joo-DEE-uh
Galilee = GAL-ih-lee
Samaria = suh-MAYR-ee-uh

Despite the news of threats to Paul's life, the community thrives and enjoys a deep inner peace that's not the victim of circumstances.

READING I Acts of the Apostles 9:26–31

A reading from the Acts of the Apostles

When **Saul** arrived in **Jerusalem** he tried to join the **disciples**,
    but they were all **afraid** of him,
    not **believing** that he was a disciple.
Then **Barnabas** took charge of him and brought him
        to the **apostles**,
    and he **reported** to them how he had seen the **Lord**,
    and that he had **spoken** to him,
    and how in **Damascus** he had spoken out **boldly** in the name
        of Jesus.
He moved about **freely** with them in Jerusalem,
    and spoke out **boldly** in the name of the Lord.
He also spoke and debated with the **Hellenists**,
    but **they** tried to **kill** him.
And when the brothers **learned** of this,
    they took him down to **Caesarea**
    and sent him on his way to **Tarsus**.

The **church** throughout all **Judea**, **Galilee**, and **Samaria** was
        at **peace**.
It was being built **up** and walked in the fear of the **Lord**,
    and with the **consolation** of the Holy **Spirit** it grew
        in **numbers**.

READING I One of the most dramatic moments in the storyline of the Acts of the Apostles is the conversion of Paul. Luke sees it as such a significant event that he offers three accounts of it: Acts 9:1–19; 22:3–16; 26:2–18. By the time he wrote Acts (around AD 85, about twenty years after Paul's martyrdom), Luke saw Paul's conversion and subsequent thirty-year mission to the Gentiles as the key to understanding the birth of the Church.

In the storyline of Acts, Paul, whose Semitic name was "Saul," encountered the resurrected Christ on his way to the city of Damascus, where he had intended to continue his persecution of Christians. This event changed Paul's life forever and set the early Church on a course that would eventually result in countless numbers of Gentiles professing faith in Jesus as the long-awaited Jewish Messiah and Son of God. Paul himself writes about this experience in his Letter to the Galatians (see

Galatians 1:13–24). What is heard in today's reading is Luke's account of the early stages of Paul's missionary work following his conversion.

There is good reason why the disciples' initial reaction to Paul was fear and mistrust: "They were all afraid of him, not believing that he was a disciple." In Acts, prior to his conversion, Luke describes the terrible deeds of Paul: "Saul [also known as Paul], meanwhile, was trying to destroy the church; entering house after house and dragging

For meditation and context:

TO KEEP IN MIND

Separating units of thought with pauses: Identify the units of thought in your text and use pauses to distinguish one from another. Running words together blurs meaning and fails to distinguish ideas. Punctuation does not always indicate clearly what words to group together or where to pause. The listener depends on you for this organization of ideas.

This is the fourth of six consecutive weeks we read from John's first letter.

The salutation suggests a loving parent saying it like it is: that is, "Don't be all talk and no action!"

The meaning of the second section is obscure. John is saying: "No matter what our hearts or consciences accuse us of, we can be sure that we abide in Christ." The tone is reassuring.

Let "Beloved" set the tone.

Because we "keep his commandments," we can be confident in our relationship with God.

Imagine a young person you love deeply and speak these words to him or her as if to save their life.

Use the words marked for stress.

Christ sent us his Spirit to configure us more completely to his image.

RESPONSORIAL PSALM   Psalm 22:26–27, 28, 30, 31–32 (26a)

R. I will praise you, Lord, in the assembly of your people. orR. Alleluia.

I will fulfill my vows before those who fear
 the LORD.
  The lowly shall eat their fill;
they who seek the LORD shall praise him:
 "May your hearts live forever!"

All the ends of the earth
 shall remember and turn to the LORD;
all the families of the nations
 shall bow down before him.

To him alone shall bow down
 all who sleep in the earth;
before him shall bend
 all who go down into the dust.

And to him my soul shall live;
 my descendants shall serve him.
Let the coming generation be told of
 the LORD
 that they may proclaim to a people yet to
  be born
 the justice he has shown.

READING II   1 John 3:18–24

A reading from the first Letter of Saint John

Children, let us **love** not in **word** or **speech**
 but in **deed** and **truth**.

Now this is how we shall know that we **belong** to the truth
 and **reassure** our hearts before him
 in whatever our hearts condemn,
 for God is **greater** than our hearts and knows **everything**.
Beloved, if our **hearts** do not **condemn** us,
 we have **confidence** in God
 and **receive** from him whatever we **ask**,
 because we keep his **commandments** and do what
  pleases him.
And his commandment is **this**:
 we should **believe** in the name of his **Son**, Jesus **Christ**,
 and **love** one another just as he **commanded** us.
Those who **keep** his commandments **remain** in him, and **he**
  in **them**,
 and the way we **know** that he remains in us
 is from the **Spirit** he gave us.

---

out men and women, he handed them over for imprisonment." Allowing Paul to infiltrate the church in Jerusalem would have been considered very dangerous. It was only by Barnabas's witness and testimony of Paul that the disciples welcomed him.

In the immediate aftermath of his conversion, Luke reports, Paul was still not well-received by many of the Jews in Jerusalem. In fact, "the Hellenists" (Jews who spoke Greek) tried to "kill him." Fearing Paul's safety, the disciples helped him escape to Tarsus, returning Paul to the city where he

grew up. According to Luke, with Paul no longer persecuting the Church, and he himself safe from harm (at least for the time being), the Church enjoyed a period of "peace," was guided by the Holy Spirit, and grew in numbers.

READING II In today's excerpt from the First Letter of John, the "Presbyter" (as the author identifies himself in a later letter) urges the members of his congregation to "love...in deed and truth"—

which is embodied in obeying God's commandment: "We should believe in the name of his Son, Jesus Christ, and love one another just as he commanded us." "Word or speech" alone are insufficient for the level of love demanded from the community of believers.

In discerning for oneself how to act in "deed and truth," the Presbyter appeals to individual conscience: "If our hearts do not condemn us, we have confidence in God." By knowing the truth of our faith, loving one another, and examining our conscience,

Jesus is making an analogy that won't work if the details are rushed or not heard. Despite the repetitions, move slowly and deliberately through the text.

Addressed to the disciples to reassure them of their right relationship with God, Jesus also speaks to us through these words.

The analogy of vine and branches expresses powerfully the need to remain attached to Christ.

By identifying himself as "vine," Jesus asserts his responsibility for our care and nurturance.

Failing to cling to Christ can have dire consequences. Employ a warning tone to communicate the seriousness of becoming a withered, rejected branch.

Resume a hopeful and encouraging tone.

Let the assembly know these words are meant for them by sustaining eye contact and delivering the line from memory, if you are able.

TO KEEP IN MIND

Pray the Scriptures: Make reading these Scriptures a part of your prayer life every week, and especially during the week prior to the liturgy in which you will proclaim.

GOSPEL   John 15:1–8

A reading from the holy Gospel according to John

Jesus said to his **disciples**:
   "**I** am the **true vine**, and my **Father** is the vine **grower**.
He takes away every **branch** in me that does not bear **fruit**,
   and every one that **does** he **prunes** so that it bears **more** fruit.
You are **already** pruned because of the word that I spoke to you.
Remain in me, as **I** remain in **you**.
Just as a branch cannot bear fruit on its **own**
   unless it remains on the **vine**,
   so neither can **you** unless you remain in **me**.
I am the **vine**, **you** are the **branches**.
Whoever **remains** in **me** and I in **him** will bear **much** fruit,
   because **without** me you can do **nothing**.
Anyone who does **not** remain in me
   will be thrown out like a **branch** and **wither**;
   people will **gather** them and throw them into a **fire**
   and they will be **burned**.
If you **remain** in **me** and my **words** remain in **you**,
   ask for whatever you **want** and it will be **done** for you.
By this is my Father **glorified**,
   that you bear much **fruit** and **become** my **disciples**."

---

believers can be assured that they "remain" in Christ and Christ "remains" in them.

GOSPEL | The Gospel readings for the three remaining Sundays of Easter are taken from John's "farewell discourse" (John 13–17) in which Jesus shares his final meal with the disciples. Jesus's metaphor of the Father as the "vine grower," himself as the "true vine," and the disciples as "branches" would have likely resonated with the disciples. After all, images of vines and vineyards abound within the prophetic texts of the Old Testament as metaphors for

Israel itself (see, for example, Isaiah 5:1–7; Jeremiah 2:21; Ezekiel 17:5–10; Hosea 10:1). Throughout the various times in Israel's history, from the eighth-century BC threat of the Assyrian invasion to the sixth-century impending attack from Babylon, the prophets returned to the image of Israel not properly caring for itself as God's vineyard.

For John, Jesus as the "vine" and believers as the "branches" was an effective image for communicating the idea that believers must "remain" in Christ. But simply *remaining* in Christ was not enough for believers; the branch must "bear fruit."

Within John's community, as heard in the Second Reading from the First Letter of John, bearing fruit means professing faith in Jesus as the Christ and the Son of God to others, as well as loving one another.

Members of John's congregation learned that God the Father, the "vine grower," was "glorified" when they were bearing "much fruit" and being counted among Jesus's "disciples." Just as Jesus "glorified" the Father through his Death and Resurrection, so too, followers of Christ have an avenue for glorifying the Father.

SIXTH SUNDAY OF EASTER

LECTIONARY #56

READING I   Acts of the Apostles 10:25–26, 34–35, 44–48

A reading from the Acts of the Apostles

When **Peter** entered, **Cornelius** met him
  and, falling at his **feet**, paid him **homage**.
Peter, however, **raised** him up, saying,
  "**Get** up. I myself am **also** a human being."

Then Peter proceeded to speak and said,
  "In **truth**, I see that God shows no **partiality**.
Rather, in **every** nation whoever **fears** him and acts **uprightly**
  is **acceptable** to him."

While Peter was still **speaking** these things,
  the Holy **Spirit** fell upon all who were listening to the word.
The **circumcised** believers who had accompanied Peter
    were **astounded** that the gift of the Holy Spirit
    should have been poured out on the Gentiles **also**,
    for they could hear them speaking in **tongues** and
      glorifying **God**.
Then Peter **responded**,
  "Can anyone withhold the water for **baptizing** these people,
  who have received the Holy **Spirit** even as **we** have?"
He **ordered** them to be baptized in the name of Jesus **Christ**.

Cornelius had a vision that resulted in the encounter with Peter. As a Gentile, he brings some superstition to the meeting.

Cornelius = Kohr-NEEL-yuhs

Peter is not scolding, just clarifying for the well-intentioned Roman.

It is Peter who learns the most in this encounter. He is yielding to Paul's contention that even the uncircumcised can be baptized into Christ.

Begin "While Peter" with an awareness of the divine manifestation about to unfold.

The "circumcised believers" are the Jewish Christians.

Gentiles = JEN-tīls

They are awed and humbled by this unexpected event.

Commanding attention, Peter calms the assembly with his authoritative declaration. Pause after his question, and then announce his firm command.

READING I Acts 10–11 narrates the descent of the Holy Spirit onto the Gentiles. Both Peter and Cornelius (a Gentile centurion who believes in Christ) receive visions that lead to Peter baptizing Cornelius and his household. This is a significant development in the plot of the story, as well as in the life of the early Church. In Acts, the Holy Spirit facilitates the spread of Christianity. Luke tells of the Holy Spirit descending not only upon Jewish followers of Jesus (Acts 2:1–4) but also on Samaritans (8:14–17) and Gentile followers (10:44–48), as heard in today's reading.

The role of the Spirit remains integral throughout Acts, in the early missionary work of Peter and John, especially in Paul's mission to the Gentiles (see, for example, 16:6–10; 20:17–24; 21:7–14). For Luke, the descent and presence of the Holy Spirit onto Jews, Samaritans, and Gentiles emphasizes the universal aspect of salvation, for the God of Israel now offers it to the world. The reason for this shift is best explained by Peter's words: "In truth, I see that God shows no partiality. Rather, in every nation whoever fears him and acts uprightly is acceptable to him."

One of the many issues that Luke needed to explain about the early decades of the Church was the high number of Gentiles who were joining. Jesus and most of his original followers were Jewish. Many wondered, at the time when Acts was written, around AD 85, what accounted for the Jewish-Gentile mixture of Christians. Luke believed it was important to show how the two leading Apostles, Peter and Paul, were open to including Gentiles. This openness was already evident in some of Paul's own letters written in the AD mid-50s. Both Galatians 2:6 and Romans 2:11 speak of

For meditation and context:

> **TO KEEP IN MIND**
>
> **Narrator:** Knowing the point of view that the narrator is "rooting for" will help you more fully communicate the meaning of the text. The narrator always has a viewpoint, often speaking as a believer, not as an objective reporter. For this reason, the narrator is often the pivotal role in a passage. Using timbre, pitch, rate, and energy can help you convey the narrator's moods or meanings.

This is the fifth of six consecutive weeks we read John's letter.

The text is short and classic. A slower pace, for the right reason, will help you communicate. The right reason? To persuade us of God's infinite capacity to love even us!

Speak compassionately of those who have not known love.

This is the core of the Gospel: Christ died and rose for us. Speak with gratitude.

This poetic text can't sound like everyday speech. Think of someone you know who needs this message and imagine them as you proclaim.

> **TO KEEP IN MIND**
>
> **Using the Microphone:** Know your public address system. If it echoes, speak even more slowly. If you hear "popping," you're probably standing too close to the microphone.

RESPONSORIAL PSALM   Psalm 98:1, 2–3, 3–4 (2b)

R. The Lord has revealed to the nations his saving power. orR. Alleluia.

Sing to the LORD a new song,
    for he has done wondrous deeds;
His right hand has won victory for him,
    his holy arm.

The LORD has made his salvation known:
    in the sight of the nations he has revealed
        his justice.
He has remembered his kindness and his
    faithfulness
    toward the house of Israel.

All the ends of the earth have seen
    the salvation by our God.
Sing joyfully to the LORD, all you lands;
    break into song; sing praise.

READING II   1 John 4:7–10

A reading from the first Letter of Saint John

Beloved, let us **love** one another,
    because **love** is of **God**;
    everyone who **loves** is **begotten** by God and **knows** God.
Whoever is **without** love does **not** know God, for **God** is **love**.
In this way the love of God was **revealed** to us:
    God sent his only **Son** into the world
    so that we might have **life** through him.
In **this** is love:
    not that **we** have loved **God**, but that **he** loved **us**
    and sent his **Son** as expiation for our **sins**.

God's impartiality to all who have faith. In Acts, with Peter's own words and eyewitness to the descent of the Holy Spirit onto the believers in Cornelius's household, Gentiles were welcomed into the Church by its two great Apostles, Peter and Paul.

| READING II | Throughout the writings associated with the Johannine community, the Gospel of John and the three letters of John, the theme, "love one another," is prevalent. In the

opening words of today's reading, we hear the plea of the author (who, in a later letter, calls himself Presbyter): "Beloved, let us love one another." In fact, the Presbyter defines the essence of God as love: "God is love." Also prominent in the Johannine writings is the idea that God's love is most clearly revealed in Christ: "God sent his only [begotten] Son into the world so that we might have life through him." (Compare with John 3:16.) In this regard, scholars often speak of John's "incarnation theology." The incarnation of the God in the world, in and of itself, is a divine, saving act.

First John also bears witness to the early Christian belief in Christ dying for our sins: God "sent his Son as expiation for our sins." For the Presbyter, God's love was revealed in both the incarnation of his Son into the world and in the sacrifice of his Son on the Cross. From this divine initiative, believers are called to respond in a very concrete way: "Love one another."

GOSPEL   John 15:9–17

A reading from the holy Gospel according to John

Jesus said to his **disciples**:
"As the **Father** loves **me**, so **I** also love **you**.
Remain in my love.
If you **keep** my **commandments**, you **will** remain in my love,
    just as **I** have kept my **Father's** commandments
    and remain in **his** love.

"I have **told** you this so that my **joy** may be in you
    and your joy might be **complete**.
This is my commandment: **love** one **another** as I love **you**.
No one has greater love than **this**,
    to lay down one's **life** for one's **friends**.
You are my friends if you do what **I command** you.
I no longer call you **slaves**,
    because a slave does not **know** what his master is doing.
I have called you **friends**,
    because I have told you **everything** I have heard from my
        Father.
It was not **you** who chose **me**, but **I** who chose **you**
    and **appointed** you to go and bear **fruit** that will **remain**,
    so that **whatever** you ask the Father in my **name** he may
        give you.
This I **command** you: **love** one **another**."

Jesus is the only speaker and his goal is to assure the disciples of his love.

So often, Jesus equates "love" with obedience to the "commandments," that is, love of God and neighbor.

Speak Christ's great love for his friends as if he were addressing one disciple at a time.

We can rely on Christ's love to help us love each other.

"Friends" has a theological meaning; Jesus does not mean those with whom he socializes.

In Scripture, Moses, Elisha, and David were called "servants" or "slaves" of the Lord.

But only Abraham was called a "friend of God." Here Jesus applies the word to his disciples and to us.
God always takes the first step. But he expects a fruitful and abundant response.

How do you command love? Try a pause after "command" and then just say it like you mean it.

TO KEEP IN MIND
Read all three commentaries.
Suggestions in each can give you insight into your own passage.

GOSPEL   Today's reading is a continuation from last Sunday when Jesus spoke metaphorically of himself and his disciples as "the vine" and "the branches." The challenge to "remain" in Christ is now developed a little further: "Remain in my love." The avenue for remaining in the love of Christ is clearly defined: "Keep my commandments." In the farewell discourse of John's Gospel account, the foundation of Jesus's commandment is simple: "Love one another as I love you."

Foreshadowing his own impending suffering and Death, Jesus speaks of his motivation for choosing the way of the Cross: "No one has greater love than this, to lay down one's life for one's friends." That Jesus refers to his disciples as his "friends" is a feature unique to the Gospel according to John. In fact, John uses two terms, *agapaō* ("love") and *phileō* ("friendship"), interchangeably. This occurs again in the Resurrection narrative in a dialogue between the resurrected Christ and Peter when Jesus asks Peter three times, "Do you love me?" (See John 21:15–17.)

The vine and branches section in the farewell discourse concludes with Jesus returning to the command for his disciples to "bear fruit." Jesus pointedly states that for this reason, he "appointed" them. Earlier in the discourse, the bearing of fruit was connected to professing faith in Jesus as the Christ and the Son of God to others and connected also to loving one another. Jesus ends the discourse by emphasizing the core of his commandment to his disciples: "Love one another."

THE ASCENSION
OF THE LORD

LECTIONARY #58

READING I   Acts of the Apostles 1:1–11

A reading from the Acts of the Apostles

In the **first** book, Theophilus,
   I dealt with all that Jesus **did** and **taught**
   until the day he was taken **up**,
   after giving **instructions** through the Holy **Spirit**
   to the **apostles** whom he had **chosen**.
He presented himself **alive** to them
   by many **proofs** after he had **suffered**,
   appearing to them during **forty** days
   and **speaking** about the kingdom of **God**.
While **meeting** with them,
   he enjoined them not to depart from **Jerusalem**,
   but to **wait** for "the promise of the **Father**
   about which you have heard me **speak**;
   for **John** baptized with **water**,
   but in a few days **you** will be baptized with the Holy **Spirit**."

When they had gathered together they asked him,
   "**Lord**, are you at this time going to restore
   the **kingdom** to Israel?"
He **answered** them, "It is not for **you** to know the **times**
   or **seasons**
   that the Father has established by his own **authority**.
But you will receive **power** when the Holy **Spirit** comes
   upon you,

This is a faith document, not a news-journal entry. Read with reverence for all you describe.

Theophilus = thee-AWF-uh-luhs

Luke always stresses the work of the Spirit, here in guiding the fledgling Church and spreading the Gospel. So highlight his two mentions of the Spirit.

Imagine yourself teaching the faith to someone as you speak these words. "Forty days" is not just a length of time, but a sacred period Jesus shared with the disciples after the Resurrection.

Pause after "not to depart from Jerusalem" and speak what follows in the persona of Jesus.

The announcement of the coming of the Spirit should be spoken with hopeful energy.

They remain unaware that Jesus did not come to establish an earthly kingdom.

Ever the teacher, Jesus responds patiently.

Jesus paints a picture of what the future will be despite his impending departure.

Today options are given for the readings. Contact your parish staff to learn which readings will be used.

READING I The opening verse to the Acts of the Apostles serves as a bridge between Luke's Gospel account and Acts: "In the first book, Theophilus, I dealt with all that Jesus did and taught until the day he was taken up." The "first book" is the Gospel according to Luke, and "Theophilus" is the patron to whom Luke was originally writing. In producing this two-volume work (commonly referred to today as "Luke-Acts") for Theophilus, Luke had expanded traditions he received about Jesus from the story of Jesus to the story of the early Church. In other words, with Luke-Acts, Luke was not just telling us about the life, Death and Resurrection of Jesus; he was telling us the story of Christianity. In this regard, Luke is considered by many scholars as an ancient historian.

Luke is not, however, a modern historian who is writing "objective" history for his readers. He is writing a continuation of biblical history rooted in the Old Testament, and his focus is on the God of Israel and God's historic intervention in human history. The life of Jesus and the history of the early Church are reported from the perspective of Luke's theological outlook, which posits that the mission to, and inclusion of, the Gentiles in Christianity are not historical accidents, but have been directed by God.

Scholars have debated over the years about the identity of "Theophilus," the person to whom Luke is writing. There is no external evidence of Theophilus's existence beyond the fact that his name was common among Jews and Gentiles. Some have

No need for overdramatizing, but be mindful that this is an incredible moment for the disciples.

and you will be my **witnesses** in **Jerusalem**,
throughout **Judea** and **Samaria**,
and to the ends of the **earth**."
When he had said this, as they were **looking** on,
he was **lifted** up, and a cloud **took** him from their **sight**.
While they were looking **intently** at the **sky** as he was going,
suddenly two **men** dressed in white **garments** stood
beside them.

"Suddenly" breaks the mood. Speak of the "two men" with awareness of who they are. They are not just any two men.

They said, "Men of **Galilee**,
why are you **standing** there looking at the **sky**?
This **Jesus** who has been taken **up** from you into heaven
will **return** in the same way as you have seen him **going**
into heaven."

Their message is blunt: you have work to do; get to it!

The word "return" should remind us to be ready and keep watch.

For meditation and context:

RESPONSORIAL PSALM   Psalm 47:2–3, 6–7, 8–9 (6)

R. God mounts his throne to shouts of joy: a blare of trumpets for the Lord. orR. Alleluia.

All you peoples, clap your hands,
  shout to God with cries of gladness.
For the Lord, the Most High, the awesome,
  is the great king over all the earth.

God mounts his throne amid shouts of joy;
  the Lord, amid trumpet blasts.
Sing praise to God, sing praise;
  sing praise to our king, sing praise.

For king of all the earth is God;
  sing hymns of praise.
God reigns over the nations,
  God sits upon his holy throne.

TO KEEP IN MIND

Go slowly in the epistles. Paul's style is often a tangle of complex sentences; his mood can change within a single passage.

READING II   Ephesians 1:17–23

A reading from the Letter of Saint Paul to the Ephesians

Ephesians = ee-FEE-zhuhnz

You begin with a prayer that should sound like a prayer, but don't speak too slowly. Prayer requires energy and enthusiasm. Note all three persons of the Trinity are named.

Brothers and sisters:
May the **God** of our Lord Jeus **Christ**, the Father of **glory**,
  give you a Spirit of **wisdom** and **revelation**
  resulting in **knowledge** of him.

---

suggested that since the name "Theophilus" (*Theo-phile*) in Greek translates as "beloved of God," it is symbolic of all believing Christians who were open to catechesis. Others believe Theophilus may be Luke's patron, the one sponsoring his time and effort to write Luke-Acts. Patron-client relationships in antiquity were common and involved two parties of unequal social rank. Patrons were socially high-ranking people who had the means to grant "favors" to less socially privileged people. It was not uncommon for authors to dedicate literary works to the patrons who sponsored them.

This may be the case with Luke-Acts, that Theophilus is the patron and Luke, his client. In both Luke (1:3) and Acts (1:1), Luke refers to Theophilus in the prologue, even calling him "most excellent Theophilus," in his Gospel account.

Luke begins recounting the history of the early Church with the Ascension of Jesus into heaven, Acts 1:1–11. Curiously, this is exactly how Luke ends his Gospel, with the Ascension of Jesus, in Luke 24:50–53. The double narration of this event points to the importance that Luke

ascribes to it. Jesus's Ascension closes an important chapter in salvation history, marking the end of Jesus's earthly ministry. But the Ascension also begins a new chapter in salvation history, the descent of the Holy Spirit. For Luke, the Church begins its mission to tell the world the Good News of Jesus Christ once it has become Spirit-filled.

The final words of the resurrected Christ to the disciples reveal the basic plot of the story line of Acts: "You will receive power when the Holy Spirit comes upon you, and you will be my witnesses in Jerusalem, throughout Judea and Samaria,

The prayer continues asking for three things: "hope," "riches," "power." This sentence extols the risen Christ who helps us see with our hearts what our eyes fail to see: the riches that belong to those who believe.

May the **eyes** of your **hearts** be **enlightened**,
  that you may know what is the **hope** that belongs to his call,
  what are the riches of **glory**
  in his inheritance among the holy ones,
  and what is the surpassing greatness of his **power**
  for us who **believe**,
  in accord with the exercise of his great **might**,
  which he worked in **Christ**,
  raising him from the **dead**
  and seating him at his right hand in the **heavens**,
  far above every **principality**, **authority**, **power**, and **dominion**,
  and every **name** that is **named**
  not only in **this** age but also in the one to **come**.

Christ now sits at God's right hand wearing a mantle of glory and reigning over every rank of angel. "Principality," "authority" "power," and "dominion" are four distinct ranks. Don't rush them together.

Christ, the Lord of heaven and earth, is also "head" of his body the Church. Tell us this is something to rejoice over.

And he put all things beneath his **feet**
  and gave him as **head** over all things to the **church**,
  which is his **body**,
  the **fullness** of the one who **fills** all things in every **way**.

Or:

READING II   Ephesians 4:1–13

A reading from the Letter of Saint Paul to the Ephesians

Ephesians = ee-FEE-zhuhnz

Paul is a prisoner when he writes. The word "urge" suggests the manner of your reading.

This text is a spirited and elegant plea for unity. Think of your own parish as you pray these lines.

This is a classic litany that should sound like a prayer; don't rush it. No need to emphasize the word "one"; instead, stress each new word it accompanies: body, spirit, hope, Lord, etc. Be sure to attend to all the commas.

Brothers and sisters,
I, a **prisoner** for the **Lord**,
  urge you to live in a manner worthy of the **call** you
    have received,
  with all **humility** and **gentleness**, with **patience**,
  bearing with one another through **love**,
  striving to preserve the **unity** of the spirit
  through the bond of **peace**:
  one body and **one** Spirit,
  as you were also called to the one **hope** of your call;

and to the ends of the earth." Luke then narrates how the disciples began their witness in Jerusalem (Acts 2–8), spread the message throughout Judea and Samaria (Acts 8–9), and began the outreach to the Gentiles (Acts 10–15). Luke concludes with the carrying of the mission to Rome (Acts 15–28), "the ends of the earth." With Acts then, Theophilus and the rest of Luke's intended audience now have a detailed explanation of how the early Church, originally a Jewish messianic movement in Jerusalem, grew into a religion that embraced the Gentiles and began to spread throughout the Roman Empire.

READING II | **EPHESIANS 1:17–23.** Paul's Letter to the Ephesians opens with an extended prayer of thanksgiving, and much of it is seen in today's reading. Part of Paul's prayer is for the Ephesians to receive "wisdom and revelation" from God in order to know him better. He also prays for the Ephesians to have "enlightened" hearts to see more clearly God's saving work in Christ.

In this latter prayer Paul expounds upon God's "power" and "might," seen most visibly in the Resurrection of Christ and his Ascension and enthronement in heaven. Christ's rule over the universe, with all its powers and principalities, solidifies the "hope," the "riches," and the "surpassing greatness" for believers. Scholars often note the parallels here between Ephesians and Colossians 1:3–20, leading many to conclude that Ephesians has a literary dependency on Colossians.

We share according to what we have received from Christ.

Paul is quoting Psalm 68:19. The same Christ who came from God ("descended") to share our humanity has returned to God ("ascended") to intercede for us.

Each has a role to play within Christ's body, but only together can we manifest the fullness of Christ. "Evangelists" are missionaries, not gospel writers. "Pastors and teachers" are the leaders of congregations.

Until we achieve harmonious unity, we will be children in the faith. Unity requires maturity.

> TO KEEP IN MIND
> **Separating units of thought with pauses:** Identify the units of thought in your text and use pauses to distinguish one from another. Running words together blurs meaning and fails to distinguish ideas. Punctuation does not always indicate clearly what words to group together or where to pause. The listener depends on you for this organization of ideas.

one **Lord**, one **faith**, one **baptism**;
one **God** and Father of **all**,
who is **over** all and **through** all and **in** all.

But **grace** was given to **each** of us
according to the measure of Christ's gift.
Therefore, it says:
*He **ascended** on high and took prisoners **captive**;*
*he gave **gifts** to men.*
What does "he **ascended**" mean except that he also **descended**
into the **lower** regions of the earth?
The one who **descended** is also the one who **ascended**
far above all the **heavens**,
that he might **fill** all things.

And he gave some as **apostles**, others as **prophets**,
others as **evangelists**, others as **pastors** and **teachers**,
to **equip** the holy ones for the work of **ministry**,
for **building** up the body of **Christ**,
until we all attain to the **unity** of faith
and knowledge of the Son of God, to mature **manhood**,
to the extent of the full **stature** of **Christ**.

[Shorter: Ephesians 4:1–7, 11–13]

The prayer ends with Paul referring to Christ as the "head" over the Church, which is his "body." Only in Ephesians and Colossians is Christ described as "head" of the "body" of the Church. This appears to be a development in thought beyond what is seen in Paul's earlier letters to the Corinthians (1 Corinthians 12:12–26) and Romans (Romans 12:4–8), where Christ is equated with the body of believers. This different concept about the Church is one reason why Ephesians is often considered a deutero-Pauline letter; that is, a letter written in Paul's name and with Paul's authority, about a generation or two after Paul's death.

EPHESIANS 4:1–13. Much of the Letter to the Ephesians focuses on the importance of Church unity. Because Jesus's Death, Resurrection and Ascension reconciled Jew and Gentile (see Ephesians 2:13, 14, 16), we hear in today's reading the call for believers to "preserve the unity." Also in today's reading we hear the list of seven unities that bind all the faithful: one body (that is, Church) and Spirit; one hope; one Lord, faith, and Baptism; and one God.

These seven unities of believers became the basis for many creeds professed by the early Church.

Another source of unity for the Church was to be found in its leadership structure, endowed with the "grace" and "gifts" of Christ. Ephesians acknowledges a developing apostolic tradition by first identifying as leaders in the Church the "apostles" and "prophets," showing clear deference to the first generation of witnesses to Jesus's Resurrection and Ascension. Other Church leaders—the "evangelists" (missionary preachers), and

In typical Marcan style, the passage begins abruptly and is instantly in full gear.

In the verse immediately preceding this pericope Jesus rebukes the disciples for failing to believe those who attested to his Resurrection (Magdalene and the disciples from Emmaus). It is that same "hardness of heart" that he condemns here.

Speak joyfully (and quickly) of the signs that will flower in the lives of believers.

The early Fathers interpreted these signs metaphorically—poison of false doctrine; the serpents of evil deeds.

Healing the sick is the most significant sign listed.

"So then" shifts the tone of the scene. Contrast Jesus going "up to heaven" with the disciples going "forth" to preach and serve.

Stress "signs" even this last time, for they are still among us.

TO KEEP IN MIND

The closing: Pause (three beats!) after ending the text. Then, with sustained eye contact, announce from memory, "The word [Gospel] of the Lord." Always pronounce "the" as "thuh" except before words beginning with a vowel, as in "thee Acts of the Apostles." Maintain eye contact while the assembly makes its response.

GOSPEL   Mark 16:15–20

A reading from the holy Gospel according to Mark

Jesus said to his **disciples**:
  "Go into the **whole world**
  and proclaim the **gospel** to every **creature**.
Whoever believes and is **baptized** will be **saved**;
  whoever does **not** believe will be **condemned**.
These **signs** will accompany those who **believe**:
  in my **name** they will drive out **demons**,
  they will speak new **languages**.
They will pick up **serpents** with their **hands**,
  and if they drink any **deadly** thing, it will not **harm** them.
They will lay hands on the **sick**, and they will **recover**."

So then the Lord Jesus, after he **spoke** to them,
  was **taken** up into **heaven**
  and took his **seat** at the right hand of **God**.
But they went **forth** and preached **everywhere**,
  while the Lord **worked** with them
  and **confirmed** the word through accompanying **signs**.

"pastors and teachers" (leadership within individual congregations)—point to a developing Church structure that was viewed as a unifying force for believers in "building up the body of Christ."

Through the seven unities of the faithful and the divinely guided Church leadership, the community of Christians in Ephesus was assured of "unity of faith" and shared "knowledge of the Son of God," the fruits of a "mature" congregation.

 GOSPEL Mark's account of the commissioning of the Apostles and the Ascension of Jesus is widely held by scholars as a later addition to the Gospel according to Mark that originally ended starkly with the empty tomb, Mark 16:1–8. However, the entire secondary ending (16:9–20) is found in nearly all the earliest manuscripts, indicating that it was likely a second-century appendage.

Mark's Resurrection and Ascension narrative contains elements found in the Resurrection narratives of Matthew (28), Luke (24), and John (20). But the distinctive vocabulary and style of 16:9–20 suggests that an entirely different, later author added these verses. This person apparently knew and made use of the other canonical Gospel accounts and perhaps made the addition as a reaction against Mark's abrupt ending with Jesus's empty tomb and as an explanation of how Jesus's Resurrection and Ascension became known to others. The addition also harmonizes the closing of Mark's account with the other three.

SEVENTH SUNDAY OF EASTER

LECTIONARY #60

TO KEEP IN MIND

Names of characters: Often the first word of a reading. Lift out the names to ensure listeners don't miss who the subject is.

"Peter" and "the brothers" command the utmost respect. The number of believers steadily grows.

While Peter speaks with confidence, he's discussing the tragic demise of one who was a friend.

That Judas was one of them and yet squandered his "ministry" must be a painful memory.

Scripture has given Peter direction on how to proceed. Speak the quote solemnly.

In a weighty tone, Peter enumerates the qualifications for joining the company of the Eleven. It must be a man who was with them from Jesus's baptism by John until his Ascension.

Let your tone attest to the fitness of each man.

Barsabbas = bahr-SAH-buhs
Justus = JUS-tuhs
Matthias = muh-THĪ-uhs

READING I   Acts of the Apostles 1:15–17, 20a, 20c–26

A reading from the Acts of the Apostles

Peter stood up in the **midst** of the **brothers**
— there was a **group** of about one hundred and twenty persons
in the one place—.
He said, "My **brothers**,
the **Scripture** had to be **fulfilled**
which the Holy **Spirit** spoke beforehand
through the mouth of **David**, concerning **Judas**,
who was the **guide** for those who **arrested** Jesus.
He was **numbered** among us
and was allotted a **share** in this ministry.

"For it is written in the Book of **Psalms**:
*May **another** take his **office**.*

"Therefore, it is necessary that one of the men
who **accompanied** us the whole time
the Lord Jesus came and went among us,
beginning from the baptism of **John**
until the day on which he was taken **up** from us,
become with us a **witness** to his **resurrection**."
So they proposed **two**, **Judas** called **Barsabbas**,
who was also known as **Justus**, and **Matthias**.

READING I   Today's reading from Acts describes why and how the Apostles replaced Judas. Both Matthew and Luke discuss the death of Judas. Matthew reports Judas's suicide within the context of his Passion narrative: as Jesus stands on trial before Pilate, Matthew tells us that Judas "hanged himself" (27:5) out of deep regret for betraying Jesus. Matthew sees the events surrounding Judas's death as fulfilling prophecy, specifically the prophets Jeremiah and Zechariah. (See Matthew 27:3–10 for his full account of the death of Judas.)

Luke, on the other hand, offers his account of the death of Judas after Jesus's Resurrection and Ascension. Like Matthew, he sees Judas's suicide as fulfilling prophecy: two lamentation psalms from King David (Psalms 69:26 and 109:8). Luke offers no motive for Judas taking his life, though Matthew's assertion of profound remorse is implied as Luke says that Judas fell "headlong" to his death (Acts 1:18–19, excluded from today's reading).

While Matthew and Luke present two different versions of the means by which Judas took his life, they share in common the tradition that Judas died in a field called the "Field of Blood." Matthew tells us this was a potters' field (27:7). Because potters worked with clay, the name "Field of Blood" may have originated with the red clay of the field. But it is also possible that the name "Field of Blood" derives from Judas's own blood, which was spilled there, according to Luke.

Peter and the other Apostles felt compelled to replace Judas as they set out to fulfill Jesus's final commandment to bear witness to the world of his Death, Resurrection, and Ascension. The fact that

You are narrating their prayer, not praying it. Note that Judas and his fate are mentioned once more.

Then they **prayed**,
　"**You**, Lord, who know the hearts of **all**,
　　show which **one** of these two you have **chosen**
　　to take the place in this apostolic ministry
　　from which Judas turned **away** to go to his **own** place."
Then they gave **lots** to them, and the lot fell upon **Matthias**,
　　and he was counted with the eleven **apostles**.

You have three clauses to announce the selection of the new Apostle. Don't rush them.

For meditation and context:

RESPONSORIAL PSALM　Psalm 103:1–2, 11–12, 19–20 (19a)

R. The Lord has set his throne in heaven. orR. Alleluia.

Bless the LORD, O my soul;
　and all my being, bless his holy name.
Bless the LORD, O my soul,
　and forget not all his benefits.

For as the heavens are high above the earth,
　so surpassing is his kindness toward
　　those who fear him.
As far as the east is from the west,
　so far has he put our transgressions
　　from us.

The LORD has established his throne
　in heaven,
　and his kingdom rules over all.
Bless the LORD, all you his angels,
　you mighty in strength, who do
　　his bidding.

> **TO KEEP IN MIND**
> **Pace:** The rate at which you read is influenced by the size of your church, the size of the congregation, and the complexity of the text. As each increases, rate decreases.

READING II　1 John 4:11–16

A reading from the first Letter of Saint John

This is the last of six consecutive Sundays that we read from I John.
Try delivering the first line from memory.

Beloved, if **God** so loved **us**,
　we **also** must love one **another**.
No one has ever **seen** God.
Yet, if we **love** one another, God **remains** in us,
　and his love is brought to **perfection** in us.

John is not lecturing about theological fine points. He's making a heartfelt assertion: those who love see the invisible God.

This is how we **know** that we remain in **him** and he in **us**,
　that he has given us of his **Spirit**.
Moreover, we have **seen** and **testify**
　that the **Father** sent his **Son** as **savior** of the world.

You are both comforting your assembly and calling forth their agreement.

Jesus chose "twelve apostles" among his many disciples, a public symbol of his ministry reuniting the twelve tribes of Israel as foretold by the prophets, likely motivated Peter to replace Judas. In doing so, they would reconstitute the original group of "twelve" Apostles. After casting lots between two disciples, Justus and Matthias, who followed Jesus in his public ministry from the beginning, Matthias was chosen to replace Judas and join the other eleven in their "apostolic ministry" to bear witness to the world of the Good News of Jesus Christ. Now the leadership of the fledgling community was whole again, ready to move on with the mission.

READING II　Throughout the Easter season, we have heard from the First Letter of John for the Second Reading. Recurring themes in this letter, such as the imperative to love one another and the necessity to believe that Jesus is the Son of God and Savior of the world, have become familiar, and these themes are prominent once again in today's reading.

We learn of the two critical benefits that are realized in the community loving one another and confessing Jesus as the Son of God. First, the community is assured that "God remains in us," And second, God's love "is brought to perfection in us." Faith in Christ and fidelity to his love commandment are essential characteristics—habits of heart and mind—for the members of Christian congregations. When believers cultivate this disposition, God's abiding presence and love are ensured within the community.

GOSPEL　The Gospel readings for the past three Sundays have been taken from Jesus's farewell discourse (John 13–17). Jesus concludes his discourse

John's repetitions deepen the impact of his message. Don't rush his words.

Another line worth memorizing! Deep truth, like deep waters, makes little noise, so speak the line softly.

Whoever **acknowledges** that Jesus is the **Son** of God,
    God remains in **him** and he in **God**.
We have come to **know** and to **believe** in the love God has for us.

God is **love**, and whoever **remains** in love
    remains in **God** and God in **him**.

GOSPEL   John 17:11b–19

A reading from the holy Gospel according to John

The entire text is a prayer of Jesus who typically prays with eyes uplifted and addressing God as Father. This is not everyday speech; it is elegant and stylized speech that requires slower pacing and a lofty tone.

Is Jesus lauding himself or teaching us about how to care for one another? Jesus's unemotional mention of Judas reveals his resignation

Jesus anticipates and longs for his return to the Father.

In stylized speech we run into repetition that we don't encounter in everyday speech. Don't gloss over the repetition, but instead speak the second "They do not belong . . . " with greater urgency than the first.

To "consecrate" means to set aside for a divine purpose, to "make holy."

As God sent Jesus so Jesus sends his disciples. Think of how you "send" various ministers in your parish.

Lifting up his eyes to **heaven**, Jesus **prayed**, saying:
    "Holy **Father**, **keep** them in your name that you have
        given me,
    so that **they** may be **one** just as **we** are one.
When I was with them I **protected** them in your name that you
        gave me,
    and I **guarded** them, and **none** of them was **lost**
    except the son of **destruction**,
    in order that the Scripture might be **fulfilled**.
But now I am **coming** to you.
I speak this in the world
    so that they may share my joy **completely**.
I gave them your **word**, and the world **hated** them,
    because they do not **belong** to the world
    any more than **I** belong to the world.
I do not ask that you take them **out** of the world
    but that you **keep** them from the **evil** one.
They do not belong to the world
    any more than **I** belong to the world.
Consecrate them in the **truth**. Your **word** is truth.
As you sent **me** into the world,
    so I sent **them** into the world.
And I **consecrate** myself for them,
    so that they **also** may be consecrated in **truth**."

---

with a prayer of petition to his heavenly Father for himself (17:1–5), his disciples (17:6–19), and for all future believers (17:20–26). Today we hear Jesus's prayer for his current disciples, those who followed him in his earthly ministry.

At this moment ("But now I am coming to you") Jesus presents three specific requests. First, he prays, "Holy Father, keep them in your name." In Jewish tradition, the divine Creator's name was too sacred to be pronounced out loud. It was written as YHWH or *Adonai* (translated as "the Lord.") But Jesus, as the Son, revealed the Lord as "Father" and invited his disciples to

"remain" in the intimate relationship between Father and Son, "so that they may be one just as we are one." Solidarity among the disciples would be essential for the mission given to them after Jesus's Death and Resurrection.

Second, Jesus prays, "keep them from the evil one." Having already lost Judas ("the son of destruction"), Jesus sought to keep the remaining eleven from the trappings of the devil. In the Gospel according to John, the "evil one" was operative in the world, and most clearly seen in the world's "hatred" of them for believing and following Christ. Disciples could take comfort, how-

ever, in knowing that neither Jesus nor they "belong to the world."

Third, Jesus finally prays, "Consecrate them in the truth," adding the assurance, "Your word is truth," thereby highlighting the fundamental portrait of Jesus in John's account: Jesus as "the Word [who] became flesh" (John 1:14). They will be consecrated in him. Sending the disciples "into the world," Jesus blesses them with the truth so that they can begin their mission of evangelization: "For God so loved the world that he gave his only Son, so that everyone who believes in him might not perish but might have eternal life" (John 3:16).

PENTECOST SUNDAY: VIGIL

LECTIONARY #62

READING I   Genesis 11:1–9

Genesis = JEN-uh-sis

Speak with the sense that this oneness no longer exists.

Let your tone suggest a hardening of hearts among the people.

Shinar = SHI-nahr

Their tone is arrogant and defiant.

Bitumen = bih-TYOO-m*n

Because of self-interest, they are defying God's order to "fill the earth." Their self-reliance is pure arrogance: "We don't need God."

A new narrative beat. God views the city with disapproval.

This is God's tough love, not malice; God is protecting humanity from itself.

The author of Genesis views this diversity as the consequence of disobedience.

A reading from the Book of Genesis

The whole **world** spoke the same **language**, using the same **words**.
While the people were **migrating** in the east,
   they came upon a valley in the land of **Shinar** and **settled** there.
They **said** to one another,
   "**Come**, let us mold **bricks** and **harden** them with **fire**."
They used bricks for **stone**, and bitumen for **mortar**.
Then they said, "**Come**, let us build ourselves a **city**
   and a **tower** with its top in the **sky**,
   and so make a **name** for ourselves;
   otherwise we shall be **scattered** all over the earth."

The LORD came down to **see** the city and the **tower**
   that the people had built.
Then the LORD said: "If **now**, while they are **one** people,
   all speaking the **same** language,
   they have started to do **this**,
   nothing will **later** stop them from doing whatever they
     presume to do.
Let us then go down there and **confuse** their language,
   so that one will not **understand** what another says."
Thus the LORD **scattered** them from there all over the **earth**,
   and they **stopped** building the city.

Today, options are given for the readings. Contact your parish staff to learn which readings will be used.

READING I   **GENESIS 11:1–9.** The story of the tower of Babel (today's reading) belongs to the cycle of stories of Genesis 1–11. These include the two creation accounts, the six-day creation and the creation of Adam and Eve (Genesis 1–3), plus the stories of Cain and Abel (Genesis 4), Noah and the flood (Genesis 5–10), and the tower of Babel (Genesis 11). Today's story of the tower is often classified as one of the "pre-history" narratives that set the framework for understanding the story line of the Bible. A pattern of creation-sin-destruction-recreation emerges in these stories and repeats itself throughout the Old Testament until God sends his own Son, Jesus Christ, who breaks the pattern and restores fallen humanity.

Thought to have originated around the time of the United Monarchy (around 950 BC), the story of the tower of Babel taught two important lessons to the ancient Israelites, one theological and one cultural. Theologically, it warned against humanity arrogantly dismissing its dependency on God. Set within the narrative context of Genesis 1-11, it showed how the growing spread of sin adversely affected all parts of the world. Culturally, it provided Israel with an explanation for the origin of the different languages they encountered.

If scholars are accurate in dating this story to the time of the Monarchy (1020–922 BC), a period of unprecedented

That is why it was called **Babel**,
  because there the Lord **confused** the speech of all the world.
It was from that **place** that he **scattered** them all over the earth.

Or:

READING I   Exodus 19:3–8a, 16–20b

A reading from the Book of Exodus

Moses went up the **mountain** to **God**.
Then the Lord **called** to him and said,
  "**Thus** shall you say to the house of **Jacob**;
  tell the Israelites:
  You have seen for **yourselves** how I treated the **Egyptians**
  and how I **bore** you up on **eagle** wings
  and brought you here to **myself**.
Therefore, if you **hearken** to my voice and keep my **covenant**,
  you shall be my **special possession**,
  dearer to me than all **other** people,
  though **all** the earth is **mine**.
You shall be to me a **kingdom** of **priests**, a **holy** nation.
That is what you must tell the **Israelites**."
So Moses went and **summoned** the elders of the people.
When he set before them
  all that the Lord had **ordered** him to tell them,
  the people all answered **together**,
  "**Everything** the Lord has said, we will **do**."

On the morning of the **third** day
  there were peals of **thunder** and **lightning**,
  and a heavy **cloud** over the mountain,
  and a very loud **trumpet** blast,
  so that all the people in the camp **trembled**.

Speak with regret, not because God *acted* this way, but because humanity *required* such action.

Exodus = EK-suh-duhs

God calls Moses; Moses goes to meet God face-to-face: momentous realities that can't sound like being called into the boss's office.

That God favors Israel is stated unapologetically.

Despite God's special love, there are conditions set: "*If* you hearken . . . and keep."

The whole nation will play a priestly role: they will mediate God to the foreign nations as the priests mediate God to Israel.

This joyful acclamation of assent is similar to the celebrant's joyful declaration after we recite the Creed: "This is our faith. This is the faith of the Church. We are proud to profess it, in Christ Jesus our Lord."

You don't need theatrics to relate the manifestation of God's overwhelming presence, but you do need conviction and awe.

prosperity in Israel's history, the tower of Babel served as a reminder that the promised land upon which the Monarchy was built was a gift from God and partial fulfillment of his covenantal promise. Israel would have, in fact, "no name for ourselves" apart from God's fidelity, mercy, and forgiveness.

The story of the tower of Babel can also be read in light of the feast of Pentecost as presented in Acts 2:1–11. As the Holy Spirit descended upon the Apostles, the curse of the tower of Babel—confusion in languages—was reversed. The Apostles began to proclaim the Good News of the Death and Resurrection of Christ and all on the streets of Jerusalem heard the Apostles speaking in their "own language."

EXODUS 19:3–8A, 16–20B. God's giving of the Law to Moses and the Israelites at Mount Sinai, around 1225 BC, was one of the most defining moments in Israel's history. Within the story line of the Book of Exodus, Israel's arrival at Mount Sinai occurred early in their journey to the promised land. Memories of God's dramatic rescue from Egyptian slavery were still fresh in their minds. From the perspective of the ancient worldview, where the strength of a nation was directly connected to the strength of its gods, many Israelites were likely stunned by their witness of the Lord's defeat of the mighty Egyptian gods. Enslaved people were widely held to have weak gods of war. The God of Israel proved otherwise.

From the Exodus experience, Israel adopted three important cultural and ethnic markers. First, because God rescued Israel from slavery in Egypt, Israel began to

The people remain at the "foot" of the mountain.

Fire and smoke, as in the Pentecost story, are seen as manifestations of God.

"Trumpet" likely refers metaphorically to a strong, driving wind. Remember, you are describing a divine manifestation, not a natural storm.

God is about to give the commandment to Moses. Speak of his being summoned with great dignity.

But **Moses** led the people out of the camp to meet **God**,
   and they **stationed** themselves at the **foot** of the mountain.
Mount **Sinai** was all wrapped in **smoke**,
   for the LORD came down upon it in **fire**.
The smoke **rose** from it as though from a **furnace**,
   and the whole mountain trembled **violently**.
The **trumpet** blast grew **louder** and **louder**, while Moses
      was **speaking**,
   and God **answering** him with **thunder**.

When the LORD came **down** to the top of Mount Sinai,
   he **summoned** Moses to the **top** of the mountain.

Or:

Ezekiel = ee-ZEE-kee-uhl

You will proclaim richly stylized language that differs radically from everyday speech. Learn to enjoy the repetition and treasure the profound, though bizarre, imagery. Take additional time to prepare this classic text.

Ezekiel is transported "in the spirit" to this stark plain of desolation. Don't read like he was taken to the mall.

This question tests his faith. Ezekiel's tone betrays a mood of hopelessness.

NOTE: prophesy = PROF-uh-sī
God is not asking but ordering Ezekiel to speak.

READING I   Ezekiel 37:1–14

A reading from the Book of the Prophet Ezekiel

The hand of the LORD came upon me,
   and he **led** me out in the **spirit** of the LORD
   and set me in the center of the **plain**,
   which was now **filled** with **bones**.
He made me **walk** among the bones in every direction
   so that I saw how **many** they were on the surface of the plain.
How **dry** they were!
He **asked** me:
   Son of **man**, can these bones come to **life**?
I answered, "Lord GOD, you **alone** know that."
Then he said to me:
   Prophesy over these bones, and **say** to them:
   Dry **bones**, hear the word of the LORD!
Thus says the Lord GOD to these **bones**:
   See! I will bring **spirit** into you, that you may come to **life**.

---

see itself as "chosen": "You shall be my special possession, dearer to me than all other people." Second, Israel's election and status as God's Chosen People would hold the Israelites to a high ethical standard: to be "a holy nation." Third, Moses's receiving of the Law at Mount Sinai became Israel's unique feature among all the other nations. The Law separated and defined Israel as distinct from the Gentiles.

By the time of the New Testament period, the Jewish people were identified with certain practices and beliefs such as circumcision, election, covenant, and Law.

This was Israel's national identity, grounding them in a storied past and offering them hope in times of uncertainty.

EZEKIEL 37:1–14. The prophet Ezekiel was witness to some of the most traumatic events in Israel's history. He was a priest living in the city of Jerusalem when King Nebuchadnezzar of Babylon attacked the holy city in 598 BC. Along with the other religious and political leaders of Jerusalem, including Jehoiachim, king of Judah, Ezekiel was part of the first deportation to Babylon. Separating the leaders from their people was a tactic the Babylonians employed as a means of subjugating the captured citizens

of a nation. It proved to be a very effective means of ruling over conquered lands.

While in exile, Ezekiel received his call to be a prophet to his fellow captives in 593 BC. Five years after his prophetic call, Ezekiel received the news that the Babylonians had destroyed the city of Jerusalem and the holy Temple that had stood for nearly 400 hundred years. Soon afterward, the second and final deportation to Babylon occurred, bringing many more Israelites. With all of Israel now in exile, Ezekiel received the vision of the dry bones heard in today's reading. This vision offered

Your energy and intensity will proclaim more forcefully than the specific words of the text.

Ezekiel speaks with confidence of his compliance. Without overdramatizing, fill these lines, spoken at a brisk pace, with a driving energy. It's not the anatomical specifics that matter, but the miracle of new life!

Prophesying = PROF-uh-sī-ing

Remember the special nature of this oratory: repetition is essential to it power, so don't rush past the repetitions. Use them like the refrain of a song that engages us with each recurrence.

Not till they receive God's spirit do the bones come to life. Again, Ezekiel speaks with pleasure of his compliance with the divine will.

Take note: this *was* their song, but now it is ended.

Speak these promises in the compassionate voice of God.

When they see God's merciful promise fulfilled they will know God is Lord.

God's fidelity is eternal, no matter how unfaithful the people.

Distinguish the two declarations of the last line: "I have promised" and "I will do it."

I will put **sinews** upon you, make **flesh** grow over you,
　　cover you with **skin**, and put **spirit** in you
　　so that you may come to **life** and know that **I** am the LORD.
I, Ezekiel, prophesied as I had been **told**,
　　and even as I was **prophesying** I heard a **noise**;
　　it was a **rattling** as the bones came together, **bone** joining **bone**.
I saw the **sinews** and the **flesh** come upon them,
　　and the **skin** cover them, but there was no **spirit** in them.
Then the LORD said to me:
　　Prophesy to the **spirit**, **prophesy**, son of man,
　　and **say** to the spirit: Thus says the Lord GOD:
From the four winds **come**, O spirit,
　　and **breathe** into these **slain** that they may come to **life**.
I prophesied as he **told** me, and the spirit **came** into them;
　　they came **alive** and stood **upright**, a vast **army**.
Then he said to me:
　　Son of **man**, these bones are the whole **house** of **Israel**.
They have been saying,
　　"Our bones are **dried up**,
　　our hope is **lost**, and we are cut **off**."
Therefore, **prophesy** and **say** to them: **Thus** says the Lord GOD:
　　O my **people**, I will open your **graves**
　　and have you **rise** from them,
　　and bring you **back** to the land of Israel.
Then you shall **know** that I am the LORD,
　　when I **open** your graves and have you **rise** from them,
　　O my **people**!
I will put my **spirit** in you that you may **live**,
　　and I will **settle** you upon your **land**;
　　thus you shall **know** that I am the LORD.
I have **promised**, and I will **do** it, says the LORD.

Or:

Israel hope for a future beyond captivity in Babylon.

　In this vision, Ezekiel is led to a plain with countless human bones scattered before him, representative of the many Israelites who died in captivity. The vision itself gave Israel hope for a new beginning in which the community itself would have an inner renewal and a new spirit. Here Ezekiel witnesses Israel's collective resurrection from the dead. He hears God's commitment to one day raise the people from their "graves" and return them "to the land

of Israel." He bears witness to God's promise to the exiled Israelites: "From the four winds come, O spirit, and breathe life into these slain that they may come to life."

　The early Christians came to see the fulfillment of Ezekiel's prophecy in the Death and Resurrection of Jesus. And on Pentecost, when the disciples receive the indwelling of the Holy Spirit, the followers of Jesus come to life in a new way, proclaiming the Good News of Jesus Christ, risen and ascended into heaven.

　JOEL 3:1–5. One of the first events related in Acts is the descent of the Holy

Spirit onto the disciples. Peter, now Spirit-filled, delivers his first speech in the streets of Jerusalem. It is the first of many speeches that Peter gives in the first half of the Acts of the Apostles. Luke tells us that Peter quotes Joel 3:1–5 at the start of his speech, seeing the descent of the Holy Spirit as the fulfillment of Joel's prophecy.

　Joel was a prophet active in the period after the return of the Israelites from Babylonian exile, around 400 BC. He is counted among some of the final prophets

READING I   Joel 3:1–5

A reading from the Book of the Prophet Joel

> **Thus** says the LORD:
> I will pour out my **spirit** upon all **flesh**.
> Your **sons** and **daughters** shall **prophesy**,
>   your **old** men shall dream **dreams**,
>   your **young** men shall see **visions**;
> even upon the **servants** and the **handmaids**,
>   in those days, I will pour out my **spirit**.
> And I will work **wonders** in the **heavens** and on the **earth**,
>   **blood**, **fire**, and columns of **smoke**;
> the **sun** will be turned to **darkness**,
>   and the **moon** to **blood**,
> at the coming of the **day** of the LORD,
>   the **great** and **terrible** day.
> Then everyone shall be **rescued**
>   who calls on the **name** of the LORD;
> for on Mount **Zion** there shall be a **remnant**,
>   as the LORD has said,
> and in **Jerusalem survivors**
>   whom the LORD shall **call**.

Joel = JOH-*l

Echoes of this text resound in Peter's Pentecost Homily (Acts 2:17–21).

prophesy = PROF-uh-sī

There is no lead-in to the heart of this message, so signal immediately that you are announcing something extraordinary: God's spirit speaking through young and old, the great and the *least*.

God's use of even "servants" makes a significant statement.

These wonders will be worked to get our attention. Don't let them sound terrifying but awe-inspiring.

"Great" and "terrible" are essentially synonyms; "terrible" means "awesome," like in childbirth.

One need only call on God's name to be spared on that "terrible" day.

"Zion" and "Jerusalem" are venerable metaphors representing the nation. Combined with "remnant" and "survivors" they evoke joyful hope.

TO KEEP IN MIND

Pronunciation: Mispronunciations can be distracting for your listeners. Pronunciation aids are provided in the margin notes (see the key at the end of this introduction). You may also want to consult the LTP publication, *Pronunciation Guide to the Lectionary*.

---

to be sent to Israel before the arrival of John the Baptist. One of the main themes of his prophetic message was "the coming of the day of the Lord" at the end of time. Because of this, Joel is commonly referred to as an eschatological (*eschaton* = end-time) prophet. One of the signs of the end-time, according to Joel, is God's pouring of his "spirit upon all flesh." We hear in today's reading some of the apocalyptic events associated with the sending of God's Spirit: "The sun will be turned to darkness and the

moon to blood, at the coming of the day of the Lord, the great and terrible day."

Although some of his imagery may be startling, Joel's message was ultimately one of salvation for Israel. God would one day send his Spirit to "save" his people. It would, in fact, be an experience of joy, when men and women, young and old, slave and free, would "prophesy," "dream dreams," and "see visions." The early Church saw Joel's prophecy fulfilled in the Holy Spirit's descent and indwelling of the Apostles.

READING II   One of the structures in Paul's theological framework was his firm belief in the *imminent* return of Christ. Paul seemed convinced that the Second Coming of Christ would occur soon, perhaps even within his own lifetime. But until such an event happened, all people were still affected by sin. Paul even saw creation itself "groaning in labor pains" in anticipation of that day when Christ returns and we experience "adoption" as children of God and enjoy "the

For meditation and context:

TO KEEP IN MIND

Sense lines: Scripture in this book is arranged (as in the Lectionary) in sense lines, one idea per line. Typically at least a slight pause should follow each line, but good reading requires you to recognize the need for other pauses within lines.

Paul means "labor" as in giving birth, not working hard. Don't waste that image.

Even we who are privileged to know the Gospel also "groan" as we await the fullness of our adoption as God's children.

Don't render this as courtroom argumentation. It is the logic of faith shared among believers. Paul is saying: You can't *hope* for what's already *visible* in front of you; you can only *hope* for what you *don't* yet see.

Our goal is to let the Spirit pray in us, especially when we don't know how to pray.

We needn't fear not knowing *how* to pray. God, who searches hearts, understands the prayers inspired within us by the Spirit. Speak with joyful confidence to persuade us to be confidently joyful.

RESPONSORIAL PSALM   Psalm 104:1–2a, 24, 35c, 27–28, 29bc–30 (30)

R. Lord, send out your Spirit, and renew the face of the earth.
or
R. Alleluia.

Bless the LORD, O my soul!
 O LORD, my God, you are great indeed!
You are clothed with majesty and glory,
 robed in light as with a cloak.

How manifold are your works, O LORD!
 In wisdom you have wrought them all—
the earth is full of your creatures;
 bless the LORD, O my soul! Alleluia.

Creatures all look to you
 to give them food in due time.
When you give it to them, they gather it;
 when you open your hand, they are filled
  with good things.

If you take away their breath, they perish
 and return to their dust.
When you send forth your spirit,
 they are created,
 and you renew the face of the earth.

READING II   Romans 8:22–27

A reading from the Letter of Saint Paul to the Romans

Brothers and sisters:
We **know** that all **creation** is **groaning** in **labor** pains even
  until **now**;
 and not only **that**, but we **ourselves**,
 who have the **firstfruits** of the **Spirit**,
 we **also** groan within ourselves
 as we wait for **adoption**, the **redemption** of our **bodies**.
For in **hope** we were **saved**.
Now **hope** that **sees** is **not** hope.
For who **hopes** for what one **sees**?
But if we hope for what we do **not** see, we wait with **endurance**.

In the **same** way, the Spirit **too** comes to the aid of our **weakness**;
 for we do not know **how** to pray as we **ought**,
 but the Spirit **himself** intercedes with inexpressible **groanings**.
And the one who searches **hearts**
 knows what is the **intention** of the Spirit,
 because he **intercedes** for the **holy** ones
 according to God's **will**.

redemption of our bodies." Paul believed that "hope" and "endurance" were two virtues that believers in Christ needed to nurture and cultivate in this period of waiting.

During these in-between times, after Jesus's Resurrection and Ascension and before his return, Paul saw the gift and the presence of the Spirit among the community of believers as a source of strength to help "our weakness." As he wrote his Letter to the Romans, a congregation he had yet to meet personally, Paul encouraged believers to rely on the Spirit which

"intercedes" for us in our prayers. While Paul saw those who have faith in Christ as possessing "the firstfruits of the Spirit," he also recognized the fragility of human nature still affected by sin, needing to rely on the power of God's Holy Spirit.

GOSPEL The first half of John's Gospel narrative presents many of Jesus's words and deeds in the context of select Jewish feast days: Passover (2:13; 6:4; 12:1); Dedication (possibly 5:1; 10:22); and Booths or Tabernacles (possibly 5:1; 7:12). Today's brief Gospel

Reading is set within the context of the feast of Tabernacles. This day (also called Sukkot) commemorates the forty years that the Israelites wandered in the desert, having fled Egypt in search of the promised land. (See Deuteronomy 16:13–16.) Experiences of thirst and hunger were common for the Israelites during their desert years.

Because of these Jewish roots, John is fond of three symbols in particular associated with Jesus: bread, water, and light. References to water are seen throughout the Gospel (see, for example 3:5;

Your tone tells us he gripped the crowd and spoke with authority.

Eye your assembly as you say, "Let anyone."

The quote doesn't match exactly any Old Testament text. Stress the preposition "within."

"He said this" is an important clarification. Don't rush it.

Jesus was "glorified" through his death, Resurrection, and Ascension.

The "feast" in this text is the Feast of Tabernacles that commemorated Israel's desert wanderings and celebrated the gathered harvest. Water was carried from the Pool of Siloam for each of seven days to symbolize the miraculous water that flowed from the rock in the desert. It also signified hope of messianic deliverance. Jesus rose to speak on the eighth day.

TO KEEP IN MIND

Gestures and Posture: Using gestures is not part of the task of proclamation; within the liturgy, gestures are an unnecessary distraction. However, your body language is always communicating. Avoid leaning on the ambo or standing on one foot. And don't let your face or body contradict the Good News you announce. Readers are allowed to smile!

GOSPEL   John 7:37–39

A reading from the holy Gospel according to John

On the **last** and **greatest** day of the **feast**,
   Jesus stood up and **exclaimed**,
   "Let anyone who **thirsts** come to **me** and **drink**.
As Scripture says:
   *Rivers of **living** water will flow from **within** him who*
      ***believes** in me.*"

He said this in reference to the **Spirit**
   that those who came to **believe** in him were to **receive**.
There was, of course, no Spirit **yet**,
   because **Jesus** had not yet been **glorified**.

4:10–15; 5:2–7; 7:37–39; 9:7; 13:3–10; 19:34). Jesus even refers to himself as "living water" (4:4–4:10, v. 10). We hear in today's reading the connection between water and the Spirit.

Jesus spoke of the Spirit itself as "living water" which believers receive. In John's Gospel account, Jesus and the Spirit have very distinct roles. Jesus speaks of the Spirit as *allon paraklēton* ("another Paraclete"), which can be translated as "Advocate," "Counselor," or "Comforter." In John, Jesus is the "first Advocate" sent from the Father in heaven. But Jesus reveals the "second Advocate," the Holy Spirit. The Paraclete comes *only* because the Son goes back to the Father: "There was, of course, no Spirit yet, because Jesus had not yet been glorified." It is in Jesus's Death and Resurrection that he is "glorified" by the Father. Among the earliest followers of Christ, it was also in the descent of the Holy Spirit and the presence of the Holy Spirit in their midst that they, too, saw the glory of God.

In Acts, Luke narrates the ascent of Jesus into heaven and the descent of the Holy Spirit onto the disciples as the triggering events that brought about the birth of the Church. Empowered by the Holy Spirit, the disciples were to carry out their mission of evangelization to the world.

PENTECOST SUNDAY: DAY

LECTIONARY #63

READING I   Acts of the Apostles 2:1–11

A reading from the Acts of the Apostles

When the time for **Pentecost** was fulfilled,
   they were all in one place **together**.
And **suddenly** there came from the **sky**
   a noise like a strong driving **wind**,
   and it **filled** the entire **house** in which they were.
Then there appeared to them **tongues** as of **fire**,
   which **parted** and came to **rest** on each **one** of them.
And they were all **filled** with the Holy **Spirit**
   and began to speak in different **tongues**,
   as the Spirit **enabled** them to **proclaim**.

Now there were **devout** Jews from every **nation** under heaven
   staying in Jerusalem.
At this **sound**, they gathered in a large **crowd**,
   but they were **confused**
   because **each** one heard them speaking in his **own** language.
They were **astounded**, and in **amazement** they asked,
   "Are not all these people who are speaking **Galileans**?
Then how does **each** of us hear them in his **native** language?
We are **Parthians**, **Medes**, and **Elamites**,
   inhabitants of **Mesopotamia**, **Judea** and **Cappadocia**,
   Pontus and **Asia**, **Phrygia** and **Pamphylia**,

Begin without signaling the excitement that will soon unfold.

Pause after "suddenly," then continue with enthusiasm.

The fire appears, parts, and rests. Stressing the three separate moments will keep you from rushing or speaking like this is "normal."

There's a "too good to be true" quality to these lines.

Subordinate (lower energy) "Now there were" and then renew energy on "At the sound."

Don't labor over the names of the nations; many no longer exist. It is their sum that communicates the universality of the Gospel. The goal is to read them all with a sense of marveling at what God was doing.

Galileans = gal-ih-LEE-uhnz; Parthians = PAHR-thee-uhnz; Medes = meedz; Elamites = EE-luh-mīts; Mesopotamia = mes-uh-poh-TAY-mee-uh; Judea = joo-DEE-uh; Cappadocia = cap-uh-DOH-shee-uh; Pontus = PON-tuhs; Phrygia =FRIJ-ee-uh; Pamphylia = PAM-fil-ee-uh; Libya = LIB-ee-uh; Cyrene = sī-REE-nee

---

Today options are given for the readings. Contact your parish staff to learn which readings will be used.

READING I Within the Judeo-Christian history and tradition, Pentecost celebrates two different events. For ancient Israel, it commemorated the giving of the Law to Israel at Mount Sinai. For Jews, Pentecost was one of the central and defining moments in their history and in their relationship with the LORD. The Law was understood as a free gift given by God

intended to make Israel a great and holy nation. It defined and separated Israel among the many other nations of the world. For Christians, Pentecost celebrates the descent of the Holy Spirit onto the disciples, an event regarded as the birth of the early Church. As with the Mosaic Law, the presence of the Holy Spirit in the Church was a free gift, empowering the disciples to begin their mission: to bring the Good News of Jesus Christ to the world.

In Acts, Luke records the descent of the Holy Spirit as fulfilling both the prophecy of John the Baptist (see Luke 3:16) and

the promise of the resurrected Christ (see Acts 1:8). Luke tells us the Holy Spirit descended from above and "came to rest" on each of the disciples, appearing to them as "tongues as of fire." For Luke, fire was not a destructive force but rather an element that symbolized transformation. As the disciples were "filled with the Holy Spirit," their very nature was changed. No longer frightened, the disciples were now able to boldly proclaim the good news of the Death, Resurrection, and Ascension of Christ on the streets of Jerusalem. They openly bore witness to "the mighty acts of

Egypt and the districts of **Libya** near **Cyrene**,
as well as travelers from **Rome**,
both **Jews** and **converts** to Judaism, **Cretans** and **Arabs**,
yet we hear them **speaking** in our own **tongues**
of the mighty **acts** of **God**."

For meditation and context:

RESPONSORIAL PSALM   Psalm 104:1, 24, 29–30, 31, 34 (30)

R. Lord, send out your Spirit, and renew the face of the earth. orR. Alleluia.

Bless the LORD, O my soul!
  O LORD, my God, you are great indeed!
How manifold are your works, O LORD!
  The earth is full of your creatures.

If you take away their breath, they perish
  and return to their dust.
When you send forth your spirit,
    they are created,
  and you renew the face of the earth.

May the glory of the LORD endure forever;
  may the LORD be glad in his works!
Pleasing to him be my theme;
  I will be glad in the LORD.

TO KEEP IN MIND
Lists: Whether proclaiming a genealogy or one of Paul's enumerations of virtues and sins, avoid the extremes of too much stress (slowly punctuating each word with equal stress) or too little (rushing through as if each item were the same).

Corinthians = kohr-IN-thee-uhnz

Despite appearances, there is more passion than logic in this text. This is an infallible formula for community harmony. As you read, long for it like Paul did.

The word "different" doesn't need stress; instead emphasize "service," "Lord," "workings," and "God."

"To each individual" is the powerful summary of Paul's teaching. We all have something to offer!

As above, the word "one" need not be stressed on each recurrence. Be sure you know what Paul is saying, then *use* the multiple clauses to make his point. You can't rush them; they are like bullet points supporting his thesis.

READING II   1 Corinthians 12:3b–7, 12–13

A reading from the first Letter of Saint Paul to the Corinthians

Brothers and sisters:
No one can say, "**Jesus** is **Lord**," except by the Holy **Spirit**.

There are different kinds of spiritual **gifts** but the same **Spirit**;
  there are different forms of **service** but the same **Lord**;
  there are different **workings** but the same **God**
  who produces **all** of them in **everyone**.
To each individual the **manifestation** of the Spirit
  is given for some **benefit**.

As a body is **one** though it has many **parts**,
  and **all** the parts of the body, though **many**, are **one** body,
  so also **Christ**.

God" that they experienced in Jesus during his public ministry.

In Luke-Acts, the Holy Spirit plays a leading role not only in the birth of the Church but also in the events associated with the birth and ministry of Jesus. In the opening chapters of Luke's Gospel account, the Holy Spirit "filled" Zechariah, Elizabeth, and Simeon (Luke 1–2), "overshadowed" Mary, resulting in the conception of Jesus (Luke 1:35), led Jesus into the wild to be tempted by the devil (Luke 4:1), and remained present to Jesus in his ministry (Luke 4:18). More so than any other Gospel

writer, Luke is attentive to the workings of the Holy Spirit that were integral to the life of the early Christians.

READING II   **1 CORINTHIANS 12:3B–7, 12–13**. Much of what contemporary Christians know and believe about the Holy Spirit is grounded in First Corinthians 12. Within the context of his letter to the Christian congregation in Corinth, Paul devotes a large amount of space (7:1–14:40) to answering specific questions and concerns expressed by the Corinthians. In chapter 12, Paul discusses at

length the proper use of gifts from the Holy Spirit. With an emphasis on the unity and diversity of all gifts from the Holy Spirit, Paul says love (*agapē*, divine love) should be used to guide the exercise of all spiritual gifts.

Paul begins chapter 12 by listing the gifts of the Holy Spirit: wisdom, knowledge, faith, healing, mighty deeds, prophecy, discernment of spirits, speaking in tongues, and interpreting tongues (12:8–11). He employs the metaphor of a body with its many parts working together to demonstrate how the various and different gifts of the Spirit work together to unify the Church

For in **one** Spirit we were all **baptized** into **one body**,
  whether **Jews** or **Greeks**, **slaves** or **free** persons,
  and we were **all** given to **drink** of one **Spirit**.

Or:

READING II   Galatians 5:16–25

A reading from the Letter of Saint Paul to the Galatians

Brothers and sisters, **live** by the **Spirit**
  and you will certainly not **gratify** the desire of the **flesh**.
For the **flesh** has desires **against** the Spirit,
  and the **Spirit** against the **flesh**;
  these are **opposed** to each other,
  so that you may **not** do what you **want**.
But if you are guided by the **Spirit**, you are not under the **law**.
Now the works of the flesh are **obvious**:
  immorality, **impurity**, **lust**, **idolatry**,
  sorcery, **hatreds**, **rivalry**, **jealousy**,
  outbursts of **fury**, acts of **selfishness**,
  dissensions, **factions**, occasions of **envy**,
  drinking bouts, **orgies**, and the like.
I **warn** you, as I warned you **before**,
  that those who **do** such things will not **inherit** the kingdom
    of God.
In **contrast**, the **fruit** of the Spirit is **love**, **joy**, **peace**,
  patience, **kindness**, **generosity**,
  faithfulness, **gentleness**, **self-control**.
Against **such** there is **no** law.
Now those who belong to Christ **Jesus** have **crucified** their flesh
  with its **passions** and **desires**.
If we **live** in the Spirit, let us also **follow** the Spirit.

No matter how different we are from each other, it is the Spirit who bonds us together because our unity is greater than our diversity.

Galatians = guh-LAY-shuhnz

Begin with a humble tone that says God can make such living possible.

The need is not to sound judgmental but to reveal the sadness of being mired in such a life.

"But if you are" requires deep-seated conviction.

Your task is to persuade us that these things are poison to the soul and will end in destruction. You are warning us of danger!

Paul warns because he loves us. Even loving parents must warn their children.

"In contrast" signals a tone shift. Speak of the "fruit" with energetic joy. Speak of them as *one idea* (healthy choices!), not as items on a list.

Christ's Death and Resurrection make possible the shedding of "passions and desires." Speak with authority. But end on a note of hope.

---

and serve the congregation as a whole (12:12–26).

  In this way, the Christian community is to function as "Christ's body, and individually parts of it" (12:27). Paul's body metaphor evokes the intimacy and interdependence he envisions for the community at the same time that it honors the individuals within it. The gifts given to each person are for the benefit of the whole community. This makes each individual gifted and responsible to the entire body. For Paul, although each gift and each individual is essential, they are hierarchically

ordered in accordance to their functions: "first, apostles; second, prophets; third, teachers; then, mighty deeds; then gifts of healing, assistance, administration, and varieties of tongues" (12:28).

  GALATIANS 5:16–25. Paul was not in a good mood when he wrote his letter to the Christian congregations of Galatia in the late fall of AD 55. He was upset that the male Gentile believers in Christ were submitting to circumcision. For Paul, this historic mark in the flesh (circumcision) that identified Jews and separated them from the nations was no longer compatible with

life in Christ. Jews and Gentiles were now "one" in Christ, enjoying both a new freedom and a new responsibility grounded in the Spirit. Much of Paul's language of "Spirit versus flesh" is grounded in this conviction.

  In this regard, Paul presents a list of virtues and vices that represent the tension between Spirit and flesh. There is nothing particularly Pauline in this list of virtues and vices, however. They reflect the Hellenistic cultural norms of the day. Paul sees no need for the Law for those who live according to the fruit of the Spirit: "love, joy, peace, patience, kindness, generosity,

For meditation and context:

TO KEEP IN MIND

Narrator: Knowing the point of view that the narrator is "rooting for" will help you more fully communicate the meaning of the text. The narrator always has a viewpoint, often speaking as a believer, not as an objective reporter. For this reason, the narrator is often the pivotal role in a passage. Using timbre, pitch, rate, and energy can help you convey the narrator's moods or meanings.

SEQUENCE   Veni, Sancte Spiritus

Come, Holy Spirit, come!
And from your celestial home
    Shed a ray of light divine!
Come, Father of the poor!
Come, source of all our store!
    Come, within our bosoms shine.
You, of comforters the best;
You, the soul's most welcome guest;
    Sweet refreshment here below;
In our labor, rest most sweet;
Grateful coolness in the heat;
    Solace in the midst of woe.
O most blessed Light divine,
Shine within these hearts of yours,
    And our inmost being fill!

Where you are not, we have naught,
Nothing good in deed or thought,
    Nothing free from taint of ill.
Heal our wounds, our strength renew;
On our dryness pour your dew;
    Wash the stains of guilt away:
Bend the stubborn heart and will;
Melt the frozen, warm the chill;
    Guide the steps that go astray.
On the faithful, who adore
And confess you, evermore
    In your sevenfold gift descend;
Give them virtue's sure reward;
Give them your salvation, Lord;
    Give them joys that never end. Amen.
    Alleluia.

GOSPEL   John 20:19–23

A reading from the holy Gospel according to John

On the evening of that **first** day of the week,
    when the doors were **locked**, where the **disciples** were,
    for fear of the **Jews**,
    Jesus came and **stood** in their midst
    and said to them, "**Peace** be with you."
When he had said this, he showed them his **hands** and his **side**.
The disciples **rejoiced** when they saw the Lord.
Jesus said to them **again**, "**Peace** be with you.
As the **Father** has sent **me**, so **I** send **you**."
And when he had said this, he **breathed** on them and said
        to them,
    "**Receive** the Holy **Spirit**.
Whose sins you **forgive** are **forgiven** them,
and whose sins you **retain** are **retained**."

Or:

John's Gospel account presents the Resurrection, Ascension, and conferral of the Spirit as occurring on a single day. This Gospel is also read on the Second Sunday of Easter.

These are important details that reveal the disciples' mindset.

His offer of peace stands in direct juxtaposition to the news of their "fear."

Pause before speaking his greeting of peace.

Jesus volunteers the sign of his wounds. In Luke, Jesus shows his "hands and feet"; here, it is his "hands and *side*," which in this account were pierced.

Don't stress "saw" the Lord, because they don't rejoice till he proves who he is.

A second offer of peace precedes the imparting of the Spirit.

Can you speak Jesus's final words without awareness of the overwhelming privilege being imparted?

---

faithfulness, gentleness, self-control." There is no need for circumcision either, as "those who belong to Christ Jesus have crucified their flesh with its passions and desires." Paul emphatically urged the Gentile Christians of Galatia to "live in the Spirit" and "follow the Spirit."

GOSPEL   **JOHN 20:19–23.** While all four Gospel accounts report on Jesus's empty tomb and the first witness of Mary Magdalene to the resurrected Christ, much of the remaining Resurrection material is unique to each Gospel. For exam-

ple, only Matthew contains the report of the guards to the chief priests (Matthew 28:11–15). Luke alone tells of the resurrected Christ's encounter with the two disciples on the road to Emmaus (Luke 24:13–35). Mark's original ending to his Gospel does not even contain a Resurrection narrative, ending instead with simply the empty tomb (Mark 16:1–8). And John actually has two separate Resurrection narratives and endings to his Gospel (John 20–21).

The Resurrection narrative heard today is the first encounter between the risen Christ and the disciples in the Gospel

according to John. Jesus has a twofold message to his disciples who are frightened and in hiding. The first is a message of comfort twice repeated: "Peace be with you." The second is a message of commission: "Receive the Holy Spirit. Whose sins you forgive are forgiven them, and whose sins you retain are retained." Just as Luke reports on the descent of the Holy Spirit onto the disciples in Acts (today's First Reading), John, too, offers his own version of Pentecost, the birth of the Church.

JOHN 15:26–27; 16:12–15. Today's reading from the Gospel according to John

---

GOSPEL   John 15:26–27; 16:12–15

A reading from the holy Gospel according to John

Jesus said to his **disciples**:
  "When the **Advocate** comes whom I will send you
      from the **Father**,
  the Spirit of truth that **proceeds** from the Father,
  he will **testify** to me.
And you **also** testify,
  because you have been with me from the **beginning**.

"I have much **more** to tell you, but you cannot **bear** it now.
But when he **comes**, the Spirit of **truth**,
  he will **guide** you to **all** truth.
He will **not** speak on his **own**,
  but he will speak what he **hears**,
  and will **declare** to you the things that are **coming**.
He will **glorify** me,
  because he will take from what is **mine** and **declare** it to you.
Everything that the Father has is mine;
  for this reason I told you that he will take from what is **mine**
  and declare it to **you**."

Speak in a reassuring tone. Note that "the Spirit of truth" is in apposition to the main clause, shedding light on its meaning. The key idea is at the end: "He will testify to me."

Make eye contact as you stress "you *also*."

The tone becomes more intimate and urgent on "I have much more." The undivided Trinity speaks in one accord. This is *information*, but much more. Speak in an upbeat tone.

Clearly, Jesus is not boasting. He is saying: "When you see me, you see the Father." The Spirit comes to open our eyes to that truth.

THE 4 STEPS OF *LECTIO DIVINA* OR PRAYERFUL READING

1. *Lectio:* Read a Scripture passage aloud slowly. Notice what phrase captures your attention and be attentive to its meaning. Silent pause.

2. *Meditatio:* Read the passage aloud slowly again, reflecting on the passage, allowing God to speak to you through it. Silent pause.

3. *Oratio:* Read it aloud slowly a third time, allowing it to be your prayer or response to God's gift of insight to you. Silent pause.

4. *Contemplatio:* Read it aloud slowly a fourth time, now resting in God's word.

---

presents an extended discussion on the Holy Spirit by Jesus during his farewell discourse with the disciples (John 13–17). The farewell discourse itself covers a remarkable range of activities (for example, Jesus washing the feet of the disciples) and topics (such as the vine and branches parable). But the subject that Jesus most frequently returns to is that of the coming "Advocate" (in Greek, *paraklētos*). The term actually has a wide range of meanings from advocate and mediator to counselor and comforter. Each of these meanings is applicable, given how Jesus speaks of the "Advocate."

Jesus speaks at length about the role of the Holy Spirit in the lives of the disciples. He initially refers to the Holy Spirit as "another Advocate" (14:16), with Jesus himself being the first Advocate. Throughout the discourse, Jesus frequently refers to Advocate as "the Spirit of Truth" (14:17; 15:26; 16:13)—a phrase which points to the intimate relationship between the Father and the Son and the Spirit.

Jesus announces that the Holy Spirit will have four main functions: to witness, guide, announce, and glorify. First, just as the disciples will bear witness to others about Jesus, so, too, the Spirit "will testify"

to the risen Christ to others. Second, the Spirit "will guide" the disciples "to all truth." Third, the Spirit "will declare to you the things that are coming." Fourth, the Spirit "will glorify" Christ by providing for the disciples all that the Son has. Set within the context of his final meal with the disciples, Jesus hopes to assure the disciples that they will not be without divine guidance and assistance after his Death, Resurrection, and Ascension.

THE MOST HOLY TRINITY

LECTIONARY #165

Deuteronomy = doo-ter-AH-nuh-mee

This is elegant oratory, as you might hear from the best speaker at a national convention, meant to stir emotions and move people to action.

Be sure your listeners understand *who* is speaking.

These rhetorical questions are meant to make listeners think. Don't rush them. Moses makes allusions to several key moments in Israel's history: God's thundering voice on Sinai; God's choice of Israel as the Chosen People; Israel's deliverance from Egypt by ten plagues; destruction of the Egyptian army.

This litany is not just history, but enumerates the undeniable signs of God's enduring love.

"This is why" shifts the mood. Moses calls for a response to God's abundant mercy: unwavering fidelity (remember, idolatry was Israel's consistent failing) and obedience to God's Commandments.

Everything hinges on their fidelity—not only prosperity, but even life itself.

READING I Deuteronomy 4:32–34, 39–40

A reading from the Book of Deuteronomy

Moses said to the **people**:
    "**Ask** now of the days of **old**, before your time,
    ever since God created **man** upon the earth;
    ask from **one** end of the sky to the **other**:
    Did **anything** so **great** ever **happen** before?
Was it ever **heard** of?
Did a people ever hear the voice of **God**
    speaking from the midst of **fire**, as **you** did, and **live**?
Or did any god venture to go and take a nation for **himself**
    from the midst of **another** nation,
    by **testings**, by **signs** and **wonders**, by **war**,
    with strong **hand** and outstretched **arm**, and by great **terrors**,
    all of which the LORD, your God,
    did for **you** in **Egypt** before your very **eyes**?
This is why you must now **know**,
    and **fix** in your heart, that the LORD is **God**
    in the heavens **above** and on earth **below**,
    and that there is no **other**.
You must keep his **statutes** and **commandments** that I **enjoin**
        on you today,
    that **you** and your **children** after you may **prosper**,
    and that you may have long **life** on the land
    which the LORD, your God, is **giving** you **forever**."

READING I | This excerpt comes from the Book of Deuteronomy, which contains a series of speeches that Moses delivers to the Israelites on the plains of Moab, just east of the Jordan River. In the storyline of the Pentateuch (the first five books of the Bible), the Israelites have finally reached the end of their forty-year journey through the desert, and are on the brink of entering the Promised Land. It is a time of great anticipation for the people who have waited so long to arrive at their destiny. The group to whom Moses was speaking was largely composed of the children born in the desert, those who never experienced slavery the way their parents had in Egypt. Much of what Moses has to say is intended to remind them of the lessons learned by their parents while in the desert.

Moses uses the arrival to remind the Israelites of the history they have shared for nearly a generation. Foremost on Moses's mind is the LORD, the God of Israel, who called him to lead Israel out of Egyptian slavery. The dramatic events, associated not only with Israel's rescue from slavery but also with the many perils faced over the forty years in the desert, were Moses's most effective means of teaching the Israelites about God. Historians date these events of the Exodus to around 1200 BC, a period in history when the people of the Near East believed in many gods. Moses's insistence that there are "no other" gods except the one "Lord" is the theme in today's reading and throughout his speeches in Deuteronomy. Odd as it may seem, monotheism (belief in one God) was a relatively foreign concept to Israel and the other nations of that region.

For meditation and context:

TO KEEP IN MIND

Who really proclaims: "When the Scriptures are read in the Church, God himself is speaking to his people, and Christ, present in his own word, is proclaiming the gospel." (General Instruction of the Roman Missal, 29)

Reading I and the Gospel focus on God the Father and Jesus the Son. Here we contemplate the Spirit, who assists us to claim our birthright as God's children.

After the declaration of the opening sentence, pause briefly, then launch into an explanation of what you just proclaimed.

Speak with patience and understanding, as if explaining an obvious truth we've failed to grasp.

Paul's point is simple: if we are God's children, we are also "heirs" of all God has in store.

RESPONSORIAL PSALM Psalm 33:4–5, 6, 9, 18–19, 20, 22 (12b)

R. Blessed the people the Lord has chosen to be his own.

Upright is the word of the LORD,
  and all his works are trustworthy.
He loves justice and right;
  of the kindness of the LORD the earth
  is full.

By the word of the LORD the heavens
    were made;
  by the breath of his mouth all their host.
For he spoke, and it was made;
  he commanded, and it stood forth.

See, the eyes of the LORD are upon those
    who fear him,
  upon those who hope for his kindness,
to deliver them from death
  and preserve them in spite of famine.

Our soul waits for the LORD,
  who is our help and our shield.
May your kindness, O LORD, be upon us
  who have put our hope in you.

READING II   Romans 8:14–17

A reading from the Letter of Saint Paul to the Romans

Brothers and sisters:
Those who are led by the **Spirit** of God are **sons** of God.
For you did not receive a spirit of **slavery** to fall back into **fear**,
    but you received a Spirit of **adoption**,
    through whom we cry, "**Abba**, **Father**!"
The Spirit himself bears **witness** with **our** spirit
    that we are **children** of God,
    and if **children**, then **heirs**,
    heirs of **God** and **joint** heirs with **Christ**,
    if only we **suffer** with him
    so that we may also be **glorified** with him.

Moses saw the Promised Land as a precious gift from God. His desire for the Israelites was that they would "prosper" and "have long life on the land." To do so, the Israelites need to meet two conditions. First, they must believe only in the one God of Israel: "Fix in your heart" that there is "no other" God in heaven or on earth. Second, be faithful to the Law received by God at Mount Sinai: "Keep his statutes and commandments."

READING II Today's Second Reading comes from a section of Paul's Letter to the Romans in which he is speaking about the dichotomy between flesh and Spirit. (See Romans 8:1–27.) He is discussing "the Spirit of God." Paul held the conviction that faith in Christ provides believers with a new freedom that breaks us away from the trappings of the flesh, from what he called "a spirit of slavery." Those who live by the Spirit and have faith in Christ are no longer slaves to the flesh but, in fact, "children of God."

For Paul, "the Spirit of God" unites believing Jews and Gentiles alike as God's children and, therefore, as "heirs of God and joint heirs with Christ." As heirs, believers now receive all the blessings that God bestowed on his own Son, and so Paul challenges them to "suffer with him" in order to be "glorified with him."

Proof of the presence of the Spirit of God in one's life is the confession of faith: "Abba, Father" ("Abba" being an Aramaic word expressing Jesus's intimate relationship with God). Mark reports Jesus using this term during his agony in the garden (Mark 14:36), and twice Paul uses the phrase (here in Romans 8:15 and in Galatians 4:6). For Paul, it is the expression

Set the scene by sharing clearly the important data: "*eleven*," "Galilee," "mountain."

"Worshiped" and "doubted" shouldn't appear in the same sentence, but they do. Help them make sense.

Jesus asserts his divine kinship and universal authority, and then commissions the disciples.

Their orders are fourfold: go, make, baptize, and teach. Don't rush the Trinitarian formula.

We need this assurance today as much as the disciples did. Speak with conviction and joy.

TO KEEP IN MIND
Ritardando: refers to the practice, common in music, of becoming gradually slower and expanding the words as you approach the end of a piece. Many readings end this way—with a decreased rate but increased intensity.

GOSPEL   Matthew 28:16–20

A reading from the holy Gospel according to Matthew

The **eleven** disciples went to **Galilee**,
    to the **mountain** to which Jesus had **ordered** them.
When they all **saw** him, they **worshiped**, but they **doubted**.
Then Jesus **approached** and **said** to them,
    "All power in **heaven** and on **earth** has been **given** to me.
Go, therefore, and make **disciples** of all **nations**,
    baptizing them in the name of the **Father**,
    and of the **Son**, and of the Holy **Spirit**,
    teaching them to **observe** all that I have **commanded** you.
And **behold**, I am with you **always**, until the **end** of the **age**."

---

of the Spirit dwelling within believers and of our "adoption" by God.

GOSPEL | This reading is the final episode in the Gospel according to Matthew—the scene in which the resurrected Christ commissions the disciples to evangelize and baptize "all nations." Here we find the clearest expression of the Trinitarian formula in the New Testament: "Go, therefore, and make disciples of all nations, baptizing them in the name of the Father, and of the Son, and of the

Holy Spirit." With this great commission, Matthew is able to bring his Gospel account full circle, ending with what scholars refer to as an *inclusio* (Matthew 10:5–6). The mission, once limited to Israel, now includes all nations.

One of the curious features of Matthew's account is his characterization of the disciples as people "of little faith" (see 6:30; 8:26; 14:31; 16:8). In this final scene between the risen Christ and the disciples, Matthew tells us that when the disciples saw Jesus raised from the dead, "they worshiped, but they doubted." Yet in

spite of their doubt, in the next sentence we hear that Jesus approaches and commands them to "make disciples," to baptize, and to teach. Their doubt apparently does not deter Jesus from entrusting them with his mission. Perhaps because Jesus understands their human weakness, he promises to be with them in this work. What ordinary disciple would not be heartened to hear that even the Apostles had doubts, and still, with Jesus's help, were empowered to carry out the mission?

THE MOST HOLY BODY AND BLOOD OF CHRIST

LECTIONARY #168

READING I   Exodus 24:3–8

A reading from the Book of Exodus

When **Moses** came to the **people**
    and related all the **words** and **ordinances** of the Lord,
    they all answered with **one** voice,
    "We will do **everything** that the Lord has **told** us."
Moses then **wrote** down all the words of the Lord and,
    rising **early** the next day,
    he erected at the **foot** of the mountain an **altar**
    and twelve **pillars** for the twelve tribes of **Israel**.
Then, having sent certain young men of the Israelites
    to offer **holocausts** and sacrifice young **bulls**
    as **peace** offerings to the Lord,
    Moses took half of the **blood** and put it in large **bowls**;
    the **other** half he splashed on the **altar**.
Taking the book of the **covenant**, he read it **aloud** to the people,
    who answered, "**All** that the Lord has said, we will **heed**
        and **do**."
Then he took the **blood** and **sprinkled** it on the people, saying,
    "This is the blood of the **covenant**
    that the Lord has **made** with you
    in **accordance** with all these words of his."

TO KEEP IN MIND

Context: Who is speaking in this text? What are the circumstances?

Exodus = EK-suh=duhs

The people are enthusiastically assenting to all the "words" and "ordinances" of the Lord. Distinguish the two words; they are not synonyms.

The Law was God's gift; writing it down was Moses's great service to Israel.

Moses is preparing for a great ritual. Don't speak of his work as preparation for a mundane activity like a barbecue.

From "Then, having sent" until "to the Lord" can be spoken at a quickened pace, but slow your reading as you describe "half of the blood."

Such graphic rituals are alien to us, but let it speak for itself The imagery is powerful: the altar symbolizes God; sprinkling symbolizes union.

Now the blood is liberally sprinkled on the people. This bold sign manifests the eternal union between God and Israel.

READING I   The Book of Exodus tells of God's call of Moses to lead his people out of Egyptian slavery and form them into the nation of Israel. God established a new covenant with Moses, a binding relationship, but not intended to be with him alone (as was the case with Abraham); rather, with an entire nation (Israel). It was to be centered on the Law (the Torah, or "teaching," "instruction") that Moses received from God on Mount Sinai. (See Exodus 20–23.) As we hear in this reading, the Israelites readily accepted the terms of the covenant: "We will do everything that the Lord has told us."

While other cultures at that time lived by similar codes, Israel's understanding and practice of the Law helped define it. For Israel, the Law (Torah) was more than a code of conduct. The Torah, the five first books of the Old Testament (Genesis, Exodus, Leviticus, Numbers, and Deuteronomy), also recounted the stories of Israel's ancestors such as Abraham and Sarah, Joseph and his brothers, and the Israelites' forty years of wandering in the desert. There were lessons to be learned and instructions to be given from all of these people and events in Israel's history.

For Israel, one of the central aspects of living the Law was the practice of offering sacrifice to God, including animal sacrifice, such as young bulls, as a "peace offering" and as a means of maintaining a covenantal relationship with God. Integral to animal sacrifice were the rituals associated with blood. The blood was carefully drained from the slain animal, some of the blood was "splashed on the altar" on which the animal was slain, and the rest was poured into large bowls and then sprinkled on the people. The animal's blood on the people sanctified the Israelites, cleansing

For meditation and context:

TO KEEP IN MIND

Echoes: Some words echo words
that went before. For example, "You shall be a glorious
crown . . . a royal diadem"
(Isaiah 62:3). Here "diadem" echoes
"crown" so it needs no stress.
In such cases, emphasize the new
idea: royal.

Find at least one other translation of this text
to get a clearer sense of its meaning. Like a
guide through a complex building, you'll need
to walk your listeners through this text. Pay
close attention to the punctuation and the
words marked for stress.

The sense of these lines is: Jesus came to
earth through the perfect "tabernacle,"
heaven, which obviously is not made with
human hands, and he entered that sanctuary
to remain eternally. What's more, he gained
access to the sanctuary not with the blood of
animals, but through his own blood.

Here you have a logical assertion: "if the
blood of goats . . . can sanctify . . . how
much more will the blood of Christ."

Animal sacrifice brought legal purification,
but the blood of Christ accomplishes much
more: new life in the Spirit and access to the
living God. This is joyful Good News.

RESPONSORIAL PSALM   Psalm 116:12–13, 15–16, 17–18 (13)

R. I will take the cup of salvation, and call on the name of the Lord. orR. Alleluia.

How shall I make a return to the Lord
    for all the good he has done for me?
The cup of salvation I will take up,
    and I will call upon the name of the Lord.

Precious in the eyes of the Lord
    is the death of his faithful ones.
I am your servant, the son of your
    handmaid;
    you have loosed my bonds.

To you will I offer sacrifice of thanksgiving,
    and I will call upon the name of the Lord.
My vows to the Lord I will pay
    in the presence of all his people.

READING II   Hebrews 9:11–15

A reading from the Letter to the Hebrews

Brothers and sisters:
When **Christ** came as high priest
    of the **good** things that have come to be,
    passing through the **greater** and more **perfect** tabernacle
    not made by **hands**, that is, not belonging to **this** creation,
    he entered **once** for **all** into the **sanctuary**,
    not with the blood of **goats** and **calves**
    but with his **own** blood, thus obtaining **eternal** redemption.
For if the blood of **goats** and **bulls**
    and the sprinkling of a heifer's **ashes**
    can **sanctify** those who are **defiled**
    so that their flesh is **cleansed**,
    how much **more** will the blood of **Christ**,
    who through the eternal Spirit offered himself **unblemished**
        to God,
    cleanse our consciences from dead works
    to **worship** the living God.

---

them spiritually and allowing them to be
near God's holy presence.

This ritual became known as "the
blood of the covenant" and served to ratify
the terms of the covenant between God
and Israel. Following the Law, which often
involved animal sacrifice, would become
the foundational doctrine that defined
Israel's national identity.

READING II While the author of the
Letter to the Hebrews is
unknown, the audience was almost certainly comprised of Jewish Christians, since

so much of the theology presented in this
letter presupposes a Jewish worldview and
a thorough familiarity with the Old
Testament. One of the aims of this letter
was to make sense of Jesus's Death on the
Cross, the sacrifice of his body and blood.
Language heard in today's reading such as
"high priest" (in reference to Christ), "tabernacle," "sanctuary," and "blood of goats
and calves" provided a deeper understanding of the mystery of the Cross among the
earliest followers of Jesus.

Hebrews draws a sharp contrast
between the "blood of goats and calves,"

which was a Jewish ritual required to be
repeated often and annually, and the blood
of Christ, his "own blood," that secured for
believers, once and for all time, "eternal
redemption." The "blood of Christ" not only
offers believers salvation, it also serves to
"cleanse our consciences from dead works
to worship the living God." Secure in the
belief that the body and blood sacrifice of
Christ on the Cross redeems and restores
our relationship with God permanently, followers of Christ could better understand
how God's covenantal relationship with
Israel was now fulfilled. (And this teaching

"A death" refers to Christ's Death. The verse that follows this passage in Hebrews clarifies the author's meaning that an inheritance can be received only after the death of the one who wrote the will. This sentence is saying: Jesus had to die in order for us to receive the inheritance he willed us. Since he did die, we can now claim our inheritance: forgiveness and eternal life.

For this reason he is mediator of a **new** covenant:
    since a **death** has taken place for deliverance
    from transgressions under the **first** covenant,
    those who are **called** may receive the promised
        eternal inheritance.

GOSPEL   Mark 14:12–16, 22–26

A reading from the holy Gospel according to Mark

It is not Holy Week, so these details are important for setting context. The sacrificial lamb anticipates the fate of Jesus.

Your tone for both the disciples and Jesus should be positive.

On the **first** day of the Feast of Unleavened **Bread**,
    when they sacrificed the Passover **lamb**,
    Jesus' **disciples** said to him,
    "**Where** do you want us to go
    and **prepare** for you to eat the **Passover**?"
He sent two of his **disciples** and said to them,
    "Go into the **city** and a **man** will **meet** you,
    carrying a jar of **water**.
Follow him.

The details are less important than the fact that Jesus has anticipated this crucial meal.

Wherever he **enters**, say to the **master** of the house,
    'The **Teacher** says, "Where is my **guest** room
    where I may eat the Passover with my **disciples**?"'
Then he will show you a large upper **room** furnished and **ready**.
Make the **preparations** for us **there**."
The disciples then went off, **entered** the city,
    and found it just as he had **told** them;
    and they **prepared** the Passover.

Their surprise at finding Jesus's words so thoroughly fulfilled underscores his anticipation of this special time with his disciples.

The text jumps and thus the mood suddenly shifts. You already know and love these words. Speak them from memory directly to your assembly.

While they were **eating**,
    he took **bread**, said the **blessing**,
    broke it, **gave** it to them, and said,
    "**Take** it; this is my **body**."

---

would be of particular interest to Jewish Christians.)

In light of the Death and Resurrection of Christ, Jesus could now be understood as the "mediator of a new covenant." His Death on the Cross took away the sin (a "deliverance from transgressions") that separates us from God, so clearly defined in the "first covenant." The blood of Christ offers believers the "eternal inheritance" promised by God.

GOSPEL | The events associated with the final meal that Jesus

celebrated with his disciples before his suffering and Death (commonly referred to in Christian tradition as "the Last Supper") belong to the earliest stages of the written Gospel accounts. Scholars believe that prior to the composition of the Gospel according to Mark in AD 70, the first of the four written Gospel accounts in the New Testament, the sequence of events from Jesus's final entry into Jerusalem to the discovery of the empty tomb comprised the original oral (and perhaps written) Gospel among the original followers of Jesus.

We see in even Paul's letters, written in the years AD 50–60, a full ten to twenty years before the Gospel accounts were written, evidence that certain aspects of the final week in Jesus's life were carefully preserved and recorded. Chief among these were Jesus's words at "the Last Supper." Paul tells the Christians in Corinth, in the spring of AD 55, about the tradition he received of Christ's institution of the Eucharist at the Last Supper (see 1 Corinthians 11:23–26).

In both First Corinthians and the Gospel according to Mark (repeated in the accounts of Matthew and Luke), we hear

As before, speak from memory with clear eye contact.

Jesus's final words anticipate the new wine of the Kingdom.

Note that they go off singing hymns.

Then he took a **cup**, gave **thanks**, and **gave** it to them,
  and they all **drank** from it.
He **said** to them,
  "This is my **blood** of the **covenant**,
  which will be **shed** for **many**.
Amen, I say to you,
  I shall not drink **again** the fruit of the **vine**
  until the day when I drink it **new** in the kingdom of **God**."
Then, after singing a **hymn**,
  they went out to the **Mount** of **Olives**.

TO KEEP IN MIND

Tell the story: Make the story yours, then share it with your listeners. Use the language; don't throw away any good words. Settings give context; don't rush the description. Characters must be believable; understand their motivation. Dialogue reveals character; distinguish one character from another with your voice.

Jesus's fourfold action of taking the bread, blessing it, breaking it, and giving it to his disciples. Jesus then tells them, "Take it; this is my body." In a similar way, he took the cup of wine, blessed it, and gave it to the disciples with the words: "This is my blood of the covenant, which will be shed for many." Christians from the very beginning celebrated this event as a perpetual memorial of the Death of Christ.

Unlike Paul's account of Jesus's words at the Last Supper, Mark provides a narrative context for the institution of the Eucharist rather than simply a report of the received tradition as heard in First Corinthians. Two details in particular are important for their history and their symbolism.

First, Mark informs us that Jesus's Last Supper occurred on the "first day of the Feast of Unleavened Bread." This Jewish feast begins the next night after the Passover and celebrates Israel being delivered from slavery in Egypt. In a similar way, Jesus's Death on the Cross was about to deliver believers from slavery to sin. Second, Mark connects this feast to the Passover lamb about to be "sacrificed." The blood of the sacrificial lamb was sprinkled on the doorposts of the Israelites enslaved in Egypt. The angel of death would "pass over" these homes marked with the lamb's blood, sparing the life of the firstborn, the tenth plague to hit Egypt for the Pharaoh's refusal to release the Israelites. Likewise, Jesus's body and blood about to be sacrificed would spare the life of all who come to faith in Christ.

ELEVENTH SUNDAY IN ORDINARY TIME

LECTIONARY #92

Ezekiel = ee-ZEE-kee-uhl

Throughout, the tone is assertive and self-confident. The final line summarizes the tone of all the text.

"Crest of the cedar" refers to the House of David; "tender shoot" alludes to a future leader God will raise up.

This new leader will rule over Israel.

These are poetic lines, but not of the Hallmark variety. They soar with vision and divine strength.

God is sovereign Lord who rules the earth and all that's in it. Highlight the contrasts ("low"/ "high" and "green"/ "withered").

Try a deliberate delivery of the final four words: "so / will / I / do"

> **TO KEEP IN MIND**
> **Poetry** is gourmet food, eaten slowly and savored. Go slowly. Pay attention to the sounds, rhythms, and repetitions.

READING I   Ezekiel 17:22–24

A reading from the Book of the Prophet Ezekiel

Thus says the Lord **GOD**:
  I, **too**, will take from the **crest** of the cedar,
    from its topmost branches tear off a **tender** shoot,
  and **plant** it on a **high** and lofty **mountain**;
    on the mountain heights of **Israel** I will plant it.
  It shall put forth **branches** and bear **fruit**,
    and become a majestic **cedar**.
  Birds of every kind shall **dwell** beneath it,
    every winged thing in the shade of its **boughs**.
  And all the trees of the field shall **know**
    that **I**, the **LORD**,
  bring **low** the **high** tree,
    lift **high** the **lowly** tree,
  wither up the **green** tree,
    and make the **withered** tree **bloom**.
  As I, the **LORD**, have **spoken**, so will I **do**.

READING I Today's poetic prophecy of God's life-giving intentions for the future comes through the prophet Ezekiel. He had grown up in Judah and was one of the 3,000 Jews deported to Babylon in 597 BC. There in captivity he received his call to be a prophet. Today's reading comes from this period. It is among the oracles that Ezekiel spoke to his fellow captives while in exile, before the Babylonian siege on the southern kingdom of Judah in 587 BC. Among the warnings of the coming destruction of Jerusalem is this vision of hope for the exiled Israelites. Images of towering, majestic cedar trees bearing fruit, peacefully growing with birds nesting in their branches, conjured up memories of the days of King David and the united monarchy from nearly 400 years earlier, when the kingdom was strong and faithful to God. Here God promises to restore the people to their land under a faithful king he will choose when the time is right.

Although Ezekiel bore witness to some of the most traumatic events in Israel's history, he also helped shepherd the people through the dark days of exile and captivity in Babylon, offering a vision of the restoration of the Davidic kingdom.

READING II Paul wrote his Second Letter to the Corinthians shortly after his first letter, in the fall of AD 55. Written about twenty-five years after the Death and Resurrection of Jesus, Paul still remains committed to his belief in the imminent return of Christ. This creates for Paul a sort of tension between the present time and the impending future time. We hear this tension today when Paul speaks of the believers' desire to "leave the body

For meditation and context:

TO KEEP IN MIND
Know who wrote the letter and who received it. Discover the circumstances. **The intent of each letter dictates the tone.** Often Paul is the writer; he is motivated by multiple concerns: to instruct, console, encourage, chastise, warn, settle disputes, and more. When reading from one of his letters, be aware of what he's trying to accomplish.

Corinthians - kohr-IN-thee-uhnz

This is an uncomplicated text. Speak it to your neighbors as if it were a truth you've pondered and wish to share in loving dialogue.

"We walk by faith" is a classic line and a supreme Christian insight.

"At home or away": our "home" is heaven; here on earth we are "away" as in exile.

The ending is a bit sobering; each of us will make accounting before Christ, our ruler and udge. Let your tone suggest the urgency of living in right relationship with God and others.

RESPONSORIAL PSALM   Psalm 92:2–3, 13–14, 15–16 (2a)

R. Lord, it is good to give thanks to you.

It is good to give thanks to the LORD,
    to sing praise to your name, Most High,
to proclaim your kindness at dawn
    and your faithfulness throughout
        the night.

The just one shall flourish like the palm tree,
    like a cedar of Lebanon shall he grow.
They that are planted in the house of
        the LORD
    shall flourish in the courts of our God.

They shall bear fruit even in old age;
    vigorous and sturdy shall they be,
declaring how just is the LORD,
    my rock, in whom there is no wrong.

READING II   2 Corinthians 5:6–10

A reading from the second Letter of Saint Paul to the Corinthians

Brothers and sisters:
We are **always courageous**,
    although we know that while we are at home in the **body**
        we are **away** from the **Lord**,
    for we walk by **faith**, not by **sight**.
Yet we **are** courageous,
    and we would rather **leave** the body and go home to the **Lord**.
Therefore, we aspire to **please** him,
    whether we are at **home** or **away**.
For we must all appear before the **judgment** seat of **Christ**,
    so that each may receive **recompense**,
    according to what he did in the **body**, whether **good** or **evil**.

and go home to the Lord." He even draws upon of the idea of people in exile, "whether we are at home or away." The language and memory of exile were part of Israel's storied history and fit well with Paul's own experience of living in what he believed was the end-time, the eschaton.

It seems this eschatological tension created some degree of fear for both Paul and the Christians in Corinth. Paul speaks of being "courageous" awaiting the return of Christ. Closely connected to Jesus's Second Coming is the judgment that awaits the world. Paul saw the risen Christ not

only as Lord of the universe but also judge of all. Living a moral and ethical life also required courage as the earliest Christians sought to make their way in uncertain times. Focusing on the soon-to-come heavenly judgment and life with God gave strength for discipleship in the interim.

GOSPEL To understand today's Gospel Reading, it's helpful to look back at the first words of Jesus in the Gospel according to Mark. They are centered on the Kingdom of God: "This is the time of fulfillment. The kingdom of God

is at hand. Repent, and believe in the gospel" (1:15). For Mark, the centerpiece of Jesus's public ministry and message was the inbreaking of the reign of God into the world. Sometimes Jesus spoke about God's Kingdom in parables, such as the parable of the mustard seed. Other times Jesus showed what the reign of God looks like, as when he shared table fellowship with people from all levels of the social ladder.

In teaching about the Kingdom of God, Jesus often drew upon images and experiences that Jews living in the rural areas of Galilee could easily relate to. Planted seeds

GOSPEL   Mark 4:26–34

A reading from the holy Gospel according to Mark

Jesus said to the **crowds**:
   "This is how it is with the kingdom of **God**;
   it is as if a man were to scatter **seed** on the land
   and would **sleep** and **rise night** and **day**
   and through it all the seed would **sprout** and **grow**,
   he knows not **how**.
Of its own **accord** the land yields **fruit**,
   first the **blade**, then the **ear**, then the full **grain** in the ear.
And when the grain is **ripe**, he wields the **sickle** at once,
   for the **harvest** has come."

He said,
   "To what shall we **compare** the kingdom of God,
   or what **parable** can we use for it?
It is like a **mustard** seed that, when it is **sown** in the ground,
   is the **smallest** of all the seeds on the earth.
But once it is **sown**, it springs up and becomes the **largest**
      of plants
   and puts forth large **branches**,
   so that the **birds** of the sky can dwell in its **shade**."
With many such **parables**
   he spoke the word to them as they were able to **understand** it.
Without parables he did not **speak** to them,
   but to his own **disciples** he explained **everything** in **private**.

Imagine Jesus before the crowd conjuring images that will express deep truths they don't yet understand. His solution is stories.

Keep the pacing brisk and upbeat.

It's not the specifics that matter, but the sense of incremental steps that lead to fulfillment. The farmer has no recourse but to wait and trust.

Let your tone signal the end of the parable.

Jesus is searching for another image. Survey your assembly as you speak this line (perhaps, from memory).

He finds an image! Make your voice "small" to suggest the seed.

Here, enlarge your voice to match the narrative.

The "tree" of the Kingdom provides shelter for many.

Jesus adjusted his methodology to the capacities of the crowds.

But he reserves theological reflection to his inner circle.

---

and harvested fields were tangible images for the disciples and the crowds that would help them better understand Jesus and his worldview. The example of the mustard seed in particular was a useful metaphor for God's coming reign in the world. The mustard seed aptly communicated the manner in which God's Kingdom grows in the world. Parables such as the mustard seed also signaled that Jesus's public ministry was fulfilling the prophecies of Israel, as heard in the reading today from Ezekiel.

One of the more interesting features about the Gospel according to Mark is the secrecy motif that runs through the story line. Jesus will often command the demons, his disciples, and even those he heals to be silent. (See, for example, 1:34; 1:44; 3:12; 8:30.) In today's reading, we hear that Jesus often spoke in parables to the crowds. According to Mark, Jesus did not interpret the meaning of his parables to the crowds, preferring them to ponder their application, in effect, keeping the meaning of the parable a secret. But Mark tells us that Jesus employed a different strategy with the disciples: "To his own disciples he explained everything in private."

Scholars have long puzzled over Mark's use of the secrecy theme. One conclusion drawn from modern scholarship is that Mark was not only preserving a received tradition about Jesus, he was also carefully crafting his own theological perspective on Jesus—that the mystery of Jesus's identity was so deep, it could not be understood by ordinary means. Jesus would try to tutor his disciples in it, but ultimately only God could reveal the secret—in Christ's Death and Resurrection.

TWELFTH SUNDAY IN ORDINARY TIME

LECTIONARY #95

Job = johb

God speaks to Job from "out of a storm," not a "window." God's voice is awesome and majestic.

With poetic imagery, God claims control over all the forces of the universe.

God is not intimidating Job, but reminding him that God is God and Job is not.

The questions continue to the end. The sea is vast, but God is infinitely greater. Though not angry, God's question is bold and immodest.

God's powerful voice can calm the ocean and a trembling human heart.

For meditation and context:

TO KEEP IN MIND
Word value: Words are your medium, like a painter's brush or a sculptor's chisel. You must understand the words before you can communicate them. Most words have a dictionary meaning (denotative) and an associational meaning (connotative). "House" and "home" both mean "dwelling," yet they communicate different feelings. Be alert to subtle differences in connotative meanings and express them.

READING I   Job 38:1, 8–11

A reading from the Book of Job

The Lord addressed **Job** out of the **storm** and said:
  Who shut within doors the **sea**,
    when it burst forth from the **womb**;
  when I made the **clouds** its garment
    and thick **darkness** its swaddling bands?
  When I set **limits** for it
    and fastened the bar of its **door**,
  and said: Thus **far** shall you come but no **farther**,
    and **here** shall your proud waves be stilled!

RESPONSORIAL PSALM   Psalm 107:23–24, 25–26, 28–29, 30–31 (1b)

R. Give thanks to the Lord, his love is everlasting. orR. Alleluia.

They who sailed the sea in ships,
  trading on the deep waters,
these saw the works of the LORD
  and his wonders in the abyss.

His command raised up a storm wind
  which tossed its waves on high.
They mounted up to heaven; they sank to
  the depths;
  their hearts melted away in their plight.

They cried to the LORD in their distress;
  from their straits he rescued them.
He hushed the storm to a gentle breeze,
  and the billows of the sea were stilled.

They rejoiced that they were calmed,
  and he brought them to their
  desired haven.
Let them give thanks to the LORD for
  his kindness
  and his wondrous deeds to the children
  of men.

READING I The compelling and sometimes disturbing Book of Job, from which this reading comes, is the product of Israel's wisdom tradition. In ancient Israel, among the majority of common people of the land, there were also three groups of people who could speak with authority: the priest, the prophet, and the sage. The priest's main duty was to instruct in covenant Law (Torah). The prophet's function was to convey God's "word." The sage was to provide wise advice. While the author of the Book of Job is unknown, he would have been counted among the sages of ancient Israel.

The Book of Job is probably the best known of the Old Testament's "wisdom books." Archaeological discoveries reveal that long before Israel came into existence, thinkers in Egypt, Mesopotamia, Edom, and Phoenicia had produced "wisdom literature." Israelite writers and thinkers likely borrowed and adapted from those wisdom traditions, but brought a unique element to the table: monotheism, belief in the one God of Israel.

The one God of Israel speaks in today's reading, an excerpt that comes toward the end of the book. The plot has unfolded as a dramatic dialogue between Job and his three friends (Eliphaz, Bildad, and Zophar) about the relation of suffering to human behavior. Is suffering always a punishment? Why do the innocent suffer? From the midst of great suffering, yet still faithful, Job lays his question and his sense of outrage directly before God. Today's reading begins toward the very end of the story line, when God finally speaks to Job. Images of the sea and raging waters were common metaphors in ancient Israel, used to depict the power and omniscience of God. God's dramatic, poetic response, the beginning of which you will proclaim today, will extend

READING II 2 Corinthians 5:14–17

Corinthians = kohr-IN-thee-uhnz

The text begins with a clarion call: God's love motivates, persuades, urges, and obliges us! Speak with conviction.

When Christ died, we all died with him. Now it is possible for each of us to live.

A reading from the second Letter of Saint Paul to the Corinthians

Brothers and sisters:
The love of Christ **impels** us,
    once we have come to the conviction that one died for **all**;
    therefore, all have **died**.
He **indeed** died for all,
    so that those who **live** might no longer live for **themselves**
    but for **him** who for their sake died and was **raised**.

Christ's Death and Resurrection changed everything. We can't judge with the same criteria anymore.

Consequently, from now on we regard no one according to
    the **flesh**;
    even if we once knew **Christ** according to the flesh,
    yet now we know him so no longer.
So whoever is in Christ is a new **creation**:
    the old things have **passed** away;
    behold, **new** things have come.

The last sentence of this passage would be Scripture enough for today. It is a profound and joyous revelation. Announce the news slowly, a phrase at a time.

TO KEEP IN MIND
Dialogue imitates real conversation, so it often moves faster than the rest of the passage.

GOSPEL Mark 4:35–41

Jesus is tired and seeks a respite from the crowd.

A reading from the holy Gospel according to Mark

On that day, as **evening** drew on, Jesus said to his disciples:
    "Let us cross to the **other** side."
Leaving the **crowd**, they took Jesus with them in the boat just as
    he was.
And **other** boats were with him.

The peace of the opening is soon broken by the "violent squall."

A violent **squall** came up and waves were **breaking** over
    the boat,
    so that it was already filling **up**.
Jesus was in the stern, **asleep** on a cushion.

Speak with the incredulity of the disciples of Jesus sleeping.

They **woke** him and said to him,

---

to chapter 42 and can be summarized in this way: the wise person finds meaning in suffering and trusts that the Lord governs the universe with purpose and fidelity.

READING II When Paul wrote his Second Letter to the Corinthians in the fall of AD 55, conditions had significantly deteriorated in that congregation since the writing of his First Letter (what we call First Corinthians) a few months earlier in the spring of AD 55. Paul had to answer charges and accusations leveled by other teachers who had made their way into the Corinthian congregation since Paul left. (See later in

the letter, 11:5, where he says, "For I think that I am not in any way inferior to these 'superapostles.'") He had to win back those believers in Corinth who no longer saw Paul as their authoritative voice and leader. In this sense, Second Corinthians is best understood as an apologetic letter, that is, a letter defending a position.

Paul's desire to heal the rift that developed between him and the Corinthians was consistent with his message as a whole in Second Corinthians: his missionary work is a "ministry of reconciliation" (5:18), and he and Timothy are "ambassadors for Christ" (5:20). Today's reading lays a foundation for

that assertion with its focus on "the love of Christ" and the fact that Christ "died for all." Paul is pointing to unity in Christ that can transcend their current divisions. Paul was convinced that in their united faith in Christ, he and the Corinthian community were "a new creation." "Old things have passed away" (division, rivalries), and "new things have come" (Jewish and Gentile believers united by faith).

GOSPEL An interesting feature of the single episodes in the Gospel accounts selected as readings (called "pericopes," or cuttings) is that the

For a storm to panic these experienced seamen, it must have been a powerful one.

They've been holding back; now their blunt complaint bursts out like a missile from a silo.

Try an intense whisper rather than a shout to quiet the storm.

Take time announcing the aftermath of Jesus's command.

They've witnessed miracles before, so Jesus is surprised and disappointed by their fear. His questions are pointed and embarrassing.

Aware they stand in the presence of a terrifying and enthralling mystery, they ask, who can this be?

> TO KEEP IN MIND
> **The closing:** Pause (three beats!) after ending the text. Then, with sustained eye contact, announce from memory, "The word [Gospel] of the Lord." Always pronounce "the" as "thuh" except before words beginning with a vowel, as in "thee Acts of the Apostles." Maintain eye contact while the assembly makes its response.

"Teacher, do you not care that we are **perishing**?"
He **woke** up,
    rebuked the wind, and said to the sea, "**Quiet**! Be **still**!"
The wind **ceased** and there was great **calm**.
Then he asked them, "Why are you **terrified**?
Do you not **yet** have faith?"
They were filled with great **awe** and said to one another,
    "Who then **is** this whom even **wind** and **sea** obey?"

evangelist is often presenting multiple messages. Today's reading of Jesus's calming of the sea offers a prime example.

The dramatic story of Jesus saving the disciples from a "violent squall" that suddenly popped up on the Sea of Galilee is layered with multiple meanings. This nature miracle of Jesus calming the sea and wind was likely recorded by Mark to point to Jesus's divinity. As heard in the First Reading from Job, the Lord alone controls the sea.

On another level, Jesus's reaction and question to the disciples, "Why are you terrified? Do you not yet have faith?" rein-forces one of the major themes of Mark's Gospel account: without faith, you are blind to Jesus's identity as the Messiah and Son of God. Those whom Jesus encounters in the Gospel according to Mark are frequently portrayed as individuals who either believe in Jesus (for example, 1:40–41; 5:28–29) or who lack faith in him (such as, 3:20–21; 6:6). Only with the eyes of faith can one see Jesus's true identity.

A third layer is also at work in this miracle at sea. It is found as the story concludes with the disciples asking the question: "Who then is this whom even wind and sea obey?" By this time in Mark's story line, the disciples have been witness to many of Jesus's powerful deeds, his teachings to the crowds, and even private lessons by Jesus (see 4:34). That the disciples themselves still are uncertain about Jesus's identity points to their lack of faith and perhaps to the long process involved for many of us in coming to faith. This rather unflattering portrayal of the disciples will continue in future episodes as they misunderstand the meaning of Jesus's Passion predictions and even abandon him on the way to the Cross.

THIRTEENTH SUNDAY IN ORDINARY TIME

TO KEEP IN MIND

Read all three commentaries. Suggestions in each can give you insight into your own passage.

Don't assume a defensive tone; God doesn't need our apologetics. Just state the truth simply.

God created only life and all God made is good! That's the infallible truth you proclaim.

First you state God's original intent: human beings were to be "imperishable."

Then you tell us how death entered the world and *who* experiences it.

For meditation and context:

TO KEEP IN MIND

Pauses are never "dead" moments. Something is always happening during a pause. Practice will teach you how often and how long to pause. Too many pauses make a reading choppy; too few cause ideas to run into one another.

LECTIONARY #98

READING I   Wisdom 1:13–15; 2:23–24

A reading from the Book of Wisdom

God did not make **death**,
   nor does he rejoice in the **destruction** of the **living**.
For he fashioned all things that they might have **being**;
   and the **creatures** of the world are **wholesome**,
and there is not a **destructive** drug among them
   nor any domain of the **netherworld** on earth,
   for **justice** is **undying**.
For God formed man to be **imperishable**;
   the image of his own **nature** he made him.
But by the envy of the **devil**, **death** entered the world,
   and they who belong to his **company experience** it.

RESPONSORIAL PSALM   Psalm 30:2, 4, 5–6, 11, 12, 13 (2a)

R. I will praise you, Lord, for you have rescued me.

I will extol you, O LORD, for you drew
      me clear
   and did not let my enemies rejoice
      over me.
O LORD, you brought me up from the
      netherworld;
   you preserved me from among those
      going down into the pit.

Sing praise to the LORD, you his
      faithful ones,
   and give thanks to his holy name.
For his anger lasts but a moment;
   a lifetime, his good will.
At nightfall, weeping enters in,
   but with the dawn, rejoicing.

Hear, O LORD, and have pity on me;
   O LORD, be my helper.
You changed my mourning into dancing;
   O LORD, my God, forever will I give
      you thanks.

READING I   The Book of Wisdom, written about fifty years before the birth of Jesus, contains some of the clearest Old Testament references to belief in afterlife. By this time the emerging Jewish view of resurrection, focused primarily on renewal of God's people, had sometimes incorporated the Greek idea of immortality. Emerging only about 160 BC, belief in everlasting life with God for the righteous still was not held by all Jews. The author of Wisdom, however, uses these concepts to offer hope and comfort to

Jews living in Alexandria, Egypt, who were suffering oppression and persecution, at times even from apostate fellow Jews.

Their hope is founded in God, source of all life, who will not allow the power of death to have the last word. The "netherworld," the world of the dead, could never overcome the power of the living God. In the Hebrew mind, sin and death were commonly intertwined, for both alienated or separated one from God. Thus the author asserts that death will not reign over God's creation, and that justice also will never die. In this passage "justice" refers not only

to a single virtue but to God's entire plan for how human beings are to live. The Old Testament often refers to a way of life based on God's teaching as the path of justice or way of righteousness. Failure to live according to that plan was described as injustice, unrighteousness, or sin. Wisdom asserts that neither death nor sin holds ultimate power; that belongs only to God, the giver and source of all life.

Part of God's plan, the writer further proclaims, is that humankind, created in the divine image (Genesis 1:26–67), would

Corinthians = kohr-IN-thee-uhnz

Paul begins with upbeat praise and encouragement.

"The gracious act" Paul calls for is a charitable collection for the Christian community.

As Christ performed a "gracious act"—forsaking divine privilege to take on human flesh and become weak like us—so you should be generous in imitation of him.

Paul softens his position a bit by saying that helping others shouldn't impoverish you. Sharing, so none go hungry, is his goal.

Paul is not impractical; he's saying: the help you give now may return to you in *your* time of need.

Paul's allusion is to the daily collection of manna during Israel's desert wanderings that left no one with too much and no one with too little.

READING II   2 Corinthians 8:7, 9, 13–15

A reading from the second Letter of Saint Paul to the Corinthians

Brothers and sisters:
As you **excel** in every respect, in **faith**, **discourse**,
    knowledge, all **earnestness**, and in the **love** we have for you,
    may you excel in **this** gracious act also.

For you **know** the gracious act of our Lord Jesus **Christ**,
    that though he was **rich**, for **your** sake he became **poor**,
    so that by his **poverty** you might become **rich**.
Not that others should have **relief** while you are **burdened**,
    but that as a matter of **equality**
    your **abundance** at the present time should supply their needs,
    so that **their** abundance may also supply **your** needs,
    that there may be **equality**.
As it is written:
    Whoever had **much** *did not have* **more**,
        and whoever had **little** *did not have* **less**.

Jesus has shuttled back and forth across the lake, clinging to the shore to avoid being inundated by the crowd.

Jairus, an "insider," comes to the quintessential outsider, Jesus. Your tone should suggest the daring nature of his request.

He forsakes his dignity, falls at Jesus's feet, and begs.

GOSPEL   Mark 5:21–43

A reading from the holy Gospel according to Mark

When **Jesus** had crossed again in the boat
    to the other **side**,
    a large **crowd** gathered around him, and he stayed close
        to the **sea**.
One of the synagogue **officials**, named **Jairus**, came forward.
Seeing him he fell at his **feet** and pleaded **earnestly**
        with him, saying,
    "My **daughter** is at the point of **death**.

share in God's life forever. Death originated not with God, but with the devil—and the One who created all things always wields greater power than the powers of sin and death.

| READING II | Today we hear the second of three excerpts from Paul's Second Letter to the Corinthians, proclaimed on the Twelfth, Thirteenth, and Fourteenth Sundays in Ordinary Time. In last Sunday's excerpt, Paul stressed the love of Christ as the impetus for his ministry and, by implication, for all Christian service.

Today's reading calls for concrete action rooted in such love.

Paul's efforts to collect funds from the churches he founded to aid the church in Jerusalem form the immediate context for today's passage. According to Acts 11:27–30, a prediction of widespread famine reached the ears of Christians in Antioch, prompting them to call for a collection to aid the church at Jerusalem. Paul exhorts the Corinthians to contribute to this relief fund with an appeal to imitate the love of Christ, who gave life itself for others. Urging

the Corinthians to similar selfless giving, the Greek text twice uses the word *charis*, literally "gift," usually translated "grace" and commonly used by Paul to refer to the unearned gift of God's own life offered to all through Jesus. Unfortunately, the English translation does not and perhaps cannot adequately bring out that connection ("gracious act").

Paul states that he is not asking the Christians at Corinth to impoverish themselves, but to give of their comparative abundance so that the needs of others may be met. He adds that there will doubtless

A new narrative beat is inserted within the previous beat. The first story will be continued. For now, narrate the woman's history with compassion.

Please, come lay your **hands** on her
    that she may get **well** and **live**."
He went **off** with him,
    and a large **crowd** followed him and **pressed** upon him.

There was a **woman** afflicted with **hemorrhages** for twelve
    years.
She had suffered **greatly** at the hands of many **doctors**
    and had spent all that she **had**.
Yet she was not **helped** but only grew **worse**.
She had heard about **Jesus** and came up behind him in the crowd
    and **touched** his **cloak**.

Out of her desperation shines this ray of hope.

She said, "If I but touch his clothes, I shall be **cured**."
Immediately her flow of blood dried **up**.
She felt in her body that she was **healed** of her affliction.

Make Jesus's awareness credible. His question is full of curiosity and admiration for one of such faith. He wants to meet the person, so there's no reproach in his question.

Jesus, aware at once that **power** had gone out from him,
    turned around in the crowd and asked, "**Who** has touched
    my clothes?"
But his **disciples** said to Jesus,

The disciples' dialogue is natural and animated. They think he's being foolish.

    "You see how the crowd is **pressing** upon you,
    and yet you ask, 'Who **touched** me?'"
And he looked around to **see** who had done it.

The disciples have made enough of a fuss that she's gown fearful. Speak from her point of view.

The **woman**, realizing what had **happened** to her,
    approached in **fear** and **trembling**.
She **fell** down before Jesus and told him the whole **truth**.

Jesus hears her story and responds with compassion.

He said to her, "**Daughter**, your **faith** has **saved** you.
Go in **peace** and be **cured** of your affliction."

The pace quickens with the arrival of the people from the official's house.

While he was still **speaking**,
    people from the synagogue official's house arrived and said,
    "Your daughter has **died**; why trouble the teacher any **longer**?"
Disregarding the message that was reported,
    Jesus said to the synagogue official,
    "Do not be **afraid**; just have **faith**."

Perhaps, as with Lazarus, Jesus is glad of the opportunity to upend their expectations regarding this "impossible" situation.

He did not allow anyone to **accompany** him inside
    except **Peter**, **James**, and **John**, the brother of James.

---

be opportunities to receive in their own time of need from other local churches. His point is not "equality" in the sense of everyone having the same; rather, Paul exhorts the Corinthians to help meet the needs of all. This is the implied meaning of his reference to Exodus 16:18 at the end of the reading ("As it is written . . . "). In this text Moses urges the Israelites who have been fed with manna during their desert journey to gather it together and then give an equal measure to each. The verse following this directive, not quoted by Paul, states: "They gathered as much as each needed to eat."

GOSPEL Early in Mark's Gospel account, Jesus's first public words proclaim that God's final rule, the "kingdom of God," is beginning in his person and action. Jewish faith expected that God's full and final reign would bring the power of God to bear on all that was afflicting humankind, overthrowing the rule of all evil forces. Demons were very real in the ancient mind; Jesus's contemporaries believed that ills such as poverty, oppression, and every kind of sickness were caused by one or more evil powers. As

seen in the First Reading, they also considered the devil to be the source of humankind's ultimate disorder, death.

To demonstrate Jesus's proclamation that the rule of evil must, through him, begin to give way to the ultimate power of God, Mark describes Jesus's first public acts as a series of healings and exorcisms. Such stories have the same fundamental intent: to clearly demonstrate the truth of Jesus's words: in Jesus the Messiah, God's mighty power is now breaking into this world, overcoming the sovereignty of evil in all its forms. Today's Gospel presents what

The mourners have created a great din around the official's house.

Jesus challenges their view of reality and unceremoniously dismisses them all.

In the New Testament, death is often equated with sleep.

Employ softer volume for this intimate scene.

Speak *Talitha koum* (tah-lee-thah-KOOM) and its translation in the soft and gentle tone you imagine Jesus would have used with the girl.

Jesus tends to two needs—for secrecy and for the child's nourishment.

When they **arrived** at the house of the synagogue official,
  he caught sight of a **commotion**,
  people **weeping** and wailing **loudly**.
So he went in and said to them,
  "**Why** this commotion and weeping?
The child is not **dead** but **asleep**."
And they **ridiculed** him.
Then he put them all **out**.
He took along the child's **father** and **mother**
  and those who were with him
  and entered the room where the **child** was.
He took the child by the **hand** and said to her, "**Talitha koum**,"
  which means, "Little **girl**, I say to you, **arise**!"
The girl, a child of **twelve**, arose **immediately** and
    walked **around**.
At that they were utterly **astounded**.
He gave strict **orders** that no one should **know** this
  and said that she should be given something to **eat**.

[Shorter: Mark 5:21–24, 35b–43]

THE **4** STEPS OF *LECTIO DIVINA* OR PRAYERFUL READING

1. Lectio: Read a Scripture passage aloud slowly. Notice what phrase captures your attention and be attentive to its meaning. Silent pause.

2. Meditatio: Read the passage aloud slowly again, reflecting on the passage, allowing God to speak to you through it. Silent pause.

3. Oratio: Read it aloud slowly a third time, allowing it to be your prayer or response to God's gift of insight to you. Silent pause.

4. Contemplatio: Read it aloud slowly a fourth time, now resting in God's word.

---

is known as a "raising story," intended to proclaim an insight fully perceived only after God raised Jesus from death. The insight is that through the life, Death and Resurrection of Jesus, even the power that brings death into the world is fully defeated. The God of life now truly reigns over all.

The miracle story preceding today's Gospel recounts Jesus's healing of a man so afflicted that he lives among tombs, at times shackled to be restrained. As is common in Mark, the evil spirits recognize who Jesus is—the Anointed One who bears

God's power, the only power able to break their hold over human beings. Immediately after this exorcism, Jesus encounters Jairus. The man expresses astounding faith in Jesus, asking him to heal his dying daughter. Jesus underscores the importance of faith when Jairus hears that his daughter is already dead: "Do not be afraid; just have faith." In the healing story sandwiched between parts of today's Gospel, Jesus reassures the woman relieved of hemorrhages that her faith has brought healing, thus reinforcing the necessity and power of human faith in God's mighty rule.

In describing what happens to the girl, Mark uses two different Greek words (though translated with the same English word); Jesus tells her to awaken, or get up. But Mark announces that the girl "arose," using the same word with which the New Testament describes the power of God in raising Jesus from death.

FOURTEENTH SUNDAY IN ORDINARY TIME

LECTIONARY #101

READING I   Ezekiel 2:2–5

A reading from the Book of the Prophet Ezekiel

As the LORD **spoke** to me, the **spirit** entered into me
> and set me on my **feet**,
> and I heard the one who was **speaking** say to me:
> Son of **man**, I am sending you to the **Israelites**,
> rebels who have **rebelled** against me;
> they and their ancestors have revolted against me
> > to this very **day**.
Hard of face and **obstinate** of heart
> are they to whom I am **sending** you.
But you shall **say** to them: Thus says the Lord **GOD**!
And whether they **heed** or **resist**—for they are a
> **rebellious** house—
> they shall **know** that a **prophet** has been **among** them.

RESPONSORIAL PSALM   Psalm 123:1–2, 2, 3–4 (2cd)

R. Our eyes are fixed on the Lord, pleading for his mercy.

To you I lift up my eyes
> who are enthroned in heaven—
as the eyes of servants
> are on the hands of their masters.

As the eyes of a maid
> are on the hands of her mistress,
so are our eyes on the LORD, our God,
> till he have pity on us.

Have pity on us, O LORD, have pity on us,
> for we are more than sated with contempt;
our souls are more than sated
> with the mockery of the arrogant,
> with the contempt of the proud.

Ezekiel = ee-ZEE-kee-uhl

Everything builds up to the main message in the last line. God is saying: At least they will know I tried to warn them.

Ezekiel's difficult mission will be to alert Israel to the consequences of their infidelity.

Keep in mind that Ezekiel is given this difficult mission after being filled with the *spirit*.

The nation's rebellion against God has been both serious and chronic. God's uncompromising tone is motivated by a desire to call the people back to fidelity.

God's stark description.

[This needs to go next to: "Hard of face . . ."

God speaks again of their rebellion. Say it with an uptick of energy.

Speak the last line with determination. God wants them to know he made every effort to win them back, because a "prophet" is God's mouthpiece, God's active love enfleshed, God's mercy personified. what prophets among us have we missed?

For meditation and context:

READING I | Ezekiel was a priest from Jerusalem who was taken prisoner among the early deportations leading up to the final destruction of Judah. At the time, the kingdom had begun its eleven-year disintegration: Judah became a vassal to Babylonia, which started deporting captives into its land. But even in exile, the Chosen People were given a prophet to speak the word of the Lord, though they had previously refused to listen to many of his predecessors. In today's First Reading, Ezekiel becomes the first prophet called to speak for God in a country outside the Promised Land.

As is typical of a prophetic call, with the divine commission comes God's Spirit, empowering the prophet to carry out his service. God addresses Ezekiel as "son of man," here simply referring to a human being; the phrase connotes human weakness and mortality, emphasizing the prophet's need for divine Spirit. God calls Ezekiel to a most difficult task: to prophesy to a people who have long ignored God's word, rebelled against the divine plan, even attempted to kill prophets whose message they did not wish to hear. Though recognizing the people's obstinacy, God calls the prophet to speak the Word of the Lord to them, whether they accept or not. Ultimately, they will recognize Ezekiel as truly sent from God, for the true test of a prophet was whether his words proved true. Only in the aftermath of total destruction of Judah and captivity of those who survived it will God's people recognize that a true prophet spoke God's own word.

READING II | Rather uncommonly, today's Second Reading

Corinthians = kohr-IN-thee-uhnz

Previously, Paul presented his special "revelations" as credentials to refute his opponents. Now he takes the opposite tack, explaining how God also humbled him to balance his unique privilege.

The special favors he received were so "abundant" that God ensured Paul didn't become prideful.

Jesus's words to Paul become a theme throughout Paul's ministry.

Ponder this countercultural wisdom: when we ourselves are "weak," then God's power can shine through us.

He's saying: when *I* am weak, then I am strong *in Christ*! Speak this profound insight with humble conviction.

TO KEEP IN MIND

Narrator: Knowing the point of view that the narrator is "rooting for" will help you more fully communicate the meaning of the text. The narrator always has a viewpoint, often speaking as a believer, not as an objective reporter. For this reason, the narrator is often the pivotal role in a passage. Using timbre, pitch, rate, and energy can help you convey the narrator's moods or meanings.

READING II   2 Corinthians 12:7–10

A reading from the second Letter of Saint Paul to the Corinthians

Brothers and sisters:
That I, **Paul**, might not become too **elated**,
    because of the abundance of the **revelations**,
    a **thorn** in the **flesh** was given to me, an angel of **Satan**,
    to **beat** me, to keep me from being too **elated**.
Three **times** I **begged** the Lord about this, that it might **leave** me,
    but he said to me, "My **grace** is **sufficient** for you,
    for **power** is made **perfect** in **weakness**."
I will rather boast most gladly of my **weaknesses**,
    in order that the power of **Christ** may **dwell** with me.
Therefore, I am **content** with **weaknesses**, **insults**,
    hardships, **persecutions** and **constraints**,
    for the sake of **Christ**;
    for when I am **weak**, then I am **strong**.

---

seems to relate to the other two readings for this Sunday. Like Ezekiel and Jesus, Paul must carry out the work he believes God has given him in the face of resistance, threats, and difficulties. Like Ezekiel and Jesus, Paul receives God's own Spirit, a powerful divine presence within, to carry out his mission despite such hardships. He even acknowledges that some struggles might have a divine cause, illustrating that it is God's power, not his own, that empowers his ministry. The precise nature of Paul's "thorn in the flesh" is unknown, but its purpose is clear: he must never congratulate himself, but give thanks to God's grace, for any success of his mission.

Paul's further reflection might repel ancient and modern hearers as much as did Ezekiel's words. He recounts begging God to remove his affliction, only to be told that his experience of weakness can become the path to strength: God's power at work in him. It is divine power that Paul—and we—must rely upon, even to the point of rejoicing in our weakness so that Christ may live and work in us, accomplishing far more than our human limitations allow. Paul's final statement, "when I am weak, then I am strong," can meet with much resistance in an age that glorifies personal strength and accomplishment—as much resistance as Ezekiel, Paul, and Jesus faced in their times.

GOSPEL   Today's Gospel follows immediately from last Sunday's account of Jesus raising the synagogue official's daughter. Here the people continue to be astonished at him: he not only works wonders—often associated with prophets—but he teaches in the synagogue. Normally, only a man educated in

This important text shows how Jesus's ministry came up against a most insidious form of opposition. It is not enemies who oppose him, but those whose lives had been the playground and the classrooms of his youth.

The opening is festive and hopeful. The return of the native son turned celebrity brings a crowd.

It is his success that turns them against him. Avoiding the use of his name, the neighbors ask, "Where did this man . . . " They seem to be saying, "How dare he climb so high . . . What wisdom, what mighty deeds! He needs to be brought low!"

Recall the family's recent effort to bring him home for fear he had gone mad (Mark 3:21). Perhaps his use of the familiar proverb about prophets is for their benefit as well as for the crowd's. The irony of the words will speak for itself, so you needn't overplay them, but take brief pauses after "native place," "kin," and "house."

Jesus would not storm away and embarrass his mother and family. But his disappointment is palpable, as is his sadness. Tell us that in the way you speak the final line.

TO KEEP IN MIND

Go slowly in the epistles. Paul's style is often a tangle of complex sentences; his mood can change within a single passage.

GOSPEL   Mark 6:1–6

A reading from the holy Gospel according to Mark

Jesus departed from there and came to his **native** place, accompanied by his **disciples**.
When the **sabbath** came he began to **teach** in the synagogue,
    and many who heard him were **astonished**.
They said, "**Where** did this man **get** all this?
What kind of **wisdom** has been given him?
What mighty **deeds** are wrought by his hands!
Is he not the **carpenter**, the son of **Mary**,
    and the brother of **James** and **Joses** and **Judas** and **Simon**?
And are not his **sisters** here with us?"
And they took **offense** at him.
Jesus said to them,
    "A **prophet** is not without **honor** except in his **native** place
    and among his own **kin** and in his own **house**."
So he was not **able** to perform any mighty deed there,
    apart from **curing** a few sick people by laying his **hands**
        on them.
He was **amazed** at their lack of **faith**.

---

the Hebrew Scriptures by one or more rabbis would be able to do so. But the people perceive this man as an unschooled carpenter and "son of Mary." This title is highly unusual, since Jewish custom referred to a man as the son of his father. The usage might reflect that Mary is at this time a widow, or indicate the low esteem in which some held Jesus; alternatively, some scholars suggest that Mark here expresses his belief that Jesus's true father is God. Clearly, onlookers can hardly accept that this man who appears all too common and ordinary could teach them anything about

the meaning of Scripture, which communicates God's will to the people, and so "they took offense at him." Resistance to God's word takes many forms.

Jesus clearly indicates that he sees himself as one who speaks for God in applying a commonly known saying to prophets. He seems all too aware of how his people rejected previous spokesmen for God. Mark also might be foreshadowing Jesus's coming Passion and Death, since Jews knew well their history of attempts to kill prophets with an unpopular message.

The people's resistance to Jesus indicates lack of faith, and so Jesus cannot perform further mighty deeds, that is, healings and exorcisms. Jews understood a "mighty deed" or miracle as an act of God's power working through a wonder-worker. In the New Testament, sometimes faith appears to be a prerequisite, at other times the result, of a miracle. This passage clearly indicates the former; who could believe that God would teach and act in such a common man?

FIFTEENTH SUNDAY IN ORDINARY TIME

LECTIONARY #104

Amos = AY-m*s

Amaziah =am-uh-ZĪ-uh

As in Jesus's rejection by his neighbors in Nazareth, the hostility here is born of jealousy. It's all personal, not professional. They resent this country farmer who lacks credentials and authorization coming to Bethel and making trouble. Amaziah speaks "visionary" with malice and disdain.

Amaziah suggests Amos prophesies for profit, not for God. His words are full of scorn.

Amos says, "I didn't ask for this; I was drafted by God and *told* to prophesy!" His voice is not whiny, but convincing.

READING I   Amos 7:12–15

A reading from the Book of the Prophet Amos

Amaziah, priest of **Bethel**, said to **Amos**,
  "**Off** with you, visionary, **flee** to the land of **Judah**!
There earn your bread by **prophesying**,
  but never again prophesy in **Bethel**;
  for it is the king's **sanctuary** and a **royal** temple."
Amos **answered** Amaziah, "I was no **prophet**,
  nor have I belonged to a **company** of prophets;
  I was a **shepherd** and a dresser of **sycamores**.
The LORD took me from following the flock, and said to me,
  Go, **prophesy** to my people Israel."

For meditation and context:

RESPONSORIAL PSALM   Psalm 85:9–10, 11–12, 13–14 (8)

R. Lord, let us see your kindness, and grant us your salvation.

I will hear what God proclaims;
  the LORD—for he proclaims peace.
Near indeed is his salvation to those who
    fear him,
  glory dwelling in our land.

The LORD himself will give his benefits;
  our land shall yield its increase.
Justice shall walk before him,
  and prepare the way of his steps.

Kindness and truth shall meet;
  justice and peace shall kiss.
Truth shall spring out of the earth,
  and justice shall look down from heaven.

TO KEEP IN MIND
Separating units of thought with pauses: Identify the units of thought in your text and use pauses to distinguish one from another. Running words together blurs meaning and fails to distinguish ideas. Punctuation does not always indicate clearly what words to group together or where to pause. The listener depends on you for this organization of ideas.

READING I   The conversation we hear in this reading between Amaziah, a priest of the sanctuary of Bethel, and the prophet Amos, takes place in the northern kingdom (called Israel). The king who had established Israel after seceding from the united monarchy had placed an idol at Bethel, where the people offered sacrifice to God. For this reason, the shrine was frequently associated with idolatry. Amos was a prophet of the southern kingdom (called Judah), and was the only biblical prophet from Judah to come north and prophesy in Judah. Amos understood that the word of the Lord was addressed to the entire Chosen People, and he had chastised the people for their hypocritical worship at Bethel (4:4–5).

Amos, as did the other prophets, sharply criticized people who observed external rituals meticulously but tolerated social injustice. He warned that such hypocrisy was false worship—a mockery of worship, which was supposed to be a wholehearted response to God. In today's reading, Amaziah has had enough of Amos's criticisms, and orders him to go back to the southern kingdom of Judah and earn his living there.

Amos, who never minces words, defends his vocation as a prophet by reminding the priest that he never belonged to a group of professional prophets or a prophetic guild, people whose physical needs were usually cared for by others. He had another occupation, but God's call changed his life course. He speaks at God's call, with divine directive, not seeking gain for himself. His entire goal is to proclaim God's message to the covenant people who continue to ignore or damage that sacred relationship.

READING II   Ephesians 1:3–14

A reading from the Letter of Saint Paul to the Ephesians

Blessed be the God and **Father** of our Lord Jesus **Christ**,
  who has **blessed** us in Christ
  with every spiritual blessing in the **heavens**,
  as he **chose** us in him, before the foundation of the **world**,
  to be **holy** and without **blemish** before him.
In **love** he destined us for **adoption** to himself through
    Jesus **Christ**,
  in accord with the favor of his **will**,
  for the praise of the glory of his **grace**
  that he granted us in the **beloved**.
In him we have **redemption** by his **blood**,
  the **forgiveness** of **transgressions**,
  in accord with the **riches** of his grace that he lavished
    upon us.
In all **wisdom** and **insight**, he has made known to us
  the **mystery** of his will in accord with his favor
  that he set forth in him as a plan for the fullness of times,
  to sum up **all** things in **Christ**, in **heaven** and on **earth**.

In **him** we were also **chosen**,
  destined in accord with the **purpose** of the One
  who **accomplishes** all things according to the intention
    of his **will**,
  so that we might exist for the praise of his **glory**,
  we who first **hoped** in Christ.
In him you **also**, who have **heard** the word of truth,
  the **gospel** of your salvation, and have **believed** in him,
  were sealed with the promised Holy **Spirit**,
  which is the first installment of our inheritance
  toward **redemption** as God's **possession**, to the **praise**
    of his **glory**.

[Shorter: Ephesians 1:3–10]

Ephesians = ee-FEE-zhuhnz. This is the first of seven consecutive weeks we read from Ephesians.

The text is a song of praise whose words flow quickly, phrase upon phrase. Paul tells us much about ourselves in these lines, so use the rhythms and images of the text to paint a portrait of the believer.

As you read, don't leave out Paul's joyful tone of praise.

While the sound of these lines is upbeat and joyful, the sound alone won't be enough. To communicate the meaning, pace your way through the many phrases using inflection to distinguish one thought from another.

The mercies of God are overwhelming. Speak with deep gratitude.

By "we" Paul refers to Jewish Christians, but you are also speaking of yourself and your neighbors, and of the profound privilege of knowing Christ.

By "you also" Paul means the Gentile believers in Christ. Note: they "heard," they "believed," and they were "sealed."

The knowledge of Christ we are now privileged to have is but a foretaste, a "first installment," of what we will have in the glory of God's Kingdom.

READING II Though addressed to the church at Ephesus, this Pauline letter actually speaks to the entire Christian community, the worldwide Church of its time. For various reasons many scholars date the letter some decades after Paul, but the writer clearly knows and develops the Apostle's vision. Some think Ephesians was a circular letter meant to be distributed and read to various local churches in Asia Minor.

After a customary opening, the author omits the usual greetings and inserts what is often called a "hymn of the Church" (1:3–14). Its poetic language apparently draws upon liturgy and prayers already in use among Christians. The hymn opens by praising God "who has blessed us in Christ." Throughout the letter, the author presents Christ as the origin and uniting force of the Church. It was God's will and plan from all eternity, the author stresses, to form a holy people. In Hebrew thought, "holy" meant "set apart," usually for a purpose. Hence the Church, as the newly created people of God, is destined to reveal and embody the gracious love with which God made us sons and daughters of one Father, the Father of our brother, Jesus Christ. In the Church, God has revealed the "mystery"—God's eternal plan—to bring all things into oneness in Christ. An important aspect of that oneness is not mentioned here, but will be repeated later in Ephesians: the unity of Jews and Gentiles in one redeemed, recreated People of God, the Church.

GOSPEL Today's passage from Mark begins immediately after last Sunday's reading, in which Jesus expressed regret at the people's lack of faith. Here, after continuing to teach in various villages, Jesus turns to the Twelve, the inner circle of disciples whom he will send

Don't rush the opening. Speak of the "Twelve" with respect and affection.

Speak the instructions in the voice of Jesus giving clear, but not stern directions.

The instructions may seem overly specific, but they make the point that the Apostles must not rely on human favors or earthly goods to sustain their ministry.

"Until you leave" means "leave for *good*." Let your stress fall on "there" in "stay *there* until."

Jesus prepares them for inevitable rejection.

Pause at the end of the instructions. Their ministry is distinguished by repentance and driving out demons. Let your tone tells us they will be successful in their mission.

TO KEEP IN MIND

Gestures and Posture: Using gestures is not part of the task of proclamation; within the liturgy, gestures are an unnecessary distraction. However, your body language is always communicating. Avoid leaning on the ambo or standing on one foot. And don't let your face or body contradict the Good News you announce. Readers are allowed to smile!

GOSPEL   Mark 6:7–13

A reading from the holy Gospel according to Mark

Jesus summoned the **Twelve** and began to send them out
>   **two** by **two**
> and gave them **authority** over unclean **spirits**.
He **instructed** them to take **nothing** for the journey
>   but a **walking** stick—
> no **food**, no **sack**, no **money** in their belts.
They were, however, to wear **sandals**
>   but not a second **tunic**.
He said to them,
>   "Wherever you enter a house, **stay** there until you **leave**.
Whatever place does not **welcome** you or **listen** to you,
>   **leave** there and shake the **dust** off your feet
>   in **testimony** against them."
So they **went** off and preached **repentance**.
The **Twelve** drove out many **demons**,
>   and they **anointed** with oil many who were **sick** and
>   **cured** them.

---

forth to spread his message by word and deed. In Mark, the "Twelve" are a representative group comparable to the patriarchs of the twelve tribes of Israel. They are to carry on the mission of Jesus in order to help create the new Israel of the age of salvation, the Church.

With those he commissions, Jesus shares authority over unclean spirits (forces of evil), but cautions them also to support one another, undertaking their work in pairs. They are not to be overly concerned about material needs such as food and clothing, but to rely on the power of God. Perhaps echoing the necessity of faith in last Sunday's reading, Jesus instructs the Twelve not to linger in places that refuse to listen. Rather, they are to confront such a response with a sign of dissociation, shaking the dust from their feet. In Israel's history, refusal to listen to God, who spoke through the prophet, was often presented as a major reason for downfall and exile.

The brief statement that the Twelve went abroad proclaiming a call to repent carries great significance. The English words "repent" and "repentance" translate a Hebrew word, often used by Old Testament prophets, that meant "to turn," involving a complete about-face in perceiving, judging, and acting. In Mark, Jesus's first public words proclaim the nearness of the Kingdom of God, followed immediately by a call to repent (1:15). It is *because* God draws near in Jesus, the Messiah, that people are able to turn their lives around, and this is the message the Twelve are to proclaim. It is a message that still asks to be welcomed and heard.

SIXTEENTH SUNDAY IN ORDINARY TIME

LECTIONARY #107

READING I   Jeremiah 23:1–6

A reading from the Book of the Prophet Jeremiah

Woe to the **shepherds**
    who **mislead** and **scatter** the flock of my pasture,
    says the LORD.
Therefore, thus says the LORD, the God of Israel,
    against the shepherds who shepherd my people:
    You have **scattered** my sheep and **driven** them away.
You have not **cared** for them,
    but **I** will take care to **punish** your evil deeds.
I myself will gather the **remnant** of my flock
    from all the lands to which I have **driven** them
    and bring them back to their **meadow**;
    there they shall **increase** and **multiply**.
I will appoint shepherds for them who **will** shepherd them
    so that they need no longer **fear** and **tremble**;
    and none shall be **missing**, says the LORD.

    Behold, the days are **coming**, says the LORD,
        when I will raise up a righteous **shoot** to David;
    as **king** he shall reign and govern **wisely**,
        he shall do what is **just** and **right** in the land.
    In his days Judah shall be **saved**,
        Israel shall dwell in **security**.
    This is the **name** they give him:
        "The LORD our **justice**."

Jeremiah = jayr-uh-MĪ-uh

Like the parent of a victimized child, God speaks with righteous anger.

Instead of gathering and protecting the sheep, the shepherds have "scattered . . . and driven them away."

God's voice rings out across the lands where the sheep are scattered, reassuring them of safe return. God will find good and *worthy* shepherds who share God's love for the neglected flock.

The final paragraph shifts tone; here we have a prophetic oracle about the coming Messiah.

God's voice rings with pride because this *faithful* servant will honor and *accomplish* God's will.

Speak "The Lord our justice" as if he will bear all of the world's pain and all the world's hopes.

READING I This First Reading, which will be contrasted with the Gospel, comes from the prophet Jeremiah, who was given the difficult challenge of proclaiming God's word to the covenant people as they degenerated toward downfall and exile. At this point, the prophet is certain that the destruction of Judah is inevitable, but he must convey hope for the future even as he proclaims that message.

For centuries the LORD's people had been governed by kings who, ideally, were religious as well as political leaders, ruling as God ruled and seeking to establish peace and freedom from oppression for all. The Bible's religious history, however, indicates that most fell short of that goal, some to an extreme. Since Israelite kings were often called shepherds, the prophet's condemnation here addresses the kings of his era who have failed repeatedly to care for, guide, and nourish God's people. This failure of religious leadership is one significant reason for Judah's demise.

The prophet boldly proclaims that in the unknown future, after the cleansing disaster of destruction and captivity, the LORD's flock will have a true shepherd: their God, who will restore the people and give them a new, truly righteous shepherd, a king of the line of David. This new shepherd-king will finally rule as God always intended.

For meditation and context:

TO KEEP IN MIND

Go slowly in the epistles. Paul's style is often a tangle of complex sentences; his mood can change within a single passage.

RESPONSORIAL PSALM Psalm 23:1–3, 3–4, 5, 6 (1)

R. The Lord is my shepherd; there is nothing I shall want.

The LORD is my shepherd; I shall not want.
  In verdant pastures he gives me repose;
beside restful waters he leads me;
  he refreshes my soul.

He guides me in right paths
  for his name's sake.
Even though I walk in the dark valley
  I fear no evil; for you are at my side
with your rod and your staff
  that give me courage.

You spread the table before me
  in the sight of my foes;
you anoint my head with oil;
  my cup overflows.

Only goodness and kindness follow me
  all the days of my life;
and I shall dwell in the house of the LORD
  for years to come.

Ephesians = ee-FEE-zhunz. This is the second of seven consecutive weeks we read from Ephesians.

The text speaks of God's will for universal salvation. Those "far off" (the Gentiles) and those "near" (the Jews) will have a common destiny in Christ.

The blood of Christ has evened the playing field, making Jew and Gentile coheirs of God's promises.

Paul asserts that Christ knocked down the wall that divided Jews and Gentiles "through his flesh," through the shedding of his blood. We are no longer subject to "commandments and legal claims" because we are justified in that blood. Out of "two" Jesus has fashioned *one* people ("one new person") in whom all have access to the Father.

The final sentence summarizes what went before. Use the repetition to deepen our experience of the truth Jesus came to share: God wants all people for himself. Speak as if you were Jesus drawing listeners to your bosom where the "Spirit" waits to open the door to the "Father."

READING II   Ephesians 2:13–18

A reading from the Letter of Saint Paul to the Ephesians

Brothers and sisters:
In Christ **Jesus** you who once were far **off**
  have become **near** by the **blood** of Christ.

For he is our **peace**, he who made both **one**
  and broke down the dividing wall of **enmity**, through his **flesh**,
  abolishing the law with its commandments and legal claims,
  that he might create in himself **one new person** in place
    of the **two**,
  thus establishing **peace**,
  and might **reconcile** both with God,
  in one body, through the **cross**,
  putting that enmity to **death** by it.
He came and preached peace to you who were far **off**
  and peace to those who were **near**,
  for through him we **both** have access in one **Spirit**
    to the **Father**.

READING II Today's Second Reading continues Ephesians, which, as noted last week, focuses on the unity of the Church. In this letter and elsewhere, Paul refers to Christ, directly or indirectly, as head of the Church, his Body on earth. Today's usage tends to use "head" in the sense of leader or ruler; while that meaning is not absent in Paul, he most likely intends the more common meaning of his time: source and origin.

Hence this passage focuses on the work of Christ in creating peace (which includes notions of wholeness and right relationships) and breaking down barriers of division to create one new, unified body, the Church. Although here the author does not name the major division to be overcome, this and other letters deal with the necessity of bringing together Jewish and Gentile followers of Christ into one body. It is very clear who breaks down "the dividing wall of enmity": it is Christ. He alone reconciles all through the cross, uniting his followers in one Spirit. Overcoming enmity, hostility, and divisions among numerous groups remains an urgent task for the Church today; and today, as in the early Church, the source of oneness is Christ, the head.

GOSPEL Last Sunday we saw Jesus commissioning the Twelve to go out and proclaim his message by word and deed. Like Jesus, they were to announce the inbreaking Kingdom of God with its call and empowerment to conversion of heart and life. In today's Gospel, they return to report their missionary activity to Jesus. This is the only time that Mark refers to the Twelve as "Apostles." The word literally means "those who are sent."

This is a tale of human need and divine compassion.
Jesus wants to know of their labors and successes. Speak with vibrant energy.

Jesus desires to draw them away so they can share and *reflect* on their experience.

The narrator may betray some annoyance at the insensitivity of the crowd.

There is humor and irony in the crowd reaching the "deserted" place first.

Pause before the last sentence.
The mood changes as Jesus sees the crowd and immediately senses the depth of their neediness. The simile is poignant all on its own; no need to punctuate it. Pause again before announcing his compassionate decision to "teach them."

TO KEEP IN MIND

Each text contains **three kinds of content**: intellectual-theological, emotional, and aesthetic. The plot and details of the story and the theological teaching behind them comprise the intellectual-theological content. How the author or characters feel (or want us to feel) is the emotional content. Elements that make the writing pleasing—rhythm, repetition, suspense, and picturesque language—are the aesthetic content.

GOSPEL   Mark 6:30–34

A reading from the holy Gospel according to Mark

The **apostles** gathered together with **Jesus**
    and reported all they had **done** and **taught**.
He **said** to them,
    "Come away by **yourselves** to a **deserted** place and **rest**
        a while."
People were coming and going in great **numbers**,
    and they had no opportunity even to **eat**.
So they went off in the **boat** by themselves to a **deserted** place.
People **saw** them leaving and many came to **know** about it.
They **hastened** there on **foot** from all the towns
    and arrived at the place **before** them.

When he **disembarked** and saw the vast **crowd**,
    his heart was moved with **pity** for them,
    for they were like **sheep** without a **shepherd**;
    and he began to **teach** them **many** things.

Like a caring shepherd, Jesus urges the Twelve to rest and restore needed energy after their days of travel and missionary efforts. Mark and other evangelists show Jesus himself periodically taking time for solitude and prayer in the midst of his ministry of preaching, teaching, and healing. The first attempt to escape from the crowds for needed rest is fruitless; indeed, even greater numbers gather, so that Jesus and the Twelve cannot even share a meal. A more concerted effort to gain respite also fails; though they take to a boat for refuge, word spreads and they are met by multitudes as they approach land.

At this point, the reading reaches its climax. Jesus, the Good Shepherd, puts aside his own desire for rest and tends to the people's need, for he recognizes that they are "like sheep without a shepherd," and he first meets their need for sound teaching. With one brief phrase, Mark draws a parallel between Jesus's situation and that of Moses in the Exodus journey, who asks God to give the people a leader and guide so that "the Lord's community may not be like sheep without a shepherd" (Numbers 27:17). In this passage Mark also calls to mind a prophecy of Ezekiel in which God promises that in Israel's future restoration, "I myself will give them rest." Thus in a few words, Mark underscores the identity of Jesus the Messiah: the fulfillment of Israel's hopes, the beginning of God's final rule, and the agent of new creation for God's people.

SEVENTEENTH SUNDAY IN ORDINARY TIME

LECTIONARY #110

You must give the reading time to make its impact; focus on the details without becoming artificially slow.

Baal-shalishah = BAY-uhl SHAHL-ih-shuh

Elisha = ee-LĪ-shuh

READING I   2 Kings 4:42–44

A reading from the second Book of Kings

A man came from **Baal-shalishah** bringing to **Elisha**,
   the man of **God**,
   twenty **barley** loaves made from the **firstfruits**,
   and fresh grain in the **ear**.
Elisha said, "Give it to the **people** to eat."
But his servant **objected**,
   "How can I set this before a **hundred** people?"
Elisha **insisted**, "Give it to the **people** to **eat**.
For thus says the LORD,
   'They shall **eat** and there shall be some left **over**.'"
And when they had **eaten**, there **was** some left over,
   as the LORD had **said**.

While the numbers here are dwarfed by those in the Gospel, they merit emphasis.

Because his tone was almost mocking, Elisha "insisted" in the following line.

Sense the meaning beyond the literal in this line: God will provide for all the needs of his people, and always with abundance.

RESPONSORIAL PSALM   Psalm 145:10–11, 15–16, 17–18 (16)

R. The hand of the Lord feeds us; he answers all our needs.

Let all your works give you thanks, O LORD,
   and let your faithful ones bless you.
Let them discourse of the glory of your
      kingdom
   and speak of your might.

The eyes of all look hopefully to you,
   and you give them their food in
      due season;
you open your hand
   and satisfy the desire of every living thing.

The LORD is just in all his ways
   and holy in all his works.
The LORD is near to all who call upon him,
   to all who call upon him in truth.

For meditation and context:

TO KEEP IN MIND
Dialogue imitates real conversation, so it often moves faster than the rest of the passage.

READING I The Second Book of Kings contains what is often called the Elisha cycle, a series of stories about the successor of Elijah. Both of these great early prophets proclaimed God's word to various kings who allowed or even encouraged idol worship and social injustice among God's people. At the time, working wonders was one mark of a genuine prophet; today's reading is one of a series of such wonders meant to testify that God was truly and powerfully at work

in Elisha. Previous to the account in today's reading, God had been working through Elisha when the prophet multiplied a poor widow's oil, raised another woman's deceased son, and cleansed a pot of poisoned stew.

The man described in today's Scripture has twenty loaves, which suggests that he probably enjoys more security than many of his neighbors. The prophet's command to share his bread is met with some resistance and the objection that it could not possibly feed the number of those lacking

bread. (Bread was a staple of the ancient Mediterranean diet.) In words that echo in several Gospel accounts, the prophet repeats the command to share what little food there is, with the assurance that God will work yet another miracle through the prophet. The small amount will prove to be more than enough. And true to the powerful word of God spoken through the prophet, that promise is fulfilled. The focus is less on Elisha than on the power of God's word, speaking and acting through the prophet.

READING II   Ephesians 4:1–6

A reading from the Letter of Saint Paul to the Ephesians

Brothers and sisters:
I, a **prisoner** for the Lord,
   urge you to live in a manner **worthy** of the call
     you have received,
with all **humility** and **gentleness**, with **patience**,
bearing with one another through **love**,
striving to preserve the **unity** of the spirit through the bond
   of **peace**:
one **body** and one **Spirit**,
as you were also called to the one **hope** of your call;
one **Lord**, one **faith**, one **baptism**;
one **God** and **Father** of all,
who is **over** all and **through** all and **in** all.

Ephesians = ee-FEE-zhuhnz.

This is the third of seven consecutive weeks we read from Ephesians.

Paul writes from prison and he uses the word "urge." Both details suggest the tone of your reading.

Imagine using these words of Paul to persuade two siblings who have stopped speaking to each other.

When you announce the seven "unities," don't stress the word "one," but rather each new noun.

You don't often get to do it, so enjoy stressing the three prepositions in this final line.

GOSPEL   John 6:1–15

A reading from the holy Gospel according to John

Jesus went across the Sea of **Galilee**.
A large **crowd** followed him,
   because they saw the **signs** he was performing on the **sick**.
Jesus went up on the **mountain**,
   and there he sat down with his **disciples**.
The Jewish feast of **Passover** was near.
When Jesus raised his **eyes**
   and saw that a large **crowd** was coming to him,
   he said to **Philip**,
   "Where can we buy enough **food** for them to eat?"
He said this to **test** him,
   because he himself **knew** what he was going to do.

Jesus's "signs" demonstrated his divine power, but they also helped open eyes and hearts to the Good News.

Jesus intends some time alone with the disciples.

The proximity to Passover is not insignificant.

Before the crowd has even arrived, Jesus anticipates their need.

Jesus seems to be having some fun with the disciples.

READING II The Second Reading is the third of several Sunday Scriptures from Ephesians, the Pauline letter that repeatedly emphasizes oneness in the Church as the body of Christ with Christ as head. Previous readings have stressed the crucified and risen Christ as origin and principle of unity in the Church, the one whose abiding presence heals all divisions. It is important for modern Christians to realize that in the New Testament the "Spirit" does not yet indicate a third "Person" in God; the Church would not define that understanding for nearly three centuries. In the Old Testament, reference to the "spirit" of God indicates the powerful presence of God experienced within and among a person or persons, usually enabling them to carry out a God-given role or task. One Hebrew word means breath, wind, and spirit; hence the "spirit" of God signified divine presence as interior, powerful, and life-giving—as is one's own breath. The earliest Christians understood this presence of God as now being lavished on all people through the risen Christ.

Immersed in his Hebrew way of thinking, the author of Ephesians can urge the community to imitate the attitudes and actions of Christ, for he now gives access to God's powerful spirit. At Baptism, this divine spirit breathes in each and every member, enabling them to overcome all divisions and so create and preserve a community of love, peace, and unity. The goal of oneness and the spirit of Christ that empowers Christians to strive for it are two tightly interwoven strands in this reading.

GOSPEL Today's Gospel begins a lengthy section on the meaning of Christian Eucharist in John. The

If Philip thinks Jesus serious, he would respond with alarm; if not, his response would be dismissive.

Several times in the Gospel accounts, Andrew brings someone to Jesus without realizing what results will follow. He goes against logic in bringing forth this boy who has so little.

As narrator, you are interested in emphasizing the details that will heighten the drama of the story.
Don't fail to spotlight the Eucharistic allusions.

The bounty of God must not be taken for granted, nor wasted.

The number of baskets contrasts sharply with the original number of barley loaves.

In many, this miracle inspires genuine faith.

But Jesus knows that soon greed and self-interest will corrupt their genuine insight, so he eludes their efforts to hail him king.

> **TO KEEP IN MIND**
> You'll read more naturally if you read **ideas rather than words**, and if you share **images rather than sentences**.

Philip **answered** him,
　"Two hundred days' **wages** worth of food would not be enough
　for each of them to have a **little**."
One of his disciples,
　Andrew, the brother of Simon **Peter**, said to him,
　"There is a **boy** here who has five **barley** loaves and two **fish**;
　but what good are **these** for so **many**?"
Jesus said, "Have the people **recline**."
Now there was a great deal of **grass** in that place.
So the men **reclined**, about five **thousand** in number.
Then Jesus **took** the loaves, gave **thanks**,
　and **distributed** them to those who were reclining,
　and also as much of the **fish** as they **wanted**.
When they had had their **fill**, he said to his disciples,
　"Gather the fragments left **over**,
　so that nothing will be **wasted**."
So they **collected** them,
　and filled twelve wicker **baskets** with fragments
　from the five barley loaves
　that had been **more** than they could eat.
When the people **saw** the sign he had done, they said,
　"This is truly the **Prophet**, the one who is to come into
　　the world."
Since Jesus **knew** that they were going to come and carry him off
　to make him **king**,
　he **withdrew** again to the mountain **alone**.

multiplication of loaves is the only miracle story included by all four Evangelists, but as usual, John employs some of his own unique approach in this account. John does not use the term "miracle" but "sign"; he uses certain wondrous acts of Jesus to reveal who Jesus truly is: God's own Word incarnate. The Fourth Evangelist also frequently depicts Jesus fulfilling, or even replacing, certain practices and institutions of Judaism. In this passage, references to the story of Elisha are obvious, though Jesus is shown to be much greater than he.

The time setting, near Passover, also anticipates John's later interpretation of Jesus as the new Passover Lamb. The great abundance of food also suggests the overflowing richness of the banquet in the final age of salvation.

While it is impossible to determine what actual event might have given rise to this account, as presented by the Evangelists, it clearly carries strong overtones of Christian Eucharist. Key elements in the early celebration of the Lord's Supper are often summed up in four words: take, bless (or give thanks), break, give. Though

not all these precise words appear in John, the actions are clearly indicated. Further, the Greek word used here for "fragments" was commonly used for the bread of Eucharist by the early Church. At this point in John, however, the sign only partially reveals Jesus's true identity to fellow Jews. They recognize him as "the Prophet" (that is, the final prophet expected when the age of salvation dawns)—but they do not yet see what John wishes them to perceive. They do not yet understand that the Christ given in Eucharist is his very life, given that we may have life to the full.

EIGTHTEENTH SUNDAY IN ORDINARY TIME

LECTIONARY #113

Exodus = EK-suh-duhs

READING I   Exodus 16:2–4, 12–15

A reading from the Book of Exodus

As narrator, you want to suggest, with disapproval, the adolescent tone of those who "grumbled."

The whole Israelite community **grumbled** against **Moses**
   and **Aaron**.
The Israelites **said** to them,

They are whining, like ungrateful children who can only see as far as their bellies.

   "Would that we had **died** at the LORD's hand in the land
      of **Egypt**,
   as we sat by our **fleshpots** and ate our fill of **bread**!

Amidst the uncertainty of the desert, memories of Egypt awaken desire. They'd give up freedom for comfort!

But you had to lead us into this **desert**
   to make the whole community die of **famine**!"

God doesn't respond to their capriciousness, but instead speaks with guarded patience. They are to gather only a "daily portion" ("enough for that day") and no more.

Then the LORD said to Moses,
   "I will now rain down **bread** from **heaven** for you.
Each **day** the people are to go out and gather their daily **portion**;
   thus will I **test** them,
   to see whether they follow my instructions or **not**.

Is God lavishing this goodness or granting it grudgingly? Clearly, the people should, by now, have more confidence in God's providence.

"I have **heard** the grumbling of the Israelites.
Tell them: In the evening **twilight** you shall eat **flesh**,
   and in the **morning** you shall have your fill of **bread**,
   so that you may **know** that I, the LORD, am your **God**."

Don't speak of the quail and manna in the voice of the people, but as the narrator wishing they had trusted more.

In the **evening quail** came up and **covered** the camp.
In the **morning** a **dew** lay all about the camp,
   and when the dew **evaporated**, there on the **surface**
    of the desert
   were fine **flakes** like **hoarfrost** on the ground.

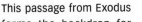 This passage from Exodus forms the backdrop for today's Gospel, in which the Evangelist John continues his extended treatment of what is commonly called the "Bread of Life discourse." Both readings emphasize that all true food or nourishment has one ultimate source: God. While Exodus focuses on physical food, John stresses bread for fullness of life in Christ, given in the Lord's Supper.

The First Reading presents the Israelite community, recently delivered from Egyptian bondage, in the early stage of their long journey to freedom in Canaan. In a pattern repeated often in the Scriptures, they soon forget what God has already done for them, and complain about their current hardship. They even have second thoughts about leaving a life of slavery—at least in Egypt they had sufficient food and drink. Perhaps that life was better than their present uncertainty and need.

Through Moses, the Lord promises to supply food and drink in the wilderness, adding that the people's trust (faith) will also be tested: each day they are to gather only enough food for that day's sustenance. In response to the people's grumbling, quail and manna appear; their question "What is this?" has a double meaning. On one level they simply don't recognize this new kind of food; on a deeper level, they do not understand its

They can't recognize the miracle that's right before their eyes.

Moses identifies what God has done and simultaneously tells them what to do with it.

For meditation and context:

> **TO KEEP IN MIND**
> **Sense lines:** Scripture in this book is arranged (as in the Lectionary) in sense lines, one idea per line. Typically at least a slight pause should follow each line, but good reading requires you to recognize the need for other pauses within lines.

Ephesians = ee-FEE-zhuhnz

This is the fourth of seven consecutive weeks we read from Ephesians.
Paul opens with urgency ("I declare and testify") and follows this immediately with an imperative ("you must no longer").

"The futility of their minds" means they clung to reason instead of yielding to faith and praise.

Paul is less interested in critiquing Gentiles and more in calling the believers to a clear sense of who they are. They are not Gentiles enslaved to their desires.

The imagery of clothing oneself in the "new self" given in Baptism is central to Paul's theology.

Paul wants to convince us that we can be made new and live the holiness of God.

On **seeing** it, the Israelites asked one another, "What **is** this?"
   for they did not **know** what it was.
But **Moses** told them,
   "This is the **bread** that the **Lord** has given you to eat."

RESPONSORIAL PSALM   Psalm 78:3–4, 23–24, 25, 54 (24b)

R. The Lord gave them bread from heaven.

What we have heard and know,
   and what our fathers have declared to us,
we will declare to the generation to come
   the glorious deeds of the LORD and
    his strength
   and the wonders that he wrought.

He commanded the skies above
   and opened the doors of heaven;
he rained manna upon them for food
   and gave them heavenly bread.

Man ate the bread of angels,
   food he sent them in abundance.
And he brought them to his holy land,
   to the mountains his right hand had won.

READING II   Ephesians 4:17, 20–24

A reading from the Letter of Saint Paul to the Ephesians

Brothers and sisters:
I declare and **testify** in the Lord
   that you must no **longer** live as the **Gentiles** do,
   in the **futility** of their minds;
   that is **not** how you learned Christ,
   assuming that you have **heard** of him and were **taught** in him,
   as **truth** is in **Jesus**,
   that you should put **away** the old self of your **former** way
    of life,
   corrupted through deceitful **desires**,
   and be **renewed** in the spirit of your minds,
   and put on the **new** self,
   created in **God's** way in **righteousness** and holiness of **truth**.

true source, which Moses must tell them: it is food provided by the God who continues to care for them.

READING II Previous readings from Ephesians have emphasized the unity of the Church, centered in one Christ, one faith, and one Baptism. Today's Second Reading stresses the changed way of life that should mark each member of the Church as one Body of Christ. The caution not to live like Gentiles

probably reflects this letter's setting. Ephesus at the time was a large port city populated and visited by a great array of people who followed various gods and religions; further, social stratification, daily violence, and freewheeling sexual practices were common.

But for the baptized, who have learned about Christ and his life-giving Death and Resurrection, all such attitudes and behaviors must be put aside. At the time, Baptism was a serious adult commitment for complete conversion of life, and Paul calls for nothing less. The unity and witness of the

Church very much depends upon its baptized members, each of whom must live as the new person they were created to be in Baptism.

GOSPEL Today's Gospel continues John's unique treatment of a feeding story, presented in some form by all the Evangelists. As already noted, these accounts indicate a Eucharistic setting; they do not simply recount a miracle but offer reflection on the meaning of the Lord's Supper for the early Church.

GOSPEL   John 6:24–35

A reading from the holy Gospel according to John

When the **crowd** saw that neither **Jesus** nor his **disciples**
    were there,
  they **themselves** got into boats
  and came to Capernaum **looking** for Jesus.
And when they **found** him across the sea they said to him,
    "**Rabbi**, when did you get here?"
Jesus **answered** them and said,
    "Amen, amen, I **say** to you,
    you are looking for me **not** because you saw **signs**
    but because you ate the **loaves** and were **filled**.
Do not work for food that **perishes**
    but for the food that endures for eternal **life**,
    which the Son of **Man** will give you.
For on **him** the Father, God, has set his **seal**."
So they **said** to him,
    "What can we do to **accomplish** the works of God?"
Jesus answered and **said** to them,
    "**This** is the work of God, that you **believe** in the one he
        sent."
So they said to him,
    "What **sign** can you do, that we may **see** and **believe** in you?
What can you **do**?
Our ancestors ate **manna** in the desert, as it is written:
    *He gave them bread from **heaven** to eat.*"
So Jesus said to them,
    "Amen, amen, I **say** to you,
    it was not **Moses** who gave the bread from heaven;
    my **Father** gives you the **true** bread from heaven.
For the bread of **God** is that which comes down from heaven
    and gives **life** to the world."

Jesus has walked on water to cross the sea, leaving the crowds befuddled about how he got where he is. The opening suggests their confusion and their eagerness to find him.

Given the signs he's been performing, the crowd has kept close watch on Jesus. How *could* he have eluded them?

Jesus tells them their hearts are not moved to faith by his "signs" but by the fact that he filled their stomachs.
Jesus takes the opportunity to warn them not to settle for "junk food," but to seek instead the bread of eternal life.

The crowd seems to take his meaning, but quickly reveals the shallowness of their insight as they demand signs.

In response to Jesus's call to believe in him, they ask him to top Moses with an even more dramatic sign.

Jesus does not respond with anger but calmly seeks to enlarge their understanding. They respond like the woman at the well, as literalists expecting him to satisfy physical hunger.

In today's reading, John shifts from the multiplication of food for the crowds to major meanings of this "sign," and these meanings overlap with several of his particular emphases. For John, Jesus is the one sent from the Father to reveal the Father, and the signs are a major mode of that revelation. But to truly see the import of a sign, one must have faith. The significance of believing for John is evident in the fact that he uses the term nearly one hundred times, always as a verb. Seeing, often nearly equivalent to believing for this Evangelist, requires at least a minimal level of faith, an openness to what a sign might reveal about God, Jesus, or even oneself.

At the beginning of the reading, Jesus points out that the sign proved ineffective for his questioners, for they did not truly "see" it. That is, they did not come to any level of believing in Jesus, but perceived only physical food. Jesus then calls them to believe that he is truly the one sent from God, but the crowd still calls for a sign—an indication that they have failed utterly to perceive the true meaning of Jesus's providing food for the multitude from a few loaves and fish. Referring to the account in our First Reading, they seem to be urging Jesus to perform a similar or even greater wonder that might convince them to believe in him.

Here, too, their "give us" reply echoes the woman at the well in John 4.

Jesus speaks bluntly, as he did with the woman at the well, but here the truth of who he is will send many packing, not to return.

> TO KEEP IN MIND
>
> **Tell the story:** Make the story yours, then share it with your listeners. Use the language; don't throw away any good words. Settings give context; don't rush the description. Characters must be believable; understand their motivation. Dialogue reveals character; distinguish one character from another with your voice.

So they said to him,
  "**Sir**, **give** us this bread **always**."
Jesus said to them,
  "**I** am the bread of life;
  whoever comes to **me** will never **hunger**,
  and whoever **believes** in me will never **thirst**."

Jesus reminds his hearers—and us—of Moses's own statement: not he, but God, has given them bread (which means, more broadly, food or nourishment). John then presents Jesus speaking as directly as possible: bread from God gives life to the full. John here uses the Greek word *zoe*, which means fullness of life for the whole person, not merely physical existence (*bios*). This usage implies that such life can begin in the here and now. Jesus then proclaims that he himself is the bread that nourishes believers for fullness of life. This is the bread of the Lord's Supper, which fed Christians at the end of the first century and now nourishes believers in the twenty-first century for life to the full.

NINETEENTH SUNDAY IN ORDINARY TIME

TO KEEP IN MIND

Read all three commentaries.
Suggestions in each can give you
insight into your own passage.

Elijah = ee-Lī-juh

Elijah is being pursued by Queen Jezebel
who seeks his death; he is angry, depressed,
and fatigued.

Elijah is so depressed he asks for death
rather than deliverance.

God uses his exhaustion to dramatically
intervene.

The first effort was not enough for Elijah,
so God makes a second attempt.

The angel of God persists and now *orders*
Elijah to "get it together!"

Take time with the final sentence to suggest
the gradual transformation that comes over
the prophet. Like his ancestors who traveled
forty years, Elijah journeys forty days to
Horeb, the mount of the covenant.

LECTIONARY #116

READING I 1 Kings 19:4–8

A reading from the first Book of Kings

Elijah went a day's journey into the **desert**,
  until he came to a **broom** tree and sat **beneath** it.
He **prayed** for **death**, saying:
  "This is **enough**, O LORD!
Take my **life**, for I am no better than my **fathers**."
He lay down and fell **asleep** under the broom tree,
  but then an **angel** touched him and ordered him to **get** up
    and **eat**.
Elijah **looked** and there at his head was a **hearth** cake
  and a jug of **water**.
After he **ate** and **drank**, he lay down **again**,
  but the angel of the LORD came back a **second** time,
  touched him, and ordered,
    "**Get** up and **eat**, else the journey will be too **long** for you!"
He **got** up, **ate**, and **drank**;
  then **strengthened** by that food,
  he walked forty **days** and forty **nights** to the mountain
    of **God, Horeb.**

READING I This Sunday we are taught
again that all sustenance
and nourishment for fullness of life comes
from God. Last Sunday's First Reading
recounted the story of God feeding the
Israelites on their desert trek with quail
and manna; today we find the great
prophet Elijah also in need of food for body
and spirit.

In the two chapters before today's passage, the author of Second Kings recounts
Elijah's struggle with King Ahab of Israel,
described as more evil than any of his royal
predecessors. With the complicity of his
foreign wife, Jezebel, Ahab worshipped the
fertility deities Baal and Asherah. Jezebel
murdered the LORD's prophets, while Ahab
consulted prophets of Baal. Immediately
before today's reading, Elijah slew these
prophets, and so found himself under the
threat of Jezebel who promised that he
would meet the same fate.

Weary of the struggle, Elijah seeks rest
under a broom tree and begs God to take
his life. The exhausted prophet falls asleep,
but is awakened by God's messenger bidding him to gather strength from food and
water laid before him. After doing so he is
about to return to sleep, when the messenger, now identified as God's angel, commands him to take further nourishment.
When Elijah does so, he discovers that this
food and drink must indeed be of divine origin, for it strengthens him to journey forty
days and nights toward God's mountain.

READING II The series of readings from
Ephesians continues this
Sunday with further instruction about how
those joined to the Church by Baptism are
to conduct themselves. The author reminds
his hearers that Baptism marks them with

For meditation and context:

TO KEEP IN MIND

Echoes: Some words echo words that went before. For example, "You shall be a glorious crown . . . a royal diadem" (Isaiah 62:3). Here "diadem" echoes "crown" so it needs no stress. In such cases, emphasize the new idea: royal.

Ephesians = ee-FEE-zhuhnz.

This is the fifth of seven weeks we read from Ephesians.

Paul warns that it is possible, through hardness of heart, to stifle the Spirit to such a degree that we begin bearing rotten fruit.

This listing names real problems in the Ephesian community––problems that still rage within our hearts.

Distinguish the various sins from each other, and then shift your tone for the upbeat listing of Spirit-led behavior.

Speak directly to the assembly. Our willingness to forgo our anger and resentments becomes a sweet fragrance that rises to the throne of God.

RESPONSORIAL PSALM   Psalm 34:2–3, 4–5, 6–7, 8–9 (9a)

R. Taste and see the goodness of the Lord.

I will bless the LORD at all times;
    his praise shall be ever in my mouth.
Let my soul glory in the LORD;
    the lowly will hear me and be glad.

Glorify the LORD with me,
    let us together extol his name.
I sought the LORD, and he answered me
    and delivered me from all my fears.

Look to him that you may be radiant
    with joy,
    and your faces may not blush with shame.
When the afflicted man called out, the
    LORD heard,
    and from all his distress he saved him.

The angel of the LORD encamps
    around those who fear him and
    delivers them.
Taste and see how good the LORD is;
    blessed the man who takes refuge in him.

READING II   Ephesians 4:30—5:2

A reading from the Letter of Saint Paul to the Ephesians

Brothers and sisters:
Do not **grieve** the Holy Spirit of **God**,
    with which you were **sealed** for the day of **redemption**.
All **bitterness**, **fury**, **anger**, **shouting**, and **reviling**
    must be **removed** from you, along with all **malice**.
And be **kind** to one another, **compassionate**,
    forgiving one another as God has forgiven **you** in **Christ**.

So be imitators of **God**, as beloved **children**, and live in **love**,
    as **Christ** loved us and handed himself over for us
    as a sacrificial **offering** to God for a fragrant **aroma**.

---

the "seal" of the Holy Spirit. This language, used elsewhere in the New Testament, was derived from Roman slave owners' practice of placing a brand or tattoo on their slaves to publicly signify the slave's owner. For Paul, those who choose Baptism are marked as slaves of Christ, belonging to and serving him alone.

Serving Christ as members of his Body means, above all, imitating his self-giving love, even to the point of giving life itself. In Christ's community, this kind of love takes shape in mutual compassion and forgiveness. The baptismal code of conduct fol-

lows the pattern of Christ, who surrendered himself to God even to the point of death and so was raised by God. All the baptized are to live in the powerful presence, the "spirit," of this Christ.

| GOSPEL | Today's Gospel is the third portion of the Bread of Life |

discourse, which concludes next Sunday. At this point, John turns more specifically to the disbelief of "the Jews." This and other parts of the Fourth Gospel must be handled very delicately, perhaps with the help of the homilist, in order to avoid any impression

that all Jews of all time are to be condemned. John composed his Gospel account at a time when Jews who followed Jesus struggled to clarify their own beliefs in relation to mainstream Judaism. Negative portrayal of "the Jews" reflects John's time, when the two groups were beginning to draw sharp distinctions between themselves.

In today's Scripture, John depicts "the Jews" as rejecting one of his major convictions about Jesus: that he was sent from God and was with God from the beginning (John 1:1). To those who object to Jesus's words, he is simply another ordinary Jew,

GOSPEL   John 6:41–51

A reading from the holy Gospel according to John

The Jews **murmured** about Jesus because he said,
  "I am the **bread** that came down from **heaven**,"
and they said,
  "Is this not **Jesus**, the son of **Joseph**?
Do we not know his **father** and **mother**?
Then **how** can he say,
  'I have come down from **heaven**'?"
Jesus **answered** and said to them,
  "Stop **murmuring** among yourselves.
No one can come to me unless the **Father** who sent me
      draw him,
  and I will **raise** him on the last **day**.
It is written in the **prophets**:
  *They shall all be taught by **God**.*
Everyone who **listens** to my Father and **learns** from him **comes**
      to me.
Not that anyone has **seen** the Father
  except the one who is **from** God;
  he has seen the Father.
Amen, amen, I **say** to you,
  whoever **believes** has eternal **life**.
I am the **bread** of life.
Your ancestors ate the **manna** in the desert, but they **died**;
  this is the bread that comes down from heaven
  so that one may **eat** it and **not** die.
I am the **living** bread that came down from heaven;
  whoever eats **this** bread will live **forever**;
  and the bread that **I** will give is my **flesh** for the life
      of the **world**."

The word "murmur" suggests more than ill-mannered grumbling; it is the murmuring of a heart that has closed itself to truth and wants to hear no more of it.

Jesus falls victim to the familiar-prophet syndrome: How can this local boy talk of heaven like he's been there?!?

Jesus scolds the people for blocking the truth and tells them to stop. He then commences teaching. In stark contrast to his usual calls for secrecy about his identity, Jesus makes shocking claims about himself that will lead many to abandon him.

Speak the quoted Scripture in a distinctive tone.

Jesus claims that anyone who remains open to God's prompting will be drawn to Jesus. God calls, but we must listen; and if we do, and hear the Father, then we will seek out the Son.

Jesus is not scolding here, for he wants them to see that he himself will be bread that truly satisfies and brings eternal life.

Though he knows many will leave him, he speaks with energy and passion. His tone is full of authority and a desire to give them every good reason to cling to him.

---

whose parents some even claim to know. But John has presented Jesus's true identity at the beginning of his account: Jesus is God's own Word (or Wisdom) incarnate. In the Old Testament, Wisdom teaches those who will listen how to live rightly, and she shares herself in a rich banquet (the biblical personification of Wisdom is always feminine). For John, Jesus, who is Wisdom made flesh (1:14), fulfills the prophecy that he has Jesus quote: *They shall all be taught by God.* (Versions of this prophecy can be found in Isaiah 54:13 and Jeremiah 31:33–34.) God

will carry out this teaching through Jesus in the banquet of the Lord's Supper.

John reiterates his conviction that Jesus is sent from God and can truly reveal God because he has "seen" the Father (the Greek here can mean spiritual as well as physical perception). Those who believe this have "eternal life"; here John describes *zoe*, life to the full, specifically as everlasting life. The climax of the passage arrives in the contrast between the bread from God of Judaism's past and Jesus, Wisdom made flesh, who nourishes believers with his own person. The English word "flesh" translates

the Greek word *sarx,* which points to a whole human person seen from the perspective of weakness and mortality. In his prologue John describes Jesus as God's Word/Wisdom made flesh: God's Word/Wisdom shares in every aspect of full humanity in Jesus. Here John looks toward Jesus's Death, when he will give his whole self (flesh, *sarx*) for the life of the world. And John tells us that he does so also whenever Christians celebrate the Lord's Supper.

ASSUMPTION OF THE BLESSED VIRGIN MARY: VIGIL

LECTIONARY #621

READING I   1 Chronicles 15:3–4, 15–16; 16:1–2

A reading from the first Book of Chronicles

David assembled all **Israel** in **Jerusalem** to bring the **ark** of the
   Lord
   to the place that he had **prepared** for it.
David also called together the sons of **Aaron** and the **Levites**.

The **Levites** bore the ark of God on their **shoulders** with **poles**,
   as **Moses** had **ordained** according to the word of the Lord.

David commanded the **chiefs** of the **Levites**
   to appoint their **kinsmen** as **chanters**,
   to play on musical **instruments**, **harps**, **lyres**, and **cymbals**,
   to make a loud **sound** of **rejoicing**.

They **brought** in the ark of God and set it within the **tent**
   which David had **pitched** for it.
Then they offered up burnt **offerings** and **peace** offerings to God.
When David had **finished** offering up the burnt offerings and
      peace offerings,
   he **blessed** the people in the **name** of the Lord.

Chronicles = KRAH-nih-k*ls

The lavish ceremony and liturgical splendor, lush with music, demonstrate Israel's awareness of God's great love for them, manifested by the contents of the ark (the Commandments and the manna).

The sacred ark could not be touched by those who carried it.

Enumerate the various instruments and singers as a sign of the dignity of this ceremony for which no expense was spared.

Not even Michelangelo's *Pieta* would evoke such reverence as is reported here. They are bringing into their midst great symbols of God's presence.

Here we see a primary significance of the ark and elaborate ceremony: the ark brings *blessing* to all the people.

It is admittedly difficult to choose Scriptures for this solemnity, since Mary's Assumption is mentioned nowhere in the New Testament. Although the Assumption did not become a dogma until 1950, it was celebrated by the universal Church as early as the sixth century. As with many other aspects of the faith, the Church draws upon both Scripture and tradition to arrive at this belief. The Scriptures for the solemnity revolve around the traditional symbolism describing the role of the mother of

Jesus and the development of the teaching that at her death, Mary's body suffered no decay but immediately shared in the glory of her Son's Resurrection.

READING I In Catholic tradition, one of the many titles of Mary is "Ark of the Covenant." In ancient Israel, the ark was an ornate container (carried on poles) in which the tablets of the Ten Commandments were placed. After ratification of the covenant between God and

Israel, in which the people promised to live according to divine instruction, the Lord instructed Moses on how to construct this ark, which was to be carried with them on their trek toward freedom (Exodus 25:10–22). It became an important symbol of God's enduring presence and of the people's covenant commitment.

Today's First Reading, from one of the Old Testament's books of religious history, recounts how King David brought the ark into Jerusalem, which he had chosen as the

236

For meditation and context:

TO KEEP IN MIND

Narrator: Knowing the point of view that the narrator is "rooting for" will help you more fully communicate the meaning of the text. The narrator always has a viewpoint, often speaking as a believer, not as an objective reporter. For this reason, the narrator is often the pivotal role in a passage. Using timbre, pitch, rate, and energy can help you convey the narrator's moods or meanings.

Corinthians = kohr-IN-thee-uhnz

Gradually build energy from the first line through the end of the scripture quotation (Hosea 13:14).

Speak the lines from Hosea with a deep sense of peace and confidence. Those who have returned from near-death experiences know the meaning of these words.

With great peace explain that the reason we need not fear death is Christ: he has removed the "sting" of death which is "sin."

TO KEEP IN MIND

Word value: Words are your medium, like a painter's brush or a sculptor's chisel. You must understand the words before you can communicate them. Most words have a dictionary meaning (denotative) and an associational meaning (connotative). "House" and "home" both mean "dwelling," yet they communicate different feelings. Be alert to subtle differences in connotative meanings and express them.

RESPONSORIAL PSALM   Psalm 132:6–7, 9–10, 13–14 (8)

R. **Lord, go up to the place of your rest, you and the ark of your holiness.**

Behold, we heard of it in Ephrathah;
    we found it in the fields of Jaar.
Let us enter into his dwelling,
    let us worship at his footstool.

May your priests be clothed with justice;
    let your faithful ones shout merrily for joy.
For the sake of David your servant,
    reject not the plea of your anointed.

For the LORD has chosen Zion;
    he prefers her for his dwelling.
"Zion is my resting place forever;
    in her will I dwell, for I prefer her."

READING II   1 Corinthians 15:54b–57

A reading from the first Letter of Saint Paul to the Corinthians

Brothers and sisters:
When that which is **mortal** clothes itself with **immortality**,
    then the **word** that is **written** shall come **about**:

> *Death is swallowed up in victory.*
> *Where, O death, is your victory?*
> *Where, O death, is your sting?*

The **sting** of **death** is sin,
    and the **power** of sin is the **law**.
But thanks be to **God** who gives **us** the victory
    through our **Lord** Jesus **Christ**.

capital city of the Israelite kingdom. David intended to make this city the religious and political center of the monarchy. To accomplish this, he brought this important symbol of the ark into Jerusalem, where it was to be enshrined as a constant reminder of God's continuing presence and the people's promise to worship the LORD alone. As the ark bore the Law, Mary bore Christ.

READING II Paul devotes all of chapter 15 of First Corinthians to questions concerning the resurrection of the dead. Since the predominant expectation of Judaism at the time of Jesus envisioned a resurrected community, the first Christians understood Jesus's Resurrection as the beginning of that end-time event. In Paul's thought, all believers who are "in Christ" already begin to share that new life,

beginning in the present and ultimately brought to fullness in immortality.

Before today's brief excerpt from this chapter, Paul urges the Corinthians to waste no time speculating on exactly what a "resurrection body" is like. The most important thing for them to realize is that in raising Jesus from the dead, the power of death and its partner, sin, has been fully

Be sure your assembly is well settled before you begin.

The woman's voice rings out over the din of the crowd to catch Jesus's ear. Likely a mother herself, she speaks with admiration of the one who brought this amazing man into the world.

Some feared that Jesus drove out demons because of a bond with Satan; the woman sees he is a man of God.

With as much affection as we heard from the woman, Jesus speaks of those who live God's Word, and none did it better than his mother, Mary.

TO KEEP IN MIND

The closing: Pause (three beats!) after ending the text. Then, with sustained eye contact, announce from memory, "The word [Gospel] of the Lord." Always pronounce "the" as "thuh" except before words beginning with a vowel, as in "thee Acts of the Apostles." Maintain eye contact while the assembly makes its response.

GOSPEL   Luke 11:27–28

A reading from the holy Gospel according to Luke

While **Jesus** was **speaking,**
    a **woman** from the **crowd called** out and said to him,
    "Blessed is the **womb** that **carried** you
    and the **breasts** at which you **nursed.**"
He replied,
    "**Rather, blessed** are those
    who **hear** the word of God and **observe** it."

---

overcome. This is one of the New Testament texts used by early Christians to arrive at belief in Mary's Assumption; Jesus's mother immediately shared in the gift of Resurrection as a sign and foretaste of what awaits all believers.

GOSPEL | This very brief passage from Luke underscores a major reason that from earliest Christianity, Mary became a symbol of the faithful Church.

While physically carrying the Savior in her womb was indeed a remarkable privilege, recognized by Elizabeth (Luke 1:39–45), it is Mary's constant attitude of listening for, and responding to, God's word that marks her as the first and foremost believer.

THE ASSUMPTION OF THE BLESSED VIRGIN MARY: DAY

TO KEEP IN MIND
Read all four Scriptures for your assigned Sunday. Because all were chosen for this day, it is important to look at them together.

You are recounting a dramatic mystical vision, not a favorite television show. "Temple" and "ark" are Israel's greatest symbols of God's presence. Speak with reverence.

The best way to relate these awesome, striking images is without overdramatizing, but with great sincerity and belief.

While the woman is majestic, she is in the midst of painful labor.

Mention of the "dragon" shifts the mood, for great threat looms over the woman. Let that color your tone without become melodramatic.

Speak slowly of the dragon that stares down on the woman, ready to menace her child.

Announce the "birth" with confidence to let us know that the great beast will have more to fear than this special child.

LECTIONARY #622

READING I   Revelation 11:19a; 12:1–6a, 10ab

A reading from the Book of Revelation

God's **temple** in heaven was **opened**,
    and the **ark** of his **covenant** could be seen in the temple.

A great **sign** appeared in the sky, a **woman** clothed with the **sun**,
    with the **moon** under her **feet**,
    and on her **head** a **crown** of twelve **stars**.
She was with **child** and **wailed** aloud in **pain** as she labored to
        give **birth**.
Then **another** sign appeared in the sky;
    it was a huge red **dragon**, with seven **heads** and ten **horns**,
    and on its heads were seven **diadems**.
Its **tail** swept away a third of the **stars** in the sky
    and **hurled** them down to the **earth**.
Then the dragon **stood** before the woman about to give birth,
    to **devour** her child when she gave birth.
She gave birth to a **son**, a **male** child,
    destined to **rule** all the nations with an iron **rod**.
Her child was caught up to **God** and his **throne**.
The woman herself **fled** into the **desert**
    where she had a place prepared by **God**.

READING I   The First Reading for this solemnity comes from the last book in the New Testament: Revelation. The Greek name for this work, Apocalypse, signals that it focuses on God's work in bringing the divine plan of salvation to completion. Apocalyptic literature of Israel and early Christianity usually appeared in times of threat and danger; its major purpose was to assure readers that God holds ultimate power and will bring all things to completion, with just recompense for good and evil.

Since the danger faced was often persecution, this type of writing frequently uses symbolism understood by those for whom it was intended but indecipherable for the persecutor. Revelation was written at a time when Christians who refused to worship the emperor as a divinity were persecuted in the Roman Empire. Already at this time, near the end of the first century, Mary had come to symbolize the faithful Church.

In today's reading we find a symbolic description of this dire situation: the woman enduring birth pangs pursued by a fearsome dragon attempting to devour her child.

The luminous woman, who represents the Church, faces an immensely powerful dragon. In the Bible, the numbers seven and ten are associated with perfection or completeness, and the horn was a symbol of power. Thus the dragon's power appears to be the epitome of ruling might, signified by its ten horns and seven diadems; the dragon is later identified as Satan. The son about to be born represents Christ and the growing Church, which are currently under threat of Roman persecution, instigated by the forces of evil. But the reading reaches

The text ends on a note of regal joy. God's Church, symbolized by the "woman," is under God's constant care. The words echo divine power and hope.

For meditation and context:

> **TO KEEP IN MIND**
> **Pace:** The rate at which you read is influenced by the size of your church, the size of the congregation, and the complexity of the text. As each increases, rate decreases.

Corinthians = kohr-IN-thee-uhnz

Paul uses progressive reasoning to present his argument, but his words are leavened with good news. Help us hear it.

Don't lose the heart of his message: A "man" caused death, but a "man" also brought new life; because of Adam we all die, but because of Christ we live.

The significance of the "proper order" is that though Christ is "first" we, too, will get our turn.

"Those who belong to Christ" are those who, because of their faith and obedience, have come to resemble Christ.

The struggle between good and evil won't be consummated until the very "end."

But in the end, it will be Christ who reigns over everyone and everything, including the greatest enemy—death.

Then I heard a loud **voice** in heaven say:
"Now have **salvation** and **power** come,
    and the **Kingdom** of our **God**
    and the **authority** of his **Anointed** One."

RESPONSORIAL PSALM   Psalm 45:10, 11, 12, 16 (10bc)

R. The queen stands at your right hand, arrayed in gold.

The queen takes her place at your right hand
    in gold of Ophir.

Hear, O daughter, and see; turn your ear,
    forget your people and your father's house.

So shall the king desire your beauty;
    for he is your lord.

They are borne in with gladness and joy;
    they enter the palace of the king.

READING II   1 Corinthians 15:20–27

A reading from the first Letter of Saint Paul to the Corinthians

Brothers and sisters:
Christ has been **raised** from the **dead**,
    the **firstfruits** of those who have fallen **asleep**.
For since **death** came through **man**,
    the **resurrection** of the dead came **also** through man.
For just as in **Adam** all **die**,
    so too in **Christ** shall all be brought to **life**,
    but **each** one in proper **order**:
    Christ the **firstfruits**;
    then, at his **coming**, those who **belong** to Christ;
    then comes the **end**,
    when he hands over the Kingdom to his God and **Father**,
    when he has **destroyed** every **sovereignty**
    and every **authority** and **power**.
For he must reign until he has put all his **enemies** under his **feet**.
The **last** enemy to be destroyed is **death**,
    for "he subjected **everything** under his feet."

---

its high point with the consoling proclamation that even the power of evil has been overcome by Christ, the risen Messiah, who holds ultimate authority over evil and its offspring, sin and death.

READING II   Today's Second Reading, like that for the vigil of this solemnity, is part of Paul's discussion of resurrection. His reference to Christ as the "firstfruits" indicates the Jewish belief that resurrection would bring about a transformed people of God. Paul thus compares the risen Christ to the first fruits of harvest, which in Jewish culture indicated the entire crop. Thus when God raised Jesus, his followers understood that their own resurrection would soon follow.

Paul develops this view by presenting Christ as a new Adam, in whom all share his new life of Resurrection. The Hebrew word *adam* refers to humankind, and the Old Testament, Paul's Bible, sometimes portrays a personified Adam, much like Americans speak of "Uncle Sam"—a single character representing the whole. God's intention for the first Adam was that humankind would be a living image of God (Genesis 1:26–27), but this first Adam never reached that goal. Speaking of Christ as the new Adam of the final age, Paul presents him as finally fulfilling God's purpose for humanity.

As was common in the first decades of Christianity, Paul seems to look toward an imminent completion of the age of salvation, heralded by God's raising of Jesus, thus beginning the final transformation of his followers. At the completion of God's plan, the power of God that raised Christ and those who "belong to" him will be revealed in full power and glory. The climax

GOSPEL   Luke 1:39–56

A reading from the holy Gospel according to Luke

Mary set out
and traveled to the **hill** country in **haste**
to a town of **Judah**,
where she entered the house of **Zechariah**
and greeted **Elizabeth**.
When Elizabeth **heard** Mary's greeting,
the infant **leaped** in her **womb**,
and **Elizabeth**, **filled** with the Holy **Spirit**,
cried out in a loud voice and said,
"**Blessed** are you among **women**,
and blessed is the **fruit** of your **womb**.
And how does this **happen** to me,
that the mother of my **Lord** should come to me?
For at the moment the **sound** of your greeting reached my **ears**,
the **infant** in my womb leaped for **joy**.
Blessed are you who **believed**
that what was **spoken** to you by the Lord
would be **fulfilled**."

Mary hurries because she trusts the angel's news that Elizabeth is with child.

Couched in the joyful encounter of two cousins is the beginning of two world-altering lives. Elizabeth is immediately aware that there is much more than her young cousin standing before her.

The extraordinary nature of these people and events is underscored by the infant leaping in the womb and Elizabeth being "filled" with the Holy Spirit.

What has been enshrined in our beloved "Hail Mary" was first uttered as a spontaneous exclamation.

Elizabeth already senses the special nature of the child in Mary's womb whom she calls "Lord."

Mary is exemplary in her trust; she believes without seeing.

TO KEEP IN MIND

Word value: Words are your medium, like a painter's brush or a sculptor's chisel. You must understand the words before you can communicate them. Most words have a dictionary meaning (denotative) and an associational meaning (connotative). "House" and "home" both mean "dwelling," yet they communicate different feelings. Be alert to subtle differences in connotative meanings and express them.

---

of the reading presents Paul's most important claim for today's solemn feast: the power of God, revealed through the life, Death, and Resurrection of Christ, irrevocably overcomes the ultimate enemy of humankind—death.

GOSPEL   It is natural that the Church uses a passage from the Gospel according to Luke for today's solemnity, since Luke's infancy narrative emphasizes Mary much more than Matthew's account. In today's Gospel, Luke presents Mary as following a pattern in the Old Testament: mothers of important biblical figures appear to be infertile, some of them childless even into old age, when God intervenes. (Think of the mothers of Isaac, Jacob/Israel, and Judah.)

In the immediate context for today's reading, Luke applies this motif to Mary's cousin, Elizabeth, as well. When the angel Gabriel appears to Elizabeth's husband, the priest Zechariah, announcing that the aged couple will have a son, Zechariah not only questions but doubts. Gabriel reprimands Zechariah for his lack of faith; because of it,

he will remain mute until the child's birth. Luke then contrasts Mary's response to Gabriel's announcement to her. The young girl also questions Gabriel's message—that she is with child—not because of old age but because she has had "no relations with a man" (Luke 1:34). But unlike Zechariah, the uncomprehending Mary responds with complete trusting faith, asking only that God's Word be accomplished in her. This contrast forms the important backdrop for Elizabeth's blessing of Mary in today's Gospel.

In this passage, found only in Luke, the pregnant Mary journeys to see her cousin

Mary's canticle needs to be set apart. Pause before you begin, then maintain a brisk but joyful tempo throughout.

Mary sees herself as a "lowly servant"; her "blessedness" is pure gift from God.

"Fear" of the Lord is a genuine biblical virtue on which we build our relationship with God. It means a desire to be in right relationship with God.

God's justice is part of God's mercy; they operate simultaneously. Hence, expectations and worlds are turned upside down.

Jesus's ministry will confirm the upending thrust of God's Kingdom.

Mary's song is not focused on herself but on God's mercy to Israel. End on a note of gratitude.

Pause, and then read the postscript that tells us Mary stayed to witness (and help with) the birth of John.

TO KEEP IN MIND
Each text contains **three kinds of content**: intellectual-theological, emotional, and aesthetic. The plot and details of the story and the theological teaching behind them comprise the intellectual-theological content. How the author or characters feel (or want us to feel) is the emotional content. Elements that make the writing pleasing—rhythm, repetition, suspense, and picturesque language—are the aesthetic content.

And Mary said:

"My **soul** proclaims the **greatness** of the Lord;
　my spirit **rejoices** in God my **Savior**
　for he has with **favor** on his lowly servant.
From this day all generations will call me **blessed**:
　the Almighty has done **great** things for me
　and **holy** is his **Name**.
He has **mercy** on those who **fear** him
　in **every** generation.
He has shown the **strength** of his arm,
　and has **scattered** the proud in their **conceit**.
He has cast down the **mighty** from their **thrones**,
　and has **lifted** up the **lowly**.
He has filled the **hungry** with **good** things,
　and the **rich** he has sent away **empty**.
He has come to the **help** of his servant **Israel**
　for he has **remembered** his promise of **mercy**,
　the promise he made to our **fathers**,
　to **Abraham** and his children for **ever**."

Mary **remained** with her about three **months**
　and then **returned** to her **home**.

Elizabeth, also awaiting a child by the action of God. Like her son, who will be forerunner to Jesus, Elizabeth points not to herself but to Jesus's mother. The infant in her womb leaps with recognition of the one he will later announce: the infant Savior, present in Mary. Elizabeth then proclaims why Mary is to be "blessed" (which can also mean "thanked" and "praised") above all women: with deepest trust in God, she believed that the divine Word would be fulfilled. Luke thus presents Mary as the first and foremost disciple, who became the model and symbol of the Church.

The magnificent canticle that Luke then places on Mary's lips may have been an already existing Jewish Christian hymn of praise. A mosaic of Greek Old Testament texts, this passage praises the work of God above all. In the past, Israel's God often brought about divine intent through the most unlikely persons and events. In Mary, that divine design begins its final act, for she will bear the Son of God who will complete that plan of salvation, culminating in God's final rule over all things (see Luke 1:31–33).

Throughout the readings for this solemnity, we hear that through Mary's son even the power of death is overcome forever. The Church celebrates its belief that she who utterly trusted God's Word is the first to fully share in that reality.

TWENTIETH SUNDAY IN ORDINARY TIME

LECTIONARY #119

READING I   Proverbs 9:1–6

A reading from the Book of Proverbs

> **Wisdom** has built her **house**,
>   she has set up her seven **columns**;
> she has dressed her **meat**, mixed her **wine**,
>   **yes**, she has spread her **table**.
> She has sent out her **maidens**; she **calls**
>   from the **heights** out over the **city**:
> "Let whoever is **simple** turn in **here**";
>   to the one who lacks **understanding**, she says,
> "**Come**, eat of my **food**,
>   and drink of the **wine** I have mixed!
> **Forsake** foolishness that you may **live**;
>   **advance** in the way of **understanding**."

You are reading an extended metaphor that personifies wisdom as a woman preparing a meal. Obviously this requires a lofty tone; it is not a passage from a cookbook.

"Her house" is the world supported by "seven columns" that represents an ancient understanding of how world and sky are supported.

A sense of urgency enters as Wisdom hurries to find guests for her table.

Wisdom seeks the "simple" who are open to truth; they are honest and pure of heart, not simpletons.

Wisdom competes with a rival, who seeks to lure the simple to her table of poisonous sweets. So Wisdom implores those passing by to pass up "foolishness because our very lives depend on this choice!

For meditation and context:

RESPONSORIAL PSALM   Psalm 34:2–3, 4–5, 6–7 (9a)

R. Taste and see the goodness of the Lord.

I will bless the LORD at all times;
   his praise shall be ever in my mouth.
Let my soul glory in the LORD;
   the lowly will hear me and be glad.

Glorify the LORD with me,
   let us together extol his name.
I sought the LORD, and he answered me
   and delivered me from all my fears.

Look to him that you may be radiant
   with joy,
   and your faces may not blush with shame.
When the poor one called out, the
   LORD heard,
   and from all his distress he saved him.

TO KEEP IN MIND
Stress (Bold Print): identifies words that are more important or expressive than others and require more stress. Use your judgment about the amount of stress so as to avoid an artificial delivery.

In the Sunday Lectionary, the First Reading and Gospel Reading are usually related, but today the relationship is more profound than usual. Last Sunday's commentary alluded to John's use of the Old Testament figure of Wisdom to interpret Jesus; today, this usage will become more evident.

 READING I Like most ancient civilizations in the biblical world, Israel had a wisdom tradition that sages passed on through the centuries. That wisdom consisted of the practical knowledge of how to live well, gathered from genera-

tions of shared experience and reflection upon the experience. For Israel, wisdom ultimately comes from God, and at times is almost equated with divine teaching in the Torah. Wisdom came to be understood as the way God acts in the world, and by the time of Jesus, wisdom had become virtually interchangeable with God's Word (the Hebrew word translated into English as "word" means both word and action). Further, divine wisdom was sometimes personified, always as a feminine figure.

In several Old Testament books, Woman Wisdom invites the foolish, or any-

one who seeks wisdom, to partake of her wealth at a banquet rich with food and wine. As in today's Scripture, she is generous and even insistent in her invitation, for her teaching is a necessary source of life. But choosing to feast at Wisdom's table also requires letting go of false ways, the way of the foolish who turn to sources other than God for guidance in how to live rightly. Those who come to her table must leave behind foolish (unwise) ways in order to be truly fed by Woman Wisdom.

Ephesians = ee-FEE-zhuhnz

Like the Woman Wisdom, Paul pleads that we abandon foolishness and cling to wisdom.

Paul's words are straightforward. He moves from caution ("watch carefully") to strong advice ("live not as foolish persons") and ends with motivation ("[make] the most of the opportunity").

Because Paul understands that when we make room for vices like "debauchery" there is no room for the Spirit, he urges forcefully.

Paul expects that joy will infuse the lives of the disciples. Let it show on your face.

READING II   Ephesians 5:15–20

A reading from the Letter of Saint Paul to the Ephesians

Brothers and sisters:
Watch **carefully** how you live,
  not as **foolish** persons but as **wise**,
  making the **most** of the opportunity,
  because the days are **evil**.
Therefore, do not continue in **ignorance**,
  but try to **understand** what is the will of the **Lord**.
And do not get **drunk** on wine, in which lies **debauchery**,
  but be filled with the **Spirit**,
  addressing one another in **psalms** and **hymns** and
    spiritual **songs**,
  singing and **playing** to the Lord in your **hearts**,
  giving thanks **always** and for **everything**
  in the name of our Lord Jesus **Christ** to God the **Father**.

THE 4 STEPS OF *LECTIO DIVINA* OR PRAYERFUL READING

1. *Lectio:* Read a Scripture passage aloud slowly. Notice what phrase captures your attention and be attentive to its meaning. Silent pause.

2. *Meditatio:* Read the passage aloud slowly again, reflecting on the passage, allowing God to speak to you through it. Silent pause.

3. *Oratio:* Read it aloud slowly a third time, allowing it to be your prayer or response to God's gift of insight to you. Silent pause.

4. *Contemplatio:* Read it aloud slowly a fourth time, now resting in God's word.

READING II   For the fifth Sunday in a row, we hear from Paul's Letter to the Ephesians. Here the Apostle, like other New Testament writers, may be alluding to Christ as the personification of Old Testament wisdom. In last Sunday's reading, Paul urged the community to imitate God by loving as Christ loved; he implies that Christ's self-giving to the point of death was God's revelatory Word/Wisdom made visible, a word in action to be imitated. In today's Scripture, which follows in a few verses, the Apostle encourages them to live as wise persons who understand the divine will. As in the First Reading, he teaches that wise action requires Christians to set aside some behaviors in order to walk the path of wisdom, focused on praise and thanksgiving "in the name of our Lord Jesus Christ."

GOSPEL   Today's Gospel continues the lengthy Bread of Life discourse, which includes many facets: John's interpretation of Christ, discipleship, meanings of the Eucharist, and his contemporary situation of increasing tension between Jewish Christians and mainstream Judaism. Evidence of that tension often appears in what is sometimes called the "replacement theme," in which John casts Jesus himself as the replacement for major institutions of Judaism, including the Word of God, Passover, and Temple.

For John, Jesus is the divine Word or Wisdom of God "made flesh," that is, completely one with full humanity, subject to suffering and death. In other words, it is precisely in the kind of human being that Jesus is that God is revealed and made present. Because Jesus is totally one with the Father and sent from the Father, he can

GOSPEL   John 6:51–58

A reading from the holy Gospel according to John

Jesus said to the **crowds**:
"**I am the living bread** that came down from **heaven**;
whoever **eats** this bread will live **forever**;
and the bread that **I** will give
is my **flesh** for the life of the **world**."

The Jews **quarreled** among themselves, saying,
"How can this man give us his **flesh** to eat?"
Jesus **said** to them,
"Amen, amen, I **say** to you,
unless you **eat** the flesh of the Son of Man and drink his **blood**,
you do not have **life** within you.
Whoever **eats** my **flesh** and **drinks** my **blood**
has **eternal** life,
and I will **raise** him on the last **day**.
For my **flesh** is true **food**,
and my **blood** is true **drink**.
Whoever **eats** my flesh and **drinks** my blood
remains in me and I in **him**.
Just as the living Father sent **me**
and I have life **because** of the Father,
so also the one who **feeds** on me
will have life **because** of me.
This is the bread that came down from **heaven**.
Unlike your **ancestors** who ate and still **died**,
whoever eats **this** bread will live **forever**."

How do we proclaim words that defy human logic and assert what both our senses and our sense of propriety would deny? How do we do so with the awareness Jesus had that his words were controversial and that they needed to be said anyway? Don't try to persuade with these words, just let them express your own deep faith.

Obviously *some* believe or there would be no argument.

The double "Amen" signals important teaching.

Jesus could not possibly make reception of his body and blood more important: only in them is eternal life found.

Note the echoes in these lines from today's Wisdom text.

This profound analogy should be proclaimed with direct eye contact.

Don't rush; give your listeners time to recall the desert manna. Unlike that earlier bread, the bread of life will empower those who eat it to live forever.

---

teach and act with God's authority. For disciples, Jesus's oneness with God means that those united to Jesus are, through him, also one with God. To express this mutual indwelling of the believer and Jesus, John uses a word variously translated as "stay," "remain," or "abide." In this passage, John emphasizes that one way in which disciples are united with Jesus is in the Lord's Supper.

Today's Gospel proclaims that Jesus, fully present in the Eucharist, replaces the bread from heaven of old, the manna in the desert. Those who ate this bread still died, but those nourished by Jesus, who becomes one with believers through food and drink, will live forever. As John stated at the beginning of his Gospel account, Jesus does not simply speak God's Word; he *is* God's self-revealing communication incarnate. In today's Scripture, Jesus does not simply invite people to Wisdom's banquet; he *is* God's Wisdom made flesh, and he himself *is* Wisdom's banquet, the sustenance they need to live God's way and to enjoy fullness of life. By sharing in the Lord's Supper, the mutual indwelling of believer and Jesus is deepened, and so disciples "remain" in him.

"The Jews" object to Jesus's claim that he gives his flesh and blood to eat and drink; they seem to take his statement too literally. However, in Jesus's world "flesh and blood" referred to the whole person (Matthew 16:16–17). Jesus promises that in the Eucharist, he gives his entire person, divine Word or Wisdom made flesh, so that we might have fullness of life through union with him.

TWENTY-FIRST SUNDAY IN ORDINARY TIME

LECTIONARY #122

READING I   Joshua 24:1–2a, 15–17, 18b

Joshua = JOSH-oo-uh

This is a momentous gathering, like convening Congress, the Supreme Court, and the Joint Chiefs of Staff.

Lift your voice for this challenge to the people. He knows what he will do and invites them to make their choice.

"As for me" is a beloved text inscribed on many plaques. Inscribe it today in the hearts of your listeners.

The people are not so presumptuous as to think they can abandon the Lord.

They recount their history with humility and great gratitude.

Their knowledge of God is firsthand, and therefore deeply felt.

Pause before the last sentence, and then with sincerity and conviction make the final declaration.

A reading from the Book of Joshua

Joshua gathered together all the tribes of **Israel** at **Shechem**,
  summoning their **elders**, their **leaders**,
  their **judges**, and their **officers**.
When they stood in **ranks** before God,
  Joshua **addressed** all the people:
  "If it does not **please** you to serve the Lord,
  decide today whom you **will** serve,
  the gods your **fathers** served beyond the River
  or the gods of the **Amorites** in whose **country** you are
    now dwelling.
As for **me** and my **household**, we will serve the Lord."

But the **people** answered,
  "Far be it from us to forsake the Lord
  for the service of **other** gods.
For it was the Lord, our **God**,
  who brought us and our fathers up out of the land of **Egypt**,
  out of a state of **slavery**.
He performed those great **miracles** before our very **eyes**
  and **protected** us along our entire **journey**
  and among the **peoples** through whom we passed.
Therefore we **also** will serve the Lord, for he is our **God**."

READING I   The Book of Joshua forms the opening to a large portion of Israel's religious history, beginning with the Israelites entering the land of Canaan. At the end of Deuteronomy, Moses, realizing that he will die before entering the Promised Land, commissions Joshua as his successor to lead the people into the land of freedom. Canaan was already occupied by various peoples, each with their gods, and so as the Israelites begin settling into their new circumstances, Joshua calls them to remember who they are: a people in covenant with the one God, the Lord. Today's reading is, in essence, a renewal of covenant promises as Israel begins a new stage in its life as God's people.

Immediately before today's reading, God, through Joshua, has reminded the people that their own ancestors did in fact worship other gods. There follows a recitation of the Lord's mighty deeds on their behalf: deliverance from Egypt, protection from enemies in the wilderness and in this new land, and plentiful sources of food. Then God calls for a choice: will you choose the gods of your early ancestors and of the peoples in this new country, or will you continue to serve the Lord? In Hebrew, the word used here means both "serve" and "worship." Thus God asks, in effect will the people recommit themselves to keeping the teaching, summarized in the Ten Commandments given when they first accepted the Sinai covenant and promised to worship the Lord alone.

Decision is the major focus here. In the desert, Israel made a choice to serve only the Lord; in a new world of freedom, will they make the same choice? At this point in their history, they affirm they will

For meditation and context:

TO KEEP IN MIND

Separating units of thought with pauses: Identify the units of thought in your text and use pauses to distinguish one from another. Running words together blurs meaning and fails to distinguish ideas. Punctuation does not always indicate clearly what words to group together or where to pause. The listener depends on you for this organization of ideas.

Ephesians = ee-FEE-zhuhnz

This is the last of seven consecutive weeks we read from Ephesians.

The central message is here: "subordination" is mutual and done for the sake of Christ.

Wives subject as the Church is to the Lord, who is all love and compassion.

Emphasize the need to imitate the Church's submissive love of Christ. To the cultural expectations of the day Paul very deliberately adds the obligation to love.

Establish eye contact and pause after the word "Husbands." Then share unreservedly the responsibilities of husbands to their wives.

"Cleansing her by bath" is an allusion to Baptism.

Christ, who willingly sacrificed himself for the sake of his bride, is the model for every Christian.

Because they are bonded into "one flesh," when spouses care for each other they also care for themselves.

RESPONSORIAL PSALM　Psalm 34:2–3, 16–17, 18–19, 20–21 (9a)

R. Taste and see the goodness of the Lord.

I will bless the LORD at all times;
　　his praise shall be ever in my mouth.
Let my soul glory in the LORD;
　　the lowly will hear me and be glad.

The LORD has eyes for the just,
　　and ears for their cry.
The LORD confronts the evildoers,
　　to destroy remembrance of them from
　　　the earth.

When the just cry out, the LORD hears them,
　　and from all their distress he
　　　rescues them.
The LORD is close to the brokenhearted;
　　and those who are crushed in spirit
　　　he saves.

Many are the troubles of the just one,
　　but out of them all the LORD delivers him;
he watches over all his bones;
　　not one of them shall be broken.

READING II　Ephesians 5:21–32

A reading from the Letter of Saint Paul to the Ephesians

Brothers and sisters:
Be **subordinate** to one another out of **reverence** for **Christ**.
Wives should be subordinate to their **husbands** as to the **Lord**.
For the husband is **head** of his wife
　　just as **Christ** is head of the **church**,
　　he himself the **savior** of the body.
As the **church** is subordinate to **Christ**,
　　so **wives** should be subordinate to their husbands
　　　in **everything**.
Husbands, **love** your wives,
　　even as **Christ** loved the **church**
　　and **handed** himself over for her to **sanctify** her,
　　cleansing her by the bath of **water** with the **word**,
　　that he might present to himself the church in **splendor**,
　　without **spot** or **wrinkle** or **any** such thing,
　　that she might be **holy** and without **blemish**.
So also husbands should **love** their wives as their own **bodies.**
He who loves his **wife** loves **himself.**

---

serve this God alone, for no other has redeemed, delivered, and nourished them.

READING II Before considering this particular passage, it should be noted that the Pauline writer generally thinks in Jewish thought patterns. (Scholars debate whether Paul himself or a follower wrote Ephesians, but the thinking is clearly influenced by the Apostle.) The English words "body" and "flesh" can lead to inaccurate conclusions about Pauline views, because many westerners are influenced by early Greek thought which conceived

the human person as body and soul. This notion is alien to Jewish perspectives, since the Hebrew language had no word to designate the physical body alone. In biblical thought, a human being is a unity, thought of as inspirited flesh or embodied spirit— but always a single whole. In this reading, "body" and "flesh" indicate a whole person, not a part of a human being.

Today's Second Reading is similar to a common literary form used in the Greco-Roman world: a household code delineating proper relations between wife and husband, children and parents, and slaves and

slave-owners. For the Church, however, such relationships must be ruled by faith in Christ, in whom all were baptized. At the beginning of this chapter, the author lays the foundation for his instructions: followers of Christ are to imitate God, as revealed in Christ's self-sacrificing love. Hence there is a greater degree of mutuality in this household code than in those of the Empire. The pattern for Christian relationships is the love of Christ for the Church, his body, a mutual love by which people nourish and cherish one another. Such attitudes and behaviors should characterize

For no one **hates** his own **flesh**
    but rather **nourishes** and **cherishes** it,
    even as **Christ** does the **church**,
    because we are **members** of his body.
*For this reason a man shall **leave** his father and his mother*
    *and be joined to his **wife**,*
    *and the **two** shall become **one** flesh.*
This is a great **mystery**,
    but I speak in reference to **Christ** and the **church**.

[Shorter: Ephesians 5:2a, 25–32]

GOSPEL　　John 6:60–69

A reading from the holy Gospel according to John

Many of Jesus' **disciples** who were **listening** said,
    "This saying is **hard**; who can **accept** it?"
Since Jesus **knew** that his disciples were murmuring about this,
    he said to them, "Does this **shock** you?
What if you were to see the Son of Man **ascending**
    to where he was **before**?
It is the **spirit** that gives life,
    while the **flesh** is of no avail.
The words I have spoken to you are **Spirit** and **life**.
But there are **some** of you who do not **believe**."
Jesus knew from the **beginning** the ones who would not believe
    and the one who would **betray** him.
And he said,
    "For this reason I have told you that no one can **come** to me
    unless it is **granted** him by my **Father**."

Marginal notes (left column):

Your tone needs to signal that you are quoting another text, here from Genesis.

Paul himself frees us from literalism that leads to misunderstanding; his teaching is a "mystery" understood fully only through the example of Christ.

Let your tone suggest the frustration and even anger of the bewildered disciples.

Jesus had steeled himself against their doubts and astonishment. But he knows they will face an even greater challenge to their faith when he hangs on the cross.

Without defensiveness, Jesus takes up his teacher's mantle and instructs them.

"But there are some" casts the shadow of betrayal over his comments.

Speak as a sympathetic narrator who understands the burden Jesus carried of knowing one of his own would betray him.

---

spousal relationships in particular, so that, as is written in Genesis 2:24, husband and wife become as one flesh.

While modern Western culture resists the call for wives to "be subordinate to" their husbands, the writer does not simply mandate unthinking compliance of wives, nor unlimited dominance by husbands. Marriage partners are to "Be subordinate to one another out of reverence for Christ." Mutual love and reverence leads to mutual surrender, in imitation of the love between Christ and the Church. As Christ "handed himself over for" the Church, wives are to respond to their husbands. Husbands are to love their wives as their own person ("flesh"). Through such mutual self-giving, *the two shall become one flesh.*

GOSPEL　Today's Gospel follows immediately upon Jesus's misunderstood reference to eating and drinking his flesh and blood. (Some scholars think that John might have been countering such false notions among some Jews in his own time, around AD 90–100, thus leading even disciples astray.) Some of the disciples appear to be dismayed, even bordering on unbelief. Such reference to lack of faith recalls John's prologue in which he sounds many of his favored motifs. One of these themes reflects a dualistic stance: in response to an encounter with Jesus, God's Word or Wisdom made flesh, people will either believe or not believe, choosing to belong to darkness or light. In John's view, believing in Jesus will flower fully in personal relationship with him, so those disciples who choose to leave Jesus's side at this point clearly lack faith.

We don't know the fate of those who left him, but they clearly leave hurt and disenchanted.

Jesus asks with resignation, ready for their reply.

Here is Peter at his best. His honesty is poignant. He has found the path and won't abandon it. Instead of his fears or insecurities, he focuses on Jesus.

As a **result** of this,
 many of his disciples returned to their **former** way of life
 and no longer **accompanied** him.
Jesus then said to the **Twelve**, "Do you **also** want to leave?"
Simon **Peter** answered him, "**Master**, to **whom** shall we go?
You have the words of eternal life.
We have come to **believe**
 and are **convinced** that you are the **Holy** One of **God**."

TO KEEP IN MIND
Each text contains **three kinds of content**: intellectual-theological, emotional, and aesthetic. The plot and details of the story and the theological teaching behind them comprise the intellectual-theological content. How the author or characters feel (or want us to feel) is the emotional content. Elements that make the writing pleasing—rhythm, repetition, suspense, and picturesque language—are the aesthetic content.

Jesus emphasizes that belief or unbelief involves a decision, and directly poses the question to the Twelve: "Do you also want to leave?" Peter's response resembles that of the Israelites in the First Reading; having witnessed the saving, life-giving action of God in Jesus, divine Word in the flesh, how can the disciples choose any other? Divine Wisdom stands before them in the full humanity of Jesus, feeding them with his own person.

TWENTY-SECOND SUNDAY IN ORDINARY TIME

TO KEEP IN MIND

Names of characters: Often the first word of a reading. Lift out the names to ensure listeners don't miss who the subject is.

Deuteronomy = doo-ter-AH-nuh-mee

Moses = MOH-zis

Lift out the name of Moses.

Moses is making a grand address to the entire assembly of Israel, so a lofty tone commensurate with the dignity of the event is necessary.

Before anything else, God's Law is a divine gift that commands utmost respect. And it cannot be diluted or augmented.

In both Old and New Testaments, observance of the Law is a sign of love. Imagine giving this advice to a young person going off to school or to a career in a new city.

Speak this line from the vantage point of the nations that envy the privilege of Israel.

God's Law is always viewed as a gift, not as a burden or restraint.

Note, Moses sets the Law "before" them, not *upon* them as a weighty burden.

LECTIONARY #125

READING I   Deuteronomy 4:1–2, 6–8

A reading from the Book of Deuteronomy

Moses said to the **people**:
    "**Now**, Israel, hear the **statutes** and **decrees**
    which I am teaching you to **observe**,
    that you may **live**, and may enter in and take **possession**
        of the land
    which the Lord, the God of your **fathers**, is **giving** you.
In your **observance** of the commandments of the Lord,
        your God,
    which I **enjoin** upon you,
    you shall not **add** to what I command you nor **subtract** from it.
Observe them **carefully**,
    for thus will you give evidence
    of your **wisdom** and **intelligence** to the nations,
    who will **hear** of all these statutes and say,
    'This great nation is truly a **wise** and **intelligent** people.'
For what great nation is there
    that has gods so **close** to it as the Lord, our God, is to **us**
    whenever we **call** upon him?
Or what great nation has **statutes** and **decrees**
    that are as **just** as this whole law
    which I am setting before you today?"

Today all three readings revolve around proper hearing and responding to God's laws and commands. In ancient Israel, the Law was understood to provide guidelines for how to live well in all relationships, and, as such, was considered a gift of God. But our ancestors in faith, like us, sometimes forgot that divine teaching in the form of commands is always rooted in, and oriented toward, right relationship with God, others, and the physical world. Without that purpose, laws can restrict instead of free us for right living.

| READING I | In Deuteronomy, God speaks to the Israelites through Moses in preparation for entering into covenant and giving them the Law. Since the Law—Torah or teaching in Hebrew—comes from God, the people are cautioned not to alter it in any way. As usual in the Bible, a call to hear divine teaching is accompanied by a summons to act upon what is heard; in Hebrew, one word (*shema*) commands the people to both "hear" and "obey." A response of true obedience will bear in mind the purpose of the Law: not merely external observance for its own sake, but a response of the heart that intends to foster right relationships with God and the community. When the Lord's people obey God's commands in

For meditation and context:

TO KEEP IN MIND

The opening: Establish eye contact and announce, from memory, "A reading from . . . ." Then take a pause (three full beats!) before starting the reading. The correct pronunciation is "A [uh] reading from" instead of "A [ay] reading from."

James is not sharing information, but rejoicing in God's bountiful goodness. (And yes, the song "All Good Gifts" from the musical *Godspell* is inspired by this text.)

James tells us God never varies and God's light is never dimmed or overshadowed.

James likens us to the "firstfruits" that traditionally are reserved for, and offered to, God.

"Be doers" is a direct admonition not to lull ourselves into thinking we can get away with lip-service. The line is both a plea and a command.

Pure religion, says James, boils down to caring for the needy and not succumbing to the allurements of the world. Be direct, but not harsh.

RESPONSORIAL PSALM   Psalm 15:2–3, 3–4, 4–5 (1a)

R. The one who does justice will live in the presence of the Lord.

Whoever walks blamelessly and does justice;
    who thinks the truth in his heart
    and slanders not with his tongue.

Who harms not his fellow man,
    nor takes up a reproach against
        his neighbor;
by whom the reprobate is despised,
    while he honors those who fear the LORD.

Who lends not his money at usury
    and accepts no bribe against the innocent.
Whoever does these things
    shall never be disturbed.

READING II   James 1:17–18, 21b–22, 27

A reading from the Letter of Saint James

Dearest **brothers** and **sisters**:
All **good giving** and every perfect **gift** is from **above**,
    coming down from the Father of **lights**,
    with whom there is no **alteration** or shadow caused by **change**.
He **willed** to give us birth by the word of **truth**
    that we may be a kind of **firstfruits** of his creatures.

Humbly **welcome** the word that has been **planted** in you
    and is able to save your **souls**.

Be **doers** of the word and not **hearers** only, **deluding** yourselves.

Religion that is **pure** and **undefiled** before God and the Father
        is **this**:
    to care for **orphans** and **widows** in their affliction
    and to keep oneself **unstained** by the world.

---

this spirit, it will be evident to other nations that this teaching is "just." In most cases, and certainly here, the biblical language of "justice" and "righteousness" refers to right relationships, once again emphasizing the true meaning of the Law given to God's covenant people.

READING II   Today's liturgy begins a series of readings from the brief but important Letter of James. While in the form of a letter, this document is primarily an exhortation for ethical Christian conduct. It is distinctly Jewish in character and addressed to Jewish Christians, though it may have been intended for wider distribution to other churches as well.

At the beginning of his composition, the writer urges anyone who lacks wisdom to petition God for it, certain that it will be given. For several centuries before Jesus, the Jewish people often identified wisdom with divine Law (Torah). For James, of course, the life, Death, and Resurrection of Jesus provides the full interpretation of the Law, and is to be found in the Gospel, the "word of truth."

Rooted in Jewish thought, the author urges those who truly hear this word to put it into practice; anything less is self-delusion. The admonition to care for widows and orphans also reflects a Jewish perspective: those who live in right relationships ought to attend to each other's needs, particularly in the case of the most vulnerable. In a society in which women and children depended upon a male provider, widows and orphans represented its most needy

The fussy Pharisees keenly observe the disciples and are immediately scandalized.

Mark's aside provides interesting information that can be read briskly. Mark points to the dichotomy on which Jesus will focus—the Pharisees worry more about man-made "tradition" than the Law of God.

Elaborating what requires purification helps set up Jesus's diatribe against the Pharisees.

Their tone must have been harsh to immediately evoke such a stern rebuke from Jesus.

TO KEEP IN MIND

Word value: Words are your medium, like a painter's brush or a sculptor's chisel. You must understand the words before you can communicate them. Most words have a dictionary meaning (denotative) and an associational meaning (connotative). "House" and "home" both mean "dwelling," yet they communicate different feelings. Be alert to subtle differences in connotative meanings and express them.

GOSPEL   Mark 7:1–8, 14–15, 21–23

A reading from the holy Gospel according to Mark

When the **Pharisees** with some **scribes** who had come from **Jerusalem**
   gathered around **Jesus**,
   they **observed** that some of his **disciples** ate their meals
   with **unclean**, that is, **unwashed**, hands.
—For the **Pharisees** and, in fact, **all** Jews,
   do not eat without carefully **washing** their hands,
   keeping the **tradition** of the **elders**.
And on coming from the **marketplace**
   they do not eat without **purifying** themselves.
And there are many **other** things that they have traditionally
      observed,
   the purification of **cups** and **jugs** and **kettles** and **beds**.—
So the Pharisees and scribes **questioned** him,
   "Why do your disciples not **follow** the tradition of the elders
   but instead eat a meal with **unclean** hands?"

---

members. In light of the Gospel, care for one another called for self-sacrifice like that of Jesus.

 GOSPEL   Disputes between Jesus and various religious leaders of Judaism appear with some frequency in the Gospel accounts. In today's reading, Mark describes a conversation that Jesus and his disciples have with some scribes and Pharisees who question their faithfulness to Jewish Law. Scribes were the

Scripture scholars of the day, and the Pharisee party was particularly concerned to observe all the specific commands of the Torah, which they had determined numbered 613. Some of these commands, such as Jewish purity regulations, were not part of the Torah given at Sinai (also called Horeb), but had developed through religious tradition. However, at the time of Jesus, they were considered an important part of religious observance; touching any

unclean object, person, or anything that had been in contact with them prevented one from participating in ritual worship until one had undergone purification.

Referring to the prophet Isaiah, Jesus attempts to recall his questioners to the original intention of the Law: right relationships with God, others, and material things. The quotation is sure to capture attention, for the prophet spoke these words to the people of Judah in the context of threatened destruction, a punishment for their

Jesus lets Isaiah (29:13) do his work for him—holding up a mirror before their hypocrisy.

Jesus's anger is directed at their usurpation of God's authority, placing their laws ahead of God's.

Jesus seizes the opportunity to liberate the people from some of the false notions the Pharisees have imposed on them.

Now in full swing, Jesus teaches the people about what really matters and what really defiles a person. The list of evils is long intentionally. It's as if Jesus were saying, if you want to talk about what *really* defiles, I'll *tell* you what defiles.

The final line calls the Pharisees to see clearly and focus on more important matters.

He responded,
   "**Well** did Isaiah prophesy about you **hypocrites**, as it
      is written:
   *This people honors me with their **lips**,*
      *but their **hearts** are **far** from me;*
   *in **vain** do they worship me,*
      *teaching as doctrines **human** precepts.*
You disregard **God's** commandment but cling to
      human tradition."
He summoned the **crowd** again and said to them,
   "**Hear** me, **all** of you, and **understand**.
Nothing that enters one from **outside** can **defile** that person;
   but the things that come out from **within** are what **defile**.

"From **within** people, from their **hearts**,
   come **evil** thoughts, **unchastity**, **theft**, **murder**,
   adultery, **greed**, **malice**, **deceit**,
   licentiousness, **envy**, **blasphemy**, **arrogance**, **folly**.
All these **evils** come from **within** and they **defile**."

TO KEEP IN MIND
Lists: Whether proclaiming a genealogy or one of Paul's enumerations of virtues and sins, avoid the extremes of too much stress (slowly punctuating each word with equal stress) or too little (rushing through as if each item were the same).

---

repeated acts of false worship, among other things. They had paid only lip service to the Law without true understanding of, and interior commitment to, its purpose. Jesus applies Isaiah's message to his opponents, who substitute human teaching for divine commands.

Jesus then teaches the principle underlying his actions: those who truly obey God's Law must hear and act; but even action, by itself, avails for nothing unless it comes from a heart truly attentive to God and the good of others. In Jewish thought, the heart represents the core of a human person; one thinks and decides with the heart. Thus Jesus insists that good or evil springs from the heart, and it is the heart that must be attuned to God's Law and its true purposes.

TWENTY-THIRD SUNDAY IN ORDINARY TIME

LECTIONARY #128

READING I   Isaiah 35:4–7a

A reading from the Book of the Prophet Isaiah

Thus says the **Lord**:
  Say to those whose hearts are **frightened**:
    Be **strong**, fear **not**!
Here is your **God**,
  he comes with **vindication**;
with divine **recompense**
  he comes to **save** you.
Then will the eyes of the blind be **opened**,
  the **ears** of the deaf be **cleared**;
then will the lame **leap** like a stag,
  then the tongue of the mute will **sing**.
Streams will burst forth in the **desert**,
  and **rivers** in the **steppe**.
The **burning** sands will become **pools**,
  and the **thirsty** ground, **springs** of **water**.

Isaiah = Ī-ZAY-uh

Poetry is gourmet food meant to be savored and consumed slowly. Or another image: this text is like mood music played to enliven the mood of listeners.

You have two imperatives at "Be strong"; the second requires even greater energy than the first.

The *reason* we are to let go of fear is here: God come to vindicate us!

A new beat with a new mood begins at "Then will." Share this Good News with abundant energy.

God will do the impossible, and even nature will be transformed. These are metaphors, of course, but they speak of God's power to save and renew.

TO KEEP IN MIND
Proclaiming the **words of the prophets** requires intensity and urgency. With equal passion, they spoke threat and consolation, indictment and forgiveness. You must do the same for the chosen people you call "parish."

READING I Biblical scholars generally believe that the lengthy book of Isaiah represents the work of three different prophets, each speaking to God's people in different historical situations. Today's First Reading comes from First Isaiah (chapters 1–39), when Judah's greatest threat was the powerful and war-like empire of Assyria. About 700 BC, the Assyrians moved to overtake the tiny Israelite kingdom of Judah, seizing all the towns surrounding Jerusalem. When they laid siege to the capital city, however, they failed to take control, which Isaiah attributed to God's promise that a descendant of David would rule forever in Jerusalem.

Today's Scripture is placed shortly before Isaiah's description of the Assyrian onslaught of Jerusalem. Like other prophets, even in the face of foreign attack, he boldly proclaims the Lord's ultimate victory. Even if God's people face fall and captivity, in the end, God's faithfulness will triumph. Primarily through the ministry of the great prophets like Isaiah, the Israelites began to look toward a future, final completion of the divine plan of salvation, when God would overcome all the evils that afflict humankind. Here Isaiah looks toward that era of God's definitive rule, when every kind of illness will be abolished, human beings will be made whole, and the earth itself will be perfected. What the prophet describes here, Jesus would later name the Kingdom of God.

READING II Last Sunday's excerpt from the Letter of James focused on putting the teaching of the Gospel into practice; today, the author begins to

For meditation and context:

RESPONSORIAL PSALM   Psalm 146:6–7, 8–9, 9–10 (1b)

R. Praise the Lord, my soul! or R. Alleluia.

The God of Jacob keeps faith forever,
    secures justice for the oppressed,
    gives food to the hungry.
The LORD sets captives free.

The LORD gives sight to the blind;
    the LORD raises up those who were
        bowed down.
The LORD loves the just;
    the LORD protects strangers.

The fatherless and the widow the LORD
        sustains,
    but the way of the wicked he thwarts.
The LORD shall reign forever;
    your God, O Zion, through all generations.
        Alleluia.

TO KEEP IN MIND

Who really proclaims: "When the Scriptures are read in the Church, God himself is speaking to his people, and Christ, present in his own word, is proclaiming the gospel." (General Instruction of the Roman Missal, 29)

This is the second of five consecutive weeks we read from the Letter of James.

Martin Luther disliked this letter because of its insistence that faith and works *must* go together. James argues the case, but with great love for his readers.

James's tone is direct and unpretentious.

James uses an example from "real life." He's making a point they will understand, though one that challenges.

Your tone signals you know that they know the answer to these rhetorical questions.

Don't overlook his tender salutation: "beloved."

READING II   James 2:1–5

A reading from the Letter of Saint James

My brothers and sisters, show no **partiality**
    as you adhere to the faith in our glorious Lord Jesus **Christ**.
For if a man with gold **rings** and fine **clothes**
    comes into your assembly,
    and a **poor** person in **shabby** clothes **also** comes in,
    and you pay **attention** to the one wearing the **fine** clothes
    and say, "Sit **here**, please,"
    while you say to the **poor** one, "Stand **there**,"
        or "Sit at my **feet**,"
    have you not made **distinctions** among yourselves
    and become **judges** with evil **designs**?

Listen, my beloved brothers and sisters.
Did not God choose those who are **poor** in the world
    to be rich in **faith** and **heirs** of the kingdom
    that he promised to those who **love** him?

---

describe such practice in concrete detail. The Christian message that Christ died and was raised for all pointed to the equality of all members of the Church. But in a world often ruled by strict social, economic, and cultural stratification, shedding such a mindset did not come easily for some new converts to the Christian community. James therefore points out discrimination still practiced even in a religious setting.

The word "assembly" here actually means "synagogue"; it should be remembered that the earliest Jewish followers of

Jesus still thought of themselves as Jews, albeit Jews fortunate enough to live in the time of God's final coming. These Jewish Christians continued to attend Temple and synagogue service; in addition, they gathered in their homes for the Lord's Supper (Acts 2:46). Paul indicates that, at times, social discrimination based on social or economic status divided even those who shared the Eucharist (1 Corinthians 11:17–34). James insists that a true hearing of the Gospel allows for no such distinctions in the Church. In fact, he reminds his hearers that those whom the world considers poor

and disenfranchised are the ones most open to the Word of God's salvation; they are foremost heirs of God's final rule.

| GOSPEL | In last Sunday's Gospel, when questioned by Jewish religious leaders about why he did not observe purity laws, Jesus taught that internal attitudes rather than external conditions are the true source of defilement. In today's reading, he continues to act on this conviction. Chapter 7 of Mark represents a shift in Jesus's public ministry. Up to this

GOSPEL   Mark 7:31–37

A reading from the holy Gospel according to Mark

Again Jesus left the district of **Tyre**
    and went by way of **Sidon** to the Sea of **Galilee**,
    into the district of the **Decapolis**.
And people brought to him a **deaf** man who had a
        speech impediment
    and **begged** him to lay his **hand** on him.
He took him off by **himself** away from the **crowd**.
He put his **finger** into the man's **ears**
    and, **spitting**, touched his **tongue**;
    then he looked up to heaven and **groaned**, and said to him,
    "**Ephphatha!**"—that is, "Be **opened!**"—
And **immediately** the man's ears **were** opened,
    his **speech** impediment was **removed**,
    and he spoke **plainly**.
He ordered them not to tell **anyone**.
But the more he ordered them **not** to,
    the more they **proclaimed** it.
They were exceedingly **astonished** and they said,
    "He has done all things **well**.
He makes the deaf **hear** and the mute **speak**."

Speak with a positive attitude toward these ancient places frequented by the Lord.

Tyre = tīr

Sidon = SĪ-duhn

Decapolis = dih-KAP-uh-lis

Don't fail to stress the initiative of those who "brought" and "begged."

Jesus's grab for privacy is somewhat unusual, though not unique.

Sometimes Jesus heals from a distance, with no direct contact. Here is a stark contrast. Don't rush the graphic details of his sacramental physicality.

Help us hear *all* that happened: his ears were opened; his impediment was removed; he spoke plainly.

The narrator does not regret their proclamation.

"He has done." This is a striking affirmation of Jesus's ministry. In Jesus, Isaiah's prophesy that the blind would see and the lame walk is powerfully fulfilled.

point, he has healed and taught among his own people; in this chapter he makes a definite turn toward the Gentiles. Scripture scholars debate whether Mark here reflects Jesus's actual behavior; by the time Mark wrote his account of the Good News about AD 70, the Church had been preaching the Gospel among Gentiles as well as Jews for more than thirty years.

Mark signals Jesus's intentional movement out of Jewish territory by describing the setting as the Decapolis, a group of ten cities in Gentile lands. Apparently there is already some level of faith among the people there, for they take the initiative to bring the man who was deaf and mute to Jesus. Jesus looks heavenward, emphasizing that the healing ultimately comes from the Father through him. Physical contact with a Gentile constituted a violation of the Jewish purity code, but Jesus acts on his own admonition: he considers the people's faith more important than the external accident of Gentile birth.

Like virtually all healing miracle stories, this one functions to demonstrate the truth of Jesus's announcement that God's final rule over all forces of evil has begun in his person. In this healing account, Mark adds two important notes. First, the divine plan for human wholeness extends to Gentile as well as Jew. Further, this particular healing indicates that Jesus and his ministry fulfill the prophecy of Isaiah: through Jesus the Messiah, even the deaf hear the message of the dawning Kingdom of God, and even the mute can proclaim it.

TWENTY-FOURTH SUNDAY IN ORDINARY TIME

LECTIONARY #131

READING I   Isaiah 50:5–9a

A reading from the Book of the Prophet Isaiah

The Lord **God** opens my **ear** that I may **hear**;
and I have not **rebelled**,
  have not turned **back**.
I gave my **back** to those who **beat** me,
  my **cheeks** to those who plucked my **beard**;
my **face** I did not **shield**
  from **buffets** and **spitting**.

The Lord **God** is my help,
  therefore I am not **disgraced**;
I have set my face like **flint**,
  knowing that I shall **not** be put to **shame**.
He is **near** who upholds my **right**;
  if anyone wishes to **oppose** me,
  let us appear **together**.
Who **disputes** my right?
  Let that man **confront** me.
See, the Lord **God** is my help;
  who will prove me **wrong**?

Isaiah = ī-ZAY-uh

The entire text is a monologue spoken by God's suffering servant. You are not "acting" the character, but you must convey the feeling embedded in his words.

The servant makes his own case: he's been faithful despite much abuse and suffering.

But his tone is not angry; rather, we sense gratitude for being able to endure "buffets" and "spitting."

The start of this new beat proclaims the central message: it is God who helps the servant endure and shields him from "shame."

The servant is emboldened, not by pride but by confidence in God's constant presence. Imagine a youth whose father is the police commissioner throwing out this challenge.

The final lines blend challenge and gratitude.

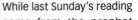

READING I While last Sunday's reading came from the prophet known as First Isaiah, who prophesied at a time of Assyrian aggression against Judah, today's Scripture comes from Second Isaiah (also called Deutero-Isaiah) who speaks God's Word to the people near the beginning of their long exile in Babylonia. A significant feature of this prophet's work appears in a figure known as the servant of the Lord, or the suffering servant. In four poems, Second Isaiah describes the mission of the mysterious, unnamed servant.

At times the servant appears to be a corporate figure, but at other times seems to be an individual. Through this faithful servant, who bears divine spirit (42:1), God will bring salvation to a suffering people. Precisely through the servant's own physical and emotional suffering, borne in trust, the covenant people will be restored and renewed.

Today's reading presents the third of four poems of the suffering servant. The opening line emphasizes that this figure is a true Israelite who allows God to open his ear to hear. In biblical thought, an open ear signified a person ready to hear and obey God's Word. In the prophetic books, sin is often described as rebellion, and the servant also states that he has not rebelled, thus signifying his right relationship to God. Even in the face of personal insult (plucking the beard) and physical abuse, the servant does not waver in his determination to respond to whatever God asks. Such steadfastness is rooted in unflinching trust that God will not fail to come to his aid.

For meditation and context:

RESPONSORIAL PSALM   Psalm 116:1–2, 3–4, 5–6, 8–9 (9)

R. I will walk before the Lord, in the land of the living. orR. Alleluia.

I love the LORD because he has heard
   my voice in supplication,
because he has inclined his ear to me
   the day I called.

The cords of death encompassed me;
   the snares of the netherworld seized
     upon me;
   I fell into distress and sorrow,
and I called upon the name of the LORD,
   "O LORD, save my life!"

Gracious is the LORD and just;
   yes, our God is merciful.
The LORD keeps the little ones;
   I was brought low, and he saved me.

For he has freed my soul from death,
   my eyes from tears, my feet from
     stumbling.
I shall walk before the LORD
   in the land of the living.

TO KEEP IN MIND
Dialogue imitates real conversation, so it often moves faster than the rest of the passage.

READING II   James 2:14–18

A reading from the Letter of Saint James

What **good** is it, my brothers and sisters,
   if someone says he has **faith** but does not have **works**?
Can that faith **save** him?
If a brother or sister has **nothing** to **wear**
   and has no **food** for the day,
   and one of you says to them,
   "Go in **peace**, keep **warm**, and eat **well**,"
   but you do not **give** them the necessities of the **body**,
   what **good** is it?
So also **faith** of **itself**,
   if it does not have **works**, is **dead**.

Indeed someone might say,
   "You have **faith** and I have **works**."
Demonstrate your faith to me **without** works,
   and **I** will demonstrate my faith to you **from** my works.

This is the third of five consecutive weeks we read from the Letter of James.
To persuade, James takes on a deferential, almost tender, tone.

James conjures a character that is more "clueless" than heartless.

This letter is best known for this single point: lack of good works makes for dead faith.

It's easy to imagine a forceful, almost confrontational delivery of this dialogue. But keeping in mind James's intent to persuade, a gentler tone will work better. He's saying: Tell me, can you prove your faith *without* any works?

READING II In today's Second Reading, James presents more of his concrete, no-nonsense ethical teaching. Last week we heard his admonition against any kind of discrimination based on social, economic or cultural status among members of the Church. Today he insists that a Christian cannot simply talk about care for other members of the community, or give verbal assurance to those community members who have physical needs; one must act, in imitation of Jesus.

But James seems to have another important point to make. Many biblical scholars view this passage as James's caution against misunderstanding one of the teachings of Paul. As is well known, the latter repeatedly insisted to fellow Jews that they were not saved by conformity to works of the Law of Moses, but by faith in God's free gift of new life through Christ (grace). It seems possible, if not probable, that some had misunderstood or misapplied Paul's emphasis on faith and behaved as if a claim of belief in Christ would, in itself, lead to salvation. James exposes such an assumption as false, insisting that faith must take concrete form in how one in fact treats others in need. A brother or sister lacking food or clothing cannot be helped by anyone's mere claim of faith; believers must act, quickly and concretely, to alleviate another's need.

GOSPEL It is often said that Mark's portrait of Jesus is drawn on the pattern of Isaiah's Suffering Servant; one reason for this view is evident in

GOSPEL   Mark 8:27–35

A reading from the holy Gospel according to Mark

Jesus and his **disciples** set out
 for the villages of **Caesarea Philippi**.
Along the way he **asked** his disciples,
 "Who do people say that I **am**?"
They said in reply,
 "John the **Baptist**, others **Elijah**,
 still others one of the **prophets**."
And he asked them,
 "But who do **you** say that I am?"
Peter said to him in reply,
 "You are the **Christ**."
Then he **warned** them not to tell **anyone** about him.

He began to **teach** them
 that the Son of Man must **suffer** greatly
 and be **rejected** by the **elders**, the chief **priests**, and the **scribes**,
 and be **killed**, and **rise** after three **days**.
He spoke this **openly**.
Then **Peter** took him aside and began to **rebuke** him.
At this he turned around and, looking at his **disciples**,
 rebuked Peter and said, "Get **behind** me, **Satan**.
You are thinking not as **God** does, but as human **beings** do."

He summoned the **crowd** with his disciples and **said** to them,
 "Whoever wishes to come **after** me must **deny** himself,
 take up his **cross**, and **follow** me.
For whoever wishes to **save** his life will **lose** it,
 but whoever **loses** his life for **my** sake
 and that of the **gospel** will **save** it."

Note the three movements in this piece: first, relaxed conversation about Jesus's identity—climaxed in Peter's remarkable confession; second, Jesus's frank teaching about his inevitable suffering and rejection of Peter's narrow vision; and third, instructing the crowd about the cost of discipleship. Each movement has its own distinct tone.

The dialogue of the disciples is animated; each is eager to contribute the latest rumor.

Without forethought, Peter speaks from the heart. He's unrehearsed and his delivery is not profound but simply honest.

Jesus's detail and striking candor will be too much for Peter.

Perhaps Peter thinks he and the others will surely shield Jesus from such a fate and is disappointed Jesus doesn't feel he can rely on them.

Frustrated by his lack of understanding, Jesus matches Peter's "rebuke" with one of his own.

Jesus extends his frankness to the crowds for he wants them to understand the true cost of discipleship. A "hard saying" like this can't be sugar-coated.

---

today's Gospel. For Mark's Christian community enduring suffering of several kinds, emphasis on the Passion of Jesus could indeed reassure them that they follow one who understands and shares their struggles. The Evangelist's unflattering portrayal of Jesus's disciples, who often close their ears to any mention of Jesus's suffering and Death, most likely intends to pose a question to his audience around the year AD 70: do you truly understand and believe who you are to follow? And are you willing to follow?

At first Peter seems to respond with accurate faith to Jesus's question about his identity, affirming that he is indeed the Christ, God's Messiah. But from the beginning, Mark has indicated that the mission of Jesus the Messiah will conform to that of the Suffering Servant. Jesus's description of his coming rejection, suffering, and Death is too much for Peter, who vehemently objects and is in turn reproached by Jesus. The word translated "rebuke" in both cases is the same word used by Jesus to cast out demons, and here he uses it to address Peter, spokesman for the disciples, as

"Satan." This word means "adversary" or "enemy," and Jesus's meaning is clear, though astounding: if you wish to deny a suffering Messiah, you set yourself in direct opposition to me and my mission.

Finally, Jesus speaks as directly as possible: if you are truly a disciple, you will follow your master in word and action, even to death, giving over your life in trust to God who will ultimately save you. Thus Mark again asks his hearers: do you truly understand who you follow—and do you truly choose to do so?

TWENTY-FIFTH SUNDAY IN ORDINARY TIME

LECTIONARY #134

READING I   Wisdom 2:12, 17–20

A reading from the Book of Wisdom

The **wicked** say:
Let us beset the **just** one, because he is **obnoxious** to us;
    he sets himself **against** our doings,
reproaches us for transgressions of the law
    and charges us with **violations** of our training.
Let us see whether his words be **true**;
    let us find out what will **happen** to him.
For if the just one be the son of **God**, God will **defend** him
    and **deliver** him from the hand of his foes.
With **revilement** and **torture** let us put the just one to the **test**
    that we may have **proof** of his **gentleness**
    and **try** his **patience**.
Let us **condemn** him to a **shameful** death;
    for according to his own words, **God** will take **care** of him.

RESPONSORIAL PSALM   Psalm 54:3–4, 5, 6–8 (6b)

R. The Lord upholds my life.

O God, by your name save me,
    and by your might defend my cause.
O God, hear my prayer;
    hearken to the words of my mouth.

For the haughty have risen up against me,
    the ruthless seek my life;
    they set not God before their eyes.

Behold, God is my helper;
    the Lord sustains my life.
Freely will I offer you sacrifice;
    I will praise your name, O LORD, for its
    goodness.

To contextualize this reading and better understand its meaning, read chapters 1 and 2 of the Book of Wisdom.

Those who plot evil see their schemes as good because they help achieve their ends. So you don't need a sinister tone; speak with conviction and urgency about the *need* to act this way.

Evil is always a liar, even to itself. Here the schemers make excuses and assume God won't let them do something their intended victim doesn't deserve.

Their resolve strengthens; they justify their malice as a "test."

Their self-delusion is complete and they place on God the responsibility that belongs on their shoulders. "God will take care of him" is an excuse, not genuine concern for the "just one."

For meditation and context:

TO KEEP IN MIND
A substantial pause always follows "A reading from" and both precedes and follows "The word [Gospel] of the Lord."

READING I Today's passage from the Book of Wisdom reflects a Jewish literary tradition that shares much in common with the suffering servant of Second Isaiah, seen last Sunday. Here we see a figure commonly called "the just one." This motif, perhaps inspired by Isaiah's Servant of the Lord, developed in a later time of crisis for God's people. In 333 BC, Judea fell under control of the Greek Empire, which first imposed Greek culture and language on conquered peoples, and then in the second century BC attempted to force Greek religion on them as well. According to the Books of Maccabees, Jewish religious customs such as circumcision and dietary practices were prohibited, and some who refused to give up their ancestral faith faced execution. Under threat of torture and death, some Jews gave up their faith, but others surrendered to martyrdom. This time period also gave birth to belief in an afterlife among some Jews.

In this time of upheaval, the just one appeared. The outlines of this literary figure are generally the same: a faithful, obedient person who does God's will, suffers ridicule, even torture and death, because of it, but is ultimately vindicated and rewarded by God. In Wisdom, written about a half-century before the time of Jesus, the just one's reward includes resurrection to immortality (Wisdom 2:22—3:5). As in today's reading, the just one is sometimes also called a "son of God," at this time referring to a person "like God," a truly faithful Jew who trusts in God in any and all circumstances. A very early, if not the earliest, interpretation of Jesus's Death and Resurrection applies to him the title "Righteous One," as seen in Acts (3:14, 7:52).

READING II   James 3:16—4:3

A reading from the Letter of Saint James

Beloved:
Where **jealousy** and selfish **ambition** exist,
    there is **disorder** and every foul **practice**.
But the **wisdom** from above is first of all **pure**,
    then **peaceable**, **gentle**, **compliant**,
    full of **mercy** and good **fruits**,
    without **inconstancy** or **insincerity**.
And the fruit of righteousness is sown in **peace**
    for those who **cultivate** peace.

Where do the **wars**
    and where do the **conflicts** among you **come** from?
Is it not from your **passions**
    that make **war** within your members?
You **covet** but do not **possess**.
You **kill** and **envy** but you cannot **obtain**;
    you **fight** and wage **war**.
You do not **possess** because you do not **ask**.
You **ask** but do not **receive**,
    because you ask **wrongly**, to spend it on your **passions**.

This is the fourth of five consecutive weeks we read from the Letter of James.

Let your experience of the harm caused by "jealousy" and "ambition" color your tone.

It's not enough to render James's listing slowly; you must read with awareness of the value and of the need for each of the virtues he lists. Consider this a prayer that these qualities infuse the hearts of your assembly.

Don't think abstractly as you read, but have in mind the dissensions within your parish or your family.

The *New Revised Standard Version* translation of the Bible makes the meaning more explicit: "You want something and do not have it; so you commit murder. And you covet something and cannot obtain it; so you engage in disputes and conflicts."

His final instruction on prayer should *be a* prayer, not an accusation. Only God can help us overcome our wrongheaded passions.

TO KEEP IN MIND

Lists: Whether proclaiming a genealogy or one of Paul's enumerations of virtues and sins, avoid the extremes of too much stress (slowly punctuating each word with equal stress) or too little (rushing through as if each item were the same).

READING II Today's Second Reading continues the exhortation of James with a turn toward internal causes of unethical behavior. In previous passages the writer pointed out unacceptable behaviors among members of the Church, including discrimination and discord in the community and failure to act on one's claim of faith. Here, James seems to follow the teaching approach of Jesus as he points out the interior dispositions that underlie such ethical lapses. First emphasizing self-centered attitudes and disordered desires as major causes of discord and conflict, he then offers alternatives.

James reminds his hearers of the wisdom of their Jewish tradition, wisdom embodied in Christ. Inner attitudes of peace, gentleness, and mercy toward others as well as a shared dependence upon God will counteract the selfish and unruly desires that lead to actions unacceptable in a community dedicated to following Christ.

GOSPEL Last Sunday we heard the first of Jesus's three predictions of his suffering and Death, and the second appears today. After the first clear reference to his coming Passion, Mark inserts the Transfiguration account, followed by a lengthy exorcism story. The disciples still focus on Jesus as a wonder-worker. They seem to think that, as his disciples, they ought to be able to perform

GOSPEL   Mark 9:30–37

A reading from the holy Gospel according to Mark

Jesus and his **disciples left** from there and began a journey
    through **Galilee**,
  but he did not wish anyone to **know** about it.
He was **teaching** his disciples and **telling** them,
  "The Son of **Man** is to be handed **over** to men
  and they will **kill** him,
  and **three** days after his death the Son of Man will **rise**."
But they did not **understand** the saying,
  and they were afraid to **question** him.

They came to **Capernaum** and, once inside the **house**,
  he began to **ask** them,
  "What were you **arguing** about on the way?"
But they remained **silent**.
They had been discussing among themselves on the way
  who was the **greatest**.
Then he **sat** down, called the **Twelve**, and **said** to them,
  "If anyone wishes to be **first**,
  he shall be the **last** of all and the **servant** of all."
Taking a **child**, he placed it in their midst,
  and putting his **arms** around it, he said to them,
  "Whoever receives one **child** such as this in my **name**,
    receives **me**;
  and whoever receives **me**,
  receives not me but the One who **sent** me."

This scene follows the dramatic Transfiguration on Mount Tabor.

Three times in Mark's account Jesus speaks of his Passion, and each time the disciples' reaction disappoints.

Jesus is in teaching mode and he knows the topic is one they don't want to hear.

It's no wonder they don't dare question, given Jesus's response to Peter in the last chapter.

A new narrative beat begins with a distinct new mood.

Of course Jesus *knows* what they had been discussing.

Their silence signals how keenly they recognize their shallowness.

Jesus knows they need this lesson; with his earlier question, he demonstrated that need to them as well.

Such physical intimacy is not seen in Jesus, except with children. Though they don't realize it, the child represents the disciples. Anyone who welcomes a servant like them welcomes Jesus, and anyone who welcomes Jesus welcomes God. Jesus invites the disciples, and each of us, to become the *anawim*, the lowly and poor in spirit who inherit the Kingdom.

---

similar deeds. As so often in Mark, the disciples fail to connect Jesus the Messiah with suffering and execution. Jesus, however, turns their attention to a need for dependence on God through prayer.

In today's Gospel, Jesus teaches again, in unmistakable terms, that he will soon be handed over to those who will kill him. A sense of his impending arrest and execution would not have required of Jesus any superhuman knowledge. Anyone claiming to be, or acclaimed as, a messiah among the Jews would be considered a threat to Roman imperial rule, for Rome knew that

the Jewish people hoped for a new Davidic king to reestablish an independent kingdom. Both before and after Jesus, other "messiahs" appeared, and all met the same fate: Roman crucifixion for treason. The reference to Jesus's Resurrection is most likely added after the fact by the Evangelist; otherwise, the women at the empty tomb would hardly have expressed fear and bewilderment (16:8). Here Mark's focus remains on a messiah in the pattern of Isaiah's suffering servant.

The disciples again give ample evidence that they do not understand Jesus's

clear teaching; they fail to grasp not only his suffering but his servanthood. Focusing on neither, they wrangle about who is most important! Jesus's further lesson is simple but profound: he places before them a child (the Greek word also means "servant"), a person with no cultural status and nothing of his or her own. To receive such a one is to receive Jesus the Messiah; to understand Jesus, the disciples must accept him in the poverty and lack of status of a servant—but the servant of God.

TWENTY-SIXTH SUNDAY IN ORDINARY TIME

LECTIONARY #137

READING I   Numbers 11:25–29

A reading from the Book of Numbers

The LORD came down in the **cloud** and spoke to **Moses**.
Taking some of the **spirit** that was on Moses,
   the LORD bestowed it on the seventy **elders**;
   and as the spirit came to **rest** on them, they **prophesied**.

Now **two** men, one named **Eldad** and the other **Medad**,
   were not in the **gathering** but had been left in the camp.
They **too** had been on the list, but had not gone out to the **tent**;
   yet the **spirit** came to rest on them **also**,
   and they **prophesied** in the camp.
So, when a young man quickly told **Moses**,
   "Eldad and Medad are **prophesying** in the camp,"
   Joshua, son of **Nun**, who from his youth had been
     Moses' **aide**, said,
   "**Moses**, my lord, **stop** them."
But Moses answered him,
   "Are you jealous for **my** sake?
Would that **all** the people of the LORD were **prophets**!
Would that the LORD might bestow his **spirit** on them **all**!"

Because they're taken out of context, Scripture passages often seem to speak of striking, extraordinary things as if they were ordinary. It is up to you to communicate that "the Lord," not some neighbor, came to speak with Moses.

prophesied = PROF-uh-sĭd. Distributing the "spirit" among the "elders" is also extraordinary news; speak with reverence.

News of the two in the camp introduces a more mundane tone, but what occurred was certainly unexpected.

Eldad = EL-dad; Medad = MEE-dad; prophesying = PROF-uh-sĭ-ing

The young man's tone tells us he thinks Eldad and Medad are insubordinate; Joshua is quick to agree and to demand censure.

Moses is as strong as his young aide as he questions the sincerity of Joshua's motivation. But then Moses longs for an outpouring of God's spirit in an almost hushed and prayerful tone.

READING I | The fourth book of the Pentateuch, Numbers, is a loose collection of accounts related to the Hebrews' wilderness journey toward the Promised Land. It includes several census lists, a "numbering" of the people that gives the book its name; several trials, including lack of food and water; and clashes with various peoples the Hebrews encountered on their way into Canaan.

Immediately before today's reading, Moses has grown exasperated with the people's unrest; tiring of manna, they have complained repeatedly about lack of meat.

Moses in turn laments to God about his own perceived ill treatment, pleading that he cannot carry the burden of the entire people by himself. After promising an abundance of meat for the people, God turns to offer aid to Moses, instructing him to gather seventy elders around him at the meeting tent.

When Moses has done so, the Lord comes down to share the power of divine presence ("spirit") already laid upon Moses with the group of elders. When two of those who had been called but were tardy in their response also receive a share of divine spirit, Joshua objects. Moses tells his young aide to make no attempt to restrict any sharing of God's spirit, regardless of whom he deems worthy. Any and all who receive a share of this powerful presence can offer assistance in carrying out a God-given mission.

READING II | Today's passage from James shifts from instruction on how to live and proper dispositions underlying a righteous life to warnings for those who ignore such teaching. Immediately before today's Second Reading, the author

For meditation and context:

TO KEEP IN MIND

Word value: Words are your medium, like a painter's brush or a sculptor's chisel. You must understand the words before you can communicate them. Most words have a dictionary meaning (denotative) and an associational meaning (connotative). "House" and "home" both mean "dwelling," yet they communicate different feelings. Be alert to subtle differences in connotative meanings and express them.

This is the fifth of five consecutive weeks we read from the Letter of James.
James's words sound like an Old Testament prophecy; they are strong, threatening, and uncompromising. Recall a time you've felt righteous anger and let that inform your controlled but intense delivery.

Sometimes we "vent" anger for our own sake; but here the purpose is the good of the other—to warn them before it's too late!

No righteous person would delight over another's loss of wealth or their destruction, so regret must color your intonation of these hard lines.

You speak *on behalf of* the exploited, not as one of them. You are their advocate.

Increase intensity from the word "condemned" to the word "murdered" and take a slight pause after "the righteous one."

RESPONSORIAL PSALM   Psalm 19:8, 10, 12–13, 14 (9a)

R. The precepts of the Lord give joy to the heart.

The law of the LORD is perfect,
    refreshing the soul;
the decree of the LORD is trustworthy,
    giving wisdom to the simple.

The fear of the LORD is pure,
    enduring forever;
the ordinances of the LORD are true,
    all of them just.

Though your servant is careful of them,
    very diligent in keeping them,
yet who can detect failings?
    Cleanse me from my unknown faults!

From wanton sin especially, restrain your
        servant;
    let it not rule over me.
Then shall I be blameless and innocent
    of serious sin.

READING II   James 5:1–6

A reading from the Letter of Saint James

Come now, you **rich**, **weep** and **wail** over your
        impending **miseries**.
Your wealth has **rotted** away, your clothes have become
        moth-eaten,
    your gold and silver have **corroded**,
    and that corrosion will be a **testimony** against you;
    it will **devour** your flesh like a **fire**.
You have stored up **treasure** for the last days.
Behold, the wages you **withheld** from the workers
    who harvested your fields are crying **aloud**;
    and the cries of the harvesters
    have reached the ears of the Lord of **hosts**.
You have lived on earth in **luxury** and **pleasure**;
    you have **fattened** your hearts for the day of **slaughter**.
You have **condemned**;
    you have **murdered** the righteous one;
    he offers you no **resistance**.

has cautioned against overly confident preparation for the future, since all things are divinely ordained. In each present moment, one ought to do God's will, and whoever fails to do what he or she knows to be right commits sin.

James addresses the warning that follows in today's Scripture to those who expend great effort amassing wealth in this world. Again he stresses that the present world is transitory, and so the attempt to store up riches for the future is fruitless. Further, those who have cheated others in order to secure luxury for themselves will

find God on the side of the poor who suffered because of their grasping for wealth. Increasing riches and pleasure for oneself at the cost of fair treatment of others is momentary; God's just recompense will last forever.

GOSPEL   Mark has quite carefully structured the middle section of his Gospel account to stress both Jesus's identity as the Messiah who must suffer and die and the disciples' failure to

grasp this reality. Peter's confession of faith in Jesus as Messiah—and his refusal to connect that identity with Jesus's impending Passion—marks the beginning of this threefold section. In each part, Jesus first announces his coming suffering and death; then the disciples give evidence that they cannot or do not wish to understand his message; finally Jesus attempts to further instruct the uncomprehending disciples.

This Sunday's Gospel follows immediately upon last Sunday's reading, which ended with Jesus's admonition to allow God to act as God chooses in sending a

GOSPEL   Mark 9:38–43, 45, 47–48

A reading from the holy Gospel according to Mark

At that time, **John** said to **Jesus**,
  "**Teacher**, we saw someone driving out demons in your **name**,
  and we tried to **prevent** him because he does not **follow** us."
Jesus replied, "Do not **prevent** him.
There is no one who performs a mighty deed in my **name**
  who can at the **same** time speak **ill** of me.
For whoever is not **against** us is **for** us.
Anyone who gives you a cup of **water** to drink
  because you belong to **Christ**,
  amen, I say to you, will surely not lose his **reward**.

"Whoever causes one of these **little** ones who believe in me
      to **sin**,
  it would be better for him if a great **millstone**
  were put around his neck
  and he were thrown into the **sea**.
If your **hand** causes you to **sin**, **cut** it off.
It is better for you to enter into life **maimed**
  than with **two** hands to go into **Gehenna**,
  into the unquenchable **fire**.
And if your **foot** causes you to sin, **cut** if off.
It is better for you to enter into life **crippled**
  than with **two** feet to be thrown into **Gehenna**.
And if your **eye** causes you to sin, **pluck** it out.
Better for you to enter into the kingdom of God with **one** eye
  than with **two** eyes to be thrown into **Gehenna**,
  where 'their **worm** does not **die**, and the **fire** is not **quenched**.'"

John is eager to "report" on the outsider whom he thinks has usurped a privilege that doesn't belong to him.

Jesus, the teacher, immediately turns the moment into a learning opportunity: "Whoever is not against us . . ." Speak that classic adage with authority.

In fact, says Jesus, anything done for the sake of my name will be rewarded.

Only perdition is worse than non-existence; Jesus's warning to those who corrupt the innocent is indeed dire. Pull no punches; these warnings are for our good, reminding us all choices have consequences, even "unquenchable fire."

This is extremely well-crafted rhetoric that uses repetition to make and deepen its point: anything that threatens our eternal relationship with God is worth cutting off and plucking out. The images are intentionally stark and strong; let them do their work.

But of course, Jesus is speaking metaphorically. Habits and weaknesses are harder to cut off than limbs. The image of blind and limping followers should jolt us into the realization that it's worth every effort to remove any obstacle to our eternal salvation.

Messiah who appears not as mighty king but as lowly servant. The disciples soon demonstrate that they would still rather dictate to God, deciding who should and should not serve as a channel of God's power in overcoming evil. Mark follows with a collection of teachings with no discernible unifying theme; many are sayings that appear in various contexts in Matthew and Luke. Several sayings gathered here seem to present God's inclusiveness as a model to be followed.

The Evangelist then adds several sayings; the first cautions against causing others to sin, and the rest vividly illustrate that disciples must surrender anything that might cause them to sin. Jesus uses a common mode of instruction, the wise saying or proverb. The proverbs here do not literally call for amputation; they are concrete examples of a larger principle: anything that might cause a disciple to sin, however indispensable it might seem, must be renounced. Reference to punishment for sin in Gehenna reflects Jewish thought of the time, which included notions of a final judgment with reward or punishment for righteous or unrighteous lives. In actuality, Gehenna was the valley of ben Hinnom below Jerusalem, which served as the city dump, continually burning. It was also the place where Israelite kings had burned their own sons as offerings to a foreign god (Jeremiah 7:30–32). Gehenna thus served as an apt image of both sin and its punishment. Jesus's major teaching, however, focuses on avoidance of all that might lead to sin.

TWENTY-SEVENTH SUNDAY IN ORDINARY TIME

LECTIONARY #140

READING I   Genesis 2:18–24

A reading from the Book of Genesis

The LORD God said: "It is not good for the man to be **alone**.
I will make a suitable **partner** for him."
So the LORD God **formed** out of the **ground**
   various wild **animals** and various **birds** of the air,
   and he **brought** them to the man to see what he would
      call them;
   whatever the man **called** each of them would be its **name**.
The man gave names to all the **cattle**,
   all the **birds** of the **air**, and all wild **animals**;
   but **none** proved to be the suitable **partner** for the man.

So the LORD God cast a deep **sleep** on the man,
   and **while** he was asleep,
   he took out one of his **ribs** and closed up its place with **flesh**.
The LORD God then built up into a **woman** the rib
   that he had **taken** from the man.
When he **brought** her to the man, the man said:
   "**This** one, at last, is **bone** of my **bones**
   and **flesh** of my **flesh**;
   this one shall be called '**woman**,'
   for out of 'her **man**' this one has been taken."
That is why a man **leaves** his father and mother
   and clings to his **wife**,
   and the **two** of them become **one flesh**.

Genesis = JEN-uh-sis

God is portrayed as possessing naïve enthusiasm, presenting the various creatures to the man as if one might become his suitable partner. Sustain a lively energy.

Naming the animals is a great privilege given the man, for it establishes his authority over God's creatures.

Speak of the naming with awareness of its significance; your tone conveys contentment and a sense of fulfillment.

As you begin "So the Lord," suggest that God has already crafted a new plan and eagerly dives into it

Your tone should suggest that God is pleased with this new creation and certain this will satisfy.

Don't rush Adam's dialogue and don't read as if he's giving her a stamp of approval. First he recognizes her as of the same stature and dignity as he, and then he enthuses that, as creatures of the same flesh and bone, they can stand side by side.

The final sentence is commentary, not story, so it requires a new attitude. Speak directly to the assembly, perhaps from memory, this ancient teaching of the bond between husband and wife.

READING I Today's account of God distinguishing male and female within humankind and their oneness when united in marriage is actually part of a second creation story in Genesis. The first story presents God forming major elements of Creation in an orderly fashion, with humankind created last. The Hebrew word *adam* signifies the human race, thus Genesis 1:27 states that God created "them; male and female." In this account, there is no further reference to distinct genders, and humans appear to be God's final creation, caretakers of other creatures.

In contrast, the second story, from which today's reading is taken, presents humans as the first of God's creation. Leading up to today's passage, God created *adam* from the clay of the earth and blew into it divine spirit or life-breath (the Hebrew word *ruah* can mean breath, wind, or spirit), and *adam* became "a living being" which God settled in the garden of Eden.

Today's First Reading continues the story by recognizing that the human creature is not meant for isolation. God creates many other living beings, and appoints "the man" to name them; the command to name the other creatures gives the human being authority in relation to them. But none of them proves to be a fitting companion to the man. Older translations of the creation of woman as "helper" to the man aroused controversy, because they seemed to suggest that she had an inferior role. Recent translations more accurately render the meaning of the original Hebrew, which points to a partnership of equals.

The story further describes the woman made from a rib taken from the man; both this image and Hebrew wordplay indicate that male and female belong to, and

For meditation and context:

TO KEEP IN MIND

When practicing, **read Scriptures aloud**, taking note of stress and pause suggestions. After several readings, alter the stress markings to suit your style and interpretation.

This is the first of six consecutive weeks we read from Hebrews.

Jesus's humanity and his suffering are signs of his love, not reasons to doubt the faith.

The author continues his lesson about why God allowed Jesus to suffer: he through whom all was created and who leads all to "glory" ("salvation") became the perfect leader of us all through obedience, that is, his willingness to endure suffering.

Like us, Jesus came from God; therefore, he is our brother and proudly wears that title.

The Pharisees come with ulterior motives. Help us hear that through your tone.

RESPONSORIAL PSALM   Psalm 128:1–2, 3, 4–5, 6 (5)

R. May the Lord bless us all the days of our lives.

Blessed are you who fear the LORD,
   who walk in his ways!
For you shall eat the fruit of your handiwork;
   blessed shall you be, and favored.

Your wife shall be like a fruitful vine
   in the recesses of your home;
your children like olive plants
   around your table.

Behold, thus is the man blessed
   who fears the LORD.
The LORD bless you from Zion:
   may you see the prosperity of Jerusalem
   all the days of your life.

May you see your children's children.
   Peace be upon Israel!

READING II   Hebrews 2:9–11

A reading from the Letter to the Hebrews

Brothers and sisters:
He "for a little **while**" was made "**lower** than the **angels**,"
   that by the grace of God he might taste **death** for **everyone**.

For it was **fitting** that he,
   for whom and **through** whom all things **exist**,
   in bringing many children to **glory**,
   should make the leader to their salvation **perfect**
      through **suffering**.
He who **consecrates** and those who are **being** consecrated
   all have one **origin**.
Therefore, he is not **ashamed** to call them "**brothers**."

GOSPEL   Mark 10:2–16

A reading from the holy Gospel according to Mark

The **Pharisees** approached **Jesus** and asked,
   "Is it **lawful** for a husband to **divorce** his wife?"
They were **testing** him.

participate in, one another (the Hebrew words for man and woman share the same root), yet are distinct. Today's passage concludes with a concise but potent image: man and woman united in marriage become one living being. The word here is the same as in the creation of *adam; "*flesh" also signifies a unit, a single living person. This powerful statement forms the basis of Jesus's response to his questioner in today's Gospel.

 READING II This Sunday begins a lengthy series of readings

from Hebrews, described by the unknown author as an exhortation, which actually resembles a sermon more than a letter. The author also emphasizes that Jesus Christ, who fully shared humanity in his suffering and Death, is now also revealed as divine Son of God.

That emphasis on Jesus's divine-human identity appears in today's reading. In the preceding chapter, the writer describes the resurrected Jesus enthroned at God's side, placed higher than the angels. Here, he focuses on the self-emptying of the Son of God in sharing the experience of all human

beings. The divine Son made himself subject to the universal human experiences of anguish and mortality; by so doing, he brought many with him to share God's life. Since both the Son and those he saved through sharing humanity have the same origin, God the Creator, the Son does not hesitate to name those being saved as brothers and sisters (the Greek word *adelphos* can mean both).

GOSPEL Last Sunday's Gospel ended with Jesus teaching several proverbs to the inner circle of his disciples.

Jesus engages in the repartee answering with another question.

Their overeager response seems well rehearsed.

Jesus, too, is ready and he stuns them with a strong, well-reasoned reply. They have fooled others and themselves too long with their distortions of God's will.

Cite the text from Genesis in a tone that suggests the holiness of the marital bond.

Here is the answer to their question, but not the one they were seeking.

The disciples wait till they're alone to ask for clarification. They, too, are likely thrown by his unnuanced reply.

This is one of Jesus's hard teachings that reminds us of our need to rely on God's mercy.

The marriage issue is left behind and a new narrative beat begins. Speak with ample energy.

Jesus is "indignant" that they fail to understand his priorities. His dialogue begins with the tension of his rebuke and transitions into words of warning spoken for the good of all.

Jesus's fondness for children clearly transcends their usefulness as images of the Kingdom. His love for them is genuine . . . as is his love for all who embrace the Kingdom.

He said to them in reply, "What did **Moses** command you?"
They replied,
　"Moses permitted a **husband** to write a bill of **divorce**
　and **dismiss** her."
But Jesus told them,
　"Because of the **hardness** of your **hearts**
　he wrote you this commandment.
But from the beginning of **creation**, *God made them male*
　　and female.
For this reason a man shall leave his father and mother
　and be joined to his wife,
　and the two shall become one flesh.
So they are **no longer** two but **one** flesh.
Therefore what **God** has joined **together**,
　no human **being** must **separate**."
In the **house** the **disciples** again questioned Jesus about this.
He **said** to them,
　"Whoever **divorces** his wife and marries **another**
　commits **adultery** against her;
　and if **she** divorces her **husband** and marries another,
　she commits adultery."

And people were bringing **children** to him that he might
　　touch them,
　but the disciples **rebuked** them.
When Jesus **saw** this he became **indignant** and said to them,
　"Let the children **come** to me;
　do not **prevent** them, for the kingdom of God **belongs** to such
　　as these.
Amen, I **say** to you,
　whoever does not **accept** the kingdom of God like a **child**
　　will not **enter** it."
Then he **embraced** them and **blessed** them,
　placing his **hands** on them.

[Shorter: Mark 10:2–12]

Today, the context changes with Jesus moving to a new locale where crowds gather around him. A Pharisee (a member of a Jewish sect that strove to live as faithful Jews by following the Law of Moses with utmost care) poses a question to test Jesus. It was a question debated by several schools of thought at the time: may a man divorce his wife? While it was true that Mosaic Law permitted divorce, views of acceptable grounds for divorce varied considerably. Following Jewish religious and cultural thought of the time, the Pharisee

inquires only about a man initiating divorce, since women were not permitted to do so.

Jesus roots his fundamental response not in Moses, but in creation itself. He quotes today's First Reading, pointing out that God's intent seems to be that husband and wife form a bond such that they become like a single living being, not a loose linkage of easily separated parts. Seeing that Jesus reaches beyond interpretation of Moses to the Creator's purposes for humankind, the Pharisee makes no response. The disciples, however, continue to question. Jesus in effect repeats his

response, adding an important detail that would likely have caused them further puzzlement. He states that either a man or a woman who divorces a marriage partner "commits adultery." With this teaching, Jesus treats man and woman in marriage as equals, with equal duties and rights. This indirectly reinforces his essential point: in marriage, the two partners are meant to create such oneness that they become an unbreakable unit.

TWENTY-EIGHTH SUNDAY IN ORDINARY TIME

LECTIONARY #143

READING I Wisdom 7:7–11

A reading from the Book of Wisdom

I **prayed**, and **prudence** was given me;
  I **pleaded**, and the spirit of **wisdom** came to me.
I **preferred** her to **scepter** and **throne**,
and deemed riches **nothing** in **comparison** with her,
  nor did I liken any priceless **gem** to her;
because all **gold**, in **view** of her, is a little **sand**,
  and **before** her, **silver** is to be accounted **mire**.
Beyond **health** and **comeliness** I loved her,
and I chose to have **her** rather than the **light**,
  because the **splendor** of her never yields to **sleep**.
Yet **all** good things together came to me in her company,
  and countless **riches** at her hands.

RESPONSORIAL PSALM Psalm 90:12–13, 14–15, 16–17 (14)

R. **Fill us with your love, O Lord, and we will sing for joy!**

Teach us to number our days aright,
  that we may gain wisdom of heart.
Return, O LORD! How long?
  Have pity on your servants!

Fill us at daybreak with your kindness,
  that we may shout for joy and gladness all
  our days.
Make us glad, for the days when you
  afflicted us,
  for the years when we saw evil.

Let your work be seen by your servants
  and your glory by their children;
and may the gracious care of the Lord our
  God be ours;
  prosper the work of our hands for us!
  Prosper the work of our hands!

Only if you have truly longed for something wonderful and truly appreciated its worth before you received it—education, love, humility—will you be able to understand and do justice to this text. This is poetry (not prose) that uses grand imagery and exaggerated speech to make its point.

"Pleaded is an intensification of the earlier word "prayed."

"Scepter and throne" are metaphors for authority and power.

"Gold" and "silver" require a positive tone because of their value, but they come off as worthless as tin compared to wisdom.

Praise of wisdom redoubles: even good *health* and good *looks* pale in comparison to her.

With wisdom comes *all* true riches. End on a note of joy.

For meditation and context:

TO KEEP IN MIND
Context: Who is speaking in this text? What are the circumstances?

READING I Today's passage from the Book of Wisdom appears near the beginning of a section presented as King Solomon's expansive praise of Wisdom and her incomparable value. By this time in Israel's history, Wisdom was commonly personified as a female figure, sometimes contrasted with a woman named Folly, hence designated "she." Jewish tradition lent authority to this late writing in the Old Testament, sometimes called the Wisdom of Solomon, by ascribing it to this ancient figure of a wise king.

In today's reading, the author presents King Solomon petitioning God for divine presence and guidance in the form of wisdom, described elsewhere in the Bible as coming from the mouth of God, mediating the Spirit of God, and the shining of eternal light into this world (Proverbs 8:12; Wisdom 9:17, 7:26). The king thus values wisdom above even his royal power and wealth of any kind. Not only material riches, but physical beauty and well-being pale in comparison to the riches of wisdom. Today's Responsorial Psalm indicates the true reason for such an exalted view of wisdom:

what Solomon values is "wisdom of the heart." Because Jewish thought envisioned the heart as the core and center of a person, one discerned, weighed, and judged in the heart, which was thus the seat of decision and action. A heart illumined and guided by God's guiding presence is what Solomon sought and praised in fervent prayer.

READING II This brief passage from Hebrews presents challenges for interpretation, as is true of other portions of this work. The author speaks of the "living and effective" word of God. Does

269

This is the second of six consecutive weeks we read from Hebrews.

Take extra care not to rush this brief reading. It was addressed to people who had grown cold in their faith. That may be true of your assembly, so use these words to rouse them.

God's word is a word of power, able to transform even the coldest heart.

God sees us exactly as we are. When speaking "naked" and "exposed" use more energy on the second word.

Rendering an account can be an intimidating endeavor.

READING II   Hebrews 4:12–13

A reading from the Letter to the Hebrews

Brothers and sisters:
Indeed the word of God is **living** and **effective**,
 sharper than any two-edged **sword**,
 penetrating even between **soul** and **spirit**, **joints** and **marrow**,
 and able to discern **reflections** and thoughts of the **heart**.
No creature is **concealed** from him,
 but everything is **naked** and **exposed** to the eyes of him
 to whom we must render an **account**.

GOSPEL   Mark 10:17–30

A reading from the holy Gospel according to Mark

The young man arrives in haste, but full of sincerity, demonstrated by his kneeling.

In questioning the young man's use of "good" (spoken with the best of intentions) Jesus seems to ask whether he really understands what he's saying or whom he's addressing.

Speak the Commandments briskly. Jesus quotes them on the way to making his larger point.

The young man responds in a tone that's more inquisitive than prideful: Is what I've done all my life sufficient?

Note Jesus's love for the young man.

"Go, sell" is Jesus's way of saying: here is what you need for perfection.

As **Jesus** was setting out on a **journey**, a man **ran** up,
 knelt down before him, and **asked** him,
 "Good **teacher**, what must I do to inherit eternal **life**?"
Jesus **answered** him, "Why do you call me **good**?
No one is good but God **alone**.
You **know** the **commandments**: *You shall not* **kill**;
 you shall not commit **adultery***;
 you shall not **steal***;
 you shall not bear false **witness***;
 you shall not **defraud***;
 honor your **father** *and your* **mother***."
He replied and said to him,
 "**Teacher**, **all** of these I have observed from my **youth**."
Jesus, looking at him, **loved** him and said to him,
 "You are lacking in **one** thing.
Go, **sell** what you have, and give to the **poor**
 and you will have treasure in **heaven**; then come, **follow** me."

the "word" here refer to the Jewish understanding of God's Word, known to bring about what it says; to wisdom, to which it was nearly equated at this time; to the Gospel; or to Christ as divine Wisdom incarnate? It is quite possible that the author, who is clearly familiar with the Old Testament Scriptures, intends any and all of these possibilities.

The beginning of the chapter speaks of receiving the "good news" of Christ, and the author also seems to refer to Wisdom 18:15–16, which compares God's word to a

sharp sword accomplishing the final plague on Egypt, thus leading to the people's deliverance. The discerning function of the word of God also connected it to wisdom, as noted above. Since the verses immediately following today's reading clearly describe Christ, the writer might also intend to suggest that Christ is the Word/Wisdom of God in the flesh. Whatever the specific or inclusive meaning of the "word of God" in this passage, the author stresses that the Word is as alive, discerning, and all-seeing as its origin, God.

GOSPEL   In today's Gospel, Mark continues Jesus's teaching after the second prediction of his Passion. Mark seems to gather together various sayings and teachings, probably originally given in diverse circumstances. Immediately before today's passage, Jesus states that only those who accept the Kingdom of God like a child (with a sense of total dependence) will enter it.

Then a man approaches, addressing Jesus as "Good teacher" and inquiring how to reach eternal life. Jesus first responds to

The young man is immediately saddened. He hadn't expected this. Speak of "many possessions" with Jesus's awareness of the weighty spiritual burden they so easily become.

Proclaim the classic "How hard it is" verse from memory.

The shock of the disciples reflects the belief that wealth demonstrated divine favor.

Jesus shares the hard saying about "the eye of a needle" without immediate commentary, leaving the disciples truly shocked.

His commentary follows in the classic line that all is possible for God.

Peter points out how *they* have made the very sacrifices Jesus calls for.

Don't rush the long litany of things "given up." Your tone should promise the bounty of God's mercy.

Jesus's news is not all good, for he promises "persecutions" along with the various rewards. Failing to highlight that word would rob your listeners of a great truth.

At that statement his face **fell**,
  and he went away **sad**, for he had **many** possessions.

Jesus looked around and said to his **disciples**,
  "How **hard** it is for those who have **wealth**
  to enter the kingdom of God!"
The disciples were **amazed** at his words.
So Jesus **again** said to them in reply,
  "**Children**, how **hard** it is to enter the kingdom of God!
It is easier for a **camel** to pass through the **eye** of a **needle**
  than for one who is **rich** to enter the kingdom of God."
They were exceedingly **astonished** and said among themselves,
  "Then who **can** be saved?"
Jesus **looked** at them and said,
  "For human **beings** it is **impossible**, but not for **God**.
All things are possible for God."
Peter began to say to him,
  "We have given up **everything** and followed you."
Jesus said, "**Amen**, I say to you,
  there is no one who has given up **house** or **brothers** or **sisters**
  or **mother** or **father** or **children** or **lands**
  for **my** sake and for the sake of the **gospel**
  who will not receive a hundred times **more** now in this
    present age:
  houses and **brothers** and **sisters**
  and **mothers** and **children** and **lands**,
  with **persecutions**, and eternal **life** in the age to **come**."

[Shorter: Mark 10:17–27]

> **TO KEEP IN MIND**
> **Pray the Scriptures:** Make reading these Scriptures a part of your prayer life every week, and especially during the week prior to the liturgy in which you will proclaim.

the man's manner of address, pointing away from himself and toward God, who alone is good. Probing further, Jesus reminds the man that he surely knows the way to eternal life, for it is summed up in God's commandments. At the questioner's statement that he has kept these commands from youth, Jesus lovingly tells him that he lacks one thing: to relinquish possessions, share them with the poor, and then follow as disciple. When the man who possesses much turns away, Jesus addresses the disciples with a shocking teaching: it is exceedingly difficult for those with riches to enter the Kingdom of God. Their amazement is most likely rooted in the long-held belief, expressed in the Old Testament, that wealth signified divine favor. But Jesus resists any claim to participation in the Kingdom based on wealth and its companions, power and status.

The essence of Jesus's teaching today seems to be the need to accept the Kingdom of God like a child. In Jewish culture of the time, children had virtually no status and no rights, and so totally depended upon others for life and sustenance. Jesus teaches that those who cannot renounce any and all perceived entitlements to sharing in the Kingdom, whether good actions, material riches, prestige, or power, cannot enter. Such total surrender may seem humanly impossible, but by dependence upon God alone, "all things are possible."

TWENTY-NINTH SUNDAY IN ORDINARY TIME

Isaiah = ī-ZAY-uh

Plucked from the midst of the longer song of the suffering servant (proclaimed each Palm Sunday) this brief excerpt requires your best effort to slow down and to use silence and pauses to convey meaning.

Try this phrasing: "The Lord / was pleased / to crush him / in infirmity. To connect with the Gospel, stress his willing self-sacrifice.

"Because of his affliction" narrates the fate of the Servant *and* of those who benefit from his selfless service. His suffering brings good to many, so speak in a hopeful tone.

For meditation and context:

TO KEEP IN MIND

Names of characters: Often the first word of a reading. Lift out the names to ensure listeners don't miss who the subject is.

LECTIONARY #146

READING I   Isaiah 53:10–11

A reading from the Book of the Prophet Isaiah

The LORD was pleased
　　to **crush** him in **infirmity**.

If he gives his **life** as an offering for **sin**,
　　he shall see his descendants in a **long** life,
　　and the **will** of the LORD shall be **accomplished**
　　through him.

Because of his **affliction**
　　he shall see the **light** in **fullness** of days;
through his **suffering**, my servant shall justify **many**,
　　and their **guilt** he shall **bear**.

RESPONSORIAL PSALM   Psalm 33:4–5, 18–19, 20, 22 (22)

R. Lord, let your mercy be on us, as we place our trust in you.

Upright is the word of the LORD,
　　and all his works are trustworthy.
He loves justice and right;
　　of the kindness of the LORD the earth
　　is full.

See, the eyes of the LORD are upon those
　　who fear him,
　　upon those who hope for his kindness;
to deliver them from death
　　and preserve them in spite of famine.

Our soul waits for the LORD,
　　who is our help and our shield.
May your kindness, O LORD, be upon us
　　who have put our hope in you.

READING I   The First Reading returns to Isaiah's figure of the suffering servant, seen five weeks ago and related to Jesus's first prediction of impending arrest and execution in Mark. Today's Scripture comes from the prophet's fourth and final poem, which is also his most extended description of the servant's suffering and its purpose. Before today's excerpt, the poem describes how the servant of the LORD silently endures the rejection and avoidance of others as well as physical abuse and unjust condemnation.

The prophet states that God has laid upon the servant the guilt of all, possibly referring to the scapegoat related to Aaron's ritual of atonement in the wilderness journey. Leviticus 20:22 describes Aaron confessing the sins of all Israel over the goat, which then carried them all into the wilderness. By the time of this prophecy, Israel had developed a belief that one person's suffering could compensate for the sin of many.

Isaiah presents the suffering servant as designated by God to fulfill such a role. It is part of the divine plan that the servant's death should serve as an offering that will bear the guilt of the people and "justify"— that is, make righteous, many.

READING I   Among several major emphases, Hebrews portrays Jesus Christ as the true and final High Priest. In Judaism, the high priest alone could enter the Holy of Holies in the Temple,

READING II   Hebrews 4:14–16

A reading from the Letter to the Hebrews

Brothers and sisters:
Since we have a **great** high priest who has passed through
        the **heavens**,
    Jesus, the Son of **God**,
    let us hold **fast** to our confession.
For we do not have a high priest
    who is **unable** to sympathize with our weaknesses,
    but one who has **similarly** been tested in every way,
    yet without **sin**.
So let us confidently **approach** the throne of grace
    to receive **mercy** and to find **grace** for timely help.

GOSPEL   Mark 10:35–45

A reading from the holy Gospel according to Mark

James and **John**, the sons of **Zebedee**, came to **Jesus** and said
        to him,
    "**Teacher**, we want you to do for us whatever we **ask** of you."
He replied, "What do you wish me to do for you?"
They answered him, "Grant that in your **glory**
    we may sit one at your **right** and the other at your **left**."
Jesus said to them, "You do not know what you are **asking**.
Can you drink the cup that **I** drink
    or be **baptized** with the baptism with which **I** am baptized?"
They said to him, "We **can**."
Jesus said to them, "The cup that I drink, you **will** drink,
    and with the baptism with which I am baptized, **you** will
        be baptized;

This is the third of six consecutive weeks we read from Hebrews.

Because of the brevity of the text, your tone will become what the assembly best remembers. Let it be upbeat and full of hope.

It is as if you were giving a toast in honor of Jesus who, as the Gospel will tell us, came to serve and to suffer for us.

Jesus's likeness to us in all things but sin is a critical teaching.

Persuade your listeners that we *can* approach God with confidence, and the *proof* is what Christ did for us.

Take time to identify the brazen brothers.

Imagine the band of Apostles on the road, and James and John catching up to Jesus and making their request as they continue walking. As he walks, Jesus responds, treating the question lightly.

Because they've rehearsed their request, the brothers speak it quickly. Jesus plays along and asks his own question to which they reply with too little thought and too much chutzpah.

Imagine that now Jesus halts the group and replies directly to James and John that indeed they will endure a fate like his. But even this won't guarantee them a special place in the Kingdom for that privilege is reserved to the Father.

---

the physical place where God was thought to dwell among the covenant people. The high priest did so once a year, on the Day of Atonement, to make an offering for the sins of the entire people. He thus represents the one who serves the most pivotal role as intermediary between God and the people. The author interprets Jesus as Son of God and the great high priest who has been raised to the fullness of God's presence, there to atone fully for all.

But in the very next sentence, the author who has just affirmed Jesus as Son of God also underscores his full humanity.

Jesus is not a High Priest who places himself above or apart from his people, but one who has shared in human suffering and weakness, tried and tested like every human being—yet he did not sin. With such a high priest, believers can also approach God, confident in an intermediary who is himself both divine and human.

GOSPEL   The immediate context for today's Gospel is highly significant, for it highlights the depth of the disciples' failure to hear Jesus's repeated message. For the third time, Jesus has told his followers of his looming arrest, torture, and execution. But now not just Peter but others among the Twelve seem to imagine Jesus only as a gloriously reigning Messiah—with themselves holding cabinet positions in his Kingdom!

Jesus asks if they can drink the cup—that is, accept the destiny planned by God—that he will drink, and in their arrogance they reply positively. Jesus's response may be Mark's reminder to his own hearers of the bitter cup they have drunk, since at the time of his writing several key Apostles

As word filters back through the other "ten,"
their hackles are raised, so Jesus takes the
opportunity to teach them all a lesson.

Jesus summons his best energies to instruct
them with patience.

"But it shall not be so" is not a reprimand but
a call to embrace a higher calling.

As always, Jesus's best lesson is the example
of his own life.

> but to sit at my right or at my left is not mine to **give**
> but is for those for whom it has been **prepared**."
> When the **ten** heard this, they became **indignant** at James
>   and John.
> Jesus **summoned** them and said to them,
>   "You know that those who are recognized as **rulers** over
>   the Gentiles
>   **lord** it over them,
>   and their great ones make their **authority** over them **felt**.
> But it shall **not** be so among **you**.
> **Rather**, whoever wishes to be **great** among you will be
>   your **servant**;
>   whoever wishes to be **first** among you will be the **slave** of all.
> For the Son of Man did not come to be **served**
>   but to **serve** and to give his **life** as a ransom for **many**."

[Shorter: Mark 10:42–45]

TO KEEP IN MIND
Dialogue imitates real conversation, so it often moves faster than the rest of the passage.

THE 4 STEPS OF *LECTIO DIVINA* OR PRAYERFUL READING

1. *Lectio:* Read a Scripture passage aloud slowly. Notice what phrase captures your attention and be attentive to its meaning. Silent pause.

2. *Meditatio:* Read the passage aloud slowly again, reflecting on the passage, allowing God to speak to you through it. Silent pause.

3. *Oratio:* Read it aloud slowly a third time, allowing it to be your prayer or response to God's gift of insight to you. Silent pause.

4. *Contemplatio:* Read it aloud slowly a fourth time, now resting in God's word.

---

had been recently martyred. Jesus then makes one last attempt to clarify by word the message he has repeatedly taught, the message his disciples have steadfastly failed to hear. After this crucial point in Mark, Jesus will enter Jerusalem, there to embody his insistent teaching that as Messiah his role is one of service to all, despite the cost of a torturous death. Today's reading focuses on Jesus calling his disciples to service rather than to seeking glory as part of a royal retinue.

In his last instruction given directly to his closest followers, Jesus contrasts modes of authority. In the Roman Empire, rulers frequently practiced complete and arbitrary power, sometimes in the most ruthless fashion. They seemed to equate authority with sheer power to work their will over others, and did not hesitate to demonstrate this power. Such behavior among "the Gentiles" must never be the model for leaders among Jesus's disciples. In imitation of their own leader, they must aspire to greatness through service to others. Mark underscores Jesus's point by using the specific word for "slave" (*doulos*) in describing the disciples' role. This word is probably meant to shock Mark's audience into hearing the reality of Jesus's instruction, since they would be well aware of the treatment and status of slaves in an empire where one-third of the population fell into this category.

Clearly referring to Isaiah's suffering servant (53:10–12), Jesus summarizes his own identity and teaching for disciples: because Jesus himself serves the needs of all at the cost of death itself, those who follow in his footsteps can do no less.

THIRTIETH SUNDAY IN ORDINARY TIME

LECTIONARY #149

READING I   Jeremiah 31:7–9

Jeremiah = jayr-uh-MĪ-uh

Jacob = JAY-kuhb

Set the stage for the Gospel miracle by rousing hope in your listeners with these poetic and elegant words of healing. God is the speaker throughout.

The reading begins with imperatives: "Shout . . . exult . . . proclaim." Speak joyfully, not like a commander.

"I will bring them back" alludes to the end of exile. God will bring them home, wiping away their tears and making them whole.

Speak with tenderness of the blind and lame, expectant mothers, and those who still shed tears.

"I will lead" requires a tone of authority and tenderness.

The image of God as "father" gives you your dominant image for the entire text. Ephraim represents the nation as God's beloved child.

Ephraim = EE-fray-im or EF-r*m

A reading from the Book of the Prophet Jeremiah

Thus says the LORD:
Shout with **joy** for Jacob,
    exult at the head of the nations;
    proclaim your **praise** and say:
The LORD has **delivered** his people,
    the **remnant** of Israel.
Behold, I will bring them **back**
    from the land of the north;
I will **gather** them from the ends of the world,
    with the **blind** and the **lame** in their midst,
the **mothers** and those with **child**;
    they shall **return** as an immense **throng**.
They departed in **tears**,
    but I will **console** them and **guide** them;
I will lead them to brooks of **water**,
    on a **level** road, so that none shall **stumble**.
For I am a **father** to Israel,
    Ephraim is my **first-born**.

READING I Today we hear part of Jeremiah's promise of future restoration for God's people, a renewed life beyond any previously known. Even as the kingdom of Judah continues its dissolution, nearing its final end, the prophet, relying on an ever-faithful God, promises that beyond destruction and exile lies a recreated people. All this will be solely a divine work beyond human power. When the scattered people of Israel are again gathered into one, their deliverance will call forth shouts of joy and praise for the LORD, the only source of hope and deliverance. Their covenant God will continue to act as a loving father who never abandons a wayward child, but continues to give life in any and all circumstances.

On the one hand, the prophet anticipated God's rebuilding a people after destruction and exile; on the other, this and similar passages from Jeremiah and other prophets expanded into new meaning in the following centuries. God's people were not restored as an earthly kingdom, but they began to look forward to a new and definitive act of God that would renew all creation. In God's future age of salvation, wholeness, healing, and peace in all relationships would reign, ending all human ills of body and spirit. This is Jeremiah's ultimate vision of a God who would bring final salvation to a sinful, scattered people, treating them as a favored firstborn and renewing all creation.

For meditation and context:

TO KEEP IN MIND

The opening: Establish eye contact and announce, from memory, "A reading from . . . ." Then take a pause (three full beats!) before starting the reading. The correct pronunciation is "A [uh] reading from" instead of "A [ay] reading from."

This is the fourth of six consecutive weeks we read from Hebrews.

This is a teaching text, but also more. Your listeners should be left with a feeling of gratitude for the role Christ plays in God's plan of salvation.

First the author speaks of the human high priests of the old covenant: because they are also sinners they must offer sacrifice for us *and* for themselves.

The role of high priest is given, not taken onto oneself.

Christ, too, accepted his role; he did not take it upon himself.

The Scripture quotations express the Father's love for his Son. Jesus is both "Son" and "priest" and therefore the consummate intermediary between us and God.

Melchizedek = mel-KEEZ-ih-dek

RESPONSORIAL PSALM   Psalm 126:1–2, 2–3, 4–5, 6 (3)

R. The Lord has done great things for us; we are filled with joy.

When the LORD brought back the captives of Zion,
   we were like men dreaming.
Then our mouth was filled with laughter,
   and our tongue with rejoicing.

Then they said among the nations,
   "The LORD has done great things
     for them."
The LORD has done great things for us;
   we are glad indeed.

Restore our fortunes, O LORD,
   like the torrents in the southern desert.
Those that sow in tears
   shall reap rejoicing.

Although they go forth weeping,
   carrying the seed to be sown,
they shall come back rejoicing,
   carrying their sheaves.

READING II   Hebrews 5:1–6

A reading from the Letter to the Hebrews

Brothers and sisters:
Every **high** priest is taken from among **men**
   and made their **representative** before **God**,
   to offer **gifts** and **sacrifices** for **sins**.
He is able to deal **patiently** with the **ignorant** and **erring**,
   for he **himself** is beset by **weakness**
   and so, for **this** reason, must make sin offerings for **himself**
   as well as for the **people**.
No one takes this honor upon **himself**
   but only when called by **God**,
   just as **Aaron** was.
In the **same** way,
   it was not **Christ** who glorified himself in becoming
     high priest,
   but rather the one who said to him:
     *You are my **son**: this day I have **begotten** you;*
   just as he says in another place:
     *You are a priest **forever***
       *according to the order of **Melchizedek**.*

READING II | Last Sunday's reading from Hebrews declared the full humanity of Jesus, tested in every way that we are but never choosing sin. Today the author again insists that Christ intimately experienced the struggle and weakness shared by all human beings. But he also attests that the totally human Jesus is Son of God as well, and so becomes the final High Priest, the perfect mediator between humankind and God. Jesus knows human trial and weakness by experience, and so understands human failings and treats them with patience. Called by God to do so,

he brings all humankind with him to God for healing and restoration. As the exemplar of full humanity recreated by divine power, he also gives glory to God who has made him Son as well as High Priest. One Jesus Christ, truly human and truly divine, stands revealed as the perfect high priest who makes the self-offering that fully unites humankind and God forever. In the biblical mind, such oneness is the ultimate purpose of all sacrifice.

GOSPEL | Today's Gospel serves as an important transition in

Mark's account of the Good News. As previously noted, Mark writes for a community suffering confusion, loss, and persecution, and so he emphasizes Jesus as the Messiah who inaugurates God's final rule in the pattern of Isaiah's suffering servant. This healing account, like other miracle stories in Mark, serves to demonstrate that the Kingdom of God truly has begun in Jesus, since through him God overcomes the evil of every kind of illness and suffering. The story of Bartimaeus also closes the important three-part section of Mark in which Jesus attempts in vain to clarify his

GOSPEL   Mark 10:46–52

A reading from the holy Gospel according to Mark

As Jesus was leaving **Jericho** with his **disciples** and a siz
 able **crowd**,
   Bartimaeus, a **blind** man, the son of **Timaeus**,
   sat by the roadside **begging**.
On hearing that it was Jesus of **Nazareth**,
   he began to **cry** out and say,
   "**Jesus**, son of **David**, have **pity** on me."
And many **rebuked** him, telling him to be **silent**.
But he kept calling out all the **more**,
   "Son of **David**, have **pity** on me."
Jesus **stopped** and said, "**Call** him."
So they **called** the blind man, saying to him,
   "Take **courage**; get **up**, **Jesus** is calling you."
He **threw** aside his cloak, **sprang** up, and **came** to Jesus.
Jesus said to him in reply, "What do you want me to **do** for you?"
The blind man replied to him, "Master, I want to **see**."
Jesus told him, "Go your way; your **faith** has **saved** you."
Immediately he received his **sight**
   and **followed** him on the way.

Jericho = JAYR-ih-koh

The size of the crowd explains Bartimaeus's need to shout.

The identity of the blind man is well established.

Suggest the great effort it took for him to get Jesus's attention.

He keeps calling even over the crowd's rebukes.

Pause briefly before speaking, "Call him."

Now the crowd vies to help him to Jesus.

Note the verbs "threw," "sprang," and "came" that suggest a sudden commotion.

Bartimaeus's request is urgent and moving.

Note that here Jesus never touches the man to heal him.

With sight comes the responsibility to "follow."

TO KEEP IN MIND
The closing: Pause (three beats!) after ending the text. Then, with sustained eye contact, announce from memory, "The word [Gospel] of the Lord." Always pronounce "the" as "thuh" except before words beginning with a vowel, as in "thee Acts of the Apostles." Maintain eye contact while the assembly makes its response.

mission as Suffering Servant of God rather than triumphant earthly king. Immediately after this miracle story, Jesus enters Jerusalem to begin the final act in the drama of the Suffering Servant-Messiah; here, Jesus will fully reveal this identity in word and deed as he willingly enters into his Passion and Death.

Mark employs a technique called "framing," which sets off important content with a similar account at the beginning and end of a section. The elements of the frame serve as a kind of commentary on what appears within it. Two stories of Jesus heal-ing a blind man punctuate Mark's tripar-tite portrayal of Jesus proclaiming his impending suffering and execution, repeat-edly followed by the disciples' lack of understanding and acceptance of this real-ity. Last Sunday's Gospel revealed the depth of the disciples' failure to comprehend Jesus's message and identity. Their blind-ness was evident as they bickered over who would hold the position of greatest authority in Jesus's Kingdom.

The beginning of Mark's frame (8:22–26) indicated that the process of coming to see happens only gradually and in stages. Even so, the disciples could not—or would not—see the reality of a Messiah who would suffer and die. With the healing of blind Bartimaeus, Mark places before us one who quickly comes to see through the persistence of faith. In Jesus's words, "your faith has saved you," we perceive the real-ity of God's Kingdom: the blind man sees Jesus with the eyes of faith, and so is saved, healed, made whole (the Greek word includes all these meanings). He fol-lows Jesus as a true disciple, on "the way," the earliest term used to describe the fol-lowers of Jesus.

ALL SAINTS

LECTIONARY #667

READING I Revelation 7:2–4, 9–14

A reading from the Book of Revelation

I, **John**, saw another **angel** come up from the East,
  holding the **seal** of the living **God**.
He cried out in a loud **voice** to the four angels
  who were given power to **damage** the **land** and the **sea**,
  "Do **not** damage the land or the sea or the trees
  until we put the **seal** on the foreheads of the **servants**
    of our God."
I heard the **number** of those who had been marked with the seal,
  one **hundred** and forty-four **thousand** marked
  from every **tribe** of the children of **Israel**.

After this I had a vision of a great **multitude**,
  which no one could **count**,
  from every **nation**, **race**, **people**, and **tongue**.
They stood before the **throne** and before the **Lamb**,
  wearing white **robes** and holding **palm** branches in
    their hands.
They cried out in a loud **voice**:

  "**Salvation** comes from our **God**, who is seated on the **throne**,
  and from the **Lamb**."

TO KEEP IN MIND
Context: Who is speaking in this text? What are the circumstances?

From word one, let your tone signal that you are describing an extraordinary vision.

These are cataclysmic events you are describing. In the midst of the terror, the voice of an angel calls for a halt, so God's people can be "marked" for protection.

The number is less important than your solemn tone. Those sealed are protected by the one whose mark they bear.

"After this" signals the start of a new, more expansive vision. "Every nation, race" means every sector of humanity is represented.

The white robes and palm branches signify the victory of God's elect.

Lift your voice to give this acclamation a joyful chant-like quality.

READING I Today the often misunderstood Book of Revelation presents a great vision of those saved in and through Jesus Christ, the Lamb of God who died but now lives forever as witness to God's life-giving power (see Revelation 1:17–18). This last book of the New Testament originates in apocalyptic thought, which often appears in times of distress or persecution. Apocalyptic literature intends to give hope to suffering people by presenting God bringing the divine plan to completion, often with a final battle between forces of good and evil, ending with God's triumph over the twin evils of sin and death. In the first century, apocalyptic visions commonly culminated in a final judgment and due reward for good or evil conduct in this world. The author of Revelation wrote at a time of Roman persecution of Christians when he himself was imprisoned for his witness to Christ. As is common in apocalyptic writings, he used multiple symbols.

Immediately before today's reading, John described 144,000 persons to be marked with a seal as servants of God. This symbolic number is derived by repeated multiplication of the numbers ten, symbolizing perfection or completion, and twelve, representing the twelve tribes of Israel. Since the Christian community considered

All of heaven joins the exuberant hymn of praise.

Give us a sense that the cry of praise filled the heavens.

All the **angels** stood around the throne
and around the **elders** and the four living **creatures**.
They **prostrated** themselves before the throne,
worshiped God, and exclaimed:

"**Amen. Blessing** and **glory**, **wisdom** and **thanksgiving**,
honor, **power**, and **might**
be to our God **forever** and **ever. Amen**."

The "elder" knows the answer to his own question. His tone is gentle and wise.

Then one of the **elders** spoke up and said to me,
"Who are these wearing white **robes**, and where did they
come from?"
I said to him, "My **lord**, **you** are the one who knows."
He said to me,
"These are the ones who have **survived** the time
of great distress;
they have **washed** their robes
and made them **white** in the **Blood** of the **Lamb**."

The elder speaks with pride and admiration of those who survived persecution and trial.

That these multitudes entered the heavenly sanctuary not through their own merit but because of the work of the Lamb should fill us with expectant hope.

For meditation and context:

RESPONSORIAL PSALM   Psalm 24:1bc–2, 3–4ab, 5–6 (6)

R. Lord, this is the people that longs to see your face.

The LORD's are the earth and its fullness;
the world and those who dwell in it.
For he founded it upon the seas
and established it upon the rivers.

Who can ascend the mountain of the LORD?
or who may stand in his holy place?
One whose hands are sinless, whose heart
is clean,
who desires not what is vain.

He shall receive a blessing from the LORD,
a reward from God his savior.
Such is the race that seeks him,
that seeks the face of the God of Jacob.

> **TO KEEP IN MIND**
> **Eye contact** connects you with those to whom you minister. Look at the assembly during the middle and at the end of every thought or sentence.

itself the new Israel of the final age, 144,000 persons sealed stands for the entire community of faithful believers saved by God. They wear white and carry palms, symbolizing joy, glory, and victory. The victory, of course, is not their own but that of God and the Lamb, the risen Christ, to whom they offer praise and thanks. They have remained faithful, even in the face of suffering and death for their faith in Christ, and so at his coming in glory they share in God's final

salvation. In and through the sacrificed Lamb of God, now raised to fullness of life, they too pass through death to greater life.

READING II A great deal is compressed into the simple opening sentence of today's Second Reading. Scholars debate whether the author of this letter and that of the Gospel account attributed to John are the same person.

Regardless, the two writings share a similar perspective. The Gospel according to John indicates that those who believe in, and enter into personal relationship with, Jesus as the Incarnation of God's own Word can become children of God (John 1:12–13); that is, share a oneness with God similar to that enjoyed by Jesus. For both Jesus and the believer, the motive and cause of such union is divine love, freely given. Both writers view this mutual indwelling of God and

The passage is full of wonder at the love of God who makes us his beloved children. Focus on that love before you begin.

Look at the assembly as you make this solemn affirmation.

Regret tinges this admission that the world rejected Christ.

Pause briefly after "beloved" before continuing. While some things are *unknown*, John confidently asserts that "at least we know *this* much . . . "

This hope we have requires action on our part—to purify ourselves of all that pollutes the mind and heart.

TO KEEP IN MIND

Lists: Whether proclaiming a genealogy or one of Paul's enumerations of virtues and sins, avoid the extremes of too much stress (slowly punctuating each word with equal stress) or too little (rushing through as if each item were the same).

READING II   1 John 3:1–3

A reading from the first Letter of Saint John

Beloved:
See what **love** the Father has **bestowed** on us
   that we may be called the **children** of God.
Yet so we **are**.
The reason the **world** does not know us
   is that it did not know **him**.
Beloved, we **are** God's children **now**;
   what we **shall** be has not yet been **revealed**.
We **do** know that **when** it is revealed we shall be **like** him,
   for we shall see him as he **is**.
Everyone who has this hope based on **him** makes himself **pure**,
   as **he** is pure.

the believer as a present reality, but one that will also continue and expand in ways yet unknown when Christ is fully revealed at the culmination of God's plan of salvation.

GOSPEL   Today's Gospel, commonly referred to as "the Beatitudes," opens the first of five sections of Jesus's teaching in Matthew. This first discourse, usually called the "Sermon on the Mount," presents many of the key elements of Jesus's instruction regarding

behavior expected of those who accept and belong to the Kingdom of God. Throughout this segment and Matthew's account as a whole, the Evangelist portrays Jesus as the true and final interpreter of the Law of Moses. As is the case in this reading, Matthew, generally believed to be a Jew who came to faith in Jesus, often has a distinctly Jewish perspective.

The formula "Blessed are" appears often in the Old Testament, especially in

Psalms and Wisdom, and is used frequently to describe the wise, who understand and follow God's teaching. Several of the beatitudes underscore righteousness, which in Matthew commonly means right conduct that conforms to God's will. The evangelist emphasizes righteousness that belongs to the Kingdom of God (in Matthew, Kingdom of heaven), which signifies the divine plan that will be brought to full flower.

There are many effective ways to proclaim this familiar Gospel text. You can pause after each "blessed"; or prior to each "for they"; or you might forgo pauses and deliver each Beatitude like a dart flying toward the bull's-eye. What is critical is that you keep a clear image of what (or better, whom) each Beatitude names. Have someone in mind for each of the eight "blesseds" and let their unique goodness color the way you proclaim.

These statements are meant to comfort those who live the Beatitudes and those who think they can't.

The message of these provocative statements is countercultural. How would your delivery be affected if some in your assembly got up and left in the middle of your speaking?

Leave time for silence between the Beatitudes so each can sink in.

Don't shy from emphasizing the word "Blessed" each time it recurs.

Speak the final Beatitude with awareness that some in your pews have indeed been insulted and slandered for the sake of the Kingdom.

Though the passage ends with an imperative, let your tone make it an invitation to God's Kingdom.

GOSPEL   Matthew 5:1–12a

A reading from the holy Gospel according to Matthew

When Jesus saw the **crowds**, he went up the **mountain**,
    and after he had **sat** down, his **disciples** came to him.
He began to **teach** them, saying:

"**Blessed** are the **poor** in **spirit**,
    for theirs is the Kingdom of **heaven**.
Blessed are they who **mourn**,
    for they will be **comforted**.
Blessed are the **meek**,
    for they will inherit the **land**.
Blessed are they who **hunger** and **thirst** for **righteousness**,
    for they will be **satisfied**.
Blessed are the **merciful**,
    for they will be shown **mercy**.
Blessed are the clean of **heart**,
    for they will see **God**.
Blessed are the **peacemakers**,
    for they will be called **children** of God.
Blessed are they who are **persecuted** for the sake
        of **righteousness**,
    for theirs is the Kingdom of **heaven**.
Blessed are **you** when they **insult** you and **persecute** you
        and utter every kind of **evil** against you **falsely** because
        of **me**.
Rejoice and be **glad**,
    for your **reward** will be **great** in **heaven**."

The Beatitudes, like other aspects of Jesus's teaching, focus on inner motivations and attitudes as the core of right conduct. Lack of material goods alone does not guarantee upright behavior; but poverty that includes a spirit of total dependence upon God can lead to right conduct. Similarly, lack of food and drink implies no necessary virtue, but inner hunger and thirst for righteousness can result in right action. Avoiding what is considered unclean may or may not represent righteous behavior; a clean heart, signifying single-minded focus on Jesus and his teaching, must guide a disciple's action. Likewise, suffering insult and persecution in itself does not necessarily conform to God's will, though rejection that results from following Jesus's instruction does. Those whose interior attitudes and motivations are formed by Jesus's teaching in word and deed follow the way of righteousness, and thus are truly blessed.

THE COMMEMORATION OF ALL THE FAITHFUL DEPARTED (ALL SOULS' DAY)

LECTIONARY #668

READING I   Wisdom 3:1–9

A reading from the Book of Wisdom

The **souls** of the **just** are in the hand of **God**,
 and no **torment** shall touch them.
They **seemed**, in the view of the **foolish**, to be **dead**;
 and their **passing** away was thought an **affliction**
 and their going **forth** from us, utter **destruction**.
But they are in **peace**.
For if before men, indeed, they be **punished**,
 yet is their hope full of **immortality**;
chastised a little, they shall be greatly **blessed**,
 because God **tried** them
 and found them **worthy** of himself.
As **gold** in the **furnace**, he **proved** them,
 and as sacrificial **offerings** he took them to **himself**.
In the time of their **visitation** they shall **shine**,
 and shall dart about as **sparks** through **stubble**;
they shall judge **nations** and rule over **peoples**,
 and the Lord shall be their King **forever**.
Those who **trust** in him shall understand **truth**,
 and the **faithful** shall abide with him in **love**:
because **grace** and **mercy** are with his holy ones,
 and his **care** is with his **elect**.

TO KEEP IN MIND
Eye contact connects you with those to whom you minister. Look at the assembly during the middle and at the end of every thought or sentence.

In the opening line we find the intent of the passage: to assure those left behind that their beloved dead are safe with God.

We are the "foolish," so speak that word with understanding, not scorn.

Speak this affirmation from the depth of your own conviction.

"Chastised" alludes to purification that may come after death; not a punishment but a gift from God that readies one to stand before God's judgment seat. Speak with reassuring authority.

"Gold" is *purified* in fire.

Here is the ultimate destiny of the just. Quicken your pace for this good news that they will shine like sparks and judge the nations.

The final sentence speaks of us as well as of those who've gone to God. Take time to emphasize the "grace," "mercy," and "care" that accompany God's elect.

Today options are given for the readings. Contact your parish staff to learn which readings will be used.

READING I The Book of Wisdom, written within the century before the birth of Jesus, intends to encourage faithfulness in Jews living outside of Palestine. Long exposed to other cultures and religions, some of which dismissed or even ridiculed Jewish belief and practice, God's people often struggled greatly to maintain their religious identity in such circumstances. Today's First Reading comes from the first section of the book, which contrasts both righteous and wicked people, and their final destiny.

Immediately preceding this passage, the author has described how faithful Jews might be tested by others, even by fellow Jews who regard the behavior of the just in the face of persecution as a judgment on their own laxity. The author exhorts the righteous to remain so, for even if they suffer persecution that leads to death, their ultimate reward lies with God. Today's reading represents one of the clearest affirmations of belief in resurrection in the Old Testament. By the last century before Christ, and in part due to exposure to Greek thought, some Jews expanded their view of resurrection to include the notion of immortality.

The reading opens with reference to the righteous who endured even death. To "the foolish," that is, the unrighteous, it seems a final, fruitless end. However, the author assures the faithful, persecution and death represent a testing in which just

For meditation and context:

TO KEEP IN MIND

Word value: Words are your medium, like a painter's brush or a sculptor's chisel. You must understand the words before you can communicate them. Most words have a dictionary meaning (denotative) and an associational meaning (connotative). "House" and "home" both mean "dwelling," yet they communicate different feelings. Be alert to subtle differences in connotative meanings and express them.

This is a bold statement to share with people who have lost loved ones. Speak from the knowledge of God's love within your own heart.

This is a bedrock Christian conviction: Christ died for us not when we were deserving but when we were steeped in sin!

Even if one might die for a "good" person, the fact is Christ died for the undeserving—us.

If God showered mercy on us during our time of alienation, how can he not shower even more on us now that Christ has "reconciled" us?

RESPONSORIAL PSALM   Psalm 23:1–3a, 3b–4, 5, 6 (1)

R. The Lord is my shepherd; there is nothing I shall want. or R. Though I walk in the valley of darkness, I fear no evil, for you are with me.

The LORD is my shepherd; I shall not want.
　In verdant pastures he gives me repose;
beside restful waters he leads me;
　he refreshes my soul.

He guides me in right paths
　for his name's sake.
Even though I walk in the dark valley
　I fear no evil; for you are at my side
with your rod and your staff
　that give me courage.

You spread the table before me
　in the sight of my foes;
you anoint my head with oil;
　my cup overflows.

Only goodness and kindness follow me
　all the days of my life;
and I shall dwell in the house of the LORD
　for years to come.

READING II   Romans 5:5–11

A reading from the Letter of Saint Paul to the Romans

Brothers and sisters:
Hope does not **disappoint**,
　because the love of God has been poured out into our hearts
　　through the Holy **Spirit** that has been **given** to us.
For **Christ**, while we were still **helpless**,
　died at the appointed time for the **ungodly**.
Indeed, only with **difficulty** does one die for a **just** person,
　though perhaps for a **good** person
　one might even find **courage** to die.
But God **proves** his love for us
　in that while we were still **sinners** Christ **died** for us.
How much **more** then, since we are now **justified** by his **Blood**,
　will we be **saved** through him from the **wrath**.

Jews prove themselves worthy members of God's people. Having demonstrated their faith in God and in God's power even over death, they will be vindicated and taken into the divine presence forever. Their trust and utter reliance upon God, in the face of ridicule, torture, and death, will be rewarded by dwelling in God's eternal love.

READING II **ROMANS 5:5-11.** The Letter to the Romans, written near the end of Saint Paul's life, represents his mature thought and offers the most systematic explanation of the Apostle's understanding of salvation through faith in

Christ. Preceding today's reading, Paul has insisted that no one can be placed in right relationship to God by his or her own adherence to the commands of the Mosaic Law. For the great Apostle to the Gentiles, the revelation offered in Christ is that God's own freely given, unearned love stands as the primary source of human salvation. For Paul, this gracious gift of love is most manifest in the sacrificial Death and Resurrection of Christ; faith consists in accepting and responding to God's life-giving love that is freely given in Christ and remains with believers through the Holy Spirit.

Today's Second Reading begins with focus on the graciousness of enduring divine love. While it does not appear in this particular passage, Paul often used the Greek word *charis*, literally meaning "gift" but usually translated as "grace," to speak of God's love given through Christ and remaining as constant presence in the Spirit. Paul stresses the depth and breadth of divine love, offered to all, regardless of merit: Christ died for sinners as well as for the just, bringing reconciliation with God. And Christ, now raised to a new kind of life, shares that transforming life with those

End as joyfully as you began. The purpose of the text is not to argue a point but to comfort with the truth of God's merciful love.

Indeed, if, while we were **enemies**,
　　we were **reconciled** to God through the death of his **Son**,
　　how much **more**, once **reconciled**,
　　will we be saved by his **life**.
Not only that,
　　but we also **boast** of God through our Lord Jesus **Christ**,
　　through whom we have now received **reconciliation**.

Or:

READING II   Romans 6:3–9

A reading from the Letter of Saint Paul to the Romans

Brothers and sisters:
Are you **unaware** that we who were **baptized** into Christ Jesus
　　were baptized into his **death**?
We were indeed **buried** with him through baptism into **death**,
　　so that, just as Christ was **raised** from the dead
　　by the glory of the Father,
　　we **too** might live in **newness** of life.

For if we have grown into **union** with him through a **death**
　　like his,
　　we shall also be **united** with him in the **resurrection**.
We know that our **old** self was **crucified** with him,
　　so that our sinful body might be done **away** with,
　　that we might no longer be in **slavery** to sin.
For a **dead** person has been **absolved** from sin.
If, then, we have **died** with Christ,
　　we believe that we shall also **live** with him.
We know that **Christ, raised** from the dead, dies **no more**;
　　death no longer has **power** over him.

Paul jolts us to attention with a rhetorical question: don't you know that by being baptized in Christ you were baptized (initiated) into this death?

The joyful consequence of that dying in Christ is heralded here: we were "buried" like Christ so we could rise like him to "newness of life"!

"A death like his" refers to our Baptism. Paul is repeating his point to ensure we get it. Be sure your tone is gentle and reassuring.

"If then we have" is a repetition. But let your energetic tone keep it from sounding redundant.

The last two lines make the same assertion twice, so give greater stress to the second iteration. "We know" means "we are convinced!"

thus reconciled. It is the boundless, unmerited love of God revealed in Christ and continuing in the Spirit that brings believers to new life, now and in eternity.

　　ROMANS 6:3-9. The Letter to the Romans, written near the end of Saint Paul's life, represents his mature thought and offers the most systematic explanation of the Apostle's understanding of salvation through faith in Christ. For the great Apostle to the Gentiles, the revelation offered in Christ is that God's own freely given, unearned love stands as the primary

source of human salvation. Paul sees this gracious gift of divine love made manifest in the sacrificial Death and Resurrection of Christ.

　　In today's Second Reading, Paul stresses that through Baptism believers are fully immersed in and must imitate Christ's passage through death to greater life. The Apostle describes union with Christ as both source and cause of the Christian's ability to die to a former way of life. The baptized must make a conscious choice to lay aside the old self, enslaved to sin, and so share

in Christ's Death. Paul, following Jewish thought that views the human person as a unity, uses "body" (Greek *soma*) to signify the whole person. Because Jews thought of human physical reality as a primary mode of relationship, Paul may have used the word "body" to emphasize that, for the Christian, whatever is sinful in any and all relationships must be laid aside. Through a chosen death to all that is not of God, the believer dies with Christ. The Christian's oneness with Christ, however, further means that the baptized will also be raised

Pause after the introductory phrase to shift to the compassionate and reassuring tone of Jesus.

Jesus's assertion that none be "lost" means we must weigh the evidence of our own experience against the infinite mercy of God. Stress "*this*" here as in the previous sentence. God wants what we want—for everyone who has known Christ to share God's eternal life.

Make eye contact and, from memory, share the hope-filled final line.

TO KEEP IN MIND

Gestures and Posture: Using gestures is not part of the task of proclamation; within the liturgy, gestures are an unnecessary distraction. However, your body language is always communicating. Avoid leaning on the ambo or standing on one foot. And don't let your face or body contradict the Good News you announce. Readers are allowed to smile!

GOSPEL   John 6:37–40

A reading from the holy Gospel according to John

Jesus said to the **crowds**:
"**Everything** that the Father **gives** me will **come** to me,
    and I will not reject **anyone** who comes to me,
    because I came down from **heaven** not to do my **own** will
    but the will of the one who **sent** me.
And **this** is the will of the one who sent me,
    that I should not **lose** anything of what he **gave** me,
    but that I should **raise** it on the last day.
For **this** is the will of my Father,
    that everyone who sees the **Son** and **believes** in him
    may have eternal **life**,
    and I shall **raise** him up on the last **day**."

---

to transformed Resurrection life in and with him.

 GOSPEL This passage from John is embedded in the "Bread of Life discourse," which follows upon the sign of Jesus walking on the sea. John presents this account as a clear indicator of Jesus's identity as divine Word in the flesh. Like so many parts of John, today's passage builds upon the author's introduction of Jesus's identity and mission in the prologue (John 1:1–18). At the beginning of his work, John tells the reader that God's own Word or

self-communication was sent to humankind to become incarnate in Jesus. As Word made flesh, Jesus reveals God and God's will for humankind: on returning to God, Jesus brings with him all those who believe, that is, who choose to live in Jesus as he lives in the Father. In other words, those who come to mutual indwelling with Jesus can participate in God's own life through Jesus. This chapter of John emphasizes Eucharist as one major mode of union with Jesus, Word incarnate.

Today's reading emphasizes Jesus as the one sent from God, choosing the divine

will rather than his own. That will of God, noted above, desires that all human beings share in divine life. Such participation in God's own life, however, requires a decision to "believe in" Jesus as Word made flesh. The Greek here literally means "believe into," signifying a chosen oneness with Jesus. It is this oneness with Jesus that brings fullness of life, union with God, now and forever.

THIRTY-SECOND SUNDAY IN ORDINARY TIME

LECTIONARY #155

READING I 1 Kings 17:10–16

Elijah = ee-LĪ-juh

Zarephath = ZAYR-uh-fath

God told Elijah that a widow would care for him. When he sees her, he recognizes God's chosen instrument. His dialogue is not of one on the verge of collapse; his request is polite.

He waits till she's turned away to call after her for bread, so lift your voice a bit.

The woman immediately confesses her dire situation. She seems resolved, not pathetic; even in her need she's able to care for another.

Elijah's is the compassionate voice of God. We see now why God sent him to *her*: Elijah *and* the woman will receive God's compassionate mercy.

A reading from the first Book of Kings

In those days, **Elijah** the **prophet** went to **Zarephath**.
As he arrived at the **entrance** of the city,
   a **widow** was gathering **sticks** there; he called **out** to her,
   "**Please** bring me a small cupful of **water** to drink."
She left to **get** it, and he called out **after** her,
   "Please bring along a bit of **bread**."
She **answered**, "As the LORD, your God, lives,
   I have nothing **baked**; there is only a handful of **flour** in my **jar**
   and a little **oil** in my **jug**.
Just now I was collecting a couple of sticks,
   to go in and **prepare** something for **myself** and my **son**;
   when we have **eaten** it, we shall **die**."
Elijah **said** to her, "Do not be **afraid**.
Go and do as you **propose**.
But **first** make me a little **cake** and **bring** it to me.
Then you can prepare something for **yourself** and your **son**.
For the LORD, the God of **Israel**, **says**,
   'The jar of **flour** shall not go **empty**,
   nor the jug of **oil** run **dry**,
   until the day when the LORD sends **rain** upon the earth.'"
She **left** and **did** as Elijah had said.

READING I | Today's First Reading underscores the tremendous trust of both Elijah and the widow of Zarepath. Elijah spent much of his life as a prophet preaching against the policies and actions of King Ahab and his wife Jezebel who ruled the northern kingdom of Israel. Together, they not only worshipped idols in Israel, but led the people to imitate them, thus earning the author of First Kings' judgment that Ahab angered the Lord more than any previous ruler. For her part, Jezebel, daughter of the Sidonian king, had

commanded that all the prophets of the LORD be killed.

Thus when God instructs Elijah to seek refuge from drought with a widow of Zarepath in Sidon, the prophet knows he is moving into dangerous territory. Further, this woman seems a most unlikely helper for the prophet for two reasons. First, she does not belong to the covenant people of the LORD, and second, she is a widow. In ancient Israel, women completely depended upon their husbands for life's basic survival needs, and a woman with no husband and a dependent child was very likely to

lack even bare necessities for herself and her child.

However, the prophet obeys God's word, and though the woman provides water, at his request for food she acknowledges that she has scarcely enough for a last bit of bread for herself and her child. In fact, she expects that after eating their last morsel, they will die. Elijah tells her that if she first feeds him, the God of Israel will ensure that her flour and oil will not fail until the drought ends. At the word of a God she does not worship and a prophet she does not know, the woman does their bidding,

Your tone says she complied without hesitation. Then announce the miracle with a peaceful sense that we can always rely on God's mercy.

She was able to eat for a **year**, and he and her son as well;
  the jar of flour did not go **empty**,
  nor the jug of oil run **dry**,
  as the LORD had foretold through **Elijah**.

For meditation and context:

RESPONSORIAL PSALM   Psalm 146:7, 8–9, 9–10 (1b)

R. Praise the Lord, my soul! or R. Alleluia.

The LORD keeps faith forever,
  secures justice for the oppressed,
  gives food to the hungry.
The LORD sets captives free.

The LORD gives sight to the blind;
  the LORD raises up those who were
  bowed down.
The LORD loves the just;
  the LORD protects strangers.

The fatherless and the widow he sustains,
  but the way of the wicked he thwarts.
The LORD shall reign forever;
  your God, O Zion, through all
  generations. Alleluia.

TO KEEP IN MIND
Names of characters: Often the first word of a reading. Lift out the names to ensure listeners don't miss who the subject is.

READING II   Hebrews 9:24–28

A reading from the Letter to the Hebrews

Christ did not enter into a sanctuary made by **hands**,
  a copy of the **true** one, but heaven **itself**,
  that he might **now** appear before God on our **behalf**.
Not that he might offer himself **repeatedly**,
  as the high **priest** enters each year into the **sanctuary**
  with **blood** that is not his **own**;
  if **that** were so, he would have had to suffer **repeatedly**
  from the foundation of the **world**.
But now **once** for **all** he has appeared at the **end** of the ages
  to take away sin by his **sacrifice**.
Just as it is **appointed** that human beings **die** once,
  and after this the **judgment**, so also **Christ**,
  offered **once** to take away the sins of many,
  will appear a **second** time, not to take away **sin**
  but to bring **salvation** to those who eagerly **await** him.

This is the fifth of six consecutive weeks we read from Hebrews.

The author continues to compare and contrast Jesus and his once-for-all sacrifice with the repeated sacrifices of the old law. Don't judge the former sacrifices negatively; but suggest that, good as they were, what we have now is so much better.

The Temple "sanctuary" is a "copy" of the true sanctuary, heaven.

Jesus comes at the end of a long and venerable tradition to replace the old sacrifices with his own perfect sacrifice. Speak this as a declaration of faith, not a courtroom argument.

You move from logic to *joyful* declaration. Be mindful you are making an analogy from us to Christ.

Every Christian must assume the joyful stance of *eagerly* awaiting Christ's return.

and her act of total trust is rewarded by complete fulfillment of the LORD's promise.

READING II Hebrews continues to describe the crucified and risen Jesus as the final High Priest of the age of salvation. The author stresses that in offering his life itself to God, Jesus's self-sacrifice is complete and unrepeatable. No one can die more than once, and so his sacrifice puts an end to the repeated cycle of sacrifices offered by the high priest of Judaism. Because of its incomparable

worth, the total sacrifice of Jesus Christ, both fully human and divine Son of God, heals human sin once and for all; further, it cannot and need not be repeated.

The second part of today's reading indicates that the author of Hebrews shares the Jewish expectation that God acts to bring human history to its culmination. Now, "at the end of the ages," the divine plan reaches fulfillment in the self-sacrifice of Christ. Jesus Christ, himself both sacrifice and High Priest, has finally and fully brought healing and reconciliation between sinful humanity and God. The

author's language here is most likely drawn from the last song of the suffering servant, described by Isaiah as the one who bore the sins of many (53:20). In both Isaiah and Hebrews, one word can mean both "take away" and "bear," a dual meaning probably intended by the author. In both cases, "the many" in Semitic usage means "all." Hebrews looks forward to an imminent return of Jesus, the ultimate High Priest whose self-sacrifice effects final oneness of God and humankind.

GOSPEL   Mark 12:38–44

A reading from the holy Gospel according to Mark

In the course of his teaching **Jesus** said to the **crowds**,
   "Beware of the **scribes**, who like to go around in long **robes**
   and accept greetings in the **marketplaces**,
     seats of **honor** in **synagogues**,
     and places of honor at **banquets**.
They devour the houses of **widows** and, as a **pretext**
   recite lengthy **prayers**.
They will receive a very severe **condemnation**."

He sat down opposite the **treasury**
   and observed how the crowd put **money** into the treasury.
Many **rich** people put in **large** sums.
A poor **widow** also came and put in two small **coins** worth
     a few **cents**.
Calling his **disciples** to himself, he **said** to them,
   "**Amen**, I say to you, this poor **widow** put in more
   than all the **other** contributors to the treasury.
For they have all contributed from their **surplus** wealth,
   but **she**, from her **poverty**, has contributed **all** she had,
   her whole **livelihood**."

[Shorter: Mark 12:41–44]

Jesus always speaks harshly of hypocrisy. Here is no different. Because hypocrisy is contagious, he *warns* lest the healthy become infected.

Jesus takes great risks speaking so boldly in the Temple precincts.

Jesus's strongest indictment is reserved for those who, in the name of God, take from the needy to satisfy themselves.

A new narrative begins. Jesus takes time to observe the Temple worshippers.

Don't speak negatively of the "rich," but signal immediately that the "widow" is a sympathetic character.

He quickly gathers the disciples so they don't miss this object lesson.

Jesus's words are both instructive and full of admiration for the widow.

Clearly, Jesus senses she has given God more than her little wealth; she has also given the riches of her heart.

TO KEEP IN MIND

Ritardando: refers to the practice, common in music, of becoming gradually slower and expanding the words as you approach the end of a piece. Many readings end this way—with a decreased rate but increased intensity.

GOSPEL   The poor widow of today's Gospel serves as a counterpoint to hypocritical scribes denounced by Jesus in the preceding brief passage. He does not present all scribes in a negative light; rather, hypocrisy is the major subject of rebuke. Those whom Jesus condemns merely play the role of observant scribes; while relishing privileges and marks of honor accorded to pious religious leaders, in fact they "devour the houses of widows." In Jesus's time, scribes fulfilled some of the duties of modern lawyers, and so could serve as trustees of a widow's estate; often the fee would be paid with a share of the estate. Scribes with a reputation for piety, perhaps demonstrated by reciting long prayers, were considered good candidates for such transactions. It is such pretense of virtue while in fact taking advantage of the most vulnerable that Jesus censures.

On the other hand, he commends the genuine faith and generosity of one potential victim of scribal hypocrisy. Jesus observes those who come into the portion of the Temple complex known as the court of the women, where the treasury was located. At Passover time, many pilgrims would have come to make their offerings for upkeep and renovation of the Temple of the Lord. But among the multitude, one poor widow stands out among wealthy contributors. Though one of the poorest members of Jewish society, she contributes two coins of the smallest possible denomination. She offers far more than the rich, for she gives generously from the depths of her poverty.

THIRTY-THIRD SUNDAY IN ORDINARY TIME

LECTIONARY #158

READING I   Daniel 12:1–3

A reading from the Book of the Prophet Daniel

In those days, **I**, **Daniel**,
   heard this word of the **Lord**:
"At that time there shall arise
   Michael, the great **prince**,
   guardian of your **people**;
it shall be a time **unsurpassed** in **distress**
   since nations began until that time.
At **that** time your people shall **escape**,
   everyone who is found written in the **book**.

"Many of those who sleep in the dust of the **earth** shall **awake**;
   some shall live **forever**,
   others shall be an everlasting **horror** and **disgrace**.

"But the **wise** shall shine **brightly**
   like the **splendor** of the **firmament**,
and those who lead the many to **justice**
   shall be like the **stars forever**."

Read the introduction with awareness of the dramatic vision that will follow.

This prophecy is serious and dire; it is not meant to terrify but to alert, so no one is caught unaware.

Speak of "Michael" with great reverence.

The news is partially good: "people will escape," but only those who are "written in the book."

This very important verse expresses Scripture's *first* affirmation of belief in life after death. Contrast those who "live forever" with those who will be eternal "disgrace."

Look at your assembly as you announce the Good News that the "wise" (those who conform their lives to God's will) will live forever. Speak not as with exploding fireworks but with fire in your heart.

READING I   Though the Book of Daniel is named for its main character, a prophet, it is actually a work of apocalyptic literature. The unknown author describes a historical setting during the Babylonian captivity, but the book was written centuries later, most likely during the religious persecution of Jews under the Selucid King Antiochus IV, 167–164 BC. Like all apocalyptic writings, this work seeks to give believers hope by looking forward to God's definitive intervention in human affairs, which puts an end to the domination of all evil powers. Part of apocalyptic thought includes expectation of conflict and distress that signals God's coming, a final battle between powers of good and evil, and a final judgment at which the righteous and unrighteous will be rewarded according to their deeds. Several phrases were used in the Bible's apocalyptic works to refer to the entire event in which God would bring the divine plan to its intended end, including "on that day," "in those days," and "at that time."

Today's First Reading makes ample use of language and images of apocalyptic thought. Daniel, portrayed as a prophet, receives the word of the Lord describing the nearness of God's final act. As the last battle between good and evil approaches, the archangel Michael will appear to protect God's people. While not named an angel in this passage, this figure is usually identified with the mighty angel who battles Satan in Revelation 12:7. Names "written in the book" imply final judgment, recalling a previous scene in the heavenly court (Daniel 7:9–18). The lines that follow clearly describe the separation and appropriate fate of the unjust and the just; the

For meditation and context:

TO KEEP IN MIND
Who really proclaims: "When the Scriptures are read in the Church, God himself is speaking to his people, and Christ, present in his own word, is proclaiming the gospel." (General Instruction of the Roman Missal, 29)

RESPONSORIAL PSALM   Psalm 16:5, 8, 9–10, 11 (1)

R. You are my inheritance, O Lord!

O LORD, my allotted portion and my cup,
   you it is who hold fast my lot.
I set the LORD ever before me;
   with him at my right hand I shall not
      be disturbed.

Therefore my heart is glad and my soul
      rejoices,
   my body, too, abides in confidence;
because you will not abandon my soul to the
      netherworld,
   nor will you suffer your faithful one to
      undergo corruption.

You will show me the path to life,
   fullness of joys in your presence,
   the delights at your right hand forever.

READING II   Hebrews 10:11–14, 18

A reading from the Letter to the Hebrews

Brothers and sisters:
Every **priest** stands **daily** at his ministry,
   offering **frequently** those same sacrifices
   that can **never** take away sins.
But **this** one offered **one** sacrifice for sins,
   and took his seat **forever** at the right hand of **God**;
   now he waits until his **enemies** are made his **footstool**.
For by **one** offering
   he has made perfect **forever** those who are being **consecrated**.

Where there is **forgiveness** of these,
   there is no longer **offering** for sin.

This is the last of six consecutive weeks we read from Hebrews.

The text contrasts the "daily" sacrifices (sacrifices offered again and again) that can't "take away sins" with the "one" sacrifice that took away all sins. Speak with knowledge and authority.

Speak with pride of how the saving work of Christ earned him a seat of glory at God's right hand.

"These" refers to sins. Explain joyfully that God has already forgiven us, making further sacrifices unnecessary.

TO KEEP IN MIND
You'll read more naturally if you read **ideas rather than words**, and if you share **images rather than sentences**.

just are "the wise" who follow and trust in the LORD's teaching. This text represents one of the clearest Old Testament references to belief in eternal life for the righteous; it is this trust that offers hope to Jews suffering persecution and to faithful believers to this day.

READING II   In this last of a long series of readings from Hebrews, the author continues to portray Jesus as the final High Priest whose sacrifice need never be repeated. He again contrasts the Jewish priesthood and sacrificial system,

with their repeated sin offerings, with Christ, whose self-sacrifice on the cross is the perfect and therefore last sacrifice for sin. This writer also refers to Jewish apocalyptic thought by describing the crucified and risen Messiah as exalted to the heavenly level with God.

Previous Sundays have indicated that the author of Hebrews shares the early Church's expectation of an imminent return of Christ, completing the age of salvation when God's enemies (powers of evil) are fully dethroned. As the verses immediately

following today's reading make evident, Hebrews believes that the sacrifice of Christ, the High Priest, fulfills the Jewish expectation of complete forgiveness and a new relationship with God in the dawning age of salvation.

GOSPEL   Today's Gospel appears near the end of a chapter often called "Mark's apocalypse." The chapter bears most of the earmarks of apocalyptic thought, still popular in the first century AD. This mode of thinking among Jesus's followers is not surprising, since

GOSPEL   Mark 13:24–32

A reading from the holy Gospel according to Mark

Jesus said to his **disciples**:
"In **those** days after that **tribulation**
    the **sun** will be **darkened**,
        and the **moon** will not give its **light**,
    and the **stars** will be **falling** from the sky,
        and the **powers** in the **heavens** will be **shaken**.

"And then they will see the 'Son of **Man** coming in the **clouds**'
    with great **power** and **glory**,
    and then he will send out the **angels**
    and gather his **elect** from the four **winds**,
    from the end of the **earth** to the end of the **sky**.

"Learn a **lesson** from the **fig** tree.
When its branch becomes **tender** and sprouts **leaves**,
    you know that **summer** is near.
In the **same** way, when you see **these** things happening,
    know that **he** is near, at the **gates**.
Amen, I say to you,
    this **generation** will not pass **away**
    until **all** these things have taken place.
Heaven and **earth** will pass away,
    but my **words** will **not** pass away.

"But of that **day** or **hour**, **no** one knows,
    neither the **angels** in heaven, nor the **Son**, but only
        the **Father**."

The meaning of Jesus's apocalyptic vision resides not only in the words but in the tone of your proclamation.

The collapse of moon and stars is meant to be an arresting, even terrifying image. Don't weaken its power.

Jesus uses the image he most often applied to himself, "Son of Man," to introduce a ray of light into the former scene of doom. His angels will select out the "elect."

Jesus introduces the analogy of the fig tree to concretize the forgoing imagery.

The call for vigilance is urgent and requires stress.

"Amen" intensifies the import of what Jesus is saying.

Only the Lord of heaven and earth could make this claim.

The final sentence is not a disclaimer about his lack of precise knowledge; it is instead a call for vigilance so that when the Son returns he can lead us to the Father.

TO KEEP IN MIND
Eye contact connects you with those to whom you minister. Look at the assembly during the middle and at the end of every thought or sentence.

Jesus devoted his life and ministry to inaugurating God's final rule, the Kingdom of God, in his person and action. Further, the "Son of Man," one of Mark's favored references to Jesus, was an apocalyptic figure who appeared as a human being, accomplished God's work on earth, and was raised to the heavenly (divine) level in God's final reign. Today's Gospel begins with Jesus describing some of apocalyptic literature's typical cosmic signs that God's plan is nearing its culmination. He then quotes

Daniel's description of the glorious appearance of the messianic Son of Man (7:13), the same text Mark will have Jesus give in response to the high priest's question, "Are you the Messiah?" (14:61).

Jesus then shifts to urging the disciples to attend to signs of the Messiah's arrival. As they can read nature's indications that summer draws near, they must also become adept at perceiving that God's final rule over all things, accomplished through a chosen Messiah, is at hand in their lives and world. As the liturgical year approaches its end, the Church focuses on

a threefold coming of Christ: in history, in the present, and in glory at the completion of the final age. In this reading, Jesus tells his contemporaries that they must be constantly waiting and watching for divine presence and action, for the time of completing God's plan of salvation is known to none but God alone. Those who trust in that final coming must be always awake and watchful, listening to the Word that does not pass away.

OUR LORD JESUS CHRIST, KING OF THE UNIVERSE

LECTIONARY #161

READING I   Daniel 7:13–14

A reading from the Book of the Prophet Daniel

As the **visions** during the night **continued**, I saw
    one like a Son of **man** coming,
      on the clouds of **heaven**;
    when he reached the **Ancient** One
      and was **presented** before him,
    the one like a Son of man received **dominion**, **glory**,
      and **kingship**;
    all **peoples**, **nations**, and **languages serve** him.
His dominion is an **everlasting** dominion
    that shall not be taken **away**,
    his **kingship** shall not be **destroyed**.

RESPONSORIAL PSALM   Psalm 93:1, 1–2, 5 (1a)

R. The Lord is king; he is robed in majesty.

The LORD is king, in splendor robed;
    robed is the LORD and girt about with
      strength.

And he has made the world firm,
    not to be moved.
Your throne stands firm from of old;
    from everlasting you are, O LORD.

Your decrees are worthy of trust indeed;
    holiness befits your house,
    O LORD, for length of days.

Introduce the reading and then pause long enough for all to become attentive.

You begin in the midst of the vision, so your tone immediately signals you are relating extraordinary images.

The "Son of man" evokes a sense of both the human and divine.

The "Ancient One" requires a tone of grand authority.

The Son of man receives a litany of awe-inspiring gifts; don't enumerate them like a list of groceries.

Read the final declaration in a tone worthy of the eternal King of kings.

For meditation and context:

TO KEEP IN MIND

As you are becoming familiar with your passage, read it directly from your Bible, **reading also what comes before and after** it to get a clear sense of its context.

READING I | On this Solemnity of Our Lord Jesus Christ, King of the Universe, the Church again invokes the Old Testament's apocalyptic expectation of a messianic figure called the Son of Man. The First Reading, like that of last Sunday, envisions the final intervention of God in human history acting through an anointed one or messiah. In the last several centuries BC, Judaism thought of the messiah as a function rather than as a particular figure. There were, in fact, a number of different expectations about how the anointed of the Lord would appear. The role of the messiah, however, was singular: to act as God's agent in bringing about the final age of salvation in which God would rule over all things. One such messianic figure, as noted last Sunday, was the Son of Man. The phrase originally simply meant "human being" but in several apocalyptic works, canonical and non-canonical, "Son of man" came to refer to a messiah figure who would do God's bidding on earth as a human being, then be raised to the heavenly level, implying some kind of divinity. God's final reign over all things, and often the final judgment, would be carried out through the messianic Son of Man.

This is the vision of Daniel in today's First Reading; having accomplished his task as the anointed one, the Son of Man is raised to the throne of God (the "Ancient One") who begins his final, definitive reign through the exalted messiah.

READING II   Revelation 1:5–8

Because the reading is praise from the start, let your heart swell with gratitude as you approach the ambo. Don't run together, but distinguish, the various attributes you extol.

The first sentence resolves into an earnest prayer of praise. Help us pray with you.

"Behold" signals a new beat. Avoid a melodramatic exclamation as if he were coming through the window; instead, speak with quiet intensity to persuade us his arrival will be unannounced and unanticipated.

When he comes, those who rejected Christ will tearfully regret their decision.

"Alpha" and "omega" are the first and last letters of the Greek alphabet.

Employing the divine "I am," the Christ announces who he is—the beginning and end of all our longings, the all-powerful Lord of the universe.

A reading from the Book of Revelation

Jesus **Christ** is the faithful **witness**,
    the **firstborn** of the **dead** and **ruler** of the kings of the earth.
To him who **loves** us and has **freed** us from our sins by
        his **blood**,
    who has made us into a **kingdom**, **priests** for his God
        and Father,
    to him be **glory** and **power** forever and **ever**. **Amen**.

    Behold, he is coming amid the **clouds**,
        and every eye will **see** him,
        even those who **pierced** him.
    All the peoples of the earth will **lament** him.
        Yes. **Amen**.

"I am the **Alpha** and the **Omega**," says the Lord God,
    "the one who **is** and who **was** and who is to **come**,
        the **almighty**."

TO KEEP IN MIND

Word value: Words are your medium, like a painter's brush or a sculptor's chisel. You must understand the words before you can communicate them. Most words have a dictionary meaning (denotative) and an associational meaning (connotative). "House" and "home" both mean "dwelling," yet they communicate different feelings. Be alert to subtle differences in connotative meanings and express them.

READING II Continuing several apocalyptic themes of the First Reading, Revelation opens by introducing the book with a vision of the crucified, now resurrected Christ, the Messiah who has begun God's age of salvation. Since the author writes for Christians facing persecution and perhaps even death for refusal to worship the Roman Emperor as divine, it is important to introduce Jesus as "firstborn of the dead" who exerts power over all human rulers. The resurrected Christ as firstborn implies siblings—daughters and sons of God who, though they might suffer death as Jesus did, will be raised through faith in him. Such brothers and sisters of Jesus form his Kingdom, where the power of God rules through him, conquering the enemies of sin and death.

In Greek, alpha and omega are the first and last letters of the alphabet. Chapter 1 later repeats this image of the risen Jesus, with the emphatic addition, "Once I was dead, but now I am alive for ever and ever" (Revelation 1:18). This focus on Jesus's passage through death to greater, everlasting life reveals the ultimate ruling power of God at work. It is this life-giving power now acting through Christ that holds sway over all things forever.

GOSPEL This portion of John's account of Jesus before the Roman governor, Pilate, must be understood on several levels: Pilate's perspective, that of Jesus, and that of the Evangelist. It is important to be aware that the Fourth Evangelist speaks primarily of Jesus in glory, as understood near the end of the first century. John presents religious rather than historical meaning.

Don't read today as when this text is part of the Passion narrative. Here, Jesus's words affirm the cosmic visions of Daniel and Revelation, which tell us to watch the skies; Jesus affirms this by declaring his Kingdom is not of this world.

Today, Pilate stands in the shoes of anyone who seeks to know who Christ really is. Ask his question without malice.

Leave out the tension and urgency of Good Friday. For today, this is just an effort to understand.

Jesus's question to Pilate, "Do you say this on your own?" could as easily be addressed to each of us.

On this day, this dialogue ("My attendants *would* be fighting") establishes the unique kind of king Jesus came to be.

"So you are" is Pilate's effort to get a straight answer. He thinks he's gotten it.

But Jesus responds with only a half affirmative. Deliver the final line from memory, looking right at the assembly to assure them this affirmation comes directly from the King of kings.

GOSPEL   John 18:33b–37

A reading from the holy Gospel according to John

Pilate said to **Jesus**,
   "Are you the **King** of the Jews?"
Jesus answered, "Do you say this on your **own**
   or have **others** told you about me?"
Pilate answered, "I am not a **Jew**, am I?
Your own **nation** and the chief **priests** handed you over to me.
What have you **done**?"
Jesus answered, "My **kingdom** does not belong to this world.
If my kingdom **did** belong to this world,
   my attendants would be **fighting**
to keep me from being handed over to the Jews.
But as it is, my kingdom is not **here**."
So Pilate said to him, "Then you **are** a king?"
Jesus answered, "**You** say I am a king.
For this I was **born** and for this I came into the **world**,
   to **testify** to the **truth**.
Everyone who **belongs** to the truth **listens** to my voice."

THE 4 STEPS OF *LECTIO DIVINA* OR PRAYERFUL READING

1. *Lectio:* Read a Scripture passage aloud slowly. Notice what phrase captures your attention and be attentive to its meaning. Silent pause.

2. *Meditatio:* Read the passage aloud slowly again, reflecting on the passage, allowing God to speak to you through it. Silent pause.

3. *Oratio:* Read it aloud slowly a third time, allowing it to be your prayer or response to God's gift of insight to you. Silent pause.

4. *Contemplatio:* Read it aloud slowly a fourth time, now resting in God's word.

In John and all the synoptic narratives describing Pilate's interrogation, the governor's first question is the same: "Are you the King of the Jews?" For Pilate, a positive answer would seal the prisoner's fate, because any threat to the absolute power of the Roman Emperor merited a death sentence. For the governor, the query is political. Jesus shifts the dialogue to his own point of view; he pursues not an earthly kingdom, but a heavenly one—God's rule over all. Pilate rephrases the question in a manner that seems to expect a positive response. Such irony is typical of John; the character in his account does not realize that he has correctly described Jesus, though hearers do so immediately. The careful phrasing of Jesus's response indicates agreement, but with qualification: the title is accurate, but it would not have been Jesus's own primary self-description. He has come from the Father to reveal God's truth, not to seize political power. At the very beginning of his account, the evangelist proclaimed to his hearers that grace and truth have entered the world in the divine Word sent from God, made flesh in Jesus (1:14–17). Further, in his last instruction to disciples, Jesus described himself as the truth (14:6).

For John, Jesus crucified and raised presents the full truth of a self-giving God who now rules forever through him. The power of Jesus's Kingdom is the strength of such love, far greater than the authority of one who sends him to execution. This truth stands unrecognized in the flesh before Pilate, but embraced by those who listen to Jesus's voice.